THE NEW ENGLAND MIND

The Seventeenth Century

THE NEW ENGLAND MIND: THE SEVENTEENTH CENTURY
[FIRST PUBLISHED, 1939; REISSUED, 1954]

THE NEW ENGLAND MIND: FROM COLONY TO PROVINCE
[1953]

THE NEW ENGLAND MIND

THE SEVENTEENTH CENTURY

PERRY MILLER

HARVARD UNIVERSITY PRESS
CAMBRIDGE, MASSACHUSETTS

1954

DISTRIBUTED IN GREAT BRITAIN BY
Geoffrey Cumberlege
OXFORD UNIVERSITY PRESS
LONDON

PRINTED IN THE UNITED STATES OF AMERICA

For

KENNETH

FOREWORD

The title which I have given this work may appear presumptuous in the light of its actual contents, for the book is rather a topical analysis of various leading ideas in colonial New England than a history of their development. I must plead in extenuation that I offer this as the first volume in a projected series upon the intellectual history of New England to extend through the eighteenth and early nineteenth centuries, that I conceive of it as setting the stage or furnishing points of departure for the subsequent account, and that in the portion to follow I shall begin the narrative with the decade of 1660 and there undertake a more sequential tracing of modifications and changes. The present work, therefore, is to stand as a preliminary survey, as a map of the intellectual terrain of the seventeenth century, disregarding for the moment occasional and chronological phases. I am herein concerned with defining and classifying the principal concepts of the Puritan mind in New England, of accounting for the origins, inter-relations, and significances of the ideas. The next volume will partially overlap this, but herein I have not considered chronology so much as structure, nor the morphology so much as the anatomy of the Puritan mind. I have limited the field to the seventeenth century and not overstepped the second decade of the eighteenth, which seems to me the furthest extent to which one may say that the original system of Puritanism survived without drastic alteration.

My project is made more practicable by the fact that the first three generations in New England paid almost unbroken allegiance to a unified body of thought, and that individual differences among particular writers or theorists were merely minor variations within a general frame. I have taken the liberty of treating the whole literature as though it were the product of a single intelligence, and I have appropriated illustrations from whichever authors happen to express a point most conveniently. Seldom have I exhibited a passage from one Puritan writing which could not be paralleled by several more that assert the same thing in different words. Since this volume is of necessity concentrated upon the content of the thought, since it aims at a descriptive analysis of what the New England mind took to be truth, it is offered as a chapter in the history of ideas; the design has called for large excursions into the background of English and European opinion, particularly in questions of dialectic and rhetoric, but I have deliberately avoided giving more than passing notice to the social or economic influences. Investigation of these factors in the English setting would obviously lead too far afield, while the correlations of American environment with intellectual growth will, I trust, be more specifically treated in subsequent volumes. In order that a beginning may be made, even though by main force, I have taken Puritanism for granted, and starting from the fact of its existence, however it may have come into being, have sought to discover what it held, what spirit and what thoughts inspired it and to what it aspired, what combinations it made of older ideas and what it added of its own, and what finally, in the broadest terms, it can be said to have meant or still to mean as a living force. I assume that Puritanism was one of the major expressions of the Western intellect, that it achieved an organized synthesis of concepts which are fundamental to our culture, and that therefore it calls for the most serious examination.

At every point I have phrased the ideas first of all in the language of the times, and undoubtedly employed many quotations, for I know no other way in which the terminology of seventeenth-century thinking can be made accurately intelligible to contemporary appreciation. It ought to be unnecessary in a work of history for the historian to advertise his impartiality, but Puritanism has recently become the center of so many critical storms that any writer upon the subject is greeted at once with the question of whether he be friend or foe. At the risk of appearing too conspicuously before the curtain and stating baldly what ought to be visible in the performance, I should like to make clear that I wholeheartedly admire the integrity and profundity of the Puritan character but that I am far from sharing in its code or from finding delight in its every aspect. Yet I can honestly say that my interest in Puritanism has not been a matter of liking or disliking. Regardless of the repute in which it may be held today, Puritanism is of immense historical importance: it was not only the most coherent and most powerful single factor in the early history of America, it was a vital expression of a crucial period in European development, and those who would understand the modern world must know something of what it was and of what heritages it has bequeathed to the present. Undoubtedly a more direct attack upon the subject might be made by writing upon Puritanism in England or Calvinism in Europe rather than upon the New Englanders, who were a small and often peculiar group, who were not called upon to deal with some of the greater issues, and who produced no writer comparable either to Milton or Bunyan. My concentration upon these provinces is to some extent justified by my larger intention, since I am a historian of a portion of America, but even in terms of the seventeenth century there are incalculable advantages to be gained from considering New England intensively and alone. What may be lost in extensiveness or range is compensated by the virtues of limitation; the colonies supply, as it were, a laboratory where the experiment can be studied under more controlled conditions than in the mother country. When the thought of New England is regarded not from a New England or even from an American point of view, but is seen as what in truth it was, a part, and an important part, of the whole thought of the seventeenth century, exemplifying the essential characteristics and struggling with the most importunate problems of the epoch, then and only then can both the provincial and European scene be illuminated. Quite apart from the adventitious interest that attaches to New England Puritans as founders of an American nation, they are also spokesmen for what we call the Renaissance, and I believe that the principal value of this volume will prove to be that it makes some contribution to our study of general intellectual history.

Because the pages are loaded with quotations, the problem of annotation has proved exceedingly difficult. The number of titles by New England writers, or by English Puritans whose works need to be considered along with them, are legion; were I to supply a footnote indicating the exact source of every direct quotation or the inspiration for many remarks which are not literal citation, I should republish the complete bibliography of early New England, with various additions, not merely once but many times over, and the documentation would run to as many pages as the text. In most instances, it is a matter of complete indifference or chance that a quotation comes from Cotton instead of Hooker, from Winthrop instead of Willard; all writers were in substantial agreement upon all the propositions which I am discussing in this book, even though they differed among themselves upon some of the issues I shall take up in the sequel, and only an occasional student actively engaged in research would profit from knowing the sources for particular passages. Consequently, I have assumed the power to omit such annotations, and to supply through the remaining notes only the sort of marginal comment or bibliography that may be of value to more general readers. Meanwhile, an annotated copy of this volume has been filed in the Harvard College Library along with a bound set of complete notes, in which references are given to the provenience of each quotation and often to other instances of like utterances in the New England writings. For two topics alone has it seemed necessary that bibliographies be furnished in this publication; at several points where I have relied upon particular bodies of literature I have listed the chief titles in corresponding notes.

It might be well to point out that in order to formulate the contents of the New England mind, in addition to their own publications and unpublished manuscripts, I have drawn upon three kinds of material not composed by New Englanders, and have often illustrated colonial positions or attitudes with the words of English and continental writers. Particularly I have used the textbooks which were employed in Puritan education, for the thought was so directly based upon the propositions of the liberal arts that the textbooks may justly be viewed as an integral part of the intellectual life, as containing the premises of all Puritan discourse. My frequent appeal to his authority on all these matters reveals that I have depended heavily upon Professor Samuel Eliot Morison's *Harvard College in the Seventeenth Century,* and a full list of the relevant titles can readily be consulted in his excellent chapters on the curriculum. Secondly, I have made little distinction, for the purposes of defining and illustrating the ideas, between the writers of New England and the particular English theologians and preachers of the early seventeenth century under whom New Englanders studied, whom they read and digested before their migration and continued to read for over a century thereafter. Though these men never set foot in America, they exerted so deep and pervasive an influence upon the colonial intellect that their books must be treated to all intents and purposes as though they were productions of that intellect. As my constant mention of their names will suggest, three great teachers in particular were responsible for much of the New England creed: William Perkins, William Ames, and John Preston. My exploration of this "background" material would have been infinitely better managed had I had the advantage of Professor William Haller's *The Rise of Puritanism,* which came to my hands only after the completion of my manuscript; the reader can there find a superb orientation in the vast literature which, for the settlers of New England, was as much theirs as any they created of themselves. Thirdly, I have sometimes used certain books by English Puritans and Nonconformists that postdate the migration as though they too were of a piece with contemporaneous New England works. A certain caution must be exercised in construing the ideas of any Englishmen after 1640 as wholly synonymous with those of New Englanders, for Puritanism at home expanded and proliferated rapidly with the beginnings of the Civil Wars, and was obliged to take stock of innumerable questions which never arose in the colonies. Nevertheless, on general theological points at least, Richard Baxter and John Owen can be interpreted as saying what any orthodox New Englander would have said, or did say, upon the same themes.

Not least among the pleasures of scholarship are the incurred indebtednesses, and it is a particular pleasure for me to express my large obligation to the John Simon Guggenheim Memorial Foundation, which made possible a year of freedom and travel without which this work could never have been undertaken. I gratefully acknowledge the many services of the Harvard College Library, the Massachusetts Historical Society, the Boston Public Library, the British Museum, and the Bibliothèque Nationale. I found not merely assistance and coöperation but much needed instruction at Dr. Williams' Library. I thank Dr. Urs Schwarz of Zürich for his help in furthering these researches as well as for much else, and the authorities of the library of the University of Zürich, who provided free access to their invaluable stores. I have profited frequently from the counsel of Dr. Richard B. Schlatter, and from the kindness of Mr. Granville Hicks, who went beyond the limits of his official duties as the publisher's reader to subject some chapters to his searching and fruitful analysis. The book would have been improved throughout had I been guided at all points, as I have been explicitly at several, by my colleague, Professor Theodore Spencer. Miss Eleanor Wiles has assisted materially in the preparation of the manuscript. Elizabeth Williams Miller has worked with me at every stage of the research and writing.

PERRY MILLER

February 25, 1939
Harvard University

NOTE TO THE SECOND PRINTING

An author is always happy to heed the call for a second issue. I am particularly pleased that over the years since 1939 *The New England Mind: The Seventeenth Century* has proved useful in a variety of fields — literature, philosophy, political theory, and theology — in none of which can I pretend to special competence but on all of which my material touches. The high cost of reproduction gives the present publisher no choice but to use means that prohibit changes beyond a correction of the more egregious misprints. Indeed, were I writing the book afresh, I would alter many emphases; I would have to avail myself of the scholarship which has used it as a point of departure or object of rebuttal. However, what value it possesses lies in such coherence as it achieved at the time of composition. I am by no means certain that I could improve upon it by rewriting, although other students have advanced beyond it and still others will, I trust, go even farther.

As work on the sequel, *The New England Mind: From Colony to Province,* progressed, despite the long interruption of the Second World War, I discovered that my project for commencing with 1660 required revision; the second book is obliged, on several points, to reach back to 1630, but the main emphasis is upon the later decades of the seventeenth century and the first three of the eighteenth, when the ideas, the cosmology, the schematic values set forth in this volume underwent a transformation which nobody in the community deliberately advocated, yet to which everybody somehow, and generally with reluctance, contributed. Further investigation and much meditation have at least confirmed my youthful insight into the effectiveness of New England as a laboratory for testing how, if not always why, the modern ethos emerged out of this Protestant scholasticism.

P. M.

August 1, 1953
Harvard University

CONTENTS

BOOK I

RELIGION AND LEARNING

CHAPTER I

THE AUGUSTINIAN STRAIN OF PIETY

Four hundred years after Christ, Augustine of Hippo enacted an arduous pilgrimage, driven by his insatiable quest for satisfactions that nothing of this earth was ever able to supply him. Even while deluding himself with Manichean palliatives, he cried out,

O Truth, Truth! how inwardly even then did the marrow of my soul pant after Thee, when they frequently, and in a multiplicity of ways, and in numerous and huge books, sounded out Thy name to me, though it was but a voice . . . I hungered and thirsted not even after those first works of Thine, but after Thee Thyself, the Truth . . . Yet they still served up to me in those dishes glowing phantasies, than which better were it to love this very sun . . . than those illusions which deceive the mind through the eye.

Twelve hundred years later, in a rude wooden structure by the Connecticut River, built in a newly cleared field that had just been named Hartford, Thomas Hooker preached to faithful Englishmen who had crossed an ocean that they might have the privilege of hearing him. He did not speak in the first person, for he was not uttering *Confessions,* but he spoke of what he and every one of his congregation could attest from their own experience. In his words sounded once more the accents of St. Augustine.

Sin is truly cross and opposite . . . to the Nature of the soul in a right sense: Look at the soul in respect of the end for which it was created, and that impression which is enstamped and left upon it unto this day, whereby it's restlessly carried in the search, and for the procurement of that good for which it was made . . . The soul was made for an end, and good, and therefore for a better than it self, therefore for God, therefore to enjoy union with him, and communion with those blessed excellencies of his . . . this impression remains still upon the soul, though the work thereof is wholly prejudiced . . . Being possessed with sin, the Judgment is blinded and deluded that it mistakes utterly, and perceives not this good, and so pursues other things in the room of it, yet restless and unsatisfied in what it hath, and attains, but it hath not that for which it was made.

Thus, when the wave of religious assertion which we call Puritanism is considered in the broad perspective of Christian history, it appears no longer as a unique phenomenon, peculiar to England of the seventeenth century, but as one more instance of a recurrent spiritual answer to interrogations eternally posed by human existence. The peculiar accidents of time and place did indeed entice Puritanism into entertaining a variety of ideas which were the features of its epoch, yet it was animated by a spirit that was not peculiar to the seventeenth century or to East Anglia and New England. The major part of this volume will necessarily be occupied with local and temporal characteristics, but these were not the substance or the soul of the movement. As Puritanism developed it became more and more encased in technical jargon and increasingly distracted by economic and social issues; as it waned it partook more of the qualities of one age and became less of a gospel for all time. But as long as it remained alive, its real being was not in its doctrines but behind them; the impetus came from an urgent sense of man's predicament, from a mood so deep that it could never be completely articulated. Inside the shell of its theology and beneath the surface coloring of its political theory, Puritanism was yet another manifestation of a piety to which some men are probably always inclined and which in certain conjunctions appeals irresistibly to large numbers of exceptionally vigorous spirits.

I venture to call this piety Augustinian, not because it depended directly upon Augustine—though one might demonstrate that he exerted the greatest single influence upon Puritan thought next to that of the Bible itself, and in reality a greater one than did John Calvin—nor because Puritan thought and Augustine's harmonize in every particular. Some aspects of his work, his defense of the authority of the church and of the magical efficacy of the sacraments, were ignored by Puritans as by other Protestants.[1] I call it Augustinian simply because Augustine is the arch-exemplar of a religious frame of mind of which Puritanism is only one instance out of many in fifteen hundred years of religious history. For a number of reasons many persons in late sixteenth-century England found themselves looking upon the problems of life very nearly as Augustine had viewed them, and, for reasons still difficult to expound, the number of such persons increased during the next six or seven decades. In the 1630's some twenty thousand of them, avowedly inspired by their religious views, settled New England and thus served to leave the impress of Augustine upon the American character. In England, as these spirits became more numerous, they came into conflict with other

Englishmen, some of whom were certainly no less pious and no less Christian, but in very different fashions. When Puritans debated with Richard Hooker, the apologist of the Anglican church, they spoke at cross-purposes, for his intellectual affinities were entirely with Thomas Aquinas and scholastic tradition. The Puritans also were scholastics, but though they and Richard Hooker might use the same terms, their emphases were irreconcilable, and as between the two there can be no doubt that in the writings of Hooker's enemies we shall find the turn of mind and sense of values, even sometimes the very accent, of Augustine. There survive hundreds of Puritan diaries and thousands of Puritan sermons, but we can read the inward meaning of them all in the *Confessions*.

Puritan theology was an effort to externalize and systematize this subjective mood. Piety was the inspiration for Puritan heroism and the impetus in the charge of Puritan Ironsides; it also made sharp the edge of Puritan cruelty and justified the Puritan in his persecution of disagreement. It inspired Puritan idealism and encouraged Puritan snobbery. It was something that men either had or had not, it could not be taught or acquired. It was foolishness and fanaticism to their opponents, but to themselves it was life eternal. Surely most of the first settlers of New England had it; in later generations most of those who did not have it pretended to it. It blazed most clearly and most fiercely in the person of Jonathan Edwards, but Emerson was illuminated, though from afar, by its rays, and it smoldered in the recesses of Hawthorne's intuitions. It cannot be portrayed by description; to be presented adequately there is need for a Puritan who is also a dramatic artist, and Bunyan alone fulfills the two requirements. But in order that we may pursue the story of expression in New England, that we may find larger meanings in the formal intellectual developments, it has seemed advisable to attempt a description of this piety. The subsequent narrative will, I hope, take on added significance as an episode in the history of humanity if we can first of all conceive, even though we do not share, the living reality of the spirit that motivated this particular group of men. Thus I am here endeavoring to portray the piety rather than the abstract theology in which it was embodied, to present it not in the dry metaphysics of scholastic divines, but in such plain statements, thrown deliberately into the present tense, as the most scholastic of the clergy could utter, fortunately, in their less controversial moods. I shall undoubtedly do the material a certain violence by speaking of the sharply defined concepts of systematic divinity in the looser and vaguer language of human passion; yet the great structure of the Puritan creed, ostensibly erected upon the foundation of logic, will have meaning to most students today only when they perceive that it rested upon a deep-lying conviction that the universe conformed to a definite, ascertainable truth, and that human existence was to be had only upon the terms imposed by this truth.

Such a chapter as I am now attempting could never have been written by any true Puritan, for I am seeking to delineate the inner core of Puritan sensibility apart from the dialectic and the doctrine. In Puritan life the two were never so separated; they were indeed inseparable, for systematic theology, now become wearisome to the majority of men, provided Puritans with completely satisfying symbols; it dramatized the needs of the soul exactly as does some great poem or work of art. The religious emotion could not have existed, for them at least, except within the framework of dogma. Although we, starting from other assumptions and thinking as historians rather than as Puritans, may now ask what underlay the doctrine of predestination before we undertake to trace its evolution through the next two centuries, for Puritans themselves such a dissociation of the meaning from the formula was inconceivable. They saw no opposition between the spirit of religion and the letter of theology, between faith and its intellectualization, and they would have found no sense whatsoever in modern contentions that the words and parables of Christ may be understood without reference to an organized body of abstractions. It should also be confessed at once that many of the statements made in this chapter will be found at variance with the later sections. This is not to be wondered at when the nature of theology, and more particularly of theologians, is considered. Puritan sensibility was truly unified and coherent; but it was articulated only in dogmas and logical deductions. Dogmas can easily become severed from their emotional background, even by those who believe in them most passionately, whereupon they often become counters in an intricate intellectual chess game and lose all semblance of their original meaning. The effort to trace these permutations is triply difficult because transformation may come through a subtle shift in emotional connotation, or the same connotation may be preserved within a gradual reformulation of the doctrine, or else there may be a step-by-step progression in both signification and doctrine. It is not surprising, therefore, that among the basic assurances of early seventeenth-century Puritanism, after the Protestant cause had already been argued for a century, there should have been some that did not wholly correspond to the verbal symbols. Finally, we must remember that religion was not the sole, though it was indeed the predominant interest of the Puritans. They were skilled in many sciences besides theology, and they inevitably drew ideas from these sources, sometimes deliberately, more often unwittingly. We shall find that such ideas existed in their minds in more or less happy fusion with their religious convictions, and that when there was latent opposition among them, the Puritans themselves were at best only dimly aware of it. These considerations are almost too elementary to need restatement; still, they indicate cautions to be observed as we seek for a definition of Puritan piety, of the temperamental bias behind the thought, before we undertake to examine the thought itself.

It would, however, be a grave mistake to regard Puritan piety solely as an affair of temperament. We may declare that Puritans universalized their own neurasthenia; they themselves believed that their fears and anxieties came from clear-eyed perception of things as they are. We may say that they derived their ideas from the Bible, from Augustine and Calvin, Petrus Ramus and William Perkins, and that they were influenced by such and such factors in the environment. They believed that, the facts being what they are, one deduction alone was possible. The facts were in the Bible, which was of course the Word of God, but they were also in experience, and a man did not need the sermons of a godly minister to perceive the terms upon which all men struggle through existence; he needed merely to look about him. "Look," says the Puritan preacher, the doctrine is "as in nature, reason teacheth and experience evidenceth"; to deny it "is to go against the experience of all ages, the common sense of all men." It is obvious that man dwells in a splendid universe, a magnificent expanse of earth and sky and heavens, which manifestly is built upon a majestic plan, maintains some mighty design, though man himself cannot grasp it. Yet for him it is not a pleasant or satisfying world. In his few moments of respite from labor or from his enemies, he dreams that this very universe might indeed be perfect, its laws operating just as now they seem to do, and yet he and it somehow be in full accord. The very ease with which he can frame this image to himself makes reality all the more mocking; the world does give men food and drink, but it gives grudgingly, and when "the world says, peace, peace, then suddenly destruction comes upon them as a whirlwind." It is only too clear that man is not at home within this universe, and yet that he is not good enough to deserve a better; he is out of touch with the grand harmony, he is an incongruous being amid the creatures, a blemish and a blot upon the face of nature. There is the majestical roof, fretted with golden fire, and likewise there is man, a noble work that delights not himself. It is certain that the works of God "were all Good and Beautiful as they came out of his Hands," but equally certain that some deed of man "has put all out of Order, and has brought Confusion and Desolation on the works of God." There are moments of vision when the living spirit seems to circulate in his veins, when man is in accord with the totality of things, when his life ceases to be a burden to him and separateness is ecstatically overcome by mysterious participation in the whole. In such moments he has intimations of rightness, of a state of being in which he and his environment achieve perfect harmony, just as in his imagination he has fancied that once he did dwell in paradise. When these moments have passed he endeavors to live by their fading light, struggling against imperfection in the memory of their perfection, or else he falls back, wearied and rebellious, into cynicism and acrimony. All about him he sees men without this illumination, exemplifying the horrors of their detached and forlorn condition. They murder, malign, and betray each other, they are not to be relied upon, they wear themselves out in the chains of lust, their lives have no meaning, their virtues are pretenses and their vices unprofitable. What wonder that we see exorbitancies and confusions in human societies, "when fools and madmen have gotten the reins in their necks, and act all their own pleasure without any control"? Mortals pursue illusions, and success inspires only disgust or despair. They seek forgetfulness in idolatries and narcotics, or delude themselves in sophistical reasonings, and they die at last cursing the day they were born or clutching at the clay feet of their superstitions. Puritans did not believe that they saw things in these terms merely because they were victims of melancholia, but because such things were there to be seen. The so-called "Five Points" of Calvinism were simply a scholastical fashion of saying this much, and to living Calvinists they did not signify five abstract dicta, but a description of the plight of humanity.

The ultimate reason of all things they called God, the dream of a possible harmony between man and his environment they named Eden, the actual fact of disharmony they denominated sin, the moment of illumination was to them divine grace, the effort to live in the strength of that illumination was faith, and the failure to abide by it was reprobation. The heart of this piety was its sense of the overwhelming anguish to which man is always subject, and its appeal to anguish-torn humanity has always been its promise of comfort and of ultimate triumph. The Augustinian strain of piety flows from man's desire to transcend his imperfect self, to open channels for the influx of an energy which pervades the world, but with which he himself is inadequately supplied. It takes flight from the realization that the natural man, standing alone in the universe, is not only minute and insignificant, but completely out of touch with both justice and beauty. It cries out for forgiveness of the sins by which he has cut himself off from full and joyous participation. It proceeds upon the indomitable conviction that man, a part of created being, must once have been happy, though now he is everywhere miserable. It draws sustenance from the moments of exaltation in which glimpses of the original happiness are attained, a bliss which, though seen but faintly, extinguishes by contrast all other delights. It finds the infinite variety of the world's misery reducible to a concrete problem, the relation of the individual to the One. The substance of Augustine's message is this: "Deum et animam scire cupio. Nihilne plus? Nihil omnino." If man once achieved knowledge of God and of his soul, the answer to all other questions would soon follow. The irrepressible demand of the soul for this knowledge is the driving force of the piety. On the one hand, the facts are those ordained by a just God; on the other hand, there are the desires of the soul. The soul must be satisfied, but the facts cannot be denied. There can be no separating the attainment of happiness from the attainment of truth. Solutions which pass lightly over the unpleasant or ignore intractable realities are doomed to failure; so also are those in which the aspirations of the spirit are given insubstantial answers. Wherever the spokesmen for this strain of piety appear, whether in fifth-century Rome or seventeenth-century New England, this is the burden of their sermon, the substance of assertion and the problem for resolution. To the extent that the Puritan generations in New England were able to think and to express their thought, this was the inevitable preoccupation of their discourse.

Long before the seventeenth century, theologians had discovered that the endeavor to formulate this piety centered upon certain fundamental conceptions: God, sin, and regeneration. Each of these ideas received elaborate exposition in the creeds, confessions, and institutes that streamed from the inexhaustible inkwells of Protestant writers; each of them was divided into sub-doctrines, which in turn were sorted into still further theological ramifications. Meanwhile, the basic ideas in their essential meanings remained simple and inviolate. "God" was a word to stand for the majesty and perfection which gleam through the fabric of the world; He was Being, hardly apprehensible to man, yet whose existence man must posit, not so much as *a* being but as *The* Being, the beginning of things and the sustainer, the principle of universal harmony and the guide. "Sin" was in effect a way of setting forth disharmony, of describing man's inability to live decently, his cruelties and his crimes, and also a way of accounting for the accidents, the diseases, and the sorrows which every day befall the good and the bad. On the definition of "regeneration" Protestants expended their greatest ingenuity and differed among themselves most furiously, exemplifying in their controversies all the vindictiveness which they deplored in other men as an evidence of innate depravity. Yet to all Protestants the general conception was the same; it meant substantially that there existed a way in which supernal beauty could be carried across the gulf of separation. It was an inward experience in which the disorder of the universe was righted, when at least some men were brought into harmony with the divine plan. It was the solution to the double problem of religion, reconciling the soul to fact and yet satisfying its desires. It joined God and man, the whole and the particle. God reached out to man with His grace, man reached out to God with his faith. Regeneration meant the repose and the happiness toward which all men grope, because God "is the most pure, perfect, universall, primary, unchangeable, communicative, desirable, and delightfull good: the efficient, patterne, and utmost end *of all good;* without whom there is neither naturall, morall, nor spirituall good in any creature." All men seek the good, but only those who in unforgettable moments are ravished by it ever come to know it.

Since these three conceptions may be called the essentials of any Augustinian and Puritan point of view, our discussion of the piety can perhaps proceed most advantageously by considering them in turn. Once again, at the risk of needless repetition, I should remark that we are not here dealing with the verbal propositions through which the ideas were embodied in technical handbooks, but for the moment we are seeking to understand, as far as we can without resorting to sanctimonious and hackneyed phrases, with what emotional connotations the three beliefs were invested, what they meant, not so much as speculation, but as ever present realities to men of this particular piety, and especially to men in seventeenth-century New England.

GOD

Puritan thinking on the subject of the Deity always confronted the initial difficulty that in one sense thinking about Him was impossible. The Puritan God is entirely incomprehensible to man. The Puritan system rests, in the final analysis, upon something that cannot be systematized at all, upon an unchained force, an incalculable power. God can never be delineated even momentarily in any shape, contour, or feature recognizable to human discourse, nor may His activities be subjected to the laws of reason or of plausibility. He is a realm of mystery, in whom we may be sure that all dilemmas and contradictions are resolved, though just how we shall never in this world even remotely fathom. He is the reason of all things, and though men can "explain" the behavior of things, they cannot pretend to expound the reason of reasons. The seventeenth-century theologian, like the modern scientist, was perpetually explaining his world without being able to give the reason for its being precisely the kind of world which he explained.

The theologian was no more deterred than is his successor the scientist from the labors of exposition by this confession of fundamental ignorance. Time and time again a textbook or catechism begins with the incomprehensible God, and then proceeds to dogmatize confidently about His character and behavior. Some Puritans pay no more than lip service to the doctrine, and Cotton Mather in his heart of hearts never doubted that the divinity was a being remarkably like Cotton Mather. Yet, though individual Puritans might forget its implications, to Puritanism itself the idea was fundamental that God, the force, the power, the life of the universe, must remain to men hidden, unknowable, and unpredictable. He is the ultimate secret, the awful mystery. His essence "is capable properly of no definition"; all we can say is that He "is an incomprehensible, first, and absolute Being." He cannot be approached directly; man cannot stand face to face with Him any more than the stubble or the wax can draw near the fire: "He is a consuming fire to the sonnes of men, if they come to him immediately." His thoughts go beyond man's thoughts, "as much as the distance is betweene heaven and earth." We stand before Him, said John Preston, as a man upon the shore of an infinite sea:

> If he goes into the deepe, he is drowned: You may looke into *Gods* Essence, and see and admire it; but to think that thou couldest comprehend *God,* is, as if a man should think to hold the whole sea in the hollow of his hand.

The metaphors of the sea and of the sun were favorites with Puritan writers. Thomas Shepard used them both at Cambridge in Massachusetts Bay: the glory of God no man or angel shall know, "their cockle shell can never comprehend this sea"; we can only apprehend Him by knowing that we cannot comprehend Him at all, "as we admire the luster of the sun the more in that it is so great we can not behold it." At the end of the century Samuel Willard began his gigantic tome on the "compleat" body of divinity, in which over a thousand folio pages are required to tell what man may comprehend, by declaring that all reason is too finite to comprehend the infinite, "too shallow to contain the deep, the bottomless; too narrow to grasp the boundless; too little comprehensive to include this incomprehensible Object."

Men who could lose sight of this doctrine, who could say that God is such and such a being or that He conforms "of necessity" to these or those rules, could not be Puritans. "What God is, none can perfectly define, but that hath the Logicke of God himselfe"—this might well serve by itself for a definition of the Puritan spirit. However, it was also clear that no men, not even Puritans, could worship, much less obey, an illimitable mystery. Should human beings be required to contemplate forever an incomprehensible essence, their religious life might become an anarchic surrender to ineffable impulses, and no result was further from Puritan intentions. Therefore Puritan textbooks hastened to assert that while we cannot define God we may piece together "an imperfect description which commeth neerest to unfold Gods nature." This imperfect description was achieved by enumerating in logical sequence what were called God's "attributes." Strictly speaking the attributes have no existence outside the human intellect. God is one, indivisible, timeless act, but as such He is utterly meaningless to us: "we must needs have a diversified representation of it." The attributes are representations of the divine essence in terms with which the human reason can deal; they are "divine Predications, or Titles." They are not "divers things in God, but they are divers only in regard of our understanding, and in regard of their different effects on different objects." Diverse aspects of the divine essence cannot in fact be separated; yet from the human point of view they must be distinguished, and in thinking of them men are compelled to separate one from another "notionally." "They are not distinguished at all in God, but onely to us-ward, according to our manner of conceiving." Religion is what man believes about God, not necessarily what God in Himself is.

The doctrine of attributes is designed "to help our understanding the better to conceive of the Essence of God." The very method by which the list of attributes is reached shows that they are not really characteristics of God but creations of the intellect. If there is a God, the reason feels confident that He must be perfect; if He is perfect, then there are some things that He is *not*. Thus the reason arrives first at those attributes known as the "negative" ones, those which "remove from God all imperfection," which are simplicity, eternity, immensity, immutability. Furthermore, the reason continues, though God is indeed outside time and space, He must still stand in some relation to the spatial-temporal world; ergo, He must possess "relative" attributes, such as creation, providence, lordship, benignity, mercy, justice. Finally, while the mind cannot say what God is in Himself, it nevertheless has certain connotations inevitably attached to the idea of perfection, by which "our understanding is helped in our meditation of God"; since God must be perfection itself, the mind invests Him with the "positive" attributes of wisdom, will, holiness, liberty, and omnipotency.

The theory of attributes saved the doctrine of an incomprehensible God from resulting in folded hands and nerveless contemplation of Nirvana; it gave the mind something to go upon and furnished foundations for theology and the sciences. At the same time it did not, at least theoretically, curtail the infinite perfection of God or lessen human awareness of the mystery. After God has been described as the sum of the attributes, He becomes in fact all the more difficult to imagine pictorially, since He is now envisaged as constantly active in a number of thoroughly contradictory directions. He possesses all the attributes and in Him they balance perfectly, one against another. John Preston, from whom the New England Puritans derived a large measure of their instruction—and upon this point in particular—wrote at the beginning of the century in England:

> All the Attributes of God are equall among themselves, not one higher than another, or larger than another; for if hee be *simple,* and there are not two things in him, then his Attributes, and his essence, and himselfe are the same; and if so, one cannot exceed another; his *mercy* is not beyond his *justice,* nor his *justice* beyond his *wisedome.*

At the end of the century Samuel Willard in Boston was still declaring:

> The Divine Attributes in God are *not contrary one to another.* There is no clashing between them; but they do perfectly agree in their Essence. . . . God is all Justice, and yet he is all Mercy too; neither doth his being all just, hinder his being all merciful, or contrarily.

Here was a statement which the pious might accept but never understand. The mind will never fathom how these qualities exist side by side in one consistent being; though men speculate to the end of time they will never conceivably reconcile plenary forgiveness with implacable righteousness. We must regard the balance of the attributes as both a fact and a logical necessity, but we must not expect to know how the balance is maintained. We can conceive of God only through His effects, which are varied, or through our reason, which is discursive and therefore must distinguish; hence in our ideas of God the attributes will not only become separated, but some will be emphasized more than others. Thereby we merely illustrate the limitations of intelligence: "we ought to believe that the divine Attributes are one with the Essence, and one with another." If we allow theology to be swayed by our emotions, if we are led by our own sternness into exalting His justice above His mercy, or are lured by our tenderness into pleading His mercy at the expense of His justice, we are guilty of "a gross and dangerous error." Over the entrance to the mansions of Puritan theology might have been inscribed an injunction to all who entered there to abandon partiality.

Puritans did not invent this reasoning. The discovery that man can conceive of God only by clustering the attributes, culled from the meadows of philosophy, around an unknowable essence had been fully exploited by scholastics. In Puritan thought the doctrine received a renewed importance because they, in common with Augustinians of every complexion, medieval or Protestant, accused other theologians of abusing it. With the correctness of their charge we are not now concerned, but rightly or wrongly they believed that for centuries philosophizing divines had mistaken the limitations of the mind for the limits of reality. Theorists had endeavored to confine the unconfinable within artificial distinctions. Thomistic theologians had erred by making God too rational—an error of which Anglicans like Richard Hooker were still guilty—nominalists had exaggerated His irrationality, Lutherans His mercy. The various "Calvinist" groups started from a fresh realization that to fix too narrow limits or too explicit tendencies upon the principle of the cosmos was to court disaster. The world is not governed by reason, or power, or love, but by "I am," who is a jealous God and wreaks vengeance upon those who idolize His titles instead of worshiping Himself. Puritans reasserted the divine simplicity and warned men to guard their thinking lest they again identify God's essence with whichever of the attributes seemed most attractive to them. They were endeavoring to reach truth about God by deductions from the content of their conception of Him, whereas most of their predecessors, they believed, had arrogantly pretended to extract deductions from His inscrutable essence.

The first generation of New England writers repeatedly insisted that the attributes are modes of human understanding rather than of the divine nature, and they displayed admirable caution in speaking of the essence. As Thomas Hooker told his congregation, "In these Secrets and depths of

Gods Spiritual Dispensations with the souls of men, we must learn *to be wise to sobriety,* and adore the waies of God which are too wonderful for us." He would employ human learning when he felt that "it makes way for the understanding of the thing in hand," but he would observe a healthy moderation: "Curious we should not be, careless we must not be." Yet enemies were prompt to point out that, for all their protestation, Puritans committed the very sin they condemned, and to an exorbitant degree. It is difficult to determine the justice of this charge. If we took Puritan writers literally we should exonerate them, for they dilated continually upon the balance of the attributes and the impenetrable mystery of the Godhead. Still, in the history of thought what is spoken is less important than what is felt. We must take account not so much of systematic theology as of piety. If the Puritans, for all their admonitions to impartial perceptions of the divine Being, nevertheless emphasized certain conceptions of Him at the expense of others, and even came close to identifying these conceptions with His essence, it was because they were impelled by the spirit which informed their articulated creed.

The very terms in which they posed the problem made it inevitable that they should end by putting more emphasis upon one attribute than upon any other—upon that of sovereignty. For to them the visible world was not the final or the true world; it was a creation of God and it was sustained by Him from moment to moment. Deeper than their belief in the more obvious articles of their creed lay their sense of the world as a created fabric, held together by a continuous emanation of divine power, apt to be dissolved into nothing should the divine energy be withheld. They fastened with particular avidity upon the doctrines in which Christian thinkers had embodied this view. Puritan sermons dwelt incessantly upon the theme of "concursus dei." The world could not make itself, so neither could it continue itself in being; if the power which made all creatures did not preserve them, they would presently return to the first nothingness. "The frame of nature would be dissolved the next moment, if there were not an hand of Providence to uphold and govern all." It was not enough to imagine that God organized a mechanical world and merely set the first wheel in motion:

> As He *predetermins* Second Causes, so He *concurres* with them in their Operations. And this *Praedetermination,* and *Concurse* is so necessary; that there can be no real Effect produced by the Creature without it.

God must be more than the original designer of the creation, He must continuously create it anew out of His infinite stores of being. "All Creatures are dead Cyphers, of no signification, except the Influence of God adds a Figure to them." Wherever the heirs of Augustine appear, they are men for whom a sense of the continuous dependence of matter upon the spirit takes precedence over all other values, and always they verge so close to pantheism that it takes all their ingenuity to restrain themselves from identifying God with the creation.

The Puritans' defense against mere blind vitalism was their conviction that God not only gives being to the world, but, Himself the supreme intelligence, directs it to intelligible ends. This conviction was expressed in the doctrine of "providence." God's government must by definition consist not only of "sustentation" but also of "Direction . . . whereby he orders everything to its right end." Contemplation of this theme provided occasion for some of the loftiest flights of New England rhetoric:

> His hand has made and framed the whole Fabrick of Heaven & Earth. He hath hung out the Globe of this World; hung the Earth upon nothing; drawn over the Canopy of the Heavens; laid the foundation of the earth in its place; Created that Fountain and Center of Light, Heat, & Influence in this lower World, the *Sun*. . . . The Seas, the vast Mountains also, and the Wind so undiscernable in its motions, and other strange Meteors, they are His Work. . . . Those notable changes in the World in the promoting or suppressing, exalting or bringing down of Kingdoms, Nations, Provinces or Persons, they are all wrought by Him. . . . The Yearly seasons, also Seed-time and Harvest, Summer and Winter, binding up and covering the earth with Frost, Ice and Snow, and the releasing and renewing of the face of the Earth again, it's His work.

As men view the world it is full of contingencies, but, though they cannot account for them, they must never forget that "the Lord has an over ruling hand of providence therein." To our eyes time and chance occur to all things, "but in respect of God it is not so: There can Nothing fall out either besides his Knowledge or Intention." Events divinely foreordained invariably come to pass, even those which require the fortuitous convergence upon a single place or moment of a diversity of creatures seemingly acting in complete independence. Many of these creatures are "reasonable," and therefore voluntary agents, nourishing secret intentions and deliberating their measures in their own minds. Their freedom is no illusion, and yet in autonomous pursuit of their sovereign choices they contrive to bring about predetermined consequences. In practice Puritan theology did not engender a nerveless surrender to "fate," but it did contain one tenet which, taken by itself, supported an inexorable fatalism:

> He has decreed when and where every man that comes into the World shall be Born; and where he shall live, in what Country, and in what Town; yea, and in what House too . . . He has decreed when every man shall dy . . . All the Circumstances attending every mans Death, the place and the manner of it, whether he shall dy by Sickness, or by any other Accident, all is determined in Heaven before it comes to pass on the Earth.

The ground for the Puritan objection to card games and dice-throwing was not primarily that these pastimes were sinful because enjoyable, or that they wasted men's estates—though this was a secondary consideration—but that they prostituted divine providence to unworthy ends. Lotteries are appeals to providence, said Increase Mather, and so they "may not be used in trivial matters." God determines the cast of the dice or the shuffle of the cards, and we are not to implicate His providence in frivolity. It was a symptom of the waning of piety in the eighteenth century that the colony engineered lotteries, with clerical blessing, for the benefit of Harvard College; devoted as the founders were to that school of the prophets, they would never have regarded it a sufficient excuse for making profits out of divine determinations.

If the power that created the universe now governs it, then it must be clear that He wills what happens in it. Puritan theology did not consciously exalt the will of God above His reason or His goodness; it was simply that the Puritan's intense belief in unremitting supervision by a supernatural power, coupled with his equally intense awareness that the power was beyond human comprehension, made it difficult for him to speculate about the reasons for God's actions or to discover clearly wherein they were always good. Meanwhile, what befell him in life—accidents, earthquakes, shipwrecks, and deliverances—furnished tangible evidence of the operation of God's will. What God decreed no man could fail to perceive; the reasons for His decreeing one thing rather than another had to be guessed or, as often as not, foregone. Divines were compelled to confess that they could find no reason beyond the mere enactment of God when "Men of shallow heads grow rich and get great Estates, when men of understanding can thrive at no Hand." The reasons why God created such a world as this and none other are far beyond our ken; meantime the world which He has created and still governs is an ever present reminder of His will. The most we can know is that by His almighty power He has ordered things as they are. Sometimes in the world of nature He uses instrumental causes, which we can trace, but if the reason of the being of things be followed to the top, "this Will of God, is the First Cause of all things," and we cannot understand it or trace its logic. Had God created the world "of necessity," it would have been eternal; but since it was obviously created in time, God must have brought it forth by a free act of choice. The decree of God, said John Norton, is "His eternal purpose of working all things according to the counsel of his will." Thus, while Puritan piety insisted upon the undecipherable nature of God, and warned against affixing a disproportionate importance to any one of the ideas which we employ in thinking about His unthinkable essence, nevertheless it did focalize human emotions. Had Puritans been cloistered hermits or contemplative sages they would have found time perhaps to marvel as much at God's wisdom as at His sway, but since they led exceedingly active lives, it was His rule with which they had most frequently to deal. Since God was not bound by any logic that man could discover, He generally appeared in these contacts to be exceedingly arbitrary, and the speculative certainty that God was good became secondary to the pragmatic certainty that He was sovereign.

That God is arbitrary may be perceived not only by the outward lives of men, but also by their inward histories. The Gospel is preached to thousands; some give it little heed and some strive to obey, but whether this or that man receives a renewal of spirit obviously depends on something outside himself. He cannot work it in himself by his own efforts, no matter how hard he tries. The doctrine of predestination seems harsh and unreasonable when viewed simply as a doctrine. When we consider it as a description of experience, we see at once that just as the rewards of rank or wealth depend upon the apparent chance of birth or opportunity, and wisdom upon the accident of intellectual ability, so the achieving of spiritual illumination depends upon whether or not it is given. "The greatest number of mankind are groping in the dark, seeking an object in which to find their happiness"; those to whom He does show Himself are no whit better men than those to whom He does not appear, "so that his meer good pleasure is herein displayed." The creatures have been made like pots for the maker's purposes:

> But *God,* being the first cause, may have what end hee will in governing his creatures, and no man can say, why doest thou so? he may make some vessels of honour, and some of dishonour, and all for himselfe, and his own glory.

The intensity with which the experience was desired, the reality of it when it came, the impossibility of correlating its coming with any antecedent desert—these were not abstract dogmas but the issues of life or death. Belief in predestination was for the Puritan the penetration of God's sovereignty into his personality. Therefore it was a necessary corollary from the attribute of sovereignty that "God doth not visit all alike in the world, whose sins are alike, but picks and chuseth as he sees meet, some to be monuments of his severity, while others are left." And for the Puritan both articles were more than mere doctrines, they were first and foremost descriptions of fact.

Piety is not dialectic, and what men believe in their hearts does not need to be logical. Yet the strong emphasis which Puritanism placed upon the absolute sovereignty of God made it necessary for theologians to keep an eye on consistency, lest they be compelled to admit with their adversaries that they had sacrificed other attributes to their glorification of the one. Consequently the writings of English and American Puritans devoted considerable space to asserting, and as far as possible proving, that the arbitrary will of God must also be good. At the end of the century Samuel Willard intimated that congregations were growing weary of endless dispute over whether God wills things because they are good or whether things are good because God wills them; Willard endeavored to silence the debate by awarding judgment to both contentions at once. Since all the attributes are one, he said, "then God both wills the things because they are good . . . and also they are good because he wills them, his Active Will put the actual goodness into them." Willard's disposition to compromise is indicative of his period; earlier in the century the theologians, while far from denying that the things God wills must be good, unhesitatingly founded the goodness upon the fact of their having been willed. William Perkins said roundly, "A thing is not first of all reasonable and iust, and then afterward willed by God: but it is first of all willed by God, and thereupon becomes reasonable and iust." John Preston said that the creatures must seek for perfection out of themselves, but God is the first cause and all perfection is in Himself:

> In our judging of the waies of *God,* we should take heed of framing a modell of our owne, as to thinke because such a thing is iust, therefore the *Lord* wils it: the reason of this conceit is, because we thinke that *God* must goe by our rule; we forget this, that every thing is just because he wils it; it is not that God wils it, because it is good or just. But we should . . . finde out what the will of *God* is; for that is the rule of justice and equity; for otherwise it was possible that the *Lord* could erre, though he did never erre: that which goes by a rule, though it doth not swarve, yet it may; but if it be the rule it selfe, it is impossible to erre . . . What *God* wils is just, because he is the rule it self; therefore in the mysteries of predestination, we are to say thus with our selves; Thus I finde the *Lord* hath set it downe, thus hee hath expressed himselfe in his Word. such is his pleasure; and therefore it is reason, and just, such against which there can be no exception.

Deriving their instruction from such teachers as Preston, the New Englanders enshrined it in sermons and catechisms: "God's good pleasure is the first and best cause of all things." Consequently, though the poor creature is naturally "loth to be damned," yet "he yields this to God, that he may with all equity do it." The will of God is just because it is itself the source of justice.

Also in the interests of consistency, the Puritans were led to a further deduction: if the creation is ruled by God's will, and His will is itself the norm of justice and equity, the universe must be essentially good. They may be described as cosmic optimists. On this score they again show their affinity with Augustine rather than with scholasticism; where Thomas spends years of dialectical effort to prove the justice of fact, Augustine depends on the moment of aesthetic vision; he, and the Puritans after him, seek for those perspectives of vision in which evil becomes resolved into the design of the whole, like shadows in a picture. They rest their trust that whatever is is good upon the *a priori* conviction that it must be good, not upon dialectical proof. Augustine concluded, "So long, therefore, as they are, they are good . . . Thou didst make all things good, nor is there any substance at all that was not made by Thee." The Puritan preacher exhorts his flock:

> And therefore, I say, when you see such a vanitie and emptinesse in the Creatures, labour to see the more fulnesse in *God* . . . to think with thy selfe there is not the least thing without this providence, there is not the least Creature that makes a motion, this way, or that way, but as it is guided and directed by him.

Augustine argues the goodness of the world from considering its creation, while his Puritan successor argues from its government, but both agree that what flows from goodness must be good. When the world's wrong is looked upon "with the eye of Reason," Satan seems to hold sway, "but whilest you look upon it in the Scripture, you shall find its motions ordered exactly by, and subservient unto Gods will." His dispensations are various and mysterious, "many times past our finding out: yet in the end, the righteousness of his Government shall be manifest." Labor expended, as with the scholastics, in proving dialectically that God is both wise and equitable in His dealings with men will be fruitless; we should therefore with faith and patience "wait for a good issue," secure in our assurance that it is bound to come.

Yet men are indeed frail. They could never bear up with nothing more to sustain them than an assurance that there must be somewhere a reason for their agony. The disproportion between the wisdom of God and the knowledge of man would be a torment were there no bridge thrown across the chasm:

> As when the members of the body are reached and stretched beyond their compasse, it chaseth away all sleep and rest: so when the minde is set upon the rack by such transcendent meditations, it rendeth the soul with vexation and restlesse disquietnesse.

Therefore the sovereign God, who is also merciful, has patiently explained all that we really need to know in a language we can understand. He does not leave us to the delusive light of natural reason, but gives us a law, not "in more obscure termes, or so as only to be drawn by Consequence, but this shall be expressed in so many words"; it is "written as in Capitall Letters, that every one that runneth may read it, and none may plead excuse or exemption." That Protestantism appealed to the authority of the Bible against the authority of the Pope is a platitude of history. That the Calvinists were vehement asserters of its finality is also common knowledge. What is frequently forgotten is that without a Bible, this piety would have confronted chaos. It could not have found guidance in reason, because divine reason is above and beyond the human; not in the church, because

God is not committed to preserving the orthodoxy or purity of any institution; not in immediate inspiration, because inward promptings are as apt to come from the Devil as from God; not from experimental science, because providence is arbitrary and unpredictable; not from philosophy, because philosophy arises from the senses, which are deceptive, or from innate ideas, which are corrupted, or from definitions of the attributes, which are mental creations. Unless the formless transcendence consents, at some moment in time, to assume the form of man and to speak "after an humane manner," men will have nothing to go upon. In the Bible God has so spoken. He has not therein uttered the naked truth about Himself, He has not revealed His essence; His secret will remains secret still, as we witness daily in the capricious orderings of providence. The Bible contains His revealed will, tells men what is expected, but does not explain why, for even if it were explained men could never understand their relation to the whole drama of creation.

That the Bible is the inspired word of God rested for the Puritans upon absolute conviction. They did not reject the help of historical confirmations, but when speaking most characteristically they did not stop to argue. The Mahometans, John Davenport declared, "have no Word for their beleeving in *Mahomet,* but the lying *Alchoran,* but we have the Scripture." The proof which a Christian has, said Cotton Mather, "is of that sort, that assures him, The *Fire* is indeed the *Fire;* even a *Self-evidencing, and scarce utterable Demonstration.*" The Bible is fiat, it cannot be questioned, it alone is authority. "If the word speake for thee, it is no matter though all men and Angels speake against thee; and if the word condemne thee, it is no matter who speakes for thee." We must not shape our rule to suit men but must align men by the rules: "Crook not God's rules to the experience of men, (which is fallible, and many times corrupt,) but bring men unto the rule, and try men's estates herein by that." No sense or feeling nor any reasoning has the slightest validity "but that which is from and according to the Word of God." Any proposition asserted by Scripture is true: "When I am sure that God has said it, I believe it, for in things Divine there can be no sublimer proof then the testimony of God himself." Throughout the seventeenth century New England ministers reiterated this teaching, and there was hardly a man in the whole community who doubted it.

Consequently, as we endeavor to trace the history of Puritan thought in America we must remember that the Puritan looked upon discoverable truth as already discovered, set down in black and white, once and for all, by the supreme wisdom. There was nothing essential to be learned outside revelation. Puritan thought was incurably authoritarian and legalistic. Every proposition had to be bolstered by chapter and verse, and the margins of books, whether of divinity or politics, science or morals, the margins even of love-letters, had to be studded with citations. But one further consideration must at the same time be borne in mind, and it is of no less importance: the authority to which the Puritan thinker appealed as final and decisive was not itself the ultimate authority, and though the Puritan may have forgotten to distinguish between the two on occasion, he never did so for very long. The soul of Puritan theology is the hidden God, who is not fully revealed even in His own revelation. The Bible is His declared will; behind it always lies His secret will. His secret purpose "hee hath in himselfe, before al worlds, and hath not discovered it to the creature"; His revealed will is the purpose "which he hath made known to us by his word." His secret will is His decree of what shall be, His revealed will is His command of what ought to be. By the former, "God disposeth of all the affairs of his Creatures, according to his infinite wisdom, and good pleasure"; by the latter, He "prescribes to us our Duty, and how we ought to carry towards him in all things." Undoubtedly the two are not in fact opposed, but "in our manner of conception and expression," especially according to our experience, they come "under a diverse consideration," and can often seem thoroughly contradictory. We must obey the commanding will; we must pray for the things revealed, not for things according to His secret will, "for so we cannot guide our actions." We must not be wise "above what is written"; if we inquire further into the mystery of the Godhead than what is revealed, we will attain not knowledge but blindness. The visible church is not founded upon the secret intention, "but onely his revealed will signified in the Scriptures."

Thus the Puritan conception of God resulted in a Puritan habit of mind which must be called literalism. And yet, by the very terms of the conception, it was literalism up to a point; there was a reservation, however theoretical. The reservation may not seem very significant; to us it may appear quite superfluous, when there exists only one authoritative source for human knowledge, to give thought to a further realm of absolute knowledge beyond the explicit realm, since that region remains forever inaccessible to man. Yet the space between revelation and the inconceivable absolute, between the revealed will and the secret will, between the command and the decree, between knowledge and the searing flame, was from the point of view of orthodox apologetics the one fissure in the impregnable walls of systematic theology; from the point of view of history, it was the portal through which ran the highway of intellectual development.

SIN

Puritan divines counted that day lost in which they did not spend ten or twelve hours in their studies. They sacrificed their health to the production of massive tomes which demonstrated beyond the shadow of a doubt that man, created upright, fell of his own untrammeled choice into a corruption so horrible as to deserve the worst of punishments and so abject as to preclude all hope of recovery by his unaided efforts. Imposing though the sheer bulk of this literature may be as a monument to clerical industry, it probably never convinced anyone who was not already in profound agreement. The doctrines of original sin, of the depravity of man, and of irresistible grace were not embraced for their logic, but out of a hunger of the human spirit and an anxiety of the soul.

On this score the Puritans exhibit most clearly their descent from Augustine. The same subjective insight, the same turning of consciousness back upon itself, the same obsession with individuality, the same test of conclusions not so much by evidence or utility as by the soul's immediate approbation or revulsion—these qualities which appear in Augustine almost for the first time in Western thought and give him his amazing "modernity," reappear in force among the early Puritans. Like his, their meditations are intensely introspective, and in their own breasts they find the two fundamental issues: the natural emptiness of the heart and its consuming desire for fullness. From the depths of imperfection the soul conceives of God as flawless perfection, whom it cannot hold responsible for its own desolation: "Because my soul dared not be displeased at my God, it would not suffer aught to be Thine which displeased it." The soul must therefore conclude that it is itself the cause for its plight; becoming further aware that the will nevertheless deliberately persists in evil, the soul cries out in anguish, "O rottenness! O monstrosity of life and profundity of death! Could I like that which was unlawful only because it was unlawful?" From such an insight flows the piety of Augustine, from the double conviction that in a world emanating from all-good, all-perfect Being, man lives at odds with it, and that nevertheless the maimed soul, even while persisting in evil, longs for deliverance from the body of this death, for reinstatement in the created harmony.

The similarity of mood between Augustine and the Puritans could be illustrated merely by the frequency with which he is quoted in Puritan writing. Thomas Hooker begins a discussion of regeneration thus:

> There is an old phrase, which Saint *Austin* propounded in his time, and Divines take it up with one consent in this case, and that is this, *that God of an unwilling will, doth make a willing will.*

The high estimation in which Puritans held the name of Augustine is revealed when Hooker continues to call him "Saint," though this use of the word was generally proscribed as a Popish corruption. But even when they were not directly borrowing Augustine's phrases, the Puritans were speaking out of the same spirit. New England diarists had not the literary genius of the author of the *Confessions* and the *Soliloquies,* nor could the divines put autobiographies into their sermons; still at their more pedestrian pace they followed his example in relying for the demonstration of original sin and innate depravity upon an analysis of the soul. If the soul, which is a spiritual substance, is ever to find peace, it must return to its creator: "Its rest must bee in God; as the Rivers runne into the Sea, and as every body rests in its center." Even souls that have never been touched by compunction still betray the soul's desire; even those too blind to know that they lack sight exhibit an unconscious craving for vision:

For, looke what the Soule is to the body, the same is the grace of Gods Spirit to the Soule. When the Soule is deprived of Gods Spirit, there followes a senselesse stupidnesse upon the heart of a man. . . .

Goaded by his appetite for happiness, man ranges over the world, glutting his senses with enjoyments which give no relief beyond the delusive moment; in his inability to find enduring comfort in a surfeit of pleasures man exhibits at once the desperateness of his present condition and the loftiness of his origin:

The eyes and the eares are the inlets or doores of the soule, through which innumerable objects enter, yet is not that spacious roome filled, neither doth it euer say it is enough, but like the daughters of the horsleach, crys giue, giue! and which is most strang, the more it receius, the more empty it finds it self, and sees an impossibility, euer to be filled, but by him in whom all fullnes dwells.

A "Leprous person" can have little use for a gold chain, and rich apparel is wasted upon "a dead carkasse." Unless he find forgiveness, unless he be reinstated, man cannot overcome separateness; his appetites will grow only the more exorbitant by feeding upon substitutes.

The want of this takes off the sweetness of al the comforts, contentments, the sap and rellish of al priviledges, and the confluence of all Earthly Excellencies that can be enjoyed in this Pilgrimage, when the soul is under the pressures of Gods displeasure, and the tyranny of his own distempers, which carries him from God, and keeps him under the dreadful indignation of the Almighty, present him then with the beauty of al the choycest blessings that ever any man had on Earth, yea, what ever others hoped for, but in vain. Put them into his hand, conceive him possessed of the fulness of al worldly perfections, Crowns, Kingdoms, Honors, and preferments, the broken heart tramples al under foot with neglect, what is that to me, saies the soul? had I al the Wealth to enrich me, al Honors to advance me, Pleasures and Delights to content me, and my sins stil to damn me? miserable man that ever I was born in the midst of al these falsly conceived comforts. This sowr Sawce spoils al the Sweetmeat, this dram of poyson makes deadly al the delights and pleasures that possibly can be attained or expected.

Terrifying though such a prospect is, the ultimate horror is not merely the vanity of the worldly quest, but the willfulness with which man persists in it. "We not only have these lusts, but we love them." We are swaggerers who reply to correction by exaggerating our faults; because we are unable of our own power to escape the tools of desire, we refuse the offered help.

> There is an incapability in our minds to receive this spiritual light by which we might be enabled to come to the right discovery of our Corruptions . . . The sinner at first would not see his sinnes were it in his power and might he have his own mind, he would have the ghastly visage of them gone out of his sight.

Yet even such defiance is a sham, a piece of bravado, springing from a secret knowledge that though mercy and salvation "were laid downe upon the naile for believing and receiving of it," a man cannot do it of himself. As long as the heart continues cross to the Almighty, as long as it is separate from Him, the burden will remain insufferable and insupportable. Again and again analysis of the heart reveals that "as long as this remains unsubdued, there is no end of his sorrows, nor end of his prayers in suing to the Almighty for succor and relief." The lesson does not have to be learned by reading the history of Adam or by memorizing the logic of predestination; it is familiar to all men in their terrors, their inferiorities, and their insecurities; no sentence of reprobation can visit them with more condemnation than they themselves know they deserve, at least in the awful moments of honest self-recognition which no man can escape.

At the same time, while the conception of original sin is made vivid by inward knowledge of a man's self, it is reinforced by what a man observes of humanity in general. Even if he be undisturbed by an innate grief of spirit, a man may behold in the spectacle of the race enough to convince him that no created being could have been intentionally assigned the rôle which he sees men enacting every day of their miserable existences. Reason alone, said Willard, "will say that he could not be made such as he is now become, consistent with the wisdom and goodness of his maker." Since there can be no suspicion of the maker's wisdom or goodness, the present plight of mankind cannot have been a part of His original design. When we look over the world, when we see therein the children of men born to affliction as surely as sparks fly upwards,

> when we see Sicknesse, Diseases, Deaths, Perplexities, Disappointments, Discontents, and all manner of Miseries, let us stand still and enquire, How a Creature so excellent in his Creation, is become so Sorrowful and Miserable in his present condition; and to satisfy our Minds about it, let us look back to Man's Apostacy.

Puritan theologians cited testimony of this sort ostensibly to corroborate revelation; they did not expect that in itself the force of such reflections would be sufficient to humble sinners. Even in the face of indisputable facts men persist in their blindness and refuse to make the inescapable inferences. The degradation of man will be realized to the full extent only when viewed with the light of grace, and without that light no amount of factual perception will lead to spiritual understanding. Yet, for all that, the theologians themselves continued to press upon men not yet regenerated the arguments from common knowledge, and their persistent appeal to experience may be taken by us as a sign that the piety was derived as much from it as from Biblical instruction, that the doctrine came not only from the book of Genesis but also from the lesson of mortality. To any objective scrutiny man as he exists seems "like an old House gone to decay"; yet the observer must infer that the ruinous heap indicates "what a famous Structure it once was, but is now nothing but Rubbish." From the miserable fragments can be imaginatively reconstructed the nature with which man was created, "like a fair House, new built, fit to entertain the King of Glory, fit for a Temple for the Holy Ghost to dwell in." Certainly He who created man could not have marred His own handiwork; the fault must lie entirely with man himself. The edge of the doctrine of innate depravity was made sharp on the whetstone of human responsibility. It was obvious that men had contrived to bring upon themselves all the anguish they suffered; it was still more obvious that neither this awareness nor the anguish itself liberated them from the trammels of perversity. A being who brought such a destiny upon himself could hardly expect to find within himself the power to master it. The force of this conclusion gave the Puritan cry for deliverance through the grace of God its urgency and its poignance.

REGENERATION

In a handbook that was widely used in New England John Ball defined faith as "the gift of God, and the act of man: a wonderfull and supernaturall gift of God, and a liuely motion of the heart renewed by grace, and powerfully moued by the Spirit." The moment of regeneration, in which God, out of His compassion, bestows grace upon man and in which man is enabled to reply with belief, was the single goal of the Augustinian piety. Without it individual life was a burden, with it living became richness and joy. Other people have found other names for the experience: to lovers it is love, to mystics it is ecstasy, to poets inspiration. Even ordinary men have their ups and downs, know seasons when they are filled with something more than their usual vitality. That there is some such phenomenon hundreds have testified, though their explanations have varied from calling it a merging of the self with an all-pervading substance to taking it for a physiological crisis caused by the excess secretions of a ductless gland. To the Puritans there was of course only one interpretation. It was the act of communion in which the infinite impinged upon the finite, when the misery of the fragmentary was replaced by the delight of wholeness. Regeneration was the receiving by man of "the fulnesse of the infinitenesse of all perfections which are in the Lord," who alone is "able to fill up all the emptie chinks, void places, the unsatisfied gaspings & yawnings of the spirit of a man." It was the resolution of the problem of sin, and of all other problems that torture humanity.

No other subject in the repertoire of theological debate was more bewritten and no other riddle so exercised the ingenuity of the clergy and the patience of the laity. We shall have occasion to sympathize with the Sysiphean labors of the divines as we behold them again and again almost finishing exhaustive systematizations of the doctrine, only to have their structure collapse because some obstinate fact simply will not fit in. As Thomas Hooker rightly said, "The point is difficult, and the mysterie great." Yet we must not be deceived by the mass of black-letter type devoted to the elucidation of regeneration into thinking that it was not a real conception to Puritan sensibility, that it did not correspond to a vivid experience. Throughout all the laborious analyses the fundamental idea remained clear, and if Puritans could never satisfactorily define faith they were not therefore hindered from living by it.

Theological formulation was difficult because regeneration is a mystery. Those who have it, or think they have it, cannot tell exactly how it was wrought or precisely what happened, and those who do not have it cannot conceive what it might be; furthermore, there are some who are never quite sure whether they have it or not, and they make the problem exceedingly difficult. We have little right to patronize the Puritans for their ignorance. With all the laboratory facilities now at hand and all their clinical study, modern psychologists differ among themselves no less than did the theologians in their diagnosis of what occurs to human beings during the seizure; the layman of the seventeenth century becomes the patient of the twentieth and overhears his case as hotly disputed among doctors of the mind as formerly he beheld his symptoms argued among doctors of divinity. The result once more is a tribute to the bewildering variety of the religious experience. No one can deny that some such psychological event does take place; dispute arises over the nature of the theoretical frame in which the explanation is set. For Puritans the frame was inevitably theological; its outlines were predetermined by the system of belief inherited from the past, from Augustine in particular, to which a renewed precision had been given by the Reformation.

The Puritan theory of regeneration began with the premise of an omnipotent God and an impotent man. It seemed obvious that a man, bound in the slavery of sin, could not liberate himself; before he could stand once more erect the effects of his sin had to be canceled and the transgression pardoned. Regeneration therefore must begin with an act of absolution, performed before the divine tribunal, an act in which man himself could take no part. A change must be wrought in his status before any could be made in his nature. In theological parlance this first act of regeneration was known as "justification," and it meant that God, having decided to acquit a particular individual, says to him, in effect, "that his Iustice and Law is fully satisfied, that hee will lay nothing upon your score, require no satisfaction at your hands, but he will fully and freely discharge you of all your sins which you have committed." Thereupon divine grace reaches forth to the prostrate man in two ways: first it comes as a call to new life, a summons from above—which was called "vocation"—and then it penetrates his being and there it generates—or, in view of Adam's original nature, "re-generates"—a power to respond. John Milton's tutor at Cambridge, William Chappell, compiled a bibliography of theological works for the guidance of divinity students, and under the heading "Treatises on True Conversion" he listed only New England writers; the divines of the Puritan colonies excelled as analysts, and of them all Thomas Hooker was esteemed the most profound. He illustrated justification and regeneration by the simile of a sick apprentice: to make a free man of him there must be a double change; his master must tear up the indenture, thus working a "moral change," and then the physician must cure him, working a "real change."

> Just so it is in this change of the soule: there is a morall change in justification, a man is bound to the Law, and liable to the penaltie of it, and guiltie of the breach of it: now God the Father in Jesus Christ, acquits a man of this guilt, and delivers him from this revenging power of the Law, and thats not all, but withall hee puts holinesse into the heart, and wisedome into the minde . . . & this is called a naturall change, because there are new spiritual abilities put into the heart.

Therefore grace is to be understood as something inward and spiritual, and when it has wrought upon a man in regeneration "it leaves an impression upon the most inward motions of the soul, as they meet with God in the most retired and refined actions thereof." It is a renewal of man out of sin, a resurrection from death. It regenerates not merely his mind and his will, but the whole man, giving him a new inclination, a new heart, a completely new life.

The one bedrock certainty about the matter is that grace is a supernatural power and that no man can enact regeneration by his own exertions. The natural disposition is not only bound by sin, it cleaves to sin; though the soul may cry out for deliverance it fights against the deliverer. Grace must pursue the soul, forcibly seize upon it, violently reverse the will. It is "a marvellous strong work, when the Spirit of God comes to act things contrary to nature." Man instinctively wishes to do for himself and to rely upon his own prowess; faith "is the going out of the soule to another, and to see all-sufficiencie in another, and to fetch all from another." So we cannot properly say that in regeneration a man comes to possess Christ but rather we must say that he is possessed by Christ, "because the worke lies on Christs part." The peace that passes understanding must come from above the understanding. Only a supernatural power can withdraw the natural heart "from all those secret bosome distempers . . . which breed . . . discontentment within a man," and compel the soul to "resigne up it selfe to the good will of God." Regeneration must be done "by an irresistible power" or else it will never succeed in overturning the dominion of sin.

Consequently, the initial requirement for a description of regeneration is a rigorous distinction between the effects of divine grace and all behavior elicited by natural causes. This distinction was not always an easy one for the Puritan to establish, because in fallen men there are faculties which can sometimes produce actions remarkably similar to those that result from faith, even at times seeming to excel them. The presence of these faculties argues no saving worth in man, it only proves the fiendish subtlety of his corruption. Sin does not always manifest itself as violence and rapine, but masquerades as virtue itself, thus setting a trap by which the unwary may be betrayed into resting content with a performance that has nothing of God in it. For example, certain natural influences or physical causes will work a life of seeming virtue; fear of punishment, "the good Temperament of the Body," a decent education will often lead to well-regulated conduct and everyday probity. But all such effects come from mechanical and comprehensible causes, the results are temporary and relative. Grace is absolute and supernatural. It is, Hooker said, "a holy kind of violence." It is not wrought by "morall perswasion" but by "his powerfull operation, and omnipotent hand put forth for such a purpose." Faith is not a thing "which our nature can attaine to with outward helpes," there are no seeds of belief within us. "Neither education, nor examples of others, nor our own resolutions, can settle our hearts upon God, till we find an inward power and authority causing divine truths to shine into our hearts." A child may have the "most towardly natural disposition" and "be advantaged by the most likely way of education"; he may have instilled into him arguments to convince the most obdurate mind, and "yet till the heart be changed and over-poured by a work of supernatural grace, the life will alwayes be found barren of any good fruit, void of holiness, and sincere obedience."

It is also true that in natural man there exists an internal conflict which to the uninitiated seems to be the struggle of grace and sin. There is in man something of a conscience; he was created with it, exactly as he was created with eyes or limbs, and no more could it have been obliterated at the fall. It is now extremely unreliable, but still strong enough to restrain most men from the more extravagant vices. It accuses men of their sin, and it can make them so uncomfortable that some will fly to religion for refuge. A few may even fight and die for the truth, but if their motive is no more than self-preservation, if they are driven by nothing more than a haunting conscience, they commit in effect an act of suicide; "this is but a principle of nature, not an inward principle of life, whose property is to seek the subversion of corrupt nature, as natural conscience seeks the garnishing of it and the actions thereof." In wicked men the conscience is at odds with the will, and because all men are compounded of spirit and matter they are torn by a never ending contention between the soul and the body. But in them the conflict is natural, mechanical, all on the same plane; it is a crossing of one faculty by another, each wanting its own advantage. When grace is poured into the reluctant soul, the inward struggle takes on vastly more complex dimensions. Grace injects into every faculty a new element, by which each learns to judge its own sinfulness and thereupon commences a civil war with itself:

> In the Saints the Controversie is between every faculty and it selfe, between the understanding and it selfe, betweene the whole Soule, as it is compared with it selfe, there is something good in every part of it, and something ill, and these two contend.

Natural men alternate between joy at one moment and sorrow at another; gracious persons are filled simultaneously with exultation and grief. They are elevated by the glory of grace and cast down by the knowledge of sin, and therefore only they can at one time be both diligent in worldly business and yet untainted by the world.

> Where ever the heart of a man is sanctified by the Spirit of grace; where you have the life of sanctification in a Christian, you shall finde variety of graces in them, some of them of such diversity and opposition one to another, that in nature the like temper is not to be found in one person at the same time, and in the same businesse.

Grace comes from God, who is, as we have seen, possessed of attributes which in nature are not compatible with each other, and it makes man in some measure capable of the same supernatural balance of qualities.

It was difficult enough in practice to keep from taking some of the natural perturbations of the unregenerate for the stirrings of authentic grace; it was still more difficult to distinguish accurately between the powers of natural reason and those of divine grace. If there are remnants of conscience in the progeny of Adam there are also fragments of the intellect, for without a mind man would cease to be. When the Puritan spoke of "the light of reason" or of "the light of nature" he meant these ruins of the image of God; the phrases signified the amount of innate rationality that descendants of the first man still retain, though in a sadly dilapidated condition.

> The light of nature, remaining in *Adams* posterity, since the lapse: is so little as that it is not to be mentioned the same day, with what was in *Adam,* before the fall. The light of nature, consists in common principles imprinted upon the reasonable soul, by nature: inclining man, to assent unto some naturall, and manifest trueths upon the representation of them; without waiting for any proofe; that is, as it were by instinct, without argument. Viz. *that it is impossible for the same thing, at once, for to be, & not to be.*

By the same tokens, even before the mind begins to think, it already knows that there is a God, that parents are to be honored, that there is a difference between good and bad. Consequently some men, for example Seneca or Plutarch, guided solely by the light of reason, building upon merely natural principles, are able to acquire the "morall virtues" inculcated by supernatural light. Puritans did not deny that such virtues had their uses—in fact, they allowed them rather too much utility—but they were positive that such were not the stuff of divine grace and contributed nothing toward salvation. Men can learn some things from "the book of creation," from the arts and sciences, by the light of nature, but not what the elect learn by the light of glory. Rational conviction at best makes things appear but as they seem, whereas spiritual conviction presents them as they really are. The holy spirit may use argumentation, but it goes much farther and enables the soul to see intuitively as well as through the point-by-point demonstrations of logical discourse.

> Reason can see and discourse about words and propositions, and behold things by report, and . . . deduct one thing from another; but the Spirit makes a man see the things themselves, really wrapped up in those words. The Spirit brings spiritual things as well as notions before a man's eye; the light of the Spirit is like the light of the sun—it makes all things appear as they are.

The life of reason, though lived never so well, "is but a dead life." Faith "exceeds the most lively and heroicall performances of the best of the Heathens that ever was," because what they did was from their own strength; their finest actions "are but so many dead works, because the heart is dead." Knowledge will not cure a wounded spirit, and though a man "bee acquainted with all the motions of heaven, they cannot bring him to heaven: With all the secrets of nature, they cannot bring him out of the dreggs of nature." There was for the Puritan a hierarchy of comprehension, what Preston called a "three-fold kinde of Truth": on the first plane there was natural truth within the heart of men; on the second there was the common knowledge that natural men could acquire from theologians and books; on the third was spiritual knowledge. All men had the first, all might gain the second, only grace could give the third; yet on that level alone was redemption to be secured. The life of the Christian was not sustained by wisdom, or brilliant abilities, or by philosophical fortitude, but by faith.

The danger that the natural convictions of reason might be mistaken for the supernatural impress of the spirit was real enough. To the Puritans the danger was made the more threatening as they recognized the existence of a species of belief which accepts not merely natural religion but revelation as well, which nevertheless is merely a belief of the mind, not of the soul. It is what the seventeenth century called "historicall faith"—"a beleeving, not of the stories of the Bible onely to be true, but a beleeuing of the whole Word of God, the articles of the faith; but beleeved onely in a historicall manner generally, not applyed particularly to himselfe." It is not saving faith for all its confession of Christianity. Like heathen morality, it is a thoroughly natural product; under favorable circumstances it can be cultivated in any by good teachers. Men can be instructed in the meaning of Scriptural words and be made proficient in its logic, but in order that they may "see the spiritualnesse of the work that is manifested and communicated in that reason there," they must be instructed by the spirit. It is as though, Hooker explained, an ignorant man should be shown a clock and be told how it was put together; he might understand the words and the reasons, but he could not on the spot acquire the art of clock-making.

> There is a curious frame in the soule of a Christian, of grace, of faith, of repentance, of holinesse, of love, patience, and the like . . . but I that read what he hath written of these things, being a naturall man, though happily I understand the sence, and apprehend the meaning of the words, yet the true knowledge of the nature of repentance, or faith, or hope, I cannot possibly attain to, so long as I remain a meer naturall man . . . When I finde my own heart wrought upon, then I can best discover it to another, then doe I know that which before I never understood; though happily I could discourse something concerning such things, and understand the outside as it were, yet that was all, I never knew the bottom, as I doe now.

Most of the divines were ready to admit that in extent of knowledge a wicked man might go as far as any saint under heaven, and all agreed that religion learned by rote was not the religion of the heart, that an understanding of theology was not an experience of grace.

Natural reason could not be expected to reach so high as grace because by definition it had been corrupted. It had shared in the general contagion of sin; Adam no doubt was created as upright in his reason as in his will, but what now remains as the light of reason is almost certain to prove a will-o'-the-wisp. No matter how successfully reason may upon occasion contrive actions that resemble those of grace, so long as it remains unregenerate it is not only incapable of true excellence but vigorously hostile to it. Reason will bend the arguments of Scripture and wrest the words to devious meaning; when a man is first accused of sin he gets reason, like a hireling lawyer, to defend him before the court of God, "to plead against the word of God lest it should prevaile, or his sins should lie so heavy upon him as to tire and weary him out of them." In many men of great ability "for depth of brain and strength of understanding" the sway of reason becomes so firm that they can never be brought to the truth; where there is "wiliness, depth and subtilty of wit, large reaches of carnal reason," there is apt to be but little faith. For the Puritan further and conclusive proof of the enmity of reason to faith was the Papacy and its teachings; the principles of the Roman church were in their eyes eminently satisfactory to human reason, and the institution deserved damnation if for that sin alone. Faith demands the acceptance of things above reason, grace fills men with the power to believe the impossible. Up to a certain point rational arguments may be used to prepare and confirm, but they cannot serve for persuasion. Even when reason is legitimately employed, its conclusions must always be tested by the proposition of faith, and whatever reason turns up to the contrary must be at once discarded. "Almost all the sin and misery that hath filled the World, hath broke in at this door, hearkening to reason against Institution." We should note in passing that it was not reason itself, conceived in the abstract, that the Puritans condemned, but reason as men employed it. The light of pure reason, said John Norton, is "an effect proceeding from the Word," but man, endowed with no more of it than remains in him after the fall, is in virtual darkness. Pure reason is therefore inaccessible to man, like the essence of God; man has only "carnal reason," a mere caricature of that which he once possessed as the badge of his lordship over all other creatures.

> Star-light, cannot make it, otherwise then night. The light of nature since the fall, compared with the light of the image of God, before the fall, hath not the proportion of Star-light, to the bright Sun-light at noon-day. This indeed is but darkness. But, if compared with the light of the Gospell, it is worse then gross darkness.

As we pursue the story of New England thought we must bear in mind the complete separation which the founders made between supernatural grace and all its natural simulacra. Puritanism could exist only on condition that it maintain the distinction, and when we shall find the division closing up, we shall perceive the dwindling of piety.

The effort to set off supernatural grace from natural morality and reasonable conduct involved also a metaphysical difficulty which was to become of great importance, down even to the time of Emerson. Grace was to be distinguished from natural powers; but was it not true, according to the doctrine of concursus, that God created and sustained all natural processes, and that by the doctrine of providence He directed and controlled all the operations of mind and body? To say that grace was supernatural seemed to say therefore that it was above God Himself, or that there was a division of the Deity into an ordinary self and an extraordinary self. Most of the issues that were so hotly contested among seventeenth-century theologians were connected with attempts to resolve this discrepancy between the God of everyday providence and the God who dispensed His grace according to no rule but His own pleasure, who then condemned to damnation those who, never receiving the grace, lived as well as they could in the strength of natural conscience, unregenerate reason, and historical faith. For the orthodox Puritan there was no way out except to keep the two activities of God, providence and regeneration, on separate planes. God diffuses Himself through space to create and sustain the world, but there is a second emanation, over and above the original one, which is grace. When He puts grace into the heart of a man it is as though He made a new and gratuitous concretion of his substance in addition to that already precipitated in creation. The omnipotent Being fills all space, controls all actions, directs all destinies; out of Him comes all life, and without the constant play of His sustaining power physical being would disintegrate into nothing. He fills heaven and earth with His presence, says Hooker, "His infinite Being is every where, and one and the same every where in regard of himself; because his being is most simple, and not subject to any shadow of change, being all one with himself." There is, says Shepard, an essential presence of the spirit "that is in every man, as the Godhead is every where, in whom we live and move." The spirit lives in the most wicked men, in "the vilest creature in the world." Therefore the presence of God in the regenerate soul must follow upon a second act of creation, a new radiation reaching directly across to man, overleaping the regular channels of influence. "Yet he is said to take up his abode in a special manner, when he doth put forth the peculiar expression of his Work." Our union with the spirit in faith, while we live in a world sustained and governed in every detail by that spirit, is not with that aspect of it which regulates the course of events or our everyday life, but that which comes to us of itself. Natural life is common to all, "but this special Presence of God, he affords only to his Redeemed, Chosen and Called." It is not enough that God has spoken once; the fall of man has made it necessary that He speak again. He must re-create those He would redeem, He must bring them under more than the government of His providence, even under the dominion of grace.

The distinction between God's energy put forth in governing the universe and in regenerating the saints furnished metaphysical grounds for a theological distinction between God's decreeing will, as seen in the events, and His commanding will, as seen in the Bible. As we study this distinction we come close to the Puritan's innermost sense of the living process. It is as though a pulsating energy were continuously pumped through creation's veins by the beat of a mighty heart, which yet at irregular intervals, by an exceptional contraction of the ventricles, sends forth a stream of still more tremendous force. Out of the same being have proceeded the stars, animals, men; but in some incarnations the being has taken forms superior to others. "The least spear of grass has the same power to make it that made heaven and angels," says the Puritan, but he does not then chant with the author of *Leaves of Grass* that the least thing in creation is equal to any other. A fly is above the cedar because it has another life which the cedar has not, "so the meanest believer is better than the most glorious hypocrite." In the regenerate, the author of all life ordains yet another life superior to the other forms, giving them something which the others have not. In the course of providence God often provides men with powers and gifts, bridles their violence, overcomes their pride, teaches them the truth of Scripture. But these things He does by managing secondary causes, sending men to the right teachers, instructing them through their experience or through science. What is achieved in this fashion is a work of "common grace." Supernatural grace is a work peculiar to the elect, which comes upon them with irresistible force and depends upon no antecedent conditions or preparations. This conception, that for the relation of God and man a new line of communication must be opened over and above the relation of creature to creator and of life to the source of life, a special contact, a designation by name and a specific bond, is the very heart of Puritanism. To the Puritan, cosmic optimism was not enough. The scheme of perfection became monotonous if restricted to flawless regularity; the human quest, the deep longings of the soul, went unsatisfied if the wheels of the world ground slowly, justly, and implacably. There must be room in the universe for a free and unpredictable power, for a lawless force that flashes through the night in unexpected brilliance and unaccountable majesty. It was better in Puritan eyes that most men be passed over by this illumination and left to hopeless despair rather than that all men should be born without the hope of beholding it, or that a few should forgo the ecstasy of the vision.

CHAPTER II

THE PRACTICE OF PIETY

In no society are the formal or official tenets those which necessarily determine action, yet many observers find in the Puritan community a discrepancy between profession and practice that seems abnormally wide. Critics at the time, and since, have argued that the piety, with its degradation of man and its exaltation of God, should have driven its votaries in solitary flight to the desert and attired them in the hair shirt of repentance, after the example of the more straightforward saints of the Middle Ages. But the only desert into which Puritan saints fled was New England, where such as could afford it wore crimson waistcoats and expensive cloaks. Later generations have been puzzled, as was young William Ellery Channing, over the spectacle of their fathers pronouncing approval upon the morning's sermon—"Sound doctrine, Sir"—and then going whistling home to a warm house and a good dinner. The conclusion seems to them inescapable that the Puritans were arrant hypocrites.

This judgment proceeds upon an assumption concerning the nature of the piety. When critics accuse Puritan society of glossing its avarice with sanctimoniousness, or of taking solid satisfaction in the things of this world while pretending to despise them, they presuppose that the piety was a gloomy, otherworldly, and tragic conception of life, which ought to have forbidden such relaxations. Yet I think it very doubtful that any seventeenth-century Puritan so interpreted his creed. There can be no denying that Puritanism did give rise to Pharisaism and accentuated the complacency of men like Cotton Mather; it was also ruthless in inflicting its will upon dissenters and those whom it judged sinners. Yet in everyday life Puritanism did not mean that because Puritans were virtuous there should be no more cakes and ale. It was only after the piety had abandoned the essentials of true Puritanism, only after it had turned to the newer, more extravagant, and less scholastical positions of eighteenth-century evangelicalism that it began to indulge in wholesale denunciations of the senses, of the acquisition of wealth or the wearing of such finery as was appropriate to the social station of the wearer. The divorce between conduct and belief was probably as wide in Puritan society as in any other, but certainly no wider; that the behavior of Puritans did not excessively belie their words becomes more apparent when we ascertain exactly what standards of behavior were professed.

Definition of these standards is difficult since Puritans entertained many which were not necessarily connected with the piety, but were merely the common notions of the day. The idea of man's unhappy lot does not always proceed from a sense of internal discord; as uttered even by the ministers it is sometimes simply such an observation upon the caprices of fortune as was a standard theme in Renaissance literature. There is always an element of Stoicism in the piety, which amounts to urging stalwart souls to endure misfortune with resolution. When Thomas Hooker illustrates original sin by pointing to little children—who before they have learned anything, "yet they wil easily take in naughty words and tattle them when they know not what they talk"—or when John Cotton assures the godly that they will not escape pain by leading a holy life—"it never fell out otherwise, but as sure as thou are sprinkled with the water of Baptisme, so sure thou shalt be drenched in affliction"—they are not so much Augustinians as men of ordinary worldly wisdom. Furthermore, it is clear that the doctrine of human depravity was often a metaphysical convenience rather than the reflection of a vivid sense of sin; it offered easy solution of theological difficulties. The assertion that creation must be intrinsically good could the more readily be made if all responsibility for what seems amiss could be placed upon man:

> When therefore we see all things out of frame, remember it is not from the Unskillfulness of the Workman, but the Confusion which Sin hath hurled upon the Works, that the curious Instrument is so disordered; which hath broken some, and displaced other of the Wheels of it, whereby it is now full of Confusion.

Man has spoiled the beauty and comfort of the world and he therefore is to blame for its becoming "a place of Briars and Thorns, of Troubles and Sorrows, and a Valley of the shaddow of Death." God is no more the cause of sin, said John Cotton, "than the Sun is the cause of the stench of a Dunghil." "If men will Sin, and ruin themselves," asked Increase Mather, "what Obligation is there on God to hinder them?"

Thus in the Puritan conception of sin there were strains that did not arise directly out of the piety; the importance of these more formal or conventional motifs must not be minimized, for they were eventually to give rise to important modifications in thinking and in practice. Still, the evidence not only of the sermons but of the history and the whole tone of the early seventeenth century goes to show that to the first settlers of New England the conviction of human depravity was not merely a metaphysical concept or a sage comment upon the sorrows of humanity. Consequently, the charge that their conduct was patently inconsistent with their creed demands first of all an examination of what the doctrine of sin in its original context actually did demand from men. It is not accurate, for example, to call the Puritan sense of life "tragic," or to find the bustling energy which Puritans exhibited in war and commerce inconsistent with their theology of predestination. They did feel that life was certainly grim, and never for a moment did they lose sight of its harshness, pain, and brutality; Puritanism failed to hold later generations largely because the children were unable to face reality as unflinchingly as their forefathers. But though Puritans confronted horror without shirking, they never perceived that any failure or defeat added up to a tragedy. They never doubted the ultimate outcome, there was never a time when they said with Hamlet that the rest is silence. They remembered their cosmic optimism in the midst of anguish, and they were too busy waging war against sin, too intoxicated with the exultation of the conflict to find occasional reversals, however costly, any cause for deep discouragement. "No day, but God calls us to warre with some crosse, or some temptation or other." The Christian life was indeed strenuous, but the more desperate the situation, the more action it evoked. Joshua Moody said that we are like soldiers landed in a hostile country, whose commander has burned their ships behind them and told them they must either eat up their enemies or drink up the sea. Urian Oakes's eloquent sermon before the Ancient and Honourable Artillery Company in 1672 described the Christian engaged in continual resistance to both sin and affliction, so that he must not only work with a weapon in his hand, "but he must actually use his Weapon whilest he is working; fighting with one hand, and building or labouring with the other." Far from making for tragedy, the necessity produced exhilaration. The title of Oakes's sermon was *The Unconquerable, All-Conquering, & more-then-conquering Souldier;* the doctrine of original sin did not lead to apathy, but to victory.

Furthermore, the fight was a good fight. For those who fell there was the future life in which they would be fully rewarded, and those overwhelmed in this world would have opportunity to exult over their foes at the day of judgment. Yet I find it difficult to believe that the conception of the afterlife was as vivid to most Puritans as was their realization of sin or their experience of divine grace; there are but few sermons specifically devoted to immortality compared with the tremendous number drawing out the lessons of depravity or analyzing in minute detail the processes of regeneration. Perhaps the expectation of immortality was so axiomatic that little discussion was needed, but I am inclined to suspect that because their energies were so intensely concentrated upon the problems in hand they had few left for doubts about those to come.[1] In any event, the belief was real enough to wipe out the sting of earthly defeat with the promise of heavenly triumph. As for those who fought on the wrong side, in the livery of Satan or Antichrist, there was nothing tragic in their fate, since they got precisely what they deserved. Furthermore, quite apart from the rewards which were to be distributed in heaven, the warrior of the Lord had made up to him, here and now, all that he lost in active service. One of the best discussions of this theme in New England writings, Samuel Willard's *The Child's Portion,* points to the glory which is reserved for the child of God, but also insists upon his bliss and security in the midst of persecution or present distress. All ordeals are tests to be met with delight; God has provided true believers with "consolations strong enough to hold up their heads above water when the waves rise highest, and the raging billows make the greatest noise"; all the world and its creatures are under the government of providence, "but these Children are under his special inspection and care"; that worldly men hate them is an argument for their "sonship," because it discovers "that enmity which God hath put between the seed of the Serpent & of the Woman"; though the children must confront many enemies, men and devils, "yet all these being over-ruled by the power and wisdom of God which stand on his peoples side, are made beneficial to them." Willard promises the usual compensatory bliss in heaven, and adds as a special enticement that there we shall at last have perfect comprehension of the "Divine Riddles" of theology, but he insists also that in this world the faithful "have not only their assurances, but also sometimes their extasies." And though individuals may be destined to hear the shout of victory only in heaven, for the people of God as a whole success is promised on this side of the grave. By the year 1600 Puritans in England were growing more confident of this assertion; the settlers of New England said again and again that the concursus Dei "is for his Churches sake," and that by His providence He so disposes the world "as maketh most for his glory, and the good of his Elect." So far was the Puritan spirit from being itself tragic that it was actually incapable of perceiving tragedy. This deficiency is by rights the accusation which ought to be leveled against it, and constitutes a much more telling charge than that of being over-gloomy or dismal. Precisely because Puritanism lacked this insight, by the turn of the eighteenth century, as the sense of sin became less urgent, cosmic optimism often lapsed into smugness, and the doctrines of depravity and election gave rise to snobbery. The tragedy of Puritanism may be that it could not always retain a vivid sense of the fall of man, but certainly while Puritans did have such a sense they could not look upon life itself as tragic.

The indestructible optimism contained within the grim Puritan creed is apparent in the theoretical explanation of affliction. Seeming contradictions between the creator's goodness and the creation's visible evils necessitated no denial of either; they merely reinforced the distinction between God's revealed and secret wills. Providence was the expression of His inner determination, and though the lesson of some "divine providences" could be read with ease, the teaching of others remained obscure. God frequently causes things to fall out contrary to what seems to us fitting and proper, contrary even to His own uttered Word. Wise men ought to get estates, but it does happen "that some understanding Men cannot thrive in the World and grow rich, notwithstanding all their Endeavours"; the ways of providence are exceedingly intricate, so that "not only wise but good men have sometimes been put to a non-plus here." There are occasions indeed when Puritanism seems to exact an unbearable toll from human fortitude. It requires not only that men endure afflictions, but that they find positive goodness in the worst of them: "If we speak evill of Gods ordinances or providences, as for a man to say, would to God I had never known such a woman, it is blasphemy; Gods wisedome and righteousnesse hath ordayned it." No matter how exasperating, no matter how disastrous, because all experience is given of God, it must have some reason behind it. There can be no prospering that is not of God's appointment, "nor is there any evill hapneth but according to the determination of *the only wise God*." Nothing can happen merely from blind chance, from mechanical causes, or from the irresponsible malice of voluntary agents. Whether a man be tortured by a disease or a devil, the providence of God is "the Supream Governing Efficient cause of those Afflictions." It is our duty "to look beyond second causes in all the troubles that we undergo in this world." In some crises the hand of God may be "wrapt up in a Cloud," but our spiritual sight should penetrate into it, "and God should not be concealed from us by the crowd of immediate *Agent*[*s*], which are the Instruments of our Vexations." Therefore, no trial should be unduly softened or explained away; it is as sinful to minimize an evil as to exaggerate it. True faith must show itself able to stand up under punishment. God would not have made men capable of grief had He not expected them to grieve, but sorrow must be "more for Gods displeasure apprehended therein" than for the loss itself, and it should never exceed the proportions warranted by the cause. We may lament as much as the calamity justifies, but no more. There was in the piety a strange tendency to calculate and measure human miseries, in almost a Benthamite spirit, because it was necessary for the child of God to know how much he was being disciplined and at what point he should put off sackcloth and ashes that he might be up and doing the Lord's work. The basic certainty was that no adversity could be so immense as to cause complete despair. God has set limits to every malignity. Facts are often intractable or desolating, but nevertheless to Puritans justice and fact were really one, though they might appear now and then to be separated. Reality was as yet unsundered from value, though humanity was unable to perceive the value of all realities. The world was indeed full of confusion and vanity, "but not simply, so that no order and good at all lyeth hid, and is found in that confusion." Whatever their sufferings or however painful their ordeals, Puritans could take heart through the darkest moments in the confidence that all things are ordered after the best manner, that serene and inviolate above the clouds of man's distress shines the sun of a glorious harmony.

Puritanism has been called not only tragic but "other-worldly," and disliked as much on the one score as on the other. The doctrine of sin seems clearly to involve condemnation of the world and all its works; there are innumerable passages which, taken by themselves, confirm this deduction. Thus Joshua Moody moralizes in Jacques' vein upon the spectacle of economic enterprise:

> The Product of the Toyl and Travel of many a Day, is only a little Earth. Let a Man search up and down the World, compass Sea and Land, ransack the Bowels of the Earth for the hidden Treasures that are there, tire out himself in the Multitude of his Way, waste away his Time, and wear away his Strength, rise up early and go to Bed late, and eat the Bread of Carefulness; and when all is done, what hath he gained? Why a very small Portion, a poor Pittance, that which is so far from deserving the Name of Profit that is a meer Vanity and Vexation of Spirit.

Yet Moody was preaching these words to a congregation in which were many assiduous accumulators of merchandise, many sharp traders and shrewd investors. Is not this proof positive that the Puritans were hypocrites?

Moody's elegy upon the vanity of the profit-motive must be read with reference to the whole symmetry of Puritan belief. Christianity has always insisted that the creature is subject to change, but Protestantism, particularly the "Calvinistic" wing, had already given a peculiar twist to the cry of "all is vanity," and Puritanism had developed a still more special connotation. Clerical denunciations of the flesh were never intended to lead to ascetic renunciation of it, for a major premise in all Puritan thinking was the belief that God created the universe good. In spite of man's sin He has somehow kept the whole undefiled; He has even contrived that human depravity, though fatal to men, should enrich the beauty of the cosmos with the added drama of redemption and salvation. The fall has put the curse of vanity upon the creatures—but only in their relation to man. God cannot be imagined as ever having cause to repent the creation; therefore it must still be intrinsically and positively good. God continues to will it, and the creatures within it must, while they are here, live according to the terms God originally appointed for them. The doctrine of sin does not mean that men should no longer propagate or cause the wilderness to blossom. They are indeed to repent, but without ceasing to delve and spin. The unknowable and inscrutable God has, out of His sovereign liberty, erected a world on certain knowable and circumscribed laws; on the day of judgment He will roll up the work like a scroll and the laws will be annihilated, but meanwhile they endure. Human beings, as a part of this world, must obey the requirements set them and fulfill the rules of their nature. They must, for example, live in civil societies "as members of this or that City, or Town, or Commonwealth, in this or that particular vocation and calling," and they must live the life of the senses, "by which we eate and drinke, by which we goe through all conditions, from our birth to our grave, by which we live, and move, and have our being." *Per se* these activities are not unlawful. And also, the God who made men must have made whatever men require in order to live. All that supports life, preserves or restores health, feeds natural hungers, is to that extent good. A thing becomes dangerous when it hinders life or health, when it proves disagreeable to "the nature of Man for whose use it was made." Works "of Necessity and of Compassion" were always permissible on the Sabbath, though there was often difficulty in deciding what was necessary or compassionate. The ultimate purpose of man is the glory of God, but that he may achieve his final end he must also pursue his subordinate ends. Hence he may "lawfully seek his present comfort, and use the approved means for the obtainment of it." No seventeenth-century Puritan ever said that food, love, and music were intrinsically bad or that recreation was inherently sinful. On the contrary, he said, "God hath given us Temporals to Enjoy . . . We should therefore suck the sweet of them, and so slack our Thirst with them, as not to be Insatiably craving after more." Sin lies not in them, but in a sinful use of them, in employing what God designed for the relief of natural wants merely for their pleasurableness, in eating not to maintain life but solely for the savor of the food, in loving not for procreation but for sensuous gratification, in ruling not to benefit society but from a lust for power. Actions are never sinful simply because they are enjoyable; if their felicity remains subordinate to their utility, they are beyond criticism; they become reprehensible the moment they are practiced for their delectability alone. The people of God are free to use the things of this life, "not only for their necessity, but also for their convenience & comfort: but yet he hath set bounds to this liberty, that it may not degenerate into licentiousness." To speak properly, no created thing and no act of a created being can ever be in itself "evil"; it acquires an evil character only in relation to man, when he abuses it to the hurt of his immortal soul. The innocence or criminality of a deed depends on circumstances. Killing is admirable in war, but murder is crime; the marriage bed is blessed, but adultery is damnable. The Puritan's attitude toward worldly joys flowed from his deepest sense of the cosmic process. The fundamental constitution of the universe had to be forever good and remain forever inviolate; otherwise there would be a curtailing of the infinite perfection of God. The derangement wrought by sin therefore was held to have disturbed not the order of nature, but the orderliness of the human will.

Thus what is generally characterized as "other-worldliness" in Puritan theology was in fact a recognition of the world, an awareness of a trait in human nature, a witness to the devious ways in which men can pervert the fruits of the earth and the creatures of the world and cause them to minister to their vices. Puritanism found the natural man invariably running into excess or intemperance, and saw in such abuses an affront to God, who had made all things to be used according to their natures. Puritanism condemned not natural passions but inordinate passions, not man's desires but his enslavement to them, not the pleasures found in the satisfaction of appetites, but the tricks devised to prod satiated appetites into further concupiscence. "You might meddle with all things in the world," said John Preston, "and not bee defiled by them, if you had pure affections, but when you have an inordinate lust after any thing, then it defiles your spirit." Increase Mather observed concretely that drink is itself "a good creature" to be received with thankfulness, "the wine is from God, but the Drunkard is from the Devil." The disobedience of Adam must be corrected by the salvation of the spirit; at the same time the children of Adam must eat and drink, perform civil duties, pursue a calling, bear arms, pay or receive wages, increase and multiply. The irony of man's predicament is that in his present condition he is not released from natural necessities, and yet he is incapable of satisfying them without adding to the enormity of his sin.

Consequently a staple moral of Puritan discourse is that men must love the world with "weaned affections." They must be completely in it, but not of it. You may use things, "but not be wedded to them, but so weaned from them, that you may use them, *as if you used them not.*" Puritanism sees illusion in the visible universe; it requires men, as long as they are in the flesh, to act as though the illusion were real; it punishes them if they take illusion for reality.

> Hee doth not forbid mercy or love to Beasts or Creatures, but hee would not have your love terminated in them, bounded in them, hee would not have you rejoyce or delight in the Creature, before you have part in the Creator, for if you affect these things for themselves, the love of God is not in you.

The inward meaning of Puritan commercial ethics, the explanation of its peculiar mixture of profit-taking and soul-saving in the single act of a business transaction, lies in this passage of John Cotton's:

> There is another combination of vertues strangely mixed in every lively holy Christian, And that is, Diligence in worldly businesses, and yet deadnesse to the

world; such a mystery as none can read, but they that know it. For a man to [take]. all opportunities to be doing something, early and late, and loseth no opportunity, go any way and bestir himselfe for profit, this will he doe most diligently in his calling: And yet bee a man dead-hearted to the world. . . . though hee labour most diligently in his calling, yet his heart is not set upon these things, he can tell what to doe with his estate when he hath got it.

With the passage of time, as the profession of dead-heartedness became a stereotyped formula, uttered on the Sabbath and forgotten in the counting-house, hearts inevitably were the more wholly set upon "these things," and as estates accumulated men forgot what they should have done with them. The gulf between the formal creed and the social reality widened because, for decades after many New Englanders had ceased to read the mystery in humility of spirit, a confession of humility was publicly retained.

Yet these later developments should not blind us to the fact that in the seventeenth century philosophy was more consonant with practice. There can be no denying that in Puritanism as in all Protestantism there was an economic motive, that the creed had its origins in society as well as in the Augustinian temperament, and that its ethic was adapted to such considerations. Weber and Tawney have shown how far the teaching of "weaned affections," though seemingly a spiritual ideal, also jibed with the disposition of a rising middle class, that it was in effect a fine psychological assistance to the growth of capitalism. A glib popularization has resulted—and with some degree of correctness—that Puritan piety is ultimately to be explained as no more than a rationalization of economic change. Of course, this deduction is over-simplification. It is obvious that Protestantism did thrive frequently in centers of commerce and industry, that there were many profound connections between the new opportunities for profit and the spread of the new piety, and we shall, I trust, be able to trace some of the interactions of business and religion on the New England scene through the later stages of this narrative. Nevertheless, it is eminently worth pointing out for the moment that though some Puritan doctrines may appear to us marvelously suited for the needs of adolescent capitalism, to Puritans they were all logically consistent with the cosmology. Furthermore, in this cosmology were certain dogmas which proved obstacles rather than helps to the bourgeois economy. The practice of pious industry, the code which required of men that they labor in the vineyard without acquiring an inordinate love of the grape, followed from the natures of things as Puritans conceived them; it grew from the premise, not that the combination of diligence in the world and deadness to its seductions would fill coffers, but that upon such terms all men must live. The world of time and space is not ultimately real, yet in it men must dwell for the time being as though it were real. Hence the saints must do the work of the world more diligently than worldlings. They may not be useless monks or unnatural celibates, for they were appointed by God to fulfill the plan of creation by doing the tasks assigned them and raising their families.

> Faith drawes the heart of a Christian to live in some warrantable calling; as soone as ever a man begins to looke towards God, and the wayes of his grace, he will not rest, till he find out some warrantable Calling and imployment . . . He would have his condition settled in a good calling, though it be but a day-labourer.

The Christian could not be an elegant gentleman of leisure, even were he able to pay the bills: "If thou beest a man that lives without a calling, though thou hast two thousands to spend, yet if thou hast no calling, tending to publique good, thou art an uncleane beast." Adam was required to tend the garden; the fall has made man's task more arduous, but it has not altered the requirement. "God sent you not into this world as into a Play-house, but a Work-house." All labor, no matter how homely or hazardous, is a worship of God provided it is done in the proper frame of mind. The difference between orthodox Puritanism and the enthusiasm of the sects cannot be better illustrated than in Thomas Shepard's advice to an over-zealous simpleton who complained that religious perplexities assailed him while he was plying his trade and interfered with his business efficiency:

> When there is a season of God's appointing for civil things or business, it is not season now to be molested or perplexed in it, by the injection and evocation of those thoughts which we think to proceed from the Spirit of God . . . for as it is a sin to nourish worldly thoughts when God set you a work in spiritual, heavenly employments, so it is, in some respects, as great a sin to suffer yourself to be distracted by spiritual thoughts, when God sets you on work in civil (yet lawful) employments.

The Christian may sojourn in a strange land, his true home may be outside this life, and sin may have spoiled almost all the delights of the temporary dwelling-place; nevertheless, while he abides here, the Puritan must be "serviceable" to the worldly community, to the family, the church, and the commonwealth. It is true, therefore, that the sense of sin did cause the Puritan to center his hopes upon heaven, but it is altogether untrue that Puritanism required him to withdraw his attention from the earth.

If the doctrine of original sin did not mean either irreparable tragedy or unrelieved asceticism, the question now remains of what we can say it did signify. We are, of course, interested in what it meant to seventeenth-century Puritans in New England; undoubtedly it had been and was still being variously interpreted by many sorts of Christians, yet to these men it seems to have entailed two outstanding corollaries: what I might describe as a perpetual judgment of all things by the loftiest conceivable standard, and an unflagging intensity of purpose. The latter result is connected more properly with the doctrine of grace, but the former goes hand in hand with the doctrine of original sin. Puritan thought incarnates a double-edged paradox: the abasement of man points to a supreme ideal of perfection, and the sense of a possible perfection makes man appear by contrast immeasurably abased. The peculiarly Puritan element in the conception is the insistence that no specific content may be attached to the standard; it is, in fact, synonymous with God, who is the incomprehensible sum of all perfections, not to be understood in His essence, not to be prefigured by man-made images, at best to be suggested by a series of abstract logical definitions. The standard of beauty and excellence is therefore above and beyond any physical beauty or human excellence, not to be represented by any triumph of art. Yet Puritanism demanded of Puritans that they remain always conscious of this divine norm, even if they could not formulate it, that they judge the finite by the infinite, though the infinite was beyond human grasp, that they be content with nothing short of absolutes, though man was unable to attain to anything absolute. It gave them no peace, it allowed them to make no shift with the merely good-enough, it permitted no relaxation because they had done their best. English Puritanism was one of the most rigorous products of the Reformation, and those who came to New England were the most logical and consistent of Puritans; in America, removed from the mollifying influences of an old and complex society, beginning anew where all things could be ordered not as they might like them but as God demanded and perfection required, their rigor was proportionally intensified. They went as far as mortals could go in removing intermediaries between God and man: the church, the priest, the magical sacraments, the saints and the Virgin; they even minimized the rôle of the Savior in their glorification of the sovereignty of the Father. Puritanism allowed men no helps from tradition or legend; it took away the props of convention and the pillows of custom; it demanded that the individual confront existence directly on all sides at once, that he test all things by the touchstone of absolute truth, that no allowance be made for circumstances or for human frailty. It showed no mercy to the spiritually lame and the intellectually halt; everybody had to advance at the double-quick under full pack. It demanded unblinking perception of the facts, though they should slay us. It was without any feeling for the twilight zones of the mind, it could do nothing with nuances or with half-grasped, fragmentary insights and oracular intuitions. It could permit no distinctions between venial and mortal sins; the slightest of them was "against the Great God, can that be a *little Evil?*" It was all or nothing, white or black, God or the Devil.

Thus Thomas Hooker argues that for virtues to be praised merely because they are superior to the ordinary run is a false estimation; by the same token, a man might conclude, the coursest cloth that is to be fine; because, if you compare it with a Rug, it makes a faire shew; will not comparisons make those things that are naughty in themselves seeme good? Let that alone be held for good, that is good in it selfe, whose goodnesse is to be found in the nature of the thing, not in the respective reference onely to that which is worse then naught.

The Puritan was required to love truth for its own sake, "yea to love it when it shall condemne our practises and persons also." He who seeks God for ulterior motives is damned, like Balaam, who "would feather his nest with Immortality." A soul begins the ascent to holiness "when it labours that in all things something more then human excellency may appear"; if in our deeds and prayers anything of ourselves is discerned, "wee fall short of Gods *Name.*" Virtue is not, as Aristotle and the scholastics said, a mean between two extremes, but an extremity itself: "Can you then be too pure and holy? No, you cannot, though you were as full of grace and holinesse as Christ himself." It is not enough for a people to have the right forms of worship and the true church polity if the living God is not to be found in them. Puritan opposition to the Church of England, though grounded theoretically upon the ecclesiastical prescriptions supposedly derived from the New Testament, actually seems to owe more to the Puritan conviction that the beauty of ceremony and ornaments causes men to mistake aesthetic pleasure for supernal grace. By rituals men charm their consciences and then imagine that God is pacified "and all is clear above head"; by musical instruments the mind is stirred, but by a natural and not a spiritual influence, "which they that commend them as an help partly natural and partly artificial, to the exhilarating of the spirits for the praise of God, may do well to consider." Therefore, in their four-square timbered churches they chanted the Psalms as translated in the Bay Psalm Book, where it was proclaimed that God's altar needs not man's polishing and that a literal translation is worth more than all the embellishments of style. Certainly, their temples were not defiled by any strains that would stir their minds to delight rather than frame them to a right disposition.

Mr. George Santayana, writing out of his urbane hostility and the elegance that comes with detachment, has defined Puritanism as "the natural revolt against nature." The seventeenth-century Puritan would not have agreed that the revolt was "natural," but otherwise he would certainly have gloried in the description. He would have asked in reply, what are the results of not revolting against nature? To show what enormities follow he would have pointed, not at Mr. Santayana himself, who might in his own person be uncomfortable refutation, but to the world and the generality of men in it. Not to revolt against nature seemed to him to sit back content with imperfection, to resign life into the power of vice and to turn society over to tyrants, madmen, or money-changers. A favorite commonplace of the Puritan preacher was that the mind is great if the object of its desire is great; "as the things and object are, great, or mean, that men converse withall; so they are high or low spirited." If men esteem small things they will be small, and there is no final determination of what is small except by comparison with the immeasurable. God alone can redeem the mind from meanness. Therefore, Thomas Hooker said, it was a "sweet speech" of him who said that man should lose the creatures in God.

> So, I would have you do, loose your selves, and all ordinances, and creatures, and all that you have, and do, in the Lord Christ. How is that? Let all bee swallowed up, and let nothing be seene but a Christ . . . As it is with the Moone and Starres, when the Sunne comes, they loose all their light, though they are there in the heavens still; and as it is with rivers, they all goe into the Sea, and are all swallowed up of the Sea: and yet there is nothing seene but the Sea. . . . When a man is upon the Sea, he can see no fresh water, it is all swallowed up: So let it bee with thy Soule, when thou wouldest finde mercy and grace.

In order that they might be protected from false values and easy acceptances, Puritans condemned all natural standards and affixed their judgment to a norm so far above any known yardstick that it remained forever indefinable, albeit forever present. It was the Puritan conviction, proceeding from the realization of innate depravity, from the certainty that the natural man could not possibly be a good man, that man must therefore set his course by the one fixed star in all the heavens, although it lay always beyond his horizon.

Recent writers on New England history have tended to minimize the importance of abstract theology and of the pulpit, to point out that whatever the theology, Puritan conduct can be explained without it. This conclusion has the advantages of appealing to an age that has no relish for theology, and of making the task of writing about New England appreciably simpler. It would perhaps be unkind to suggest that historians, particularly those known as "social and economic," are not prone to be themselves conspicuous examples of the Augustinian piety and are therefore the more inclined to discount spiritual motives. Whatever the reason, many students of Puritan journals and behavior, finding both preoccupied with "cases of conscience," conclude that the essence of Puritanism was its morality and that its theology was no more than an unnecessarily elaborate rationalization. If such a view is entirely correct the story of thought and expression in New England should pass over the abstract ideas more hurriedly than the present work is disposed to do.

No doubt the importance of the creed can be over-stressed; unless the sermons and the tracts are read with constant reference to social backgrounds and economic trends, there is every danger that the doctrine will be held responsible for traits which are simply those of the age in general, of the culture of middle-class Englishmen, or of physical adjustments to the new environment. The Puritans were middle-class Englishmen engaged in New England in an eminently practical task of settlement, and they were men rather of action than of contemplation. None of them can be called original thinkers. Their thought was inherited and transported; their intellectual energies were devoted to learning what others had taught or at best to making novel combinations of ideas already enunciated. The writers achieved some startling effects by this method, but not until Jonathan Edwards was there a mind capable of sustained independent speculation. The standard textbook survey of theology used by New England students, William Ames's *Medulla,* said frankly that divinity is not a speculative discipline but a practical one. It admonished young preachers to treat lightly the "naked finding out and explication of the truth" and to concentrate on "use." John Preston said that the end of theology was action, and in his sermons would apologize if he stayed too long "in the doctrinal part." Thomas Hooker was impatient of metaphysical argument: "While we are parlying and disputing what we should do," he said, "we omit so long to do what we ought, and unfit our selves to do what we intend"; and Samuel Willard insisted that "the end of spiritual Principles is for spiritual Performances." The Puritan does not seem ever to have deliberately chosen to spend long hours unraveling theological knots; he was forced to become proficient in dividing a hair 'twixt north and northwest side by the necessities of a highly controversial age.

It is also true that much of the preaching was given over to the inculcation of sobriety and self-control. In the early half of the century, when the tempo of religious zeal was mounting, the clergy strove continually to hold their followers in check. In New England occasional outbursts of enthusiasm, particularly the emotional excitement aroused by Anne Hutchinson, called forth still more ministerial counsels of moderation. Sermons demanded discretion and prudence: "Prudence doth not abate diligence, but guides it in its worke." Thomas Hooker told his people that their souls should be under the spirit as the hand of a child learning to write is guided and controlled by the teacher. In a sentence that speaks volumes for the Puritan character he says, "I know there is wilde love and joy enough in the world, as there is wilde Thyme and other herbes, but we would have garden love and garden joy, of Gods owne planting." Because the Puritan ideal was one of intensity but not of emotional abandon, and because religious passions were constantly threatening to get out of hand, much of Puritan preaching and of the introspection recorded in Puritan diaries is necessarily ethical.

Yet in their own eyes morality, however important, was secondary to the issues of salvation and regeneration. It may be that as a matter of historical fact many Puritan actions were largely determined by environment and economic interests, but Puritans themselves believed they followed from the condition of their souls. Ethics was a corollary of piety, it did not precede and prepare for belief, but was the temporal aspect of faith. In theological terms this idea was phrased: *"Sanctification* flowes from *Iustification;* Being justified, we are sanctified," which meant simply that virtue and morality were useless if there was no regeneration. The important quest was grace; if men once had it, they would endeavor the good life as a consequence. In justification the believer is freed from the guilt of sin; then in sanctification he is freed from its power. "Where ever fire is, it will burn, and where ever faith is, it cannot be kept secret." Grace will inevitably manifest itself in "conversation." But it was essential that the improvement in behavior follow regeneration; what preceded could have no value. The gulf between sin and morality could be bridged only by grace; when New Englanders were tempted at last to overleap it, trusting in their natural strength, and sought ethical results without first securing the heart, they had ceased to be Puritans.

There was, however, one consequence of the original doctrine of regeneration that was eventually to accelerate the development of moralism: Puritans contended that regeneration was usually an ascertainable experience, that men could tell whether or not they were in a state of grace. With this conclusion they went beyond Augustine, for he would never have said point-blank that the presence of grace could be verified by external symptoms; he would never have claimed that a man himself could positively know whether he had it or not, much less that a set of impartial examiners could discover the true state of his soul. Yet Augustinian theology, in other hands than Augustine's, tends toward this deduction which the Reformation made explicit. Protestantism was definite on the point chiefly because in the doctrines that faith was recognizable and that assurance of salvation could be obtained the reformers found serviceable weapons against the Church of Rome. Papal tyranny seemed to Protestants maintained by the withholding of these truths. The devout trudged upon an endless treadmill of anxiety and uncertainty, with no promise of relief; their religion was made a nightmare so that they would the more desperately cling to the church, burn candles, say their beads, and contribute to the support of the priests. Protestant leaders were determined to put a stop to what they deemed this sacerdotal profiteering. They were convinced that to require men to pursue faith endlessly, and yet to give them no hope of knowing when they had definitely reached it, was to prevent their ever seriously undertaking the search.[2] As Preston put it, men will not set themselves upon a work which they know they can never finish; "for every one loves to goe about things of a finite nature, which may be accomplished." The Catholic doctrine that God gives grace as a reward for good works seemed to Protestants to throw upon sinful man a greater burden than he could bear:

They finding people in trouble of mind, doe hold them in doubting and by their doctrine leave them in desparation, because they teach them not to looke for salvation by the free mercy of God, and the merits of Iesus Christ, but partly (at least) by their owne workes. . . . And hereof it commeth to passe, that they seeing their sinnes many, and deserving certaine damnation, and their workes imperfect, are ever afraid they have not done enough, and so fall to despaire; the proper fruit of this doctrine.

If only for the opportunity it gave to undermine the foundations of Rome, Protestants would have preached assurance of election, but they were at the same time convinced of it on other grounds. Logical deduction from the principle of election can demonstrate that to each individual's question there must be an answer somewhere, and the theory of regeneration will indicate that the answer must be made known to him in time. There is a goal to be won, a release from ceaseless striving, a chord of rest. Consequently an indispensable element in all Protestantism was the equating of faith with the certainty of salvation. "The life of faith doth not onely bring us on to justification, but in time it brings us to the assurance of it." By the beginning of the seventeenth century the connection was made explicit; hundreds of theologians had written in "just refutation of that Popish Doctrine, that thinke it impossible for a man to know that he is in an estate of grace." By the time the migration sailed for New England, Puritan divines were engaged in drawing up the "signes of Faith," by which a man or his pastor might ascertain whether he were among the elect of God. Once in New England they preached that though a man may not be able to name the precise moment of his conversion,

yet every one should, and if gracious, he can give such proper and special evidence, such never failing and infallible fruits of this work, that they may undoubtedly discover to others, and ascertain to his own soul, that the stroke is struck indeed.[3]

At the end of the century Samuel Willard, summarizing the principal facts to be learned from each of the sources of information available to man, concluded thus:

Of all knowledge, that which concerns our selves is the most profitable, and of our selves, that which informes us about our eternity is the most desirable: The souls immortality is discovered by a beam of natures light, the happiness of some, and misery of others in their immortality is evident by Scripture revelation; the uncerteinty of our present condition here, is known by constant experience: He therefore, and only he can enjoy solid comfort, who hath an hope grounded in knowledge that it shall at last go well with him.

Of all the knowledge man can derive from the light of nature, from revelation, and from experience, the crown and glory of all is the certainty of his election and the assurance of his ultimate ascension into heaven.

The Puritans were never so simple as to set up a hard and fast rule by which at one stroke the sheep could be separated from the goats. They believed that there were certain signs of true regeneration; they did not hold that all the regenerate always exhibited them. They recognized that the process of regeneration was a mystery, that it might last over a period of time as well as be wrought in the twinkling of an eye, and that many might really have true faith while not yet sensible of it. But making allowance for all such particular cases, the Puritans were certain that in the majority of instances the translation from sin to grace was so abrupt that a man could tell when it happened to himself, and others could recognize the outward evidences. Textbooks such as Ames's *Marrow* listed the tests, while the ministers asserted that though no man can discover the secret windings of the heart, yet God lays down in His Word "infallible signes, whereby people may know whether they are in the truth of grace." Chief among these signs was the inward impact of true grace itself, a spiritual sense which believers must have in themselves and which they cannot fail to recognize, though they may be unable to describe it in words.

> For saints have an experimental knowledge of the work of grace, by virtue of which they come to know it as certainly—as we dispute against the Papists—as by feeling heat, we know fire is hot; by tasting honey, we know it is sweet.

A person must know whether he has grace first of all by his own experience, "as a woman that is breeding a Child feels such qualmes and distempers, that shee knows thereby shee is with Child." Also, there are other signs, and among them, not altogether as reliable as the first, but still within measure trustworthy, is conduct. If a man has been regenerated the fact will show in his moral life: "sound sorrow is ever accompanied with sound reformation." If justification entails sanctification, then conversely sanctification becomes an evidence of justification.

> If men keep Gods Commandements, which is to perform good works, . . . wee may come to know that wee know Christ . . . though this doth not justifie us, yet wee say, they do justifie the truth of our Estate and that is no small matter. . . . Wee grant much comfort from good works, for though they do not justifie us, yet hereby wee know that we are justified.

A Christian's sanctification may be used as a ground for concluding his justification only if he has first discerned the faith within him, "for though true sanctification be an evidence of a mans justification, yet it selfe must be first evident." Still, granting a subjective event which may very well have been regeneration, it then follows that obedience to the precepts of religion becomes, as the phrase of the time had it, a "scientifical argument" of fellowship with Christ.

Therefore the absorbing preoccupation with problems of morality exhibited in Puritan sermons and casuistry, the never-ending siftings of every day's doings which fill the Puritan diaries, must be read in the light of the doctrine of regeneration. The chief value of a Puritan's actions in his own eyes was symbolical; they were emblems of his election rather than ethically commendable deeds. He did not propose, or at least should not have proposed, discovering a moral code while he was putting his life under the microscope. His principal interest in behavior was its source. Guilt or innocence consisted not in what was done but in what was intended. Here was no estimate to be made by a simple rule of thumb, for, as we have seen, a host of natural causes could produce effects practically identical with those that follow upon grace.

> To distinguish in men between that Sanctification which floweth from the Law, and that which is of the Gospel, is a matter so narrow, that the Angels in Heaven have much ado to discern who differ.

Therefore it is no easy matter "to make such use of Sanctification, as by it to beare witnesse unto Justification." Because natural conscience frightens men, because reason calculates that honesty is the best policy, because men want approbation or fear hellfire, because they have been well educated, because they are aided by some "common grace," by the example of a father or a pastor, for any of a thousand such reasons, men will take on the cloak of sanctification. "It will behove Christians to be wary, for even Eagle-eyed Christians will have much adoe so to discerne of sanctification in themselves, before they see their justification, as to cut off all hypocrites from having the like in them." So conscious were the ministers of the dangers and difficulties that in addition to lecturing their people on the signs of faith they also added rules for detecting "the difference between the natural affection of hope and this spiritual gift of hope in God." In their eagerness that every yeoman and merchant understand the difference they frequently delivered what amount to tirades against morality. John Preston had taught them that God's wrath is set against "the free, civill men, that carry themselves soberly, deale justly with men, that doe well in many things" while actuated by the wrong principles, by their own strength and not by the glory of God; such men, he said, "are as abominable to God, as those that run into the greatest outrages." Thomas Hooker in New England thundered damnation upon hollow righteousness: "Such a one as is outwardly just, temperate, chaste, carefull to follow his worldly businesse, will not hurt so much as his neighbours dog, payes every man his owne, and lives of his owne." Thomas Shepard, preaching before the students of Harvard College, sneered at those who are kept virtuous by their "civil education, whereby many wild natures are by little and little tamed, and like wolves are chained up easily while they are young." For a sinner to think he can achieve moral excellence without a call is very great folly: it is as though a poor milkmaid were loved by a king "and shee should put it off and refuse the match, till she were a Queene, whereas, if she will match with the King, hee will make her a Queene afterwards." When Puritans begin to content themselves with pious works, arguing from an ability to perform them the certainty of their election, and neglect to make certain of the regeneration itself, when they become good citizens and churchmen without a previous "experimental knowledge" of an intoxicating and ravishing faith, they do in truth become moralists whose philosophy is based upon social and economic considerations. But by that time they have ceased to be Puritans.

This much, consequently, is clear: the doctrine of regeneration caused the founders of New England to become experts in psychological dissection and connoisseurs of moods before it made them moralists. It forced them into solitude and meditation by requiring them continually to cast up their accounts. The Lord will not make his way to the heart in the throng of a city, "but in a solitary Desart place, he will allure us, and draw us into the wildernesse, from the company of men, when he will speak to our heart." Thomas Hooker compared meditation to "Perambulation"—"when men goe the bounds of the Parish, they goe over every part of it, and see how farre it goes; so meditation is the perambulation of the soule." Characteristic of Puritan exhortations is this of Jonathan Mitchell's:

> Pursue and follow home in frequent self-examination, by applying and considering the Scripture-evidences of a state of Salvation, and searching whether they be found with thee; so shall you come acquainted with your own estate, and the spirit breaths in that way to help us to know the things that are freely given us of God.

Before his regeneration the sinner must scrutinize his soul each day for the first stirrings of grace; afterwards the saint must not relax his vigilance, for not only is the working of grace within the soul a strange and wonderful occurrence which must be studied intently, but after it has appeared the soul will still encounter dejection. It will not always be rapt in ecstatic illumination, and when the moment has passed it will seem as though the glory has departed. It is often difficult to see how Puritan divines could believe that they offered battered humanity any more of a haven than the priests, for in practice he who was justified by faith was taken from the rack of fear only to be strapped to the wheel of doubt. The Augustinian piety lives by its moments of exaltation; it requires that they who have great moments live afterwards in the memory of them, but no man on his black days can be certain that it was the finger of God which touched him the day before yesterday—particularly when his minister tells him that Satan can simulate an angel of light and lead men to destruction by giving them false confidence. The emotional alternations to which all believers in a supernatural influence are already liable were aggravated among the Puritans to a frenzy by their apprehension lest they be swindled of true grace with a premature and natural counterfeit. Yet the clergy were never inhibited from denouncing Catholic theology merely because their own created appallingly similar effects. They had another theory which satisfactorily explained this matter, a doctrine that was to be of great importance in the intellectual development of New England. For lack of a better name it may be dubbed the doctrine of imperfect regeneration. When a man is chosen, clearly he must be irrevocably elected; the grace of God, being of God, must *ipso facto* be effectual and irresistible. Hence when a man is once truly justified he is certainly saved, no matter what thereafter happens to him or what he does. Yet in this life the regenerated man is not at once made perfect; he still retains his body and sensual desires; his sin is not expelled, but grace is given him to resist it and defeat it. The struggle is a hard one, sin is not vanquished in a day or in a month. Communion with God admits of no degrees "properly so called, but it is together and at once perfect in one only act, although in respect of the manifestation, sence, and effects, it hath divers degrees." In the last respect, the degree objectively exhibited may indeed be very slight. It is not to be wondered at, therefore, that the truest of saints should at times have doubts about himself, that he should fall into his old lusts, or even commit worse crimes than the unregenerate themselves. He could conceivably be hanged for murder and yet have his election sure. The strongest assurances will waver, and there will be times when the called will lose hope more dismally than ever they did before their vocation. Yet all this time the final issue is settled could they but know it. Defects in their sense of security arise not from a defect in grace, but from the corruption which still adheres to physical being. "It is not the office of faith to cherish and maintaine such feares and doubts, but to resist them, to fight against them, and so much as is possible to expell them, and driue them out." Time and time again faith will subdue them, but so long as we dwell on earth it cannot completely expel them. The graces of God in the soul, like the trees of the field,

> have their spring, wherein they in their glorious hue are comparable to *Salomon* in his royalty, so haue they their winter, wherein their sap retireth to the root, the branches seeme to be withered, as if they were not the same, no life in them: so is it with the graces of God in mans soule, they have their spring and summer seasons, they have also their winter, wherein they seeme cleane blasted and decayed, as if there were no seeds of grace in their hearts; and as we must not call in question the vegetative power and life that is in plants and hearbs, by reason of the little appearance thereof in the dead time of the yeere; no more must wee make question of the truth of grace in our hearts.

Communion with heaven must necessarily be intermittent on earth. Worldly occasions intrude upon spiritual joy. By the time the heart is well "warmed" at the church service, "and you begin to see its good being here," the Sabbath is over and on Monday there is dull labor again.

To hearten the pious through such fluctuations the ministers used several devices for encouragement. The most obvious was the exhortation to bear up with the reflection that when they reached heaven there would be "no Interruption, no breaking off, a full spring-tyde without any Ebb." A more useful counsel was to remember in times of temptation that a totally depraved mind would be unable to frame enough imagination of holiness to realize its lack. A fairly reliable test was perseverance; if the grace was not of the right stamp it would wear thin, whereas in true saints it would endure. Yet this test was not infallible, because hypocrites might maintain a façade of righteousness all their lives, and saints might be overcome by sin a hundred times a day. The one sure certification of true faith was to be made from an examination of what the soul desired: whether it craved holiness for holiness' sake or merely for the release from pain. If it wanted the former, all was well; if the latter, then indeed what had seemed like vocation was not by the voice of God.

> Suffer mee to expresse my selfe after this manner, that every one may understand: Conceive two women, the one sicke . . . desires the Physitian, to bee healed by him, the other desires him not so much to be healed, but shee is desirous to be married to him. So it is with the soule that is carried in a kinde of love and affection to godlinesse, hee would not have Christ onely to heale him, but he would be married to Christ.

Unfortunately this touchstone was not easy to apply. The metaphor of Hooker's eloquence is deceptive in its simplicity, as is the nature of metaphors. To tell whether one desires grace for itself alone and not for the benefits accruing from it is a hard point to establish. A Puritan was forced to go through life thinking that if what he had supposed was his regeneration was authentic, he was secure; if it was not, he was worse off than ever. Therefore it behooved him to make as certain as he could. The only way to tell was meticulous and unceasing self-examination.

Much depended on what technique he employed in this psychological vivisection. The Puritan was plagued by repeated discoveries that there is no principle known to man which sinful nature cannot misuse or Satan contrive into a snare. Man can undertake self-search, perceive his sin, pray for repentance, and then wax secretly so satisfied with himself for becoming humble as to spoil the whole enterprise. "Therefore you had need pray for the repentance of your repentance; and to beg the pardon of all your prayers." As soon as the will attains resignation to God, it turns about and self-consciously congratulates itself upon its own cleverness: "the secret passage of the Soule is most subtle here." The distinction between humiliation and discouragement is extremely difficult to make, yet only the former is a sign of true regeneration. Only a sinner despairs. A minister must indeed be a skillful doctor of souls, "and so experienced that he might be able in some measure to find out the nature of the disease"; he must have learned compassion on the same sea on which sinners now are tossing, but he must not bend the truth to fit men's humors, "nor answer the desires of their hearts in speaking what they would have him." The search of soul must be impersonal, meditation must be thorough. Hooker employs another simile, this one recalling the scrutiny to which ships plying to and from the Bay were subjected by the agents of Archbishop Laud: just as the customs officer unlocks every chest and "romages every corner," so meditation must take into consideration "all the secret conveyances, cunning contrivements, all bordering circumstances that attend the thing, the consequences of it, the nature of the causes that work it, the several occasions and provocations that lead to it, together with the end and issue that in reason is like to come of it." The true saint, as was said of Thomas Hooker, is one "vers'd in digging into the Mines and Veins of Holy Scriptures, to find how they agreed with his own Experiments"; his soul has "traversed the intricate Meanders, and the darkened (through temptations) windings of this narrow passage and entrance into Life *(and few there be that find it)*." By deep reflection upon every step and every aspect of God's procedure with him, by carefully checking his every response with the written word of God, the saint learns little by little to avoid the crooked by-ways in which darkened men go astray. To navigate such reefs and shoals successfully the soul must be piloted by the spirit peculiar to the elect, but in so hazardous a passage the members of the crew do not lounge on the decks, trusting the pilot to sail the ship; they stand by every line and stay to do his instant bidding. The true saint, though under the guidance of the spirit, applies himself the more intently, the more assiduously, to probing every recess of his being, to leaving no place unexplored in which sin might hide, to unmasking every disguise which nature puts on in its frantic effort to pretend holiness without actually surrendering its lusts.

Much of this introspection, as we now read it, makes doubly strange the many declarations that only the true Puritan doctrine gave the peace which Papal teachings denied. Surely if ever a theology tortured its votaries it was that taught by New England divines, and if ever mortal was driven to distraction it was the mother who, as Winthrop tells, drowned her child that it might escape damnation. As John Cotton succinctly put it, "From doubtings, ariseth trouble of mind, and terror of conscience." To some extent Puritan boasts that the assurance of salvation will give men relief from despair was a device for propaganda, promising that in addition to being true, the doctrine offered the gratuitous charm of happiness. To a still greater extent, however, the Puritan argument must be interpreted in terms of the religious intensity characteristic of the early seventeenth century. The

English Puritan was only one among many individuals in the age to whom the most profound truth ever uttered was the prayer of Augustine, "O God, thou has made us for thyself, and our hearts are restless until they find rest in thee." [4] At a time when salvation was the all-engrossing issue, when men were slaughtering each other on German battlefields for their religious differences, even while new skepticisms threatened the foundations of all certainties, then, no matter how many practical difficulties attended the doctrines of election and reprobation, the assurance that in the mind of God the fate of all men was definitely settled became an immovable cliff above a tempestuous sea. That emotional tension was not confined to New England, and that some measure of Augustinian piety was expressed by other than Puritans, will appear at once by comparing Puritan thought with that of a John Donne or a Pascal. In point of sheer earnestness, the journal of William Laud is fully the equal of any Puritan diary. When Puritanism is seen in relation to the epoch the grounds for many of the more superficial charges against it disappear. Puritans did not put an abnormal stress upon the religious life as against all others, nor were they fanatics on the subjects of salvation and damnation.

Yet it is also true that, when compared with analogous contemporaneous movements, Puritanism shows some unique features. We cannot properly say that it was more intense than the others, but it was certainly as intense as any, and in a particular fashion. Its peculiar ferocity came from its absolutism, its refusal to make allowances for circumstance and weakness, from its judging by the highest possible standard, its unremitting measurement of the human by the divine. Its requirement that men disregard all advantages to be gained from truth in order to follow truth itself was both majestic and pathetic; it was both the strength and the limitation of Puritanism that it permitted no discharge in the holy war. If a man's religious life were to follow the course mapped out by the clergy, it would begin with turmoil at the first realization of sin:

> A broken battered Soule, that hath beene long overwhelmed with the weight of his corruptions, the Lord brings him to a marvellous desperate low ebbe: You may see a man sometime in the torment of Conscience, that nature and naturall parts begin to decay; his understanding growes weake, and his memorie failes him, and he growes to bee marvellously distracted, and besides himselfe; so that the partie which was (before) a man of great reach and of able parts, and was admired, and wondred at for his wisedome, and government; he is now accounted a silly sot, and a mad man, in regard of the horror of heart that hath possessed him.

From the initial onset he must struggle not merely to escape the horror of heart that possesses the unregenerate, but to pass beyond all human weakness: "In all services: a man should not bee quiet in his affections & endeavours till he come to the highest pitch, that is Gods glory." There is no stopping halfway. When grace lends aid, the intensity does not lessen; those who allow it to slacken prove that they have not received grace but an imitation of it. Hooker, who again is the most eloquent on the subject, uses a figure which was worked for all it was worth by many preachers:

> Looke as it is with a Gold-smith that melteth the metall that hee is to make a vessell of, if after the melting thereof, there follow a cooling, it had bin as good it had never beene melted, it is as hard, haply harder, as unfit, haply unfitter than it was before to make a vessell of; but after he hath melted it, hee must keepe it in that frame till hee come to the moulding and fashioning of it: So meditation is like fire, the heart is like a vessell.

"Deadness of heart" was the most insupportable curse the Puritan was called upon to bear. How often from the diaries of those who seemed to have little outward cause for complaint does the cry go up: "Today much deadness of heart." Dullness, coldness, emptiness were more to be lamented than any specific sin; loss of estate, even of friends, was an occasion for thankfulness if thereby the floodgates of being were opened and the spirit once more flowed freely. The sermons denounce enemies and libertines and hypocrites, but they scale the heights of vituperation and scorn when they descant upon the "glozing neuters of the world." Puritan writing by and large makes dull reading, but not when the preachers launch into the theme of spiritual mediocrity. When discussing those who halt midway between good and evil they let themselves go:

> These are they that halt betweene two opinions, your faire fooles, that would harme no man, so no man would harme them: the highest pitch that these come to is this, that they may get respect and credit among the best, and they say, He that meddles least is happiest; these are pretty good civill neighbours, and will sometimes doe a man a good turne, provided that they may not hurt themselves: they will bee of all straines; if a wretched man come, they will bee like him, and now and then strew forth faith and troth, and they will not reprove others, because they shall not censure them . . . If the Minister will bee onely generall, they commend him highly, and say, Oh hee is a very wise discreet man, and knowes how to carry himselfe; yes, and he knowes not how to meddle with them, you must marke that: and if he will preach Doctrinall things, and take five or sixe Doctrines in a Sermon, Oh then hee is a judicious man, and takes the very creame of the Scriptures; but if hee come to discover their basenesse, and to meddle with their corruptions, Oh then he falls to reading that he may not heare, and wisheth that the man would keepe him to his Text. . . . He accounts zeale in a good course like the hot fit of a feaver, very dangerous, and therefore he likes best of a cold lukewarme temper in his profession. . . . Lukewarmnesse is loathsome to the stomacke, therefore appeare in your colours what you are, that you may be known either a Saint or a Divell; lukewarme water goes against the stomacke, and the Lord abhorres such lukewarme tame fooles.

Puritan orators did not usually thump the rostrum or gesticulate like their successors in the camp-meeting and the revival. Their tone was restrained and their manner surgical, but among the first generation the sermons glowed therefore with all the whiter heat. The ministers grappled with the metaphysical problems of free will and foreordination, but in their pulpits, when they thought the occasion demanded, they put aside all such abstruseness and, regardless of logic, demanded of their followers wholehearted, continuous, and heroic exertions. "You must not thinke to goe to heaven on a feather-bed; if you will be Christs disciples, you must take up his Crosse, and it will make you sweat." The imagery used in such passages was the homeliest and most direct, as when Cotton says,

> If a cloth be foully stained, it is not a little rinsing in cold water that will get it out, but it will take much rubbing, batting, and scouring; it is not a few teares, but washing throughly that you must looke for.

As might be expected, the figures of speech were often military; congregations who trained on militia days, marched against the Pequods and fought King Philip's braves, were told that the moment a man becomes converted enemies beset him, that he must either fight or die, that the way to heaven lies through a hostile country, full of ambushes, and that he "must dispute every step at the *Swords point*." There are probably a number of causes that account for the decline of Puritanism, for its various transformations, for the ever-widening circles of rebellion against it that have characterized three centuries of American intellectual history. Economic and social forces contribute much to the change, the development of science dissipates the Puritan cosmology, humanitarianism protests vehemently against Puritan harshness. Yet there are times when to the reader of the words left by the founders these objections lose their force. When the belief and the temper which the first settlers brought to America is examined, when the piety is estimated on the emotional and non-theological level, it seems obvious that the reason later generations ceased marching to the Puritan beat was simply that they could no longer stand the pace.

For over a century those in revolt against the piety have been accusing it of a pathological gloom. The majority of men today, if ever they have occasion to think of the matter, undoubtedly agree that what they understand to be Puritanism takes no stock of ordinary enjoyments, needlessly stifles innocent pleasures, and generally makes a nuisance of itself. They applaud the healthy wisdom which Ben Franklin exhibited by shaking the dust of Boston and of innate depravity from his shoes and setting up shop in the city of brotherly love. Some recent historians have sought to counteract these impressions by showing that they are not always borne out from the known facts of seventeenth-century society. They have demonstrated that even in the shadow of their creed the Puritans were not sexually inhibited, that they read secular poetry, played musical instruments, cracked jokes, and imbibed prodigious quantities of alcoholic beverages. Our interest, however, being not to judge what was done but to narrate what was thought and said, whether it be sad or cheerful, need not be concerned in this controversy. Yet in the light of the Puritan's own words, I am inclined to suspect that both those who attack and those who defend have been speaking beside the point in that they have equally tended to measure the level of lugubriousness by modern standards. Some blame the Puritan way for a harshness which was characteristic of the age or for an asceticism which was then a part of the Christian tradition; meanwhile others, in order to prove that Puritans were not so bad as they have been pictured, seize upon actions which were commonplace in the seventeenth century and adduce them as evidences of an unsuspected jollity. In the heat of the dispute the Puritan's own avowed intentions are virtually ignored.

Even after it is proved that Puritans had more fun out of life than is usually supposed, the fact remains that theirs was a somber way. The versifier's prayer that God would

> grant that I may serious be
> In and about things of Eternitie

was the one request made by New Englanders with which a capricious Deity unfailingly complied. In their own day there were critics who said that "to sit moping in a corner" and to "smoak out their dayes in a melanchollick pressure and pensiveness of spirit" was "a silly kind of sottish behaviour unbecoming persons of a generous spirit." It is important to note that the Puritans were fully aware of the figure they cut. They did not, like some of their modern apologists, argue that a man can have a "good time" even though a Puritan. Living was serious business, and those who took it gaily here would come to a reckoning hereafter. What made it supportable to them was not the incidental amusements along the way but the one engrossing joy of the saints' communion with the God who had made them and had redeemed them.

Joy was only in part an assurance of personal survival. Some divines did say that "the doctrine of Predestination is ungrateful to none that are converted; and that of Election is most precious to all that know themselves to belong to it," but the greater preachers dwelt more frequently upon the impersonal beauty and the sheer loveliness of regeneration.

> The Communion the Saints have with God in his Ordinances here: Oh how sweet is it. . . . The World knows not, nor can they well express the sweet incomes they have; the heart-raising, yea ravishing Communion, the Quicknings, Gracious Breathings, the Comforts they meet with in Prayer, sometimes in Hearing the Word . . . in Meditation . . . in Gracious Spiritual Conference . . .

In the Sacrament of the Supper, where they are refreshed as with new Wine. Why if dark glimpses through these glasses of the Ordinances be so sweet and Glorious . . . what then will the sight face to face be?

Hooker's volume, *The Soules Exaltation,* is a sustained dithyramb on the theme, "Get you into Christ, I say, and you shall bee safe enough, I will warrant you; your soules shall be transported with consolation to the end of your hopes." His contempt for nonentities is no more eloquent than his celebration of the felicities of holiness.

The life of the beleever, is the life that hath most ease with it, and brings most delight with it; there is no life under heaven more free from tediousnesse, and hath more ease and liberty than a Christian course; let a mans condition bee what it will bee, faith makes a mans life most easie: I use to compare the conditions of them that want faith, to the cart that is from his wheeles; they draw heavily, and they are in great extremitie, and they tug and toile, but it will not be drawne with any ease or good successe: so unfaithfull soules sinck in their sorrowes upon every occasion, and their lives are tedious and wearisome; but faith sets the cart upon the wheeles, and carries all away easily and comfortably: you must know thus much, it is the hardest matter in the world to get faith, when we want it; but it is the most easiest life in all the world, and hath the most delight in all the world, if wee have but skill to use it wisely when we have it, and it gives most ease and quiet to a man in all his conversation.

The Puritan would hardly thank his recent champions for their endeavor to patch up his reputation by proving that he could drink a pot of ale or fall in love with a pretty girl. He would feel that if his way of life needed defense, let defenders point to its promise of "spirituall joy arising from peace of conscience, whereby wee rejoyce in our union with Christ, with joy unspeakable and glorious."

Not that the Puritans utterly scorned the minor gratifications or failed to take them into account. Cotton said that "Life is not life, if it be overwhelmed with discouragements," and there are many pages of his sermons devoted to establishing the legitimacy of the ordinary recreations. He found it acceptable to God that we should use gladly what He has provided, eat meat and bread with contentment, "Wine, It [is] to be drunken with a cheerful heart . . . The wife beloved, and she to be joyfully lived withall, all the dayes of thy vanity." He condemned riotous feasts on four counts, each of which is as much descriptive of some banquets of the period as symptomatic of a hypochondriac hostility to well-being:

First, by Excesse in eating and drinking to gluttony and drunkennesse: Secondly, The Company, swaggering and debaucht Ruffians, Swearing and roaring Boyes: Thirdly, Instead of pleasant discourses Ribaldry, wanton songs and dances, abusing of the name of God or man. Fourthly, fallings out and quarellings: or else linking in conspiracy to doe some mischiefe.

As against this sort of repast he gave a clerical approbation to those in which there was good eating and drinking, loving and neighborly company, and "Pleasant discourse and sometimes Musick." Thomas Shepard said—though unfortunately he does not seem to have followed his own prescription—that while grace does not depend on the temper of the body, yet the exercise of it may; therefore a good dinner "and sometimes wine to a sad, melancholy (if gracious) heart" may remove physical obstructions to the working of grace. Thomas Hooker could use, as a simile for the saint's love of God, the love of a man for a woman, showing that he and his supposedly grim-visaged people understood it.

> The man whose heart is endeared to the woman he loves, he dreams of her in the night, hath her in his eye & apprehension when he awakes, museth on her as he sits at table, walks with her when he travels and parlies with her in each place where he comes . . . the heart of the lover keeps company with the thing beloved.

But in this preaching on the amenities there is always a *memento mori*. Cotton cannot tell men to love their wives without adding "all the dayes of thy vanity." Worldly pleasures, even when permissible, turn pale before heavenly ones, and unmistakable limits were set to Puritan cheer. It could not ever exceed a "seasonable cheerfulness."

The one pure, unqualified, and absolute beatitude was the inward ecstasy of regeneration. However hazardous the struggle for grace, however cruel the ordeal inflicted by the secret will of God, however narrow and strait the path, the Puritan could afford to smile at men who pretended that their easier way was also the more delectable. He had his inner sensibility, his "rellish and taste of the sweetnesse" of God's love, the "sent and savour of it, with which he was "deeply affected." No phrases were more reiterated in Puritan sermons than these. John Ball followed the definition of faith from which we have already quoted by a description which reveals still more what faith actually meant to Puritans. "Iustifying faith for nature and qualitie is a spirituall taste, howsoeuer defectiue for degree. It receiueth the word, tasteth, relisheth, and retaineth it, as the most sweet, wholsome, and delectable food." Forbidding as later generations may find that which Puritans called truth, it was beauty and sweetness to those who knew it. Those who see only the outside cannot be expected to love it or to live by it. "For this is a certain and everlasting truth, *viz.* that that truth which a man hath received without love to it, by some sense of the sweetnesse of it, in times of temptation, he will quickly cast off." According to the Puritan way of thinking, those whom God would not cast off he caused to love the truth and to experience a sense of its sweetness. We may prefer to say that those who were capable of loving this truth and believed they had tasted sweetness in it would not of themselves cast it off. In either version the connection between men and the doctrine is subjective. Men were made believers by an inward gladness, and they remained true Puritans as long as they found in their belief the supreme source of joy and an inexhaustible delight.

CHAPTER III

THE INTELLECTUAL CHARACTER

The usual connotations attached to the word "Puritanism" refer almost entirely to its piety. The first New Englanders figure in popular imagination as beings swayed by fanatical dogmas and given to thundering and disagreeable imperatives. The ordinary conception of them does not accurately reflect the true nature of their piety; yet it is probable that even were their religion more sympathetically understood, the judgment of the present age would not be materially altered. To most twentieth-century minds, particularly to many lineal descendants of the Puritans, the movement would still seem a reaction against the "Renaissance spirit," antagonistic not only to "pagan" joy in life, but to Renaissance scholarship as well, to the new learning and humanism. General discussions today, even when well informed concerning the doctrine and creed, find the Puritans interesting almost entirely as psychological studies, either as men intoxicated with God or puffed up with sanctimonious egotism. When they are described as men of piety, it appears that they regarded the Bible as fiat and held the salvation of their individual souls the supreme requirement for successful living; hence the conclusion is frequently implied and often explicitly drawn that the Puritans looked upon philosophy as a sensual indulgence, upon classical authors as contemptible heathens, upon science as a work of the Devil and a hindrance to faith. Neither the friends nor the foes of the Puritans have shown much interest in their intellects, for it has been assumed that the Puritan mind was too weighted down by the load of dogma to be worth considering in and for itself.

There is naturally some justification for this view. No doubt the strain of piety was dominant in the Puritan make-up. Values were translated into theological tenets, inward assurances were externalized into rigid dogmas. Puritans had read in the epistles of Paul that Christianity was foolishness to the Gentiles; they frequently exceeded the Pauline denunciation of reason and metaphysics and declared that religion was to be learned only from revelation and from the spirit. Were such passages to be taken merely by themselves, without reference to the whole body of thought, the conclusion would follow that however interesting Puritanism remains for the study of religious emotion, it has nothing to offer the mind but a brutal authoritarianism. There are many assertions that the Gospel "suits not with Carnal Reason," that ministers cannot teach the Christian life, that no study can attain it, that natural endeavor will never achieve it. Knowledge will not save, and the desire for knowledge, "when it is to no other end but to know," is fatal. Preachers who rely upon judgment and learning are deceivers, "for these may come from nature; but they must come perfumed with graces, to keep themselves and others from putrefaction." Because the things of divinity are above our comprehension, our assent to them is worthless if grounded upon our reasoning, "or because we see into the rational arguments to evince the Truth of them." We do not need formal training to find the essential truths. "If wee have the light of Christ by faith, it will discover all the delusions, and deceits of darkness, that Satan seeks to involve our reasonings in." We should always "have an eye to the *proposition* of Faith," regardless of what seem to be the propositions of reason.

The importance of such utterances must not be minimized. In them we hear again the voice of Augustine, proclaiming that men must first believe in order to know. The conclusions of all possible investigations were already given, and since right reasoning would at best merely arrive at them once more, men might as well forbear reasoning, since there was every probability that they would be betrayed by the fallibility of natural powers or the mendacity of the unregenerated soul. Passages in this vein were not spoken idly, the Puritans could not imagine that revealed truth would ever be completely understood in this world, or satisfactorily expounded to the human reason in the curriculum of post-graduate study.

Yet these remarks tell but half the story. In one sense their point cannot be made too strongly; in another sense it can be too exclusively dwelt upon. From the same writers, from the very same works, in which reason and comprehension are condemned, can be extracted another and as extensive a series of quotations bearing in the opposite direction. Had Puritans merely recited in order the points of dogma and not also endeavored to grasp their inner coherence, had they not set forth a philosophy as well as the assertions of the creed, there would be no accounting for the intellectual history of the last three centuries; in their zeal they were prepared to make short work of some ancient rituals and honored conventions, but they did not therefore cast aside the traditions of their age, nor did they renounce all learning save theology or lose interest in other inquiries besides the religious. They did indeed subordinate all concerns to salvation, and they did force their social and philosophical thinking into conformity with religious conclusions, but they were incapable of confining themselves solely to dogma or giving over the arts and sciences into the keeping of the unregenerate. They were first and foremost heirs of Augustine, but also they were among the heirs of Thomas Aquinas and the pupils of Erasmus.

Hence in certain aspects the Puritan appears an anti-rationalist, but in others he is exceedingly rational; he attacks with fury those misguided zealots who jump to the conclusion that religion can dispense with learning, ministers with education, saints with knowledge, or converts with the fullest possible understanding, not only of theology, but of science and philosophy. Puritan writers can pity the insignificance of human reason, and in the next breath sing the praises of the human mind: "The mind of man is a vast thing, it can take in, and swallow down Heaps of Knowledge, and yet is greedy after more; it can grasp the World in its conception." There are times when the theological sense seems close to the Pickwickian; in describing human depravity a Puritan writer explains that he is not now considering man "as the Philosophers describe him," because from that point of view he is indeed "a noble creature, endued with understanding, with a reasonable appetite, with affections capable of divine objects, with apprehensions and operations suitable to his nature, being able to compare, connect, discourse, deduct, to remember, and perform other noble parts and actions." However deplorable they find the present condition of humanity, the writers always include perfect rationality and complete understanding among the qualities of perfection, and promise the elect that full explanations of this world and its creatures, which they now "gather up something of from Arts and Sciences," will be given unto them in heaven. A saint must believe in order to know—but *after* he has believed he must endeavor to know as much as possible. An ordinary man "takes these things upon trust, and beleeves them, as others doe, but hee doth not much trouble himselfe about them," whereas the true saint never relaxes his efforts so long as a single doubt remains. Only the hopelessly unregenerate rest content with unexplained perplexities; since no man in this life can secure answers to all his questions, life for the regenerate therefore becomes unending effort to translate what they know in their hearts into what they can formulate in their minds. Faith is an act of both the will and the understanding, never of the will alone. The understanding does not assent to a thing merely because the thing is so, "but because it is enlightened to discern the Truth of it." The Puritan preacher never loses a chance to insist that "we must fortify our Understandings with all those Arguments, by which this Principle is established in the Hearts and Consciences of Men." If it is impossible to establish some principles by reason, we can at least trample "upon all those Sophisms that are brought by Men's corrupt Reasonings to enervate them." In true Puritanism, faith can never remain mere spiritual conviction; it must also be made articulate.

Even on the points about which no ultimate reason can be discovered believers do not give over the use of their minds. If explanation is unattainable there is always knowledge to be had. "Faith is grounded upon knowledge," said Samuel Willard; how then can a man choose the ways of God unless he knows what they are? "For this reason it is said, that *without knowledge* the mind of Man cannot be *good,* and that a people are *destroyed* for lack of Knowledge." John Cotton declared that a blind mind can no more grasp heavenly things than a blind eye can judge colors. Mere knowledge alone, without faith, is empty, but also, Cotton added, "zeale is but a wilde-fire without knowledge." God's wrath threatens those who are zealous without "saving knowledge." All questions should be settled by the authority of the Bible and not by human authorities; still, if a controversy is rightly managed, "much good use may be made of their writings, and by the ablest gifted." A minister must have the gifts of grace, but he must also have "prudence," which includes, according to Willard, "both an *Acquaintance* with the *History* of former Times, and Ability to Judge between Rational, and either meerly Casual, or Supernatural Events."

Thus, when the whole range of Puritan thought and writing is passed in review, the impression grows undeniably that though Puritanism was a piety, it was at the same time an intellectual system, highly elaborated and meticulously worked-out. The emotional propulsion was fitted into the articulated philosophy as a shaft to a spear-head. "The end of the Gospel," said John Norton, "is to be known, the duty and disposition of the Beleever, is to know." Conversion was seen as a humbling of the heart, but it was also construed as an enlightening of the mind, and humiliation unaccompanied by a considerable degree of information was worthless. "It is not that colliers faith of the Papists, that put out his owne eyes to see by another mans: this is a delusion and an implicite faith." An "implicite faith," an ignorant faith that believed on trust unsupported by reasons and arguments, was always scorned and attributed to Papists. A man might have much knowledge and lack grace, but a man who had grace would also have knowledge; "historical faith" alone could not save, but many had been lost because their faith was "not so fully historicall as it might be." Divinity was a science, to be mastered with labor and industry, "and the greater mysterie that is infolded in the Science, the greater labour it requireth." No one could be spared the exertion; the meanest believer must learn to give the grounds for his belief. If a Puritan sermon is compared with an evangelical discourse of the eighteenth or nineteenth century, the extremely intellectual character of Puritan religion becomes immediately apparent; though there are Puritan paragraphs that glow with emotion or reflect intense experiences, these are purple patches in an otherwise closely knit, carefully reasoned, and solidly organized disquisition. A Puritan preacher never surrenders to feeling; he does not celebrate the glories of religion in sustained paeans or bring home its terrors by shouting, but argues his way step by step, inexorably disposing of point after point, quoting Biblical verses, citing authorities, watching for fallacies in logic, drawing upon the sciences for analogies, utilizing any information that seems pertinent. He proceeds thus not only in controversy with scholars, but also in composing sermons for the populace. As far as possible he simplifies his explanations, avoids abstruse issues, demands no more of his auditors than he thinks necessary; even so, he demands a degree of close attention that would seem staggering to modern audiences and is not to be paralleled in modern churches. He does not hesitate to put his congregation through the most difficult dialectical paces and take them over lofty metaphysical hurdles. The objective of the sermon was regeneration; it was also "understanding consideration," which meant, according to one president of Harvard College,

> that a person or people syllogize well, and conclude aright concerning the end of their wayes and actions: that they do not . . . reason themselves into a mistake and errour or false conclusion about the end of their deportments towards the Lord, and put a fallacy upon their own Souls in this respect.

Religion is revealed in Scripture, but it is proposed to the mind by the ministry; grace enabling to believe is supernaturally from God, but men must receive the articles of belief "as men, that is, judge of the sense and meaning of them, discover their truth, and finding them revealed, acquiesce in the Authority of him by whom they are first revealed." Bare doctrine, naked dogma—these were not enough. When the reason faltered or sin warped the judgment, the devout could always take refuge in the fiat of authority. But they should flee to arbitrary enactment only as a last resort. "I should be very ill satisfied," says the Puritan minister, "in an irrationall Gospel." Mere zeal alone, however sincere, was not sufficient. The ideal was guidance of the heart by the mind, and while God requires zeal of his people that they may be "active and forward in the pursuit of the things [to] which they engaged," yet in order that zeal may be truly serviceable, "it had need to be well regulated with a right and clear understanding of what they do." Israel was ruined for a lack of "Counsel and Understanding"; understanding requires "an intense and industrious exercise of the mind," and counsel demands "a judicious, fixed or abiding dijudication of things." The elect must have acumen and sharpness, be able "easily and speedily to penetrate into the nature and qualities of things," have "right Ideas, notions and conceptions." The Puritan was abject and mute before "Thus saith the Lord," but once the Lord had spoken, he was ready to investigate the reasons behind what the Lord had said, and to demand of the faithful that they include such reasons in their quest for salvation. They had not only to fulfill but to understand the will of God, though both tasks were equally difficult.

Piety, therefore, is only a half of Puritanism. It is the essential part, no doubt; yet unless we consider the machinery of theory and demonstration which accompanied it, we can give no full account of Puritan thought and expression. In the seventeenth century the intellectual elements were adjuncts to faith, but in our perspective they often take on more importance; out of the philosophy came the lines of thought that continued to develop long after the religious impulse had waned. If we today still insist upon calling Puritanism an absolute authoritarianism we will be much disconcerted by its continual appeal to experience and reason. John Preston characteristically proved his points first by authority and then by reason. Thomas Hooker reinforced a dogma on the grounds that it had "reason and common-sense to put it beyond gainsaying"; he would explain a difficult text "by al the little light I have," in order to give "a savory and seasonable interpretation," and he was eulogized by his colleague, Samuel Stone, for his work in clarifying "dark Scripture" and making "the truth appear by light of reason." Later Puritans in New England continued to invoke rationality: Hubbard called reason "our most faithful and best Councellour," and Willard preached upon affliction, the most capricious manifestation of almighty power, so that believers might know "what you may rationally propound to your selves." We would seriously overstate the case did we call Puritanism a form of "rationalism"; yet the works of New England divines and of their friends in England, as well as the textbooks used in Puritan education, make it apparent that Puritanism was, if not a rationalism, then decidedly a reasonableness. Among the attributes of God was perfect rationality as well as absolute will and infinite sovereignty, and man was created in the image of God. As an English Puritan put it in an address to Parliament,

> That God who is abstract wisdome, and delights that his rationall creatures should search after it, and that his Ministers should study to propogate it, will expect that you should be Foster-fathers of knowledge.

Divine wisdom overflows the limits of human reason, and the mind of man is terribly decayed; hence the universe does not always seem to conform to the principles of human rationality. Faith must keep reason at heel. But no matter how irrational the government of God may seem to His uncomprehending creatures, it is so only in appearance. Faith is called upon to believe, not merely in redemption, but in the reason behind all things. The regenerated intellect may not understand "abstract wisdome," but it can catch at least a glimmering. By the very fact of being regenerated the intellect is duty-bound to strive for such a glimpse.

The highly intellectual character of the Puritan creed becomes more apparent if we consider it in its seventeenth-century setting. In their day the Puritans found themselves called upon to define their position against two extremes of anti-rationalism, the Catholic and the Protestant; and when confronted with either of these dogmatisms they made explicit the reasonable affirmations ever latent in their thought, though generally disguised by copious denunciations of human depravity and subordinated to a veneration for the Word. Against the rationalizing theologians of the Church of England, against Arminians, Socinians, and Erastians, orthodox Puritans exalted the arbitrary revelation, doggedly recited Biblical verses and closed their ears to Richard Hooker's temperate persuasions, but when they turned about to deal either with skeptics or with mystics—with those who sought not merely to chasten reason but to annihilate it—they took their fingers out of their ears and caught up the weapons of their erstwhile opponents. It is characteristic of the Puritan divine that he would make miserable the last hours of Chillingworth and condemn *The Religion of Protestants* for rank heresy, but when he was confronted with a Montaigne or an Anne Hutchinson, with a Dryden or a John Fox, he would speak with what seems to be Chillingworth's voice.

The Catholic attack upon reason came in the form of "fideism." Many Catholic disputants prized this argument for its great strategic value, because from the beginnings of the Reformation it had become obvious that the Protestant appeal to Biblical authority was in reality an appeal to the Protestants' interpretation of it. The various schools of thought among the Protestant churches had made abundantly clear that Scripture was not altogether self-evidencing. Protestant divines were not dismayed by this discovery, for they never doubted that their own readings were demonstrably true. In a century of debate they had gone far, in terms of the scholarship of the age, toward maintaining their various contentions. Therefore certain Catholic apologists executed a clever flank movement by giving up wrangling over specific interpretations and accusing the human mind in general of being unable to interpret. They argued with great show of logic that since the reason of man was utterly corrupted, his only hope was surrender, blind and "implicite," to the guidance of faith, and therefore of the instituted church. They seemed to be yielding with a vengeance to arguments hitherto used by Protestants, to be going them one better in literal acceptance of the doctrines of original sin and innate depravity. It is true that the sources of this fideism were not always Christian, that Greek skepticism and Montaigne contributed as much as St. Paul. It is also true that fideism was not confined to Catholic apologists; many defenders of the Anglican church discovered that it offered them the same advantages against the Puritans which Catholics found in it against Protestants in general; many Englishmen could go as far as *Religio Laici* without continuing to *The*

Hind and the Panther. But from the Puritan point of view fideism was a wile of Babylon, a Papist trick to confuse the devout and mock the truth. In self-defense the ministers were compelled to point out that the doctrine of original sin did not mean that men should utterly cast aside their reason merely because it was tainted by the sin of Adam. Though Puritan divines ordinarily declared that the mind of man is abysmally corrupt and that reason is a treacherous guide, yet when they discussed Popish arguments they assured their hearers that such pronouncements were to be taken with a grain of salt.

In New England there was no pressing necessity to counter Catholic arguments, but still the divines, being good Protestants, made occasions to contribute their share to the common front against Rome, and thereby showed that they, like their continental brethren, appealed as much to reason as to Scripture whenever they came into conflict with Catholicism. Cotton Mather's words were typical, and illustrate as well as any the tension in the Puritan mind between piety and reason: the doctrine of transubstantiation, he said, was so absurd and irrational that should we accept it we should "altogether loose all the use of *common sense,* and *Natural Reason,* in those very things which God Himself has made them judges in; and we can be sure of Nothing, all the World must Evaporate into Nothing with us." Puritanism was dogmatic up to a point, authoritarian on the essential tenets of the creed, but it was not so dogmatic as to surrender demonstration, not so authoritarian as to abandon rational comprehension. On the contrary, there was a wide field in which God had given men competence to ascertain truth by their common sense and natural reason; were men to lose this ability the intelligible world would disintegrate into chaos. Dogma and authority could exist only in conjunction with the exercise of reason and judgment.

Puritans in England naturally found the Catholic attack a more serious matter, and devoted themselves more extensively to distinguishing their belief from fideism. The New England leaders were so much in accord with the authors of the two principal works on this question that there is every reason to believe they would have written in the same vein. John Owen's *Animadversions on Fiat Lux* (1662) was a direct reply to a Catholic work,[1] and Richard Baxter's *The Judgment of Non-conformists, of the Interest of Reason in Matters of Religion* (1676) sought to prove against the Catholics, and incidentally against Anglicans who borrowed Catholic thinking, that Puritans were at one with orthodox Protestants in rejecting fideism. Baxter's book is in fact rather a party manifesto than an individual treatise, for the chief leaders among the dissenters attested their approval, and from passing references in New England sermons as well as from the whole tone of New England expression it is clear that all New England divines could have signed the endorsement. If *The Pilgrim's Progress* is a supreme statement of the Puritan spirit, these two contemporaneous works, though of infinitely less literary merit, are no less important for a definition of the Puritan mind.

Far from being dismayed over conflicts of opinion among the jarring sects of Protestantism, far from concluding therefore that truth is unattainable and that men should no longer strive for comprehension but simply cultivate a will to believe, Owen takes courage from the reflection that if men contend over the meaning of Scripture, there must exist one certain, sure, and stable meaning at which they will ultimately arrive. Though controversy is deplorable and no one should deliberately encourage disagreement, truth is not to be attained by giving over analysis, explanation, deduction, and debate, but by pressing them all the more energetically. Men can discover the sense of Scripture only by their reason; they must judge "of what is spoken to them according to that Rule which they have received for the measure and guide of their Understandings in these things." The same high confidence that whatever the imperfections of reason it was given to man for settling the positive content of faith, the same instinctive hostility to skepticism, the same dislike of easy acceptance of the incomprehensible, the same refusal to live comfortably among unknowables, is revealed in Baxter's pronouncement. The Word of God is of course the utterance of Jehovah and to be accepted whether or not we understand its whys and wherefores, but, granting this much, there remain many tasks for the reason. When Baxter has finished enumerating these tasks, we may justifiably wonder whether the original concession, the granting of an arbitrary authority to the God of revelation, is anything more than a verbal concession, for as he extends the scope of interpretation he seems in effect to make the Bible serve merely as a convenient starting point for the construction of a rational cosmology.

> We must use our best *Reason* in diligent Meditation, and Judgement, to search the *Works* of God in Nature, to know which are the true Canonical Scriptures, to discern true *Copies,* and *Readings* where the Copies differ, to *expound* the Text, to Translate it truly, to discern the *Order* of sacred Verities that are dispersed through all the Scriptures, to gather them into *Catechismes,* and *Professions* of Faith, discerning things more necessary from the less needful. . . . To gather just, and certain Inferences from Scripture Assertions: To apply general Rules to particular Cases, in matters of Doctrine, Worship, Discipline, and ordinary Practice, prudently to discern those Duties, which are but generally commanded in the Scripture, and left to be discerned by us, in particular, according to determining Accidents, Circumstances, and Occurrences, which must be considered, and compared. And when Parents, Magistrates, Pastors, Tutors, or Masters, shall so determine of such particulars in the Government of their Inferiours, which belong to their several Relations, or Offices to determine of, according to Gods general Laws, or Rules, Inferiours must obey them in such determinations; and in so doing they do obey Gods General Laws, and

obey God consequentially, in obeying such Laws of his Officers as he authorizeth them to make.

Obviously, if the function of reasonable interpretation was conceived on so large a scale, and if deductions according to reason were as authoritative as the text, then very few questions could be raised which a mere citation would be wholly sufficient to determine. Only on the broad principles of the Christian religion would there be no occasion for reason's judgment; as soon as investigation was narrowed to particulars, then reason must interpret the Word. Men like Owen, Baxter, and the New England divines did not realize that the ultimate effect of their argument would be steadily to lessen the importance of the words in the Bible while the scope of interpretation was progressively extended, yet toward such an end seventeenth-century Puritanism was deliberately traveling, for as Baxter insisted throughout this significant volume, "the *most Religious,* are the *most* truly, and nobly *rational.*"

It was not difficult for Puritan divines to maintain anything, least of all the prestige of natural reason, when opposing Catholics. A very different task confronted them when they undertook to preserve rational method and the heritage of scholarship from attack by their own followers. Protestantism always ran a hazard that through excess of zeal its doctrine might be perverted to erroneous conclusions. Unsophisticated laymen could never understand, after they had been taught that the natural mind was abysmally incompetent and that God had uttered the truth in clear and simple dicta, why they should still need ministers skilled in the sciences, in rhetoric, logic, and physics, in order to hear and comprehend the explicit word of God. They argued with a naïve plausibility that since regeneration infused God's own substance into the elect, then a regenerated man thereafter required no other mentor than the Holy Ghost, no other instruction than its ever-present promptings. "For it is *only* the *Inspiration of God,* that inables a man to know the *things of God,* and not a mans *study* or *Humane Learning*. . . . No man can know *Christ* and His *Gospel* . . . but by the most *present Teaching* and *Revelation* of God himself by his *Spirit.*" From the time of the Anabaptists at Münster, Protestant theologians strove with might and main to keep justification by faith from becoming a justification of illiteracy. Such a perversion of the doctrine was as horrible to them as the Catholic, for both came in effect to the same conclusion, that reason is to be excluded from religion, that sincerity makes knowledge superfluous, that faith can and should dispense with learning. Too much zeal was no more commendable than a lack of it, and in this world much more dangerous, not only for creedal uniformity, but for society and the ecclesiastical order, since thereby any Tom, Dick, or Harry would think he had all the requisites of a good minister when he felt himself moved by the right spirit. Catholics undermined the pretensions of the intellect by an intellectual demonstration of its fallibility; fanatical Protestants demolished intelligence at a blow by asserting the infallibility of the spirit. Catholics argued inferentially by exposing the unreliability of all other guides except faith; left-wing Puritans proclaimed the all-sufficiency of God's grace to inform and illumine His elect. Catholic anti-rationalism took refuge in the heresy of an authoritative church; Protestant anti-rationalism would have destroyed all churches, expelled learned men from the ministry, and thrown organized religion into chaos.

In England during the 1640's, in the midst of civil war, with no power capable of enforcing ecclesiastical discipline or suppressing popular outbursts, sects of enthusiasts multipled beyond number; whatever their differences or their eccentricities, these "gangraena" were united in their hostility to universities, college graduates in the pulpit, and the monopoly of religious instruction by the formally educated. They endeavored to destroy the intellect of Puritanism by separating religion and education; the Presbyterians and Independents were even then engaged in a furious combat over the form of church polity, but they both strove to remain loyal to orthodox Calvinism and to the orthodox conception of the necessary alliance between religion and learning. Thus while the orthodox ministers were quarreling with each other, they were forced to band together against extremists to defend the existence of a learned clergy. Self-appointed preachers were proclaiming, said one of their enemies,

> that Arts, Sciences, Languages, etc. are Idols, Antichristian, the smoak of the bottomlesse Pit, filth, froth, dung, needlesse and uselesse for the right understanding of the Scripture: the spirit alone (say they) is sufficient without these humane helpes.

The cooper, the tinker, the shoemaker, exhilarated by what they supposed was the grace of God, mounted improvised rostrums, became hot gospellers, and made ignorance into a theological virtue.

> Even *How* the Cobler dares the Pulpit climb.
> Belike he thinkes the difference is but small
> Between the sword o' th' Spirit and the Awle.
> And that he can as dexterously divide
> The word of truth, as he can cut an Hide.[2]

Massachusetts had already seen the beginnings of one such movement among the followers of Anne Hutchinson; as one of her partisans declared in the shocked hearing of Captain Johnson, "I had rather hear such a one that speakes from the meere motion of the spirit, without any study at all, then any of your learned Scollers, although they may be fuller of Scripture." The colony saved its learned scholars by the simple expedient of banishing into Rhode Island all those who got their tuition by way of "immediate revelation," but English Antinomians, Anabaptists, Seekers, or Fifth Monarchy Men could not be so summarily disposed of, because they had arms in their hands, had learned how to use them—and also had become indispensable to General Cromwell. Hence the ministers had no recourse but to the power of persuasion. They heaped maledictions upon the over-zealous, calling them, says one of the recipients of their abuse, libertines, blasphemers, sectaries, heretics, "and indeed what not?" The Protector would not permit forcible extermination of the fanatics, but the clergy did prevail upon him to protect the universities and to enforce the collection of tithes; meantime they demonstrated at length that authentic Puritanism had nothing in common with any anti-rationalism of the sects and repudiated all responsibility for it.

In England the situation often became sadly muddled because the Independent divines, who in speculative matters were at one with their enemies the Presbyterians, were yet forced to argue for toleration of the sects in order to gain allies against the Presbyterians during the battle over church polity. Yet even when men like Nye or Goodwin pled for toleration of Anabaptists or Antinomians—to the horror of their New England brethren—they were vehemently combating Anabaptist and Antinomian teachings, particularly the sectarian condemnation of learning. In New England there was never any such unfortunate confusion of purpose. The colonial ministers needed no assistance from sectaries, and made it clear once and for all that orthodox Puritanism and enthusiasm were as much opposed as Puritanism and Catholicism. In New England can be found in unspoiled simplicity the attitude toward reason and education which in fact characterized all Puritans, though in England the unity of front was marred by quarrels among them over questions of ecclesiastical organization.

The classic statement is the opening paragraph of the original Harvard commencement program, *New Englands First Fruits,* the splendid words which are now emblazoned upon a gate in the Harvard Yard, and officially invested with a meaning that must cause shudders among the shades of the founders:

> After God had carried us safe to *New England,* and wee had builded our houses, provided necessaries for our livli-hood, rear'd convenient places for Gods worship, and setled the Civill Government: One of the next things we longed for, and looked after was to advance *Learning* and perpetuate it to Posterity; dreading to leave an illiterate Ministery to the Churches, when our present Ministers shall lie in the Dust.

Professor Morison has shown incontestably that Harvard College was not, and was never intended to be, merely a theological seminary, that the founders provided that arts, sciences, and good literature be taught as well as eschatology, that the education was suitable for general purposes or for professional training in law or medicine as well as in preaching. This is indeed all very true, and the broad aims of the founders indicate decisively that Puritans did not reject the intellectual heritage of their age. Yet we may question whether Professor Morison has sufficiently emphasized the unquestioned premise, that the advancement and perpetuation of learning was one and the same with a succession of literate ministers in the churches. Other and more secular purposes were present in the founding of the College only insofar as in the Puritan mind there was no conflict between them and the purposes of Christianity. Certainly it is not correct to hail the statement as a disinterested dedication to the pursuit of learning in the abstract. Reading the passage in its contemporary setting, remembering that in New England recollections of the Antinomian affair were very fresh, and that leaders were then taking every opportunity to show the Protestant world their detestation of every advocate of an illiterate ministry, we can perceive that instead of being a charter for academic liberalism it was rather a manifesto of orthodoxy against radicals who had contended, or were then contending, that religion and preaching should be taken out of the control of colleges and professors. The *First Fruits* is to be read as a party assertion that the chief function of learning was to assist theology, that piety was not to be divorced from intellect, that reason and religion should forever be joined in indissoluble unity. It is one among many pronouncements written between 1640 and 1660 by those Puritans who, having achieved certain well-defined political and ecclesiastical positions, lost every vestige of their revolutionary character when the revolution threatened parts of the established order which they held in high esteem, such as universities, academic degrees, tithes, the holding of benefices by college graduates, and the syllogistic interpretation of Scripture. Among those who attacked these institutions and customs piety and piety alone held sway; the orthodox owed allegiance to the intellectual tradition as well as to such doctrines of piety as the dogmas of total depravity and irresistible grace. It is a significant commentary upon the nature of Puritanism that when enthusiasts, who emerged from the Puritan party, transformed the attack upon the Anglican hierarchy into an attack upon all human reason and secular learning, in the bitter pamphlet war that followed, Puritan divines stood shoulder to shoulder with Anglican priests.

The bibliography of the controversy is extensive, and the whole dispute has been frequently retold. On the side of the sectaries the chief writers were William Dell and John Webster,[3] against whom appeared a number of gentlemen and scholars, employing all the lore of the universities, all the wisdom of the sciences, all the stylistic resources of academic rhetoric, to defend universities, sciences, and rhetoric.[4] Even though suppression of the Hutchinsonians removed the danger of an overt attack upon learning in Massachusetts and Connecticut, even though the inhabitants were at the time making enormous sacrifices for their college and for the education of their ministers, still this controversy demands notice in an intellectual history of New England. The arguments of the defenders were endorsed unreservedly by the leaders of New England, both clerical and political, and can be paralleled by passages in New England sermons. Furthermore, the position of the orthodox Puritans in the 1640's and 1650's was to be asserted again in New England after 1670, when the cause of learning became once more endangered, not through a recrudescence of Antinomianism, but through the growing indifference of the people to the technical perplexities of theology and the increasing hunger of the crowd for a style of preaching which finally swept the backwoods in the Great Awakening, the passionate harangue that depends for nothing upon college training or book learning. But still more important for our study, this controversy illustrates the equilibrium of forces, emotional and intellectual, within the Puritan creed. The very existence of the attack betrays an inveterate tendency of this piety: whenever it has aroused the masses, to whom abstract thought is both boring and impious, for whom the fiat of revelation renders all speculation superfluous, upon whom the lesson of previous Antinomian outbursts is lost, then it almost always gives rise to a conviction that sheer emotional fervor is infinitely preferable to the least degree of intellectual discipline. On the other hand, the clerical defense is significant in the first place because it demonstrates that the Puritan movement of the seventeenth century was not simply a piety, that in the judgment of its leaders the spiritual motivation was balanced by an indispensable intellectual element. Secondly, when we come to examine more particularly the tactics of the apologists, we can perceive how Puritan theorists sought to unite in one harmonious system both science and religion, reason and faith, how they endeavored to reconcile revelation with natural learning and so to combine in one systematic belief both piety and the inherited body of knowledge. Finally, the defense shows how doggedly the clergy strove to maintain the unity, even though the rank and file were incapable of full understanding, even though some of the more devout, accusing them of stifling the spirit for the sake of the letter, broke into open revolt against their scholarship and their rational demonstrations.

Something less than justice has been done to the writings of Dell and Webster, possibly because historians, who belong for the most part to the scholarly caste, entertain the same prejudices in favor of that caste as did the Puritan clergy. Yet it must be admitted that if the assumptions of the Puritan creed be granted, if the premises dictated by the piety be admitted, then the arguments of these pamphleteers are eminently respectable. They took the formal tenets of Puritanism with a literalness embarrassing to the more circumspect clergy, and they became a thorn in the flesh of the righteous by deducing from the ministers' own utterances such inferences as repeatedly forced the prophets of the Lord to explain that Jehovah had not meant quite what He seemed to have said. Both Webster and Dell professed to have no quarrel with learning when restricted to "its *own place* and *Sphear,*" nor did they wish to do away with secular education or with research. They objected to making learning "an other *John Baptist,* to prepare the *way* of *Christ* into the *world,* or to prepare the *worlds* way to *Christ,*" to its being held the criterion of a candidate's fitness for the ministry. Up to a point, if the Puritan clergy were to remain faithful to the piety which was the soul of Puritanism, they too were compelled to agree; they had said many times that no soul could be brought to Christ by knowledge alone and that scholarship *per se* did not make a teacher. Webster laid down another principle with which his opponents were constrained to agree when he said that acquired science was something quite different from "that evidential and experimental knowledg, which men partake of, by the sending in, inflowing, and indwelling of the Spirit of Christ." Every Puritan acknowledged that not all the "*Study, Knowledge, Learning, Languages, Sciences, Degrees,* and *Ordination*" to which college graduates are exposed could of itself "change their *inward evill Nature, Mind, Will, Affections,* nor the *corrupt Disposition* and *Principle* in which they were *born.*" These admissions once secured, Webster and Dell, and with them hundreds of the New Model's hardiest troopers, could see no grounds either for any human learning in religious education or for any considerations of human reason in doctrine and belief. If the Bible is the Word of God, then it needs no confirmation from the words of Aristotle.

Must that word be *secured* by *Aristotle,* which *delivers* all the *Elect* from *sin, death* and *hell* for ever? Are *Grammar, Rhetorick, Logick, Ethicks, Physicks, Metaphysicks, Mathematicks,* the *weapons* whereby we must defend the Gospel?

The program of studies which Puritan authorities retained in the universities seemed in Webster's eyes still to consist of Popish doctors and pagan poets. Therefore was it not ridiculous for men who claimed to have purged the churches, who shut up the theaters of London on the charge of licentiousness, who bent every agency of government to punish moral lapses, to send their sons to be made "more of the *world* than they were by *Nature,* through the *high improvement* of their corruptions, by their *daily converse* with the *Heathens,* their vain *Philosophers,* and filthy and obscene *Poets*"? The unlearned were certain that college textbooks were full of the same heathenism and antichristianism "as were many hundred years ago, in the *darkest* times of *Popery.*" Surely, this sort of learning could contribute nothing to forming ministers of the Gospel. Much better would it be for pastors and people alike if all such works of the Devil were eschewed. Only the grace of God could give to a sinful mortal the power and the capacities, the will and the right, to take up the work of God.

The contention that a university training could not engender living faith seemed to Webster and Dell to be proved by the facts. No doubt an M.A. obtained great skill in the original tongues, but by that very acquisition he was made "utterly ignorant of the true original tongue, the language of the heavenly *Canaan*." Many youths went into the universities with great spiritual promise, but once there "how soon have they *ceased* from that *sense* of the Gospel, which they *once* seemed to have had? and how, *suddenly* have they been *intangled* and *overcome* with the Spirit of the *University,* and of *Antichrist,* for worldly Honour and Advantage sake?" The clergy had a base and ulterior motive in defending the schools, which neither Dell nor Webster were reluctant to expose to the people: they loved learning neither for its own sake nor for its assistance to faith, but simply because it got them special privileges and worldly power. By concealing divinity in the abracadabra of exposition and exegesis they sought "to deterr the *common people* from the *study* and *enquiry* after it, and to cause them *still* to expect all *Divinity* from the *Clergy,* who by their *education* have attained to that *Humane Learning* which the *plain people* are destitute of." As long as common folk were kept abject before a mystery which they could not themselves understand or criticize, they would meekly and fearfully pay their tithes and never dream of laying rude hands upon university endowments.

The seventeenth-century objection to learning, therefore, sprang from social causes as well as from piety. Revolt against the learned ministry was a prelude to rebellion against tax-supported and state-defended churches; condemnation of the academic curriculum pointed toward confiscation of academic revenues. The attack of the sectaries upon college graduates is a counterpart of the Levellers' attack upon social inequalities. Like all critics of established orders in the Christian centuries, the sectaries found support in the example of primitive Christianity. The Savior summoned the Apostles to forsake the world and follow Him; should not successors of the Apostles likewise trust in God to provide both their food and their convictions? Why did the village parson first obtain his religion at the university and then require that his wages be guaranteed by "the power of a compulsory Law made by a Commonwealth"? Was he afraid to rely upon "the free Gift and Contribution of those individuall persons wrought upon by that mans Ministry"? Surely he did not in his own heart believe in himself or trust in the Father; he was diverting attention from his lack of piety by demanding respect for his erudition. His argument that the people should support him while he devoted himself to study was a device for brow-beating them into footing his bills. In the writings of men like Dell and Webster appears the perennial challenge of the world to all academic institutions, the challenge which academicians, even in the twentieth century, have not yet succeeded in answering without some suggestion of secret misgiving: just what justification of its existence can a university plead with a society when its expenses must be paid from the taxes or labors of those who disapprove the whole tenor of its teachings?

The sectaries pressed this question the more boldly because they were certain that neither Oxford nor Cambridge could show any justification. If, as was universally admitted, their principal function in society was turning out able and pious ministers, then it seemed to the sectaries that far better results were being achieved every day outside academic walls, exactly as to many critics today it seems that the public is better taught and science more advanced by those who do not immure themselves in professorships. A learned clergy was not only an expense to the body politic, but an unnecessary one, because ministers, like geniuses, are not made by education but born of the spirit. The arguments of Dell and Webster always come back to a fundamental Antinomianism, to the idea that grace gives not only the ability to act but all requisite knowledge, that the child of God knows the principles of eternal truth merely out of his subjective assurances. "*All* that are *counted worthy* to receive the *Spirit of God,* do receive it *alike immediately* from him; neither hath Christ left any *Lieutenant* or *Deputy* in the world, to give his Spirit to men in his absence." A candidate for the pulpit need submit to no scholastic discipline or pass no baccalaureate examination before receiving a call to the priestly office. "The true faithfull Christians, are not onely of *God,* but also have God himself *dwelling* and *abiding* in them." In this view, divine grace is not merely a form of energy, galvanizing the will, but an indwelling of knowledge, filling the mind with an instinctive science; it gives not merely faith but the content of faith. To ascertain what he should believe the saint need not bow at "The *Throne* of the *beast* in these *Nations,*" the universities. The lowliest and most uneducated among the sheep of Christ have power and authority from Him to judge true and false doctrine, "Let Fathers, Schoolemen, Doctors, Councels, Assemblies of Divines, Universities, Ministers, propound and publish what Doctrine they please." The spirit that searches all things can by its own light and wisdom unfailingly indicate what is right and what is wrong, in complete disregard of the carnal and devilish wisdom of man. The things of God cannot at all be deciphered by "the power of Argument, the force of Dispute or Eloquence, nor the efficacy of humane Reason."

These points were exceedingly difficult for orthodox Puritans to answer, for they followed closely from the orthodox conception of regeneration. When the clergy condemned the works of Dell and Webster they ran every risk of contradicting themselves, of advocating the life of reason and disparaging the life of faith, of exalting the value of natural or acquired knowledge at the expense of that spiritual knowledge without which, by their own account, all other varieties were useless. Their pleas for learning verged upon extenuations of "historical faith," of the belief which rests upon scientific or logical demonstration rather than upon "a liuely motion of the heart renewed by grace." If, as they so repeatedly declared, natural reason is an enemy to divine truth, if reason is valid only in strict subordination to the Word, was not Dell entirely correct in arraigning teachers who "speak in the words which *mans wisdom* teacheth, and so mingle *Philosophy* with *Divinity,* and think to *credit* the Gospel with Termes of *Art*"? If John Cotton could say, "What the Lord would have us to doe, he is present by his Spirit to teach us, and to strengthen us, and so to doe it for us," was not Dell justified in saying, "They who preach the *Outward Letter* of the Word, though never so *truly,* without the *Spirit,* doe . . . wholly mistake the *Mind* of Christ in the *Word,* for want of the *Spirit,* which is the onely *true* and *infallible Interpreter* of his mind"? If the Puritan movement had been simply and solely an outburst of piety and zeal, if it had relinquished for a moment its firm hold upon the philosophical and cultural heritage of the century, if Puritans had been men whose consciousness had centered exclusively upon the dogmas of original sin, predestination, and irresistible grace, then Puritanism would certainly have gone the way of Dell and Webster, and not the way of the champions of the English colleges, not the way of the founders of Massachusetts Bay and of Harvard College.

The clergy clearly could answer Dell and Webster only by drawing upon other sources than piety. Their principal stratagem was one which the disciplined scholar almost instinctively employs for the bewilderment of the uninitiated: they called for a definition of terms. Of course, they said, a minister must have "gifts" for his calling, but what do we mean by gifts? Obviously certain essential ones must come from God. But there are other kinds of gifts besides those infused by the spirit; there are also those supplied by nature, and then those acquired by study. The universities do not pretend to furnish the first, only the providence of God can give the second, but the third sort, inferior to the other two yet still essential, can be cultivated only in the proper schools. These gifts of the schools are: "a distinct and methodicall comprehention of the severall subjects to be treated of, together with the meanes or advantages that helpe to facilitate the worke of instructing others." If these distinctions were clearly perceived, then it seemed clear to the orthodox that Webster and Dell confused one sort of gift with another, that they were merging what God Himself had put asunder.

As with the question of ministerial gifts, so also the whole question of knowledge demanded that terms be rightly distinguished and sound conclusions drawn. But on this score it seemed that Dell sinned, not in failing to recognize a distinction, but in exaggerating it. He was willing that the universities should "stand upon an *Humane* and *Civil account,*" educating youth to be "*useful* and *serviceable* to the *Commonwealth,*" but he demanded that they stand on this account alone. Webster said that human knowledge was of transcendent use "while moving in its own orb" but that it destroyed itself when it would "see further than its own light can lead it." To the orthodox, such a drastic separation of religion and knowledge was impossible; the two were indeed distinguishable realms, capable of individual description, but they were incapable of existence apart from each other. To cut the connection would be to ruin both. Dell believed that if education were discharged from all concern with religion, education would gain by the release; Puritans could see in such a cleavage only the extinguishing of culture. As Reynolds put it, all truth must by definition come from God, and all knowledge of truth be ultimately knowledge of Him; but we must recognize that "there is a knowledge of God *natural* in and *by his works:* and a knowledge *supernatural* by revelation out of the Word; and though this be the principal, yet the other is not to be undervalued." If the zealous but misguided sectaries would stop their hysterical denunciations long enough to learn the true distinctions between divine instruction and acquired information, they would see at once, not only that there is a legitimate sphere for the second apart from the first, but that the two must be cultivated together, that scientific truth is not a contradiction but an enhancement and a necessary complement of the revealed.

That the content of university education was Popish or heathen was a more difficult charge for the apologists to meet, but they did so to at least their own satisfaction. They acknowledged freely that scholastic writers were corrupt and classical moralists deficient in true doctrine, but nevertheless both had their uses. If, for example, Christians could see "the continency, justice, temperance, meekness, clemency, and other amiable moral Vertues of *Heathen* men," might they not be shamed into emulation? The knowledge of tongues was obviously necessary to discover the true sense of Scripture; so also there was a necessity "of *Logick* to understand the contexture, method, argumentation and *Analysis* of Scripture; of *Rhetorick* to understand the *elegancies* of Scripture." The apologists were the first to admit that Peripatetic philosophy was full of fallacies, but they said there was therefore no reason for casting it aside, for it also contained profitable instruction. Against the charge that learning masked the worldly schemes of a designing clergy, the apologists found it easy to ascribe the foul motives to their accusers:

> This hatred of Learning must needs proceed either from *ignorance* . . . or from *Avarice,* and out of a sacrilegious desire to devoure those Revenues wherewith the bounty of Benefactors hath from time to time endowed the Schools of Learning.

No doubt denunciations of tithes and the wealth of the colleges were "most taking with the people," but demagoguery was not Christianity. At this point some of the writers could only exclaim sadly that "unlesse Tythes, as setled by Law . . . are preserved to the Church, and all men from whom they are due, be compelled to pay them . . . I shall think the Church-man but in a bad case, and Religion unbefriended." Such *argumentum ad hominem* probably had little effect upon the Dells and the Websters, but fortunately it registered with Parliament and with the Protector.

The apologists concentrated their rebuttal chiefly upon the argument for an immediate infusion of wisdom into the elect. The economic attack might be difficult to fend off, but when the sectaries rested their case upon this contention they laid themselves open to the charge of Antinomian heresy. The scholars were seizing every advantage, and were able to draw upon the long experience of church Fathers and medieval divines for a store of weapons. The substance of their criticism was put concisely by Joseph Sedgwick in a sermon preached at St. Mary's at Cambridge in 1653:

A confident boasting of dictates from above is not sufficient warrant that the doctrine is heavenly. Without better evidence then their bare word, we may modestly suspect that they are nothing but the distempers of a disaffected brain.

The apologists took elaborate care to certify their own adherence to the piety; they cautioned as much as did Dell himself against "making our *Reason judge* of Articles of *Faith;* or setting *Humane* Learning in the *Tribunal* against *Divine* Truth." Thereupon they once more took to distinguishing terms, and proved adroitly that the sectaries' lumping together of all knowledge into the insight of regeneration was blasphemous. We must keep quite distinct the "savoury sense and inward experience and cordiall embracing of the ways of God" from the "intellectual, notional, though right knowledge of the truths of Christianity." By thus distinguishing the two methods, we are enabled to delimit their spheres: inward experience is the private discovery of each individual Christian, and is no doubt more clear and effectual than the other; but knowledge can be taught by one man to another or by a preacher to his flock only as external theory and speculation. This knowledge is not regeneration, but that which can "beget that knowledge of the Gospel, which (by the Spirits assistance) may put the soul upon a further desire of a feeling knowledge and coming under the power of truth." It may be the approach to salvation, and many of its vast domains bear fruit on which piety may feed:

To be able to search into the true and naturall sense of Apostolicall writings, to discern the excellency, consonancy and true authenticknesse of Scripture, to examine and draw consequences from it, to see the agreement of reason and revelation, to view the appearances of God among the Heathen, their self-condemnednesse, attestations to part of truth and defectivenesse, to take notice of God in the Creation, and distinguish miracles from impostures, to observe God's Providence in the World and Church, to see the severall breakings forth of light and overcastings of darknesse in the Church, to make out the Truth by full evidence, to explain and order the severall Truths of revelation, and have a distinct and more then popular notion of them, so as to be able to answer Atheisticall and unbelieving Cavills, to converse with Christians in all Ages and make use of their experiences and discoverties, to know God, our selves, and men in order to a convenient application of our selves unto them for their good: these are some of the ends of Learning, that thus and otherwise enlarges, quickens, and imbetters the naturall faculties of the Soul.

The conclusion at which the writers always arrived was put by Reynolds thus: "Sanctified *Wit beautifies* Religion, sanctified *Reason* defends it, sanctified *power* protects it, sanctified *Elocution* perswades others to the love of it." In England, wit, reason, and elocution were to be studied only at Oxford or Cambridge, and in New England Harvard was founded that the youth of the colonies might have access to them.

At every point we find the New England utterances in perfect unanimity with the apologists. In its "Declaration concerninge the advauncement of learning in New England" of 1638 the General Court of Massachusetts Bay admitted that skill in the tongues and liberal arts was not so indispensable but what the commonwealth or the churches could exist without it; "yet we conceiue that [in] the judgment of the godly wise, it is beyond all question, not only laudable, but necessary for the beinge of the same." The ministers were acutely aware of the controversy in England, and though they had nothing to fear, so it seemed after 1637, from Websters or Dells among the now well-disciplined members of the Bible commonwealths, yet they never lost a chance to cry up the cause of education and a learned ministry. In the later years of the century the ministers were to look back upon the work of the first generation with pride and satisfaction. Thomas Shepard the younger thanked God for having prompted the fathers to erect Harvard College, "that so this land might not be a land of darkness and wilderness." Increase Mather compared them to the early Christians, who ever set up schools for learning for the training of succeeding generations, and moralized in a striking phrase, "that the Interest of Religion and good Literature, hath risen and fallen together." And in New England there is to be found one of the frankest of Puritan avowals that the interests of class were protected by the cultivation of learning: a speaker at a Harvard commencement said that if the fathers had not founded the College, "the ruling class would have been subjected to mechanics, cobblers, and tailors; the gentry would have been overwhelmed by lewd fellows of the baser sort, the sewage of Rome, the dregs of an illiterate plebs which judgeth much from emotion, little from truth." The Antinomians banished into Rhode Island might still denounce the "Popish college way," and chant with Peter Folger:

They vilify the Spirit of God,
  and count School Learning Best.
If that a Boy hath learn'd his Trade,
  and can the Spirit disgrace,
Then he is lifted up on high
  and needs must have a Place.

But Rhode Island was *in partibus infidelibus,* and Harvard then as now disregarded criticism from regions of which it did not approve. For the time being Puritanism in New England remained faithful to the learned ideal.

Evidence for the opinion of Puritan New England on this issue is abundant, but the outstanding document, and a fundamental one for the intellectual history, was written as a direct contribution to the English controversy. Charles Chauncy, while president of the College, delivered in 1655 *Gods Mercy, Shewed to his People in Giving them a Faithful Ministry and Schooles of Learning for the Continual Supplyes Thereof,* in which he went after William Dell with hammer and tongs. He covered the same ground traversed by the English apologists, insisted upon a knowledge of the tongues for a true understanding of Scripture and of the liberal arts for a correct interpretation. He defended the use of heathen writers and scholastics. Though the schoolmen had made "a very hodch-potch & mingle-mangle of heathenish Philosophy and Divinity together," still we have now recovered from their errors, and because they made mistakes are we therefore to be forbidden a "sober & Christian Philosophy"? He added his condemnation of Dell's claim to immediate revelation by pointing out that if Dell pretended to be inspired by God, who had inspired the Bible, "then what Mr. D. and any other believers write or say, is of equall authority with the Canonicall Scriptures"—a conclusion that had only to be stated for its absurdity to become apparent, at least in New England. He disproved the idea that the grace of God could give the content of education by inward communication. The Bible, he said, contains many other matters in addition to the narrative of redemption; it describes all the works of God, "and whatsoever is contained in the scriptures of the works of God, and as farr as it concerns a minister to preach all profitable and Scripture trueths, the knowledge of Arts & Sciences is usefull and expedient to him to hold them forth to his hearers." Grace is indispensable to a Christian, but in one sense grace is not enough. The regenerate, by the strength imparted to them, can embrace the content of true belief, which, however, they do not discern within themselves but in the accumulated wisdom of Christendom. The perfect doctrine contained in Scripture "comprehends the doctrine of Gods works, which is called *Philosophy.*" This distinction of the realms of piety and of intellect which Puritanism maintained against its own radicals was held by the Puritans to have been ordained by God Himself, and the convergence of the two upon the same array of orthodox principles was demonstrated by His very Word. In the strength of these convictions New England leaders were enabled to be at one and the same time men of intense piety and yet men of learning.

How far the rank and file were also learned, or how far they respected learning is difficult to say. In England, for several decades before the migration, Puritan clergymen lamented the shocking ignorance of the people.

The great William Perkins enumerated some of the notions which he found at large in the 1590's, thinking it quite sufficient that they be merely stated to arouse general consternation, little dreaming that in a later age his description might be more highly prized for its flavor of Shakespeare's Merrie England than for its record of his disapprobation:

That God is serued by the rehearsing of the ten commandements, the Lords Prayer, and the Creede.

That none can tell whether he shall be saved or no certenly.

That it is the safest to doe in Religion as most doe.

That merry ballads and bookes, as *Scoggin, Beuis of Southhampton,* &c., are good to driue away the time, and to remooue heart-qualmes.

That ye know all the Preacher can tell you.

That drinking and bezeling in the ale-house or tauerne, is good fellowship, and shewes a good kinde nature, and maintaines neighbourhood.

That it was a good world, when the old Religion was, because all things were cheape.

Before the New England divines departed the mother country they too bewailed the sad state of the public mind. "I can speak it by experience," said Thomas Hooker, "that the meaner ordinary sort of people, it is incredible and unconceiveable, what Ignorance is among them." Even in London, where opportunities for instruction were plentiful, if a man should go from house to house, "he should find a marvellous poor deal of sanctifying and saving knowledge, yea, I doe assure you, of any reasonable common knowledge in matters of Religion." No doubt the Puritan parson judged his people by a lofty standard; for that very reason, however, he labored heroically to bring them up to it, assuring them that an ignorant man was like a sick man in an apothecary's shop at night:

though there be the choycest of all receipts at hand, and he may take what he needs, yet because he cannot see what he takes, and how to use them, he may kill himself or encrease his distempers, but never cure any disease.

The clergy were so far successful that by the time of the Civil Wars the mass of those who had come under Puritan influences were generally familiar with a marvelously large body of thought. The ability of Cromwell's soldiers to debate intricate theological issues around their campfires was a wonder to all beholders; so in later times the proficiency of New England farm hands in threading the mazes of free will, foreordination, and fate around the kitchen fire was a never-ending source of admiration to visitors. The evidence would seem to show that whenever a people were taught for any length of time by a Puritan ministry the level of their information was definitely raised. Leaving aside the question of whether the sort of knowledge purveyed was worth while, or whether the people were more harmed than benefited by their acquisitions, the fact remains that for better or worse the people were instructed. By the light of history it might seem that the chief function of Puritanism in the development of modern civilization was the education it gave to a segment of the British public. In New England this function was the more assiduously performed because there the people were relatively uncontaminated by non-Puritanical influences. Even the young men at sea generally served under skippers who, like the "gruff Tarpaulin," Captain Jenner, "had some smatterings of Divinity (as most of the New England Captains have) and went not only constantly to Prayers (which was a thing very Commendable) but also took upon him to Expound the Scriptures." Forecastle debates were as highly colored by theology as were social gatherings ashore. Furthermore, in the original settlement of New England the proportion of university-trained men to the total population was one to every forty-four families;[5] the church members were a picked lot, inspired to migrate in some part by their understanding of religious issues, careful readers of their Bibles, and attentive, note-taking listeners to the sermons and lectures of their learned parsons. The defection of the Hutchinsonians was the only revolt of any importance against ministerial domination during the first decades of colonial life, and even in this case, though the Hutchinsonians attacked learning, the trouble seems to have been not so much a lack of knowledge among the people as too much of it. By the spring of 1637, Winthrop says, all men's mouths were full of the arguments, and the insurgents went about making trouble at the lectures of the ministers "by public questions, and objections to their doctrines, which did any way disagree from their opinions." Puritan education did not intend that students think for themselves, but it did intend that they should take in the vast quantity of received and orthodox information. The evidence of journals and diaries, the inventories of libraries, seem to show that the average church member, during most of the century, acquired a good portion of this information by attending sermons and reading not only Scripture but many commentaries, histories, and solid treatises. He respected the prerogatives of the liberal arts, and never questioned that the rules of grammar, of logic, and of rhetoric should determine the interpretation of Scripture. Of course, it is also true that only one-fifth of the population were church members; in the court records there are evidences that some non-members were less devout, but their insubordination was apt to come from some theological scruple against an established practice, such as baptism, or from some disagreement with the minister's doctrine. Any judgment concerning what the inhabitants were able to comprehend must rest in the final analysis upon somewhat negative testimony. Still, since in the first decades there is no evidence of any extended discontent outside the Antinomians, we may conclude that the majority of the people, whether or not members of the churches, saw nothing amiss in the teachings or the methods of the clergy, paid reverence to the ideal of learning, and endeavored to the best of their abilities to come up to it. Some part of the clerical learning and the knowledge taught at Harvard, which was an epitome of the learning and knowledge of Europe, must have been impressed upon the populace, and the people learned their religion not merely as a series of flat dogmas concerning the divine transcendence, human depravity, and supernatural grace, but as it was expounded by logic, phrased with rhetoric, illustrated in physics, and supplemented by all the other arts and sciences.

CHAPTER IV

THE INTELLECTUAL HERITAGE

For the content of their belief, for the meanings which they read into Scripture or the principles they deduced from it, the Puritans both in England and New England drew freely upon the stores of knowledge and the methods of thinking which were then available to educated men. Like other persons of cultivation in the period, they profited, sometimes deliberately, sometimes unwittingly, from the advantages of their location in the intellectual history of Europe. At the commencement of the seventeenth century it seemed as though many different countries of the mind as well as of the world, many continents of thought and many trade routes of culture, lay simultaneously ready at hand for intellectual exploitation. Piety did not inhibit the Puritan scholar from adventuring upon them. True, he surveyed them in a thoroughly didactic spirit, and exercised critical wariness lest in his travels he be lured into accepting as fact what might in reality be the fancy of a depraved mind. But the circumstances of the times enabled him to retain Christian caution without sacrificing impartiality. He could be both selective and eclectic without seeming to do violence to any field of knowledge, without seeming to suppress any idea merely because it was at variance with his creed. With every show of justice and fairness, he could combine the arts and sciences into one coherent scheme of knowledge, which tended at every point to substantiate the truth of revelation; whatever teachings were incompatible with his religious beliefs he could exclude, not on the grounds merely of that incompatibility, but by objective and rational demonstration of their falsehood, demonstrations which he did not believe his enemies ever succeeded in disproving. Being a Protestant, he had the vast literature of Protestantism to supply the main outlines of his system; yet because he lived a century after Luther and Calvin he could view the first reformers in perspective, go beyond them or dissent from them when he had reason or Scripture to warrant him. Being an Englishman, on the edge of the Protestant world and always a little remote from his continental brethren, he could select what he saw fit from the works of Dutch, German, or Swiss Calvinists, and meanwhile take up from indigenous traditions, particularly from English legal and political theory, whatever supported his contentions. Like all Protestants, he had revolted against the sway of medieval schoolmen without having discarded the immense accumulation of scholastic thought, which lay before him like an Aztec city before the plunderer. He was still exhilarated by the revival of learning; Erasmus was as much his intellectual progenitor as Calvin, and he could seize upon the spoils of the heathen to furnish the trophies of Christianity. Finally, because his theology taught that whatever was practically useful was contrived in the providence of God, he could welcome without trepidation advances in logic or method, in science or invention, once these demonstrated their utility. Thus the Puritan scholar in the first half of the seventeenth century ranged at will through the spacious chambers and hoarded treasures of a rich intellectual inheritance. The fact that the conclusions of all investigation were already given in the creed did not preclude opportunities and even necessities for investigation. In the first decades of the century the Puritan devoted himself to exposition, proof, and explanation all the more intensely because he already possessed the truth; he was not content to let truth stand upon the bare authority of revelation while he turned his energies to the less abstract problems of morality or to settling parish squabbles. He was ready to appropriate whatever advanced his creed or served his piety from whatever source it might come, for his creed and his piety were living and growing. As the exigencies of the moment demanded or the need for confirmation arose he enlarged his explanations, until at last an elaborate system was constructed. By the middle of the century, as the objectives of the movement became defined, as the long controversy with the Anglicans and later the bitter conflict with the sects forced specific declarations of position on every side, the leaders of English Puritanism utilized all their resources, ran through their libraries, mastered their techniques, and formulated what must be called a philosophy of Puritanism.

This philosophy was not a deliberate or intentional creation. No committee ever gathered round a table and drew up a syllabus, no one ever wrote a comprehensive treatise upon its whole aspect. It cannot be defined in one sentence. It was the result of much disputation, many sermons, long experience with heresies, manifold discoveries of what consequences flowed from what premises, careful interpretations and reinterpretations of the Bible, critical studies of the great theologians, years of study in the colleges. Few Puritans ever agreed on every feature of it, and on some essential questions there was always difficulty in framing a formula satisfactory to all the orthodox. Many who were thoroughly sound on every other point developed erroneous notions on some particular, as when Charles Chauncy, after due and serious meditation, decided that babies were not properly baptized unless they were totally immersed. In England the party was never able to formulate the grounds for unanimity, because divergences within the ranks grew apace, and political triumph signalized the beginnings of intellectual disintegration. Yet such a philosophy did exist. The outlines of the belief upon which the majority of English Puritans concurred are relatively distinct, and those of the New England version are still more clear. During the larger part of the century the orthodox colonies remained close-knit and well-regulated; the official doctrine was one and the same for every thinking man, and never seriously questioned by the vulgar. The writings of New England divines do not set forth its every aspect in full detail, but omissions may be supplied from the works they studied or endorsed. Puritanism in New England can be isolated for the purposes of study as Puritanism in England cannot be. From the writings of New Englanders can be extracted a coherent body of belief and theory, a combination of piety and exposition, which make up the Puritan *Weltanschauung,* to which the various elements in the intellectual heritage contributed their various shares.

Of recent years much scholarship has been devoted to discovering the extent of this heritage.[1] Catalogues of libraries have been exhumed, inventories of booksellers reprinted, works cited by Puritan writers enumerated and their quotations run to earth. Very often such investigation comes to nothing more than a register of titles, most of them meaning little or nothing to any but specialists in the period. Stress is generally put upon the discovery of authors who are still held in critical regard. Hence the appearance in the library of a New England parson of one item by Milton is more prized than twenty by Manton; that a Harvard undergraduate quotes Horace is celebrated, but not that he repeats Pareus; greater significance is attached to a citation of Beaumont and Fletcher than of Burgersdicius. Such a proportionment of emphasis helps to show that the Puritans in New England were not unfamiliar with works which we call literature, that Puritanism was not in itself hostile to "belles-lettres." But from the point of view of the Puritan himself, this criterion has little relevance. Works of literary merit did not often find space on Puritan bookshelves because of their style or beauty. Even if occasional works esteemed by us turn out to have been important to the Puritan, his reasons were certainly quite different from ours; Milton and Bunyan in Puritan eyes were controversialists and theologians who loomed no larger than Owen or Baxter, John Cotton or Thomas Hooker. No doubt Spenser and Sidney influenced the poetry of Anne Bradstreet, and Cotton Mather read *Don Quixote,* but the sources of

Puritan thought are not to be found among literary masterpieces. Mere enumeration of volumes possessed by one or another seventeenth-century New Englander will not of itself declare what ideas were taken from them, still less how the appropriated material was worked into the Puritan metaphysic. It will be much better for our purposes, therefore, that we define the intellectual culture of New England, not by arraying books and authors, but by appraising the several bodies of ideas incorporated in it, by analyzing the categories of influence exerted from the inherited learning upon the writings of New Englanders. From this point of view the intellectual content of Puritanism can be traced in the main to four principal sources. One was European Protestantism, the reinterpretation of the whole Christian tradition effected by the reformers. Secondly, because at the time of the settlement of New England Protestantism was already undergoing transformations, we must consider certain peculiarly seventeenth-century preoccupations and interests. Thirdly, there was humanism, the stimulus and the challenge of the revived learning and the still fresh discovery of classical culture. Fourthly, there was the all-pervading influence of medieval scholasticism, as yet unchallenged within Puritan hearing by the new physics and the mathematical method. There were other sources of lesser importance, as will appear in the course of our narrative, but these were the four quarries from which the Puritan scholars carved out their principal ideas and doctrines.

Obviously, the major part of Puritan thought was taken bodily from sixteenth-century Protestantism. From the great reformers came the whole system of theology, definitions of terms, orientation of interests, interpretations of Scripture, and evaluations of previous scholarship. In fact, Puritan thinking was fundamentally so much a repetition of Luther and Calvin, and Puritans were so far from contributing any new ideas, that there is reason to doubt whether a distinctly Puritan thought exists. The theologians simply took up residence in a vast and already constructed mansion of theory; during their tenancy they tried neither to make additions nor to change the façade; they devoted themselves to repairing roofs, replacing foundations, and redecorating interiors. In time they did effect some drastic alterations, but they did so inadvertently, and often without conscious realization.

Thus it can be said that New Englanders took most of their beliefs from the reformers, and that their sermons were substantially restatements of positions already defined in Geneva. Nevertheless, from their own point of view, and in their daily life and meditation, they valued the reformers more for inspiration than instruction. In New England eyes the sixteenth century was inspiriting to contemplate for its heroes, martyrs, and champions of truth: "What worthy Ministers did that first age of the Reformed Churches yeeld? as *Luther, Calvin, Martin Bucer, Cranmer, Hooper, Rid-*

ley, Latymer, &c. What a wonderfull measure of heavenly light did they of a sudden bring into the Church? and that out of the middest of darknesse and Popery." But that they themselves derived their ideas from these "worthy Ministers," that the light streamed from the men and not from heaven, the Puritans would indignantly have denied. Their convictions came from the Bible, and if men in the previous century had maintained the same opinions it was because they too had sat under the same schoolmaster. All reputable theologians were merely expounders of the Word. In some ages, when the meaning had become obscured, the providence of God raised up mighty saints to recover its significance; these always seemed to inaugurate new epochs in the history of thought, but in reality they merely returned to what had been lost or concealed. Augustine's doctrine of conversion, Luther's doctrine of justification, Calvin's doctrine of predestination "were all of them thought new Doctrines in their times; and yet all of them the ancient truths of the everlasting Covenant of grace." [2] Consequently, though Puritanism appears in history as an episode in the life of Protestantism, and though the creed professed in New England is described today by the adjective Calvinist, New Englanders themselves did not go directly to Luther or Calvin for the articles of their persuasion. They studied the reformers less than they did a score or more later formulators of Protestant opinion and less than they did Augustine himself. Luther was a deeply venerated man, but there were held to be "some notorious errors of his way." Calvin's was a still more potent name, but even he was regarded as only one among many "judicious and pious" divines. The ministers did not think of him as the fountain head of their thought, nor of themselves as members of a faction of which he was the founder; they did not hesitate to "cast another Construction" from his upon any passage in Scripture. "We may oppose *Calvins* authority with reason," said John Norton, "It's not the authority of *Calvin* that concludes for; . . . but the reason . . . according to truth, that determines the question." If we were to measure by the number of times a writer is cited and the degrees of familiarity shown with his works, Beza exerted more influence than Calvin, and David Pareus still more than Beza. Yet from the very beginnings of the settlement New England divines publicly and specifically set aside the example of Calvin, Beza, Pareus, and all continental Calvinists on the crucial issue of ecclesiastical polity.[3] They went to Calvin for information or insight in about the same spirit as a modern Shakespearean scholar might go to Coleridge; they esteemed the text more highly than the annotation. They did not consider that their belief came to them from any man or any school of thought. Norton declared that the sixteenth century had abounded with notable confessions, but also with many errors. Men engaged every day in freeing the pure and certain meaning of Christ's gospel from false constructions would look upon themselves as Christians and not as Calvinists. They supposed themselves in the service of the same universal and eternal truth which Calvin had also served, but which existed apart from him and could be studied without reference to anything he had ever written or said. It was only at the end of the century, when in England Puritanism had evolved into nonconformity and in New England theocracy had been reduced to Congregationalism that the theologians accepted their doctrine as the peculiar possession of a denomination and were content to be designated "Calvinists."

Hence, while English Puritanism was a segment of European Protestantism, and its theology was that of Calvin, the immediate influence of the sixteenth-century figures was not overwhelming. There is another and more paradoxical respect in which the reformers may be said to have shaped the contours of the New England mind: the character of Puritanism was determined as much by the questions which Luther and Calvin did not solve as by those which they did. Out of both church and theology they swept whatever seemed to them corruptions insinuated by the Papacy. They ransacked philosophy and science in order to expunge whatever lent support to the pretensions of Rome, they demolished everything in medieval culture that conflicted with reformed doctrine. But they left it still unclear how much of the medieval culture was to remain, or in what fashion the purified body of knowledge was to be reconstituted. They did not discard Peripatetic physics, they left intact the medieval educational program of the trivium and quadrivium. They chastised carnal reason, but they still demanded that faith be defended by the syllogism. In order to establish the orthodox dogma they overleaped the difficulties of proof and drove home correct conclusions by the mere vehemence of assertion; wherever necessary they cut ruthlessly across laws of reason and of nature, rules of equity and justice, or the evidence of history. But they rode thus rough-shod only when it seemed to them absolutely imperative. Otherwise they left the arts and sciences unscathed, the traditional functions of reason undisturbed. It was the task of their successors to make an inventory of sound knowledge, to inscribe the proper scope of reason, to determine the relation of learning and intellect to belief. The reformers did not have time for these matters; they strained every nerve and sinew to secure essentials, the doctrine itself, and a chance to live without the swords of Catholics at their throats. The "Captaines" had not descended to particulars, William Ames said, because they "were necessarily inforced to fight alwaies in the front against the enemies to defend the Faith, and to purge the floore of the Church." By the beginning of the seventeenth century this work was done; confessions were formulated, Protestant armies had gained a degree of security and leisure for theologians, universities had been established and scholars were ready for settling the yet unfinished business of Protestant theology.

Had the scholars been at all sluggish about undertaking their task, they would have been hurried to it by their enemies. Positions which the reformers had not fortified were so many breaches in the walls through which Popish skirmishers were eagerly pressing. Calvin composed a sublime system of dogma; he sketched out the architectural framework, in broad and free strokes. He did not fill in details, he did not pretend to solve the myriad metaphysical riddles to which his canons gave rise. He wrote in the heyday of Protestant faith and crusading zeal, and at that time the ecstasy of belief made affirmation sufficient in and for itself. There was no need for elaborate props and buttresses, for cautious logic and fine-spun argumentation. For the period of Protestant beginnings, dogmatism was entirely adequate. The warriors of the Lord did not need to dissipate their energies in fruitless questions, and could concentrate on action, certain that they had the correct solutions for all the puzzles which scholastics had argued and debated to the point of exhaustion. But by 1600 warfare with Rome had become a matter of debate as well as of arms, and logic as important a weapon as the sword. As the defenders of learning frequently asked Webster or Dell, "how shall we be able to preserve the truth in its purity, to stop the mouth of a subtle Jesuite, or learned Heretick, without learning?" Calvinism could no longer remain the relatively simple dogmatism of its prophet. It needed amplification, it required concise explication, syllogistic proof, intellectual as well as spiritual focus.

The thinking of early New England as of all Puritanism was governed by this requirement. The great difference between Calvin and the so-called Calvinists of the seventeenth century is symbolized by the vast importance they attached to one word, "method." Systematic organization of the creed had indeed been of great concern to Calvin, but never the obsession it was to his followers. Richard Baxter stated succinctly the engrossing preoccupation of seventeenth-century Puritans, the service which they felt they had been summoned by God to perform for the benefit of mankind, when he said that truth should be long studied and diligently elaborated, "till it be concocted into a clear methodical understanding, and the Scheme or Analysis of it have left upon the soul its proper image, by an orderly and deep impression." Several years previously John Preston at Emmanuel College had come to the conclusion that students should "first read Summes and Systemes in Divinity, and settle their opinions and judgements" before they studied the Fathers, the schoolmen, or sermons. At the end of our period Samuel Willard, in *A Compleat Body,* which is the greatest New England monument to the Puritan veneration of "method," was still counseling students to organize and classify all doctrines methodically before they endeavored to write sermons.

The books most used by New Englanders, by which their interpretations of Scripture were guided and their general thinking most influenced, were not those of the first reformers but of later refashioners or reformulators of

Protestant doctrine. These authors taught the same theology, but they extended its scope beyond the religious creed to include all knowledge, systematized both religion and science, and reduced all principles to method. To compare the *Institutes* with William Ames's *Medulla Sacrae Theologiae* is to perceive at once the difference between the mentality of Calvin and of the Puritan. Where the *Institutes* has the majestic sweep of untrammeled confidence, the *Medulla,* though no less confident, is meticulously made up of heads and subheads, objections and answers, argument and demonstration. The preface admits that the care for "Method, and Logicall form" may seem "curious and troublesome" to some, but such persons would "remove the art of understanding, judgement, and memory from those things, which doe almost onely deserve to bee understood, known, and committed to memory." [4] The dedication to logical form exhibited by the *Medulla* grew with the years among Calvinist writers, and later textbooks far outdid William Ames. By the 1670's the *Medulla* was generally replaced at Harvard by John Wollebius' *The Abridgment of Christian Divinity,* praised for being the "most exact and compendious of any that hath been yet done by Protestant writers," [5] which told students "before all things to imprint in their memories the *Anatomie* of the Body of *Theologie,* that in the Common places, in the definitions and Divisions of heavenly doctrine, they may be exact and perfect." Throughout the period Zacharias Ursinus' *The Summe of Christian Religion* was a standard reference work, and it asserted that while human reason was not to be heeded when it "oppugned" the Word of God, yet it was not to be utterly cashiered, because by its light we must distinguish "contradictory opinions; and fully conceiving what is consonant with Gods Word, and what jarreth therewith, should applaud and embrace the one, and reject the other." [6] At the beginning of the eighteenth century Cotton Mather and the mentors of New England were enthusiastically recommending Petro van Mastricht's *Theoretico-Practica Theologia.*[7] In its 1300 pages the whole of Christian theology and morality, theory and practice, is laid out with a minuteness and precision that bring a hundred years of methodizing to a stupendous fulfillment. Beyond this limit no mortal could go. Every chapter expounds a text, analyzes it grammatically, etymologically, rhetorically, logically, comparatively, extracts all possible doctrines from it, argues all the supporting "reasons," raises and answers every conceivable objection, makes the practical applications, and points the moral of every principle. The volume commences with God and the attributes, works its way through creation, apostasy, redemption, the church, and ends with a lengthy treatise on ethics. It is introduced with an apology for method, of which the subsequent chapters are so triumphant a vindication, and methodizes the arguments for method. Method is to be cherished, according to Van Mastricht: one, because God Himself is methodical; two, because theology is also methodical; three, because method is good and beautiful in and for itself. Even if the specific doctrines of Calvinism were unchanged at the time of the migration to New England, they were already removed from pure Calvinism by the difference of tone. The authors to whom New England students went for opinion and discipline have generally been forgotten, because to later generations they make exceedingly dull reading; when they are dropped out of account the content of New England thought seems to link directly onto the teachings of Calvin, from whom ultimately Ames, Ursinus, and Wollebius derived their principal ideas. But although these writers may be less inspiring than John Calvin, it was from them rather than from him that the thinking of New England was borrowed. By them the specific tone and quality were imparted to the New England mind, and from them Harvard graduates learned that in the seventeenth century the function of the theologian, whether in the new world or in the old, was to make theology "to bee understood, known and committed to memory."

In their reorganization of all knowledge in accordance with a Protestant methodolgy, the scholars had chiefly to take into account classical literature, brought into prominence by the humanists, and the literature of scholastic science and philosphy. When they were appropriating heathen material for Christian purposes they were still faithful to the precepts of Augustine, who had said that we should "claim it for our own use from those who have unlawful possession of it," but they were all the more eager for the capture because to them it seemed that the revival of "the Gentile learning" and the reformation of religion had gone hand in hand. As always, providence was at work in the course of human history, but in this case it had managed affairs with even more than its usual dexterity:

> Incredible Darkness was upon the Western parts of *Europe,* two Hundred years ago: *Learning* was wholly swallowed up in *Barbarity.* But when the *Turks* made their Descent so far upon the Greek Churches as to drive all before them, very many Learned Greeks, with their Manuscripts, and Monuments, fled into *Italy,* and other parts of *Europe.* This occasioned the Revival of *Letters* there, which prepared the World for the Reformation of *Religion* too; and the *Advances of the Sciences* ever since.

Learning had paved the way for Protestantism and so could not be repugnant to it. God had given a whole people, who had at least professed Christianity, into the power of Mahometans, so that thereby the machinery might be set in motion to produce the true theology. There were some Puritans whose Bibliolatry made them over-jealous of other books; John Winthrop thought that Nathaniel Ward was to be censured because in an election sermon of 1641 he grounded "his propositions upon the old Roman and Grecian governments," but Thomas Shepard assured him, "Your apprehensions agaynst reading & learning heathen authors, I perswade myselfe were suddenly suggested," and recommended that if Winthrop still had doubts he discuss them with President Dunster. President Chauncy put into the code of College laws in 1655 a rule that only such authors should be read in any subject "as doe best agree with the Scripture truths," but in answering Dell he made clear that the regulation did not exclude the Greeks and Romans. His argument was the one employed again and again in the controversy over human learning: there are certain principles, he said, written so deeply into human nature that even the fall has not entirely obliterated them, and when heathen authors deliver them to us they "doe not cross the holy writ." He agreed that to deify a heathen writer, or to set his authority "cheek by jowle with the speaking in the Scriptures" was wrong, and he regretted that some Christians in the past had been thus guilty, but *"abusus non tollit usum."* The Puritan conviction, therefore, remained as Increase Mather said, "that the Interest of Religion and good Literature, hath risen and fallen together." The cultivation of the classics in New England did not begin with the Age of Reason, nor during the seventeenth century was there discovered any antagonism between them and theology. Cotton Mather said that Ezekiel Cheever, the venerable schoolmaster of Boston, "us from *Virgil* did to *David* train"; the progression from classical morality to Christian ethics was a natural one for the Puritan, and the education which he insisted should be prerequisite to preaching the Christian gospel included Plato, Seneca, and Plutarch as well as Augustine and William Ames.

By its assimilation into the intellectual heritage of Protestantism, classical culture inevitably had certain restrictions put upon it. It was always used with caution. Cotton approved quoting heathen authors for natural or moral points, but not "for divine or Evangelical." From time to time the preachers warned that mere morality would not save, that the best of heathens fell short of the least of Christians, and that none of them would be found in heaven. Occasionally they seem to have been saddened by this reflection, and secretly been of the opinion that paradise might be still pleasanter for the company of Cato, Seneca, or Aristides. If there was no way in which they could smuggle such heroes into heaven they at least moved them up as close to it as possible; Increase Mather said of these three in particular that they had lived free from the accusations of conscience, and that "their punishment in another world will not be so great, as of those that have been of a vicious Conversation." Sometimes it seems as though the ministers could use their precious knowledge of the classics only for heaping shame upon Christians. They chanted monotonously that practices such as card playing or mixed dancing, "which the Graver sort of Heathen have condemned as unlawful, Christians may well look upon as Sinful." They completed their proofs by declaring that even the heathens knew this or even the Romans acknowledged that. They tortured texts of great writers and did violence to meanings in order to prove that the agreement between pagans and revelation resulted not only from the inherent similarity of the law of nature with the Gospel, but from actual plagiarizing by Greeks and Romans of Jewish lore. They particularly interpreted Plato in this fashion, and hailed with joy Theophilus Gale's *Philosophia Generalis* for its definitive proof that the teachings of Plato were derived "traductione e limpidissimis Hebraeorum Fontibus." [8] When learning falls into the hands of men whose chief interest in it is didactic, it cannot expect to be treated with the objectivity of liberal and disinterested scholarship.

Yet teleological interpretation of the classics was a characteristic of the age, and was inculcated by other faiths than Puritanism. In spite of it, the authors were read, and if they were constrained to yield up odd meanings, they also led the Puritans into many regions where piety alone would not have brought them. The ministers reflected, for instance, that the empire of ancient Rome could not have enjoyed such long success and prosperity had it not been for the justice, temperance, and industry of the Romans, and surmised that possibly peace and plenty were God's way of rewarding well-behaved communities—a conclusion of which the implications were profound and less innocent than they might seem at first glance. Because some authors among their own contemporaries, whom they might have condemned out of hand on the grounds of heresy, were at the same time great classical scholars they gave them a hearing. Increase Mather once called Hugo Grotius "that *Socinianizing,* and at last *Papizing,* and most corrupt Interpreter," but in a calmer mood said Grotius "was one of the Learndest men that this age has produced"; many sermons quoted Grotius and many young men must therefore have read something in him. Classical orators and citations from classical philosophy helped out many sermons, and often when they were paraded as supernumerary witnesses they had in fact donated the whole idea. Two authors above all were found particularly fertile in suggestions: Plutarch, whose works Increase Mather said "Beza esteemed to be amongst the most excellent of humane writings," and Seneca, whom William Hubbard called "the best of *Heathen Philosophers.*" Passages from these two moralists are legion in New England writers; only less frequently appear Plato, Cicero, Aristotle. As might be expected, the array of classical authority and precedent is most impressive in election sermons and tracts on political theory. Influence of the classics was greatest upon the social thinking, yet it is also extremely significant that a preacher, celebrating the joys of the Christian hereafter, telling his congregation that from the achieved bliss of paradise they will look back tenderly upon the sorrows of this life, should quote to them without mentioning Virgil's name, "Haec olim meminisse Juvabit." [9]

If we were to take the pronouncements of Puritan writers at face value we should decide that they owed nothing to medieval philosophy. The ministers constantly informed their congregations that before the Reformation there had flourished a race of "schoolmen," who had corrupted doctrine by making a "mingle-mangle" of paganism and divinity, perverted the Word of God and prostituted theology to the schemes of a dissolute and worldly Pope. Even the defenders of learning called the scholastics "a Dunghill of errors," so that on the strength of his pastor's description the layman, having no first-hand acquaintance with them, must have pictured them as imps of Satan, and agreed with John Webster that "*Scholastick Theologie,* what is it else but a confused *Chaos,* of needless, frivolous, fruitless, triviall, vain, curious, impertinent, knotty, ungodly, irreligious, thorny, and hel-hatc'ht disputes, altercations, doubts, questions and endless janglings, multiplied and spawned forth even to monstrosity and nauseousness?" The laity could hardly have suspected that much of what was delivered from New England pulpits came from such a source; the ministers themselves were more aware that they had derived something from Anselm, Aquinas, or Duns Scotus, but even they never acknowledged their full indebtedness, and expended upon the schoolmen as much vituperation as did Webster. However, though the schoolmen were condemned because they "left studying of Scriptures, and read Peter Lombard, which was mentioned in Latine," the ministers, in spite of themselves, repeated sentences of the Lombard. Few men in the early seventeenth century were yet capable of stepping outside the framework of medieval belief, and the Puritan was neither a Bacon nor a Descartes; his mind was not original, and consequently the settlers of New England retained with few alterations the cosmology of the Middle Ages, even though they constantly denounced its authors.

The Puritans were wrong in believing they had left the philosophy of the schools behind them, but it is not difficult to account for their belief. The differences between Protestant and medieval thought appeared to men of that age completely revolutionary. Since the gist of any philosophy was its theological and ecclesiastical conclusions, and since that of the schoolmen concluded with a defense of Rome and the Catholic creed, it appeared to be directly contradicted by that of the Puritans. One whose every moment was engrossed in religious conflict could have no suspicion that the opposition was incomplete at any point, and no opportunity for noting that while condemning scholastic doctrines of the church and of salvation he was accepting scholastic premises in physics and astronomy, the scholastic theory of the four elements or the four causes, the distinctions between potentiality and act or essence and existence, the theory of motion, the description of human psychology, the criteria of ethics, an identical organization of the academic curriculum, with subdivisions of knowledge into the same disciplines, and the same explanation of their interdependence.

Because scholasticism lent support to Popery, Protestants damned it, but not because it ignored inductive method or contained a fallacious theory of substantial forms. Puritan criticism of scholasticism did not at first go beyond the specific issue of ecclesiastical order and the controverted points in theology; otherwise Puritans found that it contained only what all intelligent men recognized was truth.

When Puritans spoke of medieval philosophy they did not always have the same thing in mind. When ministers thundered against "the subtilty and sophistry of the Schoolmen," they generally were aiming not at the great figures of the thirteenth century but at their decadent successors, the followers of Occam, the nominalists of the century preceding Luther, whom Luther had declared the source of all mischief in the church. In them Puritans found the qualities and doctrines they most abhorred, and yet many arguments which were uncomfortably similar to their own. In them they beheld great wits set "to tie and untie school knots, and spin questions out of their own brain, in which brabbles they were so taken up, that they slightly looked to other matters." It was through their sophistry in particular that the Pope had managed to corrupt all doctrine; they supplied the ammunition used by fideists and by Socinians—two foes whom Puritans had special cause to fear. Among the late scholastics reason had turned back upon itself, and the sublime trust of earlier centuries in the nobility of the intellect gave way to agnosticism, skepticism, and a flight for refuge in submission to authority. Yet while the Puritans were beholding these errors in nominalism they recognized in it, as in its seventeenth-century offspring, several tendencies which could also be ascribed to themselves: emphasis upon the unreliability of reason and the corruption of the human mind by sin, exaltation of God's will above His other attributes and the founding of morality upon arbitrary decree, the conception of regeneration as a union with God of the will rather than of the intellect. The nominalist appeal to authority in order to settle problems found insoluble by reason was made in almost the same spirit in which Puritans invoked revelation. Hence when Puritan divines belabored "those lofty speculations of the schools (which like emptie clouds flie often high, but drop no fatnesse)," they were apt to mean this variety of schoolmen, or to act for the moment as though all schoolmen were of this opinion. Meanwhile they disregarded their own retention of formulae and methods which had descended unchanged from earlier schoolmen. They were able to escape the questions of the fifteenth century, not by succeeding where nominalists had failed in reaching rational and demonstrable answers, but by discovering satisfactory answers in revelation, and so forestalling the need for demonstration. "This is the excellencie of the Word, when all the learned Doctors and Schoolemasters shall have the tongues, but shall never humble one soule, nor purge nor convert one heart, yet the Word and the Spirit in it, will doe that which is usefull and helpfull for thee in this kinde." However, the Puritans came to revelation, not fleeing for protection while cosmology was tumbling about their ears, but with a positive and serene conviction that the regenerate reason would in some measure find revealed teachings verifiable in the natural universe. In this sense, therefore, while Puritans revolted against a particular brand of scholasticism, they became thereby all the more scholastical: with doubts which in the fifteenth century had threatened to split asunder the thirteenth-century synthesis now laid to rest—it is true, not by intellectual resolution but by Biblical authority, yet nevertheless disposed of—with all the queries which medieval reasoners had raised to the discomfort of reason and the trial of faith now settled satisfactorily both to reason and to faith, the Puritans were committed to unreserved acceptance of traditional assumptions in physics, astronomy, or metaphysics, in jurisprudence, medicine, or arithmetic. By appealing to the Bible they believed they were dispelling the disillusionment that had withered philosophers of the late Middle Ages, that they were replacing probability with certainty and reachieving the "homogeneous view of God and the world." All Puritans were once more confident of what the fifteenth century had brought into question, that natural and revealed religion agreed, that belief and an adequate degree of understanding could be reconciled together.

In estimating the scholastic cast of the Puritan mind we must remember, not only that Puritans were unaware how much they naturally and inevitably took from medieval lore, but that they seldom went directly to medieval writers. Instead they generally used restatements by writers of their own day and their own persuasion. By the beginning of the seventeenth century Protestant scholars had worked out careful reformulations, not only of theology, but of every other science as well. They had produced an immense array of textbooks, surveys, and encyclopedias, in which they reorganized and rearranged all human learning, omitting everything Catholic or heretical, closing up the gaps, filling in hitherto disputed chapters with orthodox versions, systematizing the Calvinistic culture, of which Professor Perrin has truly said that it "was real, pervasive, deep rather than broad, peculiarly consistent, like Calvinistic theology, systematic and logical."[10] Protestantism was a revolt against medieval thought, but only on a limited number of particulars; otherwise it was that same thought once more stabilized.

Two of the many works in which learning was thus reorganized and systematized for Protestant purposes were especially employed as reference works in New England, those by Johann Heinrich Alsted and by Bartholomäus Keckermann. In Alsted's *Encyclopaedia Scientiarum Omnium,* by which Cotton Mather said you could "make a short Work of all the Sciences," for it was a veritable "North-West Passage" to them, were mapped out the expanse and boundaries of all disciplines, conveniently within the compass of four folio volumes.[11] It was indeed nothing short of a summary, in sequential and numbered paragraphs, of everything that the mind of European man had yet conceived or discovered. The works of over five hundred authors, from Aristotle to James I, were digested and methodized, including those of Aquinas, Scotus, and medieval theology, as also those of medieval science, such as the *De Natura Rerum*. It first presented the *Praecognita* of learning: "Hexilogia," narrating the habits, conceptions, and faculties of the mind; "Technologia," defining the arts, demonstrating their interdependence and the essential unity of all knowledge; "Archelogia," stating the ends or purposes of the various disciplines, the final and efficient causes, and the guarantees of certainty. Proceeding then to the specific subjects, the work gave the substance of philology, grammar, rhetoric, logic, oratory, poetics, metaphysics, pneumatics, physics, arithmetic, geometry, cosmography, astronomy, geography, optics, music, ethics, political economy, political theory, education, theology, jurisprudence, medicine, the mechanical arts, chronology, and history. A student who had Alsted in his library had everything that man could or need know. Keckermann produced no systematic survey, but he compiled treatises on almost every subject, all of which were available in his immense *Operum Omnium Quae Extant* (Geneva, 1614).[12] If these Gargantuan works were not adequate—and it is hard to imagine any important respect in which they failed—the Puritan scholar had many handbooks on each discipline: surveys of physics in Johannes Magirus' *Physiologiae Peripateticae* or in Zanchius' *De Operibus Dei Intra Spacium Sex Dierum Creatis Opus,* of metaphysics in Burgersdicius' *Institutionum Metaphysicarum,*[13] of ethics in Magirus' *Corona Virtutum Moralium.*[14] If he sought still more erudition, he had the gigantic bibliographies in which were ranged the titles of every work of which the Protestant scholar might conceivably have a need. Henry Diest's *De Ratione Studii Theologici* provided a selected list, George Draudius' *Bibliotheca Classica* was an almost exhaustive bibliography of 1200 folio pages.[15] In John Molanus' *Bibliotheca Materiarum* works were grouped under the topics upon which a minister or a disputant might want a handy reference, such as Abraham, Apostasy, Colleges, Drunkenness, Debt, God, Illegitimate Children, Machiavelli, Miracles, or Paradox; in appendices was a list of Catholic works on the Bible and a gratefully short epitome of Thomas Aquinas. Knowledge was still laid out in these surveys and bibliographies in medieval patterns, as can be seen by comparing Protestant works with similar Catholic ones. Indeed, Protestants used the very compilations of their foes. Sir Kenelm Digby presented Harvard College with a copy of Antonius Possevino's *Bibliotheca Selecta de Ratione Studiorum,* and President Hoar assumed that students would use it along with the Protestant Draudius.[16] It was dedicated to Clement VIII and in many chapters furnished bibliography for exposing Protestant errors, but in chapters on philosophy or the sciences it enumerated works which were used by Protestants and Catholics alike, under rubrics in which they both were thinking.

Consequently, though Puritan literature abounds with condemnations of scholasticism, almost no limits can be set to its actual influence. At every turn we encounter ideas and themes which descend, by whatever stages, from medieval philosophy, while the forms of the thinking, the terminology, the method of logic—though this was believed to have been drastically revolutionized in the sixteenth century—were still duplications of medieval habits, modified but not transformed. Indeed, in seventeenth-century Puritanism, the scholastic influence was actually stronger than it had been in sixteenth-century Protestantism, and for the same reasons that dictated the exaltation of "method." Although John Preston recommended that students come to scholastic philosophy after they had studied a Protestant compendium, yet he was himself a great reader of Scotus, Occam, and particularly of Aquinas, "whose Summa he would sometime read as the Barber cut his hair, and when it fell upon the place he read, he would not lay down his book, but blow it off." John Cotton wrote in 1652—in a passage indispensable for the understanding of New England's intellectual history:

> The Schoolmen (though they be none of the soundest Divines) yet of late years, have crept (for a time) into more credit amongst Schools, then the most judicious and orthodox of our best new writers (*Luther, Calvin, Martyr, Bucer,* and the rest:) and their books were much more vendible, and at a far greater price.

The explanation for their preëminence, Cotton continued, lay not in their possession of the light of divine grace, nor in their skill in tongues and polite literature—for in this respect, says the Puritan humanist, "they were Barbarians"—but in "their rational disputes, with distinct Solidity and Succinct brevity." Hence, we find an avowed effort on the part of New England writers to salvage the schoolmen, to use them and their methods more freely than Protestants a century before had done. They sought deliberately to acquire the virtues of the schoolmen for the profit of the Protestant cause. Cotton praised Norton's *Orthodox Evangelist* for preserving what was "commendable and desireable" in the schoolmen, and he would unhesitatingly bring in Aquinas to settle an objection. Hooker said that the schoolmen went astray whenever they would gratify their master the Pope and so devise "a way to put out the right eye of their reason, and to crook the rule and crosse their own principles," but implied that at other times their reason was sound, their rule and their principles admirable. In his *Survey* he cited Scotus by name and throughout his writings employed the aphorisms of medieval science to illustrate his points: "The rule was of old, *Genus cum forma constituit speciem,*" or "Now it is a rule in Philosophy, that the generation of one is the corruption of another." In published sermons Cobbett, Davenport, and Jonathan Mitchell quoted Aquinas, and Davenport bolstered an opinion by claiming, "the best Schoole-men have determined and concluded it." In 1682 Increase Mather, arraying against Socinius the testimony of all Christian history, as of equal authority with the Fathers and the reformers adduced Anselm, Aquinas, Bonaventura, and Hugo de Saint Victoire. In 1687 Samuel Lee was still declaring that while the "school Divines" before the Reformation devised niceties that "have eaten out the heart of solid Divinity, till the happy dayes of the restauration of the Gospel," yet their works "in some things may be of good use to fix terms and distinctions." Van Mastricht explained the Puritan attitude: on the one hand the scholastics had developed method in excess, but on the other it was "in defectu" among Anabaptists, enthusiasts, and fanatics; only orthodox Protestant theologians, among whom the New Englanders counted themselves not the least, had hit the right moderation between extremes. Puritans were scholastics with everything omitted that seemed to support the Papacy; they believed that they had purified medieval learning of its abuses, and therefore saw no reason why it should not be retained and adopted as their own.

So scholasticism supplied content for every department of Puritan thought. The physics was traditional, and the theory of the natural world that of medieval science. As a part of physics Puritanism retained the medieval conception of man, of his physiology and his psychology; it thought of the body and soul as matter and form, and it was undisturbed by the suspicions which led Descartes to a reinvestigation of the passions or Hobbes to commence the *Leviathan* with an onslaught upon academic psychology. The definition of human reason, the description of its potentialities and its limitations, its relation to authority and revelation were essentially scholastic. But extensive as was the scholastic contribution to the content of particular arts, much more important was its influence upon the spirit in which they were conceived, upon the fundamental assumptions about their nature, origins, and inter-connections, their function and their aims. Protestants in the seventeenth century merely rephrased Peripatetics in claiming that "Philosophiam Studioso pietatis non esse negligendam," that philosophy was not only useful to theology, "necessarium etiam."[17] Divinity may transcend "the capacity of reason corrupted, but not of reason illuminated by the Word and the Spirit, which judges spiritually and even disposes things spiritual in order."[18] Charles Chauncy reiterated an ancient contention when he said that physics, politics, rhetoric, or astronomy "in the true sense and right meaning thereof are Theologicall & Scripture learning, and are not to be accounted of as humane learning," for Scripture itself supplies the grounds of their precepts. Medieval lecturers would have recognized as their own the standard theories: the Holy Ghost instilled an intuitive knowledge into the Apostles, but men now must acquire knowledge by study of the arts; in his original integrity, Adam possessed a complete understanding of them, but after the fall man can reachieve such understanding only by painful industry, and though acquired knowledge of the arts must forever remain an imperfect reconstruction of the knowledge with which Adam was endowed, it is still an approximation to the image of God.[19] In fact, as was maintained again and again in Harvard commencement theses, "The arts are radiations of divine wisdom," "The author of being is the author of the arts." Men did not invent them, they were gifts of God—"non inuentum sit hominum, sed splendidissimum Dei immortalis donum." Their rules were not tentative hypotheses but divine ordinations. God, not any general or material influence, determined the regulations of the "art of war"; consequently, men who waged battle "artificially" did so not merely for advantage's sake, but to attest the wisdom of God: "to be able to war or fight according to Art, gives much glory to him who is the Author of every commendable Art or Science." What was true of the art of war must be easily true of arts less subject to circumstance, of logic or rhetoric, or of philosophy in general. Philosophy was derived, said Keckermann, "from primary, infinite and most perfect wisdome, just as rays from the body of the sun," and this wisdom is God Himself. After the fall of Adam, the arts were constituted, in part from the vestiges of God's image still remaining in him, "in part from a peculiar inspiration of the Holy Ghost." William Ames taught that the principles of the arts were those by which the world was created and governed, that though they were learned by men from their experience in the world, yet in reality they were nothing less than the wisdom of God, and that however diverse they appeared to human comprehensions they were in reality integral parts of the single, eternal wisdom by which all things were perfectly ordered. Every art, therefore, with its limits, its contents, its rules, was a perfect structure that could not be altered or improved upon. In education the student submitted himself to the disciplines, not that he might learn, as we would say today, "to think for himself," but to acquire the habits of mind which they would impart as surely as a cause will work its effect:

> Every part of *Philosophy* contributes its share; *Logick* and *Metaphysicks,* sharpness of Judgment; *Mathematicks* Solidness and Sagacity; *Physicks* good conjecture at the Reasons of things; *Moral Philosophy* and *History,* Prudence; *Rhetorick,* Fairness and Confidence of Address; *Poetry,* quickness of fancy, and *Imagination.*

From their scholastic background Puritans acquired their assurance that the individual arts, since they emanate from God, must fit together into an harmonious edifice of knowledge. Charles Morton taught Harvard undergraduates that "there is a mutual Subserviency of Arts and Sciences like Stones in an Arch which support each other."[20] "All disciplines have some relation to each other," said one commencement thesis, and another more poetically declared, "All parts are bound to each other by a sisterly chain (sororio vinculo)." Indeed, how could they be otherwise, since "Primary being is the Alpha and Omega of the arts," since the seven liberal arts make "a circle of seven sections of which the center is God"? Hence from an ultimately scholastic source came the Puritan faith, never questioned or criticized, that all knowledge is one, that every discipline harmonizes with every other, that all human learning can be ranged in a hierarchical progression, that the mind of man, beginning on the elementary level, proceeds naturally in systematic study to higher levels, until it reaches at last the supreme knowledge of theology, the queen of the sciences, toward which all other knowledge tends and to the enthronement of which all other sciences lend full support. Samuel Willard spoke in the strength of his scholastic heritage when he declared, "It is a received Maxim, *that all Arts are Handmaids to Divinity;* and what are they but Rules to direct Man how to attain his subordinate Ends?" To the Puritan mind no more than to the mind of Anselm was it conceivable that a system of philosophy might exist apart from theology, or that theology could maintain what philosophy must deny. All knowledge was fused into one belief, all sciences were ultimately segments of a single science, all disciplines were integrated into harmonious unity. As Alsted's *Encyclopaedia* had it, "The catholic and foremost measure of all the disciplines ought to be the glory of God and our eternal salvation." The history of thought in New England is meaningless unless we remember that the intellectual tradition began with an assumption of the unity of knowledge, that men in seventeenth-century Boston entertained this basic conviction exactly as men had entertained it in thirteenth-century Paris.

To describe Puritanism simply as a piety is far from adequate. It was part of the Protestant revolt, it was a particularly intense form of revolt, but like all Protestantism it had an intellectual as well as a spiritual side. It too might be described, in the definition supplied by Professor Gilson, as a "Christian Philosophy," for it too was a belief "which, although keeping the two orders formally distinct, nevertheless considers the Christian revelation as an indispensable auxiliary to reason."[21] Puritans also had asked, "What intellectual advantages were to be gained by turning to the Bible and the Gospels as sources of philosophic inspiration?" They had answered in no uncertain tones, that everything was to be gained thus; their criticism of scholastics was that they had not turned to the Bible enough, that they had not preserved the distinction sufficiently, but subjected revelation to reason. Therefore, Puritans felt, the schoolmen had betrayed Christianity into the power of Rome. But their criticism was limited to what they considered points at issue; piety furnished energy and the motive for revolt, but the revolt never touched upon a large array of inherited beliefs and traditional doctrines. Along with piety there existed in the minds of Puritans many tenets and attitudes that had no inherent connection with it, and some that could be reconciled to it only with difficulty. They said in one moment that everything was to be gained by going to the Bible for the articles of belief, but in the next they went also to other books, to systematic treatises on divinity, to methodized tomes on doctrine and ethics, to classical antiquity, to medieval scholasticism or to monumental restatements of it. Taking their material from such various sources, they put together a coherent scheme of philosophy and science. They compiled and combined, rather than investigated or theorized anew, or they merely memorized what others had compiled; but resting secure in their conviction that all knowledge was one, they took all knowledge, as it then existed, for their province, at the same time that they were probing the inward turnings of the soul and voicing the desires of the spirit.

BOOK II

COSMOLOGY

CHAPTER V

THE INSTRUMENT OF REASON

In the Puritan view of man, the fall had wrought many melancholy effects, but none so terrible as upon his intellect: "O Grief! that most efficacious instrument for arriving at deeply hidden truth, for asserting it, vindicating it and eliminating all confusion"—that instrument was warped and twisted. Adam had been created in the image of God, possessed of perfect holiness and an intuitive grasp of the principles of right reason, but after the fall he was no longer able to tell what should follow upon what, or to perceive the interconnections of things. Had the race been left in the plight to which he reduced it, surely it would have perished. Fortunately, however, God is merciful as well as just, and He did not utterly forsake His creatures. Knowing that men now desperately required guidance from outside themselves, God gave them explicit commands through the Prophets and through revelation; in order that all aspiration might not be extinguished among them He regenerated the wills of His chosen, and in addition, out of the superfluity of His bounty, He enabled several mortals to reconstruct, to some degree, the method which Adam had possessed in his integrity of drawing conclusions from given premises. In the Puritan conception of the human saga, the art of logic was a particular gift of God, bestowed upon fallen and hapless humanity, in order that they might not collapse in the ineptitude they had brought upon themselves.

Considered therefore in the light of logic, the fall of man had amounted in effect to a lapse from dialectic; the loss of God's image, reduced to the most concrete terms, was simply the loss of an ability to use the syllogism, and innate depravity might most accurately be defined as a congenital incapacity for discursive reasoning. Regarded in this light, whatever mastery of logical methods the heathens, Plato and Aristotle, had achieved resulted simply from God's being graciously willing that a few individuals should recover certain elements of the pristine rectitude in order that the whole race might not be devastated. By the same token it followed that a return to God through His grace involved also a simultaneous return to Him through logic. Grace brought men through the direct intervention of the Holy Ghost to will the truth, but the most gracious would also stand in need of logic, which had been devised "to helpe us the rather, by a naturall order, to finde out the truthe." Both grace and logic were divine gifts, though the logic had been formulated by heathens and could be learned by the unregenerate. Pagans could not have discovered it without some divine help, as they themselves realized: their myth of Prometheus was their allegory of logic, and the fire stolen from heaven was really dialectic. Therefore Christian schools could use the texts of Greeks and Romans, and all students, elect or reprobate, could be made to learn the rules in the class-room, for the authority of logic was divine no matter who employed it. The art was not man-made, though men had written it down; it was a portion of heavenly wisdom, a replica, however faint, of the divine intelligence. Whosoever learned it approximated once more the image of God. By logic "(in some sort) is healed the wound we received in our reason by *Adams* fall: and this daily tryall teacheth, because by the precepts of Logicke, things hidden and darke, are clearly objected to our judgement." Since we have for the purposes of this study created an issue where the Puritans themselves would have denied that one existed, in the opposition or at least in the latent tension between their piety and their learning, we are compelled to ask, in accordance with the terms of our inquiry, how in Puritan thought the piety and the intellectual heritage were reconciled, how dogma and rationality were joined, how the concepts of man as fallen and the saint as regenerated by irresistible grace were made compatible with the Puritan passion for learning, for argumentation and demonstration.

No Puritan ever believed that logic of itself could redeem. Many learned doctors were obviously outside the Covenant of Grace, and many who were uninstructed in dialectic were clearly sanctified. But since logic was a fragment of the divine mind, the saints, being joined to the divinity, must become logical. According to the doctrine of imperfect regeneration they would no more achieve perfect logicality than they would come to flawless holiness; nevertheless, by receiving grace they regained something of Adam's original power to reason correctly. They learned the rules and methods of study, and they were given an ability to use them by conversion. God demands that men judge between truth and falsehood, and Scripture is not addressed to irrational beings. Puritan piety was formulated in logic and encased in dialectic; it was vindicated by demonstration and united to knowledge. "Logic does not teach fallacies," said a Harvard thesis. It did not teach fallacies because it was instituted by God Himself, and what could be proved by logic was sanctioned from on high.

This veneration of logic was in part an inheritance from the past and in part a characteristic of the epoch. Neither humanism nor Protestantism had diminished the prestige with which medieval theologians invested the art. The study of antiquity generally enhanced it, and Protestantism was, in one sense, an appeal to logic for the arbitration of belief, since logic alone could interpret the Bible. Keckermann declared truly at the end of the sixteenth century that no other era in the world's history had been so devoted to logic, produced more books, or studied it more assiduously. No sooner had humanism and Protestantism gained a foothold in England than one who was both a humanist and a Protestant brought out a vernacular textbook of logic. In *The Rule of Reason,* 1552, Thomas Wilson spoke of logic as the gift of God bestowed upon men that they might not be destroyed in the chaos of sin, that they might still comprehend the divine universe. Through the many treatises, in which Keckermann boasted the century rich beyond all previous centuries, sounded a sustained paean to the art. Alsted hailed it as the queen of the mind, the light of intelligence, the norm of judgment, the laboratory of truth, the panacea of memory, without which no man could become lawyer, physician, or philosopher. Renaissance logicians celebrated their subject with all the fervid eloquence which Renaissance poets put at the service of their mistresses. Without it, said one of them, all study is strife, all life lifeless, all study of laws stultification of laws, medicine mendacity, philosophy sophistry, "and all doctors of all arts are not doctors but seducers" ("non doctores sed seductores"). Because men are distinguished from the brutes, declared another, only by the possession of right reason, then logic, which guides and governs reason, is the most excellent and most necessary of the arts. A third declaimed that if we are to discover in all the other arts anything useful to human life, it is thanks to noble and divine logic; if we are able to think acutely and judge prudently, if we can teach young men the sage advices of good authors, if we can widen things narrow, clarify obscurities, divide universals into parts, draw out the latent, discern the ambiguous, it is because of logic; "lastly, if we excel in that by which men most excel the beasts, i.e. in reason, counsel and judgment . . . it is by the help of noble and divine logic." The necessity for logic in theology was no less than in other disciplines: "so necessary and useful to the study of theology," said Henry Diest, "that without it there is absolutely no theology, or one maimed in body and imperfect in many respects." Had we not logic we could not analyze texts, clear up controversies, defend ourselves against sophistry, protect ourselves against heresy. English Puritans swelled the Protestant chorus; in 1621 Richard Bernard wrote in his manual of pastoral care, *The Faithfull Shep-*

herd, that by logic are doctrines collected, confirmed, and proved; a sermon without logic, he said, "is but an ignorant discourse," and logic therefore must be "the sterne, to guide the course of our speech, that the sudden and stormie blasts of violent affections ouerwhelme it not."

Because logic served to restrain "sudden and stormie blasts," as well as because it was the most prominent of the "humane helps" to divinity, it became a principal target for the sectarian assault upon learning in the 1640's. Webster asserted that university men "have drawn *Theologie* into a close and strict *Logical* method, and thereby hedged in the free workings and manifestations of the Holy one of Israel." Truth, he said, should be learned from the Holy Ghost, but from theologians can be learned only "a farraginous heap of divisions, subdivisions, distinctions, limitations, axioms, positions and rules." With their logic, he continued, they make the Bible their sport—"a tennis ball to be tossed and reverberated by their petulant wits and perverse reasons"—while the simplicity of faith is forgotten in the fascination of the game. Naturally the effect upon the orthodox of these denunciations of "the Devil's Sword" was a still more hearty dedication to its use, if we can imagine them any more committed than they had been all along.

New Englanders contributed freely to the glorification of logic. Charles Chauncy said that without logic the milk of Scripture would be soured:

> Yea how shall a man know when a Scripture is wrested, or falsly applyed, or a false use is made of it, or a false consequence is drawn out of it, or a true, without some principles of logick, especially to hold forth these things to others he must needs be a shamefull workman, and many times ridiculous, neither rightly apprehending, nor dividing the word of trueth, that hath no knowledg how to interpret the Scripture.

John Eliot considered logic so important a part of Christian knowledge that he translated into Algonquin a short treatise, "to initiate the Indians in the knowledge of the Rule of Reason," wherein he taught them that as soon as they could read the Word they must learn to analyze it. Davenport exhorted his congregation to exercise their "understanding . . . the dianoetical, discoursing faculty, which is the seat of conclusions." Samuel Willard told young scholars that they must know grammar and rhetoric to read Scripture, and logic "for the analysing of the Text, and finding out the Method of it, and the Arguments contained in it." He explained to the people that "logical Analysing of the Scripture" was absolutely prerequisite to understanding it, "and do require a great deal of Time and study rightly to perform it; yea and whereof is one great reason why the Scriptures are often quoted impertinently, and besides the genuine intention of them." William Brattle, when a tutor at Harvard College, composed a manuscript synopsis of logic, explaining that the object of the art was all things knowable, and Charles Morton, when vice-president of the College, taught that

> Upon the prikly bush of Logick grows
> Of other Sciences the fragrant rose.[2]

At Harvard College, by the laws of 1646, the study of Scripture was specifically declared to involve "observations of Language and Logicke"; the laws of 1655 required that Scripture be read at morning and evening prayers and that one of the Bachelors or Sophisters "Logically analyse that which is read." The B. A. was bestowed upon those able to read the Testaments and "to Resolve them Logically."[3] Samuel Mather of the class of 1643 showed nine years later how well he had studied his lessons when he wrote in the preface to Samuel Stone's defense of Hooker, "There is no art but useth the help of Logick; nothing can shew itself to the eye of the mind of man, but in this light."

The intellect of early New England is customarily described as "theological," but in practice it was as apt to be merely logical. A great part of the creed was confessedly "not verbatim contain'd in the Bible," but was collected therefrom by deduction. In the complete body of New England divinity as many tenets were entered on the authority of the syllogism as of revelation. In a book which, though published in 1869, is replete with factual material about an earlier New England, Harriet Beecher Stowe caused a character to remark,

> If there is a golden calf worshipped in our sanctified New England, its name is Logic; and my good friend the parson burns incense before it with a most sacred innocence of intention. He believes that sinners can be converted by logic, and that, if he could once get me into one of these neat little traps aforesaid, the salvation of my soul would be assured. He has caught numbers of the shrewdest infidel foxes among the farmers around, and I must say that there is no trap for the Yankee like the logic-trap.[4]

The reign of logic in the New England mentality was an inheritance from the seventeenth century, and the rule continued unbroken until the Transcendentalists consigned consistency to the sphere of hobgoblins and Dr. Holmes wrote its epitaph in the supremely logical construction of a one-hoss shay.

The influence of logic being thus pervasive, a great part of New England thinking and writing inevitably depended upon what particular logic was studied and employed. One of Webster's charges against the universities was that therein the students were confined to a single method of dialectic, "nay even bound to the same authors, and hardly allowed so much liberty, and difference, as is between *Aristotle,* and *Ramus Logick.*" This accusation must have caused considerable puzzlement among the dons at both Cambridges, for it probably was the first intimation they had received that the difference between the rival logics of Aristotle and Ramus was not a fundamental issue or that they had not strained the limits of academic liberty by permitting their students to examine both systems together. In Protestant Europe the logic of Petrus Ramus had been the most fiercely contested of educational issues for over a century, and in the 1640's professors were still wrangling. The fundamental fact concerning the intellectual life of New Englanders is that they ranged themselves definitely under the banner of the Ramists. The Peripatetic system was indeed read at Harvard, but the Ramist was believed, and it exercised the decisive rôle in shaping New England thought. It is not too much to say that, while Augustine and Calvin have been widely recognized as the sources of Puritanism, upon New England Puritans the logic of Petrus Ramus exerted fully as great an influence as did either of the theologians.

The life of Ramus is a testimony to the immense importance of logic for the Renaissance mind.[5] His long career was unrelenting warfare, of a ferocity hardly conceivable today, over questions of method and terminology, from the year 1536, when he, a youth of twenty-one, startled the learned world by maintaining in his Master of Arts thesis at Paris, "Whatever has been said from Aristotle is forged," to the year 1572, when his colleague and bitter foe, Jacques Charpentier, closed a twenty-year argument on the third day of St. Bartholomew by setting a gang of murderers upon him. Between those years Ramus wrought, so it seemed to his contemporaries, a revolution in intellectual history, chiefly by his reform of the subject which determined all use of the mind. Aided at every step by Omer Talon—the two were pictured as another Damon and Pythias—he lectured to large audiences and published an array of works on grammar, mathematics, physics, and theology, while Talon worked out his teachings in rhetoric. In 1556 Ramus issued at Paris a compact manual of fifty pages, *Dialecticae Libri Duo,* the crucial statement of his teaching and, measured in terms of immediate influence upon the times, one of the three or four outstanding books of the age. During the earlier part of his career he was protected by the Guises, who saved him from rioting students and enraged professors. In 1554 a royal decree proscribed his works, which were publicly burned, and prohibited him from lecturing on philosophy; but with the help of the Cardinal of Lorraine the ban was lifted and he was appointed to a specially endowed chair at the Collège de France. There in the 1550's he was far and away the greatest figure among the faculties of Europe, with students thronging to his lectures and carrying his ideas to every corner of the continent. His doctrine was ideally suited to Protestant needs, but his repute among Protestants was made doubly certain in 1561 when he announced his departure from Rome. Thereby he sacrificed the favor of the Guises, and from 1568 to 1570 he found it expedient to travel in Germany. His progress up and down the Rhine was a triumph. Delegations of Ramists, coming forth to hail him as he approached each university town, were set upon by bands of Aristotelians; broken pates and lengthening disputations marked his progress. His death at St. Bartholomew sanctified his fame in Protestant circles as far away as Boston, where Increase Mather spoke of him always as "that Great Scholar and Blessed Martyr," and many pious works dwelt in detail upon his martyrdom, how he was thrown from his chamber window "so that his bowels issued out on the stones," how he was dragged through the streets, "whipt by certain young schollers who were set on by their popish Tutors," how he was beheaded on the banks of the Seine and his remains cast into the river.[6]

In the eyes of his contemporaries he died equally for the cause of logic and of Christ: "because of Ramus his Love to Protestants, and Testimony against Aristotle."[7] He had already translated his *Dialecticae* into the vernacular—significant gesture!—and shortly before his death penned for it a moving preface which, translated into Latin or into other vernaculars, acquainted all men with the meaning of his labors. As Archimedes had asked that on his tombstone be engraved his solution of the problem of spheres and cylinders, so in this preface Petrus Ramus prayed that on his mounument be graven his reform of logic. For proof that he did not exceed the bounds of modesty, he pointed to his many works, his reduction of logic to short and concise compass, the poets and orators who had praised him, the number and fury of his enemies, his long vigils of study, the sophistry he had combated. And then, he continued, when he had applied this great ardor for pure logic to the cause of religion, when he had endangered his life amid civil wars, God so shielded him that his studies had not even been interrupted! He besought God, therefore, that He would "please to illumine this light of Logic in all good spirits, studious and desirous of knowing the truth, and that He will cause it to augment from more to more, that it may embellish all the liberal disciplines, but principally that it may make clear the mysteries and celestial secrets of the sacred and divine doctrine." To his followers this dying prayer, sealed with his blood, was nothing short of a sacred trust. They took up the work where he had left it, developed his system, fought his enemies, dedicated his logic to the defense and clarification of religion.

After Ramus' death the stream of learned works expounding or defending him swelled to a torrent, and the number of attacks kept pace. Controversies lengthened from reply to rejoinder to rebuttal, and scholars expended on each other not merely arguments but an extensive command of invective and vituperation. The influence of the system varied from place to place and time to time, and was everywhere a cause for debate and tumult. Advocates were extravagant in their praises, opponents no less vehement. In England the teaching prospered along with Puritanism, with which, by the beginning of the seventeenth century, it became almost synonymous. Not all Puritans, to be sure, were Ramists, but many Ramists were Puritans. Andrew Melville studied under Ramus at Paris and carried the dialectic to Scotland;[8] it reached Cambridge in the 1570's, and there dominated the teaching of logic, primarily through the work of three great commentators: William Temple of King's, George Downame of Christ's, and Alexander Richardson of Queen's. It was opposed by Richard Hooker, by Oxford in general, and by the Laudian party to a man. Many young men responded to it as the herald of a new day. Sir Philip Sidney, to whom Temple dedicated his commentary in 1584, discussed it with his friends and wrote its figures into the *Arcadia*;[9] Marlowe dramatized the death of Ramus in *The Massacre at Paris* in terms which make clear his intimate knowledge of the doctrine, and he caused Dr. Faustus anachronistically to quote the opening sentence of the *Dialecticae;* John Milton rewrote the *Dialecticae,* probably early in his career, though his recension was not published until 1672. His was almost the last publication of importance in England upon the system, marking the close of a century during which there were always versions of Ramus available to English students and lecturers discoursing upon him at Cambridge.

The passing of the system from Cambridge, England, to Cambridge, New England, and thence to New Haven, is clearly traceable. At the end of the century both Increase Mather and John Leverett cautioned against too exclusive a cultivation of any one method, boasting that Harvard practiced the "liberal mode of philosophizing," that students consulted Aristotle, Ramus, Descartes or Bacon, "pledged to the words of no particular master." There was justice in these pretensions in that Harvard had never officially excluded the Aristotelian logic, in that scholastic handbooks, like that of Burgersdicius, had always been available. Nevertheless, these speeches must be interpreted as of the late seventeenth century, betraying an awareness, which had by then become general, that the system of Ramus had its defects. Earlier in the century there had been no such doubts, and the Ramist teaching was followed, no matter how much the Aristotelian was read. Cotton Mather said in the *Magnalia* that the Ramist discipline was merely "preferred unto the Aristotelaean," but the reason for his moderation is made apparent in the next sentence, to the effect that Harvard was now devoted to the "libera philosophia" as preached by Bacon. Had he written before Bacon and Descartes began to overshadow Ramus, he would have used words stronger than "preferred." In 1679 his father had been more emphatic as he traced the intellectual tradition of New England in the preface to James Fitch's *The first Principles of the Doctrine of Christ*— itself an unmistakably Ramist document. He then said that models of divinity, "methodically disposed, according to the golden Rules of Art," were exceedingly valuable; this phrase, "golden rules of art," was a stock one among Ramists to describe Ramus' rules for "method", and Mather revealed its provenience when he continued:

> In this way that great and famous Martyr of France, *Peter Ramus* held forth the light to others. After him succeeded the profoundly learned and godly, *Alexander Richardson,* of whom Mr. *Hooker* was wont to say, that the Lord would not suffer *Richardson* to live unto old age, or to finish what was in his heart & head to doe . . . lest the English Nation should glory too much in their own strength . . . About the same time the Lord raised up that great Champion, Dr. *Ames* . . . He in his *Medulla Theologiae* hath improved *Richardsons* method and Principles to great advantage.

The same conception of the tradition was entertained at Yale in 1714, as is shown in the manuscript synopsis compiled there by Samuel Johnson, which begins with a history of logic, distinguishes three schools of philosophy, the Platonists, the Peripatetics, and the Eclectics, and declares that of the Eclectics, "princeps fuit Ramus ille magnus," after whom followed Richardson, whom Ames followed, "whom we follow."[10]

The accuracy of this philosophical genealogy can be substantiated in full detail. Alexander Richardson died before he could complete a final résumé of all the arts according to the principles of Ramus, but his disciples were not left entirely in the dark about what had been in his heart and head to do, for manuscript notes on his lectures circulated widely in England and were carried to New England; a version of them was apparently printed in 1629, and in 1657 Samuel Thomson brought out a copy under the title of *The Logicians School-Master*. Ames applied the methodology, as amplified by Richardson, to theology in the *Medulla* and to casuistry in *De Conscientia.* His papers on philosophy were collected in a volume entitled *Philosophemata;* one of these, "Demonstratio Logicae Verae," is simply a word-for-word repetition of the *Dialecticae,* omitting the illustrations from classical authors, compressing the system to forty octavo pages, to which is appended a recapitulation in four, while another of the papers is a collection of *Theses* gathered out of Ramus and Richardson, restating the entire doctrine in propositions, thus serving as a mine for theses at Harvard commencements. Increase Mather had reason to cite Hooker in connection with the two expounders, for his *A Survey of the Summe of Church-Discipline* is composed entirely in the logical patterns of the *Dialecticae*. Harvard students owned and studied the works of Ramus, the commentaries of Downame and Richardson, Ames's *Philosophemata,* the recensions of Milton and of Wendelin, and some of the literature of the controversy.[11] In 1661, before he became president of the College, Leonard Hoar wrote from England advising his undergraduate nephew, Josiah Flynt, to take notes on his reading and to classify them according to "the method of the incomparable P. Ramus":

Get his definitions and distributions into your mind and memory . . . He that is ready in those of P. Ramus, may refer all things to them. And he may know where again to fetch any thing that he hath judiciously referred; for there is not one axiom of truth ever uttered, that doth not fall under some speciall rule of art.

Apparently unaware that Richardson's lectures were now published, Hoar told Josiah to procure a manuscript, for it "would be as an Ariadne's thred to you in this labyrinth"; he was certain that copies were available, since they "have bin continued in your colledg ever since the foundation thereof among most that were reckoned students indeed." Hoar suggested that either Danforth or Jonathan Mitchell might still have one; certainly Mitchell had owned Richardson's lectures in 1646, for his class-room disputations of that year propose and defend questions in phrases taken bodily from Ramus, and his notes contain marginal references both to Ramus and to Richardson.[12] Manuscript synopses made by later undergraduates, Thomas Shepard, A. B. 1653, or Samuel Johnson at Yale, are simply compilations of Ramus and Richardson. The book which Eliot translated for the Indians was Ramus' *Dialecticae* reduced to a basic simplicity. That the ministers did their thinking according to Ramus is shown almost without exception by New England sermons; Biblical texts were "opened" by the logic of Ramus and the rhetoric of Talon; the terms of this system can be seen in the handling of the proofs, where often ministers pause to explain technical forms in the Ramist vocabulary. The treatises upon polity were maintained, like Hooker's, upon Ramist principles; many of the Presbyterians persisted in using Aristotelian methods, and from a reading of the controversies between them and the New Englanders arises an impression which is almost a certainty that the Congregational theory developed hand-in-hand with the application of Ramus' dialectic to the Bible, that there was a deep-seated affinity between the logic and the polity. Such a conclusion rests upon more than guesswork, for Ramus himself quarreled with Beza in 1571 over this very issue. Ramus persuaded the synod of the Ile-de-France to declare that the power to elect pastors and pronounce censures should reside in individual congregations and not in a ministerial classis; Beza, representing the Presbyterianism of Geneva and the majority of the Huguenots, overruled Ramus at the national synod of Nismes in 1572, denouncing Ramus' argument as making for a "démocratique" constitution, "ne laissant au conseil presbytérial que les propositions," and being therefore "complètement absurde et pernicieuse."[13] Without admitting that Congregationalism was "démocratique," the New England divines freely acknowledged him as a discoverer of "the *Congregational way* of Church Government," and in their expositions used his logic to establish it. Samuel Stone recognized the New England bias artfully in his defense of Hooker against the Presbyterian Samuel Hudson by declaring that a particular point was admissible on the authority of Aristotle *as well as* on that of Ramist logicians, the chief of whom he called by name: "Not onely *Ramus, Berhusius, Snellius, Gutberleth,* &c., but *Aristotle* will grant it."

The most important proofs of New England allegiance to the *Dialecticae* are the logical theses maintained at Harvard commencements, which from the beginning to the year 1689 are pure and uncontaminated Ramism. The initial list, published to the world in *New Englands First Fruits,* was equivalent to an open proclamation of Harvard's alignment; thereafter at each commencement the theses followed in the order of topics set forth by Ramus, employed his phrases and catchwords, used terminology in the peculiar senses he had given it, defended his most controversial positions. President Chauncy seems to have been lukewarm toward the system; he once demurred while Increase Mather was disputing, "upon a Dislike of the *Ramaean* Strains in which our Young Disputant was carrying on his Thesis," but Jonathan Mitchell cried out that Mather might continue, for he was disputing "doctissime". In spite of this hostility, Chauncy did not alter the Ramist character of the theses during his presidency, and from the very nature of the propositions it is clear they must have been defended in "Ramaean Strains." Out of the dialectic and its amplification by Richardson and Ames grew the doctrine of "encyclopaedia" or "technologia", a systematic philosophy of the inter-connections of the arts, formulated within the terms of this logic; [14] after the commencement of 1653 theses under this heading as well as those in logic itself bear witness to the Ramist coloring of New England thought. The first sign of a change appears in the logical theses for 1689, just after Increase Mather had gone to England, when tutor William Brattle was left in charge of the teaching of logic; in the theses of this year the principles of Descartes are first distinctly introduced, as they had been formulated three years before by Brattle in his manuscript, *A Compendium of Logick.* Yet even this innovation represents no radical break with Ramist methodology, for in the *Compendium* Brattle did not utterly discard Ramus but rather rewrote the system, following the same scheme of organization, dropping the outmoded concepts and inserting instead those of Descartes, or else merely translating Ramist terms into Cartesian nomenclature.[15] The teaching of logic, as indicated by the theses, continued still to be closer to Ramus than to the versions of Aristotle, while the essentially Ramist technologia remained unchallenged for several decades, one of its theses for 1719 declaring, "The Ramist logic is not to be esteemed less than the Aristotelian."

There is but one figure of importance in the intellectual history of seventeenth-century New England who adhered to the Peripatetics, and he was a late arrival whose inclination was determined in England. Charles Morton was head of a dissenters' school at Newington Green before he came to Massachusetts Bay in 1686; he served as fellow and vice-president of Harvard until 1698, and brought with him the manuscript notes from which he had taught in England and from which presumably he continued to teach in New England.[16] His treatise on physics reflects many new developments, but his logic was a reactionary Aristotelian manual. If Morton taught from it while Brattle was tutoring on the basis of his own *Compendium,* then two diverse views were being presented to Harvard students, but there is little evidence that Morton's system was influential. It contained nothing that had not been available in the vernacular since 1552 in Thomas Wilson's *The Rule of Reason* or since 1617 in Blundeville's *The Arte of Logick;* it was no more than a repetition of texts that had long been in the hands of Harvard students, such as the *Institutionum Logicarum* of Franconus Burgersdicius (1626), which Morton specifically mentions, or as Adrian Heereboord's revisions of Burgersdicius, Ερμηνεια *Logica* (1658) and *Meletemata Philosophica* (1659), or the three or four treatises of Keckermann collected in his *Operum* (1614), or—most compact of all—Johannes Stierius' tabloid summary of all Aristotelian teachings, *Praecepta Doctrinae Logicae, Ethicae, Physicae, Metaphysicae, Sphaericaeque* (first edition 1628, seventh, 1671).

When Morton's text or these Aristotelian handbooks are put beside Ramus' *Dialecticae* the differences crystallize at once. The hallmarks of a Peripatetic treatment are the features historically regarded as Aristotle's great contributions to the art, the categories and the syllogism. After a brief definition of logic, an Aristotelian text plunges into an enumeration of the "predicables", the terminology of logical discourse, the vocabulary of disputation, what Blundeville described as "certaine titles or Tables containing all things that be in the world," what Morton called "such things as are apt to be spoken, i.e. affirmed or denied of things." Generally these books divided the predicables into three classes: the "antepredicaments", described as "something to be known by way of preface for the better understanding of the predicaments," containing definitions of terms like "perfect" or "imperfect", "different", "property", "accident", "genus" and "species", "abstract" and "concrete", and a few elementary rules, such as that what is true of the predicate is true of the subject. Then came the "predicaments" themselves, consisting of the ten categories; then the "postpredicaments", which Morton said explain "the predicaments as appendix or postscript to them," usually defined as the "affections" of things arising from their disposition in categories, including such concepts as priority and motion, cause and effect, matter and form, and the various degrees of diversity, opposition, and contradiction.

Most Aristotelian texts divided the whole of logic into three parts: simple terms, proposition, and discourse, though Morton preferred to call the first two "apprehension" and "composition". The first section contained the predicables, which were enumerated dogmatically, to be memorized by the student, not worked into any sustained scheme or pattern. After the student had learned these, he proceeded to the second part, usually the briefest, in which he learned to make propositions, to form statements for argument or denial, and discovered the meaning of "definition" and "description". The third section was always the longest, for here the student came to grips with the syllogism. He learned first the standard three figures, and then worked through a succession of chapters on all their possible variations, on sophisms and the detection of fallacies, all of which had technical denominations, and on the "elenchus". In the last chapter of the third section were customarily delivered a few directions on "method", such as that reasoning should proceed from universals to particulars and from the total to the partial. These rules were brief and platitudinous; the essence of an Aristotelian handbook was not the "method" but the predicables and the syllogism, and a student had mastered logic when he could recite the categories and argue to conclusions through middle terms.

Such was the logic taught at Paris when the penniless Pierre de la Ramée came up from Picardy, consumed with a desire for useful knowledge. To him it was all frivolity and incoherence. "When I came to Paris, I fell into the subtleties of the sophists, and they taught me the liberal arts through questions and disputes, without ever showing me a single thing of profit or service." Their logic had neither rhyme nor reason, even from the very first lessons in which they confronted the student with a series of abstruse and disconnected terms and required him to memorize them. No reason for these terms was ever offered, no philosophical justification for their number or arrangement, and so the student never suspected that a rationale for the structure of logic could possibly exist. He was given a miscellaneous aggregation of disparate concepts, none of which had any integral connection with any other, and trained to flourish them in forensic disputations, to dazzle his opponents and to give no thought to practical applications. The predicables were brute affirmations, parts of no synthesis, and the rules for method were highly unmethodical. It seemed to Ramus impossible that with this logic any underlying unities of experience could be discovered, and disputation was doomed to be for the sake of disputation alone. He determined therefore that the first requirements for reform were banishment of the predicables and the curtailment of the syllogism in the interests of utility.

He was encouraged by his conviction that the logic of the schools was based upon a misunderstanding of Aristotle himself, and so declared in his bombshell of a thesis, "All that has been said from Aristotle is forged." The first task was reform or actual abolition of the categories. Most of the concepts conventionally listed under the antepredicaments, predicaments, and postpredicaments, he said, belong in physics or metaphysics; others are tautological and superfluous. The remainder he refashioned entirely, doing away with the words "predicables" and "predicaments", and substituting the single term, "arguments", or, as they were often called among his disciples, "reasons". He defined an argument as "whatever is affected to the arguing of something else." Thus the word "cause" is an argument, because it has the affection of "arguing" its effect; so also is "subject", which argues its adjunct, and all words that have relations with others are arguments, as is, let us say, "vice", because it argues its opposite "virtue", or "high", which argues against "low". In short, by the term "argument" Ramus intended any word by which things are understood or represented in speech, any concept, any counter employed in thinking. It could be a noun like "cause", an adjective like "similar", a figure of relationship like "opposition", an abstraction like "truth" or "virtue", a definition of a thing, or the thing itself. In the statement, "fire causes heat," for example, the word "fire" is an argument, either as representing the thing itself or as the cause; the problem for the logician is not to learn an abracadabra of predicables, but to take such a statement and find out the relations that obtain among its arguments. Downame explained the Ramist connotation of argument as an affection in a thing to make its meaning clear, the reason in a thing by which it becomes intelligible, just as the word "fire" becomes an argument in relation to "heat" by serving as cause. At Yale in 1714 an argument was defined as whatever is uttered so that the agreement of things may be discovered ("quicquid proponitur ut arguatur quae coincidunt"). Ramus did not have in mind something which proves or maintains a debatable point; "heere it hath a more generall signification, and betokeneth not onely confirmations, but also declarations without any syllogisme or forme of concluding." In his vernacular *Dialectique* Ramus gave a more detailed explanation of his meaning than in the Latin: an argument is "that which is destined and proper to declare something, as is a simple and single reason considered by itself, which is comprised and declared by some exterior word, which is the sign and note of the reason and argument"; thus in grammar an argument is a word, in rhetoric a trope, in dialectic the conception. He hoped by this simplifying definition to supersede the traditional "seats" or "places"; "argument is named sometimes category, and the doctrine of them categories, and the precepts of them topics," but the abuses of such a needlessly complicated vocabulary were obvious. Hence it was maintained at Harvard in propositions that would make no sense whatsoever unless taken in the Ramist sense, "The arguments are the radii of logic," "A reason and an argument are parallel." When Samuel Willard told divinity students that they must analyze a text and find out "the Arguments contained in it" he meant that they should read the Word of God in the light of Ramus.

To Ramus' enemies his insult to the categories was blasphemous. One of them said that dialectic without predicables was like grammar without verbs; another waxed ironical: "That I may bestow something upon you, O

Ramus, whatever is congruent with the ten fundamental categories of Aristotle, that we acknowledge is true, Aristotelian and genuine; whatever is not congruent, that we leave for you." Ramists replied by still further criticism of the categories; Ramus said they were inconstant and unreliable; his followers noted that few Peripatetics could agree on the same list. In particular the Ramists declaimed against them for their inutility. William Brattle had the additional authority of Descartes behind him, but he spoke for Ramists as well as Cartesians when he called the categories "mysteries", idolatrously adored by many, "but to speak plainly they are altogether unprofitable & so far from being helpfull to pass a right judgment (which is the only Scope of logick) that they very often are prejudicial and do great harm in this respect." Among the *Theses Technologicae* of 1719 is one that might well have appeared in any year since the founding of Harvard: "Categories and predicabilia are of very little use in cognition of truth."

Once the categories had been metamorphosed into arguments, Ramus then saw the task of logic merely as providing an efficient means of classification. His aim was to arrange concepts in ordered rubrics, so that at the portal of logic would not stand a nondescript array of catchwords. "The definition of the categories is the same as the definition of art," he said, meaning that the ideas and concepts tumbled together in the conventional predicables were in substance, if resolved into arguments and properly and decently ordered, the content of any art. As Richardson put it, the predicaments "are nothing but practises of method." The logic of Ramus was, from one point of view, simply a schematic arrangement of logical terms. Its emphasis was always on laying things out in series. "Art is defined according to P. Ramus," said a commentator, "as comprehension of precepts in things useful for life, in catholic order." The standard diagram or "epitome" reproduced on p. 126, is the blueprint that always accompanied Ramist teaching; it shows at a glance how this logic was built up as an architectural unit, all its parts fitting together, represented on this chart exactly as a house may be represented in the architect's plan. No such design could be discerned until the categories were broken up. "The *Predicaments* were so untowardly ranged, that a mans minde shall not without some hesitation know where to fasten; and then when he hath pitched there, he is but engaged in a dispute." Only when the arguments were liberated from the categories, and allowed to fall into their proper places in the art of reasoning, could the whole pattern of reason be recognized. Only then could logic achieve what it had been destined to accomplish: a transcript of a unified intellect, a formal description of the image of God.

The method by which Ramus classified arguments, as the diagram will show, was "dichotomy". He defined logic as "ars bene disserendi"—"the art of disputing well"—but his contemporaries understood that his gerund was a pun, for in classical Latin "disserendi" meant also "planting seed here

P. RAMI DIALECTICA.
TABVLA GENERALIS.

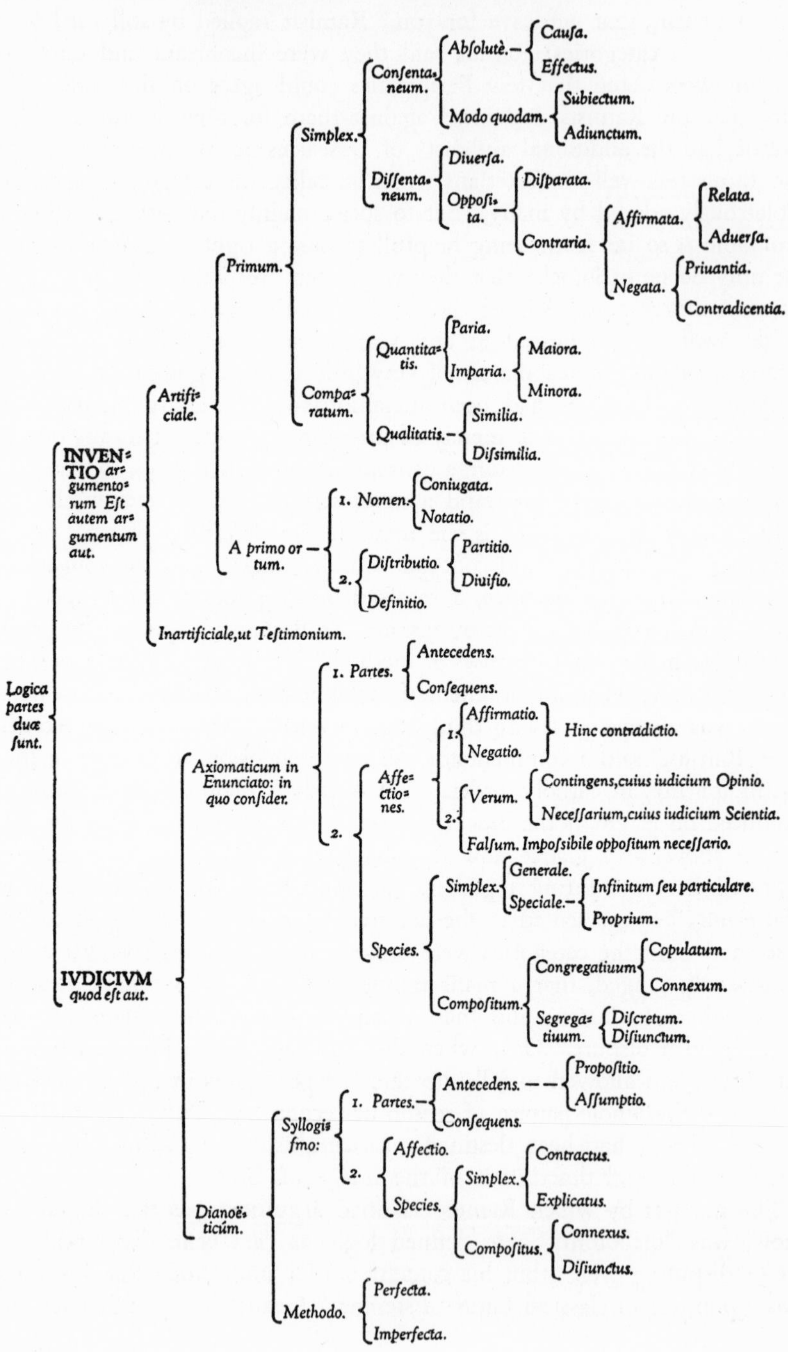

and there." So Richardson translated it "sowing asunder"; the Ramist logician, said another English expositor, "disperseth his seed in diuers places, and not confusedly throweth all on one heape, which is the natural signification of this word disserere." A Harvard thesis which declares that genesis and analysis do the work of "dissolvendis" indicates that the pun was appreciated in New England. The deliberate ambiguity of the definition showed that the material of any art, physics or medicine, could be "sown asunder" by logic, first by a division of its two component parts, then by a subdivision of each part, and then by continued bifurcations of the subdivisions, until at last, on the right-hand side of the page as shown in the diagram, the fundamental units, the indivisible "arguments" would all be enumerated. Thereafter, by running our eye backwards along the brackets we can at once establish a proper classification. Taking our statement, "fire causes heat," for instance, we find in it arguments related as cause and effect, and by consulting the diagram we find that this connection is absolute, agreeing, simple, and primary, whereas the statement, "truth is opposite to falsity," presents a connection which is contradictory, negativating, contrary, opposite, and disagreeing, before it becomes, like the connection of cause and effect, simple and primary.

Ramus contended that this method was not merely simple and clear, but objectively true, that the content of every science falls of itself into dichotomies, that all disciplines can be diagramed in a chart of successive foliations. The Ramist logic was a classification of concepts, and specifically a classification by dichotomies. The "golden rule" began with a general definition of the art, then divided the art into halves, halved the halves, and at last arrived at the indivisible entities which compose it. Ramus' enemies were not slow to attack these dichotomies; Francis Bacon summarized their objection—and also the reason why eventually the Ramist logic has been relegated to the limbo of the forgotten:

> Men of this sort torture things with their laws of method, and whatever does not conveniently fall in these dichotomies, they either omit or pervert beyond nature, so that, so to speak, when the seeds and kernels of science are springing forth, they gather so many dry and empty husks.[17]

Yet to Ramus' disciples his dichotomies were his great contribution to the age. Marlowe represents the Duke of Guise declaiming as he sentences Ramus to death:

> He that will be a flat dichotomist,
> And seen in nothing but epitomes,
> Is in your judgment thought a learned man.

If dichotomizers merited death, Harvard students should have supplied subjects for a new massacre of the innocents. Jonathan Mitchell maintained in 1646, "Dichotomy is the best distribution"; a thesis of 1663 held, "Dichotomy is the anatomy of logic," and one in 1678, "The most accurate distribution is dichotomy." The philosophical moral implicit in these assertions was pointed in Richardson's comment upon "disserendi": just as the chemist's fire makes homogeneous elements cohere and segregates the heterogeneous, so the art of "sowing asunder" sorts the arguments; "it picks out *homogenies,* it disposeth them, and layes them in several places." Dichotomy thus enables the student to "see Gods Logick in the things, and had not man faln, he might have come to have seen all the wisdom of God in the Creatures." Samuel Willard declared in 1701, "who distinguishes well, teaches well." The work of the intellect, as trained by the Ramist logic, was primarily to perceive and to distinguish, to perceive the divine order and to distinguish its parts by the method of dichotomy.

The Ramist logic was presented as a sort of universal organology of all arts and sciences. It was "the most general of the arts," applicable to jurisprudence, physics, or theology. Ramus compared dialectica to a Roman emperor administering the whole earth by universal laws: "for even if there be many provinces, various regions, dissimilar prefectures in that empire, yet all are governed by these laws." There is one reason which orders all things, and though things are administered in various disciplines, in mathematics, physics, or in history, yet all can be treated by the catholic precepts of dialectic. "And so we judge this participation of dialectic pertinent to all things"; the principles of logic can be illustrated in any subject, for all subjects depend for their form upon the precepts of cognition. "Dialectic is of all arts the most general," dutifully ran a Harvard thesis of 1643. The framework of Ames's theological and ethical writings was dichotomy; in Alsted's *Encyclopaedia* every subject was dichotomized and furnished with diagramed "epitomes" to trace the divisions. In New England, when the Word of God was "resolved logically," when a text was analyzed into its arguments, it was "sown asunder" by the Ramist method of dichotomy.

The art of logic itself was, of course, organized on the same principle. Ramus first divided it into two general parts, into what he called "invention" and "judgment", though the latter was also known indifferently as "disposition". "The integral parts of logic are two, invention and disposition," says a Harvard thesis of 1687, while an earlier one called them "intellectus gemelli." Invention is the part in which are arranged individual terms, the concepts, the arguments or the reasons, with which discourses are constructed; in judgment or disposition are contained the methods for putting arguments together. "Fire", "cause", and "heat" are the arguments separated and recognized in invention; "fire causes heat" is the axiom or discourse composed in judgment. Just as the grammarian must learn words before he can write sentences, the logician must learn arguments before he can make propositions; "the Brick-layer must first have bricks before he can make a brick-wall . . . so first we must *invenire,* and then *judicare,* that we may *bene disserere.*" Or, as Richardson varied the figure, "The Carpenter must have his timber in several pieces to square them before he can joyn them together." Downame commented less figuratively, that invention contains the places and homes of the arguments, "whence the furniture of all oratory as well as abundance of reason is drawn forth." New England writers, having learned from Richardson to embellish logic with metaphor, expounded invention as did Samuel Stone:

> *Invenire est in rem venire,* to invent is to come in upon a thing: and it is impossible to finde a thing in nature, that is not there to be found. A man cannot find fruits or flowers growing in orchards or gardens where they never grew: nor mines of gold, in places where the Sun never made any.

Samuel Mather prefaced Stone by saying that in order to comprehend him the reader must know the meaning of the arguments, you must "know the method of the first part of Logick." A novice in the Ramist method was not confronted with a meaningless array of categories, but with a comprehensible dichotomy; in his first lesson he learned the grounds for this division and the function of the two parts. Commencing with this understanding, he could then proceed systematically to learn the succeeding dichotomies, acquiring in logical progression everything which the Peripatetics piled upon him pell-mell in the categories. "Predicabilia must refer to the invention of arguments," said Ramus; Peripatetics put them "ante praecepta Logica in alieno loco et confuso modo." A fundamental intention of the Ramist logic was the avoidance of alien places and confused modes.

The next step was the dichotomization of invention. Here Ramus advanced one of his most startling innovations, at which his enemies became particularly exasperated. He divided arguments into two kinds, "artificial" and "inartificial". The artificial, he said, demonstrate themselves from the facts to any observer at any time. Thus when we call fire the cause and heat the effect we perceive at once the arguments which are "introduced into the structure of the thing itself"—"in fabrica rei," as the usual phrase had it. But men are not capable of perceiving all arguments directly; the assassination of Caesar, for instance, or the resurrection of Christ are arguments which must be taken on trust, on testimony. These are what Ramus called "inartificial". By the artificial arguments man "may see by himself"; by the inartificial, "he may see by another mans eye." Invention is a "seeking out"; the very name "tels us the Lord hath hid things secret in nature, and we must labour for the simples and so find them"; but some simples are "in artificio rei," while there are others which "other men have seen by the *artificials;* and because none can testifie of a thing before he have seen it himself, *ergo, artificiale* is before *inartificiale.*" Samuel Stone told Hudson that he might quote many authors to substantiate Congregational theory, "but those are onely inducements, not convincements, being onely inartificiall Arguments"; he professed therefore that he would confine himself to "Artificiall Arguments and reasons for the demonstration of this truth." The worth of an inartificial argument depended upon the reliability of its artificials; "inartificiall arguments," said Richardson, "have no ground but as they are backt with artificials," or as a Harvard thesis put it, "Inartificial argument is the client of the artificial."[18]

Although Peripatetics found this distinction absurd, for the Ramists it provided a place in logic for such arguments as could not be established by demonstration, particularly for revealed theology, which was the supreme example of the argument inartificial. Ramus explained that such arguments are of little use for investigating the nature of things, but are of great value in civil and human affairs, where much must rest upon testimony. As Wotton phrased it,

> The exact or perfect truth is narrowly sought for, when we desire to know . . . the reason how a thing commeth to be so; and in this inquiry no testimony can giue satisfaction. For it doth no more but say, it is so. The divine testimony is sufficient to breed certainty, yea most sufficient: but it is evidence, and cleereness we seek for in the search of truth; that we may see, how, and why it is so.

Peripatetic hostility to the doctrine of inartificial arguments sprang from a fear that it would bring all authority to the bar of criticism; Marlowe represents the Duke accusing Ramus of setting up a purely private judgment against the learned on the plea that their opinions are not artificial:

> Excepting against doctors' axioms,
> And *ipse dixi* with this quiddity
> *Argumentum testimonii est inartificiale.*
> To contradict which, I say, Ramus shall die.

Ramus having died for this doctrine, New Englanders were all the more determined to use it, to declare that the Bible, being an inartificial argument, derives its authority from "the efficient cause, or author of it; vpon whose credit, all the strength of an inartificiall argument dependeth." Among the *First Principles* James Fitch listed a belief in the divine inspiration of the Scriptures upon the testimony of witnesses, which support he called "inartificial", though he added that the wisdom, justice, holiness, and harmony of the Scripture were truly "artificial arguments" and "that kind of Argument which by the Learned is called Artificial, and argues from the Artifice, Frame, and Nature of the thing . . . must necessarily be granted the strongest way of Reasoning."

There is no necessity here for tracing in detail the subsequent dichotomies into which Ramus organized the arguments. The design can be seen in the "Tabula Generalis" on p. 126. Artificial arguments are divided into still another pair of classifications, and these in turn divided, until at the end of each progression we reach the basic terms. Thus by following the first series of dichotomies to its end we come to the kinds of artificial arguments that agree absolutely one with another, which are cause and effect; by branching off at the primary stage into the comparative arguments, instead of proceeding with the simple, we reach the arguments of equality or disparity between things, either as respects quantity or quality. By reading down the right-hand side of the page, from cause to inartificial, we can list all the fundamental concepts, all the arguments, which enter into any discourse. When the arguments have thus been classified, defined, and their position in the whole scheme made clear, the first act of logic, the "discerning", is accomplished. In the second part, "judgment" or "disposition", the arguments now discerned are put together. So Temple explained it:

> As invention treats of the precepts of inventing arguments, so judgment embraces the precepts of conjugating these arguments among themselves and of disposing what is invented. Invention invents causes, effects, subjects, adjuncts, opposites, comparatives, distribution, genus, species, definition, etc. Judgment disposes and conjugates cause with effect, subject with adjunct, opposite with opposite, comparative with comparative, the whole with the parts, genus with species, definition with definition, etc.

Richardson's lectures again illustrate the point imaginatively: the arguments, he said, are the hooks and nails in a thing, and judgment is the fastening of them together; or again, invention is like a tailor's shop, where you may see the imperfect garment, "and you may ask what it is, but let the Taylor make it up compleat with all its cuts, and jagges, then you may see it your self, and need not ask what it is for further knowledge." Simple things, individual things, are bound together in nature by affections or dispositions, as a cause is bound to its effect; these affections are the "glue", said Richardson, by which all entities in the world are held together; judgment is the pot that contains this "glue". As with invention, judgment is both a transcript of reality and a process of the intellect. Things are "glued" in nature, and the mind also glues one thing to another in thinking about them; if the mind is guided by dialectic it fastens things together in thought exactly as they are joined in fact. Hence one commentator defined judgment as "the posterior faculty of the intellect, of judging acutely and skillfully concerning the things invented, whether they are truly or falsely accommodated to arguing the nature of the thing proposed." The second book of Ramus' *Dialecticae* taught what Ramists believed to be the correct method for the exercise of this faculty, enabling the mind to come to a true picture of the method by which the objects of thought are connected among themselves.

The ways in which things are "glued" can be classified into two main varieties, either in simple axioms, or else in discursive reasonings. We have two axioms, each composed of arguments, "fire makes heat" and "heat warms the body." We put them together, exactly as we put arguments together to frame the axioms, and so achieve this discourse, "When the body is cold it is wise to light a fire." Hence Ramus dichotomized judgment into "axiomaticum" and "dianoeticum". Each of these could then be subdivided; dianoeticum obviously consists of two kinds of discourse, for we may be able to carry our point merely by speaking one axiom after another, or we may have to demonstrate it by the syllogism. We may be compelled to plead, "fire makes heat, heat makes warmth, ergo, fire makes warmth," or we may, on so obvious a matter, fashion our oration by simply listing the axioms in intelligent sequence. Therefore Ramus dichotomized dianoeticum into "syllogism" and "method". Wotton expounded the grounds for these divisions:

> No true judgment can be given of any thing according to *Logicke,* unless arguments be so disposed as art requires . . . If we would judge of truth and falsehood; we must joyne the arguments together, according to the rules of an Axiome or proposition. If we would know; what followeth vpon this or that, what doth not; we are to set downe our propositions after the rules of a Syllogisme. Would we vnderstand, whether things be orderly handled, or no? Let vs haue recourse to the precepts concerning Method.

The important point in this division, which the "epitome" does not make sufficiently clear, was the demarcation of the general rules for method from the rules for asserting or proving specific propositions, from both "axiom" and "syllogism"; sometimes the word "judgment" was used to signify merely the first two forms, while "method" was treated as a third division equal in rank to judgment and invention; in Puritan sermons, where the ministers had to give the simplest explanations and yet wished to educate the people in the basic terminology, logic was sometimes said to consist of three parts, invention, judgment, and method. In his sermons on Ecclesiastes, John Cotton so defined the "acts or exercises of Logick":

> He sought out, is the work of invention . . . He weighed (as in a ballance) is the work of judgement. He set in order, is the work of method.

But no matter how the divisions were conceived, procedure according to the Ramist logic was always the same: first we invent individual arguments; second, we dispose one with another to form an axiom; third, if in doubt, we dispose one axiom with another in a syllogism to get a conclusion; fourth, we set our conclusions in order and so make a discourse, a sermon, a poem, or an oration.

Of course, the procedure might be reversed: we may start with the finished sermon or poem, carve it into axioms, and resolve the axioms into their arguments. At the end of all Ramist dialectics was a chapter describing the complementary methods of "analysis" and "genesis", analysis in which a proposition is analyzed into its elements, genesis in which out of the elements a proposition is constructed. Ramus' innovation in pedagogy was his contention that all instruction should be by these methods and by no other. He recommended that the student first learn analysis, how to dissect a work into arguments, how to take apart some existing discourse, poem, or entire art, and that then by the method of genesis he learn how to build up axioms and discourses out of particular arguments.

Analysis is proposed first, by examples of noble and grave authors, who not only have spoken purely and grammatically, ornately and rhetorically, but also reasoned subtly, acutely and prudently on the questions proposed: so that the student is instructed in these authors concerning the rules of dialectic, that is, he explores and learns the species of arguments, enunciation, conclusion, method: then with the help of genesis he treats and exercises his learning similarly in a similar question; he conforms and forms himself to these ideas, so that at last by himself and without any example, he may dispute and explain any question whatsoever (if he wishes) with abundance of things and supply of arguments, in a clear and direct way of order and disposition.

The two methods follow equally from the structure of the *Dialecticae;* they are, in fact, the same method, the difference being merely one of direction, as was indicated by a Harvard thesis in 1647: "Synthetic and analytic method do not differ really." Aristotelians accused Ramus of pilfering this teaching and of misusing it; his adherents were certain that they alone understood it and put it correctly into practice. Consequently, by the Ramist method of analysis New England divines resolved their texts into component arguments, and by the method of genesis recombined the arguments into the doctrines of their sermons.

By the particular place to which Ramus assigned the syllogism he strove ingeniously to reduce its ancient pretensions. He gave much more importance to both "axiomaticum" and "method", and to explain this radical reversal he made still more explicit his fundamental philosophy. Before Adam lost the image of God, Ramus said, almost all of his judgments had been simply axiomatical; in his integrity he had been able to see and to pronounce sentence immediately, as when he named the animals; he had uttered what was true and perceived what was false, and had discoursed by infallible progression from one proposition to its inevitable successor. Ideally all good judgments—sermons, reflections, poems—ought to be such a series of self-evident axioms, arranged in artistic sequence. But fallen man generally comes to conclusions through love, hate, envy, or cupidity rather than through perception. Therefore today men must use the syllogism in order by its constancy to animate their judgments, "otherwise all our assertions will be levity, error, temerity, not judgment." Yet the fact remains that the stuff of judgment is not the syllogism but the axiom; the aim of an orator or preacher is a succession of sentences, not a display of deductions. When he has laid out the arguments and combined them into several axioms, he then ought to perceive from the axioms themselves what are their interconnections and what is their order; he should use the syllogism only when in doubt about formulating a particular proposition, or when incapable of recognizing the order of precedence among several statements. The student of Ramus was expressly warned to use the syllogism as sparingly as possible. When working by genesis, he should strive to invent his arguments, join them into axioms, add axiom to axiom to compose his discourse; when using analysis he should carve the discourse into its constituent axioms, and resolve each axiom into arguments. The essence of the Ramist system was exactly this belief that logic is no more than the distinguishing of entities and the joining of them together, that the function of thinking is primarily discerning and disposing, not investigating or deducing. "From the nature itself of proposition and assumption," Ramus declares, "is furnished abundant light, as though some gleam, for illuminating the complexion of art." Consequently his disciples required the syllogism only when an axiom looked dubious or when the priority of one axiom over another was not immediately apparent on the grounds of common sense: "nor indeed in the syllogism does art treat of anything else than to remove the dubiety of a proposed question by the legitimately manifested truth of one of two dispositions." Ramus did not mean to dislodge the syllogism entirely; he respected it as much as any Peripatetic and called it the very law of reason, "more truthful and equitable than all the laws which either Lycurgus or Solon ever made," but he demanded that it be kept within its proper confines, "in which the judgment of the doubtful axiom is established by a necessary and immutable sentence." Abraham Fraunce translated the Ramist contention precisely: "The first, and almost the chiefe kinde of iudgment is in axioms, yea, the very foundation of all other iudgement." All arts should consist of plain and manifest axioms, and the answers to the questions posed in logic—What is it? What parts has it? Where is it? What qualities does it have?—should always be unitary sentences. An axiom was "such a truth as is worthy credit without any discourse," or "what agrees to that which is *per se manifestum.*" But Ramists acknowledged that sometimes the answers to the questions are not immediately forthcoming, not perfectly manifested in the thing; the matter must then be referred to the syllogism, "there to be discussed." Nevertheless, in the syllogism itself, the premise is an axiom, the conclusion an axiom, so that whatever is judged by the syllogism, "it is all iudged by the help of this first and axiomaticall judgement." The basic certainties are the arguments and the axioms, not conclusions; syllogisms are built upon them, not they on syllogisms. "For if the premisses in a syllogisme bee not sometimes certayne and so iudged by axiomaticall iudgement, and graunted; there will bee no end of making syllogismes." The logic of Ramus hoped to put an end to the interminable making of syllogisms that flourished in the schools.

The explanations of Alexander Richardson generally throw the most revealing light upon the inner meaning of the system. In his account, the syllogism becomes a tool, to be employed only when a chain of thought has been interrupted; it serves as an anvil upon which the broken links can be welded together. "Dianoeticum" tells how to knit one sentence with another; "we must lay nothing by the rule of method but axioms." If we could always perceive to what rubric of invention an argument belongs, or the comparative importance of axioms, we should never need the syllogism; but since our perception is not always too clear, we must often establish an axiom before we can sift its arguments, or test an argument before we can use it in an axiom. "Syllogisms serve but for the clearing of the truth of axioms, and then afterward we return again to the rule of an axiom to judge whether it be true or false, and this is all that is required for disposing arguments, *ergo,* method is *dispositio axiomatum* onely." We call any proposition into controversy only "for want of axiomaticall iudgment"; we resort to the syllogism only to rescue ourselves from doubt and to regain the plane of indubitable axiom. "Syllogistical judgement hath for his subject *axiomas dubium.*" The whole Ramist system assumed, in short, that most axioms will show on their face whether they are true or false; when there is no doubt, then "an axiom will serve us," but when there is doubt, "we must have a candle to make it clear." This candle, the syllogism, merely makes "truth, or falshood more manifest unto us: so that clear *per se* belongs to an axiom; but perspicuity in regard of us belongs to a syllogism." All thinking, says Richardson with customary vividness, is "the running about of our reason for the finding out of truth," and we run about because we do not always see the truth at once. Varying the metaphor, he compared axiomatical judgment to a calm sea, "for there our reason is quiet, being satisfied with the truth," whereas syllogistic judgment is a troubled sea, "full of storms, winds and tempests, for there our reason beats every corner to conclude that which is doubtful." When the storm of doubt is passed we sail once more serenely forward on a smooth surface of progressive axioms. William Ames formulated Richardson's teachings into the succinct lesson, "Syllogism serves axiom." He explained his rule in words borrowed from Richardson:

> Whenever the truth or falsity of an axiom is not *per se* clear, or it is obscure or dubious, either in itself or in the agent upon whose fidelity it is based, then the question is posed, about which the mind of man exercises itself by running over or transmitting from one to another, so that it makes the thing clear or brings light to it: this is the reason dianoetical of the syllogism.

Harvard theses echoed these masters: "All truth properly spoken is axiom," "Judgment is made immediately from axiom, mediately from syllogism." The New England preacher, trained on the *Dialecticae,* did not build syllogisms but composed sermons; he paused when in doubt, or when he feared his congregation might be in doubt, and only then did he turn to the syllogism; when he had removed perplexity he thereafter resumed his sermon, which was primarily an ordered sequence of axioms. Thanks to this liberation, the Puritan parson did not need to argue every doctrine from A to B to C, but could preach in straightforward propositions, each doctrine followed by its reasons, the reasons by their uses, exhortations, and the pertinent applications.

The logicians of the schools were horrified at what they deemed this lèse-majesté against the syllogism, but they were shocked still more deeply when Ramus thereupon remodeled the theory of the syllogism. They taught the syllogism in its three "figures", and called these the only legitimate modes; they discussed other forms of establishing conclusions, induction, enthymeme, example, dilemma, sorites, etc., but held them valid only so far as they could be reduced to one of the authentic figures. Ramus simplified Peripatetic teaching once more by resorting to dichotomy: he subdivided syllogism into two modes, which he called the simple and the composite. By the simple he meant the orthodox three figures; the composite he dichotomized again into the hypothetical and the disjunctive. The hypothetical meant reasoning thus: "If there are Gods, there is divination"; the disjunctive meant this construction: "It is either day or night, it is not day, therefore it is night." Ramus insisted that both configurations were every bit as respectable, reliable, and useful as the traditional ones. He was the first to admit that Aristotle condemned them, but he triumphantly pointed out that nevertheless Aristotle used them over and again. "Wherefore," said Omer Talon, "the disputation of Aristotle is refuted by the example and testimony of Aristotle." Ramus justified composite syllogisms, characteristically, as the ones most widely used in ordinary life; his followers hailed this doctrine as one of his great discoveries. Scribonius said that there were many arguments which never could be disposed and judged in the simple syllogism. Downame admitted the disapproval of Aristotle, but noted that in the very act of banishing the composite syllogisms Aristotle used them; furthermore, he added, they are employed by the best authors and by the Bible itself. With every right, therefore, "in the sermons of ordinary men and in the use of reason the composite syllogism is much more frequently employed than the simple." Richardson said that the simple syllogism is better for the clearing of doubtful axioms, "because there the question is broken in pieces, and the third argument, which is the candle or light, is laid to each part," but when the question is not hidden in obscurity—as most questions are not—"then we make but a composite syllogism." For this reason the "common Logicians never dreamed of a composite syllogism, but onely of a simple," but Ramus was not a "common Logician." On the authority of Ramus, consequently, the New England divines used the composite syllogism, and conclusions thereby established were as strong to their minds as though confirmed by Holy Writ.

Ramists stressed the disjunctive more than the hypothetical mode. The concept of disjunction was, indeed, particularly congenial to the whole dialectic. When in invention all arguments are laid out in the pattern of the "Tabula," some of them, like cause and effect, subject and adjunct, obviously "agree" with each other, but still more of them in some measure oppose each other. The historic Aristotelian logic always emphasized opposites and contraries; every textbook reproduced the time-honored "square of opposition," by which the relationship of contraries and contradictories was diagramed. Because Ramus divided logic into arguments, axioms, and method, and therefore encountered the principle of opposition on each of these three levels, he omitted the diagram of the square—an omission which immediately distinguishes a Ramist textbook from a Peripatetic. Instead he introduced the student to the principle of opposition first in the catalogue of arguments. Artificial arguments were dichotomized into the primary and those derived from the primary; the primary into the simple and the comparative; the simple into the agreeing and disagreeing; the disagreeing were then divided into the diverse and the opposed, and the opposed into the disparate and the contrary. Ramists believed that all possible degrees of dissension were thus classified in the order of increasing opposition, from the disparates, which disagree on one point only, to the contradictories, which deny each other completely. Ramus took over the ancient rule of the contradictories, "from the affirmation of one, necessarily follows the negation of the other," and for his followers his restatement within the context of the dichotomies was one of his most fruitful regulations. Downame alleged that the doctrine of diversities was deficient in all logics except the Ramist, "yet though it be neglected by the authority of men, if we wish to follow the leadership of Reason and Use, it will easily stand, and diversities must necessarily be conceeded a place in the doctrine of arguments." To know a thing, said the commentators, we must first know what it is, then what it is not, "for, by the one our knowledge is begun, and by the other our knowledge is confirmed." Richardson found in nature the grounds for this doctrine: "the creatures of God are discreet, and many, *ergo,* there is dissention, and because reason was made to behold the creatures of God, *ergo,* it was necessary that they should be handled in Logick." Hence, Jonathan Mitchell exercised his undergraduate wits on the proposition, "Diversity is from adjuncts, opposition from primary form," and at the commencement of 1643 it was held, "Of opposites, from the one affirmed the other is denied." The doctrine was interpreted in the sense in which Richardson expounded it, as is shown by a thesis of 1646: "Dissension of opposites is perpetual."

On the level of axiom, the principle of opposition gave rise to a classification (cf. the "Tabula Generalis," p. 126) of "segregating" axioms, which were divided into the "discrete" and "disjunctive". Thus the arguments "white" and "black", "right" and "wrong", are contraries; the statements, "it is either white or black," "it is either right or wrong," are disjunctive axioms. As a Harvard thesis explained, they "do not conclude but distinguish." Conclusion can be affixed to a disjunctive axiom only be completing the figure of the disjunctive syllogism: "It is either right or wrong; it is wrong; therefore it is not right." In the disjunctive syllogism "we evermore conclude from opposites"; "one contrary will conclude another." Ames put it, "Contradiction in the composite syllogism always ought to divide the true from the false." Therefore it was an especially serviceable device for New England preachers, as can be seen in a hundred sermons; over and again a point is established in disjunctive syllogisms, as when John Cotton insists that "the will of God towards the world is put forth in a disjunct axiome," or as when James Fitch proves the divinity of Scripture in the *First Principles:* "Either these Scriptures were invented by God or by some creature; . . . therefore it is apparent these Scriptures are invented by God himself." Samuel Willard proved the temporal creation of the world by the same figure: "Now that which is not Eternal, must needs be Temporary, for these two are opposites; that which is not Eternal is a Subject of Time." He concluded in another work that the righteousness of Christ is "imputed" to the elect and not "infused" in them by posing the question in disjunction:

> that the individual and personal Righteousness of Christ cannot be infused into a Believer, is a truth so plain and necessary, that to assert the contrary, is to speak a contradiction.

The way to settle all such questions, Willard further asserted, is to reduce them "to this Disjunctive"; the body of divine truth is uniform and contains no contradictories, "so that whensoever you meet with two Doctrines, between which you observe a manifest inconsistency, you may and must conclude, that both of these cannot possibly be true." In his directions to young men "designing the ministry" he summarized the logical tradition and experience of New England by telling them they must learn the wrong doctrines as well as the right ones, reduce all to the proper heads and then ascertain their opposites, being guided by this principle, "By the same arguments with which Truth is established, falsity is destroyed."

Such glorification of the disjunctive speaks volumes upon the character of the Ramist logic. The system was endeavoring to reach conclusions by laying out self-evidencing propositions in intelligent arrangements rather than by extracting one proposition from another and snarling over deductions. It was a logic for dogmatists; it assumed that decency and order prevailed both in the mind and among things. Therefore, the crowning achievement of the system was its doctrine of method. The *Dialecticae* came to a culmination in the last chapters, and this portion was not, as in

Peripatetic handbooks, a few platitudinous after-thoughts. "Our Author stayes long upon method," comments Richardson; "his reasons are, because all Logicians are very silent in the doctrine of method." The logician must learn invention, axiom, and syllogism, but without method all study will be vain; "it is infinitely more great and difficult to dispose well and collocate by this artificial method, than it is to invent and judge well by axiom and by syllogism." Ramus cited Plato to prove (inartificially!) that the man upon whom God sheds the light of method can alone be the true philosopher, that when men are tossed on the seas of opinion and custom only he who is guided by this light can pilot them to port.

Now the Judgment of method is the sovereign light of reason, in which not only the other animals have nothing in common with man, as they can have in judgment of the axiom; but see, men themselves are very dissimilar: For however much they be all naturally participants in the syllogistic faculty, nevertheless the number of them is very small who study to use it well; and of this small number, still smaller is the number who know how to dispose by good method and to judge by it; so that although man surpasses the beasts by the syllogism, yet one man excels among men by method: and so the divinity of man does not shine forth in any part of his reason so amply as in the light of this universal judgment.

Therefore "method" was a word to conjure with among the New England divines, a key word in all their thinking, as important as the words "God", "sin", or "regeneration". Willard, who told divinity students that they must learn logic to decipher the arguments in their text, also instructed them that they must find out "the Method of it"; from Ramus, said Increase Mather, the age had learned to write models of divinity "methodically disposed, according to the golden Rules of Art." As was frequently asserted in innumerable connections by the New England leaders, "Method is the parent of intelligence, the master of memory"; "Truth is methodical, Error lies latent in confusion."

The Ramist doctrine of method was peculiar in that it signified merely a consecutive collocation of axioms—"suitable arrangement of the things invented." Suppose, said Ramus, we had all the rules, distributions, definitions of grammar, each upon a tablet and the tablets shuffled together like a pack of cards; how would we learn to sort them out? Not by invention, "for all is here found"; not by axiom, "because all is here proved and judged"; not by syllogism, because here "the controversies of all singular things are disputed and concluded"; but by method, which teaches the rules of arrangement. The words "disposition" and "judgment" were used by the Ramists interchangeably, for each of them meant "a Disposition, ordering or placing and setling of these seuerall argumentes alreadie inuented, to the intent that a man may the better iudge of them." A Harvard thesis put it, "The norm of judgment is the disposition of things invented." It is difficult for us to recapture the enthusiasm aroused by such assertions; they seem to us merely the elementary laws of composition, yet their great appeal in their day was precisely their simplicity and common sense. This "one and only method of art," said one of Ramus' defenders, is "the sole way to an intelligence and most clear memory of the arts, and is most largely compendious; but the contrary way is obstructed with contrary evils, with obscurity and prolixity." To understand why contemporaries beheld such marvelous charms in Ramus' method we must compare it with the current Aristotelian instructions, particularly those in the rhetorics, for organizing discourses, with their elaborate rules for the formal divisions, their intricate devices for digression, and their complex models for exordia and conclusions. Ramus swept all this confusion aside by declaring that a coherent discourse would emerge of itself if axioms were placed one after another in their natural order. "Axioma flourishes and is animated in chains," said a Harvard thesis.

The rules for the practice of method as laid down by Ramus were extremely simple: "That which is naturally preceding, more clear and distinct (as are the causes of their effect . . .) may be put in order and declaration first, that which is more obscure may follow afterwards." The single requirement was that "Method proceeds from universals, to singulars."

> And in brief this method seems to me some long chain of gold, such as Homer imagines, of which the links are these degrees thus depending the one on the other, and all chained so justly together, that nothing can be taken away without breaking the order and continuity of the whole.

Method was observed "when as that which is best knowne is placed in the first roome, and those which bee lesse knowne of themselves, doe follow in order, as euery one is better knowne then an other." If things are marshaled in this fashion, memory will be served; the preacher can go from point to point naturally and with ease, his congregation can retain the organization in their minds. Impressions upon the eye or ear vanish quickly, "but by the rule of method we place the things in their order, as God hath done, and when our eye hath seen them once in their place, she knows where to go to find them again." Method was the "golden rule" because it was a transcription of the divine order: it "makes all things one, and we remember all things as one: and therefore it is that the world is one, namely, by method." If we wish to understand any portion of God's creation, we must set everything in its place; "and whilst the Spirit of God his mighty power that governs all things, doth place every thing in order, we see he doth it by the rule of method continually." No wonder that John Eliot told the Indians to read the Bible in order to study method; "if any wisely make or wisely teacheth, this he doth."

To guide those who wisely taught the liberal arts, Ramus laid down three "laws", three rules for organization—the "lex veritatis," "lex justitiae," "lex sapientiae." Abraham Fraunce translated them: "All preceptes of Artes are or ought to bee necessarily and alwayes true, without exception," was the law of truth; the law of justice was that "which giueth vnto euery thing his owne, in coupling those thinges together which agree naturally, wherein vsually are disposed together, the formall cause and the thing formed; the generall and his speciall; the subiect and his proper adiunct"; in the law of wisdom "arguments disposed may bee mutually affirmed one of another. So that, as the later is verified of the former, so the former may bee of the later." These laws constituted, in shortest form, the creed of the Ramists. By the first of them, Ramus said, an art achieves certainty; by the second, assurance that all its parts pertain to the whole; by the third, that all its parts are reciprocal. These laws, like so much of the system, seem no more to the modern reader than common sense, but they too must be read in the light of the background. Defined in the sixteenth century, when the schools were entangled in a decadent scholasticism, they were an exhilarating program of liberation. They still promised freedom when Richardson expounded them at Cambridge to the men who later settled New England, when William Ames used them to give order and clarity to the whole body of knowledge, and when, on the very first set of logical theses at Harvard, they were cited in Greek and declared to be the laws by which all arts ought to be formed.

Such in short was the system disputed so furiously in the universities of Europe and taught so serenely at Harvard and Yale. Most of its characteristics are obvious from even this inadequate survey, yet some of its implications do not appear on the surface and probably all of them were not completely understood by its author. Certainly the average reader of today cannot easily comprehend why the battle should have raged about such a doctrine, or how it could have molded a whole theology and determined the Puritan way of thinking. Full understanding cannot be acquired from a study merely of the tenets and principles; deeper meanings appear in the defenses offered by adherents. Among these, perhaps the most reiterated was the attribution to the system of the virtues of simplicity and utility; also prominent were the contentions that the formal dialectic was true because it was in close harmony with "natural reason," and that therefore it could be illustrated by the practice of great poets and orators; finally, probably the most important boast of the Ramists was that their logic corresponded to the true laws of nature, and so gave immediate and infallible access to things as they objectively are.

From the first proclamation of the method, Ramists magnified its simplicity and utility. Ramus revolted against what he deemed the sterility of school logic, for he says that never amid the clamor of disputation "did I ever hear a single word about the applications of logic"; he told the Privy Council in 1567 that his method "should rather explain and suggest real usage," and he constantly moralized that "the greatest and properly the only virtue of disserendi is exercise." Not art itself, he said, "but much more the exercise and practice make the artisan . . . To know only the universal rules, without knowing the particular usage, is not to know absolutely and actually." He shocked university men by suggesting that students in the liberal arts be trained as were apprentices, being taught not only to learn but to do. "It is better by far to have the usage without art, than the art without usage: For by the usage of reason without art, we see in all parts of the state many wise men and men of good judgment," whereas in the schools almost all who know the arts are unable to do anything with them. Accordingly all Ramist logicians—and Puritan theologians—emphasized the "use". Temple echoed his master: dialectic is not devoted to an inane ostentation of subtleties, but to the service of human life. The very brevity of the *Dialecticae* was celebrated by its partisans as a special virtue; the method was advertised to be so easy and delightful "that almost by thyself (yf thou haue any quicknes of spirite) thou mayest attayne in the space of two months the perfecte knowledge of the same," its fifty pages being able "to bring more profytt to thee (I speake after experience) than all thy fower yeares studie in Plato or Aristotle as they are now extant." Robert Fage published the *Dialecticae* in the form of questions and answers, as a catechism of logic, "that so my booke may even learne to stoupe to the weakest capacities," and young men in New England were taught that "all art is practice," that the "vis" of every instrument is in its use.

Ramus' enemies could find no more opprobrious epithet to heap upon him than "usuarius." The lofty contempt of the Aristotelians was most devastatingly phrased by that master of irony, Richard Hooker, who described the dialectic as a "new devised aid" promising such quick dispatch that it "doth shew them that have it as much almost in three days, as if it dwell threescore years with them." The most charitable construction, he suggested, was that the Ramists were striving to avoid the sin of intellectual arrogance, and so confined their thinking "unto such generalities as every where offering themselves are apparent unto men of the weakest conceit that need be."[19] Not all opponents were so urbane; Abraham Fraunce gives us the more usual tone when he represents the Aristotelians crying out in horror:

> Antiquity is nothing but Dunsicality, & our forefathers inuentions vnprofitable trumpery. Newfangled, youngheaded, harebrayne boyes will needes bee Maysters that neuer were Schollers; prate of methode, who neuer knew order; rayle against Aristotle assoone as they are crept out of the shell. Hereby it comes to passe that euery Cobler can cogge a Syllogisme, euery Carter crake of Propositions. Hereby is Logike prophaned, and lyeth prostitute, remooued out of her Sanctuary, robbed of her honour, left of louers, rauyshed of straungers, and made common

to all, which before was proper to Schoolemen, and only consecrated to Philosophers.

According to Fraunce, the Ramists countered that if the wisdom of the ancients were now degenerated into what schoolmen and philosophers taught, no wonder it had become odious:

Ramus doth not so rule, but that he can suffer reason to ouer rule him. Ould doating graybeards talke much of Baralipton, whilest youngheaded boyes beare away Logike. They thinke much that a boy should conceaue that in a weeke, which they could skarce perceaue in a yeare.

As for logic being "rauyshed", the graybeards were trying to conceal their inability to hold the affections of a robust mistress; they "locke vp Logike in secreate corners, who, as of her selfe shee is generally good to all, so will shee particularly bee bound to none." Only the brave deserved the fair, in logic as in love, and if the goddess of reason was now granting her favors exclusively to the young Ramists, it was because they alone were laying trophies at her feet: "the fact itself is acknowledged, and the adversaries are indignant because of it: because Ramus values having utility in view in all things."

The whole debate has for the modern ear a stirring ring, and at first sight we are tempted to hail in Ramus a hitherto neglected precursor of the scientific spirit. Yet we must be careful always to take the vocabulary of the sixteenth century in a sixteenth-century sense; although there are many scores upon which history has never given Ramus his full measure of credit, nevertheless historians of science have not been guilty of oversight in omitting his name from the praises bestowed upon Copernicus and Bacon. He and his followers were first and foremost humanists, and their understanding of "use" would never have permitted them to soil their logical fingers with the "mechanic" arts. Philosophy, said Rennemannus, is suited only to "liberos homines," who need to possess intelligence but do not need the ministrations of the hand, and therefore "reijciuntur à Philosophiae confinio omnes artes Mechanicae, & sordidae." The aim of these liberal gentlemen, as of all humanists, was to cleanse the scholarly atmosphere by opening the windows of clarity, precision, and simplicity; they contributed materially to what might be called the democratization of medieval science, but as compared with a modern scientist, they were still living in a medieval world of abstractions and *a priori* judgments. Ramus' educational program was a critique of the academic curriculum, a reform of the trivium and quadrivium, which never conceived that knowledge could be increased by experiment, inductive method, or through the verification of hypotheses in nature. The Ramist dialectic demanded that thought be put to use, but as a Harvard thesis affirmed, "The sciences are worth little for inventing new things"; it was of no value in such directions because it started with the assumption that truth exists as a single, eternal, and fully formulated essence. It never probed half so far into the abyss of doubt as did Descartes; the only purpose of doubt, said the Ramist with disarming frankness, is "that we may remove the scruple which prohibits us from understanding and that, having found the truth, we may be the better established in it." Truth itself always remained to the Ramist "vnica ac simplex"; it was external, inviolable, a unique rule "which Logic demonstrates." The stress upon use must be read in the light of these assumptions; only so does its importance in the thought of New England become comprehensible. Precisely because such philosophical premises underlay the dialectic, it was able to supply Puritans with rational justification for their concern with practice and with the regulation of conduct, and at the same time to satisfy their need for abstract, logical articulation. Both services were equally valuable and equally necessary.

With these considerations in mind, we may attribute the highest importance to a Harvard thesis of 1670: "Logic is the art of directing human reason together with the rules of the reason of things." The basic contention of the system was that logic should be derived at one and the same time both from the natural processes of the mind and from the natural order of the universe. If the dialectic had been merely methodology, containing simply the dichotomies and the laws of method, it would be of little philosophical significance; but its implications were essentially metaphysical. Ramus said that it was the art "bene disserendi," that is, of disputing, of judging, of reasoning. But all men dispute, judge, or reason, and therefore all are dialecticians, so that dialectic is in reality the "vis humanae rationis." Everything that men ever learn, they learn by dialectic: "This light of logic and dialectic is cognate and natural to men." All transitions in formal logic, said Richardson, are true because they are "true by the practise of common people." Therefore Ramus taught that logic is the formalized or regularized version of the natural intelligence. Dialectic is employed instinctively by all men, though as it is refined in the textbooks it can be employed only by the learned. The learned method should of course be more accurate and reliable than the natural, yet all learning is but an improvement upon nature. "Art always presupposes nature, as exercise does art." Two principles regulate the Ramist logic, said one expositor, reason and use, and to their tribunal he will submit the system. Logic is nature made artificial, said Abraham Fraunce:

> Artificiall Logike is gathered out of diuers examples of naturall reason, which is not any Art of Logike, but that ingrauen gift and facultie of wit and reason shining in the perticuler discourses of seuerall men, whereby they both inuent, and orderly dispose, thereby to iudge of that they haue inuented.

Every dichotomy was justified because it was congenial to native wit: "As many are the parts of logic as are the operations of the mind," says a Harvard thesis. Natural logic should be translated into artificial only in the interests of greater utility, not to create another method. "So that, Art, which first was but the scholler of nature, is now become the maystres of nature, and as it were a Glasse wherein shee seeing and viewing herselfe, may washe out those spottes and blemishes of naturall imperfection." But everything put down in logic should have a ground in nature; that painter is most cunning "who can moste liuely expresse his face whose counterfaite hee is to drawe." Aristotelians were aghast before such language. Everard Digby wrote a book to prove that logical method and natural method were not one but two; Temple replied that Digby made not merely two methods for thought but a hundred, among which the reason wandered in bewilderment. Ramists were thus reassured that all method was truly one, of which the fruits were to be gathered not in philosophy alone, "but even in all humanity, that is, in all things human, and therefore in the use of all lives."

Ramists defined reason as "the truth of divine things (as far as we are furnished with them) and of the judgment and senses of men." The use or exercise of reason was consequently "the effigy of this reason delineated by the best of all men." The precepts of artificial logic "first were collected out of, and alwayes must be conformable vnto those sparkes of naturall reason, not lurking in the obscure headpeeces of one or two loytering Fryers, but manifestly appearing in the monumentes and disputations of excellent autors." From this line of reasoning Ramus reached another of his distinctive conclusions: if logic makes deliberate what is natural in the intellect, then productions of the best natural intellects, of the great poets, orators, and historians of classical antiquity, must be unerring exemplifications of the use of logic. Each place, dichotomy, or argument, each axiom and syllogism, each law of method—all could be illustrated by the habitual practices of Virgil, Ovid, Cicero, and Livy.

> Method is not confined only to the material of the arts and of doctrine, but pertains to all things that we wish to teach easily and perspicuously; and therefore poets, orators and all writers together, as often as they publish something instructing to their audiences, intend to follow this way, even though they do not always apply themselves to it and cultivate it.

Men of letters "distill the precepts of artificial logic from the observation of native reason," and therefore Ramus joined together the study of eloquence and logic. He illustrated the places and the arguments with poetry, and interpreted poetry by logic; he was equally at home in dialectic or rhetoric and taught his system as well in the one discipline as in the other. "Reade Homer," declared Fraunce, "reade Demosthenes, reade Virgill, read Cicero, reade Bartas, reade Torquato Tasso, reade that most worthie ornament of our English tongue, the Countesse of Pembrookes *Arcadia,* and therein see the true effectes of natural Logike which is the ground of artificiall." The anatomy of poetry, of music, of the order of the planets and the combination of elements was dialectic, for it was the force that governed the universe; therefore the poets, although heathens, could not avoid expressing logical truth, and—since truth is one—expressing the same truth that is found in the revealed Word of God. In his *Commentary on the Christian Religion* Ramus outlined the Confession of French Protestantism, citing for every tenet the conventional verse-texts from the Bible, and then adding classical texts which he insisted were analogous in meaning. He reinforced the Christian doctrine of providence, for example, with passages from Anaxagoras, Plato, Virgil, Aristotle, and Cicero. Such witnesses did not, of course, add to the authority of the Bible, which was admittedly absolute, but they did show that "Christian theology is not so abstruse or so remote from the human senses that it cannot illumine all people with a certain natural light, and so its very humanity may invite and allure men to engage in divine studies with eagerness." Therefore when Jonathan Mitchell "common-placed" in a New England class-room, he quoted the *Aeneid* to prove a theological point, because "when logic is a general art, pertaining to each and all, it draws most amply upon poets and orators, in whom is the use of all arts, upon ethnic philosophers and writers of antiquity, who are universally known and accepted."[20]

All this seemed shocking dilettanteism to the schoolmen. If it was, nevertheless it bespoke a difference between the Peripatetic and Ramist mentality that was more profound than the question of their respective estimates of classical literature. The theory which justified Ramus in quoting Horace and Virgil, in the hands of his disciples if not in his own, became in effect a revival in humanist guise of the "realistic" philosophy. The division between Peripatetics and Ramists can, I believe, be said to coincide roughly with a division between nominalists and realists. The Aristotelian handbooks generally agreed that logic is a product of the mind and not of things. It is sometimes considered, said Heereboord, to be an ordered accumulation of precepts outside the mind, but it is not; it is rather "art in the mind, and is defined as a habit productive with right reason." Ramus himself, it is true, was somewhat equivocal on this point; one of his interpreters remarked, "Ramus generally calls principles constant and perpetual reasons of the soul, from which he constructed his philosophy and in which he stabilized its immovable foundations." His followers emphasized the "immobilia fundamenta" until they could no longer locate them merely within the soul. When Piscator declared that the faculty of logic "est in mente artificis," Temple replied with heat:

> By the faculty of artificial logic can not universal things be explained? These either consist in the thing itself, or are born from the figments of cognition, they

are either necessary or fortuitous. By the precepts of the science of dialectic, are not the identical things, so widely diffused, so infinite in number, so dissimilar in genus, intellected, expounded, disputed?

Thus the ancient battle over universals was renewed, with the Ramists taking up the "Platonic" chant that if general concepts are merely figments of the mind and not objective essences, then no generalization has any relevance to facts. Even if we form it in our minds, the universal is still a reality, Richardson maintained, bringing out explicitly the dogmatic realism implicit in the *Dialecticae;* "When we define, do we not lay out the thing? *ergo,* if *genus* were onely mental, it could not give essence: so *causa, effectum,* and all other arguments are things real in nature, howsoever my Logick takes hold of them." The important point was that logic does take hold on reality. Wotton said, "Truth is the aequalitie, or agreement betwixt the thing, and the vnderstanding; if wee conceiue the thing, as indeede it is; wee conceiue the truth, or truly and rightly of it." A true axiom, said Ramus, speaks "uti res est," and the Harvard theses concurred: the abstract was defined as the form of the concrete, and warning was given, "The further away an idea departs from the thing, the more it falls into error"; in 1647 it was deposed, "The art of logic is in the thing," and the same naïve realism was reiterated in 1687, "The things themselves are norms of true axioms."

Thus it appears that the appeal of this logic to the Puritan mind resulted from its satisfying one of the deepest desires of that mind. A world made up of concrete entities which conformed to no collective terms, to no laws or rules conceived by men, could never serve as the scene for the drama of salvation; Puritanism's need for a stick to beat the dog of nominalism was desperate, as is shown by the recurrence throughout the literature of New England Puritanism, in sermons, theological arguments, and above all in the treatises of ecclesiastical polity, of the insistence that universals are objectively real. Here again Thomas Hooker's *Survey* is very revealing, or perhaps still more so, Samuel Stone's defense of it, *A Congregational Church is a Catholike Visible Church.* His opponent, Samuel Hudson, argued that unless all churches were visibly organized into a national body there could be no "Church" but merely an aggregation of units; Hooker and Stone contended on the contrary that particular, independent churches were parts of the whole Church Militant, even though the church as such was not embodied in a material form. The essence did not need a visible manifestation to have an existence; it was just as real if it remained a concept. Our understanding does not create a genus, "but it is extant, and in print *in rerum natura,* whether we observe it or not." The definition of a thing is not a subjective annotation valid only for those who manufacture it; it is an immutable idea which men do not devise, "but find it made before their eyes."

They gather it up with the hands of their understandings; which they could never have gathered, if there had been no such fruit growing in the garden of nature, or *in artificio rei.*

We define the Church by deriving the idea from our experience of the churches, so that the definition is "beholding to the first Arguments for his Birth, Nativity, and Breeding; and hath derived his whole Existence and Being from them"; yet it is not, for all that, "a meer Notion, crept into the understanding of man, before it was duely entred and enrolled into the Artificial Fabrick of Reason; which is one of those *Vestigia* and Impressions which the first Being hath left behind him." Ideas are not what they are "because I discerne them; but they are existing, and therefore I discerne them." A concept is not floating in the brain, "a meere fantasme or fantastical thing, existing only in *intellectu nostro,* and no where else: but a real thing." Here was the respect that gave Puritanism such long life, for the laws of God found in the Bible were hypostatized by the logic of Ramus into never-failing realities, as endurable as facts, and from that assurance Puritanism got its strength and its confidence.

As we have said, it does not seem that Ramus himself drew out all the metaphysical implications of his system, yet they must be posited in any understanding of it. Without this realistic foundation he could not have formulated his doctrine of the "arguments" and the method for their "invention". He assumed that every object could be represented by an idea in the mind, as fire by the idea of fire, heat by the idea of heat; but he considered as equally real, and equally to be represented by an idea or an argument, any act of these objects, any relationship among them, or any description of them. Fire in relation to heat becomes the idea or argument "cause and effect". The *res,* in which the artificial or inartificial argument resided, could be indifferently a pan, a lever, the wind, justice, law, the Trinity, an act of murder, inequality, priority, or the color blue; in logic all these would become arguments. Each word would stand for something objective, even "though I thus consider it in my mind." A man is composed of arguments—hands, passions, causes, form, body, spirit, size; he is a son, a father, a prisoner, or a king; and yet he is also an argument in and by himself, as is each of these attributes when considered by itself. "As many as are the relations of ideas, so are the topics of invention," says a Harvard thesis.

If these arguments exist in space, the first task of logic is to discover them. Hence Ramus' use of "invention" in the etymological sense, to mean "coming upon" or "laying open to view," not as creating or devising. The arguments subsist, the logician comes upon them, like Columbus upon the West Indies. He detects them, and perceives the classifications into which they fall of their own accord. Things—meaning objects or their relationships—supply the arguments, and arguments correspond to extrinsic realities. To invent is "to deuize, or find out by searching and studying"; it is not "the deuizing of arguments to proue; but a declaring of the nature of seuerall arguments." Invention examines a thing and gives us its "nature" by teaching us "the places, or heades whence we are to fetch the proofe, or declaration of a thing." Therefore invention is at one and the same time an act of discovering the arguments in a thing, and the intellectual faculty by which the discovery is made, "which is suited for searching the nature of the thing proposed." Ramists gave detailed expositions of the faculty in operation; it consists of four "instruments": first, the senses, which perceive; second, "observation", which collects the sense impressions; third, "induction", which notes differences and similarities and abstracts generalizations from singulars; and finally, "experientia", which, receiving the idea after it has been collected from the perceptions of the senses and confirmed by observation and induction of various examples, pronounces what it is and what it is not. These four "instruments" were also expounded by Aristotelians, who felt that Ramus purloined them, and they are found in Morton's *Compendium,* but they were taken up with avidity by the Ramists, and in New England they were understood as interpreted by Richardson and Ames. In the process of inventing arguments the mind follows its natural bent through the acts of sense, observation, induction, and experiment, and thus extracts from the objects of experience the arguments with which it forms true ideas about the nature of things. The arguments or reasons arise from the things, "as streams from their Fountain, and children from their Parents, resembling and representing their nature." They are "as the image and shadow of the first, symbolically, tacitely, and secretly comprehending the prints and footsteps of those first arguments, wearing their badge and livery." Had Ramists known the terms, they would have allowed no distinction between the idea and the "ding-an-sich", or at least so little difference as to prevent the possibility of imperfect correspondence. The argument was the thing, or the name of the thing, or the mental conception of the thing, all at once. The charm of the system in Puritan eyes was that it annihilated the distance from the object to the brain, or made possible an epistemological leap across the gap in the twinkling of an eye, with an assurance of footing beyond the possibility of a metaphysical slip. The Puritans must be numbered among the very few men who have ever been certain that they had succeeded once and for all in performing this feat.

As Richardson expounded the elementary dichotomy of invention and judgment, he threw into still stronger relief the certitude of the Ramist that his logic came from nature and the natural mind, his strong faith that the two were in fact one and the same source. God has created the world by creating individual entities, and then by establishing them in sequences, relations, and patterns; they exist first by themselves and then in connections. "Therefore mans reason must run accordingly." God worked by the method of genesis, proceeding from the elements to the synthesis, but in our study of his handiwork we must perforce proceed by analysis. We encounter objects as they are already disposed; to comprehend them we are "to sever them, and to look at them simply"; "everything must be considered alone before it be disposed." Consequently, the acts of logical discourse were defined in New England as "to discern and to dispose"; the first was invention, which "directs the intellect in clear and distinct perception of things." Thomas Shepard the younger wrote into his synopsis what had probably become the standard doctrine in New England: the act of the mind is double: it must invent and then it must judge. The arguments therefore have a double aspect, "either as in nature they exist distributed and properly separated, or as some are disposed with others and woven or implicated together." Hence invention and disposition, "from which parts the whole Dialectic comes into being."[21]

William Ames was no less insistent than Richardson that the logic was objectively based upon things, not upon subjective fantasies. Beginning with the proposition that "Art is primarily and most properly in things," he declared that the notions of logic do not originate in the human mind any more than do the subject matters of physics or mathematics. Arguments are in things, axioms are "not first in words nor properly in the mind, but in things," and the order of the axioms set up by method is not a contrivance of human ingenuity, but "the order of things which they have in their own nature." Therefore that "ratio" which is the proper object of logic is not mere human reason, "but the reason of things, that is, the respects and habitudes of things, which they have among themselves." Moreover, the rational order of objects in the created universe, as discovered by logic, is the same order that prevails in the rightly reasoning intellect; "human reason is completed through logic, since it perceives nothing, unless under the concepts of logic, and therefore, by whatever it may the better perceive the logical concept, by that it perceives more perfectly the thing itself." Perhaps the best illustration of how New England students capitalized the teachings of Richardson and Ames is provided in Jonathan Mitchell's notes for a common-place in 1646, upon the proposition, "In logic the thing is a reason" (*Res in Logica est Ratio*).[22] He uses "ratio" here as synonymous with "argument"; in physics, he says, a ratio must be a specific, tangible object, but in logic it signifies any rational entity, whether concrete or abstract, an object or a relation. The all important question then intrudes: have we any guarantee that our chain of reasoning will so correspond with fact that when, for instance, logic declares two arguments to be in opposition, there will inevitably be the same opposition between the things themselves? Young Mitchell replies with the easy assurance which everywhere characterized the Ramists: if logic were merely a matter of words, then the disagreement of logical opposites would be a mode of the intellect; but the reasons with which we deal in logic are also the things; ergo, when our arguments dissent, the things they signify must *ipso facto* dissent! "The thing in its true genus we know is the material subject of logic (as in all art) upon which the reasons of logic are founded." The arguments stand for realities, and the relationships among them are real relationships. As Abraham Fraunce had already put it, logic is "an applying or directing of the minde to the view and contemplation of that, which of it selfe it might perceaue, if it were turned and framed therevnto"; the truth of things comprised in the arts, he continued, significantly attributing the remark to Plato, is as "naturally propounded to the viewe of the minde, as colours bee to the sight of the eye." The Ramist logician saw and comprehended, but he held that he saw and comprehended what was actually there. "The logic of Ramus is not derived from some other philosophers, but is formed by free judgment from the use and observation of nature." Logic sees arguments as the eye sees objects, or as a mock thesis of 1663 expressed it, with a humor that could have been appreciated by none but Ramists, "In respect of intellecting the species, logic is an optic nerve."

The system of Ramus thus posits the existence of an objective truth, to which it asserts man has access. It holds that this truth is made up of arguments put together in congruous designs. Scaliger commented that the Ramist theory made truth to be merely a matter of words and speech, so that it did not need to answer "to the Idea in God, but to the apprehension in man"; Richardson replied simply, "truth lyes not in the speech, but in the thing." The problem for the Ramist, therefore, was not patient inquiry but rapid survey. His chief concern was classification, for if the arguments are laid out correctly in dichotomies, the proper order among them will appear of itself, as invisible ink emerges before the fire. Truth does not need proof, but only assertion. Hence true doctrine is a series of axioms, and correct propositions are so self-evident that in almost all cases doubt can be resolved by the mere statement of alternatives in the disjunctive syllogism. Hence the glorification of method as a common-sense gradation of propositions, and hence the celebrations of simplicity and utility. The Ramist logic was in reality not at all what is usually thought of as logic, but an approach to this impersonal and abstract truth. The invocations to reason and truth, with which the writings of Ramists are studded, must be read in this light; when Ramus refuses to follow either Plato or Aristotle, and declares, "There ought to be no authority for reason, but reason ought to be the queen and ruler of authority," he is turning not to what later ages might understand by reason, but to a definite body of principle which he believes is the substance of reason. Reason to him is not an instrument but a doctrine; logic is the instrument by which the doctrine is made evident. Professor Morison has suggested that the word "Veritas" on the Harvard seal may have come from its prominence on the title page of Ames's *Philosophemata,* where is quoted the tag, "Let Plato be your friend, and Aristotle, but more let your friend be Truth." However, this injunction had received its special currency in the Renaissance because Ramus had extracted it from Aristotle and quoted it against the Aristotelians; every Ramist commentator or defender used it at least once in every work, and though it may have figured in other connections, it certainly was most often regarded as a party slogan of the Ramists. We have seen how closely the Harvard theses follow Ramus; it would not be strange, therefore, if the seal should bear the one word which Ramists used most insistently and most confidently. Later generations of Harvard men have read other meanings into the word, but by the founders "Veritas" could have been taken only in the Ramist sense.

Professor Craig finds in this logic an emblem of the Renaissance mind, which had to posit the preëxistence of truth, already finished and perfect.[23] The Puritans were still more obliged to regard truth as a body of received, inviolable, and objective dicta than were most of their contemporaries. The Ramist logic was an ideal instrument for exploring such truth, for discovering and mapping it. The Puritans could not have conceived another mode of investigation without having ceased to be Puritans. Aristotelians found the Ramist scheme too easy, too dogmatic, too nonchalant in the presence of historic difficulties. Ursinus recommended to the Elector Palatine that he prohibit the teaching because Ramus omitted essential steps in procedure, confused dialectic with rhetoric, and was irreverent to Aristotle; he prophesied that the *Dialecticae* would breed confusion and dissipation in church and state. Keckermann saw in the *Dialecticae* the twin vices, "mutilatio" and "confusio"; among the most annoying traits of the Ramists he considered their disregard of exceptions and qualifications, "since they wish all things to be necessary, true in all times and in all places, limited by no circumstances." He adjudged the illustrations of logical figures by poets and orators absurd and dangerous, and above all he felt that the system was a threat to theology, because by leaving out the categories and predicaments, by trusting to the immediate perceptions and the instantaneous recognitions of a corrupt mind, by asserting doctrine in the form of axioms, it made impossible any defense of the mysteries of religion, the Trinity, or the double nature of Christ. Therefore he warned aspiring young students: "No one will ever have a great future, to whom Ramus alone is great."[24]

However, Keckermann lived in Danzig, where Aristotle was still enthroned. In many other universities, the case was entirely altered. Probably no presentation of the system today can bring back the sense of life which in those quarters it connoted about the year 1600. Obviously no modern logician can for a moment take the system seriously, and obviously it sanctioned habits of thought which were at the least loose and questionable, for which New Englanders were to pay dearly in their subsequent intellectual life. Yet in the celebrations of the doctrine there glow a fervor and a joyousness that help explain why the system should have appealed so widely. and why in particular to Puritans. By Hercules, wrote Rodingus in 1579, if any in our day have deserved well of letters and the liberal arts, it is they who have relighted in Christian schools the torch of logic, the flame once snatched from heaven by some Prometheus, but obscured and almost extinguished by the injuries of time, the negligence of men, the fogs of ignorance and sophistry. Of all such restorers the greatest is Ramus.

And in truth, O young men! do you need a logic conducted by experience, observation, sense, induction (which Aristotle constituted the principles and foundations of all arts) and recalled to its own ends? Ramus has conducted it and recalled it. Do you need a logic delineated in precepts not false but true and perpetual, not alien but proper and homogeneous, not with precepts that are merely true and homogeneous but truly catholic, . . . that is, things general with generals, special with specials, and illustrated by the light of method? Ramus has delineated and illustrated it. Do you desire, I say, a logic not only delineated with precepts, but truly declared with examples of illustrious poets, orators and philosophers, and celebrated by use, even accommodated to all the disputes and studies which ever were, or ever will be in Theology, Jurisprudence and Medicine? Ramus has declared, celebrated and accommodated it. Do you wish to listen to a man discoursing on logic who labored in studious vigils of logic, sustained the use with daily works through thirty years, indeed almost all the days of his life? Listen to Ramus. Wherefore, O masters of the liberal arts, professors and doctors (wherever in the world you earn your stipends by educating young men) propose to yourselves for imitation this example of our philosopher; inculcate into your students in teaching the discipline of the art of logic, not vain sophistry but solid and constant precepts, the use of logic, which is master and judge of all arts and disciplines, demonstrate it with writings of approved authors and with weighty judgments.[25]

Ramists believed that their system alone could achieve the ends for which God designed logic, for their system alone was the logic He had instituted. Its preëminence could be succinctly stated:

. . . because the precepts of the arts are invented, because inventions are arranged in axioms, because axioms, disposed according to the laws of truth, justice and wisdom, are shaped symmetrically; because until now, confused and disordered, they concealed the laws of most elegant order.

Thus armed with a system that was competent to do all things required of it, the Puritan intellect could ascertain objectively the individual entities, perceive their relations, clarify doubts, and finally set everything in its proper place in elegant order; thus equipped to end all the disputes which ever had been or ever would be, Puritan logicians were prepared to inaugurate a new era in intellectual history.

CHAPTER VI

KNOWLEDGE

Although Ramus flayed the "Aristotelians" of his day, he was the first to acknowledge his own great indebtedness to Aristotle himself, and most eager to assert that he alone had read the *Organon* aright. Yet it seems probable to the modern scholar that Ramus never understood Aristotle, and while sixteenth-century Peripatetics may not have understood much more, they at least grasped enough to object to Ramus' epistemology. These Peripatetics were also entangled in the problems of cognition, of the relation of knowledge to its objects, of the guarantees for the validity of ideas, but they could not content themselves with the easy escape offered by the *Dialecticae*. They too were dogmatists, but they could never assert flatly that an argument was so precise a reflection of a thing as to be in effect the thing itself, and so feel that they had unriddled the universe.

Ramus himself does not seem to have foreseen the epistemological difficulties which he was creating for his students. He wrote "scholia" in metaphysics and physics in which he never challenged traditional theories of cognition, still assuming that from things arise intelligible forms, which the soul abstracts by its active intellect and knows by its possible intellect, and that therefore knowledge originates in the senses. Yet his contentions that words are things, that reason gives a name to objects promptly and immediately, that it is competent to deal truthfully with everything that comes within its range of vision, contradict this theory, and sooner or later his followers could not help facing that fact. His defenders were compelled to meet it, to supply more extensive metaphysical foundations; they could not indefinitely proclaim that the thing in nature becomes an argument in logic without offering some explanation of how they had eliminated the possibility of variance. How could they declare that reason contemplates an eternal and immutable "veritas" through the instrumentality of logic, when they also acknowledged that reason knows only what it encounters in sense experience? Other philosophers have come to grief over this problem, but for the Ramists it was particularly difficult because they had simultaneously to demonstrate that their teaching was compatible with a theology of innate depravity, irresistible grace, and supernatural regeneration. When Increase Mather and Samuel Johnson traced the intellectual genealogy of New England from Ramus to Richardson to Ames to Hooker, they were in effect describing a line of thinkers through whom the philosophical implications of the logic were developed into explicit statement, and the New England migration was an outcome of this development as well as of developments in English society. More important than the Ramist logic itself in the intellectual history of the colonies is the fact that when the logic came to New England these men had already constructed upon it a fully articulated philosophy, an epistemology, and a systematic body of knowledge.

The seeds of this philosophy were certainly in Ramus himself. His problem was, how can we guarantee the absolute identity of arguments and things? Without such guarantee, his whole system tumbled into a heap of rhetorical flourishes, an elegant interpretation of classical literature, but useless for practical affairs. Though he himself was exceedingly hard pressed for an answer to this question, he still remained enough of a scholastic not to seek relief in a theory of innate ideas, as did so many of the Renaissance "Platonists"; he does not seem ever to have entertained any theory that the mind contains an intuitive knowledge of the pattern of the world and therefore an innate power of understanding it without the medium of intelligible forms. But even those scholastics who had been most explicit in denouncing innate ideas had allowed the mind a natural ability to work back from the effects of God to a demonstration of His existence. By the example of the best Aristotelians Ramus was justified in ascribing to the human intellect a certain "puissance naturelle", which enables it to perceive truthfully, though it may not be provided beforehand with the content of true perception. His system was, he insisted, simply the translation into "art" of this "puissance naturelle", and he declared that his predecessors had erred by striving for the conclusions of philosophy before they had mastered the method. Once the true method was secured, he believed that content would take care of itself. Instead of conceiving of logic as the construction of tentative inferences from fragmentary and incomplete data, he preferred to describe it as a mirror which reflects the true, universal images of all things, and which would, if kept polished by careful study and exercise, reflect them clearly and unmistakably. In another metaphor—worked to the limit by his followers—he said that as the eye perceives colors, so the mind sees arguments without needing any other demonstration. The spirit may not be endowed at birth with *a priori* knowledge of the arguments, but it does have, naturally and inherently, the ability to take cognizance of them.

> For the truth of things . . . arranged in art is thus naturally proposed to the spirit, as the color is to the sight, and that which we call teaching, is not to convey wisdom, but merely to turn and direct the spirit so to contemplate that which of itself it would barely have perceived if it had been turned and addressed to it.

Of course, men are sinful and do not generally utilize their perceptions intelligently, for which reason the logician must counteract the effects of sin by training men's native wits.

Hence, although he became a Calvinist, Ramus was first and foremost a humanist. Among his followers his elevation of the dignity of the natural intellect became still more pronounced. For example, in Mulhemius' *Logica Ad P. Rami Dialecticam Conformata,* published at Frankfort in 1584—all the more interesting in this connection because it replaces the illustrations from poets and historians with Biblical verses—enhancement of natural ability goes so far that it seems no longer compatible with Protestant tenets. When God made man of the dust of the earth, says Mulhemius, He breathed the living spirit into mortal nostrils, whence comes the soul, sharing in celestial reasons and the comprehension of eternal things, whence comes the intellect, the foundation of all science, whence the innate and natural faculty by which those who have not learned a single letter of formal logic are able to distinguish acutely and prudently. Mulhemius gives a thoroughly orthodox account of the fall, of the corruption of the understanding, and of the discovery of logic through divine guidance, but in his version, this discovery, even though ordained by providence, becomes so magnificent an achievement of the natural reason that one wonders what has become of the doctrine of total depravity. As was customary in the handbooks, Mulhemius heartily invites aspiring students to the study of logic, and waxes so eloquent that logic seems in and by itself all the cure that men require for the maladies of sin, to show the way to a resurrection of the beauty and integrity of the mind without any assistance from supernatural grace.

> For what is human life, unless to be congruent to humanity, and to live conformably to nature? What in truth is it to live so congruently to humanity, and so conformably to nature, than carefully and skillfully to treat and consider by cognition things most worthy and necessary to the use of life? than diligently and skillfully to cultivate human wit and the God-given soul by that natural sustenance, namely consideration and contemplation of nature and of things? to examine by the faculty and guide of human wit the most sacred of things divine? most providently to institute and perfect the reasons and course of all life? than wisely to aid, conserve and ornament human society with the best laws and reasons? prudently to administer things public and private? . . . accurately to discern the true from the false? . . . not pertinaciously or pugna-

ciously to defend a conceived opinion or sentiment? but easily and freely to acquiesce in the better reasons? modestly to consider more the weight of truth and reason than authority? calmly and amicably to investigate the truth of things with reason brought to bear on this side and that? what lastly is more suited to nature, than rightly to use reason, than which God gives nothing more excellent to men, and by which, being distinguished from the brutes, we approach the closer to divinity? [1]

The sonorous and stately march of this passage in the original echoes still more than the translation with the mighty tread of the legions of rationalism. The whole Ramist system, with its trust in direct perception, its immediate adjudication between doubtful alternatives through the divining rod of the disjunctive syllogism, its assurance that instinctive recognitions will lead to the right practice of method, was fundamentally a glorification of nature; it was an assertion that the cultivated mind, unexalted by divine influence, is competent to gather accurate knowledge of things, and to assign particular truths to the proper place in the universal system, because the mind is fundamentally commensurate with creation.

We should have little difficulty in recognizing from what spring of inspiration flows Mulhemius' oratory. It was that which fed humanism in general, the scholarship of Erasmus, the *Utopia* of More, the educational reforms of Eliot or Ascham. But because Ramist logicians were also academicians they were compelled to fight the battle of humanism on one particular front. They had to dispose of late medieval skepticism, irrationalism, and fideism. They had to find a way out of the maze of nominalism, and the only path they could possibly follow, no matter how treacherous and hazardous it had proved to previous adventurers, was a denial that concepts are merely mental and subjective, an assertion on the contrary that they exist not in the mind but in nature. The Ramist logic was a weapon forged for humanists to hack their way through the scholastic undergrowth; the reason for its popularity was not its logical perfection but precisely its promise of escape from the fifteenth-century morass. The Puritans, as we have seen, were particularly nervous about these same nominalists, these same followers of Occam, and the especial beauty of the Ramist logic in their eyes must be explained on these grounds. Yet there was irony in the situation, as in every situation brought about by the Puritan deity: Puritan hostility to the late scholastics was aggravated by the recognition that these philosophers had embraced many true doctrines, that by them God had been properly described as an arbitrary sovereign, a hidden divinity, whose essence no man could comprehend, whose ways no reason could interpret. However, nominalists had then concluded with more than a show of logic that if God is an absolute monarch, between whose will and the creatures there stands nothing but His pleasure, there can be no intelligibility in His works, no reason for anything except that the despot has ordered it, no system in nature and nothing anywhere save the caprice of a *Deus Absconditus*. Consequently, the earnest Puritans, who also believed in the hidden divinity and worshipped Him as an absolute sovereign determining all events by arbitrary enactment, were inviting trouble for themselves when they refused to accept the universe as being without intelligibility or plan. The logic of Ramus gave them an opportunity to have their God without the chaos, the God of Calvin and yet a world that could be known and understood.

After Calvinists like Mulhemius had chanted their hymns to logic, they were faced with the unhappy necessity of explaining how natural men could arrive so unerringly at divine truth, and how men incapacitated by sin could retain such vigor. The Puritan could use his logic only after he had made certain that the method by which it directed him to recognize intelligibles lay within the confines of orthodoxy. He had to distinguish between innate ideas and innate capacities, and while not allowing enough scope to the former to inflate men's estimate of themselves, yet give the latter enough free play to keep them from over-despising themselves. Then, after he had shown that men could still sustain a "puissance naturelle" adequate to the work of perception, he was obliged to demonstrate that the fabric of nature does contain the intelligibles, so that they are veritably there to be perceived. And where could they have come from if not from the mind of God? So, his task lengthening ahead of him, before he could exercise his precious dialectic and devote himself with its help to "use," he had to preface it with a proof that it conformed to the pattern of ideas in the divine mind, though he was at the same time constrained not to forget that the mind of God is in essence unknowable and unintelligible. Nor was he, even after expending this prodigious effort, at the end of his labor, for he had at last to assure himself that with its slight natural power the human mind could apprehend *all* the intelligibles which it had pleased an omnipotent God to incarnate in nature, since a capacity that could cope with no more than a portion of them would collapse once more into nominalism and bewilderment. The Puritan expositor of Ramus, therefore, had his work cut out for him: in order to maintain the system, he had first to demonstrate that a natural mastery of the method would really enable man to perceive immediately the eternal and divine rules upon which the natural world is constructed, the sum total of which may be assumed to constitute the wisdom of God so far as His wisdom is reflected in His creation.

Richardson and Ames were not the only expositors who attempted to supply these needs. On the continent an important step in the same direction was made by Frederic Beurhusius in his commentary, *In P. Rami, Regii Professoris Clarriss. Dialecticae Libros Duos,* which was also issued in London in 1581, and was read in New England; it could very well have influenced Richardson and seems to supply an important link between Ramus and what Richardson made out of Ramus. Beurhusius found his solution by stretching the natural power to include, not quite innate ideas, but the seeds *(semina)* of things and of principles, which experience quickens into life, whereafter by cultivation according to the rules of logical tillage they may be brought to fruition. Even though man has fallen, the intellectual principle in him is still divine because it was "divinely infused" and is therefore "the faculty of perceiving and judging all cognitions, of true from false, consequents from inconsequents, and lastly, of distinguishing order from confusion; from which it is named the principle of science." This is that natural reason, that "primary dialectic," upon which the logic of Ramus is founded:

> For as sight in the eyes, so is intelligence in the spirit; and as the eyes do not carry the color of the species from the womb of the mother, but the natural power and faculty of comprehending all colors, so the soul does not carry with it the habit of innate ideas but the innate faculties.

When reason perceives a color, it forms an "argument" of it, so that an argument is "the image of a thing formed in the soul." Reason, "being excited by the senses, produces and constitutes by degrees the seeds of the various arts from its own sources." No Ramist could yet say outright that ideas are innate, but he could say that seminal principles are innate, implanted in the soul by God, and that the rain and sun of the sense experience impregnate them with the principle of growth. Sense thus remained the first teacher, as the scholastics and Aristotle had maintained; it was the initial admonitor of reason, but the reason, once instructed, thereafter could proceed by use and training to perfect ideas engendered by experience, and so come at last to discern the universals.

Because arguments are images of things formed in the soul by a divine power, they are true, and because arguments are aligned together by the same power, the axioms must be true, as we have seen Jonathan Mitchell asserting. Therefore the content of knowledge becomes a collection not of speculations and debatable deductions and unprovable theories, but of simple, straightforward, declarative axioms. And where can the whole array of these axioms be found? Where, asks Beurhusius, but in the liberal arts? If by a natural power the mind abstracts true ideas from things, the only problem that remains is classification of the ideas, so that it is in effect merely the problem of defining and delimiting the various disciplines. "Art is comprehension of proper precepts in things eternal and in order of disposition, for usefulness in respect to the purpose of life." Logic is the universal art, because it is methodology, showing the method for discovery and arrangement of the materials of the other arts. Beurhusius' preface therefore concludes not exactly with what a modern philosopher would call an epistemology, but with a theory of the arts, an explanation of the disciplines, a justification of the academic curriculum. Logic is true because it regularizes the natural faculties; it leads to true perceptions, and perceptions make up the propositions contained in the arts; the arts then are descriptions of reality, enactments of God, and knowledge of them is knowledge of Him.

Beurhusius may have influenced Richardson, or he may be of interest in this study merely as illustrating a prolongation of the *Dialecticae* parallel to that of Richardson and Ames. In either case, he defined the issue and pointed the way to solution, but Richardson worked on a much more comprehensive scale. He is a strangely obscure figure, yet unless further research will discover indebtedness which the present study has overlooked, he ought to be rated an original, daring, and immensely influential thinker, and among his virtues not the least be accounted his mastery of prose style. Laudatory prefaces in Renaissance books must always be taken with a grain of salt, but when his notes were published in 1657 Richardson had long been dead and his editor had little to gain by flattery; the wide circulation of his manuscripts and the Puritans' intense veneration for him suggest that Samuel Thomson was voicing the sincere conviction of many when he described him as a man of transcendent parts and sublime intellect, who traversed the whole of liberal and ingenuous literature and laid down "a systeme of it in most exact and methodical Precepts." In his lectures students saw "a reach beyond ordinary men"; others may have taught logic, but he dived into "the bottom of Entity," and showed logic as the key that opens "the secrets of all other Arts and Sciences."

The principal theme of Richardson's commentary is not so much the meaning of Ramus as the relation of logic to the other arts. He put it bluntly, "The purpose of Logick is to direct man to see the wisdom of God." It is, for him, the vestibule to knowledge, the guarantor of concepts, the approach to truth, the method whereby earthly reason reproduces the heavenly. And as with Beurhusius, at the end of the quest, the wisdom of God reflected in the polished mirror of logic turns out to be the liberal arts. Therefore, before Richardson discusses logic itself he surveys the arts, discovering how they are "holden together," not confused, but every one in "his rank according to the generality of the end thereof." Richardson himself pointed to this preliminary survey, this summary of knowledge, as his improvement upon Ramus:

> Indeed *Ramus* himself took no great pain about Art in general, and therefore imagined that every definition in Art was absolutely first, whereas in very truth none of them are absolutely first, but onely that rule of *Encyclopaedia.*

Richardson's contribution was this "rule of Encyclopaedia," this philosophy of the liberal arts, "Orbis ille, & Circulus Artium," a theory of their interrelations and a demonstration of their unity, the rule described by a Harvard thesis in 1670 as "a circle of seven sections of which the center is

God."[2] After Richardson, William Ames systematized the rule, as Increase Mather has told us, setting it forth in the tracts collected in *Philosophemata,* particularly in the two entitled "Technometria," in which "the limits and ends of all disciplines and faculties are accurately prescribed." The structure of Alsted's gigantic *Encyclopaedia* also incarnated the doctrine, though whether Alsted took it from Richardson and Ames or from continental Ramists like Beurhusius is not clear. Ames came at last to recognize that in this doctrine the widest limits of speculation were encompassed, and so decided that no such discipline as traditional "metaphysics" had any right to exist; he proposed to put in its place "encyclopaedia" or "technometria," and in New England accordingly, in 1653, *theses metaphysicae* disappeared, and on subsequent commencement broadsides a section was always devoted to *theses technologicae.* Thereafter it was maintained, "There is no metaphysics distinct from other disciplines."[3] Thus Puritans could appropriate Ramus' *Dialecticae* only on condition that they also appropriate Richardson's preface to it, and "technologia," formulated by him to supply the philosophical apparatus for the unification of Puritanism and logic, systematized by Ames, taught at Harvard, defended in the theses, and expounded in all sermons along with the theology, even as a part of the theology—this is the true metaphysic of Puritanism and the chief tie between its piety and its intellect. As the links must be joined together to make a chain, said Richardson, "so the Arts must be holden together, before there be *Encuclopaidia.*" Perhaps we have laid bare the innermost essence of the Puritan mind when we find that its highest philosophical reach was a systematic delineation of the liberal arts.

We have enough sources—Richardson, Ames, the manuscripts of Shepard and Johnson, Harvard theses and New England sermons—from which to reconstruct the doctrine of technologia. It is not easy for a twentieth-century mind to grasp, not because of its profundity but because of its simplicity. Its fundamental ways of regarding things being utterly foreign to our manner of thinking or seeing; to us it seems highly abstract and over-intellectualized, yet in its day the doctrine had for Puritans among its many virtues that of easy comprehensibility. It can indeed be stated very compactly. When God created the world, He formed a plan or scheme of it in His mind, of which the universe is the embodiment; in His mind the plan is single, but in the universe it is reflected through concrete objects and so seems diverse to the eye of human reason; these apparently diverse and temporal segments of the single and timeless divine order are the various arts; the principles of them are gathered from things by men through the use of their inherent capacities, their natural powers; once assembled, the principles are arranged into series of axiomatical propositions according to sequences determined by the laws of method. It must be obvious to begin with that God sent forth His wisdom to an end, and so each of the arts, being a part of that wisdom, tends toward the end; God created the arts by the method of genesis, combining arguments into the patterns of His intention, but man must find the principles of the arts by the method of analysis, discriminating the particulars within the synthesis; however, once man has formulated the rules of the arts, he should imitate God by using them, according to the method of genesis, to achieve the results for which they were predestined. In other words, technologia was an assertion that the arts direct conduct to ends enunciated by God; it was itself a science of distinguishing and defining both their contents and relations—in reality the wisdom of God—and their purpose—which was identical with the will of God. The spirit informing the doctrine emerges from one of Richardson's expositions of the concept "invention." Man, he says, was created to behold all God's creatures, "and to see his order in them"; but was the knowledge of them and their order written in his understanding? "No more than *Pauls* steeple is in my eye," for man comes into the world not furnished with grammar and logic, "but with the faculties of them," and by using his faculties finds at last the order of God in the body of the arts.

So that for Arithmetick, Geometry and nature, man was to learn them by the creatures, as he was also to learn the knowledge of Logick, Grammar, Rhetorick and Divinity. The reason is this, the *Genesis* of every thing is Gods, and man must see the rules of Art, therefore man must see them from singulars, by *analysis:* now then if man must learn these, and know them by his senses observation, induction and experience, then he must seek, and find out these, for they are not written in him: again, whereas every thing is in disposition, it is requisite that man find them out, and see them severally, therefore in this respect is this Art of reason called Invention, namely as he is sent by God to find out these things in his creatures; now if man must find them out with this act of his eye of reason, then is it fitly called invention . . . And this teacheth man thus much, that he is to seek out, and find this wisdom of God in the world, and not to be idle; for the world, and the creatures therein are like a book wherein Gods wisdom is written, and there must we seek it out.

It may be doubted if in the entire literature of Puritanism there exists a more revealing passage; it is an epitome of the Puritan mind, in which the dialectic of Ramus has blended perfectly with the theology of Augustine and Calvin. How frequently and with what different results have New Englanders posed themselves this problem, this question of how God is related to His universe, and how often have they striven to read His ideas and His intentions from "singulars by *analysis*"! The seventeenth-century Puritan "invented" technologia from reading the book of God's wisdom, but when technologia crystallized into a sterile and conventional doctrine, Jonathan Edwards came back to a fresh sense that "the beauties of nature are really emanations or shadows of the excellency of the Son of God"; when Calvinist theology decayed, Nathaniel Hawthorne, for all his skepticism, could not escape the problem of symbolism, while Emerson dedicated Transcendentalism to a new preoccupation with the old symbolism of nature and the correspondence of the thing and the word, the object and the spirit; Henry Adams, taught like all Puritans "not to be idle," sought out the singulars by an intense cultivation of analysis and endeavored to piece them together into the rules of art through the symbols of the Virgin and the dynamo. There is no evidence that any of these writers except Edwards ever heard the name of Alexander Richardson, but they did not need to; the heritage of Puritanism, as Richardson had formed it, was as strong in them as if they too, like students at Harvard in the seventeenth century, had learned to think of the basic problem of human existence in his terms, and so had been dedicated to seeking out the wisdom of God in the creatures.

Richardson guarded himself from presumptuous trespassing upon the secret essence of the hidden divinity by distinguishing between the totality of God's wisdom and the particular wisdom which God has chosen to materialize in the universe. He would ground his rules of art, not upon "Ens primum", not upon the absolute nature of God, for that can not be searched in human discourse, but upon "Ens a primo", upon that being which has proceeded from the secret essence and taken visible form before us. This distinction was of immense value to Puritans, for without it they could not even have put two and two together, and we shall encounter it in every department of their thinking. By its aid they could remain men of piety, knowing that God was unfathomable, but proceed as logicians to establish durable bases for scientific knowledge in a world created by the wisdom which could not be sounded. They could bow before the secret will, "far above all our Logick and Reason," and then preach upon the enacted will as logical and reasonable. Samuel Willard explained, for what must have been the ten-thousandth time, that if we fix our eyes upon the sun it will blind us, but "if we look on the reflected light or beams of it, we are safe, and it is comfortable." Therefore the arts enshrined the reflected beams, not the awful majesty. After making the proper obeisance before the impenetrable sanctuary, the Puritan logician was free to pierce the very secret of nature, to seize upon the eternal and universal laws of the cosmos. In relation to God, he understood, these laws would remain particular enactments, but in relation to man they would become catholic and scientific.

Technologia thus began by introducing a dichotomy into being itself: "The one from whom Art is, the other in whom it shines." Josiah Flynt, having taken his uncle's advice to heart and studied Richardson to good advantage, presented the population of New England through the *Almanack* of 1666 with a proof that the world could not be eternal. His argument was that God had impressed upon the created fabric every attribute which the creature was capable of receiving, and obviously eternity was not one of them. But the significant fact in his disquisition is his assumption that the universe is "the impression of the *Image* or *Vestigium* of those divine perfections which were in himself" [4]—the basic premise, in short, of technologia. A thesis of 1670 expresses it more poetically, "Art is a reflex apparition of divine light resplendent in intellectual night"; a mock thesis had it, "The creature is a speculum in which art is the image of eternal wisdom." The created world is by no means a revelation of the whole of God's wisdom, but it nevertheless manifests wisdom. "Ens a primo" emanates from "Ens primum", and the arts, though immediately from the created things, are derived through their medium faithfully from God Himself. Because God creates the materials of art, then the "Ens primum" is the beginning and end of the arts. God is "the alpha and omega of the arts." We may get from the arts no more than a glimpse of truth, but still it is a glimpse of absolute truth.

As it is with a torch, carry it from one place to another, and it will leave a glimpse behind, so it is in the surpassing beauty of God, hee leaves some beames behind him, that wee may say *Iustice* and *mercy* and *holinesse* its selfe have beene here.

Again and again the theses of Richardson recur at Harvard commencements: "Ens is the basis of the arts"; "All Ens is the object of technologia"; "The author of entity is the author of the arts." Always there is the distinction between entity and created entities: "Art and Ens a primo are of equal scope." One thesis puts it bluntly, "The infinite ought to be excluded from technologia"; the Puritan was committed, by his very acute consciousness of the infinite, to holding it at arm's length, to keeping it well beyond the periphery of the liberal arts, lest he and the forms of nature be swallowed up in its black formlessness.

Wisdom is by definition wise to some good end, and the radiation of Ens primum into the forms of derived being must have been toward a defined goal. "The Lord hath shot out every *ens a primo,* as it were an arrow out of his bow, to act his end." There is a purpose in the creation, and the rules of creation must contribute to its realization. "Art is the rule of the making and governing of things to their end," said Richardson; a thesis runs, "In shaping the disciplines, only didactic terms should be employed." Because the subject of the arts is "in the fabric of the thing," the arts are consequently not only descriptions of the divine plan but designations of divine intentions. For the Puritans this concept of a purpose behind the arts was expressed by the word "eupraxia". Derived from the Greek that means roughly "good conduct", and carrying the connotation of conduct not only good but appropriate to the circumstances, tactful and efficient, it became one of the principal catchwords of New England thought, freighted with both a cosmological and an ethical significance. "The Lord hath created, and governeth his creatures by the precepts of Arts, as by so many Statutes, or Commandements of things to act for his eupraxia." The arts, taken all together, make up the eternal rule in the mind of God, not merely as a draft of creation but also as a declaration of aim. "Art is the rule of eupraxia of Ens a primo," say the theses, "Eupraxia is the object and end of art." [5] If this seemed hard to follow, the authors of technologia asked the student to consider the case of physics or medicine: it is obvious that they consist "first in Theoretical rule, and secondly in Practice." By the same token, all other arts, logic, rhetoric, music, have their theory, and their theory points to their "use".[6] Technologia then demanded, when this much was made clear, that the "uses", the practices of the arts, be identified with precisely what God had previsioned, with His forecast of how the universe would function, before He had brought it into being.

William Ames, in reducing Richardson's lectures to order, sacrificed the literary charm of his teacher for the less attractive but, to the historian at least, welcome virtue of accurate terminology. At this point he devised another set of terms which came into general use in New England. He asked us to consider in chronological order the stages through which an art migrates in its progress from the essence of God to the pages of a Harvard textbook. First, it lay in the mind of God; secondly, it was positively enacted by God; thirdly, it was clothed with objects and forms; fourthly, it was extracted from the objects and forms by the mind and exists at last as a mental image or picture of the universe. Ames did not go on to trace the next steps, which were obvious, the fifth, in which it is written in a book, and the sixth, in which it appears on the printed page before the wondering gaze of young men at Cambridge. But he did conclude that our knowledge of the arts is "that effigy which either exists in the speculation of a rational creature, or in the delineation of it, which is set down in a book." Whether in the mind of God or in the book of the student, an art is always the same, but Ames thought clarity would be gained if the several stages were severally described: the first stage, the mind of God, was unnamable, since it lay outside human ken; the second, the decrees of God, could be called "archetypal"; the third, in the form of created objects, "entypal"; and the fourth, in the mind of man, might be christened "ectypal". At Yale in 1714 Samuel Johnson learned these distinctions: archetypal art, he wrote, is "the idea of the things decreed in the divine mind, which represents and therefore directs the divine eupraxia." [7] The eupraxia of the archetypal art became therefore in Puritan philosophy the phrase to denote at one and the same time both creation and providence; it was the object of abstract speculation and also the rule of concrete behavior.

When technologia had made clear that created objects manifest a pattern or platform of ideas, that the material world is the shadow or emblem of the supreme archetypal eupraxia, then the justice of Ramus' making the first act of logic an "invention" was established beyond the possibility of cavil. No art is a mere human creation; man may "invent" it but he is not the author or legislator; it is not created by the artificer, but the artificer is made by the art. "We do not form the precepts of the arts, but come upon them formed." Art records facts, and "Nature is the index of the arts." Theses repeat the point: "Nature is inchoate art; art is nature consummated"; "Nature is the nurse of art, art the assistant of nature." A mock thesis turned the relationship into a play on words: "Nature is the exemplar of art, art the example of nature." The argument is a true copy of the thing because both argument and thing are different words for one idea, the first being "entypal" and the other "ectypal". "Truth is first in God, then secondly, all things are so far forth true, as they answer to the *idaea* in God, for so God created all things"; because logic is "concrete evermore with the thing," Ramus based logic upon the invention of things, "so that first [we] look at the truth in things, which hath it from God, then at the truth of the axiom which hath it from the thing." The enacted wisdom of God may be infinitesimal as compared with His essential wisdom, but it is large enough to give us an organon of truth, for He has set up a rule, "whereunto he created things, whereby he governeth them, and whereunto they yield obedience," which rule we can ascertain. "Mark this well," said Richardson—and his students must have underlined the passage in their notebooks or drawn pointing fingers in the margins—"for the Schooles run into many absurdities, whilest they have thought that Art is in a mans head, and not in the thing." Thus Puritanism exorcised the ghost of Occam; David Hume was yet undreamed of.

The foundation of technologia was clearly the doctrine that in the mind of God there exists a coherent and rational scheme of ideas upon which He modeled the world. Outside this scheme would be the trackless wastes of His being, full of irrational horrors and sudden abysses, but within it, all was under the snug and enlightened law of eupraxia. As the similitude of a house must exist in the mind of an architect before its construction, so in the mind of any artificer, God or man, there must be a set of exemplars, prefiguring the structure and directing the work. God did not create the "entia a primo" before he had "the Idea of them in him: for he made them by counsel, and not by necessity." Every rule in art is a statute by which He governs; He could not make things by one rule and then govern them by another, else "it would not serve the turn to guide the thing to the *eupraxie,* whereunto it was made." By the necessities of our finite nature we must look upon objects first and from them extract the rules, but "the thing indeed is made to the rule, and not the rule to the thing, though we first see the thing." So technologia and theology coincided, and Ames dwelt at length upon the doctrine of the preëxistent pattern of ideas, not merely in the *Philosophemata* but in the *Medulla,* the standard exposition of the

New England creed. In every artificer, said Ames, there must exist "a platforme afore hand in the mind which when he is about to worke hee lookes into, that he may fit his worke to it"; so in God, who works not rashly or by constraint, *"such a platforme is to be conceived to praeexist before in his mind,* as the exemplary cause of all things to be done." The platform contains not only the ideas or exemplars of things, but of their connections, "whence also a certaine order ariseth of former and latter." This platform is impressed upon the creatures, as the impression of a ring upon wax; "the creatures themselves, as they are conceived in the Mind of God, are the platforme or image of that nature which they have in themselves."[8] There is a serene and inviolable pattern for the visible world which has the inestimable advantages of being both intelligible and fixed. Because the rules of the arts are the ideas of an eternal God, they are eternal and immutable; they are "radii of divine wisdom." In a world of appearances, and by men who are notoriously fallible, there can still be discovered permanent and enduring truth.

Harvard students were obviously drilled in this concept of the preëxisting pattern. "Idea is the rule in the mind of the artificer whereby he works," says a thesis, and a candidate for the M.A. affirmed that there is an idea of all being in primary being. Fitch quite rightly commenced his *First Principles* with the assertion that God rules Himself by "the idea or pattern of well acting," stamps the pattern on the creatures, "and that wisdome in the creatures is imprinted and is the impression or Image of it." Hence, Fitch concluded, in phrases that are not conventionally associated with the Calvinist view of life, the rules of art are eternal, and "the definitions of things are eternal Truths, whatever becomes of the things themselves." Samuel Willard did his best to make the idea comprehensible to the vulgar:

God contrives in his Mind an *Eternal Idea* of all things that are to be. God having a Work to do, in the Creation and Gubernation of the World; lays out the *Whole Scheme* of it in his Infinite Understanding, in which he hath a Pattern of the Whole World, and every thing in it: And this *Idea* must be *Eternal,* because Time, and all the Things of it are contrived in it.

He preached that the truth which is found in matter is a copy of exemplary truth, and defined rectitude in the creature as "Conformity unto that Idea which God had of it in himself"; he declared that the exemplary idea contains not merely the rules of creation but of providence, "by which the Creatures were to be guided to their ends, which are therefore Eternal Truths." Obligingly making clear in passing why it was necessary for Puritan theologians to put such inordinate emphasis upon this idea, he continues:

To Rule a Subject without a Rule to direct, is Tyranny, and not Government among Men; and tho' God's Will be His Rule, yet God hath in Himself an Idea of that which He will manage the Creatures by, and it is wise and just,

Piety alone could not always justify the ways of God to man; technologia established upon a cosmological basis for Puritans of the seventeenth century what Puritans of later centuries would pay a king's ransom to possess once more, the assurance that the rules by which all authority is exercised are wise and just.

The doctrine of the prëexistent platform explained not only how the universe was created, but why. Everybody knew that God had not needed to create anything; He was absolutely perfect without any additions to His perfections, and perfectly happy in Himself without any superfluous delights. But having framed a pattern of ideas which was marvelously wise and flawlessly just, He actualized it out of sheer love for its beauty. "There was a consultation in heaven, how that the Godhead might bee manifest, might bee observed, else were there none to apprehend it: I wil saith God, have my attributes expressed, therefore God would have a world wherein his goodnesse should bee discovered." He would have a world "to be a Mirrour of his Perfections." [9] As an emblem of these perfections, it was created both by an act of will and of "counsel", by almighty power according to rational design. Hence, as a thesis has it, "Art is the rule of being," and cosmic optimism rests upon the sure foundations of demonstration. "As ens and the good, so art and the true are convertible terms," and consequently, "Whatever is, is positively good," for everything has been produced by the deliberate act of that Being who framed the pattern of perfect goodness and truth.

And what, in the rational plan, could be more rational than that there should be at least one creature among the many contained within the pattern "able to read them, and acknowledge him therein"? Hence the creation of man, that some subsidiary being might behold the wisdom of God incarnated in things, and hence the logic of Ramus by which man beholds it. As a precious gem is uncovered in the earth, so the beautiful platform of God's idea must be uncovered by man, and the "entype" must parallel and reflect the "ectype". What God wrought by genesis man comprehends by analysis, "and so things are first in themselves, then they come unto the senses of men, and then to the understanding." We call the order which we perceive in the universe "science"; properly speaking "scientia" is only our knowledge of the wisdom of God as we find it exhibited, merely "ectype",[10] but Richardson, leaping once more across the gulf between the mind and the thing, declares that by "metonimy" our science may be called the true wisdom of God, since there is no break in the progression of exemplary truth from God's mind to the things and thence to the mind. The progression itself is an eminently rational procedure, because man is unable "to take this wisdom from God"—direct contact would consume him—and so it hath pleased the Lord to place it in the things, and as flowers do send out a scent, or odour that doth affect our sense of smelling, so every precept of Art doth spirare a sweet science to our glass of Understanding." Ideas radiate from the divine mind and into the human mind, being filtered through the things like sun beams "coming through a red or blew glass"; they are tinctured with the color of the thing, but in the Puritan view the white radiance of eternity had thus to be stained by the glass of matter if men were ever to apprehend it. The naked wisdom of God would blind our finite intelligences, "but the *reflections* of it that are made by the works of Creation & Providence, in which it is so admirably imprinted, will lead us by the hand to make precious discoveries of it, and most astonishing." Therefore men reconstruct the pattern of ideas that originally existed in the mind of God from the study of objects; the entire number of ideas pertaining to this pattern having been exemplified in creation, they are all present in nature, and the content of all the sciences will reproduce point by point the archetypal conceptions.

It is certain that the Arts are all of them imprinted in the *Book of the Creature;* and from thence it is that Men's Reasoning Power Collects them, by Observation and Experience, the Foundation of them is laid in the Nature of things, and is gathered from thence by curious inquiry: And such is the necessary use of them, in the Management of Human Affairs, that Mankind could not have lived without them for an Infinite space of Time.

The wisdom of God, for all that God is remote, illimitable, and incalculable Being, is not after all remote, and it can for the purposes of this world be limited and calculated. It will yield its precepts to him who analyzes, armed with the proper method.

The proper method was the logic of Ramus, because it provided the machinery for translating the entypal into the ectypal. "Logick carries from the thing to man, and speech from man to man, that which he hath seen with his Logick." To make the mechanism of this translation more explicit than it had been in Ramus, Richardson and Ames devised still another set of terms, which continued in general usage for over a hundred years in New England. The first act of the mind, according to the *Dialecticae,* is "to see the simples in things," and the power which performs this act Richardson named *"intelligentia";* when the simples are joined in axioms the mind exerts an ability which "we call . . . *scientia";* when the understanding discourses in syllogisms "it is our *sapientia,"* and when it ranges axioms in method "it is *prudentia."* Then, when the completed body of axioms is employed to direct conduct toward its eupraxia, it is *"ars,"* and when "we teach it to another it is *doctrina,* and his learning is *disciplina;* lastly as we set it down in writing or printing, it is *liber."* [11] As we ponder upon the meaning of such a passage we become aware once more that to the Renaissance mind satisfactory explanation consisted in giving satisfying names; to Puritan students Richardson's enumeration of the stages of perception, his correlation of the parts of dialectic with the "powers" of the mind, seemed so fine an analysis as to carry conviction on its face. Therefore in the science of technologia they had their much-needed preface to the *Dialecticae* and their comfort was assured; criticism was forestalled when they had shown how the pattern of divine ideas was precisely and clearly chiseled out of nature by a four-fold intellectual power, how each actuated its proper instrument in logic, *intelligentia* directing invention, *scientia* the axiom, *sapientia* the syllogism, and *prudentia* the method. The theological conclusion was impeccably orthodox: God gave man reason that man might admire God by comprehending the wisdom embedded in things, and He endowed reason with its powers that it might "promptly and readily perform its acts, as when it is prompt and ready in inventing, then it is *intelligentia,* when it is prompt in seeking out truth, then it is *scientia,* when it is ready in discoursing, then it is *sapientia.*" Ames explained that these powers were in truth the "image" of God, for they were recapitulations on a smaller scale of the stages that appear in any action of God Himself:

The Divine *Idea,* according to the variety of Notions, which are in the things, doth put on divers respects. In respect of the Principles, it is called intelligence whereby God perceiveth every severall thing in every thing: in respect of truth belonging to every severall thing it is called *Science* . . . In respect of the dependence of truths which they have among themselves, it is called *Sapience,* whereby he knoweth what is convenient for every thing, and what is disagreeable from it: In respect of the whole order to be appointed in practise, it is called Prudence, whereby he knowes, to apply the fittest occasions to every thing: Lastly, in respect of putting in practise, it is called Art, Whereby hee knowes to effect all things most skilfully.

Thus it is clear that as long as intellect exists, no matter how feeble or limited, it must be compounded of these elements, and the innate virtue of the mind, the "puissance naturelle" which is the sum total of them, could not possibly have been extinguished by the fall. As long as men are sentient they will necessarily be living exhibitions *in petto* of the cosmic intellect; hence, even in the state of sin, they have the powers that insure accuracy of perception. "The proper and formal recipient of art is the intellect," says one thesis, and another explains that the intellect receives art because it can pierce through the thing to the idea at the core: "Idea flows from the mind as effective principle, or from the object, as exemplar cause." Divine thought is the act of God in creating and governing; human thought reënacts the divine, not by creating the thing but by understanding it. Comprehension is a single act of power though it has its four stages, as a thesis of 1691 assures us: "Sapientia, Prudentia, Scientia & Ars do not really differ"; it is therefore closely analogous to the single act of creation, which, though instantaneous and eternal, can still be divided into four operations. The difference is that where God goes forth from Himself to create, man goes forth to "invent" and put into "method" what God has already created; but because our knowledge, our "ectypal" art, is "the ordered binding together of Intelligence, Science, Wisdom, and Prudence," it is a line-for-line duplication of the archetypal pattern first conceived in the divine mind.

There is of course one respect in which ectypal art must of necessity differ slightly from the archetypal. The divine prototype is single, unified, and indivisible, but when clothed in matter and diversified in time it must become multiple, so that when it is reassembled by the human mind from disparate phenomena it cannot be organized into one science. The truth which is unique in God appears, by the time it gets to *"liber,"* as the several arts, the trivium and quadrivium and the other arts, husbandry, navigation, or pharmacy. "As art is in God, it permits of a multiplex virtue, yet it is simple and one in act; but in created things, which are all concrete (as if from the refraction of rays) it comes forth multiple, and in that multiplicity is received and followed by the eye of reason." The first Being, said Samuel Stone, having all the arts in Himself, "hath left an impression of them in the frame and building of the world," but man must sever the fabric of one art from another in order to get at it. He does not actually rend the seamless unity; his abstraction is merely the concentration of a finite attention on one art at a time, dividing the different disciplines "in my understanding; not considering the other frames that are there growing together with it," as though he were plucking merely roses from a garden in which all the flowers grew together in "formal" patterns. Samuel Willard explained in the *Compleat Body of Divinity:*

> Now the reason, why this pure act must be diversly apprehended by us, is, because tho' God be to be seen by an eye of Faith, yet he must be seen by an eye of Reason too: for tho' Faith sees things above Reason, yet it sees nothing but in a way of Reason, which discerns all things by Arguments, which are conceived as distinct from the thing, and among themselves.

This Protean manifestation of truth did not disturb the Puritan confidence that truth is one; diversification was obviously a result of physical necessity, and seen in that light, the fact of multiplicity became a positive evidence for unity. When pure exemplars are called upon to direct a number of objects to their various eupraxias, they naturally must prescribe for each kind of object its appropriate regulations, yet the end of the exemplars will remain the one divine eupraxia of the whole. "The variety of art flows from the variety of the acts of the things which it governs"; the distinguishable branches of art do not indicate a pluralistic universe, but simply the wide dissemination of light from a single center. God always intended that man should reconstruct the scheme of things from his experience; even if man had not fallen he would still have required logic, he would still have invented before he judged, "and though his reason should have been so clear, as that he should have seen many things in nature, yet not all." Even in the Garden of Eden Adam used the syllogism. The apparently heterogeneous state of human knowledge, when thus considered, becomes all the stronger confirmation of its homogeneous source, and the final proof can be offered in technologia by showing how the disciplines fit together into a perfect whole. "So Art is one in God, but is various in respect of the various work it hath wrought in the creation of things, and that it acteth in their government to their end." The various bodies of precepts join one to another; "All the disciplines have some relation to each other," or, "All arts are bound to each other by a sisterly chain"—so ran the Harvard theses.

Truth is therefore collected from things by the logical method of Ramus, and arranged in the propositions of the arts; the principles of arrangement are also determined by Ramus. The body of precept was conceived as a sequence of axioms, laid out in order, the general followed by the specific, the selection and grouping of the sentences regulated by the three great laws of truth, justice, and wisdom. Ramus had said that the form of an art is "the order and collocation" of its axioms; Ramist apologists defined philosophy "ex mente Rami" as "ordered comprehension of the liberal arts"; Ames called art "Idea methodically delineated by universal rules," and said that when the rules among themselves "are ordered axiomatically, the truth may be consequential from all antecedents." Harvard theses echoed with "Method is the archetype of order," and "Art is methodical comprehension of homogeneous precepts." If the precepts collected from things are simply enumerated according to the three laws of Ramus, they must constitute true art, for they come from the God of justice, wisdom, and truth, and must be catholic precepts. The powers of the mind have each their particular logical act to perform, and so the performance of each is regulated by one of the "golden rules"; when the Puritans at last had derived from the Ramist dialectic and from technologia a complete terminology with which to explain the life of the intellect, they could demonstrate at once the correctness of the Ramist way of thinking by showing the necessary connection between the parts of logic, as Ramus had defined them, the powers of the mind, and the rules of method. What Ramus called invention was an act of the faculty of intelligence performed according to the law of truth; axiom and syllogism were performed by the powers of science and sapience according to the law of justice, and method by the power of prudence according to the law of wisdom. The schematic perfection of these correlations could not but charm any Renaissance mind, and for Puritans they had the added virtue of seeming to prove that the body of precepts which compose any art must follow inevitably both from the facts of nature and from the correct operations of the intellect. To discover truth either in things or in the Bible men had only to discover, as Thomas Bridge said in 1710, "how to dispose things into a due method and order, in the proper time and season; that matters may appear in a clear light." Behind this conception of art lay the deep sense of a cosmic order which again was made explicit by Richardson: since God who made the world, he said, is continuous, the world must be continuous, and things therefore must "appetere" to the places God has assigned them. "Hence 'tis that things ascend and descend." Samuel Stone would write, "God hath ranked things in order, that there is a subordination of things one to another, and one under another." This order cannot be ascribed to mere physical laws, said Richardson—"the efficient cause is method." In order to exhibit the variety of His wisdom God made many things, yet to show that His wisdom is single He incorporated them into one system, "and they are in one method, and so make one world." Any art, whether logic, medicine, or bee-keeping, presents a facsimile of truth by simply ranging in order the axioms which compose it. One thing follows another not primarily as the effect of a cause but because God, guided by the principles of true, just, and wise method, has ordained the particular succession.

Technologia was in many senses a wondrous construction of human ingenuity, but perhaps its most ingenious artifice was its integrating conduct with the very definition of knowledge. The platform of ideas, whether formulated in the mind of God or in the mind of man, did not remain an aesthetically satisfying object of silent contemplation, but became at once a program for action. The arts were invented in order to be used. Ames especially drove home the moral that an art is "to represent and to rule good action," that the effigy of divine wisdom achieved in ectypal art is to govern men toward their eupraxia. "Every Art," he said in the *Medulla*, "consists of rules, whereby some Act of the Creature is directed." The difference between an art and the subject-matter, a Harvard thesis said in 1708, is the difference between the rule and the thing ruled; for several decades the theses had been repeating: "Art is a method of various precepts useful for life," "The goal of discipline is direction of the intellect," "Art is idea eupraxias of catholic rule methodically delineated." Willard preached a sermon—appropriately entitled *Heavenly Merchandize*—in which he declared that the proper business of every art or science "is to lay down such Rules, Precepts, and discoveries, as may be proper and suitable means for the advancement of the genuine end of it," and that whatever is not truly "serviceable" thereunto should be ruled out. It is not difficult to read into these remarks a commentary upon the Puritan character; Weber's thesis may exaggerate the extent to which Protestant ethics subserved the needs of infant capitalism, but there can be no doubt that Protestantism in its Calvinistic form encouraged the shift of emphasis in theology and philosophy from contemplation to action, from beatitude to utility. The doctrine of technologia carried the emanations of divine energy into things, from things to the minds of men in the form of the arts, where it galvanized them into right conduct and vigorous exertions to fulfill their eupraxia.

Richardson devised still another set of terms to describe the fashion in which the arts eventuate in practical applications, and his account makes clear that the Puritan thinker regarded action not as a mere incidental advantage of the arts, but as their reason for being. Every art, he said, has its "praxis" and its "prattomenon". He defined praxis as "artis in agendo motus," the motion of art in the act of doing; he meant that the art, once formulated, inevitably generates motion, inevitably compels the artisan to doing. Thus in logic the motions inspired are genesis and analysis; the man who has studied logic can not resist using them; through this "praxis" he discovers other arts, which in turn generate a further praxis, as rhetoric the praxis of speaking and medicine of curing. "All arts come together equally in praxis and theory," was announced at Harvard in 1687. Ames took up the conception of praxis to explain many matters; it made still more understandable, for instance, why God created the world: He formulated the platform of ideas and then was propelled by the praxis to put His plan into effect. The concept also demonstrated how human comprehension of the arts was analogous to divine creation of them: man ascertains the ideas, but once he has learned them, they become in his mind what they had been in the mind of God, generators of a praxis. When either God or man harnessed an art, it ran away with them both, whether they would or no. Richardson said that genesis "begins at the simples, and so goes to the composites," but analysis "is an unwinding of a bottom of thred, which we wound up before." Ames then amplified the thesis to account for God's subtle device:

> This Image is collected artificially from the thing through Analysis of it in the first principle; afterward it is converted by the rational creature into *Idea,* which expresses a similar structure, which is called *Genesis.*

The seeds of "Idea" are, so to speak, planted in nature by God, where they flower into grain and are harvested by man with his analytical reaper; in the arts he bakes them into bread and eats them, whereupon they impart to his intellectual muscles the power to act as God had already acted, to be the source of a new genesis. Man must first analyze, but having analyzed, he has no choice but to act out the results of his analysis. "Our eupraxia begins from Analysis, is finished in Genesis."

Knowledge, therefore, leads automatically and irresistibly to results; the result, the achieved effect, Richardson called "prattomenon". Praxis is the motion flowing from the idea, the force or the radiating energy; prattomenon is the passing over of the force into accomplishment. "Praxis is the end of theory, the medium of the ultimate end." Praxis is "the cause of the prattomenon," and prattomenon is that which the art does by its praxis. Richardson illustrated the point characteristically:

So first the Shepherd hath his *prattomenon,* then the Grasier he useth the *prattomenon* of the shepherd, the Butcher useth the *prattomenon* of the Grasier, and the Cook useth the *prattomenon* of the Butcher, and they that eat the meat the Cook hath dressed use his *prattomenon.*

The commonwealth is the prattomenon of the good politician, and the universe is the prattomenon of God, as Josiah Flynt explained in the *Almanack* of 1666:

Whatever perfection was eminently in God, and the creature was Analogically capable of, was according to divine wisedome expressed (for otherwise the *Idea* or *Exemplar* would not have been consentaneous to the τό πραττόμενον).

It would be unthinkable that the prattomenon of divine action should not be consentaneous to the divine idea, and so man can truly perceive the exemplar in the created embodiment, and can proceed to produce his own proper prattomena, which will be consentaneous to the ideas or exemplars in *him*. That things do not always happen so simply and efficiently in human affairs is the effect of sin.

Many features of this doctrine tell so obvious a story that they need no comment. The question whether it was a tenable philosophy does not necessarily concern the historian, who is grateful for any philosophy. It is worth noting, however, that almost every development of thought in seventeenth- and early eighteenth-century New England can be traced in large part either to unforeseen implications in this doctrine or to efforts at smoothing out inconsistencies. The important point, speaking historically, is that through it Puritans secured everything their hearts desired in the realm of philosophy. The most obvious prattomenon of technologia was a practical system of the arts. It reorganized the medieval trivium and quadrivium. The arts were divided anew, dichotomized first into the general and the special, the general having for their subject-matter all "entia a primo", and the special devoted to particular portions of them. The general were dialectic, grammar, and rhetoric; metaphysics was abolished, according to Ames, and the special were mathematics, physics, and theology. In place of metaphysics there was now technologia, which was not another art but a preface or prologue to the arts, one of the "praecognita". Ames discussed the uses or applications of these arts in connection with the faculties of the mind; because men do not all employ the arts in the same way, the various practices must be specialized. He dichotomized the applications into the more worthy and less worthy; the more worthy into the superior, law and medicine, and the inferior, which were the seven parts of philosophy: oratory, cosmography, optics, music, architecture, economics, and politics. The less worthy applications were, of course, the "mechanic" arts, which result from the specific bearing of some one of the arts upon a limited subject, as from grammar comes calligraphy, typography, bibliography, and "bibliothecariorum"; from the precepts concerning fire in the art of physics are derived the special arts of horse-shoeing, gunpowder, and artificial illumination; from the precepts on water, irrigation and navigation; from those on earth, agriculture and horticulture; from those concerning animals, the arts of bee-keeping, fishing, and hunting.[12] Thus by the doctrine of technologia were the unity of knowledge and the divine authorship of every single particle in it brought home to the occupants of the most inconspicuous pews in New England churches.

On the larger philosophical plane, technologia made possible a release from tensions from which we have seen Puritan thought suffering at the beginning of the century, and in particular from those set up by the Ramist logic. It accounted for an intelligible universe without infringing the sovereignty of God; it showed how men could apprehend the intelligibles, even in a state of sin, by an immediate and instantaneous recognition. It proved that intelligibles exist objectively, not in man's head but in the thing. It allowed men to glory in the possession of innate powers without giving them cause to conclude that grace was superfluous. It provided a philosophical account of the visible universe, of its nature and its origin, that was thoroughly compatible with the theology, which it supplemented and supported. It demonstrated that by an innate power or an inherent habit of methodical apprehension men could perceive the eternal and divine rules upon which the natural world is constructed, and that the sum total of this knowledge was a unified and coherent organon. It provided a framework in which the Puritan, while remaining a man of piety and a believer in original sin and irresistible grace, could stabilize his intellectual heritage.

Technologia was all the more remarkable in that it contained no new ideas. It was actually no more than an elaborate restatement of the dominant medieval theory of knowledge, with a few important readjustments to suit the needs of Protestantism. It exhibits no conception that cannot be paralleled among earlier writers, no thesis but what had behind it a long and venerable history. True scholastics would no doubt regard every Puritan use of historic material as a misuse, and shudder at the naïve confidence with which Puritans cut across the bogs and quicksands of ancient disputations. Still, whether technologia be regarded as a *tour de force* and an intellectual legerdemain or as a genuine creation of philosophic genius, it served its purpose in New England for a century. Samuel Johnson completed his manuscript synopsis on November 11, 1714; a year later he recorded on the margin that he had now abandoned all this and become "wholly changed to the New Learning," by which he meant the logic of John Locke. But Johnson was ahead of his times in New England; among the more conservative technologia died a lingering death, and by the time Edwards was doing his mature work had barely become moribund. The theology of Edwards is generally taken as the supreme achievement of the New England mind, and so it is, considered philosophically and artistically, but it is a very different creation from the doctrine of the seventeenth century, if only because his theology comported with an entirely different logic, with a totally opposed metaphysic and a basically altered cosmology.

Yet if none of the ideas in technologia were new, there was something about the spirit of it, the method or the combinations, that was fresh and vivid, that made it a living symbol of the Puritan soul. It is significant that William Ames often protested that the theory of a preëxistent platform of ideas was not a species of Platonism; he felt that he had removed all such taint from "technometria" when he pointed out that in Plato ideas have an objective and Godless existence of their own, eternally uncreated, but that in his theory they exist only as the conceptions of God. They are not really ideas, in the Platonic sense, but simply "formulae in the mind of the artificer before action, formed to the action, and presenting and regulating it by presenting it." Yet the purely technical nature of this distinction, however important it may have seemed to a religious mind, is immediately apparent in terms of the history of philosophy. The essentially Platonic nature of the theory is not much affected if the ideas are thought of as ideas in a divine mind instead of self-created essences. In either case, reality is supersensuous, the visible universe is a copy of the ideal, and beauty or truth emerge not out of things themselves but from the light that shines through their opaqueness. And though Ramus would not admit outright the existence of innate ideas, and though New Englanders continued to read textbooks of physics in which the physiology of cognition was described in scholastic terms, the whole emphasis of technologia required an enhancement of innate abilities, in spite of the contrary emphasis in theology. Ramus preached the "puissance naturelle", then Beurhusius admitted the possibility of latent ideas or seminal reasons, then Richardson and Ames celebrated the achievements of intelligentia, sapientia, and prudentia—all of them powers of the natural reason—until at last it became apparent that man had not only native powers but actual concepts, not originating in the senses but merely confirmed therein. By the end of the century outspoken theses appear on the Harvard broadsides: the image of God is asserted to have been natural to man in the created state; therefore notions of God are natural to him; and finally there are innate ideas. The mere power of deriving universals from the sensibles, which was all that Thomas Aquinas would allow to man and all that Ramus thought he meant by "puissance naturelle", was not enough for Puritans, who wanted to abase man before the throne of God, but did not want to leave him wandering forlorn and distraught in a universe of which he was not competent to grasp the plan. Signficantly enough, Ramus himself had been much stirred by Plato, whom he called "the Homer of philosophers"; how well he understood Plato is a question, since it seems that no one has ever understood Plato, but Ramus apparently learned from him the principles of the Socratic method and felt therefore that he, like Socrates, was endeavoring "to raise his hearers above the senses, prejudices, and traditions of men, in order to lead them to their own natural senses of right and liberty of judgment." This sentence has the true "Platonic" ring; Ramus was hailed in his day as "the French Plato," and he frequently quoted Plato against Aristotle. His friend Hotoman explicitly identified the Platonic ideas with the Christian doctrine of divine conceptions. Hence there was a strong current of Platonism, however subterranean, in the logic of Ramus, and the fact seems to be that the implications which Richardson and Ames drew out of him are those that can be called "Platonic" without too loose a use of the word. They may not have worked in the conscious knowledge that they were Platonizing, but they did not need to know much of Plato at first hand to get their cues. In one form or another Platonic theories had been kept alive through medieval centuries, and whenever men turn to Augustine they always end by preaching something very like the *Republic.*

In New England, for example, it was frequently said, as had been said in medieval schools, "To know a thing *as it is,* is to know it in its *Essence,* and comprehend it in its definition." To medieval schoolmen, at least to those who were true Aristotelians, to know the essence was to understand the potentiality and actuality of it, to extract the intelligible form from the sensible form; but they were certain that human knowledge could not go beyond the sensible, could not come to a direct apprehension of the intelligible. But in technologia, as a legitimate outgrowth of the Ramist doctrine, the concept of potentiality almost disappears. The intelligible species were made synonymous with arguments or reasons, and in 1687 Joseph Webb won his M. A. by denying that substantial forms exist. Ramus "would not use *potentia,* and *actus,*" said Richardson, because they are "barbarous words." Potentiality was indeed reduced to nonsense in a world organized upon clear and precise ideas radiating from the mind of God, and it was likewise banished from the human intellect, which did not need to sift things through the active to the potential principle, but could seize upon essences in the single leap of penetration. Jonathan Mitchell maintained in the class-room, "Active and patient intellect are nothing else but Genesis and Analysis," and John Emerson argued for his M. A., as his descendant in Concord was to argue in print two hundred years later, though with a very different phraseology, that the form is not led from the potential of the matter.[13] Potentiality, in short, belonged only in the hypothetical realm of the divine mind outside and apart from the conceived platform of ideas, and therefore within the cosmology which embodies that platform, technologia could appear, one among the many manifestations of Platonism that everywhere characterized the sixteenth century. It was fitting and proper that Sir Philip Sidney, the earnest partisan of the *Dialecticae,* should also voice in *The Defence of Poesie* one of the classic expositions of the Platonic theory of the poet. Knowledge of the essence of things in the doctrine of technologia was perception of the transcendent idea, and if the idea had to be apprehended through the physical object, it was because refraction was necessary. Unless its blinding intensity were stepped down to the measure of our eyesight, we should never apprehend it. Also because "our intellectuals are so wounded by the Apostacy of the first man," it is "exceeding hard for us to find out the forms of things," so that even with the help of Ramus we "are forced many times to describe the forms of things by their accidents." Nevertheless, the visible world is but a veil or a screen between the intellect and the true and perfect ideas, between ectypal and archetypal art.

He that doth not see through a thing, to the other side of its Essence and Operation, comes short of knowing it perfectly: he must comprehend, in himself, all that the Being comprehends in it, and have the entire reflection of it on his Understanding.

Mistakes can be made in invention, in judgment, in method, even in the syllogism; sin makes impossible our ever fully and satisfactorily winning through to the "other side of its Essence." Yet this seeing through, this sense of "the other side," is the true Puritan theory of knowledge. In the disciplines a pious student, assisted by God but also using the methods of logic and the precepts of the arts, may understand almost everything in creation. An object is understood, said Willard,

when the whole Object is so contained in the mind, that nothing in the thing comprehended, is beyond its knowledge: all of it is so seen, as nothing escapes the eye of the mind . . . That is comprehended which is perfectly known, which is known so far as it is observable: and this knowledge doth imply an Adequation, or perfect equality of the Understanding to the thing understood.

Or, as he says again, to apprehend a thing, "I must needs have some Idea in my mind of the thing believed to be, or else I believe, I know not what, which is ridiculous." It was ridiculous to the Puritan way of life not to know what one believed; skepticism was ridiculous, fideism, doubt about the solidity of knowledge, hesitancies in reading the wisdom of God in the creatures. Therefore Puritanism maintained, in technologia, that the mind is competent to understand, adequate to the thing understood, capable of discerning, even though darkly, the pure ideas which God has formed in the recesses of His intelligence.

Probably no amount of skill in presentation can today bring back the emotional appeal, the breath-taking grandeur, of technologia. As we study it we become conscious once more of the obstacles that prevent later ages from sympathetic comprehension of the Puritan religion, particularly of its highly abstract and intellectualized formulation. Yet to Puritans themselves, technologia was one of the simpler, more concrete, more poetic doctrines in a world that gave rise elsewhere to many more closely reasoned and less imaginative interpretations. For example, Samuel Stone's defense of Hooker's *Survey* is a fair example of the Puritan mind in action; it is as gnarled a booklet as the historian, no matter what his sins, can be condemned to read, disputatious and bristling with jargon; as Stone marshals his syllogisms and his arguments "orta de primo," as he hammers at the endless distinctions between "totum essentiale" and "totum integrum," the modern reader—there have been very few—is on the point of giving him up for an incurable pedant and of going away assured that no men ever undertook heartfelt action on the strength of arguments like these. But then he turns to the preface, written by Samuel Mather of the Harvard class of 1643, who had learned from the study of Richardson and Ames the true harmony for what seems to us Stone's weary rattling of dead bones. In a passage that fairly glitters with insight, he lifts the level of the work from haggling to vision, yet the passage is in substance merely a summary of the doctrine of technologia:

> All the Arts are nothing else but the beams and rays of the Wisdom of the *first Being* in the Creatures, shining, and reflecting thence, upon the glass of man's understanding; and as from Him they come, so to him they tend: the circle of Arts is *a Deo ad Deum*. Hence there is an affinity and kindred of Arts (*omnes Artes vinculo & cognatione quadam inter se continentur:* Cicer. pro. Arch. Poet.) which is according to the reference and subordination of their particular ends, to the utmost and last end: One makes use of another, one serves to another, till they all reach and return to *Him,* as Rivers to the Sea, whence they flow.

This paragraph may not make the ensuing treatise more readable, but it makes clear that to Stone and Mather their argument, though concerned with the nature of the visible church, was part and parcel of a unified body of knowledge, and that any small question was important because every small segment of knowledge had an indispensable place in the cosmic plan. The universe, as these men beheld it, was still so magnificent and organic a unity that with no apprehension of its ever tumbling about their ears they could devote themselves to a disquisition upon this corner or that buttress, and treat it at length in the technical terminology of the workman and the student of cosmic architecture, without failing to appreciate the larger sublimity. The reader of any piece of Puritan writing must keep this reflection well in mind, for there is seldom a prefatory Samuel Mather to call it to his attention.

CHAPTER VII

THE USES OF REASON

He who undertakes to narrate any chapter in the history of the Reformation must have an appetite for paradox and an appreciation of the ironic. It was a time when the best laid plans of theologians frequently went astray, when they often brought about one result by striving for the exact opposite, when arguments advanced for one doctrine eventually gave support to quite another. Perhaps the most highly paradoxical and ironic of the doctrines was that of total depravity, for it contained on the face of it a view of life that seems to make all endeavor useless, yet in effect it aroused Protestants to fervent action; it ought to have inspired melancholy and humility, but it often gave rise to Pharisaism and sanctimonious pride; it ought to have encouraged contempt of the world and of treasure, but it proved especially congenial to thriving merchants and accumulators of worldly goods. It ought to have forced man to grovel in the dust, but instead one of its principal effects was a renewed emphasis upon the importance of his rôle in the creation, a fresh vision of the boundless possibilities of his genius.

The more theologians denounced the depravity of man, the more vividly they were obliged to describe the eminence from which he had fallen, so that while in their sermons they painted the horrors of unregenerate existence in the most lurid colors, by their implications they were continually etching a fine portrait of the original grandeur. The more the people were informed concerning the ravages of original sin, the more distinctly they came to know the lineaments of nobility and worth. For example, in order to explain the fall, the ministers had first to describe the high place for which man had been intended. From the theory of the universe modeled upon a pattern of ideas they concluded that the creatures were ranged in a great chain of being, "ranked in several Orders and Kinds of Being, and these furnished with very different Capacities." The multitude of them illustrated the divine plenitude and all were to glorify God in their various fashions; senseless objects and beasts lacking the discourse of reason praised him by their "passive obedience," moving as they are moved, knowing not why or wherefore. "But the case is otherwise in respect of Man, as to his active conformity." Puritans held it not sufficient that man merely do what God wills, "but he must do it upon choice, and as it is God's Will, that he may therein please him." Designed to fill the office of reasonable creature in the hierarchy of being, man owes to God a duty which must be reasonable. "As Reasonable Creatures are in Subjection to his special Government, so they owe him a Reasonable Service." God never intended that men should worship Him by unreflecting instinct, and Puritanism had no use whatsoever for the saint who was pure by nature and holy without struggle and temptation; Puritans could never conclude with Pascal, "Do not wonder to see simple people believe without reasoning. God imparts to them love of him and hatred of self. He inclines their heart to believe."[1] Belief without reasoning was a virtue in stones and animals, but a sad defect in humanity; Puritanism professed to regret that man had eaten of the tree of the knowledge of good and evil, but admitting that he had so eaten, it was certain that now he would triumph over Satan only after he had gorged himself, so that like Adam after being "greatly instructed" by the archangel, even though paradise were lost, he could depart with his "fill of knowledge," wondering

> Whether I should repent me now of sin
> By mee done and occasioned, or rejoyce
> Much more, that much more good thereof shall spring.[2]

Man has been summoned to an exalted rank among the creatures and invested with the insignia of his office; the fall may tarnish his epaulets but it cannot abolish his command. The exemplary pattern of divine wisdom will not miscarry, and therefore even in sin man cannot desert his post.

The service which God designed man to perform was simply "eupraxia". Adam in his integrity was a logical "artist":

> Every wise Agent always observes this method: he first propounds an *End* to himself, and fixeth upon it, and then he sets himself to study and find out proper & sutable *Means,* which he may improve in his regular pursuance of it. The Scheme, Idea, or Exemplar of the means, and the way rightly to apply them to his purpose, is that which is called his *Rule of Operation.* And such Rule is requisite in order to the practice of every *Art;* and he that is thoroughly acquainted with it, and dexterous at it, may only be called an *Artist.*

Adam was expected, alone among animate beings, to reason out his "Idea" and to put it into operation by deliberate choice. The image of God, therefore, considered either logically or theologically, consisted of reason and will. Were all things made for man," asks Richardson, "and must he see them with his reason?" Yes, he answers, and continues, therefore man must see them as good or bad and must choose the good; "*ergo*, he must have a will to imbrace them as *bona*, as well as an eye of reason to see them as *vera*." Sin no less than virtue had to be enacted by reasoned forethought and conscious will; only a being that is "a cause by counsel" could be charged with guilt. Hence, in order to expound the sinfulness of man, Puritan parsons were obliged again and again to celebrate the virtues of humanity, and their passages excite strangely conflicting emotions, on the one hand inconsolable grief over man's loss, and on the other a glow of pride in his inherent dignity:

O, Consider the Soul in its Capacities, it was made after the *Image* of God, *Auræ Divinæ particula*, endued with an *Understanding* capable of the most *Sovereign Truth*, and *Will* fitted for a Closure with the chief good, *Capacitated* for the Everlasting Fruition of God in Glory.

Urian Oakes declared that in giving men these capacities God took them "as it were, into partnership & fellowship with Himself in the way of his providential Efficiency, that they may be *Under-workers*, yea *Co-workers* with Himself." When Richard Baxter sought to establish *The Reasons of the Christian Religion* by rehearsing the *Discourse on Method* in Puritan garb, he set out to doubt everything—it is plain, his heart was not in it, but he tried hard—and the one fact he found himself incapable of denying was not, as with Descartes, "cogito," but that his senses and bodily faculties were subject "to the guidance of my Reason, and the command of my Will, as the superiour faculties." This much, he said, "is quite beyond dispute," as indeed for Puritans it always was.

However, reason is now corrupted and the will decayed, and the sure way for men to undo themselves is to think "that they have in them naturally a sufficient light to direct them in the right way." We might well ask, then, what conceivable comfort, no matter how surreptitious, can there be in thinking upon the irretrievably lost image of God? Can the remembrance of past glories bring anything but bitter repentance and self-recrimination? In one sense, of course, the ministers intended to arouse precisely this reflection, but here again we are confronted with paradox. There was in Protestant theology an article of belief which made possible a slightly more optimistic conclusion: all Protestants maintained against Catholics that the original righteousness had not been an extra grace, superadded to the natural constitution of Adam, but an inherent part of his being; the loss of God's image was not the removal of a supernatural gift but a corruption of the entire soul. The image had been woven into the very substance of humanity and was in that sense "natural" to it. Like many Protestant doctrines, this one seems at first sight immeasurably to magnify human misery, for while in the "Popish doctrine" the natural man might seem to have come out of Eden relatively unscathed, deprived merely of a gratuitous gift, in the Protestant version he has nothing good left in him. Yet the doctrine could be stated so as to leave a possibility for reassurance. The great William Perkins, for instance, defined three elements in the original righteousness: the substance of the body and soul, the faculties of reason and will, and the integrity of the faculties; in the fall the third was lost and must be restored in regeneration, so that conversion "is not the change of the substance of man, or of the faculties of the soule, but a renewing and restoring of that purity and holiness, which was lost by mans fall." Thereupon the happy thought intrudes itself: in spite of the fall, the substance of the body and soul and the faculties of reason and will remain! True, they are perverted and wicked; true, they cannot give light to direct man in the right ways, but nevertheless there they are. Righteousness is gone, integrity is gone, but "the Nature of man, as man, abides notwithstanding the Amission of it." This may seem like slim consolation, until we remember, in the language of the Harvard theses, that "Reason is the Mercury of the arts" and that "Being is equal to art." Men who loved logic with the consuming ardor of the Puritans could not resist completing this syllogism and concluding, at least by inference, that reason is the Mercury of being.

This much at least was clear: at his creation the virtues of reason and will were instilled into man, and vestiges of them must still persist. Furthermore, reason was imparted from God and is a portion of His substance; must it not originally have had some knowledge stamped upon it? "When God made man, he engraved upon his heart the Rule of his serving him; he wrote it upon his practical Understanding or Conscience." If dialectic and technologia tended to the conclusion that in spite of Aristotle there are innate ideas, they received encouragement from the theology. The frequency with which the preachers insisted upon an inherent rationality of man is truly startling. Hooker defined man as "a living creature indued with a reasonable soul: and every living creature indued with a reasonable soul, is a man"; Cotton declared that reason "floweth from the soul, or mind of man, and is not any accident to it, but of the same nature with it," and that though there is an "accidentall" reason which we acquire in experience, "there is also an essentiall wisdome in us, namely, our Reason which is naturall." Elnathan Chauncy copied in his commonplace book when he was a student at Harvard a quotation from Van Helmot:

> Truth and the rational soule are twins. For so uncessant a magnetiseme or congenerous love doth the soule hold unto the truth, that she can Know no reall or permanent satisfaction, in the fruition of any other object.

The name of God, written boldly in the heart of the first man, is still legible in the heart of his posterity, "and tho' many have used utmost endeavours to raze it out, yet they could never do it altogether." The existence of conscience proves the retention of at least a portion of righteous knowledge. Conscience operates without the aid of grace, for otherwise "there would be no civill Societies maintained in the World, but mankind must disband." Hence the "wise heathens," Plutarch and Seneca, spoke out of the remainders of the image of God within them; their belief in God, "this *Idea* in the Soul of man," was no mere tradition nor was it a politic pretense. "The Notion is as *Natural,* as tis *Powerful,"* and it is "as *General* as tis *Natural,"* for even "the Salvage Indians themselves in the most hideous and Barbarous Thickets of *America,* own a Koutantowit, as the First Cause of all." That there remains some inherent knowledge in even the most repulsive of mortals is established beyond question when traces can be found in the Indians of America.

This knowledge, kneaded into the clay of which man was molded, is called indifferently the light or law of nature, the light or law of reason. It is called the law of nature because it comes to man from "his natural Conscience, from the Nature of God, and the Relation between God and him"; "the Reasons of it are to be read in the Light of Nature, so far as it remains in him." Its content is in fact the Ten Commandments, for when the fall smirched the original pages God transcribed them on tablets of stone. Undoubtedly the law must now be read in the stone and not in the heart, for man has "knock't his head in his fall, and craz'd his understanding," and of the laws of nature there survive only "some broken fragments, & moth-eaten registers, old rusty outworn monuments," so indistinct that "there are but very few of them, that he can spell out what they mean, and in others he is mistaken." Yet blurred though the laws of nature might be, Puritans could never give over trying to spell them out. Their textbooks taught them the formal meaning of the light of nature; thus Alsted described it, as it now remains in man:

> The gleam of divine wisdom, through which light we perceive the evidentness and firmness of first principles, and of the conclusions depending from them. This we consider the light of nature by reason of first principles.

Samuel Willard would call the laws of nature moth-eaten registers, but he would base his determination of the relations that should prevail between master and servant upon "the Light of Nature, or right Reason, which is the Medium by which we are to spell out the Law of Nature." There is an internal light as well as the light of revelation, Increase Mather said, so that even if men had no written word, "yet they would know, that such and such things are Good, and ought to be done"; the drunkard does not need the Bible to stand condemned, but merely "that within him, a Candle of the Lord in his own breast." Davenport declared that the power of civil rule "is from the Light and Law of Nature, and the Law of Nature is God's Law." The Puritans did not really believe that the law of nature was extinct or useless, whatever harsh things they said in their more pious moods.

There was something left of innate knowledge, there were still the faculties of reason and will, and reason could still make out a few all-important letters in the faded text. Good civil customs and political principles, said Cotton, do not spring from the corruptions of men, "but from the law of nature, from the rudiments written in the heart," and hence it followed that "Civil Prudence, Learning, and all comely things are from him, so that we should not shun these."

It also followed that if comely things, like learning, logic, and the arts, are not to be shunned, then the rudiments of them in the heart should not be ignored. One of the most pronounced and widespread characteristics of Puritan thought in the seventeenth century is the constantly increasing emphasis put upon the remains of God's image in fallen men. It made what seems a concerted effort to salvage as much as possible from the rubbish heap. Ames, for instance, pointed out that in the midst of deterioration there are hints of truth in the hearts of men, that the image of God appears in their ability to make theoretical and practical judgments. "At least the shaddowes of vertues, are allowed and embraced of all."[3] The works of John Preston were hailed by his editors, one of whom was John Davenport, because while emblazoning the glorious attributes of God, they withal delineated "the most noble dispositions of the *Divine Nature* in us, which are the prints and imitations of those his *Attributes,* applying as a skilfull builder, the patterne to the peece he was to frame." Preston merited these encomiums, for he repeatedly describes the inclination to good and the aversion to evil which he finds an attribute of all mankind:

> There is in naturall men not onely a light to know that this is good, or not good, and a Conscience to dictate; this you must doe, or not doe, but there is even an Inclination in the will and affections, whereby men are provoked to doe good, and to oppose the Evill. And therefore the proposition is true, that naturall men have some truths, because they have this Inclination remaining, even in the worst of them.

If Preston's writings on this question of the "remains" are compared with the pronouncements of John Calvin, it will become evident how far Puritanism of the early seventeenth century had already strayed from pure "Calvinism"; what Preston says every man knows by nature, Calvin says can barely be guessed by the wisest philosophers, and to him their glimmerings are of little value. "Human reason, then, neither approaches, nor tends, nor directs its views toward this truth, to understand who is the true God, or in what character he will manifest himself to us."[4] Calvin would grant that in secular affairs and in the mechanical arts reason can discover useful principles, but his explanation again indicates the gulf between him and Preston: these achievements of reason, he declares, result from some talent bestowed upon a particular individual by a special grace of God, from a favor temporarily vouchsafed, not from any inherent abilities. Calvin was arguing, in short, for the total and complete incapacity of nature, relieved occasionally by gifts of specific powers at the pleasure of the arbitrary ruler; Preston was asserting an innate and universal capacity, even though it was imperfect and could not attain to salvation. Preston's view was transported to New England, and Thomas Hooker declared from his Hartford pulpit, "The Lord hath left in thee the remainder of many natural abilities, hath lent thee the help of many common Gifts and Graces, which by Art and Education have grown to some ripeness." Hooker asserted further that in the human will, considering it "merely as it ariseth from the power of those natural principles, whereof it is made," there are principles "which were at the first imprinted upon it," which naturally incline it "to close with God." In Increase Mather's sermons there is often an even greater enlargement of natural abilities; he told a condemned criminal that God has executed spiritual death upon mankind for Adam's apostasy, but—"he has moderated that punishment; hence men in a *natural* estate, yet close with some *practical* principles of Piety & Righteousness . . . These things shew that there are some *Remainders* of the Image of God in men." Perkins' distinction between the faculties and the integrity of the faculties became in Willard's treatment the much less sharp distinction between "Moral Powers" and "the Moral Image"; the latter was lost, "but the former abides, as belonging essentially to Humanity." Men still have reason and will, and in their reason some recollections of divinely instilled truth; there are some men who "have improved the *light of nature,* and the broken fragments of the *Law* of it, remaining in them, by the exercise of *Reason";* since the essential constitution of man is not altered, his emotions are still "moved by the impressions of reason," for "it belongs to the nature of man, that he is a reasonable creature."

There is a danger that by taking such passages out of their context we may give them greater prominence than they actually enjoyed. Of course, Puritan writers always set definite limits to the competence of reason, and held it incapable of supplying the doctrine of salvation. Yet—and once more the flicker of irony crosses the pages of theology—the very fashion in which Puritans with the aid of technologia explained the relation of the liberal arts to revelation, of the sciences collected from nature by reason to the art imposed from beyond nature and inconceivable to reason, exhibited a perverse tendency to make revelation natural and redemption rational. In a sermon entitled, ironically enough, *Morality Not to be Relied on for Life,* delivered in the year 1700, Samuel Willard inaugurated the century that was to rely more and more upon morality by defining the widest possible field in which natural reason could function: it could lead men to obey the law outwardly, to obey it conscientiously, even to take genuine delight in obedience, and "to aim at salvation this way." At that very moment the problem had become importunate of telling in particular cases whether candidates for New England churches were being motivated by grace or persuaded by reason, yet Willard and his colleagues, though worried about the growing spirit of "morality", were yet untroubled by forebodings of "rationalism". The doctrine of Richardson and Ames seemed to protect them against that danger, and technologia was so formulated that it insured them against ever taking natural light as sufficient for salvation. The authors of technologia always declared that while the liberal arts are gathered from things, the art of divinity cannot possibly be so extracted or "invented", simply because the natural world does not exemplify the pattern of ideas upon which God formed the scheme of salvation. These exemplars were precipitated in His mind *after* the creation; logic may ransack every corner and crevice of the universe, but it will never find out the arguments and axioms of theology. The doctrine of Christianity is not built into the cosmos as is the doctrine of physics, and divinity therefore remains incomprehensible to human reason. "The way for a *Sinner* to be made *Righteous,* is laid so High, that no Humane Reason could Ever have reached it." Men have something of the law in their hearts, but salvation by grace is not a "method" to be found in nature. "Then let no man think to attain the knowledge of the covenant of grace, and find out the mystery thereof by naturall understanding, by any strength of wit, learning."

However, this was not to say that the revealed Word was a violent intrusion into the texture of the arts, an explosive projectile into the serried and closed ranks of technologia. As Ames outlined the theory, he made clear that divinity had to be specially enunciated, but yet that, though not culled from things, it fitted into the organon. When man fell, the world shuddered and the mind became dimmed; thereupon, realizing that even with the gifts of invention and method still at their command, men would not any longer interpret the book of nature correctly, and not being willing to leave them to perish of their mistakes, God supplemented nature with the book of revelation. Of course, while speaking the axioms of religion He had occasion to deliver many others, ethical, political, scientific. In William Ames the Puritan dominated the Ramist, and he concluded piously that as men must go to the Bible to learn theology, so it would be better for them to take their morality from the same source rather than to attempt inventing it from nature; he argued that ethics, like metaphysics, should be eliminated from the circle of the arts, though this teaching was the only point on which he was not obsequiously followed in New England. However, even he agreed that for the discovery of all other arts men must go to the objects in nature, and use the Bible merely for confirmation of the particular axioms which happen to be enunciated therein. Thus theology took its place in encyclopedia, as an addition, a replacement, a compensation for the fall; it was an afterthought, devised for the emergency, but serving incidentally to substantiate and reinforce the pattern of ideas upon which the natural universe had been constructed. Like the precepts of the other arts, those of theology are not the essential wisdom of God but merely a segment, those which He chose to enact, but having been formulated after the universe was already in operation, they were never incorporated into its structure.

The principles of other Arts being inbred in us may be *polished and brought to perfection,* by sense, observation, experience, and induction: but the solid principles of Divinity *how ever they may be brought to perfection by study and industry, yet they are not in us from Nature.*

Following closely in Ames's footsteps, New England theorists explained that divinity was an art, unique in that "None can learn it by the book of nature, for there are some lessons in Religion which are not to be found in the book of Creation." The pattern of archetypal ideas "by which man was to be led as a Rational Agent, or cause by Counsel, to an Everlasting Estate" make for theology its "Plat-form of sound words," but it will not be found by subjecting the material universe to analysis. Because technologia assured them that reason could not possibly encroach upon faith, New England theologians could imperturbably permit the sphere of reason to be extended further than would seem to us compatible with their creed, could allow the frontiers of reason to be carried to the very boundaries of faith. There was no danger that reason would arrogate to itself the power of discovering theological truths, because the exemplars of grace, the atonement, the resurrection, and salvation by faith, were not exemplified in nature.

However, after the initial difference of theology from the other arts was established, that its source was the Bible and not the creation, it then became amenable to the same rules of formulation and articulation as the natural arts. It was to be collected by the reason from its embodiment, analyzed into arguments and axioms, difficult points settled by syllogisms, and the whole content ranged in order by the laws of method. Analysis of Scripture is accomplished, said Ames, "by right application of the precepts of Logic." Even though divinity is "not from Nature and humane invention (as others are)," but from revelation, yet intelligence, science, sapience, and prudence pertain to it, "for all these are in every accurate Discipline, and especially in Divinity." When Samuel Willard advised divinity students to study logic he explained that, as in the arts in general, the principles of theology are collected from their examples and placed in order by artificial method, except that the principles of theology must be extracted from the helter-skelter verses of the Bible instead of from the flux of phenomena. In the Bible, doctrines are not yet "digested into a Methodical System, but it is to be gathered from thence." The student must deduce from Scripture the theoretical rule of systematic divinity and the concrete "uses", "since the End of *Knowledge* is *Eupraxy*." Wollebius' textbook was popular in New England along with the *Medulla* because it contained the theories and even the phraseology of technologia according to Richardson and Ames; Wollebius thus expounded the nature of theology as an art:

That habit which apprehends the Principles, called *Intelligentia;* and that habit which demonstrates the Conclusions out of the Principles called *Scientia;* and that habit which ariseth out of the two former called *Sapientia,* are habits meerly contemplative; but for *Prudentia,* tis an active habit directing the mind in its actions, & *Art* is an effective or operative habit with right reason. Divinity then consists partly in contemplation, partly in action. Therefore Divinity may bear the name both of Sapience, and Prudence; Sapience so far forth as it apprehends the Principles by means of the Intelligence being divinely illuminated, and from thence demonstrates the conclusions by means of Science; Of prudence so far forth as it directs the mind of man in its actions.

Because the Word of God and not the creatures was the source from which theology was collected, the human reason could safely be applied to it, could extract the arguments, discern the axioms, formulate the method, all according to the eternal rules of dialectic. We need scarcely pause once more to note that in the Puritan mind confidence in the certainty of God's Word was matched by an equal confidence in the infallibility of logic.

Up to this point the Puritan philosophy hung together as beautifully as any system has ever cohered within itself. Revealed theology was correlated with the other disciplines, and the intrusion of direct revelation into nature did not disrupt but rather strengthened the natural order, so that it was not an anomaly but actually the supreme vindication of rational method. But there was a further difficulty hidden within this whole doctrine which the concept of theology as an art helped to conceal but could not entirely overcome. Technologia established the function of reason in the arts and in religion, but it still never quite settled the question of what was the exact nature of reason. If Puritans were not pressed too hard, they could speak freely of reason as the image of God and differentiate between its acts of invention and method, its powers of intelligence, sapience, and prudence. Yet if their use of the word is scrutinized closely, it becomes apparent that in all their discoursing they employed it with a double connotation, and the contradiction between its two meanings is only thinly disguised by their generalizations. The difficulty was that Puritanism could not entirely dispense with either significance; each was equally necessary in their theology, and each had been inescapably thrust upon them by their inheritance from two antagonistic traditions. From scholasticism, from Thomistic philosophy, and ultimately from Aristotle, came the conception of reason as a principle of action, a power or faculty by which truth was discovered in the sensibles, an aptitude for discovering it; from reformed theology, from Augustine, and ultimately from Plato, came the conception of reason as itself the source of truth, the container and giver of ideas through inward intuition or recollection. Much of the Puritans' thinking must be explained as an effort to relieve the tension between the two meanings by harmonizing them in logic and technologia, or as an attempt to distract attention from the issue whenever they could not resolve the opposition by fixing upon the clarity and finality of divine revelation. It may well be doubted whether theologians were fully conscious of the problem, at least as we are phrasing it, yet many of their actions remain inexplicable to us until we perceive that they were struggling to reconcile irreconcilables. The latent conflict in their theory of reason engendered conflicts in other realms as well, in their theory of human psychology and in ecclesiastical practice, and was perhaps the one glaring weakness in their otherwise perfect system, the single but fatal inconsistency in an otherwise monumental consistency.

The first conception of reason, the "Aristotelian", can be aptly illustrated in the words of Richard Baxter:

> It is true, that there is in the nature of Mans Soul a certain aptitude to understand certain Truths, as soon as they are revealed, that is, as soon as the very *Natura rerum* is observed: And it is true, that this disposition is brought to actual knowledge, as soon as the minde comes to actual consideration of the things. But it is not true that there is any *actual* knowledge of any Principles born in Man: Nor is it true, that the said *Disposition to know* is truly *a Law;* nor yet that the actual knowledge following it, is a Law: But the *disposition* may be called *a Law Metonymically,* as being the aptitude of the faculties to receive and obey a Law.

If this statement, which is strictly Thomistic, were adhered to, it would mean denial of self-evident truths, of the validity of *a priori* conceptions, of the possibility that things can be known in their eternal essences; it would limit knowledge to what man encounters in sensation and restrict reason to the faculty of making generalizations from particulars. As Ames elaborated the doctrine of technologia, he believed that he kept within the limits prescribed by this conception. He said that the arts are to be distilled from things, and he gave his approval specifically to the Baconian method of induction and experiment, recommending that it be used for ferreting out the truths of the Bible as well as of nature. The logic of Ramus purported to be nothing but the codification of the "aptitude," not of propositions native to reason; the powers of the mind, intelligence, science, wisdom, and prudence, brought to light the meanings concealed in things, and therefore logic was made up of invention, axiom, syllogism, and method, all of which constituted a methodology for collecting truths from the visible creation or from the written Bible by sense, observation, induction, and experiment.

Yet as Baxter intimates, because a methodology discovers the law, the method itself is sometimes called the law "metonymically". The Ramist method did not in truth stay within the boundaries of Aristotelian theory; even had the theologians seriously attempted to hold it back, they could not have succeeded. It so stressed the ability of the soul to recognize truths "as soon as they are revealed" that eventually it dissolved into translucence the sensible barriers between the mind and the eternal light of the divine intellect. Ames was stretching Aristotelianism to the limit when he said that the archetypal idea "is even in part in the rational creature, to whom God both gave the eye for seeing it and communicated the thing itself in his measure through sense, observation, and experience," but he exceeded the limit when he declared that though some arts originate in the senses, not all art or all propositions do so. Harvard theses, following the path opened up by the doctrine that man's original righteousness was "natural", came at last to the downright assertion that innate ideas exist. Samuel Johnson's manuscript technologia represents the extreme development of the New England "Platonism": it is obvious, he wrote, that art "has reflected its rays into the intellect of intelligent creatures since the greatest antiquity, and therefore has its reflex origin in the intelligent creature"; hence, "it seems quite beyond all doubt that our first parent, Adam, before the fall was endowed with most illustrious wisdom, of which some sparks remained after the fall." Sparks of pristine wisdom are the Christian equivalents for Plato's reminiscences, and they cannot be mere powers or aptitudes, but must be positive axioms. A Harvard thesis in 1719, asserting "The true and genuine method of philosophizing is that all conclusions are drawn from Scripture, reason, and sense," illustrates the equivocation in Puritan thinking: reason stands between Scripture and sense as the instrument by which truth is extracted from both of them—and it stands also on a level with them as one of the repositories of truth.

William Ames illustrates the second or "Platonic" theory of reason more openly in the *De Conscientia* than in the *Philosophemata,* since in the latter he was arguing in the manner of the schools and could not easily put aside traditional scholasticism, whereas in the former he was preaching practical casuistry and writing upon the one subject, conscience, in which Platonism had most frequently blended with Christian thought. He makes the customary declarations that the law "which is written and ingraven in nature," containing the premises of morality, is corrupted, that the mind is depraved, and that neither the principles "which are within the booke of the mind, are fully and perfectly legible, nor can our understanding read any thing therein, distinctly and plainly." Yet when he expounds the meaning of "synteresis", he makes assertions that hardly bear out this conclusion. Indeed, synteresis was one of the avenues by which Puritan theologians came to their rehabilitation of natural powers. The term was far from being original with them; it had come into European thought from Stoicism, where it had meant the inner judgment, the sense of rightness or wrongness, but theologians had made it signify an intuitive grasp of the highest principles. Around the year 1600 it was still a gratifyingly ambiguous concept because previous writers had never quite made certain whether it was an acquired power or an innate light of nature; they did not endeavor overmuch to clarify the meaning, but their treatment was generally inclined to bring out the second interpretation. Ames defined it in relation to the logic: synteresis, he said, is an activity of reason, reaching a conclusion through the syllogism. Thus from the premise, "He that lives in sin shall die," through the assumption, "I live in sin," conscience concludes, "I shall die"; but whence comes the premise? Is it from the senses, is it imposed from without by the "inartificial" testimony of Scripture? Or is it an inward certainty, an innate idea? Ames said at this point that synteresis gives the perennials by the light of nature, for it is the "habit of the understanding, by which we doe assent unto the principles of *morall actions.*" The understanding grasps the principles naturally; "through the goodnesse of God the knowledge of many things which wee ought to doe or shun, are still conserved in mans mind even after his fal." Synteresis therefore is the act of stating self-evident, *a priori,* moral propositions, and differs "onely in respect or apprehension from the Law of Nature, or from that Law of God, which is naturally written in the hearts of all men." To it "ought to be referred, not onely generall conclusions touching right or Law, which are deduced by good consequence out of natural principles, but likewise all practicall truths, whereunto wee give a firme assent, through the revelation wee have by faith." Hence Ames found that the real difference between a natural and a regenerate conscience was not that the regenerate had the advantage of any new methods of judging, but that its syllogisms were erected upon the principles of Scripture, while the natural could build merely upon the innate "principles of nature." In each case the body of principle would be substantially the same, yet because of innate depravity the natural axioms would be too faint and distant for the soul to pay much heed. He concluded that conscience ought, therefore, to be ruled by Scripture alone, since it made explicit all the premises which the light of nature could discover, and in addition gave the precepts of redemption; nevertheless even Ames was admitting that synteresis can build upon "morall principles that are naturally in us." As long as he granted that some precepts exist in the natural mind "so cleare, and written in the hearts of all men, that they cannot erre to obey and practice them," he could not consistently contend that all truth comes through the senses.

Life would have been pleasanter for the Puritans could they have rested with the conclusion that while some knowledge commences in the senses, some does not, but they could not be let off thus, for the question of where to draw the line, of how to distinguish sensual knowledge from the innate, was potentially a more dangerous question than whether the source was entirely external or internal. Yet if Puritanism surrendered either view it ran a risk as grave on one side as on the other. If intelligibility were held to emerge only from the senses, there loomed ahead the threat of nominalism, of a fearful world controlled by continuous arbitrary power, of an unpredictable deity and an incomprehensible universe. But if all ideas could be derived from within, by an intuition of the light of nature, out of the remains of the knowledge originally engraved upon the heart, then divine revelation was superfluous, grace was useless, the church unnecessary, and a universal Antinomianism and Transcendentalism would result. If a man in the seventeenth century had declared that he lived from within, and in reply to the objection that inward impulses might come from below and not from above, had said, "If I am the Devil's child, I will live then from the Devil," the social consequences would have been disastrous. So Puritanism tried to mediate between extremes, to take parts of each conception and yet not all of either. In this predicament, it found the doctrine of theology as a necessary complement to the body of technologia an apparently ideal solution. This kept either concept of reason from waxing too insistent to disturb the balance, and checked all suggestion of conflict. Ideas could indeed be inducted from things, but since man had fallen the book of revelation would take precedence over the book of the creatures as the text in which his most important ideas should be studied; ideas could also be innate in the mind, but since man had fallen the enunciation of them in the Bible was infinitely more reliable than the mutilated version of them in the law of reason. Furthermore, the exemplars of salvation being undeclared at the time nature and reason were created, neither in the sensibles nor in the intellect, neither by the law of nature nor by the light of reason, could the doctrine be discovered. Yet it also remained true that both the ideas collected from things and the ideas sprung up in the soul must have emanated from the single authority of God, who also, upon these proving insufficient, had devised the law of redemption; hence, if there ever seemed to be disagreement between the ideas of nature or of reason and those of revelation, then we could simply drop the whole speculation and depend entirely upon the Bible. Scripture would silence every clamor of imperfection in our philosophy.

New England theologians were therefore certain that whether reason were taken in an Aristotelian or Platonic sense, or used in an equivocal sense that was a little of both and not wholly either, it would not conflict with the Bible. The particular Christian scheme of salvation, the atonement and resurrection, could be read only in the Bible, even though cosmology could be entirely discovered by reason. Theologians of the seventeenth century, as well as those in the eighteenth, advertised that the truths of Christianity "are not contrary *unto,* yet they are *above* Reason," and strove to keep down the number that must be believed without rational comprehension. Meantime they insisted that reason was the handmaid, the support, the instrument of faith, the road to the temple, the interpreter of revelation. "Ratio sana non pugnat cum Theologia," said their textbooks. New Englanders were not alone among seventeenth-century Protestants in their eagerness to assert the coincidence of reason and doctrine; in 1628, at Geneva, the very citadel of Calvin, Nicholaus Vedelius brought out a book entitled, *Rationale Theologicum, seu De Necessitate et Vero usu principiorum rationis ac Philosophiae in controversius theologicis,* stating the position of all Calvinists, that nothing could be retained in theology which was repugnant to true reason. "Theology has much above reason and unknown to reason, but properly speaking and considered in itself, it has nothing contrary to rational truth." Fifty years later men like Owen and Baxter were again asserting, "There is no Contradiction between the natural and supernatural Revelation, or parts of Religion; for God contradicteth not himself." New England theses proclaimed, "The books of Scripture and of the creature are the mines from which this rule is excavated," and young ministers, like Nathaniel Gookin, took their M. A.'s by denying that the precepts of philosophy are contrary to the theological. The only novelty in the New England efforts to harmonize reason and religion was the help rendered by the terminology of technologia. James Fitch took over Richardson's word "prattomenon" to prove that theology fitted onto the shaft of reason as a spearhead on a javelin, "for reason in man acts upon and is conversant about only that Reason which shineth in divine Truth, but Faith is taken up with looking upon the divine goodness in them." It does not follow that reason is of no service to faith; on the contrary, reason, which reads God in the book of the creatures, "is a means to let in a light and good beyond Reason," exactly as "the senses are means to present the Reason in things to the Reason of man, although Reason is above Sense." Thus the action of sense presents to the reason its "prattomenon", and the reason in turn gives to faith its own "prattomenon".

As Reason can use the *Prattomenon* of the Rule of Sense, (namely) that which is effected by it, so Faith can use the *Prattomenon* of the Rule of Reason, that which is effected by it, and yet these are distinct acts, and have distinct Objects, and distinct lights.

The conclusions of sense are taken up by the system of reason, and the doctrine of reason is contained within the doctrine revealed by God. The sphere of reason includes that of sense, theology that of reason, and the three are as concentric circles with larger and larger diameters; the progression from sense to reason to revelation is a gradual and continuous, a jubilant widening of vision.

The efforts of Puritan theologians to harness together their two conceptions of reason, to pretend actually that the two steeds were but one horse, and to hitch them to the chariot of revelation, are amusing enough for the disinterested spectator to watch. In seventeenth-century New England, however, the ministers assumed that they had succeeded, and they put the team to galloping over every terrain that needed exploring. Three subjects in particular invited their survey: ethics, grace, and the interpretation of Scripture. On the matter of ethics, New Englanders for the one and only time rejected the leadership of William Ames, who, as we have noticed, founded morality upon the Bible instead of upon nature and reason, and endeavored to force ethics out of the body of the arts. Yet Ames did not mean that he thought ethics preached another code than did the Bible, any more than mathematics or physics presented laws at variance with revealed precepts. "The moral law of God revealed through Moses is completely the same with that which is said to be inscribed in the hearts of men." The *Medulla* and *De Conscientia* themselves give sufficient precedent for treating ethics as a self-contained system flowing entirely from natural reason or the lessons of ordinary experience. As in the exposition of synteresis, Ames constantly defines natural law as an innate principle; thus in speaking of "natural right," he calls it

> that which is apprehended to be fit to be done or avoided, out of the naturall instinct of Naturall Light; or that which is at least deduced from that Naturall Light by evident Consequence. So that this *Right,* partly consists of *Pratike Principles* knowne by Nature, and partly of *Conclusions* deduc'd from those *Principles.*

So a natural right is an "eternal" law in relation to God because it "is from *Eternity* in *Him,*" and it is natural because "it is ingraffed and imprinted in the *Nature* of man, by the God of *Nature.*" Here, therefore, in the one theologian who was so carried away by his piety as to condemn establishing the moral law upon the evidences of nature and reason, were the very elements of a rational morality and a natural ethic; the one Puritan thinker most jealous for the honor of supernatural revelation could not exalt it at the cost of denying rationality to the law of God.

A thesis of 1687 declared that ethics does not differ from theology, but one in 1670 said that it does; the authorities apparently were unable to make up their minds whether they agreed with Ames or not, but meantime, perhaps to be on the safe side, they taught ethics as a distinct science. Cotton Mather deplored the "Employing of so much Time upon *Ethicks,* in our Colledges" for a "vile Peece of Paganism"; he seems to have been on this score, as fortunately he was on most scores, decidedly in the minority. Four or five textbooks were used at Harvard, all of them versions of Aristotle, and *Theses Ethicae* rehearsed the venerable platitudes of the golden mean and the identity of virtue and happiness. One of the early texts explained that ethics was a body of precepts for honest behavior "which human reason knows is suitable to the natural man and necessary to conserving civil society," and More's *Enchiridion Ethicum,* which came into general use at the end of the century, defined virtue as pursuit of that which is best by right reason, "for that is simply and absolutely best, and is consonant with Divine reason."[5] From the foundation of the colonies the ministers argued that divine injunctions were consonant with right reason, that the crimes which the churches censured could be proved evil by the light of nature as well as by the Bible. Cotton showed the effect of his Ramist training by declaring, "Heathen Law-givers, Philosophers, and Poets have expressed the effect of all the Commandements save the tenth," and would argue that if an offense had been "condemned even amongst the Heathens, by the light of nature," then all the more cause why Christians are "bound to proceed more roundly against such." Thomas Cobbett once remarked that even though he could prove a point from Scripture, still

> a challenge is made, that laying by a little those spirituall weapons of our warfare (which indeed are mighty through God to cast downe all the specious Logismes, reasonings of the sonnes of men against Christ in the doctrine of his free grace . . .) wee should try it out at other weapons, even humane testimonies and authorities.

Puritans were confident that whenever they sallied forth onto the plain of reason the fortress of revelation remained as an impregnable refuge to which they could retreat in case they were worsted in the field; consequently they ventured boldly, and felt that they had done God a particularly valorous service when they defended a truth by their own wit without being forced to take shelter behind His ramparts.

The moral code enforced by statute in New England, as in Geneva and Scotland, was comparatively strict, because the Bible, especially the Old Testament, was taken with devastating literalness. The death penalty for adultery, for instance, was more severe than nations guided solely by the law of nature had thought appropriate. Yet if colonial laws are compared with those on the books of European communities, with those in England at the time, their standards prove generally not to be too far above the prevailing, and their reputation for harshness seems to result rather from the rigor with which they were enforced than from the unreasonableness of their exactions. In any event, the theorists made a concerted effort to prove that the moral regulations of an ideal Christian commonwealth should be wholly compatible with rational and humane conceptions, and in this argument, as in their political theory, bequeathed an important heritage to eighteenth-century America. The doctrine can be seen even in Ames: the law of God, he says, is in effect a specific enactment of the general law of nature, and all civil regulations ought likewise to be derived from universal rules.

> For that is not Law which is not just and right, and that in morality is called Right, which accords with right practicall reason, and Right practicall is the Law of Nature.

Even when desiring to abolish the science of ethics, he explicitly declares that everything in the revealed commandments except the designation of the Sabbath was previously in the law of nature, "nothing . . . which is not so grounded upon right reason, but it may bee solidly defended and maintained by humane discourse, nothing but what may bee well enjoyned from cleere reason." The law of nature had to be specifically reënacted simply because man had fallen; had he remained upright there would have been no need for the extra promulgation; the remains of natural law within us are now "like to some dimme aged picture" which God must retouch "as with a fresh pencill." The masters of New England thought, being Englishmen as well as Puritans, and humanists as well as theologians, could not avoid insisting that the laws of every sovereign, even the most absolute and omnipotent, are in fact the laws of right reason, or at least that they should be the laws of reason. Ames in exile at Franeker forecasts the scaffold at Whitehall in 1649.

The doctrine maintained in New England is best expressed in the works of Thomas Shepard. "Law natural," he asserts, "is part of the law moral." He takes care that his doctrine shall not result in a displacing of divine command by the precepts of nature, as he declares that the natural principles once impressed upon the reason "now, by man's apostasy, are obliterated and blotted out." With this condition premised, he has no hesitancy in arguing that though by His absolute power God might have issued any laws He chose, those which He has voluntarily invested with moral sanctions are exactly those which right reason finds fitting and proper; they are not good merely because He commands them, but He commands them because they are good.

> It is his will and good pleasure to make all laws that are moral to be first good in themselves for all men, before he will impose them upon all men. And hence it is a weakness for any to affirm, that a moral law is not such a law which is therefore commanded because it is good, because (say they) it is not the goodness of the thing, but the sovereign will of God, which makes all things good; for it is the sovereign will of God (as is proved) to make every moral law good, and therefore to command it, rather than to make it good by a mere commanding of it.

In keeping with the tenor of the Ramist dialectic, Shepard asserts that reason perceives what is moral, even though it does not itself determine goodness, exactly "as the wall is white before the eye see it, yet when the eye doth see it, it appears white also." Every theologian in New England thereafter found occasion to expound the coincidence of natural law or the law of reason with the law promulgated on Sinai, until there are times when the reader wonders whether Puritans had not come to regard Biblical dispensation as a corroboration to the conclusions of reason rather than the one true and perfect revelation. In *A Compleat Body of Divinity,* which always summarizes New England opinion, Samuel Willard comes frequently to two conclusions: on the one hand, the ukases of God are always inherently just, even though issued by an absolute sovereign, and on the other, the precepts are presented to man as reasonable duties for rational beings. "All the Commands of God, are highly rational; and because he treats with Men as Reasonable Creatures, he lays matter of Conviction before them, of the Reasonableness of their Obedience."[6]

Ames allowed the Sabbath to remain the one enactment of God entirely "positive", the one demand made by His mere good pleasure and adventitious to the law of nature. Had the Puritans been content to abide by the rules of an all-disposing and arbitrary divinity it does seem that they might have allowed Him to have one duty paid Him for no other reason than that He asked it. They blamed Adam for eating the apple after God had requested him to abstain merely as a token of respect, but they were not able to observe the Sabbath without trying to prove that it was logical. Shepard argued the thesis by reviewing once more the relation of natural law to revealed law; he defined the law of nature as "all that which is agreeable and suitable to natural reason, and that from a natural innate equity in the thing, when it is made known, either by divine instruction or human wisdom, although it be not immediately known by the light of nature." He remarked, in passing, that therefore even if the copy of the law in the heart of man is now blotted, still those who would cast out of theology all consideration of the law of nature, who would find the inward law "both uncertain and impertinent," do "unwarily pull down one of the strongest bulwarks." He then ran through a series of subtle logical demonstrations to prove at last that the determination of the Sabbath and its observance by man is "both suitable and congruous to natural reason and equity," that it is "according to the light of nature, even of corrupt nature." Once more, the absolute power of God and the law of reason "may kiss each other, and are not to be opposed one to another." That there were dangers of too great a rationalistic emphasis in the argument does not seem to have been suspected by any, until in the first decade of the eighteenth century Jeremiah Dummer came home from Europe and delivered his trial sermon on the then well-worn theme of the rationality of the Sabbath. His discourse would seem to us a thoroughly legitimate extension of the thesis asserted in the 1640's by Thomas Shepard, but he put it much more decisively; if even the Sabbath is an institution of reason, Dummer declared, then although the Deity is omnipotent, had He commanded anything contrary to reason, "it would have been an infinite stain and blemish on his unspotted purity." For his authorities, Dummer quoted Aristotle, Plato, Cicero, Selden, and Grotius, "most of whom I consulted on this occasion, when I had leisure, and opportunity in *Holland*." Dummer's sermon seems to me one of the most important marks of the "transition" in early New England thought; it shows us, as it were, the "Age of Reason" in the very act of emerging from the "Age of Faith," and the fact that he so trenchantly revealed the hidden rationalism in the Puritan doctrine may account for the further fact that no church would offer him a call to its pulpit.

As the doctrine of divine grace was expounded in New England certain modifications were gradually introduced which can be accounted for only as contagions from the doctrine of reason, and even before New England was settled the divines did not always describe grace as I have paraphrased them in the chapters on the piety. They never forgot the fundamentals of the doctrine, and it would be easy to gather statements from the late seventeenth century which still express the piety, which still show grace as something far different in kind from all natural principles and absolutely necessary to carry the soul to God. Yet along with such passages there are an equal number, growing more plenteous as the century progresses, in which grace is described not as a flash of supernal light blinding the recipient, but as a reinvigoration of capacities already existing by nature in the unregenerate soul. John Preston was probably as much responsible as any for setting the example; in the ruins of a palace, runs one of his favorite metaphors, the materials still exist, but the "order" is taken away. Grace reëstablishes the order by rebuilding with the same materials; grace is a supernatural power working with the natural "arguments" and realigning them according to the laws of "method". Or as he has it in another image, natural promptings—passions and desires—are like the wind, holiness is the rudder: "So Nature, the strength of nature, affections, or whatsoever they be, are like the wind to drive the ship, thou mayst retaine them, only godlinesse must sit at the Sterne." Once infused into the soul, grace itself becomes "natural", just as when a man has learned anything he was not born knowing, "as to play on a Lute, or any other Art,' the practice of it becomes, as we say, "second nature" to him; "so is this, it is planted in the heart, as the senses are, it is infused into the Soule, and then we exercise the operations of it; so that it is another Nature, it is just as the thing that is naturall." In Preston's sermons conversion is not prostration on the road to Damascus, but reason elevated. It is the sight of existing truths, exactly as a telescope is the revelation of new stars:

Faith is but the lifting up of the understanding, by adding a new light to them and it: and therefore they are said to be *revealed,* not because they were not before, as if the revealing of them gave a being unto them; but even as a new light in the night discovers to us that which we did not see before, and as a prospective glasse reveales to the eye, that which we could not see before, and by its owne power, the eye could not reach unto.

Faith is like logic: it enables men to perceive arguments and to form axioms. It does not demand acquiescence in irrationalities, but empowers us to believe thoroughly that which we find reasonable, it is not intoxication but education, not ecstasy but, in the academic sense of the word, a discipline. Logic demonstrates that "naturall things, such as *God* did not reveale *himselfe,*" which "lye before us," can be found by reason; when the exemplars are not revealed through things but through the words of God, we have faith instead of knowledge, but in either case the machinery of apprehension is the same, the mechanism of dialectic and technologia. There is reason in every article of faith as well as in the rules of art, "you can give a reason of it."

Faith addeth to the eye of reason, and raiseth it higher; for the understanding is conversant, as about things of reason, so also about things of Faith; for they are propounded to the understanding, only they are above it and must have faith to reveale them . . . As one that hath dimme eyes, he can see better with the help of Spectacles: even so doth the eye of reason, by a supernaturall faith infused. So that all the things which we beleeve, have a credibilitie and entitie in them, and they are the objects of the understanding; but we cannot find them out, without some supernaturall help.

The burden of Preston's sermon runs, "therefore faith teacheth nothing contrary to sense and reason"; man fallen and then regenerated is not either lowered or raised in the great chain of being, he "hath reason to guide him, and hee hath grace to guide reason." Not only does reason coincide with faith, but so also does the evidence of the senses, and the direct "invention" of particular "arguments" through the senses is given all the theological sanction needed:

Of all demonstrations of reason that we have to prove things, nothing is so firme as that which is taken from sense: to prove the fire is hot, we feele it hot, or honey to be sweet, when we taste it to be sweet: There is no reason in the world makes it so firme as sense: As it is true in these cases, so it is an undoubted truth in Divinity, that in all matters of sense, sense is a competent judge.

The unity of knowledge, demonstrated formally in technologia, was based emotionally upon the Puritan conviction that in God's universe "sense and reason are Gods workes as well as grace" and that "one worke of God doth not destroy another."

The faith preached in early New England was not a violent convulsion of the camp-meeting, but an exercise under divine guidance of invention and judgment, perception and reason, sapience and, above all, prudence.

Thomas Hooker, the most eloquent in portraying the abasement of sinful man and the soul's longing for peace and reconciliation, yet insisted that the much-desired grace was not a new faculty in the soul, but was "rather an assisting power," working upon the faculties already there. After grace sweeps away the obstructions of sin, "the coast is now clear that reason may be heard." Shepard declared that God does not work upon believers "as upon blocks or brute creatures," propelling them by an immediate influence, because believers are rational creatures. John Davenport preached in *The Saints Anchor-Hold* that faith is a sure anchorage because it is "an understanding grace"; when God gives us faith, "then faith seeth good reason that we should hope in him," and thus it "useth reason, though not as the ground, yet as a sanctified instrument, to find out Gods grounds." By the first years of the eighteenth century it had become common in New England to describe faith as that which "makes the law of nature more legible." Puritanism, for all its piety, for all its hunger and thirst after salvation, never doubted that the life of the elect was the life of reason, and so could never, in its earnest struggle for regeneration, let go its intellectual heritage.

Men in the seventeenth century did not see the dangers ahead, the possibility that such descriptions of faith in the terms of right reason and the rational rule of "eupraxia" could give rise to a naturalistic morality and a belief that education would achieve everything usually ascribed to grace, because they were convinced that theology would remain forever the norm of reason. Baxter and Owen denied the charge of the fideists, that Protestantism would lead to skepticism or to rationalism, by asserting the fundamental principle of all Protestantism: "the Scripture determines all things necessary unto Faith and Obedience, and . . . in that determination ought all men to acquiess." Owen held it impossible for reason to eclipse faith, for it would therefore overthrow not only faith but itself, "there being nothing more irrational, than that belief should be the product of Reason, being properly an assent resolved into Authority, which if Divine, is so also." What Owen could not foresee was the implication of his phrase, "which if Divine," for the only way by which Puritans could prove the divine authority of Scripture was by reason. Because of their untroubled assurance that faith and reason agreed, Puritan theologians were ready so to prove the Bible, and to interpret it by deductions according to reason's laws articulated in dialectic. The disciples of Ramus could not rest their belief in the divine inspiration of the Bible solely upon an inward conviction in the hearts of the pious. They insisted on adducing "additional" testimonies from reason and history, never dreaming that they were taking the first faltering steps toward what ultimately became the "higher" criticism. Preston argued that the reliability of Scripture chronicles was proved not merely by the inspiration of their narrators, but by their agreement with heathen historians, and to bear out the Old Testament he cited Alexander Polyhistor, Josephus, Cyril, "Chaldee Historians," Diodorus Siculus, Strabo, Xenophon, and "The Table of *Ptolomy,* lately founded." In 1687 Samuel Lee submitted the evidence to a more searching analysis, and concluded that there were eight rationally convincing proofs of Biblical authority, such as its antiquity, its style, the fulfillment of its oracles, and its miracles. Fortunately he had no premonitions of the day in Puritan history when, after his proofs had one by one been abandoned, the last of them, the miracles, would dissolve under the gentle scrutiny of a Harvard Divinity School Address.

Ramist logicians were always convinced that their dialectic was admirably suited for theological study. The New Englanders' devotion to it was a consequence of its already having been firmly allied with reformed doctrine. Ramus' disciples examined the Bible and found it written according to Ramist principles; some of them edited the *Dialecticae* with illustrations of the logical places and figures supplied by Scripture instead of by Cicero and Virgil.[7] William Temple gave an object lesson of its serviceableness to exegesis in a study of twenty psalms, published in 1605. The end of logic, he says in his preface, is "use"; it should teach us to contrive the frame of a discourse and to present "in the pure naturals not onely the seuerall members, but the particular structure and conformation of the same." Logic can give us the arguments for clearing a cause, direct us to that which is true, disclaim that which is inconsequent, and marshal each thing in its proper rank and place. The real meaning of the Word of God, as the real meaning of the arts themselves, will be forthcoming if the Word of God is studied by the true method; by analysis Scripture "is stripped as it were of all outward habit, and laid forth in the first and naturall lineaments."[8] The masters of New England thought, particularly William Ames, had shown New Englanders how to resolve Scripture logically, and according to the golden rules of Ramus.[9] That the Puritans would give logical formulation to their piety was inevitable because they were men of the Renaissance, but that they should have had such enormous confidence in logic came from their participation in the Ramist reform, and in particular from their being disciples of Richardson and Ames. They eagerly undertook to extract hidden meanings from the Bible in absolute certainty that the method was infallible. "Wisdome lyes in the *Rational Application* of general Rules of Scripture to our selves and our own conditions, and in the *induction of particulars,* and due Reasoning from it." Later ages have remembered Puritanism as the creed of total depravity and overwhelming grace, but there was another tenet which historians have generally forgotten:

> *A Scripture consequence; is a Trueth evidently & necessarily arising out of a proposition, held forth therein in express termes;* So that: if the doctrine conteined in the proposition held forth in express termes be true, then is the doctrine conteined therein by consequence, also true . . . The greatest part of

Scripture-trueth is revealed in Scripture-consequences. Yea many fundamentall trueths are not held forth in express termes, but by manifest consequence.[10]

There are many admonitions in the writings and sermons against "wresting" a text, against finding conclusions which it will not support, but there is also no observation more frequent than "Whatsoever is drawn out of the Scripture by just consequence and deduction, is as well the word of God, as that which is an expresse Commandment or Example in Scripture." The ministers will say, "To preferre the invention of Man before the wisedome of God were sacrilegious madnesse," but they will also say, with no sense of inconsistency, "A just deduct from the Scripture is of equall force with an expresse command." Cotton explained to his church that a preacher "speaks not the expresse words of the Scripture, but comments and explications of the Scriptures," and for that very reason the congregation must be on its guard, always ready to use "the Scripture as a rule to measure all the Sermon by." But sermons were constructed by the laws of logic, and the Scripture rule by which Cotton would have them tested was a logical interpretation of Scripture, so that his admonition amounted to the grave advice that logic should be a rule by which to measure logic.

The preachers would often explain that the light of nature is not "furnisht with ability to dive into the wonders of Gods love, or the deep mysteries of his Gospel in order to Salvation," although the use of reason should not therefore be laid aside, which properly exercised consists in "drawing Logical or Rational consequences from Scripture Assertions." Like other controversialists of the Reformation, they had become familiar with the perversity of human reason when hearing themselves charged with what their enemies considered the logical consequences of their positions, and they had joined the general cry that because reason was deceptive nobody ought to be held responsible for what others deduced from his assertions. When defending the Puritan creed against George Keith, Samuel Willard warned against making human reason the measure of divine truth; there are many passages in Scripture which "surpass our power to see through them, which yet we are to believe." But when delivering sermons on the *Compleat Body* at the Old South, unhampered by the necessities of polemic, Willard more serenely declared that the manifold uses or inferences which can be drawn from a text "are not a new sense, but consequences contained in it." The two statements are not necessarily exclusive, and yet they suggest attitudes that do not exactly accord; the first is Augustinian piety, as I have been using the phrase, but the second is—well, something for which the word "rationalism" is not too distant a term. There were critics of Puritanism in the seventeenth century who were at least partially aware of the second point of view; one Anglican writer found John Cotton saying that nothing should be practiced in church polity that could not be maintained *"rationibus cogentibus,"* and replied in amazement that if ecclesiastical laws and customs were submitted to "this feracious and pregnant *Plebiscite,*" more than the hierarchy of the Church of England would eventually be called into question, even the authority of Scripture and "the power of Kings and Monarchs with their Crownes and dignityes." Puritans were probably not unwilling that the power of kings, or at least the power of the King of England, should be called before their "feracious" plebiscite, but that they were committing an enormity in proving the authority of Scripture or interpreting it by dialectical demonstration they constantly denied. It was not possible in the weirdest of their dreams that dialectic could ever *dis*-prove the authority of the Bible, or interpret away its divinity, for the spoken Word of God was itself accommodated to the forms of logic. It was designed to be read by those who understood dialectic. Because the essence of God must remain hidden, the revealed utterances must be phrased in the language of earth:

And that is in the way of created humane Reason . . . It is impossible for us to know or understand things, but by some rule of reason or other. Reason is nothing else but the manner of a Being, whereby it is acted upon our Understanding. We know nothing of God but by putting some Logical Notion upon him. All things are conveyed to us in a Logical way, and bear some stamp of reason upon them, or else we should know nothing of them. Hence God, to fit his discovery of himself to our manner of entertaining it, takes the Rational or Logical Arguments upon himself, admits of a Distinction or a Description, utters Sentences or Actions about himself, speaks of himself as if he were an Effect & had Causes; a Subject and had Adjuncts . . . And this tells us how useful & necessary reason is to Faith; it being an instrument which is used to convey the discoveries of God unto it; and therefore Faith doth not relinquish or cast off reason; for there is nothing in Religion contrary to it, tho' there are many things that do transcend, and must captivate it. Religion is the wisdom of God, which cannot cross it self, & reason lisps out something to Faith, though this entertains more than reason is able to express.

This rich passage of Willard's vibrates with all the implications I have been endeavoring to capture in the last three chapters; it is an epitome of the Puritan theory of logic, of knowledge and of reason; founded upon the dialectic of Ramus, growing out of the technologia of Richardson and Ames, it catches precisely the elusive quality of Puritan rationalism, and might be taken for the text of still longer lectures than these upon the relations of faith and reason in Puritan philosophy. It embodies the characteristic, the deeply rooted conception of divine action, the sense of an infinite deity who has voluntarily limited Himself, taken upon Himself to be the "arguments" of our discourse, who has chosen to speak the Word that was with God and that was God in the form of the word of reason. Above all it illustrates the paradoxical consequences in practical life of the doctrine of total depravity, for though starting from the sad reflection that God has been forced to supply revelation to fallen man in order to save him from destruction, it emerges with the astonishingly cheerful discovery that once God began speaking with man, He was obliged to declare Himself in the forms of logic congenial to the human mind. God paid the highest compliment to a rationality in His creature which even the fall and centuries of sin could not extinguish. The passage helps to show, therefore, that while piety determined the cast of thought in New England, yet the particulars over which the cast was spread were found in the Bible through the applications of logic. God Himself "hath left some things to be sought out, and found by search, that so our understandings may be exercised, and our rational faculties employed about spiritual things." The Puritans may have looked upon man as a worm, as a depraved and sinful creature, but they also defined him as "a reasonable Creature, . . . able to draw inferences from inferences." They often said, "Our Saviour Christ hath taught us how to argue"; the historian, accustomed to the more conventional attributions of the "source study" method, may at first be prompted to counter that all the evidence of Puritan writing, education, and intellectual history goes to show that Puritans were taught to argue not by Christ but by Ramus, Richardson, and Ames. Yet he pauses just long enough to remember that these men were spokesmen for Protestantism and for the Renaissance, and that by appealing to the Bible both reformers and humanists did indeed seem to discover new ways of arguing, and that out of the consequent debates came, at the end of the seventeenth century, a general movement toward rehabilitation of the natural reason. Remembering these things, the historian is more content to let the Puritans' own ascription of their intellectual indebtedness stand as at least a half-truth, even though he does not often perceive an essential similarity between Puritan ways of arguing and the arguments of the New Testament.

CHAPTER VIII

NATURE

The God of Puritanism was both sovereign and wise. His attributes were so balanced that He could be at one and the same time the object of worship and the source of knowledge. The same balance was therefore thought to be extended into the realm of nature, for God's works must reflect His perfections, and the created universe must be at once the result of His decree and of His thought. It must incarnate His will and also embody the platform of His ideas. Religious doctrine and the vast accumulated store of the intellectual heritage met again in the Puritan theory of nature as they did in the theory of reason. The fusion created still further difficulties, for the New England parson was required to maintain a unified theory that would meet the requirements of both his piety and his logic; he had to force the natural universe to disclose God's supremacy in the wonderful disposition and control of all its affairs, and yet to hold it faithful to some settled order of ideas so that a consistent system of arguments might be collected from it. In the first years of the century Puritans studied physics from such textbooks as that of Alsted, in which were inextricably mingled the conceptions of arbitrary rule and rational order. "Nature is order and the connection of causes with effects in the world, which is perfect, made by the perfect, best, and most wise," declared Alsted; and then added in the next breath, with what seemed the essence of logic to the Puritan mind, that *therefore,* by the very fact that it is order, nature is the "ordinary power of God." At the end of the century Samuel Willard said, "When God wrought the works of Creation, he had a Design in every Creature"; He displayed His infinite wisdom in this design by adapting one creature to another, and His omnipotence by making all subserve His own intent. Puritan thought, in short, presupposed a natural framework in which arbitrary power was confined within inviolable order, yet in which the order was so marvelously contrived that all divinely avowed ends were swiftly accomplished.

At the time of New England's beginnings, the Puritan divines were not aware of latent difficulties in their theory of nature. They could hardly have realized the possibility of conflict between two conceptions because they could not have understood that two separate conceptions were involved. They spoke habitually of seeing God's power in the order of the universe and His wisdom in its government; it was all one to them whether nature proclaimed the power or the wisdom. "The Excellent *Order,* wherein all things are preserved, abundantly argues a God whose *Kingdom Ruleth* all." Consequently, Puritan philosophy commenced its career in America with an unperturbed confidence that even to the most sinful of men the constitution of the universe was of itself sufficient warrant for many profound truths of religion, for the nature of God and the worship which was due Him. The Puritan was no more troubled with apprehensions that naturalism would usurp the authority of revelation than he was with fears that rationalism would ever crowd out supernatural grace. Just as the Scripture was required in technologia to supplement the natural sources of truth, so in science it was needed to supplement physics, and no one could be saved by what he learned from the book of nature alone. "Tho' there is never a leaf in this Book, but hath something of God written legibly upon it, and many Characters of his Divine power, wisdom, and goodness there engraven; yet all this will leave a man short of the saving knowledge of him." With these cautions observed, the Puritans had no distrust of natural theology; it was indeed a very necessary part of their completed theory, for to deny the possibility that God could be known through the visible creation was to endanger cosmic optimism, the indispensable premise of all Puritan belief. "The creatures are good, as they come out of Gods hand," John Davenport asserted. Sinful man might indeed make them vain by abusing them, and when they are idolized, they degenerate into nothingness, but Puritanism did not, for it could not, thereupon forbid examination and even reverence of them. However depraved man might be, he must still be capable of perceiving the more obvious attributes of God from even the most casual familiarity with the universe in which he lives. "Goe into the world," Hooker commanded, "and view the height of its glory, and then conclude, If the *Creature* be thus excellent, what must the *Creator* be?" Puritanism believed sincerely that man had fallen, but in Puritan theory his lapse could never be construed as so complete a debacle that he was no longer capable of drawing deductions concerning the nature and immaculate goodness of his creator from the evidence of his senses.

Hence the textbooks used in New England all devoted chapters to natural theology. The creatures, said Alsted in the great *Encyclopaedia,* are a glass in which we perceive the one art which fashions all the world, they are subordinate arguments and testimonies of the most wise God, pages of the book of nature, ministers and apostles of God, the vehicles and the way by which we are carried to God. "A genuine reading of the book of nature is an ascension to the mind of God, both theoretical and practical." But more important than any textbook in determining the attitude of New England Puritans toward the theology of nature was the teaching of the much revered John Preston, in whose works so large an emphasis was given to the subject as to suggest that in the early seventeenth century there were particular reasons why Puritans should be obsessed with it. Even while he is declaring that something more is necessary to man than the deductions of natural wit, Preston does not view them as antagonistic to faith. Even though natural faculties are sadly decayed by the fall, yet within the sphere of demonstration the evidence of the senses is sound. Calvin had condemned all human industry, understanding, and faculties, saying, "we cannot conceive or meditate anything that is right in the sight of God," but Preston, and the Puritans after him, declared that by the experience of the senses certain right conclusions might be reached, even though they would not by themselves lead to salvation. Preston, in fact, comes startlingly close to agreeing at times with Lord Herbert of Cherbury; all that the *De Veritate* says man may know by the unassisted use of reason the Puritan author would admit:

> . . . . when such a man knowes there is an almighty power, by his naturall wit, hee is able to deduce, if there be a God, I must behave my selfe well towards him, I must feare him as God, I must be affected to him as God, I must worship him with all reverence as God; but the most ignorant man confesses there is a God, no Nation denyes it.

No nation can deny it, for "The heavens are the worke of his hands, and they declare it, and every man understands their language." Preston's sermons celebrate the "sweet consent and harmony the creatures have among themselves," "the great and orderly provision, that is made for all things." He concludes again and again, "When a man lookes on the great volume of the world, there those things which God will have known, are written in capitall letters, and such letters as every one may understand and reade." Quite apart from faith there are two important sources of truth to which man has immediate access—the remains of God's image within him and the world of his experience. Though science will not save, yet it will show us the same God who speaks in revelation:

> For, though I said before, that Divinity was revealed by the *Holy Ghost,* yet there is this difference in the points of *Theologie:* Some truths are wholly revealed, and have no foot-steps in the creatures, no prints in the creation, or in the works of *God,* to discerne them by, and such are all the mysteries of the

Gospel, and of the *Trinitie:* other truths there are, that have some *vestigia,* some Characters stamped upon the creature, whereby we may discerne them, and such is this which we now have in hand, that, *There is a God.*

Life indeed is vanity, says the Puritan preacher—but not entirely, for as Preston insists, "The workes of Nature are not in vaine."

Preston was exceptional among Puritan preachers chiefly for the eloquence with which he celebrated the charms of natural theology, not for the recognition he accorded it. In his more pedestrian fashion, Ames had said in the *Medulla* that a natural worship was possible, and that even were there no revealed law, yet by the contemplation of nature we might, "the grace of God helping us, perceive al those things which in this behalfe pertaines unto our duty." New England theologians were, like Preston, inclined to bestow passing acknowledgment upon the insufficiency of natural knowledge for salvation and then hasten to declare its value none the less great; often they seem to have forgotten Ames's qualification: "the grace of God helping us." They eloquently hailed the beauties of nature as evidences of God's being:

Can we, when we behold the stately theater of heaven and earth, conclude other but that the finger, arms, and wisdom of God hath been here, although we see not him that is invisible, and although we know not the time when he began to build? Every creature in heaven and earth is a loud preacher of this truth. Who set those candles, those torches of heaven, on the table? Who hung out those lanterns in heaven to enlighten a dark world? . . . Who taught the birds to build their nests, and the bees to set up and order their commonwealth?

In the midst of a sermon upon the other world a Puritan preacher pauses to remark that even this world is "a curious and costly piece . . . the surface of it is in the Summer-season clothed with a pleasant dress, delightful to the sense, and profitable for use." The profit might be as much emphasized as the delight, and the pleasant dress admired as much for its didactic uses as for its delectability, but nevertheless it was seen and appreciated. There was always a place in New England theology for the doctrines that men learned, or could learn, from nature. In Puritan discourses the phrase "light of nature," like the phrase "light of reason," has a double connotation: it means both the innate light that gives men naturally the glimmering ideas which in their perfection once constituted the image of God, and the body of ideas gathered from the physical universe by induction and observation. Taking the light of nature to mean either the inward light of intuition or the external light of creation, the Puritan held that though dimmed by the clouds of sin, it still gleamed not ineffectually. "And tho' Man's Apostacy hath greatly beclouded his Reason, and the exercise of it upon this account, yet those Principles are rooted in him, and cannot be totally obliterated." As long as he lives at all, as long as he is able to sustain his existence and deduce one thing from another, man must be able to apprehend some of the invisible things of God from the visible world. "If a man comes to a Place where he finds many Houses, and some of them stately Buildings," even though he sees no occupant, he must conclude that other men have been there; and so when he looks upon the world, upon the sun in the firmament and the innumerable stars, some of which being, "as Astronomers Conjecture," greater than the sun, he must perforce conclude, "Surely then there is an Eternal God to be the Creator of these things."

Certainly the very last conclusion he should draw was that he had no business concerning himself with what astronomers conjecture. Granted that knowledge of science was not saving knowledge, still when so much was to be gained from contemplating the works of God, there should be no restraints upon the study. This conclusion, by no means an original one with Puritans, but a venerable and often defended contention of patristic and medieval theologians, was reasserted firmly and unhesitatingly in New England. Science was not merely tolerated because faith was believed to be secure whatever physics or astronomy might teach, but it was actually advanced as a part of faith itself, a positive declaration of the will of God, a necessary and indispensable complement to Biblical revelation. There would be little difficulty in excerpting passages from New England writings which would seem to deny this statement; the sermons are full of injunctions to give over dwelling upon the creature and to concentrate on the eternal verities, and "schollers" are warned that they should not overvalue the knowledge which they have from natural objects. We shall not heal the crooked perversity of our natures by learning about the creation, says John Cotton, and therefore philosophers are generally "more averse and backward to embrace the Gospel then the common sort." Knowledge of the passing away of one generation after another shows us our mortality and misery, but gives us no relief; the heavens and earth are divine creations, but tell us nothing of divinity unless the spirit of God bears witness in them. Yet when he speaks in this vein without qualification, Cotton is commenting upon the Book of Ecclesiastes, and driving home the moral that all is vanity. There can be no doubt that his more considered opinion is found in another sermon, where his text called for comment upon the feasibility of predicting fair weather from the aspect of the sky at sunset or sunrise. Here he expounds the meteorological theories of the time, but reminds his listeners that these theories are incapable of establishing the invariable sequence of signs and weather. "Every man that observes them to bee evident, yet findes them not alwaies certain: And those that are best able to discerne the reason, and the naturall causes are not able to say, that event hath and will alwayes follow; but both these may fall short of an answerable successe." Thereupon he moralizes in conventional Puritan fashion that the providence of God and not the natural cause determines every event, including the weather, and even asserts that if the signs were infallible indicators of sun or rain, "and the reasons were evident," still a man should think first of his salvation. It is the nature of hypocrisy and atheism "to bee very quick sighted in points of nature, but very dull and heavy in matters of Religion and grace." Then, having guarded himself against hypocrisy and atheism, Cotton turns his argument at last serenely and surely to another conclusion than that to which he seems to have been tending, and after making sure that nature shall not be studied as an end in itself, he endorses the study of nature as a noble and legitimate occupation. For if a man looks upon the world, not as a self-contained machine, but as "a mappe and shaddow of the spirituall estate of the soules of men," then he may lawfully make observation of the weather and the face of the sky. "Our Saviour doth not reproove it in them, but onely reprooves this, in that they were better skilled in the face of the sky, and signes of the weather, then in the signes of the times . . . Hee rejects not such kind of conjectures, there is a workemanship of God in them, nor doth hee mislike the study of nature." So, even in his commentary upon Ecclesiastes, after many pages denouncing that sort of study which aims at finding felicity solely in nature, he turns about and declares, "To study the nature and course, and use of all Gods works, is a duty imposed by God upon all sorts of men; from the King that sitteth upon the Throne to the Artificer." There is "a setled order in this variety of changes, as in the motions of the Heavens," and it is the duty of the pious man to find it out if he can.

Cotton was here repeating the accepted conclusion of educated Protestantism, and the textbooks were full of precisely such injunctions. Girolamo Zanchius' *De Operibus Dei intra spacium sex dierum creatis opus,* which supplied the arguments for more than one Harvard disputation, declared that there could be nothing more worthy or suitable to the human soul than meditation upon the most beautiful and ample theater of this world, or nothing more unworthy and unsuitable than that the mind of man—by nature designed for study and knowledge, and for this purpose supplied with organs and faculties—should be constrained from its high destiny and imprisoned in ignorance of the laws of God:

> And this is the end and use of the knowledge of natural things, as they are established by God and embellished with so many excellent virtues: namely, that from the knowledge of them, we mount to knowledge and admiration of God. Therefore the usefulness is not small, which knowledge of natural things, considered piously and prudently, carries to the minds of the pious. For so our nature is constituted after sin, that, just as from ignorance of the true principles of the world and of things, and from inexperience of the nature of

them, we live in many errors against God and in many false superstitions; So conversely from true knowledge of these things we are advanced not a little to true piety.

Morton taught that "'tis naturall Theology, that men should be industrious in naturall Phylosophy,"[1] and Willard distinguished between opinion, which is mere conjecture, and science, wherein "we discover, and conclude of necessary effects from necessary Causes, & necessary causes from necessary effects." He and all true Puritans were certain that try as man will, he can never achieve perfect science about contingent events, for "there are so many casualties in the over-ruling Providence of God, that may check and over-bear this"; yet as in theology there are some immovable truths based upon revelation, so in physics there are some undeniable principles based upon the constancy of nature, such as "all natural Causes and effects, as when we say the Sun shines, Man is a reasonable Creature." There is a wide sphere of natural knowledge in which certainty can be attained, and in that sphere man should labor freely to attain it.

From the particular terms in which Puritans justified or rationalized the study of nature, certain characteristics of their science inevitably resulted. That it should be didactic is obvious. No matter what facts were observed, whether through microscopes or telescopes, they must have been ordained in the providence of God, and if any hypothesis explained them, it must necessarily have preëxisted as a law in the archetypal pattern of God. But not only were the general conclusions of physics and chemistry looked upon as emblems of God's wisdom; every single fact was a symbol, not only of the law governing things, but of the laws of the spirit. It is truly strange that the generation of Emerson and Alcott should have had to go to Emmanuel Swedenborg for a doctrine of "correspondence", since something remarkably like it had been embedded in their own tradition for two hundred years. Young Elnathan Chauncy copied into his notebooks from Samuel Purchas the truism, "There is no creature but may teach a good soule one step toward his creator," while Cotton, as we have seen, blessed the study of nature when nature was viewed as "a mappe and shaddow of the spirituall estate of the soules of men." Every particular creature was held to contain a moral import over and above the scientific laws of its particular nature, and while a Christian should study the laws, he should endeavor to "spiritualize the most Earthly objects that are before him," because there are "Numberless Lessons of *Morality,* which by the Help of the *Analogy* between the *Natural* and *Spiritual* World . . . we may learn from them." Cotton Mather indulged this penchant for allegorizing to the point of absurdity, finding the symbol of a hypocrite in a piece of leather thrown into the fire, and of the damned in the dead coals, or even a *memento mori* when he urinated against the same wall with a dog. Cotton Mather's eccentricities are of value chiefly because they illustrate extravagantly the qualities which his contemporaries possessed to a less bizarre extent, and the habit, which becomes tiresome in him, was kept within the bounds of good taste and imaginative perception by other preachers. The disposition to read sermons in brooks and morals in stones seems thereby to have become ingrained in the New England nature, and to have persisted as a habit beyond the demise of Puritan theology, until it could at length be transmuted into art by Nathaniel Hawthorne or given new philosophic expression in Emerson's assertions that "The laws of moral nature answer to those of matter as face to face in a glass," that the correspondence between mind and matter is not fancied by some poet, "but stands in the will of God, and so is free to be known by all men."

Yet if the Puritan theory of nature was hindered from viewing things as they are by the desire to behold moral lessons in them, it also set up a thoroughly utilitarian standard. Since nature was seen as the revelation of God's will in action, then whatever necessity dictated or opportunity offered could be justified on the grounds that it had been decreed by God, and whatever would work could be held to that extent ordained from on high. If Transcendentalism has roots in the Puritan past, so also has pragmatism. Samuel Mather declared that it was easy "to distinguish between such necessary things, and things indifferent; whereof there is no necessity neither from Gods Institution, nor from the nature of the things themselves." The conception that what is necessary from the nature of things is also a command of God substantiated many other Puritan ideas, such as that man while in the world must live by the laws of the world, that he must be a social animal as well as an immortal soul, that while upon this earth he must labor for his sustenance and improve all opportunities for increasing his store of creature comforts. John Dunton is not the most reliable witness that can be quoted in illustration of Puritan *mores,* but at any rate he avers that a Boston maiden, riding with him to Ipswich, assured him that "Platonick love" was of no worth at all since it was of no use.

For my part . . . whene'er I love, I will propose some End in doing it; for that which has no End, appears to me but the Chimera of a Distempered Brain: And what end can there be in love of Different Sexes, but Enjoyment? And yet Enjoyment quite spoils the Notion of Platonick Love: You must excuse me therefore . . . if I . . . declare my self against it, and oppose real Fruition, in your Platonick Notion.

If Mistress Comfort had been speaking by the book, she as a good Puritan would have insisted that love between the sexes should have procreation rather than enjoyment as its ultimate end, but her condemnation of the "Platonick" was otherwise orthodox logic.

The Puritan conception of nature also throws much light upon the connotation with which the word "beauty" was invested. Jonathan Mitchell praises the fruits of the earth because they are delightful to the sense and profitable for use; the Puritan mind was not yet capable of separating the delight from the utility. Beauty was conceived by the theologian in the truly Platonic sense; beauty was not a separable quality or an object existing by itself, but the perfection and congruence of one thing with another. It was synonymous with the good and the true. It was order and efficiency, it was beauty as applied to handicrafts and not to the fine arts. The beautiful object was the dish or the sword handle, not the statue or the poem. Preston said that beauty "consists in a conformity of all the parts," and that wherever there is not a concurrence of all constituents "Beauty is dissolved." Sin was ugly in the Puritan view for this reason, that it defaced "the beautiful frame, and that sweet correspondence and orderly usefulness the Lord first implanted in the order of things." Therefore the Puritan aesthetics contributed to cosmic optimism, because beauty "lyeth in three things met together. 1. The integrity of all the parts, none lacking or superfluous . . . 2. The symmetry or fit proportion of al the members to one another. 3. The good complexion, or colours of them al." In the *Confessions* Augustine had long before come to a similar conclusion: "And I marked and perceived that in bodies themselves there was a beauty from their forming a kind of whole, and another from mutual fitness, as one part of the body with its whole, or a shoe with a foot." This was the insight which nature could give, and this was the criterion which the natural man, even though unassisted by special illumination, even though deformed by sin, could arrive at by the study of the world, and by which he could judge the full enormity of his own deviation from the beautiful.

Therefore, though no man could achieve redemption by such insight, he could yet learn enough to perceive the justice of his condemnation. He could see that such a being as himself, lacking in integrity, marring the symmetry of the whole, spoiling the good complexion of the universe, deserved reprobation unless the redeeming loveliness of divine grace could bring him back into the beautiful frame, the sweet orderliness and usefulness, of the original plan of creation. Here was indeed a triumph in justifying God's ways to man! The knowledge supplied by nature was enough, whatever its limitations, to make men responsible. Because grace did not of itself teach any new truths, did not deliver any doctrines comprehensible exclusively to the elect, anyone could therefore grasp the essential principles. "There is no Truth we deliver to you, but an unregenerate man may understand it wholly, and distinctly, and may come to some measure of approbation." Consequently, though by understanding alone no man will be saved, any man can understand from nature that things have an eternal fitness, and he cannot plead ignorance to excuse his failure to contribute to the harmony of creation.

It is true, a man hath not power to performe these, but yet withall, I say, he hath power to doe those things, upon neglect of which, God denyes him ability to beleeve and repent: So that, it is true, though a man cannot beleeve and repent, and neverthelesse for this is condemned; yet withall take this with you, there be many precedent Acts, which a man hath in his liberty to doe, or not to doe, by which he tyes God, and deserves this Iustly, that God should leave him to himselfe, and deny him ability of beleeving and repenting.

The Puritans found it helpful, even necessary, to insist anew that as far as classical sages had gone, their teachings were parallel to divine revelation; the maintenance of Christianity paradoxically called for an appropriation of the morality of Seneca and Plutarch, while demanding the damnation of Seneca and Plutarch. The Gentiles must be proved to have known so much of God's law that "their own reason might condemn them." The defense of supernatural revelation and the necessity for supernatural grace required first of all the establishment of certain "common Principles in the Light of Nature, that are practical and improvable by humane reason, in the observation of the Works of Creation and Providence." Thus all unregenerated men could be required by the light of these common principles to judge themselves guilty and to acquiesce in the beauty of God's decrees.

The employment of nature as symbol or as doctrine was for the Puritan mind much more important than the choice of which particular system of physics was used to explain nature. The universe was to be studied and expounded because it was the providence of God in operation; the essential requirements for the study of physics were a disposition to see God's hand in events, a perception of the identity of natural order and divine decree, an ability to read the analogy between spiritual law and natural laws, and a faith in the fundamental perfection of the plan of creation. These were the goals of Puritan thinking in the natural sciences; there was only incidental concern about whether the universe were expounded according to the old or the new astronomy, whether by Peripatetic or Newtonian physics. If the religious and theological interests were protected as much by the one as by the other, then Puritanism had very few qualms over leaving to the verification of experience the determination of which was correct. The truth of this observation has been obscured because recent scholarship concerning the scientific revolution of the seventeenth century has so established its outstanding importance in modern intellectual history as to suggest that it must have been the all-engrossing concern of the time. Yet if we narrow our field from the whole of European thinking to the thinking of the Puritan colonies in New England, a very different conclusion emerges. The writings of informed New Englanders up to the end of the century demonstrate clearly that in the foreground of their consciousness was the task of explaining how God always worked in nature through a settled order and yet secured intelligible ends, how He constrained Himself to observe the laws of nature and yet contrived that whatever He decreed should inevitably come to pass. At the beginning of the century they accepted the Peripatetic theory of the order; by the end of the century they had generally agreed that mathematical method gave the better account. But this substitution was a gradual replacement of one explanation by another, made without distracting attention from what was deemed the major issue; and before the year 1700 the newly received doctrine had not yet suggested to New Englanders any problems in theology or any contradictions of accepted revelation. Hence, as it gradually came to seem true that the earth revolves around the sun, Puritan theologians were content that the fact should be admitted; as the doctrine of the four causes betrayed its inadequacy and the doctrine of efficient cause demonstrated itself capable of explaining all effects, they ceased speaking of final and material causes; as physicists denied the existence of substantial forms, the ministers omitted them from their sermons. But first of all they made certain that the Copernican system could serve the purposes of religious instruction as well as the Ptolemaic, that God wrought all effects, whether by the efficient cause or by the material or formal, that the laws of motion which now accounted for phenomena hitherto explained in terms of substantial forms were equally translatable into spiritual lessons. It was well into the eighteenth century before New England divines had occasion to wonder whether in transferring their allegiance to the new philosophy they had not raised up dangers unknown in the old.

Though the main outlines of the scientific revolution in English thought have been described, the detailed steps through which the change was accomplished have not yet been fully reconstructed, and in New England, where evidence at best is not plentiful, the precise curve of the development is hard to ascertain. In the main it seems clear that at the beginning the settlers of New England accepted without criticism prevailing notions about natural phenomena, which were still those of medieval science. Professor Hardin Craig has demonstrated the essential continuity from medieval to Renaissance thinking, and described how antipathetic to ordinary minds in the year 1600 was the habit of considering observed data apart from inherited generalizations. "The Renaissance mind," he says, "inherited or adopted generalized simplifications, formulae, for the applications of its ethical, religious, and scientific systems"; it did not take naturally or easily to the inductive method.[2] The minds of the early Puritans are fully described by Professor Craig's remarks upon the mentality of contemporary Europe. Though William Ames quoted Bacon in the *Philosophemata* to illustrate how arguments should be collected from Scripture, and though he praised by name both the inductive and experimental methods, he was thinking of them only in relation to his doctrine of technologia; he was talking about inducting ideas from things, and justifying himself, as all Ramist logicians did, by an appeal to utility. In astronomy and in physics the first generation of divines were conventional Peripatetics, and the textbooks at Harvard were of the same stripe. Zanchius' *De Operibus Dei* specifically declared that the method of Aristotle was the most excellent, the most beautiful, and the most compatible with the facts of nature; other texts, Keckermann, Burgersdicius, and above all Magirus' *Physiologiae Peripateticae Libri Sex,* were simply stereotyped versions of medieval lore, their contents arranged according to the same general plan, with the exposition proceeding from the elements, through meteors, the vegetable and sensitive souls, to the constitution of man and the rational soul. In the sermons evidences of Peripatetic science are plainly to be seen. John Preston viewed natural phenomena in the light of their ultimate purpose, as did all scholastic physicists: "All the creatures . . . have an end; the end of the Sunne, Moone and Starres is, to serve the Earth; and the end of the Earth is, to bring forth Plants, and the end of Plants is, to feed the beasts." Well after the middle of the century New England divines continued to speak the same language; Fitch explained in the *First Principles* that the creatures are composed of matter and form; John Cotton paused to refute the Copernican theory on the very solid, common-sensical grounds that if the earth were moving, when a man threw a stone in the direction of its rotation he would overtake his stone before it fell. The sermons are studded with passages in which, in accordance with the Puritan disposition to spiritualize the laws of nature and to discover theological allegories in the data of science, bits of Peripatetic theory are elaborately developed. Thus, to cite but one instance out of hundreds, Thomas Hooker explains the necessity that a sinful soul be acted upon by divine grace according to the analogy of tides:

> Looke as it is with the moone, the naturall Philosopher observes, that the ebbing and flowing of the sea, is by vertue of the moone, she flings her beames into the sea, and not being able to exhale as the sunne doth, shee leaves them there, and goes away, and that drawes them, and when they grow wet, they returne back againe; now the sea ebs and flowes not from any principle in it selfe, but by vertue of the moone, being moved, it goes, being drawne, it comes; the moone casting her beames upon the waters, it moves the sea, and so drawes it selfe unto it selfe, and the sea with it: so the heart of a poore creature, is like the water, unable to move towards heaven, but the Spirit of the Lord doth bring in its beames, and leaves a supernaturall vertue by them upon the soule, and thereby drawes it to itselfe.

This passage is significant, not merely for the charming fashion in which it illustrates how better writers and greater men than Cotton Mather practiced the art of spiritualizing earthly objects, but for its revelation of the scientific knowledge possessed by so capable and alert a mind as Thomas

Hooker. From classical times there had been controversy among the learned over the cause of tides, and long before the fall of Rome two schools of belief had existed, the majority of scientists accepting some variant of the lunar theory advanced by Posidonius and Pliny, a minority arguing for a version of Macrobius' terrestrial theory. Though the dispute had lasted for all the weary centuries, there had been little first-hand observation of tides, and some medieval disputants, like William of Auvergne, were careful to preface their arguments with a disavowal of ever having observed the phenomenon themselves—"quod ego utique non probavi." Kepler reasserted the lunar theory, and expounded it by the analogy of the magnet, but Galileo supported the terrestrial argument and accused Kepler of introducing, by his theory of "rays", the dangerous doctrine of occult virtues. At the time Hooker delivered his sermon the controversy was still unresolved; he simply took up what was the most widely received view. Not until Newton was the medieval era in the theory of tides brought to a close; meantime the Puritan preacher availed himself of what was at hand, and as long as the teaching had reputable authority behind it, he used it for his own purposes, which were rather religious and moral than scientific.[3]

The New England colonies, with their science already contained in these medieval formulae, took little part either in advancing new theories or in retarding their development. As Professor Morison says, "Harvard neither preceded nor lagged behind the academic world, which gave up Scholastic Physics with great reluctance and only when the accumulation of scientific data had become overwhelming."[4] The prevailing attitude seems to have been that of John Davenport when confronted with the Almanac prepared in 1659 by Zechariah Bridgen. Bridgen, two years out of Harvard, inserted a popular exposition of the Copernican system, and Davenport, who had learned his astronomy before the academic world commenced even to doubt scholastic doctrines, countered in a letter to John Winthrop, Jr., with one or two arguments; yet, after offering his objections, he concluded, "However it be; let him injoy his opinion; and I shall rest in what I have learned, til more cogent Arguments be produced then I have hitherto met with."[5] Davenport's reaction is all the more interesting in that he was a die-hard conservative, a man who fought literally to the death against every innovation that threatened change to the order set up in the 1630's, who resisted the union of New Haven to Connecticut because he thought that Connecticut had lost the true faith, who split the First Church of Boston over the Half-Way Convenant issue; yet the easy tolerance with which he, the stalwart of stalwarts, could regard the change in astronomical theory is a significant indication in contemporaneous terms of how the great scientific revolution figured in the eyes of orthodox Puritans.

Because the whole matter was regarded as indifferent or secondary, whatever system of physics at length proved to be backed by "the more cogent arguments" was finally entertained. Puritanism had never held any particular brief for Aristotle, as the adoption of the Ramist logic shows, and it was free to discard his theories of the natural world without disturbing a single tenet in the creed. Oddly enough, it is possible that orthodox Puritans were hastened toward their renunciation of scholastic science by the sectarians of the 1640's; at any rate, Webster and Dell berated the physics then taught in the universities for being useless and speculative instead of practical and applicable, and for being, on that account, impious. Webster, the enemy of learning in religion, invoked Bacon, by then becoming a name to conjure with; he struck not only at Peripatetic physicists but at Ramist logicians when he declared roundly that logic was ill adapted for the discovery of natural law. In science, he said, we must proceed *"a posteriore,* and from the affections and properties of things must seek forth their causes"; we need more reliable instruments than the syllogism, we must use "induction", backed "with long experience and sound observation," in order to discover "the working of mother Nature." Natural philosophy should "lead us to know and understand the causes, properties, operations and affections of nature," but that which is purveyed in the schools conceals them; natural philosophy should enable us to behold the eternal power of God, "who hath set all these things as so many significant and lively characters, or *Hieroglyphicks* of his invisible power, providence, and divine wisdome," but the physical science of Aristotle is fundamentally atheistical. The defenders of learning were in danger of being outflanked by this maneuver, and realized quickly that if "humane helps" were to be retained in theology, the obsolete physics must be abandoned. They therefore hastened to range themselves under the banner of Bacon, and Hall outdid Webster in denunciations of traditional science: he agreed that in the work of physicists he had found, not explanations of phenomena, but "contradictions, loose conceptions, and endlesse controversies." But the conclusion to be drawn, he then insisted, was not that science should be cast aside, but that religion should turn the more eagerly to the new science. If the Parliament will further the cause of learning, Hall pleaded,

> You shall see Nature traced through all her Turnings, to a cleare demonstration of her first cause, and every day bring forth varieties of experiments, either to the reliefe, astonishment, or delight of men . . . Nature which now disguises her selfe into so many shapes, forced into an open veracity and pure nakednesse . . . You shall then see Policy reconciled to Divinity, Morality, and it self, and yet better able to lay designes and prevent dangers.

About the time that Hall was composing these words Isaac Barrow, fellow of Trinity College, Cambridge, was introducing there the new or experimental philosophy, and being challenged by Edward Davenant with the prophecy, "If a new philosophy is brought in, a new divinity will shortly follow." Yet Puritans embraced it without fear, for few of them saw any threat of a new divinity, and felt either with Davenport that men could safely be allowed their liberty in such matters, or with Hall that the new philosophy would be a still greater ally of orthodox theology than the old. At Harvard the class of 1671 rebelled against further study of Magirus; newer textbooks, such as those by Adrian Heereboord, were now employed, books that presented the Cartesian critique of scholastic physics and taught the more recent discoveries.[6] Increase Mather owned copies of the *Transactions* of the Royal Society as early as 1682, and his sermons in the 80's reveal a fairly accurate appreciation of the revolution.[7] Professor Morison estimates that by 1700 the new physics had entirely displaced the scholastic at Harvard College, and though as late as 1714 Samuel Sewall thought it "inconvenient" for Cotton Mather to speak from the pulpit "of the Sun being in the centre of our System," Sewall represented only the most cautious opinion. His vague disapproval is the nearest thing to opposition to be found in the annals of early New England.

Charles Morton's *Compendium Physicae,* which he brought with him when he came to be vice-president of Harvard in 1686, represents the transition; Morton willingly admitted that at the time there were more disputes in physics than in any other part of philosophy, and endeavored to walk warily. He explained the distinction between the old and the new doctrine, in general following the old, although acknowledging on many points that the theories were under fire. He described substantial forms, for instance, but cited certain "latter men" who denied their existence, particularly Boyle. In his sermon on *The Spirit of Man,* published at Boston in 1693, Morton built an elaborate structure around the ancient theory of humors; yet he pointed out that the theory had been criticized and concluded in characteristic Puritan vein that in either case the moral of his discourse would be the same. "If any like better to have it [humor] expressed by *Matter,* more or less, moveable or moved; They may please themselves. There is no Difference in the *Thing,* however Expressions vary." Increase Mather in the 1680's seems to have gone still further toward whole-hearted acceptance of the new era; in the preface to his work on comets in 1683 he specifically castigated the Peripatetics and ranged himself with the "Learned men of these later times, wherein light in things natural as well as divine hath been admirably discovered," who have "by the help of Mathematical Instruments made ocular demonstrations." It was only "Popish Authors," he said, especially the Jesuits, who any longer strained their wits "to defend their *Pagan* Master *Aristotle* his Principles." In 1698 Cotton Mather could refer with unqualified scorn to the "Florentine Physician" who refused to look through Galileo's telescope "because he was afraid that then his *Eyes* would from *Ocular Demonstrations,* make him stagger concerning the truth of *Aristotle's* Principles, which he was resolved he would never call in Question."

Puritan receptivity to the new science was encouraged, it seems clear, not half so much by the ocular proofs through which the new methodology was established as by the concomitant attestations of its theological orthodoxy advanced by its proponents. Particularly did the strategic line taken by the defenders of the Royal Society, by Boyle, Bishop Sprat, and Joseph Glanvill, insure Puritan confidence in the respectability of the movement. In order to avoid the accusation of atheism and materialism, in order to distinguish themselves from the Hobbesians, the Academicians put great stress upon their devotion to the spirit of "Scepsis Scientifica" and wrote energetically upon "the vanity of dogmatizing"; as long as the conclusions of science could be deliberately advanced as tentative hypotheses, and as long as the scientists themselves were continually assuring laymen that more remained to be investigated than had yet been studied, so that any impressions, garnered from our present imperfect knowledge, that seemed for the moment to challenge theological axioms would undoubtedly be corrected by future discoveries, then science contained no threat of heresy. On these conditions, but primarily upon these very non-scientific considerations, New England Puritans, like many religious Englishmen, welcomed the Royal Society as an ally. The spirit of the Society was made articulate in New England chiefly by Samuel Lee, a friend of Morton, who also came to Boston in 1686 and lived on intimate terms with the Mathers. If many New Englanders were as yet a little vague about the great revolution by then being wrought in the scientific thought of the Western world, Lee's *The Joy of Faith,* issued in Boston in 1687, brought home its implications to them. The acute reasonings and finespun distinctions of the scholastics, Lee's work proclaimed, vanish into smoke "when they come to the touchstone of some solid experiments." Therefore the "Learneder part of the world" have for the time being stopped constructing systems, and are resolved for many years to come to keep their judgment upon final scientific truth in a state of suspension; they will set "all *Europe* a work to write volumns of faithful experiments before they will presume upon more Systems of natural Philosophy to gull the world." Thoroughly in the spirit of the new science, Lee predicted an unlimited future for the new method, but speaking both as a partisan of the Society and as a Puritan, he took positive comfort from the reflection that, however much the science might ultimately discover, the inexhaustible creation would always contain unsolved riddles and still further territory to be explored:

What the admirable sagacity of future ages may compass as to thousands of problems within the circle of Sciences, or in that most noble Art of Chymistry, or the Analysis of the three kingdoms of nature: the tubes and glasses of our present inventions give us no sufficient prospect . . . The learned of this age wonder at the denial of the motion of the Earth, tho now the truth of it appears clear to all the generality of the ingenious of *Europe* . . . Indeed so may posterity deride at these our ages, and the more ingenious of future times, may stand amazed at our dulness and stupidity about minerals, meteors and the cure of diseases, and many thousand things besides, about the lustre of stars and precious stones, which may be as easy to them as letters to us . . . Such rare inventions may be given in of God to beautifie the glory of the latter days. All our writings in Divinity, will be like insipid water, to what shall then appear upon the Stage . . . and the Artists that shall then be born, may discover more things in the works of God to be discust and endeavoured to be explained, then they themselves shall arrive to. The superfine Wisdom and Learned Wits of those acute times will discover vast regions of darkness and ignorance. There will be a *plus ultra* to the end of the world . . . If in millions of things we are stunted and fooled at every turn . . . we may cry out with the Satyrist—*Auriculas Asini quis non habet?* What fearful sots are we in the things before us? Then what shall dull reason do in the great sublimities and solemnities of faith, and the doctrines set forth by Infinite Wisdom?

It may well be doubted whether the new science could have made its way in English middle-class religious society had it not been thus rationalized and defended, but certainly when put forth in this guise it was not merely approved by such a society, it was eagerly embraced. The Puritans of New England were simply moving with their times, and Sherman's preface to Increase Mather's *Cometographia* indicates that New Englanders in the 1680's had already learned from Sprat and Glanvill that the way to advance the new learning was to insist upon its limitations: Mather, he says, has declared as much

as it hath pleased the Father of Lights and Fountain of all knowledge & wisdome (hitherto) to discover to poor ignorant Mortals; *viz.* the result of the judicious thoughts of the ablest and best accomplished *Artists,* who upon very many accurate, unquestionably true and exact Observations, made by the help of choicest Instruments improved by minds intensely set to search into, and find out the Mystery and Meaning of those abstruse and admirable works of him who is most High; have declared what they conceive most rationally probable. The wisest of Men know that they understand but little part of Gods wayes and works; and are not ashamed to confess that in things so much above humane Capacity, they are rather *Quaerists* then *Adeptists,* content to be ignorant of what he is pleased as yet not to discover.

Thus, though the Puritans lived in the presence of the great scientific revolution, the first consideration for them was that it should not sweep their feet off the ground of religious orthodoxy. When they were assured, by the authoritative propagandists for the Society, that the scientific innovations did not undermine, but rather supported the doctrines of piety, that the most important service of the new physics was its service to religion, the Puritans were ready to receive it.

At every point the primary requisite for any theory of nature to a Puritan way of thinking was not so much that it prove its case experimentally, but that it illustrate the orthodox doctrines of creation, of providence, and of divine concursus. The earth, a vast and heavy body, hangs in the air: "How is this done? It hath no pillars to hold it up, but the Decree and Word of that mighty God." No event can be explained fully without reference to the divine intention; there is nothing that men call accident or chance but what God ordains it, there is no necessity that is not of His enactment. To study nature is to study God in the act of willing, to marvel at the ingenuity of His plan and the minuteness of His care. "God exerts a great deal of Carefulness therein: There is no Being goes wrong, so as to miss the Design He hath about it." The textbooks imported into New England, from the beginning to the end of the century, whether of physics or of theology, whether they taught the old science or the new, repeated these doctrines in every possible guise. God has created the world, He rules it and governs the actions of all causes and all agents, said Zanchius, and yet His absolute providence does not deny true liberty to the human will or contingency and efficiency to things. Here, then, was the riddle of nature, the real problem for the Puritan theorist. In respect of the first cause, in respect of God Himself, "all things are certainly foreseen and immutably ordered and ruled, all comes about by ineluctable necessity; yet in respect of us, and of other second causes, not by coaction but according to the working of their natures." Texts that had adopted the new hypotheses nevertheless repeated Zanchius; they still argued against "Epicureanism" and against "Stoicism." Epicureans, as Urian Oakes put it, "would demonstrate that all Things in the world are rolled up and down, tumbled and toss'd about by meer Chance, and fall out as it may happen, uncertainly and fortuitously"; Stoics, as Wollebius described them, preach "fatall necessity," of a kind that "ties God to the connexion of secondary causes." The Christian doctrine, all agreed, sets forth immutable decree and yet does not take away but rather establishes second causes. "The Christian state makes a subordination of the second cause to Gods most free will of which he makes use voluntarily, not of necessity, out of indulgence, rather then indigence." Van Mastricht, writing with full perception of the scientific revolution, carefully pointed out that all the "Reformed" believed that nothing can happen outside the intention of the first cause, yet that the effects of natural agents are contingent; from these considerations, the "Reformed" concluded, "on the one hand, that the influx of predetermining providence is necessary to an action . . . on the other hand, that there are many actions, either in Scripture or in daily experience, which are truly contingent, and that predetermining influx does not deny contingency nor infer a universal necessity." Van Mastricht defended this doctrine of providence specifically against Epicurus, Aristotle, and Spinoza.

Of course, there were always theoretical difficulties in the doctrine; it seemed to assert in one clause what it denied in the other, and to some it suggested even more dreadful possibilities than those associated with the names of Epicurus, Hobbes, or Spinoza; yet New Englanders were not disturbed. To them, the doctrine, for all its complexity, seemed fundamentally simple. It meant merely that to accomplish His purposes God had set up an order which would infallibly realize them, and that this order included men with free wills and causes that were followed by effects. The operation of this order, the procedure by which free men and secondary causes worked out the divine scheme, was what Puritans called "ordinary" providence or "common" government. Ames had defined it in the *Medulla:*

Common is that whereby God doth govern all things in a like manner[;] unto this government belongeth, First, The Law of nature common to all things . . . Secondly, a naturall inclination, which is a principle of working according to that law . . . Thirdly, a naturall instinct: which is a peculiar stirring up of the living Creatures . . . Fourthly, A certaine obedientiall power, whereby all Creatures are apt to obey the command of God.

Common government is no less true government because it does not operate directly; providence still determines men's acts, though it does so by ruling their inclinations, persuading their reason, or influencing environing circumstance. Nature is a marvelous and subtle contrivance, in which all creatures are guided to ends they know not of, and yet move of their own will and volition. "He follows this Course in His Ordinary Providence to Guide and Order all Creatures according to the Inclination & Capacity of their Natures: things meerly Natural according to Instinct, and Rational Beings by Direction of their Reason." [8] He determines all actions, but not by compulsion; He decrees what happens, but the natures and wills of His creatures are not violated. They are merely inclined according to their natural dispositions and liberty.

Hence, though we have to deal with an arbitrary deity, an absolute sovereign whose will is law and whose choices are unpredictable, yet we have also to live in a world that is order and design. We need only look upon it to perceive that it has a plan. At the beginning of the century Preston preached:

When you see the wheeles of a Watch fitted one to another, when you see the sheath fitted to the sword, you say this is done by some Art, this is not by accident; Even so it is in nature, you see a fitting of one thing to another, in the body, in the Creatures, in every thing.

In *A Compleat Body* Samuel Willard wrote:

The curiousness of the composure, & exquisiteness of the fabrick, declares an exquisite workman . . . Whether we consider the composition of any one

Creature, and that the most contemptible (suppose a worm, or a pile of grass) its nature hath more wonders in it, than the greatest Naturalist that ever was, *Solomon* himself, is able to Analyse . . . Or if we consider the *harmony* of the whole in all its parts, or the admirable suting of the things that are made one to another, so that there is nothing in vain, or useless, or incapable of being serviceable in its place, its nature being every way adapted to the place it bears: every wheel in this curious watch moving aright: and what less than Infinite wisdom, could so contrive and compose this?

Therefore what we call "nature" is in reality the "art" of God; "Of all his Works this is the most Artificial and Master-piece." It is ordered as the wheels of a watch are ordered, it is arranged in hierarchies of value and form, from elements to imperfectly mixed elements like meteors, to perfectly mixed elements with bodies only, to those mixed with quickening spirits, to spirits that have only a single life like plants or the sun, to spirits that have a "compound life", and finally to men, the highest rank of physical existences, spirits with the most compounded of lives. At first the fecundity of nature seems lawless, the variety of beings innumerable, and yet every form has its place in the scale, every link its appointed function in the chain. There can be no *"Chasma* or *Vacuum* amongst them, which would tend to a dissolution of the whole." In a sense, the omnipotent God Himself is limited: He cannot violate the order of His creation, He cannot destroy the "necessity and mutual connection between the parts." Just as He cannot make truth falsehood, so He cannot do "that which is contrary to the Rule of nature, for the Rule of nature is a beam of his own wisdome." This idea persists unchanged in Puritan theory throughout the century. Ames defined the law of nature as "that order in naturall things . . . common to all things or the very nature of things." Preston declared positively, "God alters no Law of nature," and since he was writing before Aristotle had been driven from the realm of physics, he cited him freely:

Nature it cannot be altered againe, for that is the property of Nature, it still stickes by us, and will not be changed, but, as *Aristotle* observes, throw a stone up a thousand times, it will returne againe, because it is the nature of it to returne.

John Cotton, also a Peripatetic in natural science, preached concerning the providence of God that "there is a setled order and constancy in that instability, as there is in the motions of the Heavens and heavenly bodies." After the new science triumphed, Puritan preachers continued to deliver the same moral. The rules of common government are unchangeable, declares Willard, "They are setled invariable *Rules* . . . They are Ordinances made for Perpetuity." The rules of art, in natural philosophy exactly as in logic, are eternal and immutable, they cannot be nullified even by omnipotence.

But was it not clear that miracles had happened? Was not the Bible sufficient proof that phenomena existed outside and above, even contrary to, the laws of nature? And in daily life, in the experience of all men living, had there not been inexplicable occurrences, men delivered from tempests, broom-sticks that danced in the night, wounds inflicted without visible weapons, terrors that no rule of physics could account for? The pious mind might find wholly plausible the doctrine that an omnipotent providence ruled through an inviolable order, but what then became of miracles? Dialectical ingenuity might demonstrate successfully that an arbitrary God respected the integrity of common providence, but could any subtlety of argument then find a place for "special providences"? And if special providences were impossible, what after all was the difference between Christian providence and Stoic necessity?

Miracles gave very little trouble. They were out-and-out deviations from the settled order; as Willard put it, the rules of ordinary providence are unalterable, but God may if He wishes "go from or beside these Rules" in His extra-ordinary providences. Obviously God had at specific times performed miracles, and these "ought to have as much authority in our hearts, as if we had seen the things with our eyes." In order to attest the divinity of His mission, Christ had needed to prove that He was the Lord of nature. But as soon as the body of revelation had been completed, Puritans all agreed, miracles had definitely ceased. They often proclaimed this cessation with what looks suspiciously like relief; it obviated the problem of reconciling miracles with the preservation of natural law. "Miracles doe now cease, and are not to be expected in these dayes." [9] We have no promise of immediate assistance; of old, in moments of crisis, God was wont to interpose directly, as in the opening of the Red Sea; but by now He has worked enough miracles to attest the authority of His revelation and He has issued all His commandments. We now must believe the Bible on faith, not upon miraculous supports. As "the Philosopher" says, declared Cotton, *"Miracula sine necessitate non sunt multiplicanda."* "God can work miracles," preached Samuel Nowell in 1678, "but when ordinary means may be had, he will not work miracles." Therefore, though we are to believe implicitly that water became wine in Judea, we are to expect no such alchemy in New England, but are to work with the materials God has put into our hands, according to the laws of His common providence, which are the laws of nature. For this reason New England divines never had any tolerance for astrology, the philosopher's stone, or incantation, for any device by which men sought to escape the rules of nature or to circumvent the settled order of things. There were mines of gold in the earth, which God continues "by an ordinary course of his providence," but He has decreed that no magic shall ever turn the nature of one metal into another. Witchcraft was a crime, not merely because it lost the witch his soul and brought distress upon his victims, but because it was an attempt to tamper with the law of nature. The Puritan theory of nature voiced the Puritans' intense loathing for what they called explicitly "superstition".

However, special providences were another story entirely. Miracles were no longer of practical import; providences threatened to become a difficult theological problem, involving immediate consequences for the whole body politic. In New England the theory of special providences was most abundantly discussed in the 1680's and 90's, though it had been present in Puritan thought from the beginning. The essential point had been stated by William Perkins in 1595: "Sometimes he gouernes according to the vsual course & order of nature . . . yet so, as he can and doth most freely order all things by meanes either aboue nature or against nature." A special providence differed from a miracle in that God wrought it through or with means, by natural instruments, by arranging the causes or influencing the agents, rather than by forcible interposition and direct compulsion. The attitude of the early Puritans can be seen at its most characteristic in a passage from John Preston's *Life Eternall,* wherein he discusses the argument of "aetheism" that the regularity and mechanical consistency of natural law proves not the existence of God, but the impersonal and self-sufficient eternity of nature. Preston replied first by citing the miracles, but passed quickly to the special providences, occurrences that "are not contrary to Nature," yet wherein "Nature is turned off of its course." These inexplicable happenings prove, more convincingly than the miracles, that a free agent governs the world:

> Therefore this we may learne from it, the constancie of these things shewes the wisdome of God; as it is wisdome in us to doe things constantly: and againe, the variety of things shews the liberty of the Agent; for the actions of Nature are determined to one, but God shewes his liberty in this, that he can change and alter them at his pleasure.

Significantly enough, Preston goes on to declare that even better proof of God's existence is the ordinary and constant course of things, "wherein there is no such swarving," for does not lawful obedience among the creatures, especially among inanimate things, demonstrate His guidance more than irregularities and eccentricities? In the 1620's the danger was not that exceptions to the settled order would be underestimated, but that the order itself would not be sufficiently respected. By the time of Increase Mather's *An Essay for the Recording of Illustrious Providences,* peril lay in the other direction, and he, as well as others both in New England and England, felt that greater stress should now be placed upon the uncommon and the peculiar than upon the regular. The New England literature is part of a wider movement, inspired no doubt, as among the Cambridge Platonists and in the works of Joseph Glanvill, by apprehensions lest the all-conquering science result in a theory of blind mechanism or endorse the blasphemies of Thomas Hobbes. Therefore the renewed insistence upon special providences in late seventeenth-century New England is the most noticeable response of its theologians to the new science, almost the only respect in which they were compelled to reorientate their thinking or overhaul their doctrines in order to adjust themselves to the new era.

Yet this redistribution of emphasis meant no innovation in their theory. For one thing, their motive was not entirely fear of scientific atheism; the Mathers in particular found that preaching upon special providences was a strategic device for arousing the emotions of a sluggish generation. Also, as the passage from Preston shows, Puritan theologians did not need to await the triumph of mathematical physics before they faced the issue of materialism; autonomous naturalism could be and was formulated from Aristotelian physics as well as from Newtonian. To resist such deductions Puritans had always dwelt with particular fondness upon those natural events that could be explained only as contrivances of the divine intelligence. They seem to have been temperamentally uncomfortable at the thought of miracles and rather relieved that the era of violent exceptions to the law of nature was finished; but they took particular comfort in moralizing over oddities which seemed to be produced by natural causes, but in which the pious investigator could perceive the finger of God. Thus John Winthrop, who scorned "superstition" with the best of men, dwelt with particular avidity during the first years of the settlement upon those apparently natural incidents which yet bespoke the blessing of God upon His commonwealth, such as the mouse that gnawed the Book of Common Prayer but spared the New Testament, the profaner of the Sabbath whose child fell immediately afterwards into a well, or the two men of Hingham who took part with Dr. Child against the authorities and were thereafter prohibited for over a month by adverse winds from getting their raft into Boston Harbor, or the great storm which frightened all, yet by God's management did no great harm, "but only killed one Indian with the fall of a tree." After collecting a goodly number of such providences, Winthrop believed he had undeniable proof that "the Lord hath owned this work, and preserved and prospered his people here beyond ordinary ways of providence." Cotton Mather was venturing beyond the limits of ordinary Puritan prudence when he actually did *see* an angel; the more normal attitude was that by close observance of some merely natural occurrence, the presence of angels or of God Himself could be detected.

The treatments of special providences written in the later decades of the century, whatever the occasion for their composition, added nothing new to the content of Puritan theory. The difference of the later writings from the earlier is entirely one of emphasis, not only upon the importance of special providences, but upon the component aspects of them. In earlier works the ministers were more apt to explain a special providence by holding that God directed the causes toward a predetermined effect, or that he simply inhibited the effects of certain causes. "When there are causes, and the effect followes not, it is because God doth dispose of things at his pleasure, and can turne them a contrary way." In later writings the tendency becomes very marked to account for special providences, not by permitting God to meddle with causes already in operation, but by requiring Him to take the place of a cause and thus to bring about an effect through His assuming for the moment the rôle of a natural agent and binding Himself by natural law. In special providences, Fitch explained, God does not refuse to attend to the order of things, but submits Himself to it. He does not make an effect without a cause, but supplies the place of the ordinary cause and then works by natural means. He can "raise Children out of stones, which is not to produce an effect without a cause, that would be contrary to the Rule of nature and his wisdome, but he can supply the place of the cause immediately." The difference in emphasis between this and the earlier version is slight, not enough to alter the essential theory, and yet the shift is extremely significant. The later form preserves the arbitrary freedom of God, makes the peculiar event no less pointed, and yet it brings divine interposition into greater conformity with the tissue of nature, causes less of a breach in the sequential ties of one thing to another, removes the special providence further from the category of miracles. Perhaps in this small reapportionment of emphasis is to be seen a premonition of those important theological modifications which the new science was ultimately to inspire in the thought of the eighteenth century.

The principal authors on the subject of providences in later New England were the Mathers. I hope to examine their particular incentives in a later volume, but in the history of New England their works are important chiefly for providing a full and explicit account of the theory. Increase defined a special providence as any divine judgment, "tempests, floods, earthquakes, thunders as are unusual, strange apparitions, or whatever else shall happen that is prodigious, witchcrafts, diabolical possessions, remarkable judgements upon noted sinners, eminent deliverances, and answers of prayer." In the *Essay,* published in 1684, he strove to maintain what, granted the assumptions of his theory, was an objective and scientific point of view. He told of "tragical" as well as joyful providences, in which good men were maimed or killed; he tried not to blink any facts, and admitted freely "that the Lords faithful servants have sometimes been the subject of very dismal dispensations." He had explored the doctrine tentatively in 1683 on the specific question of comets; in 1684 he further expounded it in *The Doctrine of Divine Providence Opened and Applyed,* and he later devoted several works to particular varieties of phenomena in which divine providences were most apt to be found, as in *The Voice of God in Stormy Winds* and *A Discourse Concerning Earthquakes.* Cotton Mather, who ever followed with unequal steps the mighty strides of his father, wrote much that posterity will never read upon every kind of providence. The whole literature of witchcraft was, from the Puritan point of view, a department of this subject, as was also the question of angelical apparitions and the activity of angels, good or bad, carrying out God's behests or tempting men to their downfall. Throughout all these works, the position remains essentially the same; the phenomena might have come about by purely natural means, none of them are miracles; yet all illustrate the constant and unceasing government of God by showing Him, not rudely interrupting, but, as it were, insinuating Himself into nature—working not in defiance of natural law, but through skillful manipulation of it. Increase Mather refused all vague and occult explanations; he would not attribute what he could not understand to "an occult quality," and he designed "a little to divert and recreate my mind with some philosophical meditations, and to conclude with a theological improvement thereof." Where he could not find the moral, philosophical or theological, he said so, yet in all cases he tried to find morals of both sorts. The purpose of God in smiting the army of Sennacherib was clear; yet also "It is not improbable but that those Assyrians were killed with lightning." Natural causes do concur in thunder and lightning, but "nevertheless, the supream cause must not be disacknowledged"; comets happen according to the course of nature, but they are also "portentous signs of divine anger." There are eclipses every year, and not all of them are portents, but *total* eclipses must be meaningful, as one was in 1672, the day before College Commencement, which foretold the death of President Chauncy in the next academic year. Earthquakes have natural causes, but none the less they are also awful works of God: "There never happens an Earthquake, but God speaks to men on the Earth by it." God could if He wished, by merely speaking the word, engender stormy winds "without making use of Natural Causes . . . But He makes Natural Causes to serve His Providence." We should look to the causes of things, look to the vapors and the stars for the origin of storms, but also we should look "higher than the Stars when such things come to pass."

If the doctrine of illustrious providences was not incontestably proved by the treatises of the Mathers, very few New Englanders were yet capable of criticizing it, and for the time being it seemed invincible. As far as the ordinary man was concerned, from it and from the whole theory of nature emerged two particular morals that were of special relevance to his daily living: in the physical or natural world the will of man is entirely and completely free, and in the realm of nature second causes are always at work, even when the effect has been foreordained by God. The difficulties of maintaining freedom of the will in the face of the theological doctrines of depravity and inability, of the scientific doctrines of providence and concursus, were so great that many preachers contented themselves with blanket assertions, informing the people that no matter if theology and the theory of nature did make them appear impotent, they were nevertheless sufficiently free to be fully responsible for their deeds. Before Puritan theology had achieved the sophistication of its later stages, Perkins merely declared that an omnipotent first cause "doth not take away freedome of wil in election; or the nature and property of second causes; but onely brings them into a certain order." But the seventeenth-century mind, whether Puritan or Hobbesian, could not resist prying a little closer into the logic of things to find out more exactly how a free will could be brought into a certain order and yet remain free. Even in 1690, when Parsons James Allen, Joshua Moody, and Samuel Willard joined with Cotton Mather to draw up a succinct statement of *The Principles of the Protestant Religion,* they did not pause to argue, but merely announced that all creatures depend upon God, that such dependence influences their every act, that "notwithstanding this Influence upon the creature, in respect of its Action, the Creature hath its Action of its own," and that the creature therefore is morally responsible. Yet these very same gentlemen were constantly endeavoring in their pulpits and in their polemical writings to give a more scientific, a more reasonable account, and again and again retired to their nightly repose confident that they had successfully and finally reconciled free will, foreordination, and fate.

The most useful conception in their demonstrations was that of the hierarchy or chain of being. In the design of creation, as Alsted explained it in his *Physica Harmonica,* there were three stages of existence: inanimate objects, into which God has placed a "natural inclination" by which they are moved to their particular ends; animals, into which God has infused a "natural instinct" by which they are moved through the senses; and man, to whom God has given "intelligent will," the faculties of understanding and of willing to do the thing understood. As Fitch explained the idea some decades later, God has willed all creatures, but not all alike; hence some are "to be natural causes, and some to be contingent, and act as causes by counsel." As Alexander Pope was later to put it, there must be somewhere such a rank as man, because there was a necessary place for a being who thinks and who puts his thought into action, who has reason and will. Therefore, so far as the physical order is concerned, there can be no compulsion upon man; he is not moved by irresistible force, as are stones and streams, nor by brutish instincts, as are animals, but by his own deliberation and the choice of his own untrammeled will. There is no contradiction, consequently, in a man's trusting to God for supply or defense and yet "using all regular Endeavours for the obtaining of them."

Man was created to act. Hence, "The Diligent Hand makes Rich, but Sloth, and Poverty, and Rags, and Shame must be expected to go together." The problem of the depraved will was primarily a theological issue, which to the believer never became a stumbling block to the doing of God's will; but it was never for any man, believer or sinner, complicated by the doctrine of physics. The law of nature put no restraints upon man's freedom, no rational being could shirk his responsibilities by shifting the blame to God's decree, to his inheritance or to his environment, to his lack of opportunities or to the power of temptation. The study of nature revealed that by the absolute decree of God man was assigned to the place of freedom, and to speak of God's will in the natural order was to imply the existence of human liberty. God's purpose does not alter the nature of the things, Samuel Willard in 1703 explained to George Keith, in what is probably the best New England work on the question: man has been created with a rational nature, one faculty of which is his will; God has contrived that men "should act freely, and yet that they should accomplish his purposes by all their free actions." If Keith still remained unconvinced, as indeed he did, Willard could only assure him that the Puritan doctrine was "very consonant to the resentments of right reason." Willard would admit that the reconciling of God's decree and man's freedom "is a great depth, and the particular and distinct manner of it is beyond our Conception," but, like a true Puritan, he would not rest his whole case upon faith: on the authority of the Bible we should believe "the consistency of them," yet "it is commendable for us, soberly to employ our reason to satisfy us in the Compossibility of them, and thereby make it to appear that faith doth not contradict right reason." The Puritan theory of nature, like the doctrine of technologia, was one more endeavor to make faith and right reason agree, faith in the hidden God and yet rational comprehension of Him.

In its simplest form the Puritan conception of secondary cause combined neatly the ideas of order and of divine will. Cause has its effect in the ordinary course of things, and yet the cause does not of itself generate the effect; the will of God determines that when a fire burns, heat will be radiated, but God sustains and controls both the fire and the heat. There is no guarantee that fire will always give heat other than the willingness of God to maintain the sequence. "God concurs unto every operation of Second Causes, so as, immediately, and by himself, to influence upon every action of the Creature." Hence the law of causation is reliable because God works in it and by it; He can afford to give up miracles since He can secure what He wants by the means. "His hand is not shortned." There was nothing in the new scientific concept of cause that seemed to Puritan theologians to call for theological revisions. Ames had explained in the *Medulla* that God wills one thing to exist for another, as He wills the sun and stars to exist for the generation and conservation of things below; "yet the Sunne and Stars, are not a cause why God would that those things should be generated, conserved, and corrupted." Richard Sibbes agreed that the world was made as a marvelous watch, each wheel geared to another, and the whole set in operation by God, but not left to run of itself. "By a continued kind of creation, he preserves all things in their being and working . . . If God moves not, the clock of the creature stands." Later in the century, after men had ceased thinking in terms of final, material, and formal causes, Willard still found that God must concur with the efficient cause and with its effect or neither of them could exist, and that therefore "The First and Universal Cause works together, or is at work with all the actions of second and particular Causes."

From this background the Puritan use of the word "means" took on its peculiar significance. God does all things, He creates the fire and the heat, and yet in His ordinary government He makes first the one and then the other. The fire is a "means" to the heat; it does not, properly speaking, give to heat its being, yet only in a miracle would God permit of heat without the proper antecedent. Even in a special providence He will Himself supply the place of the fire rather than allow uncaused heat to exist. Men may confidently predict effects from the regularity of causes; yet we must always remember that what we call a cause is in reality a means. "Though there be men used therein, yet he is himselfe present with those meanes." Connections between things are not inherently necessary but all are appointed; "the Conditions of things are but *Media* in his Decrees, and only intend, that he will bring about such Ends, by such Means."

The idea of means, with its assumption that the relation of cause to effect is no more than a regular sequence between two phenomena, obviously served the requirements of piety. It prevented believers from being lured into the heresy of natural autonomy; it was an eternal safe-guard against atheism. It encouraged humility and patience under affliction, since all the mediate or second causes of our grief must be God's instruments. Only "pagan ignorance" would ascribe changes to mere causality. But if the doctrine was useful, it was also loaded with philosophical dynamite. It was the one point on which Puritan theologians were thoroughly at one with nominalist philosophers; yet as we have seen the Puritans were always apprehensive lest they too should come with the nominalists to skeptical conclusions, lest they find that by their doctrine of causality they had embarked upon the same voyage with Occam. They were as much concerned to establish the existence of divine order and the law of nature as to assert the absolute power of God's will, although at the end of their scientific thinking, when they came down to the practical question of causality, they were compelled to confess that the order and the law rested on no further guarantee than the condescending pleasure of a hidden, an unpredictable, and a ruthless divinity. God uses means, said Ames, "not for want of power, but through the abundance of his goodnesse: that namely he might communicate a certaine dignity of working to his Creatures also, and in them might make his efficiency more perceiveable." This was no doubt an evidence of God's graciousness, but had we any assurance that He would always remain thus gracious? Calvinism could give none, and could trust therefore only in the usual and customary procedures, the habitual limitation which the divinity had apparently taken voluntarily upon Himself. In what is perhaps the most eloquent discussion of this question in New England literature, *The Soveraign Efficacy of Divine Grace,* Urian Oakes admitted that God could bring about effects without regard to secondary causes, but assured his hearers at length that once God has determined upon a course of providence, He cannot be imagined to dispense with it. His "pleasure" is to use means "and to produce many things by the mediation and Agency of second Causes." He has set up an order by His own appointment, "whereby one thing depends upon, and receives Being from another." In everyday affairs we are not to worry about the unpredictable, the marvelous, or even the providential; we are to use the means. "The greatest probability of Success (according to an ordinary providence, and in the eye of Reason) is ordinarily on the side of Causes that are most sufficient in their kind of Efficiency." Yet the best reassurance Oakes could offer was in terms of "pleasure," "probability," divine "appointment." Was there no further guarantee of certainty, of reliability, of predictability in life and in nature, in work and in salvation? After all the ingenuity which theologians for hundreds of years had expended on reconciling God's will with natural order, after all the care and labor Puritans had consumed in appropriating these teachings and reworking them to suit the conditions of their own time, were they left at last with no other surety than this? Perhaps to the believer such certainty ought to be adequate, since it rested upon the word of God. But did it rest on the Word? Had God ever said that He would restrict Himself ordinarily to the laws of common providence? The study of nature always resulted in the posing of this question to Puritan theologians, and they, being men of their century, in spite of the tremendous solidity of their faith, could not rest without seeking to answer it. Yet the study of nature had taught them something, if not the answer itself, then a few considerations that must govern the finding. It had taught them that solution was not to be found in any particular system of astronomy or physics, that the identical question was put both in scholastic physics and in mathematical and verifiable hypotheses, but that neither system supplied the answer. Obviously the answer was not to be found in the order of nature, and with this conclusion in mind, as it had for centuries been in the minds of other Augustinians, the Puritans turned anew to the revealed Word of God and reread their Bibles.

BOOK III

ANTHROPOLOGY

CHAPTER IX

THE NATURE OF MAN

A school of Puritan writers, which included the New England divines, ultimately found in the doctrine of the Covenant of Grace the answer, which academic physics could not furnish, to the problem of securing guarantees for rational order in a universe governed by super-rational absolutism. Yet before we examine this ultimate creation of the Puritan genius, we must consider another set of preconceptions which conditioned it no less than did the physics, for the problem was posed not only in the natural universe, but more urgently in a particular portion of the universe, in the constitution and psychology of man. If the divines were forced to balance special enactment against habitual regularity in such phenomena as tides and earthquakes, they were doubly pressed to reconcile them in matters of human behavior, and above all in the process of regeneration, for the question persisted: if God enacts events in sequences within the realm of nature, must He not also ordain sequences within the realm of grace? If He establishes a succession of "means" for combustion, surely He must create one for conversion! Yet it was well understood that nowhere was the divine will more capricious, more arbitrary, than in choosing men for everlasting life; nowhere did God less heed physical causes and environmental factors than in His elections. Before the preachers turned to their Bibles to heal the imperfections of physics, they had already phrased the issue, or to speak more accurately, it had been phrased for them, in the accepted language of contemporaneous psychology. Because regeneration worked a change within the soul, they could not describe the method of grace without presupposing a certain method of the soul.

Their psychological doctrine existed ready made, and they themselves contributed no ideas or propositions to it.[1] There is no need here to review it in detail; a bare outline, more simplified than can be found in the sources, will serve our purpose. The starting point, as in all Christian science, was the assertion, "Anima rationalis creatur," that the soul is not engendered by physical transmission, but is specially and individually created by God Himself. It is, as John Norton said, spiritual, incorporeal, "created by God of nothing, immediately infused into the body as the proper form thereof, by which man is, liveth, is sensible, moveth, understandeth, willeth, and is affected." It is, of course, an integral unit, yet like God of whom it is an "image", it is also a trinity, as becomes clear when we consider its place in the great chain of being. The higher must include the lower: plants have a "vegetative soul", which contains the powers of nourishing and propagating; animals have a "sensible soul", which contains the powers of nourishing and propagating, and, in addition, the senses and animal spirits, the "interior senses" of common sense, imagination, and memory, the passions and the sinews capable of motion; men have a "rational soul", which contains all the powers and faculties of the vegetative and sensible, and, in addition, the distinguishing faculties of the rational creature, reason and will. "There are three lives in man, there is the life of plants, of beasts or sence, and the life of reason," said John Preston, and in 1678 a Harvard thesis echoed, "There are three souls in the same man." More because of this tenet than of any other, Puritans in the early seventeenth century still lived in the ordered, hierarchal, and fixed world of medieval cosmology, and by it could still glorify man as a "Microcosmos", with a body like the minerals, "a moving life as stars, a springing life as Plants . . . a sensitive life as Beasts, and . . . a rational life as Angels."

Ideally speaking, when a rational soul functions as God designed it, the powers of the three souls fall into line like disciplined soldiers, and the whole of any human action may be depicted by a symmetrical arc of motion from the impact of an object to the response. Few writers described the faculties according to such a reflex, for they usually took up the three souls in mounting succession; yet all treatments center upon a reaction that may be traced through the several stages thus: the impression of an object produces in the senses an image or replica of the thing, generally called the "phantasm" or the "species"; the phantasm is then picked up at the eye or ear by the animal spirits and carried posthaste to the common sense in the central chamber of the brain; this faculty apprehends the phantasms, distinguishes one species from another, and relays them to the imagination, fancy or "phantasy", which, located in the front part of the brain, judges and compares one phantasm with another, retains them when the objects are absent, and sways the sensual inclination by holding and vivifying the objects of desire; after meaning and intelligibility have been attached to phantasms, they are stored in the memory, which is situated in the posterior lobe of the brain, where they may be "committed to it to keepe, as to their secretarie"; the reason or the understanding, which dwells somewhere above the middle, summons phantasms before its judgment seat from either the imagination or the storehouse of memory, determines which are right and true, and sends the image representing its decision, by the agency of the animal spirits, along the nerves to the will, which lives in the heart; the will then embraces true images as the good to be pursued, and commands the "sensitive appetite," which consists of affections or passions; the proper emotions, being thus aroused, transmit the impulse to the muscles. So the bear, encountered in the wilderness, causes in the eye a phantasm of the bear, which is identified as belonging to the species bear in common sense, recognized as dangerous in imagination, associated with remembered dangers in memory, declared an object to be fled in reason, made the signal of command to the will, which then excites the affection of fear, which finally prompts the muscles of the legs to run.

Remembering that this description is shamelessly simplified, and that for every point there was a long background of dispute, we can nevertheless regard it as substantially the conception underlying all Puritan discourse about human behavior, about the sin of man, and regeneration. One quotation out of a thousand that might be instanced from Renaissance writers will indicate how the reflex was conceived in contemporaneous terms:

As soone as the Exterior sences, busied about the Obiects which are proper for them, haue gathered the formes of things which come from without, they carry them to the common sence, the which receiues them, iudgeth of them, and distinguisheth them; and then to preserue them in the absence of their obiects, presents them to the Imagination, which hauing gathered them together, to the end she may represent them whensoeuer need shall require, she deliuers them to the custody of the Memory; from whence retiring them when occasion requires, she propounds them vnto the Appetite, under the apparance of things that are pleasing or troublesome, that is to say, under the forme of Good and Euill; and at the same instant the same formes enlightned with the Light of the vnderstanding, and purged from the sensible and singular conditions, which they retain in the Imagination, and insteed of that which they represented of particular things, representing them generall, they become capable to be imbraced by the vnderstanding; the which under the apparance of things which are profitable or hurtful, that is to say, vnder the forme of Good and Euill, represents them vnto the Will: the which being blind referres it selfe to that which the vnderstanding proposeth vnto it: And then as Queene of the powers of the soule she ordaines what they shall imbrace, & what they shall fly as it pleseth her; Whereunto the Sensitiue Appetite yeelding a prompt obedience to execute her command, from the which it neuer straies, so long as it containes it selfe within the bounds and order prescrib'd by Nature, quickneth all the powers and passions ouer which shee commands, and sets to worke those which are necessary to that action, and by their meanes commands the mouing power, dispersed ouer all the members, to follow or fly, to approach or recoyle, or to do any other motion which it requireth. And shee obeying suddenly if she bee not hindred, moues, the whole body with the Organs which reside in the parts, and induceth them to fly or imbrace things according to the command which she hath receiued.

One illustration from New England writings will indicate how the reflex was understood in America: Samuel Willard did not in any chapter of the monumental *Compleat Body* delineate it so systematically as we might wish, and he often altered traditional terminology, but he described how the "Images of Things" are first received in the common sense, "as it were the *Porter,* which takes in the *Species* of things, as they are offered unto it," are then conveyed to the imagination, which lays them together, "whereby the *Sensitive Creature* as it were, doth conclude *Sensibly,*" and are finally consigned to the memory, "whereby the Creature is able to lay up, what Cogitation hath laid together; and to bring them together again unto the Fancy, when there is occasion." The reason ponders an image so sifted and stored, and having passed judgment upon its goodness or evil, "accordingly there is a natural aptitude in the Will, to embrace it or renounce it; to chuse or refuse it"; the will then issues commands, "unto the exerting whereof the Affections serve." These, Willard said, are motions of the heart responding to the meanings with which imagination and reason have invested the phantasms, "and by Vertue hereof are Sensitive Beings variously affected with Love, Hatred, Fear, Desire, &c."; at last the affections "carry the man *to* the Object that is chosen, and *from* that which is refused." Thus all Puritans conceived that the responses of men, whether to a bear, food, beauty, or the Word of God, were conclusions of such a process; the images of all things, whether of husbandry or salvation, had to run the same course to produce their appropriate responses.

This doctrine of the psychological process was a part of the intellectual heritage which Puritans accepted without criticism, almost without realizing that it was a doctrine, since to them no other concept was available. Indeed, from their point of view it was simply a fact which had never been questioned, as obvious and natural as that two plus two equals four. Few Puritans in England and none in New England wrote books directly upon psychology, whereas they composed as many on witchcraft, providences, earthquakes, and storms as upon ecclesiastical polity; clearly in their consciousness the problem of reconciling God's decrees and rational order loomed large in the natural universe, but they were hardly aware of even the existence of a similar problem within the soul. They discussed the faculties only in passing references, in incidental exegesis, but with no deliberate concentration, and a casual reader of Puritan sermons might never notice that they contain a version of human psychology unless his attention were expressly called to scattered passages. Nevertheless, were his attention once aroused, he could collect so large an anthology of these utterances as to constitute an extended treatise upon psychology, the outlines of a doctrine upon which all Puritans agreed, of a premise for all their thinking, that can be said to have influenced them all the more extensively because it was unformulated and taken as axiomatic.

Their reluctance to dwell upon it more specifically was a precaution of piety; even though the doctrine seemed to imply no conflict with their creed, Puritans must have sensed intuitively that an intensive study of the faculties might end by lessening man's realization of sin or his awareness of his dire need for grace. Calvin had voiced this apprehension when he said that while he had no quarrel with the science, nevertheless "all curious discussion respecting the faculties themselves" were better left to philosophers. The real authors of the knowledge, he noted, were pagans, who generally deduced from it "that virtue and vice are in our own power . . . that the reason of the human understanding is sufficient for its proper government"; hence even though their science be factually correct, it will "involve us in their obscurity rather than assist us," and we shall do well to let it alone.[2] The many Renaissance authors of psychological works shared some of Calvin's distrust for their own subject; La Primaudaye warned against seeking out natural causes so curiously that we "strive to finde out another beginning of all things than God," and he did not want his *French Academie* studied by those who had not previously been instructed in the fear of God. Puritan writers would base some passages of exegesis upon the psychology, but would at other moments thrust it aside and declare that since the truths about conversion are plain and incontestable, we need "not trouble our selues about the distinction of the faculties."

However, in the early seventeenth century, Protestants in general were less fearful than Calvin, and the diminution of their caution is a part of the growth of what we have called a "Protestant scholasticism." With theological doctrines codified, the problem now was to synthesize all knowledge or to integrate it into "method". Protestant scholars like Keckermann and Alsted approached physics without trepidation, and appropriated for their encyclopedias the ancient doctrine of the faculties as readily as they did the doctrine of the four causes. As a matter of fact, medieval theory was ideally suited to their purposes, for Aristotelian psychology was primarily a system of classifying acts of the soul, not for explaining them mechanically. Like all medieval and most Renaissance science, it fulfilled its task when it enumerated the components, and a science which laid out arguments in method was "veritas" for Ramist logicians and a transcript of the will of God for Puritan theologians. Because the theory was purely descriptive, it could serve Puritans as it did La Primaudaye, leading men to a better knowledge of God "by that resemblaunce and similitude of his wisedome, which hee hath vouchsafed to transferre and to imprint in mans nature." Since it was not so much a scientific hypothesis as a portrait of the image of God, the psychological theory became for Calvin's successors, in their effort to amplify the correlations between revelation and nature, an indispensable portion of knowledge, so that in a New England sermon, Thomas Hooker would elaborate the meaning of psychological terminology and conclude, "so much for these poynts of speculation, without which I could not well open the poynt." Samuel Willard, though confessing that "Our knowledge of the nature of our own Souls, is very shallow and confused," would also point out that God has accommodated revelation to the nature of man and given rules of divinity adapted to "the Understandings, Wills, Affections, and Senses of men." When divinity is preached, therefore, these "need both teaching and quickning." The faculties could not be quickened until ministers knew what they were, and the manner of teaching depended entirely upon what concept of the faculties the ministers were taught.

To ascertain precisely what New England ministers were taught we must turn to the textbooks of physics.[3] The fact that the doctrine was contained in such works explains why the theory was so much an affair of general consent, why it was so patently and universally acknowledged, why the ministers could assume that their congregations would understand the connotation of words like phantasy, animal spirits, or affections, as modern audiences understand words like carburetor or storage battery. The theory was so familiar to men of the century that they could not have stopped to consider it as theory. It is a sign of the times that in the Elizabethan period there were produced many works upon the nature of man and the diseases of the soul, yet only one Puritan author, Edward Reynolds, contributed directly to this literature. Nevertheless, in works like those of Coeffeteau, Wright, and Senault, or *The French Academie,* New England Puritans could find more extended descriptions but not fundamentally any other theories than those which were already common knowledge. Elizabethan psychologists are valuable for the light they throw upon the vocabulary of emotion, and useful to students both of Shakespeare and of Puritanism, but they were not the sources for the psychological conceptions of either dramatists or divines. The theory was a heritage from the middle ages, and had been put together by Albertus Magnus and Thomas Aquinas; yet even they were not its authors, for it was an eclectic product to which many writers had contributed, some of whom had originally been diametrically opposed to each other. The groundwork was from Aristotle, and his *De Anima* remained the basic textbook. But some tenets were in fact derived from Plato; many had descended from Neo-Platonic attempts to harmonize Plato and Aristotle; others can be traced to the Stoics, and Cicero and Seneca were quoted hardly less than Aristotle. Augustine had also contributed, as had Pliny, Plutarch, Xenophon, Avicenna, Averroes, and the major medieval theologians. Puritans had revolted against scholastic theology and its ecclesiastical teachings; they had condemned, so they believed, the logic of scholasticism, and above all they criticized schoolmen for obscuring the authority of Scripture, for concealing the true nature of divine grace and irresistible regeneration. Yet they retained without substantial change orthodox scholastic ideas of the soul, of its composition and its faculties, and were therefore faced, even though refusing to admit it, with a problem of reconciling their new doctrines of regeneration and conversion with old doctrines of human nature. Because they held fast to medieval theory in psychology, Puritans were forced to describe regeneration in the terms of a psychological mechanism as well as in the language of theology.

In the middle ages there had been countless variations among philosophers; yet in the early seventeenth century the doctrine seemed fixed and, with one important exception, wholly consistent. It was certainly simple and easily understood. When New England was settled there was as yet no indication to the Puritan view that it would prove untenable, although in the preceding years it had received more popular discussion than in any other period in European history. The Puritan version was not altered until the last decades of the century, when it was modified to suit the criticisms of Descartes, and was not really abandoned until the beginning of the eighteenth century, when the *Essay on the Human Understanding* swept it into the discard. Consequently, during the seventeenth century Puritans believed it without qualification, employed textbooks in which it was embodied, explained the Bible in its terms, and founded their whole theology and cosmology, their logic and technologia, upon this conception of man.

Though in Puritan writing there are almost enough passing allusions to each part of the psychological reflex to furnish the material for extended chapters, we need herein be concerned with merely a few points that illuminate the whole configuration of Puritan thought. To take them in the order of the reflex itself, it is interesting to note that in their conception of the phantasm Puritans ignored one element of medieval theory, the intermediary "intentional forms"; in the standard Peripatetic doctrine these were "a Sort of Spectres," detaching themselves from things and plying between them and the senses, impinging upon the senses with a substance of finer texture than the things themselves, and so more easily absorbed and digested into phantasms.[4] Like many writers of the period, like the Ramist logicians in particular—and unlike such anti-Ramists as Keckermann and Stierius—the Puritans assumed a direct transmission of the object into the image or phantasm through the act of perception; in common with philosophers like Pomponazzi[5] and Francis Bacon, with whom on other scores they would not have agreed, they looked upon sense as an activity, seizing immediately upon the thing and establishing a continuous and faithful relation between the object and the mind. Even the Peripatetic Morton explained that the intentional species were "*supposed* to be a kind of *middle things* between *body* and *spirit* . . . but indeed all this Doctrine of Species seems to be a mistake, for that which affects the outward Sense is a reall and naturall body." [6] Hence, one trained like Samuel Willard in the truly Ramist tradition would say without hesitation that though reason must work upon "Effigies", and "hence the Understanding makes use of the Imagination in this affair," nevertheless the object is known in the faculties "by the reflection of the rays and beams of it upon the faculty," that the faculties carry an exact similitude of it to the understanding, and that "knowledge is made by an assimilation between the Knower, and the thing known." The conclusion of psychology as of technologia was that truth, obtainable by the dual machinery of perception and dialectic, is the right conception of things in the understanding: "when it forms in the mind a conception of the thing, just as it is in it self, that is Truth."

There was little controversy about the animal spirits, which were defined by all schools of philosophy as "the vinculum, the tye of union between the soul and body," or as a mock thesis expressed it, "the hyphen of the rational soul and the body." There was more uncertainty in discussions of the three interior senses, though most of the "gravis disputatio" was over the fruitless question of their exact location in the brain; Puritans in general believed with Willard that the brain "is divided into so many Cells, or several Rooms, which are as it were so many *Shops,* in which the Inward Senses do work," and almost always placed the imagination in the forward room, the common sense in the middle, and the memory behind. These three senses together could receive, make intelligible, and preserve the species of things, both present and absent, and they made possible the intelligent reactions of animals without necessitating their possession of a reason or a will. The largest amount of discussion was devoted to the imagination, for its rôle was crucial; it was capable of swaying the entire being in one direction or another by the fashion in which it formed and presented the images of desirable or repulsive things to the reason, will, and affection. It could not only give significance to images handed up from the common sense, judge them and conserve them, but also do what the common sense and memory could not do, combine sense-images into synthetic phantasms that corresponded to nothing in nature. It thus performed an essential service for thought, without which reason could hardly operate, as Zanchius explained by showing that the individual phantasms of "bread" and of "the body of Christ" are received as "nudae rerum imagines" in the common sense, but in the imagination are joined into an image, "the body of Christ is bread." The "office" of the imagination, said Reynolds, is twofold: to assist the understanding in the work of invention by supplying it "with variety of objects whereon to work," and to quicken or allure the will by framing the image of desirable goals. It is therefore the freest of the faculties, less confined even than the reason, which must adhere to the truth of things and assent to what it finds in the imagination, whereas the imagination itself can indefinitely manufacture new images by combining those of the senses; "And hence it is, that in matter of perswasion and insinuation, Poetry, Mythology, and Eloquence (the Arts of rationall Fancie) have ever . . . beene more forcible then those which have been rigorously grounded on Nature and Reason."

The interior senses presented no theoretical difficulties so long as discussion was confined to the sensible soul, but when philosophers endeavored to expound the connection of the sensible with the rational soul they encountered trouble in the question of the extent to which reason is dependent upon the fancy, which question then gave rise to the further one of how much is the will dependent upon the reason. The first of these questions was posed by the apparently irresistible reflection that if reason can discharge its functions only with images received from the interior senses, is not the superior rational soul then at the mercy of the inferior sensitive soul? Cotton Mather seemed to imply as much when he said, "The *Thoughts* are properly, those *Conceptions* or *Characters* of Things, which the *Understanding* fetches out of the *Imagination,* in our Souls," and the psychologists made the dependence greater when they said, "the office of the memorie is, to preserue the fantasmes, to the end that the vnderstanding may contemplat them." Yet psychologists and ministers always denied the implication, and argued with Reynolds that while reason requires imagination and memory to provide it with species, nevertheless these "do not qualifie the *perception"*; the phantasms, he said, are "only . . . the objects . . . not the instruments of the souls working," so that the act of understanding "is immediately from the soul, without any the least concurences of the body thereunto, although the things whereon that act is fixed and conversant, require, in this estate, bodily Organs to represent them unto the soul." If this was shaky logic, there were considerations, to which we shall presently come, making further probing of the problem undesirable; at any rate Puritans were assured that reason is not placed in the body as are the other faculties: "the visive faculty must have an eye to see, the hearing facultie must have an eare to heare . . . but the understanding hath no such organ, it onely useth those things that are presented to it by the phansie." Therefore reason, free and independent, is the king and ruler of the faculties, and its consort, the will, is queen and mistress. Puritan theologians made these two the symbols of the soul's high station in the aristocratic society of the cosmos, and explained that by their voluntary coöperation the soul becomes both intelligent and responsible:

It hath an *Understanding,* which Brutes have not, by vertue whereof it is able to Read the Book of the Creature, to see into the Nature of things, to discern the Beams of Divine Wisdom shining in the Frame of the World, and treasure up the Knowledge of it within it self: By this also it can invent curious Works, having a framing as well as discerning Wisdom . . . It can govern Inferiour Creatures with Discretion . . . It is able to reflect upon it self, and read its own Knowledge . . . It can communicate that Knowledge it hath unto others: And that which is its best Advantage is, that it is capable of knowing God to Eternal Life. It hath also a *Will,* whereby it is able to chuse or refuse what it apprehends to be Good or Evil: This Faculty can set all the Powers of Soul and Body on work; it can determine concerning the Acts of them all at its Pleasure: It hath the highest Object, viz., *Goodness* it self, and the best Rule, viz., *Divinity.*

Images are approved by the reason because they are true, by the will because they are good. Therefore the office of the understanding is to judge truth from falsehood, join what should be joined, separate the separables, distinguish things that follow or are contrary, refer things to the proper rubrics—all the "acts", in short, of logic, acts of which the imagination is not capable, for it can but combine images. The reason alone can conceive of things that are not bodies, make abstractions, think from the given to the conclusion, and so "lifteth vp all the sences of man to the contemplation of the diuinity, & of the spiritual & supernatural things"; our apprehension of spiritual comfort cannot be "that which stands in the outward senses, that is not worthy the name, but the apprehension that the will and understanding hath of things."[7]

The second question, of the relation of the will to the understanding, was apparently settled in the textbooks. The will, dwelling in the heart, is necessarily blind and can see only what the reason sends down to it in the form of images. "The office of our vnderstanding . . . is to receiue, and in knowing to offer unto the will those kinds or formes, which are sent vnto it from the Imagination." Reason, the preachers frequently declared, is "the fore-horse in the teame," and as it turns, so the will must follow; it is the "governor and captaine of the soule" and "the will dependeth of it." William Ames wrote this doctrine deep into the New England tradition, and founded the whole ethical system upon it: he defined faith as an act both of the understanding, which yields assent, and of the will, which embraces the assent, but reason's act must come before the act of will; "The *Will* . . . cannot will or nill any thing unlesse *reason* have first *judged* it to be willed or nilled; neither can it *choose* but *follow* the *last practicall judgement,* and do that which *reason* doth dictate to be done." Preachers in New England repeated this doctrine throughout the century: Hooker said that it was "a rule in naturall Philosophy," and also "reason telleth us thus much," while Willard said many times, "Now the Will of man naturally *chuseth good, and refuseth evil,* according as it is resented by his

Understanding." When the will inclines to an affection of love, it is "occasioned by the report that is made to it from the *Understanding,* that the Object is good, & good for him," and in *A Compleat Body* Willard was still expounding Ames, "It is a true rule, that man's will always follows the last dictate of the practical understanding." Accordingly the Harvard theses in physics reiterated conventional statements, such as that the will never thinks, that nothing is in it which is not first in the intellect, that it is always determined by the last act of the intellect.

However, the theses also indicate that all was not so settled as these propositions would suggest, for though in 1686 John Williams affirmed for his M. A. that the will is determined by the last judgment of the mind, in 1658 Gershom Bulkeley had denied it. We have a Latin verse summarizing Bulkeley's argument: had the will always followed the intellect, even in pristine integrity, could Adam have sinned? Certainly Adam *knew* that eating the apple was wrong; his will propelled him against his reason. "Therefore the imperious will forces into vice; what the mind well dictates, it says that does not please. It stands against reason." There are several theses of like tenor, and in the sermons there are outspoken assertions that the will is not after all entirely dependent upon the mind, but is capable of taking the initiative, of being in truth the "queen" of the faculties, of swaying the intellect itself. The cause for this inconsistency in Puritan thought and in the Harvard theses is not far to seek: unless the will were granted some degree of independence, unless it were free to act or refuse of its own power, there could be no moral responsibility; otherwise, once the reason had been rightly informed, the will would have no choice but to obey, and men could be made virtuous by good education instead of requiring the grace of God. In other words, in spite of the inherited doctrine, piety demanded that the will be detached from its subordination, that it be invested with the power to force images from the memory and the imagination into the chambers of the reason, that it have the strength to breast the ordinary flow of the animal spirits and drive them backwards and upwards with their phantasms. Ames had to admit that the will can at pleasure refuse to act upon any phantasm which the reason has apprehended, that it can do so "without any *foregoing act of judgement";* Preston would forget how he had said, "the will is but the appetite that followes the understanding," or that "the will and affections hanging upon the minde, it is unpossible that the will of a man should will and affect any other thing than that which the mind is affected with," and with equal fervor would describe the will as "the very leader of the soule, the driver of all faculties, the Lady and Queene of humane acts." John Cotton seems to have been especially eager to establish this autonomy for the will; it can, he asserted, set the senses to work, force the mind to understand, the memory to keep whatsoever it chooses. "It is the will of a man, in which his goodnesse lyes, and from the will it is communicated to the rest of the faculties"; the heart is "the doore of the soule, because of that authority that the heart and will hath over the whole soule, and the power it hath to rule both soule and body." Puritanism would have lost all grounds for individual moral responsibility had it held that the psychological reflex, once inaugurated by the senses, was automatic and irresistible; there had to be a break somewhere, a power that could refuse to play the mechanically consistent part, that could deviate voluntarily from the norm. If the academic theory were taken too literally, it would enslave the soul to an internal march of sensory images, and Puritan piety could permit no such conclusion. Therefore Cotton adjured, "Keepe the heart well, and you keepe all in a good frame"; his description of the independence of the heart throws light into several dark corners of Puritan thinking:

> Set before a man any pleasant prospect, and if his mind be on another thing, all his senses take no notice of it; if the heart be not taken up with a thing, the eye minds it not; present the eare with any sweet melodious sound, and it heares and minds it not, because the heart was otherwise taken up; but upon whatsoever the heart is set, to that the eye lookes, and the eare attends, every thing acts towards it, all goes freely that way, the mind, the judgement, the invention, the affection, and what ever a man hath . . . If you have the whole man, and not the heart, you have but a dead man, get the heart and you have all.

Therefore Willard, who generally followed the standard sequence, nevertheless confessed that the will can set the understanding to work "by intending a Thing, which it will have that contrive; and so the Will is the First Mover."

Of course others than Puritans were troubled by the contradiction; all Renaissance authors tried to smooth it over, to hedge the question, to avoid it, but not to settle it, for the attempt promised merely to widen the breach. *The French Academie* said that reason rules over the will, not as absolute lord, but as "mistresse", to teach it and guide it rather than to command, that the will has liberty to do or not do "after the minde hath shewed vnto it what it ought to follow," and that the will may choose among many reasons whichever it will pursue. Harvard theses sometimes tried to voice this compromise, as in 1653: "Will follows but does not yield to the rules of the intellect"; few writers on psychology had the courage of a Casmannus, who declared forthrightly that the question, "An intellectus semper movent voluntatem ut numquam moveatur a voluntate," was insoluble.

New Englanders did not at first feel the urgency of the problem, because for them it was largely academic; the question related to man before the fall, and since they had to deal with man only after that collapse, with his will now in rebellion and his reason incompetent, they did not need to waste time speculating on what the ideal relationship might have been.

They were certain that when men regained spiritual health with the help of grace, the question would disappear: "If the minde be right, the Will will follow; and if the Will follow, be sure the affections will follow." God had intended the two to work in harmony, not to quarrel over priority; the object of reason should be truth, of the will goodness, and the true is identical with the good. "All things are made for man, the body for the soule, the understanding for the will, and the will for God; the understanding that seeth truths, and discernes the excellency that is in God, but there is nothing that relisheth and tasteth the goodnesse which is in God but the will." The will must not choose without a reason, but it is not therefore enslaved to reason:

> Nothing can affect the heart, but so farre as reason conceiveth it, and ushers it home to the soule; thereupon . . . as the King hath his Counsellors which call all matters before them, & consult about busines, and then they bring them before the King, to have a finall sentence from him . . . so the understanding is like the Councellors, and the will is the Queene; the understanding saith, this or that is good, then the will saith, let me have it: the understanding saith, these and these duties are required, and the will embraceth them.

God made man an understanding creature, and to understand means to exercise freely both the reason and will; the heart consents according to the rules of the reason, "but it is therefore said to be free, because, whether, out of a true judgment, it moves one way, or out of a false, another way; yet, in both, it moves, in a manner suitable to its own condition." So God speaks to us with reasons, not merely that our minds shall be convinced, but also that our wills may deliberate and act without constraint. It is equally sinful to understand and not act, or to act and not understand. "If a man say, I know and doe not Will it, that is folly: If a man say, I will, and have no reason for it, it is obstinacie."

The conventional doctrine of the passions offered no problem to Puritan psychologists, even though it contained a distinction that might at any moment have become troublesome. All passions were generally conceived as modes of human response, as fashions in which the organism is "affected" by some sensation, consideration, or idea toward the realization of its proper end, and the words "passions" or "affections" were used interchangeably. Reynolds' description might for the substance of it have appeared in any of a hundred discussions:

> . . . those naturall, perfective and unstrained motions of the Creatures unto that advancement of their Natures, which they are by the Wisdome, Power, and Providence of their Creator, in their own severall Spheres, and according to the proportion of their Capacities, ordained to receive, by a regular inclination to those objects, whose goodness beareth a naturall conveniencie or Vertue of satisfaction unto them; or by an antipathie and aversation from those, which . . must needs be noxious and destructive.

Tradition, however, had already distinguished between passions that are "natural" and those that are "moral", and had divided the "sensual" from the "rational". The first are immediate reactions of the body to the formation in the imagination of the phantasm of a bodily good or danger; they "go before Judgment," are instinctive and uncontrollable, entirely outside the sphere of morality. They are parts of the "law of nature," since they cause the motions which men must make for preservation, nourishment, and propagation, and without them men could not survive physically. Thus Preston spoke the Puritan discrimination between the two kinds of appetites:

The first is *Sensuall,* which apprehends things conveyed to the senses; as to the eye and eare, and so is affected to love, feare, or grieve . . . it is of objects apprehended by fantasie. Secondly, there is a *Rationall* appetite, the object of that, is that which the understanding apprehends; and from hence proceede affections to riches, honour, preferment, &c., the will being conversant about it.

Most Renaissance psychologists recognized this distinction, but preferred to dwell at greater length upon the moral than upon the natural, for the Renaissance investigation was an effort to establish bases for ethical judgments. As La Primaudaye defined the rational passions, so Puritans always conceived them: "By the affections, we meane properly those motions of the heart, which follow knowledge, and either seeke after or reiect, that which is offered vnto them: so that according to the order of nature, knowledge goeth before these motions." Puritans would have been delighted to leave to the John Donnes and the Montaignes of this world all preoccupation with passions which cannot be ruled or resisted; for themselves, "the Dignitie of Passion chiefly consists in a *Consonancie* and *Obedience* to the Prescription of *Reason.*" They were constantly preaching that in man's faculties there is "a natural *subordination,* whereby the actions of the inferior receive their motion and direction from the influence of the higher," and this lesson has, for better or worse, remained one of their principal bequests to their posterity, long after the faculty psychology has become as obsolete as the Ptolemaic universe. Reynolds even went so far as to assert that in the original design God had not intended that any passions should be aroused merely by the senses, that sense was created to present its images solely to the understanding, "upon whose determination and conduct, the *Passions* were to depend, to submit all their inclinations thereunto, and to be its Ministers." If New Englanders believed what they found in their textbooks, they must have continued to recognize the difference between sensual and rational passions as a basic decree of God Himself, but nevertheless their discussions usually pass over the sensual to draw morals and lessons from the passions that depend upon reason and will power. As Willard spoke of the affections, he meant "instruments of the will, by which it either embraceth or refuseth a thing; and they are subordinated to his *Understanding*." Had Puritans pushed their thinking upon the nature of man to its logical limits, as did the great dramatists, they too would have discovered a conflict in their theory, a possible struggle between irresistible passions and controlling reason or queenly will that would have permitted a tragic sense of life, but they never recognized it because they held to the vision of an ideal state in which all faculties harmonized, in which the passions voluntarily depended upon the will and the will upon right reason. As Urian Oakes said of the act of "consideration", though it is strictly speaking an act of the understanding, "yet it imports . . . sutable affection. It is not in the Text a bare speculation . . . but that which enwraps in it sutable actings of the Will and Affections." The faculty psychology furnished the cast of mental characters for a psychological drama of salvation, as Bunyan's embodied concepts show; long before Bunyan wrote, New England preachers were dramatically picturing the Christian's progress in terms of the faculties, and of all New England preachers, Hooker again was the most dramatic:

> The reason of this order of Gods worke, why desire comes next after hope is this; because desire is that other affection which serves the great commandresse of the soule, the *will,* for these affections are as handmaids to serve the *will.* The will saith, I will have this or that good, and therefore hope[,] wait you for it, and desire, long you after it . . . When the soule is doubting and quarrelling, and saith, will the Lord doe good to such an unworthy wretch as I am: yes saith the minde inlightned, mercy is intended towards thee, then hope goeth out to wait and looke for this mercy. Now when the soule hath waited a long time, and yet this mercy comes not, and he marvels at it . . . then the *will* sends out desire to meet with that good which will not yet come, and so desire goeth wandring from one ordinance to another, till it bring Christ home to the soule.

Puritan preachers believed that sanctification could be achieved only as a consequence of justification, that moral perfection required a previous infusion of supernatural grace, but no matter how dramatically they conceived of regeneration, we shall find again and again that their counsels of perfection were in effect hints for a rational control of the passions or for a deliberate and positive direction of emotion.

In common with previous Christian philosophers, the Puritans found themselves committed by their theory of emotion to a position that often required great ingenuity to maintain: since God created the soul with affections, these must be fundamentally good, even though they are now corrupted by sin; and the Stoic belief, that they are inherently evil and should be extirpated from the soul, is a blasphemy against God's handiwork. Even the passions of sinful and unregenerate man are not inclined towards evil and do not flee from the good; as a Harvard thesis declared,

'Evil is not desired formally." Passions may be easily misguided or they may get out of hand, but they are bound to follow what seems to them good and to eschew what seems evil. Their function cannot be dispensed with, or man would be constitutionally altered and the great chain of being broken. To prove this point Christ had assumed the whole human character, not merely reason and will, but all the passions: desire, anger, hatred, and fear. Having inherited medieval psychology, Puritan theologians also inherited the contention of classical Peripatetics against classical Stoics, that the ideal happiness of the human organism lies in a realization of its natural functions, that impediments to fulfilling its nature constitute pain and misery. "What is naturall to thee, is pleasant, because indeed all pleasure is nothing else, but a sutablenesse to our Nature"; the desire for happiness, said Samuel Willard, "is a congenerate principal of Humane nature, and can be no more separate from it than Humanity," and all men ought to aim at it. This was not to lose sight of the religious goal: happiness is our subjective end, the glory of God our objective end, "and God hath tyed these together so inseparably, that man cannot possibly make a separation of them." Consequently, though Puritan descriptions of sinful man seem very close to Stoic denunciations of the tyranny of the passions, and though the Puritan ideal of regeneration appears very similar to the Stoic ideal of rational control, the Puritans had to take elaborate precautions lest they become mere Stoics. Their position was essentially that of Thomas Aquinas: "The passions of the soul, in so far as they are contrary to the order of reason, incline us to sin: but in so far as they are controlled by reason, they pertaine to virtue,"[8] and they framed sentences which, taken by themselves, could come as well from any scholastic or Aristotelian treatise. Thus Reynolds attacked Stoicism by saying, "The agitations of Passion, as long as they serve onely to drive foreward, but not to drown Vertue; as long as they keep their dependance on Reason, and runne only in that Chanel wherewith they are thereby bounded; are of excellent service." Willard's many long passages upon the nature and government of the passions indicate how in Puritan circles discussion of the theme could proceed without too extreme or too constant an awareness of hopeless depravity and lead to a conception of moral control and rational dignity as within the reach of mere natural man. Because sin has rendered the passions unruly and exorbitant, he says, we must then "use utmost endeavour to keep them in command, under the guidance of our sanctified understanding and will." He inserts the word "sanctified" to remind us that the understanding and will must have divine help, yet there are very few other indications that he is thinking, for the time being, in religious terms; grace is not even mentioned in another paragraph that explains how "all the Affections were put into men by God when he Created them, and so they belong to the very nature of Humanity," and how "there is a rational use to be made of them, which is in it self lawful for men, yea and a moral duty; and by such an application or improvement, the Affection doth attain the moral end which it was placed in man for." The theme of human depravity in Puritan sermons is apt to have its subtleties, for in it meet the two factors that determined Puritan thinking, piety and the intellectual heritage, and though piety demanded that man be humiliated and forced to confess himself contemptible, the heritage, with its memorials of the historic Christian conflict with Stoicism, demanded that human nature be not despised too much.

Learn hence the difference between Christianity and *Stoicism*. That would hamstring nature, and cut off the Affections from their natural activity, as if they had been given to and put into men for nothing else but to be suppressed; & to make no use of; as if he could enjoy no benefit by them . . . whereas the Word of God and the rules of Religion teach us, not to destroy, but to improve every faculty that is in us, and in particular our Affections . . . and truly, whatsoever men may think, if God should lose the honour of the employment of our Affection for him, we should rob him of a great deal of his due, yea cut off the very feet of our Souls, and how then should we be able to *run the race of his Commandments*.

In theory, at least, Puritanism could never admit that any truly natural desire was, *qua* desire, sinful, and John Milton spoke the innermost meaning of Puritanism when he represented Adam and Eve before the fall enjoying "wedded love," the "sole propriety in paradise of all things common else," though he was equally the Puritan when he caused the archangel to inform Adam that the soul must not be subdued to passion, and that love "hath his seat in reason, and is judicious."

It is difficult to estimate objectively how much Puritanism owed to the traditional and inherited psychological theory, for it is next to impossible to consider Puritanism of the seventeenth century apart from that theory. Yet granting that in one sense this question ought never to be asked, we can still pose it for the purposes of our analysis: what did the psychological theory in particular contribute to the body of Puritan thinking? Furthermore, the origins of this theory, as Calvin recognized, were not Christian; it did not flow from the same sources as did the Augustinian piety. Since the whole theology was posited tacitly upon the conception of man provided by the academic theory, Puritans were hardly aware that there could be any conflict between the two, or that there were concealed fissures within the structure of their doctrine. Yet again, for the purposes of analysis, we may be justified in asking a question which they would have refused to recognize, and to join to our first interrogation a second equally artificial: did the theory accentuate or heighten any tensions within the body of Puritan thought?

Clearly it was of particular use to Puritan divines in setting forth the nature of sin and of regeneration; it was also of assistance in explaining how the will of corrupt men could still remain formally free, and finally it provided a physiological foundation for the peculiar doctrines of Ramist logic and of technologia. On the first point, the description of sin and its effects on the organism might seem one thing to us when given in the terminology of theology and quite another when couched in the vocabulary of psychology, but to Puritans the two accounts were interchangeable and synonymous. In theology they simply declared that man is corrupt, evil, and impotent; in psychology they gave those adjectives specific meaning by concrete demonstrations of how the mechanism is out of gear, how the ideal reflex created by God is now broken into as many pieces as it has parts, how each part fails to perform its designated function, how the order of the connections is reversed or disfigured, how the higher are unnaturally enslaved to the lower, and how therefore chaos and depravity become highly explicable. The parson of Westfield put the theological point into psychological language:

> The Understandings dark, and therefore will
> Account of Ill for Good, and Good for ill . . .
> The Will is herevpon perverted so,
> It laquyes after ill, doth good foregoe.
> The Reasonable Soule doth much delight
> A Pickpack t'ride o'th'Sensuall Appitite.
> And hence the heart is hardened and toyes
> With Love, Delight, and Joy, yea Vanities.[9]

Obviously the Puritan preacher as well as the poet secured certain advantages for effective speaking when able to use the psychological doctrine in expounding the articles of piety, but there was always a lurking danger, of which he was dimly aware, that if he gave too detailed a description in the comparatively mechanistic language of psychology, so that sin seemed to amount to the simple statement, "That once orderly Frame is now full of Confusion," he might inadvertently suggest that a mere setting of the machinery to rights, a mere disciplining of confusion into order, would secure all the effects attributed to spiritual regeneration. However, Puritanism in the seventeenth century was as yet not greatly troubled by this prospect, since it seemed clear that no matter how concrete the diagnosis of psychological dislocation might become, the cure of sick faculties and the realigning of the reflex could be accomplished only by God. Consequently, after the preachers had set forth the ideal sequence as God had instituted it, they could run over each of the phases, from the phantasm to the passions, pointing out how each now failed to do its share, how each rebelled against subordination, stepped out of line, established immoral liaisons with one or another, and threw the whole microcosm into pandemonium. The reflex we have been reviewing was proclaimed to be the manner in which "man proceeds in his free operations, if he will observe the order which he ought"; when all faculties "attend their destinated functions, the common-wealth of man flourisheth, when the soule is obeyed, and the body obeyeth." But "that unhappy Forefather of ours, who made us to inherit his fault," has left us an organism jangled and confused:

The body and soul suffer pain . . . The understanding hath its errors, the will her irregular inclinations, the memory her weakness . . . The senses are seduced by Objects, these help to abuse Imagination, which excites disorders in the inferior parts of the soul, and raiseth Passions, so as they are no longer in that obedience, wherein original Justice kept them; and though they be subject to the Empire of Reason, yet they so mutinie, as they are not to be brought within the compass of their duty, but by force or cunning.

Therefore, if the preacher takes the senses, the faculties, and the passions one by one, calculates the amount of imperfection and sinfulness each contains, and adds up his column of figures, the grand total will be the sum of innate depravity.

Puritan sermons seldom went about systematically to summarize the defects of all the faculties; whenever their text demanded, they developed the perversity of this or that power, and pounded home the moral on different occasions with such vehemence that whatever faculty was being discussed appeared for the moment the most sinful of the lot. In this vein the external senses, the animal spirits, common sense, and memory were all denounced for contributing to the deformation of the whole, yet in general the other four members of the reflex, imagination, reason, will, and the affections, were considered the focal points of sin, the crucial joints in the human armor through which Satan most frequently thrust his lance. The imagination was a particularly bad spot because it had never been bound to the senses and could form images beyond and in excess of nature; once it is depraved it becomes utterly lawless, and will throw up phantasms of unnatural lusts to seduce the will and affections; it can lead enfeebled reason in its train, or if the reason objects, cut short the arc of the reflex and present its perverted images directly to the will or immediately to the passions. Furthermore, it is dangerous because Satan, retaining his angelic incorporeality, can insert images into it without any agency of the senses, thus tempting the will with imaginations of such vices as could never have been conceived merely from experience. The Devil has no need "of speaking with an audible voice, or representing things to our bodily eyes, &c. but hath a closer and more secret way of access to our Imaginations, in which he can represent the Images of things, and hold them before us." Thus Satan commenced the seduction of Eve, when he was found by Ithuriel squatting like a toad at her ear,

Assaying by his devilish art to reach
The organs of her fancy, and with them forge
Illusions as he list, phantasms, and dreams.

Richard Sibbes devoted a long section of *The Souls Conflict,* which was widely read in New England, to the imagination and its crimes; it causes harm, he said, by false representation, by preventing reason and usurping judgment, by forging matter out of itself without any external sensation, by devising vanity and mischief. The most significant charge he brings against sinful fancy, again and again, is that it forms images either of happiness and delight, or of horror and terror, which are unreal, which are not in accordance with the nature of things.

The life of many men . . . is almost nothing else but a fancy; that which chiefly sets their wits awork and takes up most of their time is how to please their own imagination, which setteth up an excellency, within itself, in comparison of which it despiseth all true excellency and those things that are of most necessary consequence indeed.

Passages of this sort make clear why to Puritans what we might call "romantic" poetry, visions of supernal and unearthly loveliness, of beauties rising like Venus from the sea of imagination, were not only nonsense, but sinful. By the same token "romances" were dangerous because, as Willard said, they are "adorned with Fictions, or a representation of things according as we fancy they should be, not regarding what they are indeed." If imagination is ungoverned, Sibbes declared, it "is a wild and ranging thing; it wrongs not only the frame of God's work in us, setting the baser part of a man above the higher, but it wrongs likewise the work of God in the creatures, and everything else, for it shapes things as itself pleaseth." Because imagination is the "first wheel of the soul," it must be rigorously controlled by the reason, and if reason is incapable, then by the Word and by the spirit. Fancy is not in itself sinful, and it is necessary in the religious life to form phantasms of the truths of religion, but it must mirror only facts. "That wormwood is bitter, it is not a conceit only, but the nature of the thing itself." Things are good or evil in the Puritan view not according to our opinion but as they are in themselves. The New England divines rephrased Sibbes on countless occasions, as for example Hooker in *The Application of Redemption:*

A mans imaginations are the forge of villany, where it's al framed, the Warehouse of wickedness, the Magazine of al mischief and iniquity, whence the sinner is furnished to the commission of al evil, in his ordinary course; the Sea of abominations, which over-flows into al the Sences, and they are polluted into all the parts of the body, and they are defiled and carried aside with many noysom corruptions . . . The Imagination of our mind is the great Wheel that carries al with it.

Consequently, the first act of regeneration must be a cleansing of the imagination, an enforcement of strict conformity between the mental image and the thing, for "while the swarmes of vain imaginations keep thoroughfare in our minds," there is no hope "that the power of any meanes should come in upon the soul or prevayl with it for good." So in literature, in life, in religion, we must fight against the "natural pronitude in us to give our fansies an unlimited liberty," for fancy is "more dangerous than the glances of our outward senses." Above all in the mysterious and difficult mazes of regeneration the imagination must be held in check: "Every sinner sets up a fancie in his owne Imagination, that if Christ comes, strange matters will be wrought. Now framing this fancie in his conceit, he will take no other evidence of Christs comming." Anne Hutchinson and Roger Williams were banished from Massachusetts Bay because they were altogether too gifted with imagination.

The Puritan distinction between "opinion" and "science" was a distinction between concepts of the imagination and the understanding; when the imagination forms a hasty or false impression of facts, and passes the impression at once to the affections, a man behaves on insufficient or erroneous ideas, and reason is misled. But in the sinful state the understanding, left to itself, achieves little that is more reliable. "The Porter of the soule," as Preston called it, is now blinded by sin, and so "it mis-informes the will and affections; that is, it breeds a disorder in the soule." The natural understanding cannot abandon its office of informing the will with phantasms, but through the perversity of sin it refuses to inform the blind will correctly. "The understanding tastes things, it is as the pallate is to the stomacke, when it is out of order, it perverts the wayes of God, it sees no such beautie, nor excellencie in them." Apostasy has not demolished the faculties, but put a malignancy into them, so that merely by acting according to their natures they produce discord instead of harmony; hence the reason does not suffer from a hostility to truth, because reason, as long as it lives, must desire to conceive true images of things. Truth is still the adequate object of the natural intellect, which must be carried by a natural inclination to enquire after it; men do not embrace the lie as such, "but it must come to them under the notion and consideration of Truth." But they are not any whit better thereby; "because they are confidently built on it that it is true, this makes them to hold it tenaciously." The irony of sin is that man achieves evil by good means; he believes what he thinks to be true, and will defend it even unto death, but he knows not that the fall has so crazed his mind that he naturally calls evil good. "His spiritual Opticks are strangely discoloured, the principles of his natural reason are become corrupt, the Rules by which he measures and weighs things are depraved." He believes the lie because he takes it for truth, "his defiled understanding, proceeding according to its false reasonings, is perswaded to believe that it sees sufficient reason for it," and the remains of the original virtue, the feeble remnants of a capacity for truth, become to sinful men the actual instruments of their undoing.

The will, too, works evil by acting according to its nature, embracing the lies which the understanding delivers to it as truths, and stoutly persisting in guiding the organism to destruction. Yet also, by virtue of that partial freedom, that limited ability which in the first condition it possessed to obey reason from sovereign choice and to follow the intellect as a guide and friend rather than as an absolute lord, the will can work evil in despite of reason, so that when education and experience have tamed the imagination and taught reason the "faith of assent", the unregenerate will remains perverse. The influence of Augustine and of the late scholastics, of the nominalists against whom the Puritans struggled even while adopting their ideas, made this emphasis upon the deliberate errancy of the will, as against the informed reason, greater among Puritans than among many Protestant communions.[10] The Scotists had concluded that knowledge cannot determine the will; Puritans generally insisted that it can, but also, because they inherited some of their thinking from the Scotists and because they did not want to forego any chance to put the burden of responsibility upon the individual, they, too, had to confess that the will may rebel against the best informed understanding, that it can doggedly fly in the face of convincing evidence. The ideal supremacy of reason over will could be reëstablished only by grace, not by education. So Ames, who was reluctant to believe that in the ideal order will would ever contradict understanding, had no hesitation in insisting that a sinful will "can turne away the understanding from the *consideration* of any object, which at present it apprehendeth and judgeth to be good," and cause the mind to apprehend that which is evil as being good. Thus the will even more than the imagination is "the first cause of unadvisednesse, and blame-worthy error in the understanding." Freedom or liberty, he said—striving to reconcile the diverse tendencies of his doctrine with a scholastical distinction—is in the reason "radically", because reason propounds to the will what it understands to be true, and the will is determined by the understanding "in regard of the *specification* or kinde of thing to be willed, because it willeth nothing but that which the understanding hath first apprehended"; yet freedom also is in the will "formally", because the will may move both itself and the passions, and thus sway the mind. "And hence it is that *liberty* is in the will *formally,* which should not be true, if it were necessarily determined by the understanding." The point was, in simple terms, that the will cannot be exonerated from contributing to sin on the plea that it does only what the reason tells it; even though it be blind, and must have phantasms from the reason to work upon, it sins independently. Man is depraved not because he has a will, but because he has a will that prefers evil. Thus "the sweet Harmony and Subordination of Sense to Reason, and of Reason to God, is broken," because the will "absolutely gainsayes the Counsels, Lawes, and Directions of the Understanding."

As with many previous Christian moralists, once Puritans had made clear that they were not Stoics, they could proceed to moralize about the passions in a thoroughly Stoical vein. The motions of the soul, they would say, should be exercised in subjection to reason and will, but in ordinary life appetites are excited directly by the senses and thus thrust aside the counsels of reason and the attempted restraints of the will. They are "the vapours and mists that blinde the reason, and make a man unable to resist them, because the putting out of the eye of reason, must needs trouble a man exceedingly." The moral problem was control; the exhortation of hundreds of Puritan sermons comes to an injunction which is almost pure Stoicism: "Wee should mortifie these our affections"; "Therefore it stands you upon to keepe them under." Passions are violent perturbations, troublesome and exhausting; they must be bridled and subdued.

> When the Passions and Affections of the Soul are broken loose, having shaken off the reins of government, some thrusting the man violently forward to that which is Evil, and others forcing him to fly as fast from that which is good; when they give forth Different commands, and that he may have no leisure to think of them, they fill his Ears with clamour and importunity . . . This is the State of the Unregenerate . . . Care then should be taken to Quell this unhappy Tumult, to reduce every affection within its proper bounds.

With the background of classical literature and the issues of philosophy to direct them, secular psychologists in the Renaissance were more interested in the passions than in any other problem of the soul, and the same preoccupation is reflected in contemporaneous drama and poetry.[11] To the Puritans, the passions were no more engrossing a concern than the lawless fancy, the mistaken reason, or the malicious will, but otherwise their attitude was characteristic of the age. Yet in strict consistency, they probably ought not have agreed so easily with non-Puritanical psychologists and should have been less ready to talk of rational control. As they viewed the appetites of sinful man with the eye of piety, they saw them persuading his will to pander to their desires and bribing his reason to justify them with specious arguments; only grace could ever "Quell this unhappy Tumult." The unregenerate reason, if properly informed, and the natural will, if skillfully guided, might hold affections in check for a time, but sooner or later they were bound to slip any leash that nature could devise. Puritans had no right to demand rational control from the unconverted, for innate depravity meant precisely that the passions were "independent", that they were able to anticipate reason, "relying onely upon the judgement of *Sense,*" that among sinful men "Desire allures the Understanding to dictate Reasons and Inducements, that may perswade to the Beliefe thereof."

On the Elizabethan stage, tragedy was rightly represented by passions which escape reason and lead the hero to destruction, because the authors and their audiences assumed that the hero might possibly have restrained them; in Puritan theology, however, passions which defied reason constituted deserved damnation, although it was axiomatic that the unregenerate would never succeed in ruling them. The downfall of the reprobate through the rebellion of their affections was inevitable, yet the significant fact remains that Puritan preachers never ceased to tell all men that they should dominate their emotions with or without the help of grace.

On this matter of the government of passion there was an ever-present danger that the moral lesson derived from inherited theory might end by flat opposition to the lessons of piety, and in New England of the eighteenth century that danger became apparent. In the seventeenth century the leaders were perfectly assured that the idea of a sanctified life without a previous regeneration was unthinkable, and therefore could inculcate rational control of affection without worrying over surface inconsistencies. Meantime the conventional doctrine of the passions served with complete success what was to them a vastly more important end: it explained how the God-given passions of men might work evil, and yet not surrender the essential natures which God had bestowed upon them. It helped materially to justify God's ways to man, to uphold cosmic optimism in spite of man's depravity. According to the psychologists, once the passions were cut off from obedience to reason, they were bound to receive images directly, as Cornwallyes put it, "from a sympathysing with things," responding immediately to the object in a way which was not technically unnatural, but which was certainly unreasonable. In a sense, the passions themselves were not to blame; they were created blind and ordained to be excited by some phantasm. In the ideal state, reason would sift truth out of images in the imagination and form phantasms which were not concrete and sensual, but abstract and spiritual; passions would then react to rational images. But in the corrupted state, the imagination may drop its images into the heart instead of sending them to the understanding; the passions respond naturally to such images, and thus come innocently to disregard the reason. In this dislocation of the original reflex, man comes to be deceived by appearances, for the passions work upon images which present things, not as they really are, but as they seem to be, and the understanding is brought "to judge of things not according to their naked and natural truth, but according as it findes them bear in *Fancie* those impressions of *Pleasure,* which are most agreeable to corrupted Nature." On the "rational" level, as opposed to the "natural", the mind must "invent" the truth from things and present it to the passions as "arguments", as concepts that really correspond "uti res est", and passions must wait until reason has performed its act.

This sensuall Appetite in beasts, where there is liberty, and no superiour command to keepe them in order, the beasts are not to be blamed. But take a man where God hath set reason above the sensuall Appetite, and grace above reason to guide it; in him this sensuall Appetite rebels against reason, which it should obey, and this shewes it to be a great sinne in men, considering that reason should be the rule to guide, and keepe in the sensuall Appetite, for God hath given it for that purpose.

Consequently, logic was a corrective of sinful passions, and regeneration would take the form of a reinvigoration of rational discourse. Passion had to be chained not merely by grace but by dialectic, and technologia thus became in truth an approach to God. The only flaw in this scheme from the Puritan point of view was the contention of traditional physics—with which Puritans were compelled to agree—that there were some passions which were purely sensual in the original design, which God Himself had tied merely to the imagination; we can understand, therefore, why Puritan theorists were uncomfortable in the contemplation of these passions and contrived to center their discussions upon those affections which should always have been under the judicious direction of reason. Not upon theological grounds alone, but also because of his interpretation of the passions, the Puritan would have abhorred such a verse as this of Donne's:

Are Sunne, Moone, or Starres by law forbidden,
To smile where they list, or lend away their light?
Are birds divorc'd, or are they chidden
If they leave their mate, or lie abroad a night?
Beasts doe no joyntures lose
Though they new lovers choose,
But we are made worse than those.[12]

On the contrary, the Puritan poet puts into the mouth of an archangel a description of man's predicament: no longer able to discipline his affections, he has lost the essential of freedom, even while "Retaining still Divine similitude," still enjoying the formal freedom of intelligent discrimination and conscious choice:

Thir Makers image, answerd *Michael,* then
Forsook them, when them selves they villif'd
To serve ungovern'd appetite, and took
His image whom they serv'd, a brutish vice,
Inductive mainly to the sin of *Eve.*
Therefore so abject is thir punishment,
Disfiguring not Gods likeness, but thir own,
Or if his likeness, by them selves defac't,
While they pervert pure Natures healthful rules
To loathsom sickness, worthily, since they
Gods Image did not reverence in themselves.[13]

In the doctrine of the passions, Puritans again reached a formula by which the existence of sin could be explained and the blame ascribed to man, without necessitating an admission that God's design had miscarried or been in essence spoiled. The psychological structure of the image of God survived in all its parts, even though the passions "are become, now in the state of *Corruption,* Beastly and Sensual, which were before, by *Creation,* Reasonable and Humane."

By the same token the psychology explained how fallen man could retain sufficient freedom of will to be held responsible, even though all events, including his fall, had been predetermined, and though without grace he was utterly incapable of virtue. Philosophical proof of the "compossibility" of freedom and decree was supplemented by the psychological, and the argument then became: whereas animals have only vegetative and sensitive souls, and in them phantasms are transmitted immediately from the fancy to the affections, man has also the rational soul and in him phantasms normally travel from the fancy to the reason, to the will, and then to the passions. These various faculties, created by God, can never be wholly extinguished; therefore fallen man retains them and uses them, even though to bad effect. Sin has disarranged the dependence of one upon another, and nowadays the phantasms of the fancy may indeed draw the passions after them despite "right" reason, but the forms of the human reflex are still observed; reason estimates phantasms, though it estimates erroneously, and the will chooses after being informed by reason, though it chooses wrong. No matter how corrupted, the will is a divinely created faculty. "The Will indeed remains a Will, and hath not lost its natural power; it cannot be forced." It still commands whatever man enacts, even though seduced by fancy and passion. God fulfills His cosmic plan through the agency of men and causes without doing violence to their inherent natures, without infringing the liberty originally bestowed upon the human will, without destroying the freedom which He Himself can take away only by abolishing the order of nature.

For God accomplisheth his decrees by reasonable creatures, according to the condition of their nature, when as by objects represented and shewed to their understanding, hee inclineth and bendeth their will, that it should with free and inward motion chuse or refuse that, which seemed good from everlasting to God, and was decreed of him.

It is true that at present man is "disenabled" from choosing what is morally good, but nevertheless his understanding judges and his will chooses. He is free not only because he acts without constraint, but because "he follows the counsel of his owne will, he follows his owne judgement and reason." In the physical sense, within the psychological pattern, the will retains a free and absolute power, "so that though a man may be compelled to doe something against his liking, yet he can never be forced to doe anything against his will, at least his will cannot be forced; that like a Queene in her Throwne is alwayes free." Even God must deal with man "as with a reasonable creature," commanding by the Word and expecting a "Voluntary Obedience." The Puritan conclusion from psychology was precisely what we have seen from the logic: man does nothing by compulsion, "nor by the force of instinct," but by rational determination, by intellectual comprehension, even when he comprehends imperfectly, "so that as he doth it willingly, he also (and therefore) doth it rationally, or upon some apprehended grounds."

Psychology thus reinforced the Puritans' unremitting insistence that all conduct be rational, that men yield not to instincts and blind emotions; it underlined this moral by describing the mechanism of behavior so that the rule of reason became an inescapable factor in all actions, even the worst. Men cannot become automata, even if they wish; unless they are mumbling idiots they cannot choose something they have not rationally conceived. In the state of sin reason is enfeebled, like a palsied king misled by scheming courtiers, but it is still king and titular ruler of the faculties. Therefore it followed that the logic and the arts constructed by human reason, with some guidance from grace and revelation, out of observed experience may really correspond to created wisdom, that the ectypal can parallel the archetypal. Psychology was so interpreted that it supplied physiological foundations for the Ramist logic, and the parts of dialectic were correlated with the faculties. What is "invention" but the act of receiving phantasms? The intelligibles in nature are carried as images from the senses to the common sense and the fancy; the first operations of the soul are those "whereby it receiveth the *simple* species of some Object from immediate Impression thereof by the Ministery of the Soul." Thus when the reason works with these images, when it strips away the temporal colorations, combines them, deduces one from another, it is discourse, and what is this if not what logic calls "disposition" or "judgment"? And "method", is it not the order in which things are most efficiently committed to the faculty of memory? What logic calls the acts of intuiting arguments and disposing them in methodical order might by psychologists be called acts of the faculties, of fancy, reason, and memory. William Ames thus made explicit the correlation:

> Disposition of invented arguments tends in this either so that from them a judgment may be made, because it emanates naturally from the disposition as from a flower, or so that they may be retained in the memory; for these are the three acts of reason, to invent, to judge, and to retain in the memory, with which the three internal senses are ingrafted, phantasia, the cogitative faculty and the sensitive memory.

Richardson seems to have varied slightly from the prevailing doctrine and looked upon imagination and common sense as one, but like Ames he made essentially the same parallel between dialectic and psychology; the faculties, he said, serve dialectic: "first a fancy that serves invention; cogitation and memory that serve disposition." Physics textbooks written under the banner of Ramus always glided from the faculties to the logic with ease, particularly those by the Dutch Ramist, Rudolph Snell. His *Partitiones Physicae* follows the conventional development of the subject through the "doctrina Psychologia", describing in customary order the vegetative and sensitive souls, the external and internal senses, until he comes to the rational soul: thereupon, as he defines "mens", he suddenly swings out of the ordinary orbit of Peripatetic physics and embarks upon a summary of the *Dialecticae,* asserting that "mens" is the faculty of judging, that judging is either axiomatical or dianoetical, etc. The natural "vis" of the mind Snell identifies with the natural logic upon which, according to Ramus, formal logic is constructed, "so that the art of dialectic is the mirror and image of this faculty." In New England as late as 1702, Nicholas Noyes could combine the terminology of psychology and Ramus in a poem of which the ingenuity of the fusion helps to compensate for the crudity of the verse:

> The *Fire of Meditation* burns
> What *Sense* into the *Fancy* turns . . .
> Invention, Judgment, Memory,
> And Conscience have a faculty,
> To make *all* praise him that made *all.*

Accordingly, the Puritans were never apprehensive lest the unity of Christian knowledge be rent by a conflict between logic and physics. A distinction of faculties underlay the distinctions of dialectic, the method of thinking was founded upon the actual physiology of thought. Yet it would seem that when the two portions of knowledge fitted together so neatly, Puritan scholars ought to have been loud in their celebration of the accord and adduced it as a marvel of God's contrivance. The fact is that though they would acknowledge the agreement at times, they did not appear over-eager to dwell upon it. The reader of Puritan sermons gets the impression that the two arts, logic and physics, were studied apart rather than in conjunction. There is a suggestion that though the account of the soul and its faculties as expounded in physics was accepted as infallible truth and was discovered to be endorsed by the Bible itself, there were still some problems within it that had better not be explored too minutely lest embarrassments result in other sciences. A confession of ignorance about specific points would amount to no more than an admission of human limitations, but if there were some deeper trouble, some basic inconsistency within the psychology, some fundamental opposition between it and other essential doctrines, there would be need for extreme caution in handling any exegesis which involved explanations of the soul and its faculties.

Here we have, I suspect, another and more pertinent answer to our query of why Puritan divines who wrote upon God's handiwork in comets and eclipses did not write formal treatments of psychology. Mere instinctive jealousy, as exhibited by Calvin, for the reputation of grace and original sin would not in itself have held in check the omnivorous appetite of Puritan scholars. Calvin had also descanted upon the vanity of studying the natural universe, but Puritans in the seventeenth century moved with their age and found in natural philosophy an asset to faith. They included knowledge of the faculties in this philosophy and justified it as another transcript of the will of God, yet they explained this or that faculty only when the explanation was called for in a particular text and scarcely ever presented a complete picture of all the faculties in operation together. Was it merely because the theory was common knowledge, was it simply because the divines were concentrating on revealed doctrines and feared to become earthbound if they dwelt too long on natural wisdom, that they brought psychology into their sermons only piecemeal and by inference? Or was it possibly because they sensed, however obscurely, that there were further difficulties within it which, if exposed too openly, would raise uncomfortable queries in more important regions?

Certainly the contemporaneous psychologists, no matter how enthusiastic about their subject, confessed that there was still much *terra incognita* in the soul. "Let vs not heere looke for a sounde and perfect knowledge of that substantiall power, whereby the soule effecteth so many maruailous woorkes by the meanes of these senses," says *The French Academie;* full understanding of the soul is reserved for the time when it will be purged of corporeality. But other writers, not content with pious ejaculations, made lists of concrete problems yet unsolved, and many of these, it soon becomes clear, center about an issue which Puritanism, particularly Puritanism committed to the *Dialecticae* and to technologia, would have been happy to avoid. In 1604 Thomas Wright in his *The Passions of the Minde in General* set down as needing better answers than physicists had yet provided such questions as these:

> Whereupon commeth the difficulty we finde in Vnderstanding, proceedeth it from the obiect, or the weaknesse of the faculty, or both?
>
> How doth Reason direct or correct Sense? . . .
>
> What is Arte? what the Idaea in the Artificers minde, by whose direction hee frameth his woorkes, what is Prudence, Wisedome, the internall speech and words of the minde . . .
>
> What is evidence and certitude in Knowledge, and how they differ.

How Knowledge and perfit Science, differ from credulity and opinion, and whether feare be necessarily included in every opinion . . .

Why can we not come by as firme knowledge in Logick, Physicks, or Metaphysicks, as in Mathematicks.

Wright was once more presenting various aspects of a single query that had worried medieval philosophers and that in the seventeenth century was becoming importunate. Stated in the language of the psychological theory, it was: how accurately do phantasms mirror things? Upon the answer to this question hinged the answer to the great question of Protestant theology: what is certitude and can we be assured that we ever have it? Does the picture in the mind *always* copy the thing in nature? When the mind invents arguments, is it from the things themselves or from a distorted image of them manufactured by corrupt senses, falsified by an imperfect common sense, twisted by a depraved imagination, blurred by a feeble memory, colored by mendacious passions? If the account of human psychology usually accepted by Puritan divines were true, and the mechanism were then declared to be thrown hopelessly out of joint by original sin, if it were never fully restored to its original efficiency because of the inevitable imperfection of all regeneration, could there exist any bases of certitude in any science? Where would the logic of invention and disposition have carried us but to confusion? Even in divinity, were not arguments collected from the words of the Bible by the same process as from things, and would not this process be as fallible at one time as at another? In short, the questions posed by psychological theory in the early seventeenth century called for an examination of the very fundamentals of Protestant belief, and the Puritan reluctance to ask them or attempt answering them becomes highly comprehensible.

Interestingly enough, the issue did not present itself to the Puritan mind as one of the reliability of sense perceptions. In this respect Puritans were true disciples of Aristotle, who had apparently seen that a phantasm might not perfectly copy its cause, but had not therefore surrendered to skepticism; the laws of the phantasm were reliable enough, as he presented them, so that from our image of a thing we might attain to a definition of its essence.[14] Reynolds could define knowledge in accordance with the psychology, and yet conform to the definition required for the act of invention in Ramist logic:

Knowledge is the Assimilation of the Understanding unto the things which it understandeth, by those Intelligible Species which doe irradiate it, and put the power of it into Act: For as the beams of the Sunne shinning on a glasse, do there work the Image of the Sun: so the species and resemblances of things being conveighed on the Understanding, do there work their own Image.

Thus images are formed in the senses with enough accuracy, the spirits convey them to the internal senses with sufficient dispatch, the faculties pass them along as intelligibles to the understanding with adequate fidelity, so that even in his sinful state man can invent arguments and dispose them in art through dialectical method. The danger implicit in the psychological doctrine did not present itself to Puritans as an epistemological discrepancy between the image of a thing and the thing-in-itself. Even though corrupted, the mind still receives through the exterior and interior senses satisfactory images for transcribing the real world and justifying the dogmas of technologia, and the internal species will be in accord with the object, "uti res est." Hence, Puritan theologians encountered their difficulty in the question of whether sense impressions were the source of *all* knowledge. The psychological doctrine exemplified by their sermons is consistently Peripatetic, and traditionally the Peripatetic doctrine had been postulated upon the belief that there could be nothing in the mind except what came through the senses. "Nihil est in intellectu, quin prius fuerit in sensu," said Stierius, and the Anglican Richard Hooker, whose opinion of Ramism we have already noted, declared without reservation, "The soul of man being therefore at the first as a book, wherein nothing is and yet all things may be imprinted; we are to search by what steps and degrees it riseth unto perfection." Even if it were proved that the senses relayed to the mind a true image of the world, and that arguments could thus be truthfully extracted from things, could Puritanism rest content with a psychology that was wholly sensational? We have seen that it could not maintain technologia and certain tenets of orthodox theology if it had to confess bluntly that the senses wholly account for or produce the intellectual life.

Aristotle himself probably never said that the senses do so account for the life of the mind,[15] yet medieval Aristotelians, particularly the Arabic commentators, had made it difficult to interpret him otherwise. Consequently, there had been a long succession of philosophers who perceived a threat to Christian orthodoxy in Peripatetic psychology, and had opposed to it another theory, for which they were ultimately indebted to Plato. In the major philosophers of the middle ages the two traditions are found more or less in combination, but there is always a tendency which denies reality to phenomena and prefers to trust for the guarantees of knowledge to the transcendent and inward sanctions of the soul. The two tendencies, the Aristotelian with its empirical bases, and the mystical with its depreciation of the senses, are clearly seen in Augustine.[16] Yet the predominant theory in medieval speculation had been the Aristotelian, which made mental experiences dependent upon the reality of matter, grounded knowledge in sensation, and was concerned primarily with orderly classification. The other tendency, the subordinate and often despised mystical strain, represented in the Victorines and Bonaventura, might use the empirical classification of the faculties, yet it was not first of all interested in description, but in that which the rational soul knows without learning through the vegetative and sensitive organs.[17]

Protestantism inherited the dominant Aristotelian tradition, the empirical doctrine of the faculties, classified and defined as we have seen them in Puritan references. Yet Protestant theology made imperative a new emphasis upon a theory of conscience which had more in common with the dissenting, the mystical or Platonic tradition, than with the one transcribed in Protestant textbooks. It was supremely necessary for Protestantism to maintain that there still linger in the mind of fallen man certain inborn moral certainties, not derived from experience, and that from these come the major premises of "synteresis".[18] It was easy enough to account for such innate principles in purely theological terms: they are remains from the image of God; man in the fall lost his "moral powers", but not his "moral image"; the idea of God is therefore innate in all men, even in the savages of America; the law of nature "was perfectly wrote in the hearts of our first parents"; God has implanted within us some truths, so that all men, even heathens, "doe the things contained in the Law, their actions show it." Ergo, even the unregenerate acknowledge certain principles, and when they disobey them, they stand condemned in their own eyes. Roger Williams was legitimately banished from Massachusetts Bay, not for being in error, but for persisting in error against the light of his *own* conscience.

But it was difficult to maintain these conclusions in theology if the Peripatetic psychology was also considered a true description of man; if they were to be supported scientifically as well as dogmatically, not all knowledge could be attributed to a sensual origin. Every Puritan textbook, even those that reproduced most faithfully the Aristotelian psychology, takes occasion to deny or to qualify "quod ait Aristoteles, *Nihil est in intellectu, quod non prius fuerit in sensu.*" Even when they repeat the conventional dictum that the mind at birth is a "tabula rasa", they will still assert in other contexts that there is also some "innate light" in the mind, if not actually preëxistent ideas. Reynolds spoke for the Puritan point of view when he argued that at the moment of creation Adam did not possess "experimental knowledge," any knowledge of the future or of hidden things, but that he did have already in his mind "so much of *Moral Knowledge* as should fit him to converse in Love as a Neighbour, in Wisdome as a Father, with other men; so much of *Natural Knowledge* as should dispose him for the Admiring of Gods Glory, and for the Governing of other Creatures over which hee had received Dominion." The Platonic strain comes to the fore in the greatest preachers, who in their most eloquent flights are apt to appeal to a knowledge not gathered on land or sea:

> Looke upon bruit beasts, we see no actions but may arise from the temper of the matter; according to which their fancie and appetite are fashioned . . . It is true indeed, in a man there are fancy and appetite, and these arise from

the temper of the body; therefore as the body hath a different temper so there are severall appetites, dispositions & affections . . . but come to the higher part of the soule, the actions of the will and understanding of man, and they are of an higher nature; the acts which they doe have no dependence upon the body at all.

Furthermore, besides the inherent tendency of Protestant doctrine to father upon psychological theory an innate knowledge of moral principles and to make way for an inspiration in the soul which was not dependent upon the body, among New England Puritans the Ramist logic and the consequent technologia accentuated the Platonizing developments. From this point of view it probably becomes a fact of some significance that when the ministers speak directly upon the faculties, in the course of some technical exposition, they are consistently Peripatetic, but in logic and technologia, and in all expositions involving the language of these arts, they exhibit habits of mind which we perceive to be allied to medieval Platonism. Hence in Puritan sermons the psychological theory is paradoxically the more important the more it figures merely incidentally. In any survey of Puritan writings the theological doctrine of conscience, of the remainders of the divine image, and the logical or ethical structures erected upon the strength of intuitive perceptions will figure very largely; by contrast, the psychological theory seems a subordinate interest, never wholly articulated, never consistently spoken, yet for that very reason we must consider it the more seriously, lest we be tempted to make too much of the Platonic elements in the logic and the concept of reason. Even in technologia, Puritans strove to hold the scales between Aristotle and Plato, though that science pointed surely toward an assertion of innate ideas, of the independence of knowledge from the senses, and of the reliability of immediate perceptions. Hence the psychology played its part by redressing the balance. Though the doctrine of man admitted some Platonic features, yet in the main it held firmly to scholastic notions; logic and psychology being correlated by the identification of the acts of thought with specific faculties, Puritan allegiance to the *De Anima* was not then deterred by the Puritan revolt against the *Organon*. The Puritan predicament is, to say the least, interesting: in the realm of logic theologians were moving with the times, but in the sphere of physics and psychology they were judicious conservatives. Much of their intellectual life is explained by this anomaly, all the more because they never consciously phrased it. If the tendencies implied in the logic had not been checked by a sensational psychology, they would have led inevitably to conclusions unacceptable to orthodoxy.

Technologia might well be called a "radical" doctrine for the seventeenth century in accordance with Professor Gilson's diagnosis of the period: "A number of causes seem to have converged in the first years of the seventeenth century to determine a renovation of Platonic innatism."[19] The barren controversies of the schools had given intelligent men an intense distaste for medieval philosophy: the ethical confusion and the skepticism of nominalism forced many, both Protestant and Catholic, to conclude that entirely new bases for intellectual certainty must be found to replace those that obviously had failed. Thoughtful men were deciding that since scholasticism had sought these assurances through the senses, they must now endeavor to find them in the mind. The assumption that knowledge originates in the senses had produced chaos; could not this horror be avoided if, St. Thomas to the contrary, men could find knowledge within the soul itself? In addition, there was a widespread belief around the year 1600 that atheism was increasing; clearly the fault lay in the schools for their self-confessed inability to prove the existence of God or to supply grounds for rational conviction. Skepticism and atheism could both be silenced once and for all if confronted with indubitable demonstration that the soul possesses an innate knowledge of its creator; evil men could once more be faced down if they could be shown to be acting against the light of their own consciences.[20]

These considerations in some part account for the widespread movement, so pronounced a characteristic of the Renaissance, away from the point of view associated with the name of Aristotle—away from the metaphysic of the concrete, the science of classification and of knowledge originating in the senses, the method of biology—toward one we may legitimately describe as "Platonic"—a metaphysic of the intelligible, scornful of the sensible, a science of intuition and innate ideas, a method of mathematics. Gilson finds in Descartes the fine flowering of this Platonic renascence;[21] yet Protestantism, with its enhancement of conscience, contributed to the development, and the Ramist logic, with its emphasis upon "puissance naturelle", must have encouraged it. When William Ames could assert that though some sciences originate in the senses, nevertheless Aristotle was wrong in holding that all of them do, he had come far down the road that led finally to the *Discours de la Méthode,* though he did not foresee that end, and would have been doubly horrified could he have known that the road led also to *Le Traité Des Passions.* Alsted was on the same highway when he distinguished between innate and acquired principles, and declared that the former were everywhere the same and timeless, whereas the latter would differ from place to place and time to time. In England there were many essays toward reinterpretation which were entirely outside the Puritan sphere of influence, and these offer perhaps the most instructive parallels to Puritan thinking. Other men were struggling with the task of criticizing the schoolmen even while continuing to think in scholastic forms; and they underline the Puritan predicament because they, not being committed to so rigid a creed, were able to seek for solutions in realms where Puritans were forbidden to enter. Among these efforts Sir John Davies' *Nosce Te Ipsum* in

1599 might be cited, but even better for our purposes is Lord Herbert of Cherbury's *De Veritate,* published in 1624. These men were revolting against the schools, and for them as for the Puritan authors of technologia, the central problem was that of identifying concept with object; they too were seeking bases of certitude, they too were striving to work their way out of nominalism by their native wits. They turned inward, hoping and determined to find within the mind clear, concise, and undeniable truths, just as, at the time Lord Herbert was writing, René Descartes in Germany, "ne trouvant aucune conversation qui me divertît, et n'ayant d'ailleurs, par bonheur, aucuns soins ni passions qui me troublassent," took advantage of his freedom from emotional distraction to make himself the arch-symbol of the age: "je demeurais tout le jour enfermé seul dans un poêle, où j'avais tout le loisir de m'entretenir de mes pensées." [22] Like him, but unlike Puritans and Ramists, Lord Herbert was ready to conclude that if new guarantees of truth were to be discovered within the soul, then the empirical or sensational psychology could no longer be accepted. He perceived that no logic based even in part upon intuitive certainty would be compatible with Peripatetic psychology,[23] which permitted nothing to appear in the intellect except by leave of the senses, that compromise was impossible, and that partisans of the new views would have to commence by abandoning the faculty psychology to the Jesuits. "Let us have done with the theory that asserts that our mind is a clean sheet, as though we obtained our capacity for dealing with objects from objects themselves." Assurance of the harmony between idea and object was obtainable, in his argument, because it rested upon a divinely ordained correspondence of innate ideas with things, and in order to escape from the dilemma of late scholastic psychology, Lord Herbert turned to Plato, or rather to a species of Platonism. He reduced the sensory experience to a secondary rôle in the act of cognition, and finding that knowledge preëxisted in the mind, asserted that human knowledge did not flow inward from the senses but outward from the soul.

The result for Lord Herbert was a peculiar rationalism or naturalism, which was at the same time mystical, tinged with occultism, and, from any orthodox standpoint, highly dangerous. It might be described as a sort of seventeenth-century "theosophy". Lord Herbert is doubly useful as a comparison with the Puritans because he began his progress from many similar premises; he too was influenced by Ramus, whose dialectic he echoes in his own attempt to create a logical method, he too denounced the predicaments and defined reason in terms that might have come from Richardson: "Discursive judgments consist of forms of knowledge which proceed from the conformity of objects . . . with the faculties which are found in every normal human being." He commenced with a definition of truth which was also that of Ramus, that it is the exact correspondence of idea to thing: "The whole of my doctrine of truth is based upon the proper conformity of the faculties with their objects . . . Whatever is true, however, is readily believed, because here objects correspond harmoniously with faculties, and faculties with objects." Almost these very words were paralleled in New England again and again, as when John Cotton remarked, "all delight springeth from correspondency between the faculty and the object," in which observation is contained the very essence of technologia. For Lord Herbert as for the Ramists, the problem thus became: how could one affirm that the idea—or the argument—is really commensurate with its object? Being unhampered by theological inhibitions, he was prepared to recognize that such a correspondence could never be certified so long as the idea was defined as a phantasm, filtered through the fallible external senses and the deceptive internal senses before being presented to the reason. Thereupon he boldly established the coincidence upon the theory of a preëstablished harmony, and declared that a true copy of everything already exists in the mind, that man is the epitome of the universe, the microcosm of the macrocosm, whose inner nature reproduces by self-intuition the structure of the universe. The mind does not receive phantasms passively, but meets objects half-way, and frames ideas of them, not by abstracting ghostly copies of them, but by drawing upon its own reservoir of latent concepts, wherein is contained one that will correspond to each and every sensation. "We possess hidden faculties which when stimulated by objects quickly respond to them." Thus Lord Herbert would argue that we are frightened when we encounter a snake though we may never have beheld one before, because we know intuitively that the idea of snake is a concept of venom and danger: "We can distinguish this serpent from other animals and we perceive that we are frightened by it because of the common nature of things or the law of correspondence between man and the world as a whole." We do not imbibe meanings from sensation, but the sensation stimulates our faculties to "unfold and expand" meanings out of themselves.

Lord Herbert carried this theory to extremes, but he was not alone in his age in turning to such a solution. The sources from which he derived his ideas were open to the psychologists and the logicians. Pierre de la Primaudaye, for instance, toyed with the thesis that the impact of the senses arouses latent potentialities in the spirit; the speakers in *The French Academie* assure each other that man is born with knowledge, that even though "it is commonly said" that nothing comes to the understanding except through the senses, there is nevertheless a law written in the heart, a knowledge "which issueth from a higher spring then from the outward senses." Was it not possible, Primaudaye asked, that things encountered in the senses serve chiefly to "awaken and stirre vp the vnderstanding, which after by that vertue it hath in it selfe, proceedeth forward?" He did not permit the understanding to proceed by its own virtue so far forward as did Lord Herbert, for he too professed allegiance to Christian doctrine; he still held that the outward senses were designed by God to send to the understanding "the similitudes of things without, and be the messengers of the minde," yet he does argue that there are internal powers which may supply some ideas, which know a few truths without having to call upon the senses to supply their content.

> There is vnderstood by principles, that naturall knowledge that is borne with vs, which is the seed of all Artes, and a beame of the light of God in vs, to the end that by this meanes al Artes necessary for life, should be inuented and put in use . . . Wee may referre to these naturall principles, whatsoever God hath imprinted in mens hartes and mindes of the law of nature, which serueth all men for naturall diuinitie, the Bookes which they carry printed in their souls.

Likewise the Ramist logicians were constantly veering toward a similar conclusion, Ramus himself, with his doctrine of "puissance naturelle", disciples like Mulhemius and Rennemannus, with grandiloquent praises of "natural logic". Some of them so enlarged the scope of "puissance naturelle" that they made it rival Herbert's idea of "Natural Instinct". Beurhusius had written in 1581 that judgment is not entirely dependent upon sense, that it is superior to it; though he acknowledged that the mind must get images through the physical organs, yet he held that the intellect first directs the organs toward what it wants them to perceive, and suggested, haltingly, that in the intellect may exist the seeds of the principles of all the arts. Experience is merely a fructifying influence inciting to growth. In the reason, the "vis" or force of invention and judgment already exists, and "being excited by the senses, it produces and constitutes by degrees the semina of the various arts." [24]

Yet no psychologists or dialecticians developed this view so freely or so consistently as did Herbert of Cherbury. They, and also the Puritans—Richardson, Ames, or the New England divines—endeavored to maintain a combination of the traditions, but Herbert dissolved the union and expelled Peripateticism. He saw with startling clarity that any belief in an innate access to truth was incompatible with the traditional doctrine of the soul, and he could see no way to guarantee the correctness of ideas if ideas were images in the fancy and memory, capable of being warped and distorted by the affections. For him the intellect itself became the supreme court of judgment, wherein could be known in advance the truth about whatever the senses would some day report.

> If the sense-organ is imperfect, or if it is of poor quality, if the mind is filled with deceitful prejudices, the concept is wholly vitiated. Accordingly in addition to this truth we must postulate a truth of intellect, which alone is able to decide in virtue of its inborn capacity or its Common Notions whether our subjective faculties have exercised their perceptions well or ill.

Therefore truth is not to be winnowed from experience, but lies ready to hand in what Herbert called "Common Notions", beliefs inherent in all men, *a priori* judgments, ideas which preëxist in the soul, not born of sensation, but indispensable prerequisites for sensation. "So the Common Notions must be deemed not so much the outcome of experience as principles without which we should have no experience at all."

The Puritans also wanted to believe that some principles, at least the premises of synteresis, were inborn; it might seem that they should have welcomed the researches of Lord Herbert. But too much of a good thing is always worse than not enough. Had the noble lord attributed his common notions to the remains of a divine image, he might have become celebrated among the righteous, but he preferred to explain them otherwise. In his view they came, not from an imperfect recollection of the Garden of Eden, but from an ever-present, propulsive "Natural Instinct", a vital urge, suffusing the body, carrying with it all ideas and thrusting them into consciousness whenever the soul encountered a corresponding sensation. This natural instinct was the true image of God; it was not an abstract body of principles, not a mechanism of senses and faculties, but God's grace flowing forth as a natural power, an illumination and an influx, like that which the Puritans called regeneration except that it was not supernatural. On the contrary, it was universal and normal, it was in every man, it was life itself, or in other words, it was what the Puritans called "common grace". It was the instinct of all animals for happiness, and out of it arose the common notions, the universal beliefs of natural religion. With this conclusion Herbert inadvertently became the forerunner of English Deism; if innate ideas were supplied from within to all men by a vital force, then the external test for them, the method for arriving at a list of common notions, would be the common consent of mankind. Unanimity and universality of opinion therefore became at last for Lord Herbert "the beginning and end of theology and philosophy," and "in the last resort the sole test of truth." He might still insist that he reserved a place for divine revelation, but it was difficult to perceive. If Puritans read *De Veritate* they might have recognized themselves in the incentives and in many of the arguments, but they would emphatically have beheld in it a defense of innate ideas carried altogether too far, and would have moralized therefrom that excessive zeal for intrinsic capacities was bound to lead, sooner or later, to a subordination of the Bible to human opinion, that eventually it would find the beginning and end of theology not in the Word of God, but in the notions of men.

Here then was innatism with a vengeance, all the sadder to contemplate because Lord Herbert had begun with a fine hatred for nominalism, for this "strange and unprecedented philosophy . . . which superseded reason altogether and sought to establish its doctrines upon the basis of an implicit faith." He had turned inwards, as the Puritans had done, to contradict the schoolmen's assertions, to deny "that truth lies hidden in a well, that we know one thing only, namely that we know nothing." But at the end, he made us know altogether too much. Puritans could agree that there are some innate ideas, that mental images correspond to their objects, even that experience excites latent possibilities within the soul. Alsted could say that "intelligence assents to fundamental theoretical principles without any medium or any arguments," and in the same decade when Herbert was drawing up a list of the five fundamental principles of religion, the universal common notions which all men discover by nature, Preston and Ames formulated almost the same list in setting forth the content of "natural religion". Preston declared that man can deduce them "by his natural wit," while Ames, speaking in more Ramistic language, said that the understanding contains "principles of truth, which direct both the theoreticall, and practicall judgement," of which "all men that have any use of reason have some knowledge." These were, according to Ames:

> That which is honest, and dishonest, just, and unjust, that God is to be worshipped, that that is not to be done to another, which one would not have done to himselfe.

The body of academic physics in New England contained a thesis in 1646, "Synteresis is founded in the intellect," and the defense of such a proposition would surely have involved asserting that the light of moral truth is innate in the mind. Nor was it possible for Puritans to confine the list of innate principles to moral and religious assumptions alone; when conscience was interpreted according to the methods of the logic and technologia, when it was viewed not as "a Faculty or Power distinct from the Understanding," but as a practical syllogism, "gathering morall or divine Conclusions from a presupposed habit of Principles," then it implied the existence within man of more innate knowledge than his natural religion. In order that conscience may function upon a presupposed habit, a man's understanding must have a power, "not only to inform him in the Theory of things, but also to guide him in practice," a faculty "endued with a power of Judgment, by which it can inquire into the Nature of Things, and compare them, and discern the Connections and Consequents of them, and accordingly, commend or discommend them to the Will." Thus far were Puritans forced to enhance innate abilities, intuitive knowledge, and inborn capacities.

But they could go no further. If they exceeded these limits, then along with Lord Herbert they would find themselves so confident of an inward access to truth that they would relegate the Bible to a supernumerary; natural religion would thereupon suffice for salvation, original sin no longer be a serious blight, the criteria of religious truth become common notions and the consent of mankind. The illumination reserved for the elect would be made available for all men through their natural instinct. Religion would become naturalism or rationalism, or else—still worse—some occult and inward communication, some Antinomianism or Quakerism. Hence, though Puritans made a place in their psychology for some innate ideas and for an approach to knowledge that did not run through the senses; though in technologia they developed a naïve realism based upon an assumed correspondence between ideas and things; though they believed that the visible universe and the mind of man were dual emanations from a single creator, that the archetypal art of God was made entype when impressed upon the creatures and ectype when copied in the human mind; yet when they came to describe just how the correspondence was achieved, just what machinery of the mind extracted art from things, or just how the objective entype was translated into the subjective ectype, they dared not abandon the doctrine of the faculties. The method by which knowledge was carried from the thing to the mind, except in the relatively restricted realm of conscience, remained for them the method of Peripatetic physics: phantasms were copies of things formed at the external senses, the images were carried by the vital spirits to the reason through the common sense and the fancy, stored in the memory, handed down by the reason to the will and by the will made the objects for affection, either concupiscible or irascible. The inherent inclination of the Ramist logic was toward a further extension of Platonism, but Puritans could not sacrifice any more of the traditional Aristotelian doctrine of man, for such gains in epistemology would be secured at the expense of divine grace and supernatural revelation. If the spheres of innate capacities had been widened any further, if technologia had not been balanced by the faculty psychology, Puritanism might have become involved in a Paracelsian vitalism; theology would have centered, not upon a transcendent God, but upon an all-sufficient, all-compelling natural instinct, possessing all the characteristics of divine grace, but feeding the reason not with visions of heaven but with an ecstasy of the earth.

After all, therefore, it is not so strange that when the Emersonian generation revolted against "sensational" psychology, and hungered for a philosophy of innate ideas, direct intuitions, and the correspondence of word and thing, they could no longer derive these principles from the New England tradition. Transcendentalism might be called a remote outcropping of the same vein which in Puritanism took the form of technologia, but Transcendentalists could not go back to Richardson and Ames. Hence they resorted to Swedenborg, Plotinus, and the wonders of Oriental philosophy. These doctrines, or something like them, had been in part asserted by Puritans, and had played an important part in the intellectual life of the seventeenth century, but they had been kept in check by a psychological theory that only in one particular permitted innatism to flourish or intuition to become self-reliant. Of course, by the time of Emerson the eighteenth century had intervened, and the generation of 1830 could not reach across a whole century to recapture seventeenth-century terms; even had they been able to understand fully the language of their forebears, they would have found it of little use so long as what had been asserted in technologia was contradicted in physics. They could not resurrect one part of the original creed when that part had always been bound to the very ideas they were revolting against. They had to seek elsewhere than in New England for the accents of that Holy Ghost which New England, of all the heedless world, had come the closest to losing. Emerson and Alcott, with the help of Swedenborg and Plotinus, constructed a new and radical theory of correspondence, one that recalls, not the *Theses Technologicae,* but Lord Herbert of Cherbury, an occult monism, an immediate inspiration and a vital flux, a uniting of man and nature in the Over-Soul—all of these being conclusions intolerable to Puritanism, which Puritans would have attributed to a heretical and false, to a much too Platonic, conception of man.

CHAPTER X

THE MEANS OF CONVERSION

For Puritans of the seventeenth century, Transcendentalism lay hidden in the wallet of time, and they were blissfully unaware of any incipient antagonisms in their conception of human nature. If ever they had misgivings they could always reassure themselves that knowledge in this world is limited, and must fall short of perfection, particularly concerning so complex a subject as the nature of man, as long as man remains a hybrid of flesh and spirit. Meanwhile, the psychology was of great practical value to the divines simply because it enabled them to explain specifically what happens in regeneration. The substance of their thinking might be put briefly thus, though such a statement is more crude than any Puritan would actually have phrased: if original sin is a dislocation of the faculties, then regeneration must set them right again. If in nature the original sequence of sensation, common sense, fancy, reason, memory, will, and affection is now broken, it follows that in a converted nature the reflex must be reconstructed. When conversion was described in the vocabulary of psychology it became in effect a realignment of twisted pulleys and tangled ropes, permitting the blocks once more to turn freely and the tackle to run smoothly, in accordance with the first plan of the rigging.

Thus in Puritan philosophy the concept of spiritual regeneration, which pertained to the piety, was integrated with a concept of the physical powers of the soul, which pertained to the heritage of classical and medieval physics, because Puritans were inheritors at one and the same time of the religious and of the scientific view of man. The ministers could not keep these two concepts apart, and consequently whenever they descended from the plane of lofty piety to concrete particulars, they had to translate the process and phases of regeneration minutely into the language of the faculty psychology and of the reflex. They were hardly aware that they were expressing one idea in the terms of another, because both ideas were woven together in their thinking, and they saw no incongruity in insisting, as they did explicitly and forcefully, that the grace of God must always invade a soul through the vehicle of a sense impression. The formal creeds and professions of Puritanism seldom dwell upon this contention, but nevertheless there was a fundamental tenet in Puritan thought to the effect that all regeneration comes through the impact of a sensible species or a phantasm, that it is always attached to some spoken word or to some physical experience. In the natural estate, declared with one voice both psychologists and theologians, the human reason possesses "a natural and rational power of Discerning . . . else it were not an Understanding, but it is blind to spiritual things"; the corrupt reason must retain this power because in all human conduct an understanding of some sort must precede any act of will, and thus grace itself must act upon the understanding "first in order of Nature, and for the most part, of Time too." Though God can stretch out His arm and recover a soul in the twinkling of an eye, yet He does not ordinarily do so, "but as he applies himself in the means to men, as *Causes by Counsel,* so he proposeth things to them, and works them up to make a deliberate choice, which is not wont to be instantaneous." Hence, because reason cannot send to the will a correct judgment if it has fallacious evidence, grace endows it with an apprehension of true images. Puritan theory could not permit any belief that grace gives men an understanding different from that which is in the body; it therefore held stoutly to the doctrine that the heavenly influence merely makes the understanding, which already must have a power of discerning, capable of discerning spiritual things as well as natural things. Only the regenerate reason can perceive all things in truth, and technologia is founded upon the insights of a regenerate mind: "Rectifie therefore the apprehension, and heale the disease; labour to have judgement informed, and you shall see things as they are."

When the reason has become rectified, it then can serve in turn as the instrument by which the blind will may be led to the right choice, and an explanation may thus be offered in both religious and psychological terms for the concurrence of the dependent faculties.

> Now if the understanding be enlightened . . . it doth communicate his light by redundancie unto the rest of the faculties, then it must needs follow that the understanding being enlightened truly with grace, and the other faculties partaking thereof, they must needs be ruled by it. Every inferiour is ruled by his superiour, or at least should be so; so every facultie should be subordinate unto the minde.

Like the reason, the will does not need to be wholly replaced by another power; it still can choose among natural things, among foods and the means of self-preservation; it requires only the renewal of its power to respond to phantasms of spiritual truths, to the words of a preacher or of the Bible. Yet while the spiritual influence is necessary, that influence must be brought to the will through physical channels. No man can become either good or evil "onely because he understandeth good and evill things," since no one does anything merely by understanding, but "because he wills these things which are good and evill"; yet the gracious man must acquire a knowledge of good and evil before he can will the one and reject the other. In the saint, reason and will coöperate: "It is true, saith the understanding, and therefore that beleeves it; but it is worthy to be received saith the will, therefore that comes in, takes and accepts it." Knowledge alone, in other words, will not persuade the will, yet grace never persuades any will except through the agency of some knowledge; grace is not a formless, mystical infusion, but is tied to concrete phantasms. In order to become changed, the will requires simultaneously both a "powerfull influence" and "new light"—light which will enable the mind "to see other things, or the same truths in a more spiritual and effectual manner, those impediments being removed, which might hinder the evidence of spiritual truths, and the judgment being fully convinced, that we might *know things* not onely notionally, but practically," and an influence which, conveyed to the will within the light, sets the heart afire.

As the soul, in the bodily eye, causeth it to see, and, in the ear, causeth it to hear, and, in the tongue, causeth it to speak, . . . so the spirit, in the mind, . . . causeth it freely to choose and cleave unto Christ, and to God, in him, and, in every affection, causeth it to move towards Christ and God, in such a manner and way of working, as is suitable to its nature . . . The faculties and affections, which were by nature set upon the world and sin, and self, being now, by grace set upon things above . . . Hence every spiritual gift of grace, whereby any faculty and affection of the soul is sanctified, is called the spirit of that faculty and affection.

After the will is renovated, it commands the affections; yet even they do not yield obedience unless, like the will itself, they are directed at once both by some species of the good and by a divine influence. Passions will not embrace the good unless encouraged by grace, but grace never works upon them except through an image of the good. "Meer knowledge and discourse cannot draw the heart to trust and hope in God, except it hath a rellish of his goodnesse." The "rellish" with which grace seasons good phantasms excites holy desires, whereas the same phantasms, presented without the seasoning, will be rejected by the passions. The circle of regeneration is complete, psychologically or physiologically speaking, when affection is turned toward heaven.

The understanding, being illightened and fully convinced, closeth with God, in Christ, as the first Truth, and the will chooseth him as the chiefest good; the affections rest satisfied with him alone, and the whole soul placeth all its happinesse in its injoyment of him, and conformity to him . . . The whole soul, in all its faculties and affections, answereth.

The psychological doctrine of the physicists coincided with the theological because both were equally assured that moral instruction by itself could never restore the perfect reflex or maintain correct order among erring faculties. The secular writers agreed with divines that Stoicism was "a generous, but a useless endeavour" because it "would have us to be as well governed in the state of sin, as in that of Original Justice"; they too were Christians, and therefore knew that in order for human passions to be subjected to reason, they would need to be schooled by grace. Unaided reason or mere natural will power could not do it. The writers also professed that could knowledge alone cure the soul, knowledge was available. All men are able to read the Bible and be rationally convinced by its evidences; they can even achieve "historical faith", but if the spirit does not force home a fundamental conviction, a deep and living faith, the learned will be in no better plight than the ignorant. If physicists were so clear upon these points, it is not surprising that Puritans were doubly clear. Preston taught that a natural man can "come for substance as farre as a spirituall man, but not in a right manner"; Hooker distinguished between a moral "drawing" of the soul to God and a divine drawing, the first being external—"when a man by reason propounded, and good things offered to the understanding and the will, comes thereby to have his mind enlightened, and his will moved and persuaded, to embrace and give encouragement to the things offered" —while the second is internal, by which God not only enlightens the mind, but injects new life into the soul and all the faculties. When Hooker attempted to explain regeneration in the language of psychology, he turned instinctively to the analogy of a mechanism; a clock that is going backwards, he said, must first be stopped and then reconditioned:

The heart of a man, and the will of a man, and the affections of a man, they are the wheeles of the soules of men, the Lord Iesus made them at first to runne to heaven-ward, and to God-ward, but when *Adam* sinned, then the poyse of corruptions prevailed so farre forth over them, that they drew the heart, the mind, the will of man from God, and made it runne the wrong way to the devell-ward.

After God repairs the machine, all its wheels will run in the right direction, so that regeneration is not God's putting new faculties in the soul, but His restoring His image to those already there. Sinful man still "hath an humane Understanding, Will, Affections, Conscience, Memory," and these are "all of them the same in their essence afterwards, that they were before, but are renewed according to the gracious qualities & principles which are put into them." As with the defective clock, in order to repair wheels that are out of frame, God need not make new wheels but merely rectify old ones:

If they be foule make them clean, if they be wrong right them; so by the fall of *Adam,* all, soule and body is out of frame, and out of joynt, the minde unfit to know God, and the will unfit to close with God; . . . now when a sinner comes to be renewed, there needs not new faculties, but those he hath, to be set in frame.

Sin obscures the image of God as thick clouds the sun, but grace sweeps the mist away and shows the sun shining once more resplendent; proving that even at the darkest hour it had never been totally obliterated.

Furthermore, if grace is to work upon the soul through the faculties, it must not merely renew each one but it must penetrate to them in the proper chronological sequence. Though in essence divine grace is one and indivisible, yet "with respect to Operation," it is a separate grace for every faculty:

And this distinction and order is to be observed by us, in our considering of them; and that not meerly from the necessity of our manner of Conception, but also from the nature of the things themselves. In our Contemplation of the Divine Perfections, we are necessitated to take them asunder, though in God they are but that one absolute & *simple Being,* else we could know nothing of him; but the Graces in us have the foundation of this distinct and orderly consideration in them, being created Perfections in us, and assigned to their several uses.

Ergo, when grace comes to the soul, first the external senses are "fitted" for the service of sanctified reason; then a new inclination is put into the interior senses, so that where they "had all been the Servants of Unrighteousness, and sensually carried forth after sensible objects," they are "prest for the gracious Employments which they were made for"; next the understanding is renovated by receiving a spiritual discerning, whereupon the will is renewed by "the restoring a power to it of chusing the Good and refusing the Evil"; and at last the affections are set right again "by putting a new & spiritual byas into them, by which they are set on things above." "The last and principall thing is, the stooping of the soul, and subjection of the heart, to that which is understood and remembred." Sinful man tries all his life to see things as they are, to apprehend truth and to act by it, but at every endeavor his senses blur, his imagination deceives, his reason fails, his will rebels, his passions run riot. As soon as he receives grace, the phantasms generated by his senses go step by step through the sure and infallible route; the one combination of his faculties which he has striven in vain to achieve is suddenly achieved for him, and thereafter the species of things run the short and smooth course through his spirit, to eventuate in sanctified conduct.

From the vantage point of our analysis, we can perceive that the combination of theological and psychological conceptions accomplished certain advantages for orthodox Puritanism, but also that it gave rise to some of the more persistent problems which the divines were constantly struggling to resolve without ever being conscious of the cause. They were innocently foredoomed, for example, to encounter difficulties at the one point where psychological theory was weakest, and so were compelled in religion to deal with the dilemma posed in physics concerning the relation of the will to the reason. Obviously they, like the physicists, could not suppose that the will automatically follows a regenerated reason, because they would then make religion merely an affair of the intellect and would be reduced to accounting as the elect whatever persons happened to live under persuasive ministers. If the will always follows the understanding out of necessity, "then in Regeneration the *Will* it selfe need not be internally renewed by grace: for the inlightening of the Understanding would be sufficient." This conclusion was obviously "repugnant to Faith and Godlinesse," but equally repugnant was the alternative possibility that the natural will might remain at liberty to choose or to reject the determinations of a converted reason, for in that case the finite would be enabled to withstand the infinite grace of God, and would be powerful enough to nullify divine decrees. This was the heresy of Pelagians and Arminians, who "put a kinde of ability in the will, to take or refuse Christ and grace when it is offered." Therefore orthodoxy required on the one hand that human reason be persuaded by arguments and that the will obey the convinced reason in accordance with the scheme of nature, and on the other hand that a presence of God be discerned in both reason and will as the determiner of the natural action. "There must be this effectuall perswading, as the understanding must have the truth cleered to see a Christ, so the will must be perswaded, that it may receive power from him." It was not enough for the mind to be convinced unless the will spontaneously elected to embrace the conviction.

Thus Puritan theory held that rational comprehension of the will of God, and voluntary obedience to it, could not be secured unless the forms of the psychological reflex were observed, yet understanding and obedience could not be wrought by earthly instruments alone. There had to be an external incentive, a physical stimulus impressing a phantasm upon the senses, a satisfaction of reason, an instigation of man's will, and an arousing of his passions, as though all were being achieved by nature, and yet God had to be present at every stage of the psychological reflex, and He alone be responsible for the effect.

The Conversion of a Sinner does not depend so much on the outward Means of Grace, as on the good Pleasure, and Will of God. The Effect does not depend on the Instrument so much, as on that which is the Principal Efficient. God is able, if He be so pleased, to Convert Men without the Gospel; but the Gospel without the Power of God, will never Convert a Soul . . . It is true, that Sinners are not ordinarily Converted, without the Gospel. God has appointed the End and Means to go together.

Thus we can perceive that in the Puritan conception of regeneration there is a fascinating duality, which barely conceals an incipient contradiction, between its physical and spiritual aspects. Puritans seldom faced the issue squarely, since it never quite defined itself for them as an issue, and no one quotation from their writings will perfectly illustrate their balance of piety and physics; yet their refusal to allow either one to exclude the other appears in their use of contrary emphases when combating either Anglicans or Antinomians. Whenever they attack the Church of England—or the Church of Rome—they deplore "idolatry" and insist that grace is not to be confined to physical agents, to sacraments and rituals, but whenever they have to deal with an Anne Hutchinson, a Gorton, or a Fox, they contend with equal fervor that grace is never imparted to the soul except through the agency of a sensual impression, that it observes the orderly processes of rational psychology, and never produces an unnatural predominance of even sanctified passions over an enlightened reason. The converted reason, therefore, is prevailed upon by logic, but by logic suffused with grace; the will follows engaged reason not only by the force of proof, but by proofs radiating divine magnetism; passions yield to a sanctified will not only because she commands them, but because her commands are seasoned with heavenly "rellish". Good preachers "can set things before us *Objectively,* but not renew our Faculties *Subjectively.*" God's spirit does not always accompany the Word, or else all who hear would become saints for the listening; yet "the Lord doth appropriate the saving worke of his Spirit to goe with the ordinance; not that God is tyed to any means, but he tyeth himselfe to this meanes." God has created in man a rational machinery, and yet regeneration is neither reasonable nor mechanical. It is wholly arbitrary, though not arbitrary in the sense that it violently casts aside the psychological mechanism. "Why doth not aire nourish all, as well as meat? because onely God hath set meat apart for this purpose." In the same fashion He has set apart agencies for spiritual nourishment, and though only He "can draw and perswade, yet he does it by his word." If we have difficulties comprehending the symmetry of God and nature in the process of conversion, we may always be certain of the moral: "Therefore we must apply our selves to speak and hear, to listen to such quickning drawing Considerations." We will not be saved by the considerations alone, but we will never be saved without them.

When the Puritan theory of regeneration is placed in the frame of psychology, it appears one of the more amazing achievements of the Puritan mind, a unification of inherited science and intense piety, containing at one and the same time all the advantages of order and all the charms of caprice, all the security of an assured income and all the fascinations of a gamble. It holds in miniature almost every characteristic of Puritan thinking. It incarnates the conception of a natural world established upon an order which is fundamentally and indestructibly good, which is yet at the moment corrupted, and it makes comprehensible that essential rightness may survive in the order of things though overlaid with sin. It reinforces the all-important distinction between the universal and natural presences of God, His concurrence in all events, His sustaining influence upon every thought, deed, and object, and then shows the necessity for His special and extraordinary presence, His emanation over and above nature, His occasional interpositions, which add unto nature, lifting perfection to a still higher refinement of perfection, elevating natural felicity into heavenly excellence. Above all, the theory made it possible to regard regeneration as a process both spiritual and intellectual, to see conversion as both of head and heart. If the overwhelming glory of God should come to man as a ravishing spiritual force it would obliterate his personality; if it should come only as a logical demonstration it would be dry, sterile, and dead; but if it imparts to all the faculties an individual and appropriate "grace", then conversion is simultaneously an irresistible seizure and a rational transaction. Regeneration is "not brought forth, but in the way of morall perswasion, that is, not without the preceding judgement of the understanding, weighing on each part what is best to be done"; it follows upon "the last dictate of the Understanding," and so does not disrupt the order of nature, but still it is supernatural and not limited to the chance accident of a mechanical stimulus, not dependent upon physical circumstances. Grace is thus "both irresistible and free." Its irresistibleness may very well "stand with" the freedom of the will, for the acts of a sanctified will flow "from a reasonable perswasion; and that upon this ground, that reason lies indifferent to things opposite, that is, Reason onely is the root and foundation of all Liberty: from whence it followes, that every act of the Will, unto which Reason hath its influence, is most free."[1] The will cannot resist motions proceeding from an enlightened understanding, and yet men are not driven into sanctity as beasts to a pen, not plunged into salvation as inert stones dropped into a well.

Experience showed that even among the most assured of saints the psychological reflex was not always perfectly reëstablished. Even the holy John Eliot could make mistakes in judgment, as when he published *The Christian Commonwealth* at a most inopportune moment, just as Charles II had been restored, and so embarrassed the commonwealth of Massachusetts Bay. However, this frequently observed fact did not disturb the psychological theory, for the doctrine of imperfect sanctification accounted for it. All textbooks explained, "because our regeneration is but onely inchoate or begun, and as yet unperfect, . . . there is still much slaverie in the regenerate;

much blindenesse in the minde and understanding, much pravitie in the heart and affections, and many weaknesses and infirmities in all the powers of soul and body." As long as we are in the flesh, we can never wholly be rid of sin, and regenerate faculties will many times slip back into depravity. The finest of New England poets dramatized the incessant struggle of the regenerate in the language of all the faculties; thus he expressed it upon the level of the passions:

> My 'ffections were thy tinder in't
>   Where fell thy Sparkes by drops.
> Those holy Sparks of Heavenly Fire that came
> Did ever catch and often out would flame.[2]

But since we well understand the cause of these lapses of the saints, we can continue to believe that in regeneration God deals with men as rational creatures, converts them by an influence of grace and yet also by a rational enlightenment. The will is not forced, but led. God dispenses grace to us in a manner suitable to "intelligent creatures, made after the image of God, capable of judging and discerning the Reason and Equity of things, and of arguing one thing from another, and choosing and preferring one thing before another." We come to faith voluntarily, "Our Understanding must be eyes to our Will, and entertain the reason for our so doing." Though the Holy Ghost is "the author or efficient of this work, yet he makes use of us in the working of it." Because grace does not destroy but rectifies nature, conversion must come through the reason; to limit faith to the understanding is heresy, but to deny it any foundation in the intellect is equally fallacious.

> This we know in general, that the Understanding and Will in us must concur in every act we perform, as Causes by Counsel, or that is properly humane. And hence, both these faculties must be sanctifyed for the producing of gracious actions.

Though the grace of God is free and unpredictable, capricious and terrible, yet it does not work upon physical bodies without physical agents. It comes to men through what Puritans called the "means". Conversion is an event in nature, and as in other natural events, the will of God is worked not by miracles but by providences. God follows a sequence of causes to bring about His ends, and what may seem to us an imperfection in the effect, as in our sanctification, is God's gracious concession to the order of nature. He could sanctify us beyond the possibility of a lapse did He choose so to remake us, but He prefers to bring us back to holiness through natural agencies, and the effect of such agencies, even with the blessing of grace upon them, must necessarily be finite.

This doctrine of means made the process of grace no less supernatural, but at the same time kept it commensurate with nature. As in physics, God sustains and directs, but the effect is always appropriate to the cause. Just as He creates fire before heat, so in the elect He regenerates their reasons in order to revivify their wills, and their wills as a preliminary to renewing their affections. And not only does He abide by the forms of nature within the faculties, He also chooses to work externally through the forms of causation. The process of regeneration is initiated by an external object from which the senses derive a phantasm, exactly as in any other act of apprehension. God does not miraculously bestow vision upon the senses or imaginations of saints, though in this fashion He formerly illuminated prophets of the Old Testament. He does not mend the tangled skein of the faculties as a puppet-master unravels the strings of mannequins, but He deals rationally with men. Though grace is a cataclysm, a sudden revelation, a burst of light, though it is different from all "common providences", above the usual order of things, it is not entirely unrelated to efficient causes. A naturalistic account can be given of the supernatural, even though in many instances the same natural causes produce no regeneration. There is a logic and a preparation, a conception and a gestation. Otherwise Puritanism would have become spiritual anarchy, as indeed Anne Hutchinson and Samuel Gorton, Webster and Dell, endeavored to make it. To guard against such lawlessness God instituted the order of means, even though He Himself remains free to disregard it. In orthodox Puritan theory, grace is not thrust upon the soul unexpectedly and abruptly, but is insinuated according to the laws of psychology through means. By this doctrine were determined many aspects of the Puritan creed, and by it were ruled Puritan conceptions of the church, of the sermon, and of literary style.

The doctrine held that the means by which God commences the psychological process may be any experience, any affliction or providential deliverance, but ordinarily they are the words of a sermon and the sacraments of the church. I shall endeavor to take up the conception of the sacraments in a subsequent volume, since it became the starting-point for particular social and intellectual developments which I there hope to recount. However, whether Puritans were speaking of sacraments or of sermons as means, the essence of their theory was the same, that every conversion must begin with a specific physical stimulus. The spirit must indeed accompany the stimulus; it is God and not the means themselves that regenerates a man; as Ames phrased it, "though those doe morally concurre and operate in the preparation of man to receive this grace, yet they doe not properly confer the grace by themselves, but the spirit which worketh together with them." By operating through them, God proceeds "according to the Rules of Wisdom," said Hooker, "and the right order of causes and means"; hence the means, in his imaginative language, are "not the meat, yet they are as dishes that bring the meat, . . . these are the conduits to convey this water of life." The Puritan poet conveyed the lesson in similar imagery:

Each Ordinance, and Instrument of Grace
Grace doth instruct are Usefull here;
They're Golden Pipes where Holy Waters trace
Into the Spirits spicebed Deare,
To vivify what whithering were.[8]

The words of a minister are as arrows to wound a proud heart, and they humble the spirit, yet not by their own force, rather by the blessing of God upon them; one minister brings more men to repentance than another, and in part because of his superior eloquence, yet the final cause of a sinner's conversion is not any ministerial rhetoric but the Holy Ghost. If God "witholds His Efficacious and Irresistible operations, the ablest Preacher in the world will never be able to Convert one Soul." He "breathes" grace wherever He lists, yet usually "he doth . . . breathe the Spirit by the breath of his Word," and for all practical purposes "the word of the Gospell and the worke of the Spirit alwayes goe together." The seeming paradox in this doctrine disappears if it is considered in the light of contemporaneous psychology:

They must first heare, then learne; heare by the word, and learne by the Spirit, The hearing of the Gospell without the Spirit, is nothing else but a beating of the ayre, and a dead letter. It is true, the Lord can worke above meanes: we know also God can appoint other meanes for to call the soule, but it is not our meaning, we must not looke for revelations and dreames, . . . but in common course Gods Spirit goes with the Gospell, and that is the ordinary meanes whereby the soule comes to be called. God can make ayre nourish a man, but he doth not.

How much that is seldom recognized in the Puritan character is suggested by these phrases, "we must not looke for revelations and dreames," how much by the injunction that we must observe the "common course"! Hooker characteristically appealed to what "experience hath proved, and reason will confirme" to show that the sequence of causal means is usually God's manner. Theologians would profess that God may work by any means or without any, that He may convert men with immediate influences, with dreams, visions, or angels, but one and all they insisted that for His own holy ends He has chosen to commit the business to physical means, that thereby we behold His mercy, for did He come directly to us in His own person, "we should be overwhelmed by such an awful majesty." We see "God's gracious condescension to our present weakness, that he employs men for the benefiting our souls," that He brings us to spiritual heights by a material ascent, that He regenerates us through sacraments and sermons.

For ordinary life this theory resulted in a peculiar moral that is typically Puritan: since we receive grace *through* the ordinances we must prize them highly, but since we do not get grace *from* them we must prize them not too highly. Because God usually dispenses His favor through them, we must attend upon them. "The more we depend on a wise physician, the more we shall observe his directions, and be careful to use what he prescribes." Men are victims of "a delusory Faith" when they seek for extraordinary blessings outside the means; God becomes exceeding provoked if "a creature dares trust him in this kind, when hee hath not promised to worke." A faith that will not relie upon God "in ordinary wayes and meanes, unlesse God will shew his extraordinary power, . . . is a foule abuse of faith." The exhortation of sermon after sermon is, "Wait upon God in his Ordinances with thirsting souls: It will not be in vain"; men are not stones but rational beings, "that when they fall into a pit, labour to get out again; and make use of what help they can get from others." Yet the means alone will not serve to get them out; no sermons, no sacraments will suffice. "We may use the meanes, but there is no meanes under heaven will doe it." Therefore we must wait upon the means, and love them, but love them with those "weaned affections" which preachers so constantly celebrated. God conveys life by the means, but they themselves cannot furnish life; therefore Christians must give them their just due, "neither too little nor too much, doe not over-value them, but yet neglect them not." They lead us to God, but they "cannot give salvation to any that rests upon them," and one of the more subtle refinements of sin is a tendency to depend upon true ordinances for more than they may provide. "A man should be so painefull in the use of the meanes, as though they could do all, and yet so depend upon God above the meanes, as though all outward meanes, could not doe any good without the Lord." The less theological mind of the twentieth century might surmise from these remarks that the Puritans' devotion to the ordinances and the spoken sermon was radically checked by their circumspection, but it is of the essence of the Puritan character that it would go to the stake for that which God had ordered it to love with but half a love. While determined to hold close to the ordinances and by no means to part with them, Puritans were resolved while embracing them not to trust them; also, they were ready to migrate into New England if they could not have the ordinances in England, and to write back to their brethren at home:

> We do exhort you lovingly in the Lord . . . that neither you, nor others doe live in the voluntary want of any holy Ordinance of Christ Jesus, but either set them up, . . . or else (if you bee free) to remove for the enjoyment of them, to some place where they may be had.

An enjoyment that took the form of "while you enjoy them, trust not in them" could be comprehended only by a Puritan, and only a Puritan would hold such enjoyment adequate to repay the labor of settling a new world.

By working through means God condescends to treat with men according to their natures, not according to His, and He does not force them to meet Him, so to speak, upon His level. Hence He would have the means adapted to the physical nature of the soul; they must be devised to suit the faculties, and the instruments of supernatural regeneration must be conformed to such powers as are enumerated by Aristotelian science. Consequently, the means must be of two fundamental kinds, those addressed to the rational soul, to reason and will, and those designed to move the sensible soul, the imagination and appetite. The first must take the guise of rational persuasion, invincible proof, logical demonstration, and the silencing of objections; thus dialectic and abstract arguments were so tremendously important in Puritan writings because grace had to begin with logical conviction. "God will lay hold upon the understanding of a poore sinner, and follow him with reasons that are undeniable untill his reason shall yeeld." Of course, not even the strongest reasons will produce spiritual effects without a concomitant influence of the spirit, but the sermon has to put forth rationally convincing inducements to belief or else divine influences are materially hindered. Natural men may come to understand "the *Grammatical* and *Logical* meaning of Gospel *Theorems*" without being regenerated, yet when the spirit commences a man's vocation it imprints grammatical and logical meanings upon his intellect. Divine "drawings" are never "compulsive, but such as work upon the Rational Powers in Man"; their efficacy depends on an operation of the Spirit, but also "there is the spontaneous Operation of the Man." Therefore sermons are the chief means for salvation because they are best accommodated to God's treating with men as with rational creatures, and ministers who carry the Gospel to the world must persuade the mind of the world to believe. Their sermons are applied to the outward man and engender phantasms in the physical senses, "thro' which they are to pass to the Mind and be improved by the Rational and Moral Powers of the Soul." Ministers are to imitate God and not try to sweep their people into sanctity by force; "we must endeavour their conviction; we must first deal with their understandings." Were ministers first "to raise the affections, without informing the mind," they would be performing "a fruitlesse unprofitable labour," which "serves but to make zeal without knowledge." Christ clothed difficult spiritual truths in parables "to accommodate them the more to Humane Understandings, and to shew the rationality of them"; He did not scorn to argue *"ab Utili"*, for nothing is more comportable with reason than to consent to practical advantages, and preachers should fearlessly advance their "reasons" from "this Topick or Head of Argument" in spite of the ridicule heaped by Peripatetic academicians upon utility as a standard of value. A sermon must be constructed by the rules of dialectic, and its deliberate aim be to show things as they are. A sudden illumination, a sharp intuition, the fleeting moment of insight will not carry us far; "this sudden Blaze of Thought, tho' never so bright, will not lay open the hidden Mysteries of divine Things to our View, unless the Mind be brought by Meditation to an holy Pause upon them." Only when carefully and solidly established by logic will the truth "leave more of a transforming Power upon all the Faculties of the Soul." A Puritan sermon is to show that "a thing is not true, because I beleeve it is so, yet things first are, and then I beleeve them." As arguments are invented by dialectic, and as their arrangement is dictated by the objectively existent laws of method, so the articles of faith are proved by sermons to be not imaginary things, not phantasms of the fancy, but real things that "doe lye before the eye of reason, sanctified and elevated by the eye of faith." Puritan faith is always defined as an "understanding grace," and though reason, science, logic, or technologia cannot independently arrive at what we should believe, yet they can and must tell us the reasons for believing. "Faith useth reason, though not as a ground, yet as a sanctified instrument to find out God's grounds, that it may rely upon them." Otherwise, as Preston significantly puts it, "men were neither to be blamed nor praised for ordering their affections aright." The doctrine of means bound together Puritan piety and the Puritan intellectual inheritance; it furnished a common meeting place for irresistible grace and for reason. It made the grace compatible with nature without doing violence to nature or reducing grace to a natural influence. Augustine and Aristotle were indistinguishably fused in the characteristic Puritan moral: "There is no contradiction between God's treating men as rational agents, and yet supplying their defects and impotency of acting graciously, by renewing his Grace in those powers."

Theology thus took its place in the circle of the liberal arts, for although it required a special blessing and an extraordinary revelation, still it was gathered through sense impressions like any other art. It was a form of knowledge, and all knowledge was learned through the regular psychological channels. Ordinary science, as John Cotton explained, springs from things themselves, "from sence and experience," but knowledge of divinity comes from the Bible, from testimony, from "inartificials" and not from "artificials". For this reason the Bible needs the Holy Ghost to win from men the same degree of credence they will always accord to sense and experience, but otherwise faith is a science: it is, according to Willard, "indeed a Confidence, but it is ever built upon Knowledge." Just as rational conviction may exist without saving faith, so may literal knowledge without saving illumination, but as there can be no faith without a preceding conviction, so no illumination without adequate knowledge. Will and passion must have some species to work upon, for "Knowledg and understanding is the inlet into the soul[,] nothing comes to the heart nor can work upon it but so far as knowledg makes way, & ushers it in (as it were) into the presence of the wil and leaves an impression thereof upon it." The mere vehemence of a sermon, the eloquence of a tract, will not "sink the heart of a sinful Creature" unless his understanding thoroughly grasps the propositions. It is "opposite to all the Rules of Reason and Providence," said Hooker, "that persons should step from prophaness in the depth of it, unto the height of Christian Piety and Holiness" before the mind be informed "in the History, Matter, and Truth of the Scripture." Hence Puritan faith, being an "understanding grace," is wrought by knowledge, by knowledge of divinity in particular, but by all human learning as well, and "although an historical Faith alone, will not amount to a justifying Faith, yet there must of necessity be such a Faith in order to the other." This delicate balancing of the outward and inward means, of the causal influence of the spoken word, "in which we are treated with by men," and the regenerating influence of the spirit enabling us to learn what pastors teach, this is the subtle machinery of election, the procedure to which God in His infinite mercy has resorted in order that we might be redeemed. The outward instrument will never be effectual except "when it hath the concomitancy of the other," but the coincidence of the two "always obtains in the Elect, and is in order of means accommodated thereto." A pious heart cannot live without an inward rapture, without the quickness which God has kissed, but no matter how enraptured, it cannot exceed "the order which the Lord in the way of his providence and work of nature hath placed betwixt the mind and the heart, the understanding and wil of man." A regenerate heart never throbs a single beat except at the command of an informed mind, an enlightened intellect, an educated reason.

The means of grace must operate in order first upon the intellect, but also they must aim no less at the heart and the sensible soul, or they will fail to complete their work. Phantasms are not to rest in the brain as disembodied objects of contemplation; they are to attract the will and entice the passions. A psychologist, Thomas Wright, after arguing against Stoics that the passions are basically good, advised that divines, "who specially entreateth of our last end, and of the meanes to atchieve it, and difficulties to obtaine it," extend their study to the theory of the passions, for they need above all men to be skillful in handling human affections. No doubt the sinner will never love or hope for heaven, even when a preacher paints the most alluring prospects of it, unless divine grace guides the love and the hope, yet these passions must also have the alluring prospects in order to be set in motion. The Bible again shows ministers the way: it has some passages to inform the understanding, and others to engage the will or to move the affections; Christ used parables to make truths not merely comprehensible to reason but also attractive to the fancy. Although depending upon God's assistance, ministers still endeavor "to find out pleasant words, or words of delight." Conviction of the mind is indispensable, but "that is not the maine end of preaching, to instruct men: but to worke upon their hearts." The regenerating impulse sweeps through the whole psychological arc, as Samuel Willard thus succinctly traced it:

There is this order in such a Conveyance, *viz.* The Truths of the Word are first applied to the Understanding, by which we may know the meaning, and discern the reason of them; for here all humane Actions begin; and being approved by the Judgment, it must be past over to the Will for its Election, whereby it embraceth the Truth commended, and is won over to it; and from thence it is imprinted on the Affections, to which the Will commits the Prosecution of the choice which it hath made, and by which it performs its Imperate Actions.

God chooses whom He will, and He rejects regardless of merit, but His ministers must proceed upon the assumption that if they can drive images of doctrine deep enough into the mind, and embellish them with sufficient eloquence to call out an affection, they can then, and only then, become the means of election, and only thus fulfill God's will. They "are to do what in them lies," they are "to do their uttermost to illuminate, awaken, convince and convert sinners," notwithstanding the fact that the effectiveness of any sermon for the edification and conversion of sinners depends upon the arbitrary favor of God.

The one means above all others which was perfectly adapted to working upon all faculties, that simultaneously could carry phantasms to both reason and affection, that would impress the species of Gospel theorems upon the understanding and at the same time plunge them deep into the heart, was clearly the spoken word. "A powerfull ministery," said Hooker, "is the only ordinary meanes which God hath appointed soundly to prepare the heart of a poore sinner for the receiving of the Lord Jesus." And it must particularly be noted—for recognition of this fact is essential to our understanding both Puritan history and Puritan literature—that the minister was believed to be a thousand times more apt to become an effectual means when he spoke than when he wrote. The word as uttered and not as printed was the ordinary instrument for preparing the heart. It was well to read the sermons of a great preacher, but it was better to have heard them; the phantasms of Gospel theorems could of course be carried through the eye to the understanding and will, and occasionally sinners received their vocation through the means of a published tract, but for most mortals the call came with infinitely more persuasive force when delivered from the rostrum, when shot like an arrow from the mighty bow of a Hooker, a Cotton, or a Mather, when driven by the arm of their personalities, tipped with their eloquence and feathered with their gestures. The published writings of great divines, said Cotton, are useful "to establishment of many in the truth, and to stirre them up to stick closer to the truth," but they "do not prosper to conversion." Hence, though Christians should read sermons, and congregations that had been particularly moved by some discourse of their pastor ought to petition him to print it, and ought to pay the costs in order to have an aid to their memories and a confirmation of the impression, still psychology and the theory of the faculties made it clear that the printed word would always remain at best a pale replica of the declamation. Puritans would have scorned the comparison, but the difference between hearing and reading a sermon was for them exactly the difference others would have found between reading *King Lear* and seeing it played by Richard Burbage. The vital heat, so essential to the kindling of affections, all but evaporated when the sermon was set up in type. Because God made man of the three souls and gave him the faculties, the best means of bringing grace to a man must be the voice of a minister; the spoken words, as such, may be physically no more than aural species striking upon the ear, and like all phantasms be simply forms flowing from an object, yet "when the sound comes to the eare, and the sense to the minde, the Spirit goes with the Word when thou hearest it, either to convert thee, or to confound thee."

Thus the Lord may use misfortune and afflictions to humble a proud will, but these do not generally lead to faith; He gives the sacraments to confirm and nourish faith in those in whom it is once engendered, but they seldom supply the initial impulse. The reading of tracts will not usually batter the heart or wrest the whole soul toward heaven, nor will private study of Scripture do more than force a sinner to cry out, "What shall I do to be saved?" There must needs come a man named Evangelist to point out the wicket-gate. The absolute decrees of unconditional predestination must operate in a contingent world through the voice of the preacher, and the elect be brought home, not by an immediate and violent abduction, but by means of sermons. William Perkins, whose manual of preaching, *The Art of Prophecying,* was the basic textbook for Puritan students, said that preaching collects the church and accomplishes the number of the elect, "for this is indeed that Plexanima, that allurer of the Soule, whereby mens froward minds are mitigated and moved from an ungodly and barbarous life unto Christian faith and repentance." The spoken word alone is sharp and pointed enough to penetrate the hidden parts of the soul and barbed enough to fasten upon them; as Michael Wigglesworth proclaimed in a declamation at Harvard College, eloquence can not only review things known, "but secretly convay life into the hearers understanding rousing it out of its former slumber, quickning it beyond its naturall vigour, elevating it aboue its ordinary conception." Because the oration is the one agency by which, on the plane of nature, the innermost faculties can be reached, God once more demonstrates His determination to accommodate His workings to the order of nature by employing it most frequently in choosing His people. God dwells in every particle of the universe by virtue of His essential presence, and therefore has immediate access to the brain and heart of man, "yet hee is in a more speciall manner going with, and accompanying of his Word." He is able out of His omnipotence to call His saints in His proper person, but in practice He prefers to employ His ambassadors and to conform His grace to the process of cause and effect.

> It is true when Corne failes God can send *Manna* from heaven: God can use extraordinary meanes to bring men to life and salvation and hapinesse, but men must not looke now for extraordinary conversions, they must not expect to be miraculously saved . . . In the common course of God, if ever a soule now be converted, it must be by the ministery of the word.

The ministers acknowledged themselves mere men, as fallible and sinful as others, and they denied that they were priests with any "indelible" or sacerdotal prowess, and "yet while we are thus speaking to you, God many times conveys such a spirit of grace into us, as gives us power to receive Christ . . . The word that we speake conveyes spirit and life into [you]." Some casual phrase, the handling of an incidental point, any chance sentence in the sermon may suddenly be armed by the Lord and discharged at a particular listener with such force that, unbeknown to the preacher and to the complete surprise of the auditor, "it astonisheth and shivereth the heart of the sinner al in pieces." As in the discharge of seventeenth-century artillery, "it may be one scattred shot or splinter hitts and kils when al the rest miss; so with the splinter of a truth when directed aright." In strict theological terms, a sinner is impotent until the grace of God invigorates him, but in psychological terms, "There are none that attend a faithful Ministery but have many a pull from Christ," and Hooker could therefore advance the startling conclusion, so apparently contrary to a literal interpretation of the doctrine of natural inability that even he would not call it "absolute" but merely "a great suspicion," that those who have lived under a powerful ministry half a dozen years or so and yet have got no good from it—"it is a shrewd suspicion, I say, that God will send them downe to hell."

The figure of the pious and trembling individual closeted alone with his Bible, of the solitary walker with God, is often taken to be the true symbol of the Puritan spirit. In England, after the defeat and disintegration of the organized Puritan movement, after the collapse in 1659-60 of the Puritan political program, individual Puritans were indeed thrown back upon themselves, and *Grace Abounding* records the inward quest with no reference to the external and social scheme. Yet Puritanism in the early seventeenth century, the Puritanism that settled New England, was more properly symbolized, not by the secluded individual, but by the social tableau of the covenanted church and the public discourse. The voice of Christ was made known, according to Hooker, by the Bible, and then by the Bible as preached from the pulpit. "Whatsoever any faithfull Minister shall speak out of the Word, that is also the voice of Christ." Puritan life, in the New England theory, was centered upon a corporate and communal ceremony, upon the oral delivery of a lecture, and the effort of the Massachusetts Bay Company to set up a due form of government both civil and ecclesiastical came ultimately to the one purpose of gathering men and women together in orderly congregations that they might sit under a "powerful" and a literate ministry, that they might hear the Word of God as well as read it, and hear it not as it was written in revelation, but as it was expounded by that ministry, refashioned into doctrines, reasons, and uses. Private meditation was demanded, but meditation chiefly upon last Sunday's sermon or Thursday's lecture; reading of the Bible was required, but reading of it in the light of the exposition; attendance at the sacraments was expected of the saints, but as an adjunct to attendance upon the sermon. It was through a sermon that nine out of ten of the elect caught the first hints of their vocation, and by continued listening to good preaching they made their calling sure.

The principal theoretical justification for this exaltation of the sermon was the conception of means. Because they were armed with this theory, Puritans could view the sermon as the way and the life and could dispense with an authoritative church and a *jure divino* priesthood; instead of a miraculous communion through the Mass they had the miracle of converting grace accompanying, though not identical with, the sound of faithful words. The Christian pilgrimage set forth, not from an inn in Southwark, but from the Interpreter's House, and so journeyed not to a shrine, but to the heavenly city. Ministers were but men, and without God's blessing their most winged words were no more than any human speech, but when God chose to manifest Himself to a people, He came to them under the guise of ministerial eloquence:

> You see what businesse we have in hand, that are Preachers of the Gospell, our businesse is to make men other Creatures, which is a transcendent worke, it is the worke of God, and not of man: this is the errand we are sent about . . . You must learne to know, when you heare the Word . . . whom you have to doe with, that is, with the Almighty God, and not with man . . . We are Instruments, and the Word is an Instrument, but if there be not an influence from God, the worke will not be done.

The theory of the means, with its peculiar sense of a dual causation, of the coincidence of a natural inducement and a supernatural influence, made possible the whole social and ecclesiastical structure of New England, because it enabled members of all congregations to say of their ministers, as did Hopkins and Goodwin of Thomas Hooker, "His spirit mostly delighted in the search of the mystery of Christ, in the unsearchable riches thereof, and the work and method of the spirit, in the communication of the same unto the soul for its everlasting welfare." The ministry might be merely "an outward instrumentall cause of faith," and men living in a Puritan universe had always to remind themselves that "no outward instrumentall cause is essentiall to the effect, whether we speake of naturall or supernaturall effects," for the spirit of God could work whatever He wished without agents or instruments. Yet because the absolute sovereign of the universe was "wonted to work it by the Ministry," men had to seek their salvation by hanging upon the words of the minister, and they had to listen intently and absorbedly, even though at the same time with "weaned affections."

CHAPTER XI

RHETORIC

"Affectionate faithfull preaching and setting forth of Christ" was a means of grace because, as John Cotton said, it "stirreth up in others a saving knowledge of Christ, and hearty affection to him." To Puritanism it was quite as important that the others be stirred up to a saving knowledge as to a hearty affection, for the theory of the means was premised, as we have seen, upon the scholastic psychology and therefore required that the agents of conversion be addressed simultaneously to both the rational and sensible souls. A preacher who hoped to bring sinners to repentance would need to construct his sermons so that they appealed at every point both to intellect and passion. However, it is noticeable that whenever Puritans discuss the sermon by itself, without theorizing upon it as a means, they give the preponderant attention to arousing affection. Where there is one injunction to expound the will of God "out of soundnesse of argument, and plaine evidence," or to convey "the truth to the understanding of the meanest," there are a hundred that exclaim in more passionate accents, "O brethren, let the fire burn clear; let there not be more smoke than fire." You are not to furnish the minister's table with the "dainties" of consolation and grace, said Shepard, but are "to possess men with a sense of wrath to come, and misery"; the words of Scripture, said Cotton, are to be as sharp goads to dull spirits and as nails to fasten them to God. William Ames told New England divines that it was easier to bring the Word to the ears and understandings of men than into their hearts and hands, and Thomas Hooker, whose preaching burned with this knowledge, scorned to deliver "General Truths" unless he could also awaken the heart. "It's not enough that we be stirring in the house, and people be up, but we must knock at mens doors, bring a Candle to their bed-sides, and pinch the sluggard, and then if he have any life he wil stir." Many ministers "can tell a grave faire tale, and speake of sinnes in generall," yet mere abstractions are like arrows "shot a cock height, they touch no man; but when a Minister makes application of sin in particular, and saith, O all you drunkards and adulterers, this is your portion," then are his arrows shot "home into the hearts and consciences of men, and make them at a stand." Specific and merciless application to the sins of the very men and women before him, the skill "to hit the humor of the heart of a sinner, to make a receipt on purpose to meet with the particular distemper," these were what Hooker required in a minister, for otherwise men will "sit and sleep carelessly" under an empty noise of heaven and hell, sin and death. At the end of the century the emotional intensity of New England Puritanism had considerably slackened; nevertheless, Samuel Willard, even though lacking Hooker's fervor, declared that not only do our understandings need illumination, but much more do our wills and affections "need to be roused, quickned and drawn to their work."

Were we to consider such passages apart from their contexts, and apart from the sermons themselves, we might easily conclude that the Puritan ideal was simply an impassioned harangue, the sort of emotional evangelicalism familiar to eighteenth- and nineteenth-century revivals. Ministerial instruction seems to place sincerity above learning, zeal above knowledge, vigor above intellect. The early Puritans so felt the necessity for this holy violence in the pulpit that they were ready not merely to forbid the preacher's reading other men's sermons and to advise him against reading his own instead of delivering them *memoriter*—so that he might not lose the "inward affection"—but even to insist that none should preach who had not already undergone conversion, that however skilled in theology, a young candidate should not be ordained a pastor until his heart had become "answerable to that he communicates and delivers unto the people." William Perkins declared that "he must first bee godly affected himselfe, who would stirre up godly affected affections in other men," that before the minister attempts to arouse others he should first privately arouse himself. This impression of Puritans' standards seems corroborated when we review their comments, open or veiled, upon the preaching of their Anglican opponents, particularly upon the learned and highly ornate sermons of the Laudians, or upon such discourses as those of Andrewes and Donne. The exquisite and modulated prose of these divines seemed to their Puritan contemporaries the "carnall eloquence" of a "blubber-lipt Ministery." Perkins and Ames forbade using Greek or Latin phrases, and Ames said that a sermon should be a two-edged sword piercing inward affections, "so that an unbeliever comming into the Congregation of the faithfull he ought to be affected, and as it were digged through with the very hearing of the Word, that he may give glory to God";[1] consequently, "metaphysical" preachers, mounting their pulpits "with Metaphysical high flown Notions, or *Words of Mens Wisdom* . . . to make a Clattering with Latin, Greek or Hebrew Sentences," full of "obscure phrases, Exotick Words," "liking to hover and soar aloft in dark expressions," seemed immoral to Puritans, not merely because they blasphemously polished God's altar and adulterated the Word of God, "like as Paint doth marble, or as honey and wine in childrens milke," but also because their sermons could never become a means of grace to common men.

It's strange to see when such men have told a grave tale, and vented a heartless, toothless discourse, neither pith nor power in it; I say, it's strange to see what admiration and esteem such carnal hearts will set upon such persons and expressions; great their parts, prudence, and discretion: Oh how sweet and seasonable their discourse, how glad to hear, and how unweariable to attend such: And al the while they may sit and sleep in their sinful condition, and neither have their Consciences awakened, nor their corruption discovered. Squeamish Stomachs had rather take Sugar-sops a whol week together than a bitter Potion one day.

Hence as compared with Arminians, the Puritans seem to speak of the sermon entirely in pietistic terms, to scorn the help of art and all care for form, to open the way to fulmination and rant. When Perkins declared that a minister must preach so that not he but the Spirit speaks in him, when Preston decrees that the Bible must not be "mixt with humane Eloquence; for the pure Word should be purely delivered,"[2] when Hooker asserts, "That ministery which doth not ordinarily humble the soule, and breake the heart for sinne, doth not convert and draw home to Christ," it might seem that they intended that the minister, like Ralph, squire to Sir Hudibras, should rely wholly upon the inward inspiration which

plays upon
The nose of Saint like Bag-pipe drone,
And speaks through hollow empty Soul,
As through a Trunk, or whisp'ring hole,
Such language as no mortal Ear
But spiritual Eve-droppers can hear,[3]

rather than depend upon grammatical rules and the rhetorical periods of academic culture.

However, Puritan pronouncements upon the sermon must be read with reference to the times and to other than religious factors in the Puritan mind. When Puritans denounced eloquence as carnal they were speaking for the moment simply as men of great piety; when they heaped objurgations upon metaphysical conceits they were overstating their case merely to score off their adversaries. Just as soon as the radical fringe of their party, the Antinomian sects and the hot-gospelling enthusiasts, took the solid divines at their word and proceeded apace to deliver sermons which dispensed utterly with the "humane helps" of grammar and rhetoric, orthodox Puritans in England and New England rallied to defend these arts exactly as they upheld dialectic. Webster arraigned academic rhetoric for being at best an impertinent ornamentation, and announced in phrases that might easily have been taken from some unguarded utterance of Ames or Preston, "those which excell much in reason, and do dispose those things which they excogitate in a most easie method, that they may be cleerly, and distinctly understood, are most apt to perswade, although they did use the language of the *Goths,* and had never learned *Rhetorick.*" Confronted with such barbarity, university apologists hastened to qualify earlier statements, to explain that while they, like St. Paul, did indeed disapprove of "the glarous, painted and ranting Rhetorick of those times", the "lofty towrings of fancy, fawning words, and vainly-garnish'd expressions, neither fitting the capacity of a popular audience, nor becoming the Majesty of a God and the nobility of Divine revelation," yet that they had always advocated the studied "decorum" which could be achieved only with the help of formal rhetoric. Scripture itself, they pointed out, teaches a "true raisedness of expression, a majesticall state, and artificiall and genuine insinuation, with most patheticall captivatings of the minde." Consequently, we today cannot discover the true Puritan doctrine of style in occasional ridicule of carnal eloquence, and must turn rather to the stylistic practices of the sermons themselves, to the curriculum of Puritan education, and to more judicious discussions in the handbooks of pastoral care. Perhaps the most useful statement in the New England literature is an oration upon eloquence delivered by Michael Wigglesworth as an undergraduate exercise, which deserves notice, not so much because it is itself eloquent, but because, being an undergraduate effort, it should represent received opinion at Harvard College in the mid-seventeenth century. Defining eloquence as the "ability, fully & clearly, & gracefully & readily to express in words what the mind in thought conceives," he urges it as "one of the most effectual means to make others become good." Though he is discoursing upon eloquence in general, not specifically pulpit eloquence, yet it is the spoken word as a means that he has in mind, for it could not otherwise be conceived by Puritans, and the theory he outlines is essentially that which underlies the Puritan doctrine of the sermon. The effects of eloquence upon its auditors he describes in the phraseology of the means; he points out that it works upon the understanding, but stresses still more its use as "a fit bait to catch the will and affections." As his professors had taught him, he objects to the *"stilum poeticum,"* full of "strained metaphors, far fetch't allusions, audacious & lofty expressions"; those who "dote upon a meer ostentation of learning & empty flashes of a flourishing wit," who "daub over their speèch with rhetorical paintments," end by putting out "the very eyes of all the Reason they speak." "So many Bells hang bobbing at the end of every word, that one cannot hear sence for the gingling of Rhetorique." However, though he chides those who bewilder their auditors "amongst their winding, crooked, periphrasticall circumlocutions, & dark Allegoric mysteries," he is far from concluding that an orator must abandon all "rhetorical sweets," for as long as the sweets serve merely as baits to attract the will and affections, or to capture the imagination, they are justifiable and legitimate, even admirable, means. The ideal, he says in conclusion, is a "moderate seasoning of our speech with . . . tropical & figurative elocutions"; no orator should speak in "a bare and naked stile that hath never a ragg of Eloquence to its back, made up wholly of common and road-way expressions like ordinary table talk."[4] So far was the Puritan style removed from the unadorned simplicity and spontaneity of common speech that the modern student has his moments of wishing that more "road-way expressions" had found their way into sermons; a seventeenth-century discourse would undoubtedly seem to any modern congregation of Protestants much too highly seasoned with "tropical and figurative elocutions." Puritan hostility to the metaphysical style never became, among what we have called "orthodox" Puritans at any rate, hostility to stylistic cultivation or to the constant use of figures and tropes. In their most pious moods the divines might call eloquence a carnal deceit, but they were sufficiently of their times to believe that the faithful preaching which was to enfold the grace of God should be constructed with all possible "humane helps." They approved of sugaring bitter pills in order to facilitate the cure of souls;[5] their cry for a plain style and a simple manner was simply their protest against allowing the pill to become entirely sugar, against what they believed was the sophisticated practice of the great Anglican preachers, of covering doctrines with so heavy a coating of verbal confectionery that the bitter meanings were converted into a delightful seasoning for rhetorical gourmets. Sinful men were to be guided by logical demonstration to perceive the truth, but the way had first to be made smooth and passable by being paved with rhetoric. God having made man as he is, and having upon the completion of revelation ceased to bestow immediate revelations, it was no longer possible for any to be converted except through some means. The sermon was the chief of these means because it had the Bible from which to gather its doctrines, logic with which to prove them, and also rhetoric to make doctrines attractive, reasons convincing, and applications efficacious.

Fully to account for the theory and practice of rhetoric in New England education and in New England writings, we must once more take cognizance of the various secular elements in the intellectual heritage which the theologians were straining more or less successfully to reconcile with their piety and their creed. Had piety alone determined their literary style, as piety alone determined it among Ranters, Fifth-Monarchy men, and the early Quakers, Butler's satire would have been a factual description of New England preaching as well as of the tirades of English sectaries; but the orthodox divines formulated their doctrine of the sermon not merely from considerations of religion, but from the scholastic doctrine of cause and the consequent conception of means, from the Peripatetic psychology, and from their training in the medieval disciplines of grammar and rhetoric. Furthermore, if the weight of these inheritances was not sufficient to insure among Puritans a respect and even a great veneration for rhetoric, humanism of the sixteenth century had invested the art with a new splendor and a fresh dignity; finally, for those Puritans who had come under the influence of the *Dialecticae,* there was a still more urgent inducement not merely to high esteem for the art, but to explicit definition of its function, for Ramus and his *alter ego,* Omer Talon, had wrought as important a revolution in rhetoric as in logic, and Ramists could not give allegiance to the one without fully embracing the other. Hence William Perkins, while demanding sincerity and conviction in the preacher and castigating over-ornamentation and elaboration, nevertheless, when comparing preaching to a lady "highly mounted," required "all other gifts, both of tongues and arts," to attend her as handmaids. In New England, throughout the century, the authorities may have called upon the ministers to be "Experimentally acquainted with the power of their Doctrine upon their *own Hearts,*" but also they expected them to be "*skilful* about the Work," to possess "a sharp Insight into all the Sciences, which may accomplish them to *Divide the Word aright,* and cast a Lustre on the Scriptures of God."

With the rediscovery of classical literature humanism had come to a discovery of the majesty, the beauty, and the power of the word, in and for itself, which committed humanists to a love for rhetoric beyond even the intensity of devotion that had characterized medieval rhetoricians, to a sheer joy in words and word patterns of which euphuism and the verbal excesses of Renaissance drama were among the more extravagant expressions.[6] Just as the engrafting of the new learning upon the old trivium and quadrivium had revivified the art of logic, so it produced an almost greater flowering of systematic rhetoric. Medieval educators had defined the art, theologians had identified it with the wisdom of God, and physicists had showed it to be a means of grace, but humanists, inspired by the classical conception, endowed it with the added power of civilizing mankind and sustaining the social order. Characteristic of sixteenth-century paeans is that of Thomas Wilson in *The Arte of Rhetorique:* it was not enough that after the fall God should have repaired the ravages of sin by giving men the art of logic; at a time when "none did any thing by reason, but most did what they could by manhood," it was necessary that those who had discovered the rule of reason be also enabled "to perswade with reason all men to societie" or else their dialectic would have been in vain, and therefore God bestowed rhetoric upon them, "that they might with ease win folke at their will, and frame them by reason to all good order." Led by this means, delighted with the sweetness of imagery and the pleasantness of oratory, "after a certaine space they became through Nurture and good aduisement, of wilde, sober: of cruell, gentle: of fooles, wise: and of beastes, men: such force hath the tongue, and such is the power of Eloquence and reason, that most men are forced, euen to yeeld in that which most standeth against their will." Mere logic itself, which "plainly and nakedly" sets forth "the some of thinges, by waie of argumentacion," would not persuade the multitude into the paths of order unless it were embellished and made attractive by rhetoric, which "useth gaie painted sentences, & setteth forth those matters with freshe colours and goodly ornaments, and that at large."

> Logique by art, settes furthe the truthe,
> And doth tell what is vain.
> Rhetorique at large paints well the cause
> And makes that seeme right gaie,
> Which Logique spake but at a worde,
> And taught as by the waie.

Wherever we turn in Renaissance writings, we find similar conceptions of rhetoric as the divine instrument of civilization, the means of order and the social bond. The psychologists, for example, find their doctrines reinforcing this conclusion; the Spaniard Huarte declared that man by nature is a being capable of civility, and that his potentialities will be realized when he is taught first by logic to frame his reasons and then by rhetoric to perfect them, for the latter, by its precepts and rules, "might beautifie the speech with polished words, with fine phrases, and with stirring affections and gratious colours." [7] Speech was ordained by God, said Reynolds, "to maintaine mutuall Society amongst men incorporated into one Body," it is "the Ligament and Sinew, whereby the Body of Humane Conversation is compacted and knit into One." That the humanist estimate of rhetoric was an element in the New England opinion is proved by many utterances, not least by Cotton Mather's rhymed praise of the New England rhetoricians:

> 'Tis Corlet's pains, & Cheever's, we must own,
> That thou, *New-England,* art not *Scythia* grown.

In this humanist background, taken by itself and apart from concomitant religious influences—though in fact the two can hardly be separated—there are factors which help to account for some apparent inconsistencies in the Puritan attitude toward eloquence. Puritans were bound to discuss it, not only in the light of Aristotelian psychology, but also in that of Aristotle's

Rhetoric, for humanism had brought rhetoricians to a renewed devotion to this work as being the only begetter of their art. Since Aristotle had written of rhetoric as an instrument for the government of city-states, as the means of ruling democracies gathered in the agora, he had emphasized its social and political purpose. The second book of his *Rhetoric* authorized Renaissance writers to view the art as primarily concerned with the spoken word and as chiefly directed against the passions of men, as designed to lead the many to right decisions through a public address which made the good appear not merely good, but emotionally alluring and sensuously attractive. New England theorists like young Wigglesworth spoke as humanists as well as evangelists when they declared that oratory should be a bait for the will and passions. The obvious danger was that if rhetoric were conceived solely as "affectionum domina" and were reduced to a formula, to a set of devices for moving emotions which could be learned from any teachers by the unregenerate and the unscrupulous, it might become a means of serious mischief rather than of good. It could be pressed to make the wrong appear the better reason or to dress heresies in a more attractive garb than any in which truth could legitimately be clothed. As long as Aristotle's definition was generally received, that rhetoric is "the faculty of observing in any given case the available means of persuasion," the art was liable to be misused, particularly because his own lucid direction for working upon the feelings of a mob, delivered with scientific objectivity, might as easily play into the hands of demagogues and sophists as into the designs of statesmen and divines. Thus the Puritans, speaking as humanists, would be bound to exemplify in their theory of rhetoric a great love for it along with a nervous apprehension lest it be abused or over-worked. As long as it was kept subservient to orthodoxy and remained a natural means of grace, it was admirable, but whenever it became an end in itself, whenever it was laid on too lavishly, whenever there was elegance for the sake of elegance alone, whenever through too frequent an excitation of passion it tended to undermine the empire of reason, then it became "carnal eloquence." Rhetoric was to be used as though it were the juice of a poisonous herb, beneficent in small doses and at the right times, but deadly if taken in large draughts. If further exposition of its potentialities both for good and evil were needed, psychology afforded them: a speech is seasoned with rhetoric, said Richardson, in order that it may please the heart; hence, when too highly seasoned, it "passeth by the understanding, and so the Will takes hold of it, and whilest the Will doth hastily embrace it, the reason cannot examine it." A speech should come to an auditor like every other sensation, first to the outward senses, "then to the inward senses, and hence to the understanding, & so to the affections, and last of all to the Will," but a speech made too ravishing, even though in a good cause, will barely reach the understanding before "the affections lay hold of it, and so, tickle the Will that it may approve it: and hence it [comes] to be abused." Thus the Puritans, being disciples of Aristotle in psychology and in rhetoric, were committed like all humanists to using rhetoric as a bait for the emotions, but they too had to be on their guard lest rhetoric become an instrument of seduction rather than a means of grace, lest it betray even the truth by bringing men to it through a sinful violation of the order of nature. For a minister to lure men to an emotional reception of the creed before their imaginations had conceived it, before their intellects were convinced of it and their wills had deliberately chosen to live by it, was fully as immoral as openly to persuade them to wrongdoing.

Of course, Aristotle himself was no sophist; he called rhetoric "an offshoot of dialectic and also of ethical studies," and dedicated it solely to embellishing and popularizing that which was demonstrably right. The great orators and rhetoricians of antiquity continually affirmed their devotion to morality, as did the humanists, so that Puritans were merely echoing Quintillian, Erasmus, Sturm, or Ascham in demanding that rhetoric subserve truth and be applied to the ornamentation of that alone which theology, logic, and ethics found good and just. In the systematic scheme of the arts which New England Puritans achieved in technologia, the sphere of rhetoric was definitely prescribed, and when so constrained it was not merely innocent and useful, but like all other arts a divinely authorized body of principle, a segment of God's created wisdom, a portion of the eternal and immutable archetypal idea. It, too, had its utility, its "eupraxia", yet it was not thought of primarily as a contrivance of men for accomplishing certain ends, but as a God-given doctrine which, if humbly received and studiously mastered, would lead men inevitably through its praxis to the prattomena of a good oration and the one proper form of the sermon. Rhetoric had not been devised by Corax of Syracuse, Isocrates, or Aristotle because they had perceived a use for it, but God, having created a world wherein the existence of means was an ontological necessity, had formulated the art and revealed it to these philosophers, who thereupon fulfilled His will by putting it to its predestined work. Once more Richardson is most helpful in clarifying for us the basic concepts of Puritan theory: rhetoric, he says, is an art because like all arts "it consisteth of Precepts fitted to Eupraxy." Psychology, theology, and dialectic all contribute to elucidating its station in the circle of the arts: after the fall, man is no longer capable of seeing all things directly by his own eye, and in order that he may not be fatally imprisoned in time and space, "God hath provided Speech, to be an *Hobson,* or Carrier, between man and man; that thereby he might see all things." By the gift of logic various men can perceive various arguments, but their knowledge becomes available to all through their ability to tell it: "Logick doth act and bring the thing to my understanding & afterwards Speech is the carrier of it; therfore, it is necessary that there should be a constant rule of speech, that one man might understand another." But spoken words, describing what one has not seen or heard for himself, are to the listener "inartificial arguments", and both logic and psychology demonstrate that phantasms received at second hand are taken in with much more difficulty than artificial ones arising from a physical presence of the thing itself; therefore, "because things that are reported are not so easily received, as those which are seen by our eye of Logick," God created and revealed the two arts of grammar and rhetoric, the first to give the bare rules of speech so that one man may comprehend another, and the second the methods of "sweetning" a speech in order to expedite the understanding.

So that the Lord doth here, even as Physitians use to do with their Patients, to wit, when they have a bitter Potion to give, they use to sugar the top of the Pot wherein it is. So that Grammar may be compared to a plain Garment without welt or gard, or it is like a grave Citizen. Rhetorick may be compared to the lace, or jags on the garment, and is like a fine Courtier.[8]

The Lord shows Himself especially merciful in His gratuitous gift of rhetoric, for He might well have stopped His bounty with simple grammar; it is, however, by rhetoric rather than by grammar that we profit from the experience of the race, maintain the continuity of tradition and of knowledge, transcend the limitations of our finite selves: it not only makes communication possible because it is the "carrier from one man to another, [of] that which one man sees with his eye of Logick," but by giving the arguments "a fine suggering of them with Rhetorick, for the more easie receiving of them," it makes the interchange delectable and sure. In Puritan thinking the theory of means, posited upon Peripatetic psychology, required that in God's dispensation He vouchsafe men not the Bible alone but also the arts of logic, grammar, and rhetoric. Without these the Bible would remain sealed, but with logic the meaning of Scripture may be extracted, with grammar it may be phrased so that men may grasp it, and with rhetoric its doctrines may be insinuated into their brains and hearts. If by logic the ministers deciphered the will of God, by rhetoric they communicated their knowledge; if by logic men were rescued from the chaos of depravity, by rhetoric they were made capable of society, of an ecclesiastical as well as of a political order. Just as the Puritans, starting from the Christian doctrine of the fall, came to venerate logic as an instrument of their recovery, so they reached an equally profound respect for rhetoric as the divinely given science for making sermons powerful means of regeneration. Sermons could operate as means because their rhetoric worked upon the rational and particularly upon the sensible souls of men. Rhetoric could not be a mere collection of empirical rules for prose composition, accumulated from the experience of previous writers and speakers; it was a codification of God's eternal wisdom in a form adapted to the deepest necessities of human nature.

If there were need for further proof of the divine authorization, it existed in the Bible itself. God had uttered His revelation not alone within the constant rules of grammar but according to the forms of rhetoric, and the art was completely embodied in the tropes and figures of the Bible. Were men to lose it, they could reconstruct it from Biblical examples. Consequently, it could not be merely a human manner of speaking; no man could understand Scripture who had not been schooled in rhetoric as well as in logic. Puritan divines would often assert that the Scriptures are so plain that none can fail to grasp the syntactical and logical significances, and that we stand in need, not of a knowledge of rhetoric and dialectic, but of "the illumination of the Spirit, to help us to understand them aright"; yet in their exegeses, in their disputes and in their handbooks, they would demand that the righteous consult phraseologies, dictionaries, grammars, and rhetorics before settling upon any construction. Charles Chauncy asked Dell where he could find "such high straines of all sorts of *Rhetoricall Tropes, & figures* . . . in any Author, as there are in the writings of the *Prophets* & *Apostles*," and he defended the study of rhetoric in clerical education by inquiring how "the unlearned minister, or him that understands not rhetorick" can ever make "any tolerable sense" of such phrases as "I am the true Vine" or "Behold the Lamb of God." The divines who drew up in 1690 a New England version of *The Principles of the Protestant Religion* against the incorrigible George Keith found one of his readings hopelessly wrong because he confounded "a *Metonym. Efficientis* with a *Metonym. Signi*," and sermon after sermon resolved a text both into dialectical arguments and into rhetorical figures, arriving at the doctrine by translating into prose some Biblical "Metonimical Expression," some "Synecdoche," "an *Ellyptick* kind of expression, and very frequent in Scripture Dialect," a simile, or a hyperbole.[9] Textbooks and Puritan discourses on pastoral care repeated again and again that since Scripture is eloquent, ministers must study eloquence, first in order to expound divinity by it, and second to use it as a sanctified help in their own orations; Richard Bernard says, for instance, "Euerie where a Diuine shall meet with figuratiue speeches in holy Scripture, which without Rhetoricke hee cannot explaine," and furthermore, by observing how Scripture handles the figures, he may learn many lessons "and apply them for strengthening of faith, and for Christian consolation many times," and thus "hee may learne to speake well and perswasiuely." Rhetoricians themselves justified their subject on the same grounds, and the Puritan theory is perhaps nowhere made more explicit than in such a work as John Smith's *The Mysterie of Rhetorick Unveil'd,* first published in 1657: because, says Smith, Scripture abounds with tropes and figures, "and is like a pleasant

Garden bedecked with flowers, or a fruitful field, full of precious treasures," he who would discover what is hidden there must needs know the rules of metaphors, metonymies, and synecdoches. A bare reading of Scripture, without a searching out of its mysteries, is like gazing upon a "Treasury" when all its costly hoard is folded up, only "some ends appearing out." "Besides, the ignorance of Rhetorique is one ground (yea, and a great one) of many dangerous Errors this day," for the unlearned, taking figurative expressions literally, are betrayed into fantastic errors, and though the spirit of the Lord is indeed requisite for opening the mysteries of heaven, and though the learned whose hearts are blind cannot read them aright,

> yet, all Science, and particularly, Rhetorique, where it is reduced to a blessed subordination and conformity to the teachings of the Spirit of Truth, is a good gift of God, proceeding from the Father of lights, and very conducent to the unfolding and right understanding of the Figurative and Tropical Elegancies of the blessed Book, which abounds with most excellent and divinest eloquence.

Thus rhetoric takes its place with grammar and logic as one of the three primary arts, through which the Bible is resolved into its arguments and the body of divinity methodically established. All the arts indeed contribute to Biblical exposition, since the Word of God touches upon all aspects of human existence, but these three were the foundation of the Puritan intellectual life, as they had been the foundation of the medieval. Of all writers who determined the shape of New England thought, William Perkins was most rigorous in protecting the integrity of Scripture and most jealous of its being overlaid with artificial constructions, but his final word of advice summarized the philosophy of Puritan culture:

> First, diligently imprint both in thy minde and memorie the substance of Divinitie described, with definitions, divisions, and explications of the properties. Secondly, proceed to the reading of the Scriptures in this order, using a grammaticall, rhetoricall, and logicall Analysis, and the helpe of the rest of the Arts.

Matthew Swallow sang the praises of his pastor, John Cotton, for excelling "in the knowledge of the Arts and Tounges, and in all kinde of learning divine and humane, which made him as a Scribe, instructed unto the Kingdome of Heaven," and capped the list of Cotton's virtues with the highest attribute a Puritan parishioner could find in his parson: "Neither did he feed his people with the empty huskes of vaine discourses, but he kept the *true Patterne of wholesome words,* all his Sermons being either Meate to feede, or Medicine to heale his hearers." In order that the literate youths who were to succeed the first ministers might still merit such encomiums, the founders of Harvard College took care that they be taught the art of rhetoric, and according to this academic pattern of wholesome words the successors attempted to frame discourses that would serve, as occasion demanded, either as meat or as medicine.

Such generalities as we have so far been reviewing upon the nature and function of rhetoric were the common property of learned men in the period, and all schools and academies would substantially have agreed upon them. The reasons for such unanimity are various, but among them was the fact that though rhetoricians had added to Aristotle in order to capture rhetoric for the service of Christianity, and though they appropriated many important principles from other and later authorities, still the fundamentals of their theory came ultimately from the Stagirite. Their conception of the art as a means of persuasion and particularly of moving human affections, their perception that it gains its effects through verbal figures and formalized refinements upon ordinary speech, their assumption that the spoken word was the first subject of rhetorical embellishment, probably owe most of their currency to his authority. But when the modern student turns from the writings of the sixteenth and seventeenth centuries to a perusal of this *Rhetoric,* he finds at once that to understand many Renaissance practices he must consider more influences than can be fathered upon Aristotle, that the art of rhetoric had by this time become an altogether different matter from the comparatively simple precepts which were deemed sufficient for effective speaking in the assemblies and courts of a Greek city-state. When the historian of New England descends from the abstract theories to the specific principles and methods taught at Harvard or followed in the sermons, he soon realizes that Aristotle and all classical rhetoricians pertain at best to only a very distant background, and that the direct and decisive influence was exerted by no less a person than the preceptor of New England logic, Petrus Ramus. The history of rhetorical theory in the Renaissance is still so unexplored a field that generalizations about it are not to be advanced with any pretense of assurance, but it does seem relatively clear that, although by the end of the sixteenth century it was agreed on all sides that rhetoric was derived from God, that Aristotle and Quintillian, like the great prophets of Judea, had been essentially "scribes", merely setting down a revelation from on high, nevertheless the revelation had not proved sufficiently explicit in all its details to furnish a single and incontestable body of precepts. Students in the early seventeenth century were taught that rhetoric was a portion of eternal truth, but were forced to choose among several contending versions of it, and in particular did they have to align themselves either with the party of the so-called Aristotelians or with the faction of the Ramists. The situation, in other words, was precisely similar to that in logic, and the lines of division were drawn on the same grounds. Hence the Puritans in New England made their choice, and though with all the learned of their age they asserted the divine origins of rhetoric and expounded its uses in relation to the faculties with which the creator had endowed the soul, though in technologia they made rhetoric a part of God's universal and unvarying wisdom, and found it illustrated in His own manner of speaking, nevertheless in practice they were partisans of a particular and highly controversial opinion; though theoretically they beheld in rhetoric an ectypal reflection of archetypal doctrine, in concrete instances they appropriated the doctrines promulgated in Paris by Ramus and Talon. The fact that they were disciples of Ramus did not mean that they were less indebted to Aristotle for their general ideas, for here as in dialectic Ramus contended that he had rescued the true meaning of "the Philosopher" from the misconstructions of his followers. Naturally, Aristotelians did not agree with Ramus' reading of the *Rhetoric* any more than with his interpretation of the *Organon,* but setting aside the question of which party exhibited the greater fidelity, we can, fortunately, come to a fairly precise description of the difference between them. To discuss the background of Renaissance rhetoric as though this issue were the only one of importance, or as though all rhetorical thinking were confined to one or the other of these positions, is indeed over-simplification, yet since it seems to be true that the founders of New England thought, Perkins, Richardson, and Ames in particular, belonged to the Ramist connection in their rhetorical allegiance as well as in their dialectical, and that the dominant system in the New England colonies, even though the other was always available to students and ministers, was definitely the Ramist, and since all Ramist rhetoricians were largely concerned with vindicating their teachings against those maintained by the conventional Peripatetics, it follows that the significance of New England usages cannot be fully appreciated until the issue between these two opinions has been at least elucidated.

Exactly as in the analogous battle of the dialectics, to which in fact the rhetorical controversy was an adjunct, the conflict is epitomized by a contrast between competing textbooks. To represent the Aristotelians we might choose from among English writers Thomas Wilson's *The Arte of Rhetorique,* or Thomas Farnaby's *Index Rhetoricus et Oratorius,* first published in 1633 and continually in print at least until its fifteenth edition in 1767,[10] or else, from works available to Harvard students, the rhetorical sections in Keckermann's *Opera,*[11] or in Alsted's *Encyclopaedia,* along with his *Orator* and *Rhetorica,* his treatment of the subject having more in common with the Aristotelians even though influenced by Ramus; yet for comparison with Ramist teachings probably the most helpful work of the period is Vossius' *Rhetorices Contractae, sive Partitionum Oratorarum,* issued in Holland in 1621 and frequently republished, one edition being printed at Oxford in 1651.[12] Vossius was generally recognized as the preëminent spokesman for Aristotle, and by his partisans called the greatest of modern rhetoricians; the Estates of Holland, identifying Ramist doctrines with

Arminian heresies, ordered his rhetoric to be taught in all schools of the country. Actually his work is a composite of Aristotle, Cicero, Quintillian, and Hermogenes, but it represents what at the time was called Aristotelianism.[13] Handbooks of this complexion do not all agree on every feature or upon the plan of organization, yet they are sufficiently similar to present a united opinion, and the most conspicuous of their contentions is that the whole art of rhetoric is to be divided into five subheads, usually denominated invention, disposition, memory, elocution, and pronunciation. "Invention" covers the rules for finding appropriate matter, "excogitatio argumentorum, qua ad persuadendum idonea sunt"; and because rhetoric was ultimately addressed to the emotions—"Truly," said Vossius, "men are led not by reason alone but even by affection, indeed the great part of them almost entirely by it"—the chapters under this head often contain a long inventory of the passions, of confidence, wrath, hope, admiration, etc., and hints upon how to influence them. "Disposition" treats the form of the oration, and generally sets forth what had long since become the standard six component parts of a speech: exordium, narration, proposition, confirmation, confutation, and epilogue or peroration. Chapters on "Memory" give regulations for memorizing speeches or adapting them to the memories of auditors; those on "Elocution" contain the figures of speech, the tropes and schemes with which the oration should be embellished, and the final ones of "Pronunciation" provide instructions on the management of voice and gesture. The emphasis in all these works is almost entirely forensic; rhetoric is a science of speaking, only thereafter and consequently a science of writing. Its office is frankly to persuade—"Finis Oratoris ultimus est persuadere," says Vossius—and to this end the five branches contribute each its share: "item cum officium vocant invenire quid dicas, inventa disponere, deinde ornare verbis, post memoriae mandare, tum ad postremum agere ac pronunciare." The subject-matter of the art was declared to be always some question, hypothesis, or thesis, of which there is need that some audience be convinced. Following Aristotle's classification, the authors distinguished three general types of orations, each defined from the character of its audience, the demonstrative, the deliberative, and the judicial, though it was clear that in modern life there were many sorts of speeches that could hardly be described by these rubrics. Even so, Aristotelians clung to the classification and in their section of "disposition" so expounded the rules of the six parts that orations of all three types could be constructed at will from the one set of regulations. Elocution was conceived as a help to securing emotional effects, as an alluring raiment in which the bare arguments were clad. An eloquent man, even though but little learned, can "by shift of wordes, and meete placing of matter" more prevail upon men "then a great learned clarke shalbe able with great store of learning, wanting words to set forth his meaning." It is both "comelinesse and honestie" to adorn our bodies with handsome apparel, and so elocution is admirable because it teaches us to set forth the matter "by apt wordes and sentences together, and beautifieth the tongue with great chaunge of colours, and varietie of figures." The section on eloquence generally came down, after a few such philosophical generalities, to a recital of the tropes, the schemes, and the "colours of rhetoricke," the ways in which sentences could be spoken, such as praecisio, significatio, extenuatio, digressio, progressio, regressio, iteratio, dubitatio, and the countless other devices that grace the speech of euphuists and university wits, of Holofernes the pedant and Don Adriano de Armado—and of metaphysical divines.

To the modern eye, the first impression conveyed by these works, as by the Aristotelian logics, is their complexity and their staggering array of jargon. The divisions and subdivisions are infinite, the terminology is interminable, and the whole a riot of "the odiferous flowers of fancy, the jerks of invention." One wonders how pupils could ever learn from such texts to speak at all, much less with ease, or how their education ever came to more than having "been at a great feast of languages, and stolen the scraps." How could they, we wonder, ever achieve an "invective oration," when first they had to distinguish and memorize the many kinds: "invectiva, objurgatio, expostulatio, exprobatio, et deprecatio," and take care not to mingle one kind with another? Our query might of course be attributed merely to our modern prejudice against all formal rhetoric, but there is evidence that by the sixteenth century the rhetoric of the schools had become so intricate an affair that it could not only inspire the satire of *Love's Labour's Lost,* but also convince many scholars that reform was imperative. Ramus rallied this discontent to his side when he arraigned the teaching precisely for its useless and luxuriant elaboration. The two arts were so connected that he could not carry out his renovation of logic without also taking the occasion to simplify and clarify rhetoric, and to redeem it for "use". This part of his work was performed under his direction by his friend and colleague, Omer Talon, who in 1567 issued his *Rhetorica,* with a preface by Ramus, which work among Ramists thereafter was always an indispensable counterpart to the *Dialecticae,* in later editions the two being frequently bound together, and all subsequent treatments in the Ramist vein are simply repetitions of it, as also are the rhetorical theses printed upon Harvard commencement broadsides.[14]

Ramus reformed the art of rhetoric[15] by the simple act of amputating the sections on invention, disposition, and memory. Thus he threw the venerable six parts of the oration into the waste-basket, abolished all definitions of types, relegated discussion of the passions to physics and ethics, and left as the legitimate field of rhetoric merely the departments of elocution and pronunciation. Talon's *Rhetorica* accordingly is a systematic treatment of only these two heads, with even them reduced to schematic simplicity through the method of dichotomy. The work of the other three parts was adequately covered, Ramus asserted, in dialectic; to repeat in rhetoric the precepts of invention and disposition, and to draw up separate rules for memory when the only way to help the memory was to practice proper method, was not only tautological but confusing, not only unnecessary but a positive obstacle to both clear thinking and right speaking.

This is the true distinction between Dialectic and Rhetoric: For even if the oration be most illustrious or most ample, subtlety of invention in thinking the arguments, of truth in enunciation, of consequence in syllogism, and of order in method, is entirely, I say, a matter of dialectic and logic. But ornament and elocution in trope and figure, and pronunciation in voice and gesture is entirely a matter of rhetoric and completely pertaining to it, even if the disputation itself be mostly philosophical.

All questions of the form, structure, or disposition of the parts of a speech or a treatise were fully handled in dialectic, and the orator or writer who invented his arguments, formed his axioms, resolved his doubts through syllogisms, and arranged his material according to the laws of method, had, *ipso facto,* done everything that Aristotelians tried in vain to teach in the first three muddled and superfluous sections of their rhetorics.

What precepts soeuer the common Rhetoricians put downe for ordering of Exordiums and framing and disposing of the whole course of their speeche fitly and according to cause, auditors, time, place, and such like circumstances; all those I say, are altogether Logicall, not in any respect perteining to Rhetoricke, but as a Rhetor may bee directed by Logicall precepts of iudgement and disposition.

Artificial definitions of the parts, narrow concepts of types were futile, because every accomplished speaker will and must invent the kind of arguments he needs for his particular purpose and order them to suit his occasion. Instead of learning more rules for memorization than he can ever remember, instead of being drilled to exhaustion in distinctions between exordium and narration or confirmation and confutation, said the Ramists, let the student be taught the three laws of truth, justice, and wisdom, and the structure of his orations will be achieved. Instead of bewildering him with the multifarious abstract differences between a demonstration and a deliberation, let him study concretely the great orations of Cicero and Demosthenes by the method of analysis and imitate them practically by the method of genesis, and all questions of form will take care of themselves. Instead of forcing him to relearn in altered guise the list of affections he has already studied in physics and ethics, let him carry his previous knowledge with him and concentrate on finding out what figures of eloquence, what intonations of the voice, or what gestures, will best serve whatever purpose he has in mind, and he will be able to stir his listeners as in no other way. Ramus' reform, in essence, amounted to abolishing the separate existence of any art of oratory, because he assumed that the precepts which led to a good address could not possibly be others than those of logic, that arguments invented by dialectical laws and arrayed by the principles of method would wholly and efficiently furnish the materials and pattern of any discourse, in the fashion best suited to memorization. Affections would be moved most cogently if presented with that which is in itself true and has been proved dialectically to be as the thing is, with no other enhancement than pleasing figures of speech and appropriate gestures.

Aristotelians were ready to admit, even to demand, a dependence of rhetoric upon logic; we have already seen Wilson setting forth the theoretical relation, and he became still more explicit when he discussed the "places" of invention, for he approved taking them over from logic wherever possible. Indeed, like all rhetoricians, he required a student to have learned his logic before being permitted to take up rhetoric:

For what is he, that can cal a thing honest, and by reason proue it, except he first know what the thing is: the which he cannot better doe, then by defining the nature of the thing. Againe, how shall I know, whether mine attempt be easie or hard if I knowe not the efficient cause, or be assured how it may be done. In affirming it to bee possible, I shall not better knowe it then by searching the ende, and learning by *Logicke,* what is the finall cause of euery thing.

However, the Aristotelians felt that though many "places", such as definition, the four causes, disjunction, artificial, or inartificial, might be common to both arts, they were altogether one thing in logic and quite another in rhetoric. In rhetoric, said Vossius, "are the seats and notes of the arguments, by which is invented, whatever in any thing serves aptly for persuading." Naturally "some of them are common to rhetoric with dialectic, but others truly peculiar to rhetoric." Hence the interdependence of the arts, their sharing of terms and concepts, did not mean that their respective doctrines of invention and disposition were identical bodies of rules and precepts. Vossius argued ferociously against Ramist heresies with the aid of all the historic distinctions of scholasticism, insisting that invention and disposition could not be the same in the two arts because each has different ends, different matters, and different forms; invention in dialectic is of general truths or probabilities, but in rhetoric of "persuabilia"; arguments in logic are to prove points for the learned only, but arguments in rhetoric are to convince the vulgar. Though both arts employ the same places,

by Logic they are considered absolutely, and as far as they are useful for instructing the mind; by rhetoric they are restricted to consideration of popular notes and to the motion of the will and affections. Although Rhetoricians learn those places accurately in the Topics of Logic, yet, since no one ought to be admitted to rhetoric unless he is imbued with logic, they omit this doctrine . . . content in these places to consider in what way the arguments derived from it may be applied to moving the will.[16]

Hence the invention of arguments, even of those taken from logic, has to be taught anew in rhetoric, since here the aim is entirely incitation and not at all verification; so also must disposition be separately inculcated: logic instructs the student how rightly to dispose arguments with middle terms, how to handle single and connective questions, and how to arrange consequences after premises, but disposition in rhetoric is the rule for ordering the arguments so that they will appear most hortatory, and to secure this effect, according to the Aristotelians, the student must dispose them far otherwise than when demonstrating their truthfulness. By the same manner of reasoning, they argued, it was necessary in rhetoric to review the theory of the passions: physics considers them as the affections of a sensitive soul and expounds their natural causes; ethics treats of how they may be controlled and made virtuous; but rhetoric is concerned with them "in so far as they conduce to persuasion, and explains how they may be aroused or calmed." Once more it seemed to conservative schoolmen that Ramus, the "usuarius", was mutilating the perfection of the arts in order to manufacture a short-cut to getting results, and that not only was he irreverent of authority, but that he was bound to defeat his own intention because he so pared down the content of rhetoric as to render it incapable of meeting its obligations.

Ramists countered these charges by the same arguments with which they defended the *Dialecticae,* for since Ramus so correlated the one art with the other that neither could stand alone, they were both rationalized together. Being Renaissance scholars, they spent a great part of their energies in what is to us the pointless endeavor to prove their case through an appeal to authority, and they split countless hairs over the pages of Aristotle or Quintillian to show that Ramus alone had correctly interpreted them. Their debates take on more signification for our study when they go back to the fundamental theory of rhetoric as a divine art, and seek to prove that Talon's *Rhetorica* was the inevitable deduction to be made therefrom. We are granted a livelier insight into the meaning of the reform when Scribonius, for example, explains that God created man so that first he should reason and then speak, that after the fall God gave him first the gift of inventing arguments and placing them in method, then the gift of embellishing them so that they would be convincing, and that therefore it was the intention of God they should first be hammered out by logic and then embossed by rhetoric. Hence it would seem to be nothing less than the will of God that the two arts should be constituted and related as Ramus formed them, logic giving the invention, disposition, and memory, and rhetoric being subjoined for the sole purpose of showing how logical theorems should be adorned and orally delivered. When the two arts were taken in the Ramist sense, then, and only then, it became clear why "not only have all the best and most celebrated philosophers rightly judged that eloquence should be joined to philosophy, just as when nature is teacher it delivers the same conclusion, but even God Himself signified it and united them in a series." Thus when Ramus made rhetoric the art which comes after logic, and confined it merely to bedecking arguments with tropes and figures as an aid to their reception among the many, when he showed that the content of any oration was entirely a matter of reason and method while the style was simply a matter of garlands and festoons, then he had conformed the two arts for the first time to God's simple plan, and Ramist rhetoricians could praise their master and Omer Talon for having bequeathed a priceless legacy to posterity.

Prefaces to Ramist rhetorics resound with these assertions, but still further study of their proclamations reveals that the immense popularity of Talon must also be ascribed to the neatness, compactness, and usability of his text. Holding that the art consisted of but two subjects, and that the method for organizing the material of any art was dichotomy, he subdivided elocution into tropes and figures or "schemata", and pronunciation into the rules for voice and for gesture. The content of these four divisions was hardly any different from that surveyed in the last two books of all Aristotelian rhetorics, but the arrangement was much more systematic. Tropes were special uses of individual words through which they acquire "a signification different from that which first and naturally they had"; schemes were arrangements of whole sentences "whereby Words or Sentences are so aptly rang'd as to sound pleasingly and move Affections strongly." With rhetoric thus reduced to manageable proportions, with pupils no longer called upon to encompass the inexhaustible parade of the places, the prolix definitions of parts and types, the catalogue of emotions, the professor's task was reduced to teaching a definite list of tropes and schemes, and it is no wonder therefore that teachers of elementary schools in particular should have welcomed the Ramist reform with profound gratitude. Their hymns of praise frequently wax still more fervid than those of logicians, as for instance Charles Butler in his *Rhetoricae Libri Duo,* first published in 1597, when he asserts: "Among celebrated writers upon the arts, it is the judgment of those who, preëminent in erudition and in fairness, are able and willing to judge best," that "if you respect truth in precepts, or brevity in method, or perspicuity in examples, or use and utility in everything," you must give Ramus precedence over all others, and Butler issued his book frankly as "Rhetoricam nostram Rameam," offering it piously "hujus nomine." Ramus himself was not bashful in advertising the advantages of simplicity and utility in his system; as he asserted concerning his logic, so of his rhetoric he declared that it was both more compact and more commodious than any other because it was founded upon "nature", that the formal art was again a mere codification of "puissance naturelle", and that the true way to learn it was not to attend upon professors but practitioners. His preface to Talon, which was the manifesto of his school on the rhetorical front as his preface to the *Dialectique* was on the philosophical, vaunted that the *Rhetorica* contained the whole art, not collected out of rhetoricians, but out of close observation of great eloquence, that whatever Isocrates, Aristotle, Cicero, or Quintillian had taught was here set forth copiously and completely, because each trope and figure, each intonation and gesture, was illustrated as he had illustrated the places of dialectic with actual passages of classical poetry and oratory.[17] Talon's rhetoric was an art which presupposed nature, and was founded upon experience and practice, not upon theories and textbooks. Hence schoolmasters found it not alone concise and handy, but of tremendous assistance to the teaching of Greek and Latin writers, even of the Bible.[18] After the content of an oration or a poem, or a chapter of Scripture, had been resolved by the laws of logic into its arguments and its method, there remained for the teacher of rhetoric no more onerous work than taking up its figures, its tropes and schemes, one by one, and labeling them according to Talon's dichotomized scheme of nomenclature. "For answering the questions of Rhetoricke," said John Brinsley in 1612, "you may, if you please, make them perfect in *Talaeus'* Rhetoricke, which I take to be most used in the best Schooles."[19] Furthermore, by thus simplifying rhetorical instruction, Ramus and Talon did more than advance the teaching of that one subject: with the line severely inscribed between logic and rhetoric, it then became possible to ascertain definite boundaries for the art of grammar, and thereafter to perceive the inevitable and natural, the divinely decreed connections of all three together. To pedagogues it seemed that the supreme lucidity of Ramus' comprehensive illumination of knowledge was his bringing order into the trivium, that he at last had made intelligible and exact the rationale of the three basic arts, whereas for generations schoolmen had confused one with another and seen them all in equivocal lights. Ramus found their solid common basis in nature, and also the reason for their distinction, and he presented them as three complementary and consecutive systematizations of a single inherent capacity, as methodizations of a behavior to which all men were committed by the intention of their creator. In the design of the universe man was appointed to fulfill a certain function which, upon close examination, could be described as thinking and as embellishing what he thought. The arts contained in the trivium were formulated by Ramus with constant reference to this larger cosmological purpose as well as to "utility", and among his followers it seemed that the disciplines took on wider imports the more their outlines were made precise and rigid:

> And for determining the form of this sort of institution, P. Ramus elaborated with much contention of spirit, so that he taught that the three arts, grammar, rhetoric, and dialectic, are general, universal and finally common to all men and things; that men are rational animals, and therefore by nature are dialecticians, that men are preachers in the sermon, in which they express not alone the sense of the mind, but more various affections variously with exclamation, invective, communication, simulation, and therefore are by nature grammarians and rhetoricians.

As long as Aristotelians tried to teach the places in their incoherent predicaments, and then tried to teach them all over again in their rhetorics in a still more jumbled array, their students would perforce remain hopelessly confused and utterly ignorant of the differences between logic and rhetoric, or of their uses. This confusion was peremptorily dispelled the moment men came to the realization, in the words of Richardson, that schoolmen "have taken invention to be a part of Rhetorick, and so judgement, but when they come to explain them, they teach Logick." Thus Ramist educators joyously saw the trivium acquire an intelligible structure: grammar as the primary art of speech, dialectic as the art of the matter, rhetoric as the art of the dress. The limits of each were punctiliously drawn, and yet each complemented the others, grammar supplying the words, logic investing them with meaning, rhetoric giving them beauty. A Ramist writer spoke with the sense of this momentous revolution behind him when he said that by rhetoric he did not mean the so-called rhetoric of the schools, which was an impossible mélange of all the arts,

> but that discipline, separated from invention and disposition, which Audomarus Talaeus, aided by the observations of P. Ramus, has called back from dialectic to elocution and action, explained by genus and species, and established it with examples of orators and poets, which, finally, P. Ramus has illustrated in his writings.

For these reasons among many others, the popularity of Talon's textbook in the late sixteenth and early seventeenth century was tremendous. Naturally it everywhere accompanied the *Dialecticae,* and the academies or schools that adopted the one automatically took up the other; even in regions where Ramus' logic did not penetrate the rhetoric exerted an influence, at least by forcing Aristotelians to bring more order into their sections on invention and disposition and to insist more warily upon a close connection between the argument or proposition as an indicator of truth and as a means of persuasion. In 1611 Draudius listed sixteen editions of Talon, though there were certainly more; in addition, literally hundreds of rhetorics published by Ramist partisans were essentially reprints of Talon, and finally the school known as the Philippo-Ramists, under the leadership of Melanchthon, worked out a rhetoric which, like their logic, incorporated the gist of the Ramist doctrine and yet tried to preserve something of the older Aristotelianism. This compromise can be seen in the rhetorical portions of Alsted,[20] or in Bilstenius' *Rhetorica, ex Philip Melanchthone, Audomaro Talaeo, & Claudio Minoe selecta* of 1591; [21] the usual trick of such writers was to agree with Talon that rhetoric itself should be restricted to elocution and pronunciation, and that the arguments should be furnished by logic, but that a place must be made in the circle of the arts for a distinct art of oratory, in which must be taught the rules of the six divisions and the three types. The pure Ramist doctrine was meantime spread broadcast by many publications on the continent, and in England made available to all by a succession of rhetoricians and schoolmasters. Charles Butler's *Rhetoricae,* first published in 1597 and frequently thereafter, was practically a verbatim reprint of Talon; [22] John Hoskyns' *Directions for Speech and Style* circulated in manuscript, but was widely read; Richardson's *Rhetorical Notes* also were read widely in manuscript before they were published in *The Logicians School-Master;* William Dugard's *Rhetorices Elementa* was professedly based on Butler and claimed to improve Butler, as Butler had improved Talon, but did not substantially differ from either predecessor; [23] Thomas Blount's *The Academie of Eloquence Containing a Compleat English Rhetorique,* first edition 1654, and reaching at least a fifth edition in 1683, put the whole teaching into English and illustrated the tropes and schemes by passages from Sidney's *Arcadia,* as Abraham Fraunce had exemplified the places of logic in *The Lawiers Logike* of 1588; John Smith's *The Mysterie of Rhetorick Unveil'd* borrowed from Hoskyns' manuscript, and illustrated the figures in Latin and English, and then in the language of the Bible; [24] finally the two most important works in England during the century upon elementary education, John Brinsley's *Ludus Literarius,* 1612,[25] and Charles Hoole's *A New Discovery of the old Art of Teaching Schoole,* 1660, both emphatically supported the Ramist rhetoric against the Aristotelian. Hoole suggested once more why schoolmasters should have been so devoted to it: in order "to enter" your students into the art of fine speaking, he says, give them Dugard, Butler, or Talon, "out of either of which books, they may be helped with store of examples, to explain the Definitions, so as they may know any Trope or Figure that they meet with in their own Authors."

Textbooks of both doctrines circulated in New England, and had we no more evidence than surviving copies we should remain in doubt which of them was actually taught, though the presumption would certainly be that Ramist rhetoric was preferred along with the Ramist dialectic. Richardson's complete endorsement of Talon would point to the same conclusion, which, however, receives incontrovertible proof from the commencement theses at Harvard College. These cannot be read intelligently except when viewed as abstracted or actually quoted from Talon. Sufficient to establish this point beyond cavil, in the light of the contemporaneous background, is the frequency with which rhetoric is declared to consist of elocution and pronunciation, added to the fact that all Harvard theses are dutifully restricted to these divisions; since the whole controversy hinged upon this delimitation, the theses were in effect public declarations of allegiance. Those at the commencement of 1642 were not so explicit as were, for example, those of 1687, which contain the proposition, "The principal constituents of rhetoric are elocution and pronunciation," but the first three theses were sufficiently revealing:

1. Rhetoric differs as a species from logic.
2. In elocution, embellishment gives way to perspicacity, copiousness to embellishment.
3. Action takes first place in pronunciation.

The sequence of these assertions was in itself a manifestation of Ramism, and each of them in turn was a proposition comprehensible only as a part of the Ramist system. The first was an avowal of Ramus' distinction between the arts; the second set forth the scale of literary values as conceived by Ramists, with clarity awarded precedence over ornamentation, but ornamentation more prized than a plethora of material; the third reflected the organization of the second half of Talon's *Rhetorica*. Later theses continued to repeat the conventional apothegms of Ramist professors, particularly the restriction to elocution and pronunciation; the relationship was variously phrased: "Internal ornamentation of the sermon is designed for external pronunciation" was one version, or "Elocution is the place of the flowers of rhetoric, pronunciation the expiration of the odors" was a second, while still a third declared, "Elocution proceeds from eloquence of the soul, pronunciation from eloquence of the body." The further subdivision of the first part of rhetoric, of elocution, into trope and figure, and of the second part, pronunciation, into voice and gesture, was conveyed by a thesis of 1708: "Trope and figure respect the framing of an oration, voice and gesture its promulgating"; the function of elocution was signified with "Tropes and figures are the flowers of rhetoric" in 1653, or better in 1670 with "Rhetoric is the udder of eloquence, tropes and figures are the teats," and the work of pronunciation was set forth Ramistically with "Gesture of the body is mute eloquence," or "Pronunciation is the life of eloquence." Ramus' insistence that formal rhetoric be founded upon nature is reflected in a thesis of 1643: "Natural eloquence excels artificial," and as he had declared in his preface that Talon, "our Apelles, wishes to represent to you, as it were, the living image of eloquence," so Harvard Puritans echoed, "Rhetoric is the

Apelles of the mind." Finally, the Harvard theses concurred with Ramus in indicating the source from which the body of any oration should be derived: "Dialecticae perspicuè commendat oratorem."

At the first commencement, in addition to the three propositions quoted above, appeared a significant fourth: "The art of oratory is to conceal the art." No doubt any Harvard student, if called upon to defend this statement, would have quoted Horace, as did all Ramist logicians and rhetoricians. The assertion that "ars est celare artem" was particularly stressed by Ramists in their contentions with Aristotelians, and its appearance on the first Harvard list confirms the College's adherence to the Ramist doctrine. Yet as Ramists interpreted the concept, it did not mean quite what poets and critics have customarily read into Horace. Both in logic and rhetoric Ramus distinguished between what he called the open and the concealed "methods", and gave the greater praise to those orators and poets who did not make their use of logical places and figures, their knowledge of tropes and schemes, too awkwardly conspicuous, but who employed them without distracting from the theme, so that they seemed "natural". He did not mean that the artifice should be craftily hidden in the effect, but that the handling of stereotyped forms should not be pedantic or ostentatious; he meant that the rhetorician should observe what Puritans called "eupraxia". His assumption was always that the duty of the speaker was to make the "natural" logic appear natural; if the spoken word conformed to nature, if it followed "uti res est", it would be true by virtue of that conformity. Although Puritans were moved to embrace Ramus' rhetoric by the same considerations that made it attractive to philosophers and pedagogues, yet probably when we come to this tenet of the system we find at last the deepest motive for Puritan adherence. Ramist rhetoric was still a forensic art, it was still dedicated to implementing the spoken word and to moving affections, as is shown by the fact that half of it consisted of rules for voice and gesture. To match the definition of dialectic as "Ars bene disserendi" Ramus coined for rhetoric the definition "Ars bene dicendi," and Talon wrote that there was no kind of condiment or paint, no sort of adulation or incantation, "by which those rude and unformed auditors (of which all societies consist) may be led more easily to proper sentiments than by the ornaments of rhetoric accommodated thereunto." Puritans were always acutely conscious of rude and unformed auditors, of the constant necessity that the preacher reach the minds and hearts of the vulgar, that he employ ornament not for the sake of ornament, but for the humbling of the mass of sinners. The precepts and practices of Ramist teachers coincided with the requirement imposed upon the Puritans by their social relationships; they could find little that was useful to them in Vossius, but responded heartily to Blount's declaration that the ornaments were necessary because without them an oration would "miss of the great end of Rhetorick, which is to *persuade powerfully,*" or to Smith's definition of rhetoric as the "faculty" by which we discover what "will serve our turn concerning any subiect to win belief in the hearer: hereby likewise the end of the discourse is set forward, to wit, the affecting of the heart with the sense of the matter in hand." Harvard theses for the first decades always define rhetoric as an art of speaking, and not until 1693 does there seem to be any explicit realization that it is both "of speaking and writing ornately," though in 1708 the conventional view, "Rhetoric is the art of speaking ornately," is resumed. Many theses accentuate the appeal to the sensible soul, defining rhetoric as "affectionum domina," "affectuum hortus," "affectuum syren,"[26] and a mock thesis called gesture the personification of persuasion. To this extent, therefore, Ramist doctrine did not alter the traditional emphasis of medieval rhetoric; it was no less a device for oral incitation or for soliciting the passions. And yet, by chaining rhetoric to logic, by taking the questions of order, of selection and organization of the material, all questions of content, in short, away from rhetoric and assigning them to dialectic, the Ramist theory put just such a constraint upon eloquence as was supremely necessary for Puritans to have placed upon it. By the Aristotelian teaching, eloquence could become an end in itself, and the art of speech, instead of subserving God's original design and remaining merely a vehicle for the communication of truth from one man to another, instead of following reverently and faithfully after the discoveries of logic and confining itself to persuading men only of logical propositions, could become a glittering and sophisticated art of deception, concealing the truth with honeyed words or craftily winning men to any ends entertained by the cynical orator. The rhetoric of the schools, the ancient rhetoric of the medieval church, even its Protestant form in the textbooks of Farnaby and Vossius, was still a lawless oratory, inculcating methods for playing upon human susceptibilities without paying sufficient regard to ultimate ends, to ethical purposes and rational determinations. As long as it was intended that the analysis of propositions for their veracity should be restricted to the learned, and that the people should be nurtured upon propositions framed exclusively for their emotional appeal, as long as the "argumenta" of logic were carried over to orations and sermons, not in their logical integrity, but transformed into "persuabilia", what was to hinder rhetoric from casting off all allegiance to the good, the true, or the orthodox, and becoming sheer Machiavellian virtuosity? If rhetoric were a self-contained doctrine of invention and disposition as well as of elocution and pronunciation, did rhetoricians need ever to bother about moral or theological virtues? In that case, would rhetoric not ultimately teach how to gain effects, how to lure audiences, how to become a siren of the affections, and so come to purvey the opinions of men instead of the dicta of God?

Would not, in short, the Aristotelian system by its very nature inevitably pervert the gift of God into a sensual indulgence and a wile of Satan?

To Puritans the Ramist theory seemed to save the art from such a fate. It applied rhetoric to the work merely of adding ornaments or embellishing that which logic had invented and arranged, of uttering logical propositions with appropriate tones and bodily gestures. It preserved the forensic ideal, but prevented it from becoming too forensic. It still concentrated the art upon persuasion, but took away from it all power to determine for itself to what it should persuade. In both the Ramist and Peripatetic curricula a student would not come to rhetoric before studying logic, but in the Ramist course he would learn simply to add pleasing metaphors and harmonious phrases to his arguments, not acquire *de novo* the methods for manufacturing a new species of arguments, a kind that are pleasing before being true. Rhetoric for the Ramist, in other words, was made severely secondary to logic; the body of a discourse was to be first worked out, and only thereafter clothed with style; the logical act was always prerequisite to the rhetorical, and the art of an oration was to be not so much "concealed" as not permitted to obscure the theme. Thus Downame set forth succinctly the gist of the Ramist philosophy:

> Rhetoric alone shines opposite Dialectic, as the moon to the sun. It shines, but as the moon by the light of the sun. For whatever most ample praise is usually ascribed to eloquence, almost all of it pertains to dialectic. Is it judged preferable that these praises be proper to invention, disposition and memory, or to elocution and delivery? But the former are like to Hercules, the latter to merely the Hydra and the skin of eloquence. Now truly, invention, disposition, memory are all dialectic, rhetoric only elocution and delivery. Therefore dialectic itself affords as it were the body of oratory, rhetoric the clothing; that a spear, this a sling-shot brought into battle, that has its seat in the mind, this in the tongue, that therefore informs the reason, this oratory. As much then as the body excells the clothing, a spear a sling, the mind the tongue, reason oratory, so much does dialectic take precedence over rhetoric.

Hence in the Ramist theory, the content was all-important, the style was an afterthought, a minor consideration, a drapery, something extra and discrete, not of the essence. Rhetoric supplied only the final touches, the last graces of speech and delivery which were useful and which were not to be contemned, but which nevertheless were mechanical additions, affixed here and there like spangles or gems. The legitimate "artist" was he who "put lively colours upon common truths" in order to effect "a strong working upon the fancy and our will and affections." Edward Taylor, in his study at Westfield, submitting himself to searching examination on the eve of his monthly approach to the Lord's Supper, gave ingenious poetic expression to the Ramist and Puritan conception of rhetoric:

The Orator from Rhetorick gardens picks
  His Spangled Flowers of Sweet-breathed Eloquence
Wherewith his Oratory brisk he tricks
Whose Spicy Charms Eare jewells do commence.
Shall bits of Brains be candid thus for eares?
My Theme claims Sugar Candid far more cleare.[27]

Style in speaking or in writing meant "the tropical and figurative elocutions," the flowers which were "picked" in the garden of rhetoric, with which a discourse might be studded, which were not inherent parts of the work, but could be stripped off or fastened on at will. "The specific object of rhetoric," say the theses, "is ornamental oratory," or else "the mode of ornamenting the oration." It never was the object of rhetoric, in the Puritan view, to provide the content, the material, or the ideas, for that was the office of logic and theology.

The completeness with which New England Puritans adopted the rhetoric of Ramus very possibly throws as much light upon certain aspects of their characters as upon their academic proclivities. It would undoubtedly be absurd to attribute to all preachers who remained loyal to Peripatetic rhetoric an ability to fuse content and style, subject-matter and expression, as did John Donne or Launcelot Andrewes, but still it must be acknowledged that their kind of sermon was possible only on condition that they retained the older rhetoric. As soon as a minister became indoctrinated with Ramist ideas, he was surely forced by its inescapable tendency to divorce thought from expression, to dissever content from style; he was committed to working out his sermon structure in terms of logic, and only thereafter going over his work to punctuate it with tropes or to cast sentences into schemes. He certainly could not, for instance, any longer pour out his thought in sinuous word patterns that echoed and reëchoed the phraseology of his texts, or that coiled around the fervid imagery of the Bible in reiterative incantations. No Ramist preaching upon the metaphor, "death is the last enemy," could chant a prose poem on the image—"when I lye under the hands of that enemie, that hath reserved himselfe to the last, to my last bed, . . . when everlasting darknesse shall have an inchoation in the present dimnesse of mine eyes, and the everlasting gnashing in the present chattering of my teeth" [28]—but he would resist the seductions of these schemata and ask himself solemnly just what the Holy Ghost had meant in straightforward prose when using this metaphor. Knowing very well that "There is but one sense belongs to one Scripture . . . there is but one literal meaning," and that God Himself had in mind the one literal meaning when He covered over that meaning with a trope, the Ramist preacher first of all retranslates the rhetoric into logic and grammar.

All Rhetorical expressions must be reduced to the Grammatical sense, and accordingly interpreted. Types and figures must be allowed to the Scriptures as well as to other writings, else God had not spoken in our mode, and this way is not to obscure, but illustrate, and also to move the affections, but still we must reduce it to the Intention: Rhetorick is but an Ornament of Speech, and must therefore be brought to the Grammar of it.

If the Bible says, "God hides His face," the Puritan preacher does not paint a vivid portrait of a divinity with averted countenance, but finds what "literal" argument the figure intends to illustrate. "The Expression is *Metaphorical* and allusive, and ascribed to God after the manner of men." In plain prose, the Bible says at this point that God is displeased, and plain prose, "the Grammar of it," is the true meaning of Scripture. The rules of rhetoric should be used like the rules of dialectic for resolving the rhetoric of the Bible into grammar, not for outdoing it with fanciful conceits of our own. Even the Ten Commandments "must be opened by *Synecdoches and Metonymies; Synecdoches* to comprehend all sins of the like kinde, and all the Degrees thereof; and *Metonymies* to comprehend all the Causes and means, and occasions thereof." And so the minister imitates God's manner in the composition of his sermons; he states his meaning first, and if he can find a metaphor at hand which helps embody the meaning for a rude and unformed audience, he adds it as "a moderate seasoning," in order to win the affections of his congregation. But he never forgets that rhetoric is at best an ornament, a luxury, and that though God bestowed it and gave it a sanctified use, still no one should either read poetry in the Bible or speak eloquently in his sermons unless he has first found out "the Grammar of it." A sermon, the Puritan might have said, is not written with words but with arguments and axioms. "The work of rhetoric," says a thesis of 1678, "is to apply the dicta of reason to the fancy," and another asserts, "Rhetoric makes apparent the good." Style in the service of reason and the good, of logic and theology, was the teaching which Puritans found in the rhetoric of Ramus and Talon, and they adopted it as their own because it merged perfectly with their theory of the arts, with their doctrinal opposition to the metaphysical style, with their conception of the means, and above all with their temperamental hostility to any point of view that finds problems of technique as fascinating as problems of sense. The rhetoric, in short, although seemingly an academic and technical affair, exemplifies the spirit of the Puritan aesthetic, its dislike of any rule of beauty cherished apart from the rule of truth, its profound antipathy to every disposition that can see charms in a movement of words without first being able to say precisely what the words mean.

It is obvious that Puritans took over Ramus' system because it was of advantage to their creed; his dialectic seemed a more efficient method than the logic of the schools for interpreting Scripture, and his rhetoric more suited to preaching the unadulterated Word. But it is eminently worth noting that Puritans were herein not following a course of their own setting, but one laid out by scholars rather than by divines, and not primarily determined by piety. Ramus was spokesman for something fully as pervasive in the age as religion, for an intellectual tendency which was perhaps even more profound than any development in theology, and of which the effects were more far-reaching. Ramists and Puritans attacked Peripateticism for its complexity, and no doubt by the sixteenth century the rhetoric had become hopelessly intricate. Yet it should be remembered that medieval rhetoricians had not recapitulated the materials of invention, disposition, and memory, or the theory of the passions, merely in order to make their subject abstruse or difficult. Their rhetoric never claimed exclusive jurisdiction over these principles, but surveyed them precisely because they were common to several arts, because they were inherent in the system of universal knowledge. It ran over the precepts of logic not to contradict them or displace them, but to show how they should be used when persuasion rather than demonstration was intended; it did not deny that for their own proper ends physics and ethics should also freely expound the doctrine of the affections. Peripatetic rhetoric had originally been framed—and even in the degenerate versions of the sixteenth century it retained the impress of its origins—by selecting from the whole hierarchy of principle just those precepts which contributed to persuasive speaking, but it always assumed that the hierarchy was forever one and indestructible. Every art was but a facet of the same gem, every science a beam of light thrown in a particular direction, but each radiating alike from the single center of illumination.

Ramist doctors professed still to believe in the indivisible unity of knowledge, and in theory recognized the same foundations for it in the mind of God. All knowledge was still to them an actualizing of concepts latent in the divine intelligence, all the propositions of art were eternal rules of the creator, combining to summarize the preëxistent platform of His idea. Ramists were merely marking more incisively the boundaries of one discipline from another and putting an end to medieval confusions. Yet the very rigor with which they set off grammar from rhetoric, the very conciseness with which they divided rhetoric from logic, was in effect more than delimitation, it was an actual abstraction of one from another, a departmentalizing of the sciences, a partition of the inheritance. The Ramist reform treated the disciplines as separate particles; it strung them in order like beads upon a string. It was mechanical and divisive. It made the arts not members of an organism but a puzzle of many pieces fitted ingeniously together. The body of knowledge could no longer appear inevitable and final, the exact expression of the divine intention, so complete that it was incapable ever of having been otherwise, of being more or less, no longer the insphered wisdom and the pattern of perfection, but simply a mathematical total of separate integers, all adding up to a sum which represented what man could know, but which might easily have been any number that God chose arbitrarily to make it. The seven arts were still a circle, yet no more an endless circumference of the universe, but seven segments soldered end to end, with the joints of the patching plainly showing. Rhetoric was laid upon logic as one object upon another, as a brick upon the foundation stone. It remained discrete and separable, it could be disengaged and left standing alone, it was an affair of addition and subtraction, not a matter of necessity but of choice. The ultimate meaning of the Ramist teaching, seen in the perspective of history, is highly paradoxical: while Ramists asserted that they were not destroying the oneness of knowledge, but were only defining the inter-relations of the parts, by the very preciseness of their divisions, by doing away with overlappings and repetitions, they shut each discipline into a separate and insulated compartment. All unwittingly they were taking the first steps, although short, toward an eventual anarchy, where every science becomes an end in itself, detached from final references, where specialists in logic no longer have to be theologians, or psychologists any longer rhetoricians. When the academic innovation of Ramus and Talon is thus regarded, it presents wider significances than its authors intended, it amounts to more than an educational reform. It is a phase in that process, still not easy to describe, which we call the emergence of a modern era. Therefore it suggests that in Puritan thought the intellectual heritage was finally more decisive than the piety, that the adoption of the Ramist system, with its cleavage between logic and rhetoric, though prompted immediately by theological convenience, should in fact be ascribed to a still deeper force, to the whole intellectual drift of modern Europe, and again that Puritanism itself should be looked upon as one among many expressions of that drift rather than as a self-contained movement.

CHAPTER XII

THE PLAIN STYLE

There is a story concerning the conversion of John Cotton that was well-known in the seventeenth century and was frequently retold in New England. Before his heart was humbled, when he was one of the great lights of learning at Cambridge, he preached to large audiences "after the *mode* of the *University* at that time, which was to stuffe and fill their Sermons with as much Quotation and citing of Authors as might possibly be," but once the sense of sin came upon him he went into the pulpit for a public lecture and spoke "after the plain & profitable way, by raysing of *Doctrines,* with propounding the *Reasons* and *Uses* of the same." The scholars, who "came generally with great expectation to heare a more then ordinary learned Sermon from him that was so famous throughout the *University,"* were aghast, and perceiving his bent, "sate them downe in great discontent, pulling their hats over their eyes, thereby to expresse their dislike of the Sermon." Puritans were never troubled over the disapprobation of the critical, for those who thus rudely stopped their ears against the voice of a faithful preacher were sealing their own damnation, while those who listened were putting themselves in the path of a predestined election, as was proved in at least one instance at this very lecture, for John Preston, the future Master of Emmanuel, was present and pulled his hat over his eyes with the other scholars, but in spite of himself he heard, and immediately "was so affected, that he was made to stand up againe, and change his posture, and attend to what was spoken, in another manner than he and the rest had done." In this fashion the sermon worked upon those for whom God had ordained it a means, and hence there was a fundamental tenet in Puritanism that the learned manner of speaking, the discourse stuffed with quotations and "gingling" with rhetoric, could never become such an instrument of vocation. Persuasion of men's intellects and awakening of their hearts could not be wrought through the cadences of a sermon in "the mode of the University," but only through the plain and profitable way.

Cotton's auditors came to his address expecting the sort of sermon we now call "metaphysical"; they were given instead the standard Puritan form, and they would have needed to listen but to the opening sentences to recognize the difference. There were many kinds of sermons delivered in English in the early seventeenth century, at least as the best modern authority, Mr. Fraser Mitchell, distinguishes them; there were Anglicans like Ussher who preached in a mode very similar to the Puritan, and there were moderate Puritans like Henry Smith or Thomas Adams whose works seem to us almost "metaphysical".[1] Disregarding for the moment all the intermediate shadings, we can recognize that before the 1640's, before the sectarians appeared on the scene, there were two opposed theories of the form, style, and function of the sermon which were identified with the two parties most radically opposed in theology and ecclesiastical doctrine. When Puritans speak of abuses and extravagances in sermon style they almost always have in mind sermons of the Laudian party, the discourses of Andrewes or Donne, the preaching that symbolized in manner as well as in content the preferences of the court, the Cavaliers, and those who loved the "beauty of holiness." Against this kind of oration Puritans opposed their own conception, the plain and profitable way of doctrine, reasons, and uses, which perfectly reflected in form and style as well as in substance the mentality and tastes of Puritans, Roundheads, and lovers of the Word of God.

Opposition between the metaphysical and the Puritan sermon was a matter both of form and style. There is no occasion in this work to describe in detail the method of the metaphysicals, which of recent years has been elaborately studied and its great charms revivified to a generation that recognizes in it an endeavor to resolve problems similar to its own. To compare a sermon of Andrewes or of Donne with one of Cotton or of Hooker is to see at a glance the fundamental points of contrast; the difference of form is pronounced, for the Anglican sermon is much more an oration, much closer to classical and patristic eloquence, while the Puritan work is mechanically and rigidly divided into sections and subheads, and appears on the printed page more like a lawyer's brief than a work of art. The Anglican sermon is constructed on a symphonic scheme of progressively widening vision; it moves from point to point by verbal analysis, weaving larger and larger embroideries about the words of the text. The Puritan sermon quotes the text and "opens" it as briefly as possible, expounding circumstances and context, explaining its grammatical meanings, reducing its tropes and schemata to prose, and setting forth its logical implications; the sermon then proclaims in a flat, indicative sentence the "doctrine" contained in the text or logically deduced from it, and proceeds to the first reason or proof. Reason follows reason, with no other transition than a period and a number; after the last proof is stated there follow the uses or applications, also in numbered sequence, and the sermon ends when there is nothing more to be said. The Anglican sermon opens with a pianissimo exordium, gathers momentum through a rising and quickening tempo, comes generally to a rolling, organ-toned peroration; the Puritan begins with a reading of the text, states the reasons in an order determined by logic, and the uses in an enumeration determined by the kinds of persons in the throng who need to be exhorted or reproved, and it stops without flourish or resounding climax. Hence it was accurately described in contemporaneous terms as "plain", and the Puritan aesthetic led Puritans to the conclusion that because a sermon was plain it was also "profitable".

By the middle of the century the distinction between these two forms had become so sharply drawn, the types so exactly stereotyped, that ordinary laymen as well as Cambridge scholars would recognize the partisan sympathies of a minister by the form and technique of his pulpit utterance. Sermon style was not a matter of taste and preference, it was a party badge. Indeed, the various manners were so consciously formulated that in 1656, one Abraham Wright, an opponent of Dell and Webster, issued a book of *Five Sermons in Five Several Styles or Waies of Preaching,* in which he deliberately assumed the respective manners of "Bp. Andrewes His Way," of the Presbyterian way, and of the Independent way. These sermons are not outstanding literary examples, but because they were manufactured to order they purposely point up the typical features, and the contrast between Wright's performances in Andrewes' vein and in the Presbyterians' brings home the shock which John Cotton's auditors must have experienced as they comprehended his changed allegiance. The Andrewes-like sermon, Wright says, was actually delivered "before the late King"; it is upon the text, "And then shall they fast," which he also gives in Latin, "tunc jejunabunt." He weaves into his subject in characteristic metaphysical manner, taking up each word in the text, elaborating it adroitly with all the tropes and schemata of rhetoric, as for instance when he enlarges upon the word "fasting" by asking and answering the rhetorical questions, "cur sit?" "quid sit?" "an sit?" The sermon develops through an expanding suggestion of successive meanings, of denotations, connotations, and associations; the tapestry of elocution is assisted by a copious use of tags of Latin and Greek, by quotations from classical writers and church Fathers. But the Presbyterian sermon, which Wright delivered at St. Paul's after the Civil Wars had begun, hardly seems as though it could have been composed by the same man. It opens the text with a grammatical, rhetorical, and logical analysis, states the doctrine, gives the reasons and then the uses. There is hardly any quotation of authors, but Scripture references are affixed in the margin for every other sentence. In his Anglican sermon transitions are managed with skill, and he glides from discussion of the fast to the time of the fast with the aid of a polyglot antithesis: "And now we have got a fast for our time, let us see whether we can find a time for our fast, a *tunc* for our *jejunabunt"*; but in the Presbyterian way he pointedly makes no attempt at a rhetorical scheme, and bluntly asserts, "So much shall suffice for our first doctrinal position, rais'd from this first general part of the Text. The second observation that I shall draw from this general point of Charitie and Alms deeds, is . . ." In the first oration he comes to a swelling peroration and a chord of rest, beginning, "let us therefore who professe our selves members of the Church be like affected . . . ," but in the second he ends when he has made the last application. The outline of numbered topics and sub-topics in the Presbyterian form stands out in clear relief, and nowhere more arrestingly than in passages that might in the Anglican form furnish occasions for purple patches; when he is speaking of the joys of heaven, he reduces even the rapture of resurrection to a numerical method. "Our bodies therefore shall be endued with most unspeakable perfections, and most perfectly clarified from all imperfections, but they shall not be disrobed of their natural properties: briefly they shal be spirituall in a three fold sense," and thereupon follow the three senses. When the reader turns to the rolling and sonorous accumulations of iterative phrases and modulated clauses with which Donne or Andrewes mount to an oratorical celebration of heaven, and compares it with the Puritan tabulation, he begins to perceive the meaning of the differences in style:

> A new earth, where all their waters are milk, and all their milk, honey; where all their grass is corn, and all their corn manna; where all their glebe, all their clods of earth are gold, and all their gold of innumerable carats; where all their minutes are ages, and all their ages, eternity; where every thing, is every minute, in the highest exaltation, as good as it can be, and yet super-exalted, and infinitely multiplied by every minute's addition; every minute, infinitely better, than ever it was before.[2]

The Puritan piety was no less intense, and the ecstasy of redemption was as deeply felt, but in Puritan sermons intensity of piety was balanced by the precision and restraint of a highly methodical form, a rigid dialectical structure, and the ecstasy was severely confined within the framework of doctrine, reasons, and uses.

Abraham Wright was performing a feat of virtuosity, and his Puritan sermon is no more than a *tour de force;* many New England divines preached sermons of infinitely greater literary value, but his incarnates the form and style in which all of them were deliberately cast. His volume is important because it demonstrates how completely realized, how thoroughly *a priori,* the pattern had become. A preacher spoke as his faction dictated, and he learned in advance the method in which he should express his faction's tenets. Consequently, just as students in the schools were taught to speak or write by formal rhetoric, so ministerial candidates were drilled out of manuals of preaching. It would be exceedingly naïve, as well as pedantic, for the historian to attribute the creations of Andrewes or Donne to the textbooks, or to assert that Puritans achieved their kind of speech for no other reason than that they were students of this or that teacher. The textbooks will not account for the literary genius of either John Donne or Thomas Hooker, but they do set forth explicitly the designs which these great preachers had in mind whenever they sat down to compose. Meanwhile, lesser lights in both camps turned out their orations according to the patterns in which they were educated, and their virtues or their defects are as apt to be those of their education as of their individual talents. This observation is especially true of the majority of New England productions in the seventeenth century; except for the most prominent of the first generation and one or two gifted speakers in the second and third, New England preachers were merely competent and fairly well-educated students, who practiced in their pulpits what they had been taught in their textbooks.

The teacher from whom, above all others, Puritans learned the lesson of sermon form was William Perkins, who gave the classic exposition in his *The Art of Prophecying,* available to most students of the century in the second volume of his collected works.[3] Whether all the maxims originated with him is difficult to say, for Puritans characteristically did not recognize that any of their precepts were derived from other men, but ascribed all of them, including this of preaching in doctrine, reasons, and uses, to the universal and eternal wisdom of God. At any rate, following chronologically after Perkins, a succession of Puritan manuals reaffirmed and developed his teaching; it was set forth by Abraham Scultetus in Germany, in his *Axiomata Concionandi Practica,* 1619, and in England most notably by Richard Bernard in *The Faithfull Shepherd,*[4] 1621, by Oliver Bowles in *De Pastore Evangelico Tractatus,* 1649, by William Chappell, known to fame as having been for a short and not too happy interval the tutor of John Milton, in *The Use of Holy Scripture Gravely and Methodically Discoursed,* 1653, and in *The Preacher, or the Art and Method of Preaching,* 1656, and by William Price, an English Puritan stationed at Amsterdam, in *Ars Concionandi,* 1657. Furthermore, Richardson and Ames wrote always upon the unquestioned assumption that this way was the only legitimate order of the sermon, and for three or four decades before the settlement of New England all the divines who influenced the thought of the colonies, most of the great Puritans of the early seventeenth century, John Preston, Richard Sibbes, and John Ball in particular, followed the plan unswervingly. Hence these doctrines of the organization of the sermon and of the plain style were prominent in the intellectual inheritance of New Englanders. By them was determined the form and technique of the sermon, of the one literary type in which the Puritan spirit was most completely expressed, and if these authors can be said to have had any critical conception of artistic achievement, it was that set forth in their manuals of preaching.

There were, of course, other manuals which contained instructions for the kinds of sermons of which Puritans disapproved. When a few of these are examined in comparison with Puritan works, they disclose at once their dependence upon the Aristotelian rhetorics, and therefore those which followed the lead of Perkins must derive from some other source. Many of the Aristotelian sermon manuals are no more than wholesale transcriptions from the Peripatetic rhetorics. In an early English work, *The Preacher, or Method of Preaching,* published in London in 1576, Nicholas Heminge avowed, "I doe not forge new precepts, but doe applie the common rules of Logitians and Rhetoritians, to a certain matter." Heminge exhibited as yet no awareness of the Ramist controversy; later Aristotelians applied the common rules of their logic and rhetoric to this certain matter with a more defiant exactness. In 1598, for instance, a Dutchman, Wilhelm Zepper, in his *Ars Habendi et audiendi conciones Sacras,* studiously reproduced the conventional outline of the rhetorics even though writing wholly about preaching; he divided his book into the usual five chapters of invention, disposition, memory, elocution, and pronunciation, and found the sermon partaking of the nature of all the three Aristotelian genres, deliberative, demonstrative, judicial. He carved the sermon, like any other oration, into the conventional parts, exordium, narration, proposition, confirmation, confutation, and epilogue. The first and last of these were to be entirely devoted "ad movendos & impellendos animos," and the others "ad rem docendam pertinent." He compared an exordium to the opening bars of a piece of music, making the audience docile and attentive; in a sermon, he said, narration should treat of the causes and circumstances of the text to parallel the ordinary setting forth of the occasion in a secular oration; proposition should be a statement of the doctrine or theological position, confirmation a demonstration of its truth to the intellect, confutation a rebuttal of objections and heresies, and epilogue should restate the proposition "cum affectu," so that the theme would be fixed in the memories of listeners and their last recollection be associated with its strongest emotional impact, just as the peroration of a political orator should be his rousing climax. Alsted's chapter on ecclesiastical rhetoric in the *Encyclopaedia* repeated essentially the same instruction, though probably the most influential Aristotelian treatise among English Protestants was Keckermann's *Rhetoricae Ecclesiasticae, sive Artis Formandi et Habendi Conciones Sacras,* always available to Harvard students in the second volume of his *Operum Omnium.* Keckermann's source is evidenced by incessant citation of Aristotle, though he made some changes in the schemes and terminologies in order to adjust them to the special requirements of Christian oratory. Instead of placing under invention the general rules for finding "persuabilia," as he did in his *Systema Rhetoricae,* he declared that when we come to ecclesiastical rhetoric we find that invention is a very specialized art, being the extraction of meanings from Biblical texts and not first of all a discovery of moving considerations, that it should therefore consist of five distinct acts: "praecognitio textus quoad scopum," "partitio," "explicatio verborum," "amplificatio," and "applicatio." He reduced ecclesiastical disposition from the secular five parts to three: "exordium," "tractatio intermedia," and "peroratio," apparently feeling that narration and proposition were sufficiently covered in invention, and that in sermons the middle sections should not be too mechanically divided into confirmation and confutation, but instead should be devoted to general amplification and exposition. However, Keckermann affirmed that all these changes could be justified by the words of Aristotle, even though Aristotle himself had never written precisely upon sermonizing, and that his own modifications did not alter the basically Peripatetic character of the scheme.[5]

Mr. Fraser Mitchell suggests that the pattern of most "metaphysical" sermons, of John Donne's in particular, was taken from Keckermann,[6] and that such discourses are accordingly to be separated into the sections of praecognitio, partitio, explicatio, amplificatio, and applicatio, that they open with a formal exordium and come to a calculated peroration. Very often the artistry of a Donne completely conceals the skeleton; it is more evident in the discourses of Andrewes and protrudes distinctly in Abraham Wright's imitation of "Andrewes His Way." It is not surprising that the metaphysical sermon, the expression of men who remained loyal to scholasticism not merely in physics, as did the Puritans, but in logic and rhetoric as well, to whom the reforms of Ramus were impious and ignorant assaults upon the historic splendor of these arts in the name of a crass utilitarianism, should have had its theory couched in Aristotelian terms. It was inevitable that men of the Renaissance should look upon the sermon as a particular species in the genus of oratory, and apply to the part the laws which governed the whole, that when Aristotelians needed a treatise on preaching they should have devised one out of the general treatises on speaking. Furthermore, there were deep affinities between the Aristotelian way of thinking and religious beliefs of the Anglican party, as can be seen in the methods and arguments of Richard Hooker; therefore, certain Anglicans were bound to perfect a way of preaching that would exemplify in its very structure the qualities exhibited by Aristotelian science. Consequently, the question then arises, if the metaphysical style is to be linked to the Aristotelian logic and rhetoric, if the theory of the metaphysical sermon is to be found in an adaptation of Aristotle to the needs of the preacher, does it follow that the opposing style, the Puritan form with its doctrine, reasons, and uses, was a consequence of the Puritan adherence to Ramus?

The answer to this question will be forthcoming only when more definite information can be discovered concerning the intellectual history of William Perkins, which at the moment is somewhat obscure. If we look on the continent for parallels to his *Art of Prophecying,* we discover that Ramist writers made several attempts to translate the rules of the *Dialecticae* and the *Rhetorica* into rules for preachers. Such efforts often emerged, as did Bisterveldus' *Ars Concionandi* in 1654, with nothing more than a regular Ramist textbook, combining the logic and the rhetoric, and teaching that the content of a sermon should be discovered by invention, its order arranged by disposition, its style regulated by elocution, and its delivery dictated by pronunciation. Perkins obviously did not go about formulating his scheme of the sermon in any such slavish spirit; if he was guided by Ramist principles, he at least worked with an original insight. Perhaps the nature of his inspiration is foreshadowed by an earlier work, the anonymous translation of the *Dialecticae* published in 1574, the preface to which pointed out the value of logic for divinity in terms that seem prophetic of Perkins' achievement:

If thou be a deuine this method willethe thee that in place of the definition, thou sett forthe shortly the some of the text, which thou hast taken in hand to interprete: next to porte thy text into a fewe heads that the auditor may the better retaine thy sayings: Thirdly to intreate of euery heade in his owne place with the ten places of inuention, shewing them the causes, the effectes, the adiontes and circumstances: to bring in thy comparisons with the rest of artificiall places: and last to make thy matter playne and manifest with familiar examples & aucthorities out of the worde of God: to sett before the auditors (as euery heade shall geue the occasion) the horrible and sharpe punyshing of disobedience, and the ioyfull promises appartayning to the obedient and godlie.

This passage foretells so clearly the order which was ultimately fixed in the Puritan form as to suggest that the order might easily have been hit upon by any student of Ramus. Once the Ramist had been freed from the domination of Aristotle, once he had realized that an oration or sermon was not condemned inescapably to the five parts and that it could be arranged in any sequence which the laws of method might indicate, once he had learned that the invention of arguments and their disposition were affairs of the reason and that effective speaking was merely the delivery of disposed arguments decked out "with familiar examples & aucthorities out of the worde of God," what more natural than that he should throw aside the Aristotelian sermon and create a logical form *de novo* according to the golden rules? In that case, the laws of invention applied to extracting arguments from a Biblical text would teach him how to "open" it and how to formulate the doctrine; Ramus' rules for memory would instruct him to "porte" his text into a few doctrines; the whole of the *Dialecticae* would teach him how to prove them and how to dispose doctrines and proofs in order. Ramus' constant insistence upon "use" would show him the necessity for applying each doctrine to the auditors "as euery heade shall geue the occasion." For the embellishment with figures and tropes and for the methods of oral delivery, Talon's rhetoric would teach him that these are secondary to the analysis of arguments and the genesis of a method, that they are to be added only after the theme and the demonstration are worked out.

Perkins' teaching seems so obviously to have resulted from some such reasoning that we can hardly doubt he was a disciple of Ramus. Further confirmation of this hypothesis is suggested by the fact that he was at Cambridge University in the 1590's, as well as by the internal evidence of his book, by its vocabulary and its references. He declares in what must be Ramist phrases that the art of prophesying should be adorned "with variety and plenty of precepts," and that he has ranged the precepts "in that method, which I have deemed most commodious: that they might be better for use, and fitter for the memory"; he uses dichotomy as a principle of classification, and when he argues that doctrines must be collected from texts by logic he enumerates the "places" in a Ramist rather than in a Peripatetic order. Finally he says that memory must be cultivated

> by the helpe of disposition either axiomaticall, or syllogisticall, or methodicall, the severall proofes and applications of the doctrines, the illustrations of the applications, and the order of them all: in the meane time nothing carefull for the words, *Which* (as *Horace* speaketh) *will not unwillingly follow the matter that is premeditated.*

He expresses indebtednesses to Augustine, Erasmus, and Beza, and does not mention either Ramus or Talon; yet the phrase "disposition either axiomaticall, or syllogisticall, or methodicall" can hardly be anything but a summary of the *Dialecticae,* and his assumption that the speaker need not be too careful over words, because right words will automatically follow right matter, is the essential meaning of Talon. Certainly, if Perkins was not wholly guided by Ramus, he must have been strongly influenced, and assuredly the best of the later writers, Bernard, Chappell, and Price, were completely Ramists. We have already seen how undeniably Richardson and Ames had embraced the doctrines. Consequently this much seems clear: the Puritan form of the sermon, which was first advanced by Perkins and then expounded in Puritan manuals, was altogether congenial to Ramist ways of thinking, and hence there is good cause to suppose that Perkins arrived at it by pondering the question of form in the light of Ramus' logic and rhetoric. If this is so, our account of the genesis of the form would resolve itself into some such statement as this: Puritan theologians were committed by their continued acceptance of the Peripatetic psychology to conceiving of the sermon as a means that operates upon both the intellects and passions of men;

at the same time the Ramist dialectic supplied them with a concrete method for persuading the intellect and the Ramist rhetoric with a method for moving the passions; the concurrence of all three factors, psychology, logic, and rhetoric, resulted in their conception of the form, of the plain and profitable way of doctrine, reasons, and uses. If this statement is still too hypothetical to be taken for a factual account of origins, we cannot doubt that however the form was hit upon, even though the concurrence of these three influences may not fully account for its devising or explain all its characteristics, nevertheless Ramist theories of logic and of rhetoric, combined with Peripatetic theories of human psychology, furnished the justification or the formal rationalization of the Puritan sermon.

The three-fold convergence of these doctrines upon the Puritan sermon appears more dramatically as we examine what the preceptors had to say upon each part and upon the style in general. Thus we may note the influence of Ramus, and also a trait of the Puritan mind, when we find the authors defending the order of doctrine, reasons, and uses because it is "natural". This method, says Chappell, is "a discourse upon a Text of Scripture, disposing its parts according to the order of nature, whereby, the accord of them, one with the other may be judged of, and contained in memory." This definition is essentially the Ramist contention that all formal art is a methodizing of some "puissance naturelle", but also it suggests the concept of nature which underlies technologia, the belief that the visible world embodies the archetypal ideas of God, that these are simple, efficient, and systematic, and that all man-made works must emulate the divine perfections. The Puritan aesthetic, in other words, begins with the Ramist assumption of a natural order that has been summarized in the arts, includes the veneration for learning, demands the assistance of supernatural grace, and results in an exaltation of "method":

> Nature with her three daughters, Wit, Memory, and Vtterance, giue all attendance in him at Learnings doore. Learning, with her arts, wait as hand-mayds vpon Grace. Grace is the Lady and Mistresse, which onely can and will rightly command them all, seasonably imploy them, and will keepe them euermore doing. Method keepes all within due precincts, sets their bounds, ranketh euery thing orderly in the proper place, which Nature, Learning and Grace haue conceiued to write, or speak.

Ergo, Puritan writers condemned the exordium because it was first of all unnecessary to true believers, who should be sufficiently regardful of the preacher without any artificial capturing of their attention, and because, secondly, it offended their concept of nature. Believers who are "well instructed, acknowledging their Pastor, prepared and excited by prayers, both publike and private, to the hearing of the Word of God," do not require that their "good-will, docility and attention" be sought before they will pay heed to the doctrine; furthermore,

To seeke for Proverbs, Apothegmes, Sentences, or select Histories to make Exo[r]diums of, by the accommodating of them, doth not onely savour of something humane, unworthy the Word of God, but hath a childish kind of affectation, which is not approved in the more grave speeches of men.

If the sermon is to be a means it must impress the mind and arouse the heart, but only by thoroughly legitimate means, by the plain and profitable way; exordiums and perorations are merely occasions for an exhibition of the speaker's eloquence and hence superfluous in faithful preaching.

By the same token, the one part of the sermon in which a preacher has least need for eloquence, the one section from which he should banish it entirely and depend wholly upon unvarnished statement of fact, is the opening paragraph, the exposition of the text. Puritan instructors always demanded that this be brief. "Some speciall occasion may make the large explication of the text, or handling of the Doctrine to be necessary; but regularly, and ordinarily the principall worke of the Sermon . . . is in the use and application." The preacher should analyze his text in order to collect "a few and profitable points of doctrine out of the naturall sense." Puritans assumed that only one sense was natural to any passage of Scripture, that the Word of God was plain and explicit and did not need to be enhanced or enlarged by any words of men. Yet technologia, inspired by the Ramist dialectic, taught that the Bible should be approached exactly as should the natural world, as a welter of raw material out of which the propositions of art were to be refined by the processes of invention and disposition. The meaning of Scripture, therefore, was plain, but not too plain; it had only one literal signification, and yet it was not to be taken too literally. The divines were to collect from its random histories, songs, and preachments the axioms of theology and to dispose them in systematic, creedal order. Every sermon was an effort to abstract from a Biblical verse one or more such axioms, and the procedure, as Ramus had shown, was to take it apart by the method of analysis into its constituent elements and then by the method of genesis to recombine the elements into a succinct proposition. The first work of a preacher was always to translate the Bible into doctrines, to deliver the meaning of a parable, of the Song of Songs, of the Psalms or a prophecy, "in proper, significant, perspicuous, plaine, vsually knowne words and phrase of speech, apt, and fit to expresse the thing spoken of to the vnderstanding of the hearers without ambiguity." Sermons were to reveal that the inner structure of the Bible was the same platform of ideas outlined in the Westminster Confession of Faith, just as the arts were to show that the inner structure of the universe was the platform of ideas outlined in technologia.

Generally the analysis of a text required the help of the whole trivium, of grammar, logic, and rhetoric. "A doctrine must first be rightly found out, and then afterward hand[l]ed," said Ames; "The finding out is by

Logick Analysis, unto which Rhetoricke also and Grammar serveth." With grammar the preacher expounded the meaning of the words, and therefore he had to know the original tongues as well as the vernacular. With logic he was able to decipher the intellectual meaning and extract from the verse its appropriate doctrine or doctrines. When verses were "Analogicall and plaine," the rules of invention and axiom were sufficient; when a verse was more involved—for in spite of the supposed clarity and the assertion of one literal meaning, some texts were found to be "Crypticall and darke"—then the rules of the syllogism had to be invoked and doubtful axioms tested either by simple or composite figures. The important caution to be observed was that no doctrine be "writhen" from a text, but Puritans were supremely confident that the logic of Ramus, because it was a method for discovering or unveiling arguments concealed in matter and not a way of devising them by mere human wit, was precisely suited to collecting only such doctrines as were truthfully contained in the text. If a passage were rightly analyzed into its arguments, and these were laid out in order and considered in relation to the "places" of dialectic, they would infallibly compose themselves into axioms. Deduction of doctrines therefore was achieved "by the Logicall affection of Arguments; as from a generall to a speciall, from the whole to the parts; from the proper adiunct to the subiect; so from the cause, effect, subiect, adiunct, notation, contrary, comparat, definition, distribution." The opening of a text, said Perkins in Ramist imagery, is an action "whereby the place propounded is as a Weavers web, resolved (or untwisted and unloosed) into sundrie doctrines." Bernard illustrated again the Ramist character of these instructions by saying that once the arguments were discovered, the doctrine should be established by noting the "method" of the text, whether it be axiom, syllogism, or disposition.

Among the arguments isolated and defined by logic would be the time, place, circumstances, and context of the passage, but a different sort of analysis would be required when the passage happened to be a piece of Biblical imagery, some figure of speech, some metaphor or hyperbole. At this point the minister would turn to the rhetoric of Talon. "If by the influx of latter arts (namely Grammar, Rhetorick, &c.) into the Text, Logick cannot be immediately examined," said Chappell—that is, if the Holy Spirit spoke this or that truth in a simile or a synecdoche and therefore the logical axiom was not at once visible—"then the words are first to be stript of those arts by some general explication, and the sense to be made plain, and so the way made ready for the Logical Analysis and assignation of the axiomes that they may appear therein." Talon's rhetoric was ideally suited to just this "stripping" of figures from the logical sense, for it made tropes and schemes the secondary and subsequent wrappings of a plain speech, accidentals that could be separated from substantials, not integral parts of the thinking.[7] By this linguistic machinery Biblical syntax could be unraveled, as by dialectical invention all arguments were sifted out of concrete things. Samuel Willard, for instance, could begin with a word meaning "to bind" and argue that it signifies *"Metaphorically to chasten,* and then *Metonimically,* to *reform* or *reclaim,"* and finally state his doctrine as a proposition concerning reformation. Rhetoric was a tool with which Puritans could plane off the colors of speech from Scriptural utterances, leaving the smooth white surface of "that one entire and naturall sense." The intention of the parables, for instance, was "to explicate and clear up a Truth to the understanding by the help of the senses," to appeal to the sensible faculties by means "of sensible things, such as are obvious to our eyes, ears, &c. and so lead us to a conception of spiritual things," but the minister's task when preaching upon them amounted to what might be called unscrambling them, to give "the Reddition or Interpretation of them," thereby to bring "more light to mens understandings." Talon's rhetoric, in other words, was a godsend to men who professed to believe in a literal interpretation of the Bible, who were not gifted with poetic insight, and who were somewhat deficient in humor: "Must wee actually sell all, taking up a Gibbet daily, lend freely, looking for nothing againe, turne the other cheeke to him which smiteth one, plucke out our eyes, cut off right hands, &c.?" Fortunately we need not, for rhetoric makes us understand that these expressions are figurative, conveying an abstract truth that is much less incommodious. The groundwork of Scripture is logical, though in style it seems poetic. God chooses this way of speaking because He is adapting Himself "to the way and manner that men express themselves in, one to another"; consequently,

> The *Rhetorick* is such as men make use of, to speak in Metaphors, Metonymies, Allegories, and Similitudes, & are to be so interpreted; the *Logick* of them is such as man's Reason is wont to make use of, whether Axiomatical or Syllogistical; and hence are to be so taken, hence the word is called *Logical milk*.

When the minister had provided himself with such works as Smith's *Mysterie of Rhetorick Unveil'd,* or Hall's *Centuria Sacra,* which provided a handy "Synopsis or Compendium of all the most materiall Tropes and Figures contained in the Scriptures," he could use them as a kind of dictionary, looking up the figure or metaphor of his text and finding the meaning of it in straight-forward prose, exactly as though he were looking up words in a Hebrew lexicon to find English equivalents.[8]

Many Biblical texts contain facts or rules which touch upon other arts than logic or rhetoric; some of them exemplify principles of physics or astronomy, others of medicine or mathematics. Consequently, in order to make proper expositions, a Puritan divine needed some acquaintance with all the disciplines.

For there is occasion offered of the vse of variety of learning, as of Grammar, Rhetorick, Logicke, Physicks, Mathematicks, Metaphysicks, Ethicks, Politicks, Oeconomicks, History, and Military Discipline. The knowledge whereof are as so many lights to see into a Text by, both to find out and to lay open such variety of matter, as lye couched in the words.

But the purpose served by all knowledge of the arts was to facilitate the rewording of texts into doctrinal statements. The preacher was to use no rhetoric in phrasing any doctrine, he was to employ no art but grammar in stating the propositions of his sermons, because his first task was to sink the abstract doctrine into the minds of listeners. Viewed in the light of the theory of means, the "opening" of a text was the initial step in preaching because it was the first means of reaching the understanding. Everyone agreed that the arts "in themselves considered are not able to convert a soule," yet as Thomas Hall explained to Webster, "being spiritualliz'd and improved to the right opening and expounding of the Scripture, they may be a meanes the better to convince our judgements, and work upon our affections, and so help forward our conversion." William Perkins declared that "right cutting, or the right dividing" of a text was the means "whereby the word is made fit to edifie the people of God." Since the first stage in any human response to phantasms was intellectual comprehension, and the actions of will and affection were to follow and not precede the actions of mind, then the first endeavor of the minister should properly be "to edifie." "To fall to application before the truth be explained, and proved, is to make confusion"; so first the minister must teach the doctrine, which consists "in laying open the Truth, so as the understanding may apprehend it, and be made to give its assent to it; we must have a conception and a conviction of it, and this must go before application, being to prepare for it." Thus the Puritan interpretation of psychology as well as of logic and rhetoric determined that the initial part of a sermon be the opening of a text and the rephrasing of it in an assertion, that because the preacher's first task was to inform the intellect, his first work was to "fall into a common place; which is to handle a thing by the definition, distribution, cause, effect, by the agreeablenes with, or disagreeing from other things: all which are to be proued by Scripture, reason, and testimonies." As both Ramus and Richardson had declared, "there is nothing true or false, unlesse it be an Axiome," and therefore as soon as the arguments are isolated and defined, they must be enunciated in their "Logical directrix."

And an Axiome being a disposal of an argument with an argument, and a Syllogism of two in question with a third, and as the arguments are affected one with the other, so they actually exhibit their force in both places, it will be of much concernment here, to know well and weigh the affections of the Argument.

Here also was a reason for the Puritans' strenuous objection to the metaphysical manner of handling the text, their hostility to what they called the "Topical way of preaching," which they described as preaching "according to the series of the words, where each arguments, or Topical places, are proposed as Doctrines, or foundations of the discourse, especially when each one carryeth some kind of emphasis with it." Donne's famous sermon on the text, "The last Enemie that shall be destroyed, is Death," weaves its subtle texture by permutations upon the words "enemy," "last," "death," and finally upon "destroyed," but Chappell, whom some of his contemporaries called "a rich magazine of rational learning," declared that on Ramist grounds, Donne's method was a logical absurdity. It was taking individual "arguments," in the Ramist sense of the word, by themselves, whereas discrete and unconnected arguments are meaningless, merely serving the preacher as occasions for sensual eloquence. "For because the Argument, considered in it self, is only affected to argue, and that there is no act of judgement but where the argument is disposed with an argument, it is impossible to bring any proof, or inferre any use, of a bare argument." What Donne should have attempted, after analyzing his text into the discrete arguments of enemy, last, death, and destroyed, was to make out of them some such axioms as "At the resurrection God will abolish death," or "Death is the worst enemy of mankind," and then he should have proved and applied the axiom. The remedy for the evils of the "Topical way" was "to select, and constitute in the first place that axiome . . . which by nature is first, and contains in it self the compleat, and independent sense: and then joyn unto it that argument which may make that axiome that by order of nature is next." So Puritans saw no charms in the intricate web of the metaphysical sermon; they swept it aside as a violation of logic and a hindrance to the working of the means. Instead they would have had all preachers unravel a text by a grammatical, logical, and rhetorical analysis and then put the ravelings together into as many doctrines as could be composed out of them. If this seemed a strange procedure, Chappell replied that "none will aske me a reason of it, have he but any touch, and be never so little versed in the Dialecticks, whose judgement and memory . . . will desire an order. . . . I will rather advise you to reserve to each axiome, that which is Homogeneal to it, that the treaty may agree with the order of the axiomes."[9] It was, obviously, impossible to be a Ramist and still preach like John Donne; to English Puritans it seemed impossible, once they had become Ramists, to preach otherwise than in doctrines, reasons, and uses.

The reasons or proofs which followed the statement of doctrine in enumerated sequence were declared by the manuals to reinforce the intellectual acceptance of the doctrine and to commence the emotional reception. They were to be drawn first from confirming passages of Scripture or from some principle in systematic divinity; secondly, they could come from any principle in nature, from one of the "universall rules" of technologia; and thirdly, "from common experience and sense," because this "is euery mans certaine knowledge of the vse, nature, and quality of a thing to bee euer one and the same. . . This experience uniuersal hath these degree[s], sense, obseruation, induction, and so infallibility of the thing." The reasons were not to add to the Word of God, which of course was final and complete in itself, but for men the adducing of rational proof served at least two valuable ends: it helped the people to receive the doctrine, as the principles of psychology would explain—"This giuing of reasons is to compleate the vnderstanding of the hearers in the Doctrine, and to assure their perswasion of the equity thereof, and so make them more ready to receiue it, and more stable in beleeuing it"—and, as the principles of technologia would make clear, it helped to establish the unity of all knowledge, the continuity of theology with the arts, by showing that theological revelation could at least be substantiated by human reason.

Though no weights of reason can adde any thing to the firmnesse of that which is grounded upon divine testimony, neverthelesse Scripture being, though above, yet not against good reason, and doth not take away, but perfect it, it will not be much from the purpose sometimes to make use of reasons, and other things, as drawn from the art of Nature, if they shall be judged fitting, easie and profitable for the hearers.

Inevitably the greater part of the reasons was supplied by logic, for it was logic that demonstrated the unity of the arts in the body of technologia, and by logic alone could be maintained the harmony of revelation and reason. The other arts were used for illustrations and analogies, but next to explicit warrants from Scripture, the best reasons were always those drawn "our selues from the Doctrine Logically"; in order so to draw them,

wee must consider of the subiect and predicate of it, or the Antecedent or consequent, and marke what relation one hath to another, whether *consentanea* or *dissentanea,* whether cause and effect, subiect, adiunct, or any other topick place, and so thereafter make the reason, which reason must bee the medius terminus, in a Categoricall Syllogisme.

A doctrine must be stated in accordance with the laws of dialectic—"as that Arguments agreeing bee affirmed; that contraries bee denyed . . . that things to bee conioyned bee not seuered, and so contrarily"—and its proofs must then be framed by the same laws. Over the first two parts of the New England sermon presided the *Dialecticae* of Petrus Ramus.

The uses, however, were primarily regulated by rhetoric, for in them the preacher's intention was predominantly to move the emotions, to drive down the channel of the nerves to the heart, to the will and passions, those phantasms he had imprinted through the doctrine and the reasons upon the understanding. Proof "is for the vnderstanding, the other is for the will." The Puritan minister was to eschew rhetoric in opening his text, in stating his doctrine, and to employ it sparingly in the reasons, but in the applications he was free to call upon all the tropes and figures he knew, to modulate his voice and quicken his gestures, for here he was attempting what rhetoric was designed by God to abet, to become the means of calling men to right conduct, of arousing them to a sense of sin and an abhorrence of evil. To make applications, said Bernard, a minister "must make vse of the figures of Rhetorick . . . which haue an incredible power of attraction, & pulling to them the affections of hearers, if they bee well managed, still from the grace of the heart, and by good iudgement brought in aptly in their due places." Eight flowers of speech, he thought, were particularly efficacious: exclamation, interrogation, compellation, obsecration, aptation, prosopopeia, apostrophe, sermocination, and dialogue, and these are the devices which most frequently appear in the applications of New England doctrines. Still more occasion for the use of vigorous or arresting speech was furnished when the uses were addressed specifically to the various kinds and conditions of men. Perkins distinguished seven degrees of uses for the seven degrees of spiritual conditions, from believers to the fallen, with the intermediate gradations of those humbled, those having knowledge yet not humbled, those teachable but ignorant, and those both ignorant and unteachable; in order to set forth the fine distinctions among these states all the arsenal of tropes and schemes stored in Talon's *Rhetorica* were mobilized and set to work. Furthermore, the doctrine of the means gave an added incentive for using rhetorical embellishments in the applications, for in spite of its teaching that emotions should not be appealed to before the mind was persuaded, it held that the preacher might, after informing the mind through the doctrine and reasons, legitimately attack it a second time through the emotions. "Because the heart or will hath a great influx into the mind . . . therefore it is lawful (though it is possible and customary to falter exceedingly in this thing) . . . to insinuate something either hiddenly or openly, whereby we may possesse the hearers affections, and by them, as by setting scaling ladders invade the fort of the mind." All the more reason, therefore, why the preacher should be expert in the devices of rhetoric, particularly in the eight most telling figures!

However, if the Puritan minister was free in the uses to let himself go rhetorically, he had still to observe the limits prescribed by Ramist theory. He could not devise applications first and foremost as "persuabilia" but only as logical deductions from his doctrine. The content of his oration, here as in the earlier sections, was supplied by dialectic; rhetoric was used more copiously at this point merely to ornament and decorate the doctrine. Because the uses were addressed to the heart, said Chappell, they "doe vindicate to themselves all manner of Rhetorical preparation," but this did not mean that they were "to be undertaken without the salt of wisdom and gravity, as is befitting a sacred person and businesse." Richardson declared, "We have among us a distinction of doctrine and use," but doctrine, he explained, "is properly the first rule of Art, and use is the application thereof, or the special deducts gathered from the first." [10] The understanding of an auditor is to be exercised not only for discerning the truth, said Samuel Willard, but "also to be improved in judging of the goodness of the Truth so exhibited"; accordingly the minister must draw his uses as "practical inferences from the general truth, which are for our *Instruction.*" Thus even in the portion of his discourse where eloquence was most permissible, the Puritan minister could not indulge in the rhetoric of the metaphysical preachers, the wit and verbal play of Thomas Adams or Thomas Fuller, nor in the unrestrained emotional exhortations of Ranters and Antinomians. In order to move the heart in the one way considered proper by Puritan theorists, the preacher had not only to be learned in rhetoric, but to "have his senses well exercised in Scriptures, and be well skilled both in the art of reasoning, the nature of the humane soul, and the divers means of Gods operating." He needed always to be a theologian, a logician, and a psychologist, as well as an orator.

For this reason applications of doctrines never became full-dress oratorical perorations, for their delivery was restrained by the laws of dialectic and the method of enumeration. The authors of manuals made out a regular scheme of uses—uses for confutation, instruction, reprehension, dehortation, exhortation, consolation—and the uses in New England sermons often appear in printed texts so labeled, thus testifying to the essential supremacy of logic in Puritan thinking, even at the one point where the ministers were most intensely concentrating upon emotion. The "use of confutation," for instance, made it unnecessary that Puritan writers assign a separate section of ecclesiastical rhetoric to rebuttal; confutation could be achieved in the reasons by proposing and answering a possible "objection", though the more usual custom was to assign the first use to a declaration that the reasons have shown by inference the error of Arminians, Antinomians, or Quakers. Experienced preachers gave the novice a valuable piece of advice concerning such uses: "what error soever he brings upon the stage, let him doe it nervously, solidly, and manifestly; lest the refutation vanish away, and the error stick fast." Naturally, the phrasing of confutations was determined as much by logic or by psychological theory as by rhetoric; it was adjusted to the circumstances, in accordance with Ames's instruction that in delivering confutations "zeale and truth must be tempered with such mildnesse and moderation as becomes the cause, and as may distinguish such as erre out of simplicitie, from such as blaspheame impiously." The other uses, though not involved with polemic, required as much help from the various sciences, and in order to apply his doctrines to the people a preacher needed to "bee well studied in the cases of conscience, to be able to giue satisfaction to the weake and tender-hearted." He needed knowledge more than art, and he had to take more heed that he find applications of all types, of dehortation as well as of exhortation, that he bring the uses to bear upon specific problems of his community and his congregation, than that he phrase them with artificial eloquence.

As for style, the manuals all begin with a simple assertion that it was to be kept wholly subordinate to the Bible, to be nothing but a transparent glass through which the light of revelation might shine, to have no character of its own, to be unrelievedly plain. But even the manuals were not able to dismiss it without further discussion; the religious controversies of the period continually forced writers to more explicit statements, until at last, even though Puritans would have preferred to hold that style presented no problems, that it was merely an affair of speaking truth directly and simply, they were compelled to give much attention to it. The instructions and formal professions were all of one tenor: preachers were to make a "plaine delivery of the Word without the painted eloquence of mens wisdome, high & stately phrases of speech"; God "would have Christ Crucified to be preached in a Crucified phrase." William Ames offered no apologies for "the drinesse of the style, and harshnesse of some words," for he was ready "to exercise my selfe in that heresie, that when it is my purpose to Teach, I thinke I should not say that in two words which may be said in one"; the efficacy of the Holy Spirit, he said, "doth more cleerely appeare in a naked simplicity of words, then in elegancy and neatnesse," and "So much affectation as appeares, so much efficacy and authority is lost." An admixture of human words not only violates the purity and perfection of the Word of God, but "withall there is a scandall given to the hearers, who being accustomed to such humane flourishes, oftentimes, contracting itching eares, doe begin to lothe, the simplicity of the Gospell." The greatest of New England preachers, Thomas Hooker, foresaw that many would criticize his *Survey* for being "too Logicall, or Scholasticall," but he answered that in his compositions he sought only "plainesse and perspicuity, both for matter and manner of expression," because writings should come abroad "not to dazle, but direct the apprehension of the meanest," and that the highest achievement of any writer was "to make a hard point easy and familiar in explication." His profession is the essence of the Puritan stylistic ideal:

> As it is beyond my skill, so I professe it is beyond my care to please the nicenesse of mens palates, with any quaintnesse of language. They who covet more sauce than meat, they must provide cooks to their minde.

John Preston had taught the New Englanders that a minister must know all the arts and sciences in writing his sermons, "yet not to bring forth Eloquence, but to make us more able to Preach the pure Word"; to cover apparel with gold seemed by Puritan standards to spoil it, and so with the Bible, "though the Word may seeme to be gilded with Eloquence or Philosophy, yet it were better that it were alone, for so much of it as is covered with these, so much of the excellencie of the Word is hid." Accordingly the first classes at Harvard were ready to maintain in disputation that it is more excellent to speak aptly than ornately, and that copiousness of words should yield to ornament, and ornament give way to perspicacity.

Following upon these general principles, Puritan discussions found that the virtues of style consisted primarily in the concreteness of phrase used in applications, in the speaking of truths so that the most simple and unlearned of auditors would comprehend them, and in concealing the learning and art by which the composition had been assisted. Christ did not give men "a kind of intimation, afar off what he would," but told them "their own in English as we say. . . . He lets fly poynt blanck." The "greatest plainesse imaginable," even down-right bluntness should be cultivated when ministers "speak home to the Consciences of men."[11] The editor of Perkins' voluminous works praised him "for the manner of his deliuering the same, he condescendeth to the capacitie of the meanest of Gods children"; "my care and study," repeatedly say the New England divines, "was to accommodate it to the meanest hearer." "Let men if they please," boasted Increase Mather, "look on me as One that is . . . *Of a low Style,* which indeed is what I affect"; he thanked his creator that he was not as Cardinal Bembo, "who thought nothing but what is Ciceronian, worth Reading," and who advised authors against studying the Epistles of Paul lest these "should prove some prejudice to their Style in Writings." Any one with education, Mather once declared, would have no trouble in discoursing upon such mysterious subjects as the double nature of Chrisc "after such a Metaphysical strain as none but Scholars should have understood any thing," but it was more difficult, in addition to being more creditable, to stoop lower:

> Let the *learnedest* of us all try when ever we please, we shall find, that to lay this ground work right, that is, *to apply our selves to the capacity of the common Auditory,* and to make an *ignorant* man understand these *Mysteries* in some good measure, will put us to the tryal of our skill, & trouble us a great deal more, than if we were to discuss a *Controversy* or handle a subtile point of Learning in the Schools.

Throughout the century all Puritan manuals advised against quoting "humane testimonies" in the sermon, whether of philosophers or church Fathers, and they roundly condemned the citation of Latin, Greek, or Hebrew sentences, even though immediately translated. All the arts which a minister might use "whilest he is in framing his sermon," he "ought in publike to conceale all these from the people, and not make the least ostentation." As the current Puritan maxim had it, "So much Latine is so much flesh in a Sermon."[12] Quoting in a strange tongue "hinders the conceit of most hearers . . . it is a hiding from them what wee professe." The first requirement of Puritan writing was that it exhibit what Puritans professed, and so they felt that there was no necessity for saying more about style than that it should make the profession clear.

However, during the course of the seventeenth century, Puritans themselves learned some inklings of what is now clear to us, that a great deal depends on just what is meant by "plainness" and "naked simplicity" and "perspicacity." The fact that these are relative concepts began to dawn upon Puritan theorists with the beginning of the Civil Wars, when the hot gospellers and the Antinomians, when Tobias Crisp and James Saltmarsh, commenced to preach and their sermons to appear in widely sold volumes. It then became apparent that there were greater fidelities to Scriptural language than the orthodox Puritans had dreamed of, resulting in a florid and lurid compound of Biblical imagery that was wholly distasteful to judicious theologians; it was then revealed that while Puritans had despised those who preferred the sauce to the meat, they had always wanted at least some sauce on even the best meat, and they were far from happy at the prospect of going without it. They perceived that there were extremes in the applying of theological doctrines concretely and factually to ordinary life which they had no desire to emulate, that the sectarian preachers could practice with a vengeance all their admonitions against citing Latin and Hebrew, since these divines were totally ignorant of the languages; and as for making some things clear to the meanest, when How the cobbler had dared to climb a pulpit, he could give the learned a thousand pointers. In the light of these disclosures, it became obvious then, and it is still more obvious today, that the Puritan literary style was plain only in relation to the less plain styles of contemporaneous metaphysical preachers, of "witty" preachers like Adams and Fuller, of Senecan orators like Hall and Sanderson. It may have been less rhetorical than these modes, but it was still rhetorical; it may have been more popular, but it was still scholarly. It was still a cultivated achievement of the learned that emphasized the distinction between themselves and the "meaner sort." Why should an orator speak "after the vulgar manner, and deliver his mind as a cobler would doe?" asked Wigglesworth in his college oration; "His hearers might then have some ground to say they knew as much as their oratour could teach them." The Puritans subordinated finish to zeal, and they put the maintenance of orthodoxy ahead of the creation of works of art, but their ideal did demand discipline and much care for formal qualities. The manuals called for simplicity, but did not believe that a minister should "come into the place rawly and rudely, without very serious meditation and preparation"; they declared that the "sudden conceits of the minde, not digested, must needs be rawly deliuered, and often little to the purpose." The plain style did not preclude that a man's words "be apt and significant to expresse the matter whereof he speaketh"; since Scripture uses "a godly eloquence," men must endeavor to imitate it, "and it is a grace to speake well, and which may be attained vnto." John Eliot was conspicuous even among the pious of his generation for the simplicity of his spirit, yet "he lik'd no Preaching, but what had been *well studied* for," and he would invoke the Lord to help the ministry "always by good Study to beat our Oyl, that there may be no knots in our Sermons left undissolved." As Cotton Mather said proudly of John Cotton, his "Composures all *Smelt of the* Lamp," and so also, by deliberate intention, did those of every New England preacher in the seventeenth century.

This fact goes far to account for the additional fact that although Puritan authors gave a comprehensive allegiance to the principles of the plain style and methodical structure, there were yet some striking variations among their practices. Everything depended, in short, on how much rhetoric was thought compatible with "naked simplicity." Obviously Bishop Andrewes or Thomas Adams used too much, but nevertheless some degree of it, some embellishment with tropes and figures, some use of similes and word-patterns, at least a few devices of formal eloquence, were not inconsistent with "painful" preaching. There were also the considerations of time and place. Whether Nathaniel Ward preached in the style of the Simple Cobler is unknown; probably he did not, but when writing a secular book addressed to his warring countrymen, there was no reason in the Puritan tradition why he should not go the limit, as he did, in parading the turns of rhetoric, coining words, quoting Latin, and devising intricate schemata. Joshua Moody, preaching in 1674 before the Ancient and Honourable Artillery Company, professed that "had I been to handle the same *Head of Divinity* on another occasion and before another Auditory, I could and should have sought out other words," but since it was incumbent upon any orator to "take Measure of his Theam to cut out his Language by, and make it up something according to the mode of his Auditory," he gave the Company a highly rhetorical discourse that is possibly the most ornate and colored of all early New England writings, full of sustained metaphors and complicated schemata. The historian Edward Johnson had not been to the university, but had given himself some kind of education, in which he would inevitably have included a study of rhetoric, and therefore attempted in *The Wonder-Working Providence of Sions Saviour in New England* to write with a copious use of rhetorical flowers, though hardly with what we can call artistic success. Even among preachers of the immigrant generation, there were great differences; John Cotton adhered fairly strictly to the ideals of plain speech, whereas in Shepard or Hooker appear more freely all the tropes listed in Talon and many of the schemata. Of the later generations, Urian Oakes, for instance, followed the examples of Shepard and Hooker, and won the praise of his contemporaries for being a "Master of the true, pure, *Ciceronian* Latin & Language," which Ciceronianism he would exemplify in English in a "copious and florid Oration," whereas Increase Mather won equal esteem for keeping continually in view "plainness, perspicuity, gravity in delivering the Truth," abandoning "all Additional Ornaments whatever, betaking himself alone unto the Exercise of a sound Judgment and Spiritual Wisdom, in giving Evidence and Authority unto the Truth." Even though Puritan manuals frowned upon Latin quotations or the instancing of "humane authorities," learned New Englanders could not resist occasional exhibitions of their erudition, and the people did not seem to object. This bent toward rhetorical ornament and plentiful citation was most indulged among New England writers by Cotton Mather, who had to defend his *Magnalia* against the charge of being "Embellished with too much of *Ornament,* by the multiplied References to other and former Concerns, closely couch'd, for the Observation of the *Attentive,* in almost every Paragraph." Samuel Mather rather lamely apologized for him: "It is next to impossible, that a Man should keep from *writing learnedly,* and as if he were acquainted with Author's and their Sentiments, when his Mind is stored with their *various Ideas* and Images, and he is a compleat *Owner* of them." Other divines often yielded to the like temptation, for they also were acquainted with authors, though fortunately their range was generally more circumscribed and their taste more highly sensitive, so that they did not commit the absurdities which fill the pages of Cotton Mather. Of course, by his time the old rhetoric was waning and the earlier standards becoming less precise, so that he is not to be taken altogether as a product of genuine Puritan instruction, yet even for his day he went to extremes. His biographer acknowledged that "his Treatises were *stuck with Jewels,"* but attempted to deny they were *"burthen'd* with them"; "No, There were just eno' to render a strong and easy *Splendor."* However, Judge Samuel Sewall, who better remembered what the first generations had held, found himself "somewhat disgusted" by Cotton's filling a sermon with such expressions "as, sweet sented hands of Christ, Lord High Treasurer of Æthopia, Ribband of Humility," and was all the more sorry for them "because of the excellency and seasonableness of the subject, and otherwise well handled."

The moral would thus appear to be that even within the limits of Puritan theory considerable freedom was possible in practice. Even the division into doctrine, reasons, and uses was not absolutely obligatory; if Cotton Mather's account is to be trusted, John Wilson, the colleague of Cotton at Boston, used to preach in his younger years in the methodical way, "and was therefore admired above many, by no less auditors than Dr. Goodwin,

Mr. Burroughs, and Mr. Bridge, when they travelled from Cambridge into Essex, on purpose to observe the ministers in that county," but after becoming a New Englander he left the methodical way to his more methodical colleague, "and gave himself a liberty to *preach* more after the primitive manner, without any distinct propositions, but chiefly in exhortations and admonitions, and good wholesome councils, tending to excite good motions in the minds of his hearers." If there were many Puritans preachers like Wilson, then there were more sermons delivered than survive in print like the exhortatory utterances of the sectarians, for the hall-mark of these was generally their omission of "distinct propositions," but it should be noted that Wilson's evangelical excitations were made only "upon some texts that were doctrinally handled by his colleague instantly before." In brief, whatever the differences among Puritan writers, from the rhetoric of Nathaniel Ward and Cotton Mather to the simplicity of William Bradford, whatever the divergence in their sermon styles, from the rigor of John Cotton to the impassioned eloquence of Thomas Hooker, the guiding principle was the assurance that content was more important than form, that the essence of any composition was the doctrinal handling of the text, and that style was a secondary concern, a dress or an ornament, that could be varied to suit times and places, that could be furnished with more or less rhetoric, that could be ornamented with many or with few tropes, the only universal requirement being that the eloquence must not interfere with the major purpose of impressing a Gospel theorem upon the minds of listeners and readers, that it serve as a legitimate means for exciting good affections, and never become an artistic end in itself. Even if he had been able to answer any man's desire in daintiness of speech, said Hooker, he would not so have injured his matter; "The substance and solidity of the frame is that, which pleaseth the builder, its the painters work to provide varnish." Literary style in the Puritan aesthetic was "varnish"; it was useful, even commendable, and a good workman should know how to apply it, but his first consideration always was to secure the substance and solidity of the frame.[13]

It will be seen at once that this was exactly the conclusion of Ramist doctrine, the aesthetic moral implied by Ramus' detaching the laws of invention, disposition, and memory from the art of rhetoric and leaving as an adequate body of instruction for teaching the "ars bene dicendi" merely the precepts of elocution and pronunciation. It would, again, be attributing too much weight to an academic influence even in an age when the intellectual life centered upon universities, to argue that Puritan style resulted from the teachings of Talon. But the Puritan temperament and Talon's doctrine obviously fitted together; Puritan taste would determine that the Puritans choose his rhetoric instead of the Aristotelians', and then, once it became their textbook, it would accentuate their taste and confirm their natural inclination. When John Norton translated from Latin into English the letter he and other New England parsons had written to John Dury, he apologized because in the vernacular "much of the Elegancy" of the words was taken away; his conception of elegance then revealed itself when he said that books like bodies "are nothing so comely when arrayed with a strangers, as with their own proper clothing and habit," but nevertheless, he had so contrived it that "wherever appeared a necessity of changing the phrase, the sense is preserved whole and entire." Preserving the whole sense was all-important; afterwards the dress could be arranged. John Saffin sang the praises of Samuel Lee because although his style was "florid", yet it was also

full of Sence,
So fraught with Rhetorick, and with Eloquence
With all Accomplishments of every sort.[14]

Saffin found similar virtues in William Hubbard's "most exact History of New-England Troubles":

Such is thy modest Stile enrich'd with Sence,
Invention fine, faced with Eloquence:
Thy *florid Language* quaintly doth express
The *Truth* of matter in a comely Dress;
Couching the Sence in such a pleasing Strain
As makes the *Readers* Heart to leap again.

Reading the Bible according to this conception of rhetoric, Puritans found the Song of Songs its most eloquent book, "with more store of more sweet and precious, exquisite and amiable Resemblances, taken from the richest Jewels, the sweetest Spices, Gardens, Orchards, Vineyards, Winecellars, and the chiefest beauties of all the workes of God and Man," but they read it primarily for its "truth of matter," which was a series of propositions concerning the great love of Christ for the way of the churches in New England, and looked upon all its amiable resemblances as eloquent facing, as a comely dress, making the heart leap. When John Cotton preached upon Canticles, he analyzed its verses by the laws of invention and disposition, and he rigorously compressed its metaphors into theological prose.

Talon's *Rhetorica* aided this sort of analysis and pointed to the kind of eloquence which Puritans cultivated. Yet they had to place certain curbs even upon it. Ramus and Talon had divided elocution into tropes and figures; the metaphysical and the witty sermons depended more for their effects upon figures than upon tropes; they were built upon the schemata of balance, antithesis, parallelism, and assonance in the sentence more than upon similes and metaphors in the words. Puritan orators found a few of these schemata, like exclamation or dialogue, very effective in their applications, but they perceived that too large a dependence upon schemata always became a tendency to forget the "Sence" in the fascination of the eloquence. Therefore the Puritan doctrine demanded extreme caution in the use of figures and advised in general that preachers speak in simple indicative sentences; but tropes, being more obviously facings, more clearly supernumerary additions to the content, separable raiment merely decorating the propositions, were considered more admirable. "Trope is to the learned the sweetest part of elocution, figure to the unlearned," declared a Harvard thesis in 1678, reflecting a passage in the *Medulla* where Ames had acknowledged that the Prophets and Apostles had employed both tropes and figures, but insisted that "Figures of words, which consists in likenesse of sounds, measures, and repetions," were the less frequent. The reasons, he said, were clear, and he enumerated them in Puritan fashion: first, "the harmony of elocution is the lighter part of Rhetoricke, which more agreeth to light persons and things, then to grave, sacred and divine"; second, they serve "only for naturall delight, not for spirituall edification"; and third, they hinder demonstrations of the spirit, so that those "doe foolishly therefore which in their Sermons, affect sounds ending alike, but specially they which propound such rimes in unknowne Latine or Greeke words." The most useful tropes, in the Puritan view, were those which could be worked into the text after the abstract proposition had been posed: similes, metaphors, illustrations, and examples. By facing their doctrines with comparisons, by announcing flatly that this truth is comparable to this fact or to such and such an experience, they could achieve the ends of rhetoric, appeal to the sensible soul by a sensory image, and yet the doctrine would not be submerged in the rhetoric.

> Amongst these three wayes of teaching: Authority, Reason, & Example: the last is peculiarly accommodated to the capacitie & nature of man, as that which both inlightens & affects. Examples make difficult things plain, and doubtfull things certain . . . upon the reception whereof, all experience attests unto a perswasive & operative influence, concomitant in rational subjects.

Examples and comparisons were the best means for sugaring the pill; "it will goe downe the better," says Hooker in a metaphor. "When we read only of Doctrines, these may reach the understanding, but when we read or hear of Examples, humane affection doth as it were represent to us the case as our own." Thus if Puritan sermons are read in comparison with the sermons of other English factions, the most marked technical feature of their style appears to be the similes and examples, whereas the others exhibit a wider range of sentence figures. One or two passages taken at random will show us in the shortest possible compass the essential qualities of the Puritan style in its contemporaneous setting. The rhetoric of John Donne reveals itself in this quotation as primarily a manipulation of schemata:

Let the head be gold, and the armes silver, and the belly brasse, if the feete be clay, Men that may slip, and molder away, all is but an Image, all is but a dreame of an Image; for forraine helps are rather crutches then legs. There must be bodies, Men, and able bodies, able men; Men that eate the good things of the land, their owne figges and olives; Men not macerated with extortions: They are glorified bodies that make up the kingdome of Heaven; bodies that partake of the good of the State, that make up the State.[15]

The same dependence upon "likenesse of sounds, measures, and repetions" is manifested in the style of Thomas Adams as he portrays the hypocrite:

Hee hath a flushing in his face, as if he had eaten fire; zeale burnes in his tongue, but come neere this gloe-worme, and he is cold, darke, squallid. Summer sweates in his face, winter freeseth in his conscience: March, many forwards in his words, December in his actions; pepper is not more hot in the tongues end, nor more cold at heart; and (to borrow the words of our worthy Diuine and best Character) wee think him a Saint, hee thinks himselfe an Angell, flatterers make him a God, GOD knowes him a Deuill.[16]

And then, to take a characteristic Puritan passage, the plain-speaking John Cotton, making the distinction between a true saint and a hypocrite, illustrates it thus:

Observe when those ends part, which will be at one time or other. When two men walk together, a dog follows them, you know not whose it is, but let them part, then the dog will follow his Master.

The more eloquent Hooker shines best in his comparisons, but he shows the ultimate limit of Puritan ornamentation in typical similes; this one, for instance, in his more homely vein, is on the resurrected body:

It is in the nature of many things to increase, when as nothing is added unto them: As may be observed in an Onyon, take a great Onyon, and hang it up in the house, and it will grow bigger and bigger: what is the cause of it? not because any thing is added, but because it spreads itself further; so then there shall be no new body, but the same substance enlarged and increased.

In his happier moments his images are more moving, as when he thus explains how the reprobate are responsible for their own fate:

Looke as it is with a childe that travels to a Faire with his father, or goeth into a crowd, his eye is alwayes upon his father: he bids him doe not gaze about and lose mee, the childe is carefull to keepe his father within sight and view, and then if hee bee weake and weary, his father can take him by the hand, and lead him, or take him into his armes and carry him; or if there be any thing hee wants, or would have, his father can buy it for him, bestow it upon him; but if the childe bee carelesse and gazeth about this thing and that thing, and never lookes after his father; hee is gone one way, and his father another, he cannot tell where to finde him: whose fault is it now? it is not because his father would not be within his sight, or because hee could not keepe within the view of him, but because hee out of carelessnesse lost the sight of his father.

The contrast of these passages tells in summary the whole story of Puritan style and of the Puritan mind. Donne's balance of head, arms, and belly, with gold, silver, and brass, Adams' antithesis of March in the words and December in the actions, and then the Puritan's homely illustrations: the resurrected body is like an onion, the reprobate is like a careless child, and the appended moral in unmistakable prose—to this difference in technique the Puritan conception of logic and rhetoric, the Puritan reading of "the capacitie & nature of man," and the Puritan piety led the Puritan orator.

The supreme criterion of the style was, inescapably, the doctrine of means. Metaphors were more prized than antitheses, similes more admired than assonances, because they were better instruments for convincing the mind and moving the passions. Scripture itself used "earthly Similitudes," comparisons and parables, to convey truth "to us under sensible things, things that wee can feele, because that we are lead with senses in this life." The choice of words was subordinated to the selection of matter, because men are humbled by matter rather than manner. In preface after preface New England authors explained that their sermons were stylistically "unfit . . . for the vein of this curious carping Age," but that they always intended "to edifie more then to please, any further than pleasing is a means to edification."[17] Increase Mather "was very careful to be *understood,* and *concealed* every other *Art,* that he might Pursue and Practise that one *Art* of *Being Inteligible,*" and proudly affirmed that his *"Simple Discourses,* which they that account themselves the Wits of the World, look upon as *Babling,* will either be blessed by Christ for the Conversion and Edification of Souls, or turn for a Testimony to the Speaker." The danger that artistic cultivation might become an impediment to intelligibility lay behind the Puritan rejection of all other prose styles of the day. Richard Baxter expressed the aesthetic standard when he declared "painted obscure sermons" to be "like the Painted Glass in the Windows that keep out the Light."[18] The iconoclasm of the New Model Army was not vandalism, it was artistic criticism; neither Cromwell's soldiers nor the New England ministers could perceive anything beautiful in the sermons of John Donne or the stained glass which they tossed upon rubbish heaps: both alike "kept out the Light." Excess ornamentation in the sermon was impious in Perkins' eyes because it required "absurd, insolent and prodigious cogitations, and those especially, which set an edge upon and kindle the most corrupt affections of the flesh." It was sinful in the eyes of Bernard because it glorified man rather than God, for metaphysical preachers "weigh euery word they intend to vtter in the balance of mans corrupt imagination, marking how tuneable to the eare, how farre from offending, how expressing wit and conceits and all for an applaudite for their owne praise, not caring at all how little they shall profit their hearers, or how well before God they discharge their duties." It was damnable in Ames's judgment because it prevented understanding:

> When the speech is carried on like a swift stream, although it catch many things of all sorts, yet you can hold fast but a little, you can catch but a little, you cannot find where you may constantly rest: but when certaine rules are delivered, the Reader hath, alwayes, as it were at every pace, the place marked where he may set his foot.

And when we come to the bottom of these criticisms, we shall find always that there is a social implication which, in historical terms, may perhaps be the basic explanation for the differences in style. John Donne declared that it was good art both "to deliver deep points in a holy plainness, and plain points in a holy delightfulness," because without the first the unlearned part of our auditory will not understand us, but without the second, "another part understands us before we begin, and so they are weary." [19] Certainly one large factor in inspiring metaphysical and courtly preachers to deliver plain points with holy delightfulness was their consciousness that a large part of their audience would be bored unless regaled with rhetorical brilliance, but the Puritan asserted that the preacher should be as plain as possible so "that he may be understood by the lowest Capacities," and at the same time "so Solid and Rational as that he may be admired by the greatest Divines." The uneducated in both a Puritan congregation and in John Donne's would need deep points delivered to them with holy plainness, but in a Puritan assembly the educated would not grow weary when plain points were not made delightful; educated Puritans did not find life that dull, and they were awakened not by elocution but by solidity and rationality.

We have spoken thus far of style only in the sermon. There were, of course, other types of expression in New England of the seventeenth century, the histories, diaries, narratives of travel and of special providences, biographies, and above all the poetry. There is no occasion in this study for a review of Puritan literature; it is enough to point out that the authors of that literature, who in most cases were divines, did not conceive of themselves as writing in literary genres. They had practically no sense of what we might call belles-lettres, and all their writings were simply other ways of achieving the same ends they were seeking in their sermons; histories, poems, or tracts were treatises on the will of God as revealed in nature, experience, history, or individual lives, and the style was determined by precisely the same considerations and the same rhetorical doctrines as governed the sermons. Daniel Gookin was not a parson, but he declared that he had, "through the grace of Christ," transmitted his *Historical Collec-*

tions of the Indians in New England to the reader, "not clothed in elegancy of words and accurate sentences; but rather I have endeavoured all plainness that I can, that the most vulgar capacity might understand, and be thereby excited to praise and glorify God . . ." Histories, in other words, were first of all means, and the plain style, with its qualities determined by the requirements of a means, was as fitting for them as for orations.

It is a desireable thing, that all the loving kindnesses of God, and his singular favours to this poor and despised out cast might be Chronicled and communicated (in the History of them) to succeeding Ages; that the memory of them may not dy and be extinct, with the present Generation.

To chronicle the providence of God in the settlement of New England was the entire purpose of the New England historians, of Bradford, Johnson, Hubbard, Gookin, Winthrop, and the Mathers; consequently, for them subject-matter was primary, and a style which was basically designed for conveying the subject-matter of theology served perfectly for their narratives. Even the Puritan letter was written in the style of a pulpit discourse, and Margaret Winthrop said of one epistle from her loving husband—she was paying it the most extravagant of compliments—that it had served her in the place of a sermon.

The poetry of early New Englanders has been variously exhumed and studied in recent scholarship, and probably more attention has been devoted to it than either the intrinsic or historical value of the verse will justify. However, I do not believe that hitherto it has been connected with the background of rhetorical theory, and some tenets in the Ramist doctrine help as much as those in the religious creed to account for the Puritan attitude toward poetry. To a Ramist rhetorician, verse was simply a heightened form of eloquence, it was speech more plenteously ornamented with tropes and figures than prose, but still speech; like the oration, its function was to carry inartificial arguments from man to man. Poetry as well as prose, according to Richardson, was bestowed by God as a part of rhetoric, not because it was necessary in respect of things, but in respect of men, so that men might understand things more easily. Therefore "Rhetorick serves to deliver the matter more soberly and gravely; and Poetry yet makes it more fine where all things must be done by measure and sweet sounds." Before the fall, Richardson suggests, Adam must have spoken naturally in poetry, but now "we know some men are not delighted at all with Poetry; which if it be from their nature that they despise it, it argueth a distemperature of it, otherwise 'tis wisdom in others." This theory incorporated verse into the scheme of God's creation, among the arts arranged in technologia, but only at the cost of putting upon it the same restrictions placed upon prose style. Poetry existed primarily for its utility, it was foredoomed to didacticism, and because it was the most highly ornate of the arts, it was always in grave danger of overstepping proper limits and becoming pleasing for its own sake. "Poetry," said Richardson, "may . . . be compared to a fine Frenchman of the French fashion, or to a Courtier: Oratory to a grave Alderman." Puritans were not usually very hospitable to either fine Frenchmen or courtiers; they were at home with grave aldermen. Hence the New England parsons who put the Psalms into what they were pleased to call meter did not worry about their poetic shortcomings: "Wee have . . . attended Conscience rather then Elegance, fidelity rather then poetry. . . Gods Altar needs not our pollishings." Wigglesworth wrote verses when he was too ill to preach, proposing therein "the Edification of such Readers, as are for Truth's dressed up in a *Plain Meeter,*" and Jonathan Mitchell prefaced the versified *Day of Doom* with a religious rationalization which he borrowed from the Anglican Herbert: "A Verse may find him who a Sermon flies." Poetry in Puritan eyes, therefore, was a species of rhetoric, a dress for great truths, a sugar for the pill. Only some two persons in seventeenth-century New England have left any evidence that they were deeply imbued with a true poetic insight; the greater of these, the Reverend Edward Taylor of the frontier village of Westfield, set forth the poetical theory of Puritanism all the more arrestingly for our purposes since he phrased it in the language of psychology. The elegance, the dress and fine embellishment of poetry he conceived as the creations of fancy. A poet discoursing upon worldly topics may be permitted, even by Puritan standards, to "invent" exotic conceits and startling figures to enhance his subject or to win belief for his inartificial arguments, but when he comes to the solid truths of religion he will find the products of human ingenuity, the spawn of a finite imagination, inadequate and irrelevant. Taylor's verse combines into one motif the themes of the limitation of human faculties and of the theological necessity for a plain style even in poetry:

I fain would have a rich, fine Phansy ripe
  That Curious pollishings elaborate
Should lay, Lord, on thy glorious Body bright
  The more my lumpish heart to animate.
  But searching o're the Workhouse of my minde,
  I but one there; and dul and meger finde.

Hence, Lord, my Search hand thou from this dark Shop
  (Its foule, and wanteth Sweeping) vp vnto
Thy Glorious Body whose bright beames let drop
  Vpon my heart: and Chant it with the Show,
  Because the Shine that from thy body flows,
  More glorious it then is the brightest Rose.[20]

The other of the true New England poets, Anne Bradstreet, expressed the gist of the matter more succinctly: "I haue not studyed in this yov read to show my skill, but to declare the Truth—not to sett forth myself, but the Glory of God."

Upon reviewing the results of our study, we might reflect that any criticism which endeavors to discuss Puritan writings as part of literary history, which seeks to estimate them from any "aesthetic" point of view, is approaching the materials in a spirit they were never intended to accommodate, and is in danger of concluding with pronouncements which are wholly irrelevant to the designs and motives of the writers. Up to the point at which their rhetorical theory permitted a care for form, the form may be criticized, but hardly beyond that. We shall do nothing but misread the literature if we do not always remember how their great teacher, William Ames, had told the Puritans, "That key is to be chosen which doth open best, although it be of wood, if there be not a golden key of the same efficacy." The undoubtedly excessive number of quotations in which I have indulged this work offer enough samples of Puritan expression to enable the reader to form his own impressions of Puritan literary competence. However, if our study of stylistic theory does not lead to definite critical estimation, it does point up once more certain elements in the historical situation and the consequent effects upon the Puritan mind. In their concept of style as in their theories of nature, Puritans mingled attitudes of Christian piety with ideas inherited from secular accretions. Augustine and Ramus coöperated to produce the doctrine of the plain style; social pressure coincided with ideology to create the profitable method of organizing a sermon in doctrine, reasons, and uses. The manner incarnated the thought, it reflected the spirit of the thinkers; the technique as well as the content of the writings exhibited the combination of deep religious passion and severe intellectual discipline which is the supreme characteristic of Puritanism. The style was adapted to the dual purpose of preaching a truth revealed arbitrarily from on high, but also manifested naturally in the order of things and in the laws of reason, of showing how men were tangled in the insanity of depravity and yet could remain fundamentally logical. Aided by formal logic and rhetoric, the Puritans constructed their doctrine of style upon their assumption that beauty is the efficient order of things, and saw nothing incongruous in making the manner of their expression serve simultaneously to advance the glory of God and to cement the social or ecclesiastical order. As William Perkins said in the first of the Puritan manuals, the speech must be both spiritual and graceful, "both simple and perspicuous, fit both for the peoples understanding, and to expresse the Majestie of the Spirit." Occasional passages may even now manage to express for us something of the majesty of the spirit; granted a Puritan community, probably many that are dull to us then succeeded in being majestic, but there can be no doubt that every word uttered from New England pulpits was eminently fitted for the people's understanding.

BOOK IV

SOCIOLOGY

CHAPTER XIII

THE COVENANT OF GRACE[1]

As far as we have now surveyed it, Puritan thought has exhibited a composite of ideas originated neither by Puritans nor in the seventeenth century. That it was so little original ought not to be surprising; originality in any age is rare, and there were many reasons why Puritans should have kept an exceptionally tenacious grip upon the past. Their piety, like that of all Protestants, was understood to be no new thing under the sun but a resurrection of primitive Christianity, and they were willing, they were positively eager, that it be couched in a formal theology long since established. In philosophy, science, and literature their culture was wholly academic and traditional; even in those departments where they had taken the side of innovation, in logic and rhetoric, they had ostensibly gone no further than to reform the medieval trivium and quadrivium; by 1630 this impulse had spent itself, been stabilized in a system and become respectable in the universities to which the saints looked for guidance. No Puritan perceived that the Ramist critique of scholasticism was merely the prologue to still more fundamental revisions, that already Copernicus, Bacon, and Descartes were setting in motion forces which in a few decades would cast the inherited knowledge into limbo. Puritans had indeed appropriated the new learning of humanism, but not because it was new; it too purported to be a revival, a return to a crystalline past, and in the Puritan curriculum it was incorporated into the conventional precepts of the arts and jealously guarded against introducing new heresies. Every student in New England assumed that the entire terrain of the mind was explored in technologia's map of the disciplines. Puritans lived in a fixed, limited, and unalterable universe, appointed by God and every part of it known; they were intellectual conservatives, who constantly denounced "novelty" as a sin and held it a high tribute to any theologian that "he ever kept the ancient received Doctrine . . . nor did he . . . seek a new path in the old way." They were quite content with their universe, even though it had been the scene of man's fall; they believed that God had created it by perfect wisdom, and that it was just such a universe as men should live in. They had no conscious intention of disturbing its outlines or widening its horizons.

However, all good Puritans knew that man proposes and God disposes, and that sometimes He demands of His creatures what they of themselves would think incompatible with His own interests. Through His inscrutable providence He so ordained events in the early seventeenth century that there arose out of the reformed confessions heresies as reprehensible as the Popery against which the confessions had been framed, and thus He demanded certain extensions of orthodoxy in order that it might counteract new errors. This, after all, was a way in which He frequently worked; "though the being of heresies be a great evill," He sometimes uses them for His own ends, since "opposition begets disputation, that removes objections, and clears the trueth." Accordingly, between 1600 and 1650, English Puritans were compelled, in order to preserve the truths already known, to add to their theology at least one that hitherto had not been known, or at least not emphasized, the doctrine of the Covenant of Grace. Strictly speaking, this was no more an invention of their own than the doctrine of original sin; they cited Biblical proof to show that it had always been contained in revelation, and it had been touched upon by previous theologians; still, none elsewhere made it so all-important, so central to the whole structure of belief, as did these Englishmen. It should be said at once that only a restricted group even of English Puritans concentrated their thinking upon it; not all the party shared the sense, so keen among members of the school, that without it the whole Protestant edifice stood in danger of internal collapse, but the New England leaders were all pupils, friends, or disciples of those who formulated it. Consequently, the intellectual history of New England must commence with some notice of these covenant or, as they were then called, "federal" theologians and of the forces in the English and European background which instigated their discoveries.

The development of the theory must be viewed as a part of that seventeenth-century systematization of Calvinism on which we have already remarked. It was one result of the effort to provide reformed doctrine with the "method", the scholastical integration, which at the moment was everywhere felt to be supremely necessary, in order that the theology might, in the words of Ames, "bee understood, known, and committed to memory." It was designed to counteract certain weaknesses in the original creed, which might have required strengthening even without the heresies, but which, being particularly strained by these defections, revealed the need for reinforcement. When the Puritan movement commenced, in the 1560's and 1570's, the field of agreement between the opponents was much larger than the field of controversy; Elizabethan bishops were "sound" on the theology of depravity, irresistible grace, and reprobation, as even the arch-foe of the Puritans, Whitgift, demonstrated in his *Lambeth Articles*. As an anachronistic survival from this initial phase, the New Englanders as late as 1700 persisted in asserting their cordial agreement with the true doctrine of the Church of England and still protested that they had never "separated" from the communion, although by then such protests had become pointless. But in 1570 the only issue in dispute was church polity; Puritans entered the fray assuming that once this engagement were won, no further battles were to be fought, and they were more and more dismayed to find that the war enlarged its limits, that enemies appeared where they had assumed none could exist. The worst of it was that many of these new opponents had fought originally in their own ranks, or at least were armed with weapons from their arsenals. As controversy spread from the church to doctrine, Puritans had to defend their position not only against Anglicans but against two revolts within their own camp, against what was known at the time as "Arminianism" and against what for the sake of convenience we may call "Antinomianism". Both these errors sprang from orthodox Calvinism, both ended by repudiating certain fundamental doctrines, and both were driven to their conclusions by a sense of Calvinism's deficiencies. The group of Puritans who made up the federal school endeavored to forestall Arminians and Antinomians by their doctrine of the Covenant of Grace, believing it no essential alteration of orthodox theology but a legitimate extension of its implication. The intellectual history of the century was to prove them sadly mistaken, and their imposition of the covenant doctrine upon the system of Calvin produced at last in the New England theology an altogether different philosophy from any propounded in Geneva.

"Arminianism" is an ambiguous term, for it means both the theology developed in Holland by Arminius and his followers, and also the doctrine of the Laudian party in England, although the Anglicans did not necessarily import it from across the Channel. In both cases, certain theologians were reacting against Calvinism, and especially against what they found to be its ethical absolutism. It seemed to these critics devoid of any grounds for moral obligation: what duties could be exacted from ordinary men when everything depended upon a mysterious decree of election? Calvin himself had simply brushed aside such frivolous cavils, magisterially declaring, "Man, being taught that he has nothing good left in his possession, and being surrounded on every side with the most miserable necessity, should, nevertheless, be instructed to aspire to the good of which he is destitute";[2] but by 1600 divines were more hard pressed to answer the intensely human rejoinder, "Yes, but if I am not elected, I can do nothing, and why should I try?" They could no longer overcome this scruple by crying with Calvin, "Away, then, with such corrupt and sacrilegious perversions of the whole order of election."[3] Theologians like Perkins or Ames preached that a man must be "a meere patient in the first acte of conuersion to God," but were compelled to add that, notwithstanding, he could perform duties which "are in themselves good." What wonder exasperated laymen grew restive when divines said "that this was so from all eternity, and that God is unchangeable in his Decrees," and yet also said "that the wicked may save themselves if they will, and it is their own fault that they are damned"? How could the laymen be prevented from finding in these statements "such diametrical opposites, and contradictory sayings, as there are not clearer in the world"?[4] When Ames would announce, "The Calling of men doth not in any sort depend upon the dignity, honesty, industry, or any indeavour of the called, but upon election and predestination of God only," why should not men reply, "Then let us cast care away, let us sweare, and ryot, and drinke, and live as we list, we heare that all the duties that we can do, will not save us"? If but few are chosen no matter what their crimes and many are damned no matter what their virtues, "for what end is it then to pray to endeavour a change of life, or to repent, for if there be such an unresistable decree past against me, what hope is there?" It was not enough to silence these demurrers by flat assertions that sanctification follows justification or by rhetorical questions embellished with tropes, such as, "A Maid that knowes she shall be married such a day, will it make her the less careful to adorn her self?" Humanity could see less and less reason for caring about moral adornments if its spiritual nuptials were arranged before the courtship had begun. The divines had to discover some more explicit grounds on which to plead the necessity of "works", but to discover them without sacrificing the absolute freedom of God to choose and reject regardless of man's achievements. Otherwise, Calvin's splendid vision of God's omnipotence would become, when taught to men of weaker resolution, an excuse for their licentiousness and a justification of their indolence.

The pressure for an orthodox resolution of the problem became imperative after Arminius declared that the efficacy of grace "depends on the will of man, in regard that by vertue of its native liberty, it may receive or reject this grace, use it or not use it, render it effectuall or vain." Once this were admitted, the field would be thrown open to human initiative and a definite inducement offered to moral exertion, for according to Arminius, "if we do what we can, and improve the natural abilities we have, and the means we do enjoy God wil not deny to give us the grace supernatural we want." Of course, anyone truly imbued with Augustinian piety could see the fallacy of this argument: to suspend "the converting grace of God upon the free will of the creature," to make "Gods free grace lackey after mans free wil," was to commit both the intellectual mistake of giving the finite a veto upon the infinite and the spiritual crime of destroying all hope of salvation, "for if none should be saved but those that do what they can, its certayn never any man either in nature or grace did what he could." If men's hopes hang upon their performances, "they must needs have their lives and their everlasting condition ever in doubt and suspence, and in issue sink down in everlasting discouragement." Puritans believed literally that did all men get their just deserts, who should 'scape hanging? But human nature showed an ineradicable tendency to think better of itself. The fact that the Arminians were solemnly condemned, without a fair hearing, by the assembled pundits of the reformed churches at Dort weighed less with many Englishmen than that Arminianism made living more attractive. As John Hales listened to Episcopius, he then and there "bade John Calvin good-night." William Ames might sneer that Arminian grace "may be the effect of a good dinner sometimes," but unless he could find more persuasive deterrents than sweeping denunciations of "rank and palpable Pelagianisme and Arminianisme" or baseless accusations that Arminian viands were furnished from the Jesuits' cellar,[5] the multitude would prefer to feast with Arminians on freedom of the will than to gnaw with him on the dry bones of natural inability.

Puritan divines did not mend matters when, to confute the belief that faith is given for good works, they told the people that God "giveth himselfe first in order of nature, before he giveth any thing else accompanying Salvation . . . and with him[self,] Faith, and so worketh our wills unto himselfe." Arminius asked if a beggar, to whom a passing monarch tosses a coin, could not reach out his hand for it; Puritans replied that when Christ raised Lazarus, "now dead and smelling in the Grave," He put a soul into the body "without any causal concurrence of help of *Lazarus*." When the soul divorces its lusts, said Hooker, it is moved "as under the power, and in the vertue of the motion of the Spirit"; it is "only a sufferer and acts not, but is acted upon." Such statements might help the multitude to understand that regeneration was an inward ecstasy and not a ribbon of merit for distinguished services, but they then gave rise to a further reflection: since the recipient of grace is assured of salvation without ever doing anything to deserve it, should he not surrender to the intoxication of certainty and give no further thought to his behavior? If the elect are joined to Christ so that they move not of themselves but by the spirit within them, and if they are sure of their vocation, why need anyone study the commandments or fear condemnation for his sins?

This conclusion is substantially what was meant by "Antinomianism". In the early years of the century it was not so pressing a danger as Arminianism, being advanced only by surreptitious groups of Familists or

Anabaptists, but it became more formidable to Puritans in both Englands after Anne Hutchinson broached it in Boston. She caused a greater sensation than the numerical strength of her following might indicate, for she dramatized the heresy as a logical outcome of orthodox doctrine, and forecast what Puritan divines in England were to confront during the Civil Wars, when the sects came out of hiding and Cromwell gave them toleration in spite of the remonstrance of his New England cousins. It is no doubt inexact to label all these sects "Antinomians", yet most of them, Anabaptists, Quakers, Ranters, Levellers, or what-not, came to their various opinions from a common belief that the union of the elect with the Holy Ghost is immediate and intimate. If Arminianism resulted from a feeling that Calvin was deficient in ethical sanctions, Antinomianism came from a conviction that it did not go far enough with the doctrine of assurance.

Thus Antinomianism was one result of a movement which had long been maturing in Puritan circles. We have seen that Protestantism in general had gone beyond Augustine in asserting that the saints might come to an assurance of their election, and that theologians after Calvin had made certainty still more feasible in order to underline the error of Popery. But we have also seen that all was not plain sailing; the elect were not always certain, they had their fluctuations of doubt and their melancholy lapses from grace. The best of them were imperfectly sanctified. Calvin had wisely advised caution in promising positive assurance, since predestination takes place in the inmost recesses of divine wisdom, where the careless intruder may obtain no satisfaction, "but will enter a labyrinth from which he will find no way to depart."[6] To him it seemed unreasonable that men should scrutinize what the Lord had hidden in Himself—which was enough for men of 1550, but not for men of 1600, who wanted to know more definitely what there was in it for themselves. They could not forever be incited to faith or sustained upon the high level of intensity without the prospect of tangible reward. But the more the ministers probed into cases of conscience and the more they became versed in the mysterious ways of Jehovah the more they were forced to qualify the doctrine of assurance, to declare that "Christ may come into thy soule, and thou dost not know him," to draw metaphysical distinctions between the object of assurance as "sealed to all true believers" and "the perceiving of it, which is called a certainty of the subject," and which, alas, "is not alwayes present to all." Forthright and practical men, particularly if not trained to distinguish between artificial and inartificial arguments, grew restive when told to make their callings sure and yet were warned that "it may and often doth come to passe, either through weaknesse of judgement, or through divers tentations and troubles of mind, that he, who truly believeth, and is by Faith justified before God, yet for a time may thinke according to that which hee feeles, that he neither believeth, nor is reconciled to God."

The various forms of Antinomianism were popular revulsions against these subtleties of discrimination, asserting that if there is faith in the heart, it will not lay hidden, it will not "stagger and waver." Thomas Maule, the Salem Quaker, boasted,

> Humane Learning I have not,
>   God doth to me afford
> His Teaching by his Spirit good
>   To understand his Word,[7]

and by the light of the spirit he found it antichristian "to perswade People, that God is not willing to give Power to them that truely believe in him, to perform what he requires of his People, that is, to keep all his Commandments, according as he hath commanded, . . . that is, to be free from sin." [8] Declaring that "no imperfect thing can enter the Kingdom of Heaven," [9] and that therefore believers must be made perfect, the sectarians simplified all problems of election, regeneration, assurance, and imperfect sanctification with an absolute assurance, an immediate and personal revelation. They preached such an inward union of man with Christ "as in the root and branches, head and members," so that the man and the Redeemer became as one tree or one person. Ames had admitted that the existence of divers degrees of persuasion was a detriment to "that consolation and peace which Christ hath left to believers"; the sects wiped out the detriment at one fell stroke. Orthodox theologians were thus faced with the difficult problem of maintaining that no saints could ever become perfectly sanctified, because such imperfection was the only check upon the "strange dreams and visions" of enthusiasts and Familists, who "under the pretence of free-grace . . . destroy the grace of God in the power and operations of it, in the hearts and lives of men." They had to defend themselves against Antinomians by proving that assurance was possible, yet that the assured would doubt and would sin; they had to reconcile the certainty of salvation with a persistent inability to keep all commandments perfectly, and yet not to condone the failures. They had to find a doctrine that would adequately explain how communion was perfect in one act and yet the manifestations various, how the elect were united to Christ and yet not made one flesh with Him, why assurance was continuous but the knowledge of it intermittent, and why notwithstanding these discouragements the elect strove to be as sanctified as possible.

It is not quite accurate to look upon the Covenant as a direct reply to Arminians and Antinomians; ambiguities inherent in the doctrines of sanctification and assurance would have forced theologians to rethink them in any event, and the covenant theory developed in England before Antinomianism became a great concern. Still it was as walking between these extremes that orthodox Puritans generally pictured themselves, and in their conception of their age these opinions loomed larger than those we now associate with the intellectual history of the century, than deism, skepticism, or scientific rationalism. A preacher in 1652 recorded that "it was not long since that our great contest was against the *Pelagians,* who from the Scriptures, pressing duty, would have inferred a power in mans will to perform it," but that now we have "to do with them, who because man hath no power in himself naturally to perform it, would have no duty pressed at all"; thus, he concluded, "we ground between two milstones: But neither extream is good, when *virtus* is in the middle."[10] Even at the end of the century, Willard entertained the same conception of the situation: "the way lyes very narrow between Antinomian and Arminian errours, and therefore needs the greater exactness in cutting the threed true." It was necessary, he said in *A Compleat Body,* to "fortify our selves against the *Pelagian* and *Popish* Errors on the *one* hand, which some *Protestants* have too deeply imbibed, and the *Antinomian* and *Libertine* Frenzies on the *other,* which too sadly prevail in this Licentious Age." From our point of view we may applaud Willard's definition of the issue, for the two heresies can be regarded as separate embodiments of the halves we have discerned in Puritan thinking, the Antinomians bespeaking the piety without the intellectual accompaniment, and the Arminians effecting a subordination of piety to the intellectual tradition. Thomas Shepard once "heard an Arminian . . . say, If faith will not work it, then set reason a-work"; Arminianism, as he saw it, could inspire some men to good behavior, such as was achieved by those who "have been kings and lords over their own passions by improving reason, and from some experience of the power of nature . . . have come to write large volumes in defence of it"; though Arminians ascribed something to grace, "yet, indeed, they lay the main stress of the work upon a man's own will, and the royalty and sovereignty of that liberty." To this conclusion men who studied logic and rhetoric apart from revelation, who looked upon second causes apart from divine concurrence, who held the operation of the means merely an instance of natural causation, who studied the faculties without a conviction of innate depravity, to this conclusion such men were bound to come. But on the other hand, it was no accident that the Antinomian sects should be the enemies of learning in ministerial education, that William Dell should both attack "humane helps" to divinity and assert that in regeneration Christ Himself, not merely some created habit or gift of grace, comes into our flesh exactly as the divine nature came into the flesh that was born of the Virgin. Antinomianism was a crude grasping at the tenets of sin and irresistible grace and of the union of believers with the Godhead, apart from any logical understanding of the terms, with no comprehension of the nature of cause and effect, with no instruction in the faculties of the soul or in the method of conversion through means. Ignorant zealots like Thomas Maule could not distinguish between grace "mixed with the Creature as a part of its Essence" and grace "with every Creature as an Efficient," and so could not understand that "wee are not the same person with Christ, and therefore wee have life not the very self-same with his, but conformable to his, and fashioned after his Image." Arminianism was a kind of ethical rationalism that had lost the sense of piety, and Antinomianism was an uncontrolled piety without the indispensable ballast of reason; Puritanism looked upon itself as the synthesis of piety and reason, and the federal Puritans looked upon the covenant theology as the perfection of that synthesis.

It seemed clear to the orthodox that both heresies came to grief in the final analysis because of imperfect conceptions of God, for thus heresies had always begun. Both of them were investing the creator with too definite, too restricted a nature, re-creating Him in their own image, destroying the balance of His attributes. Arminianism made Him too rational and too human, altogether too amenable to what man thinks is just and equitable. Antinomianism made Him a vital, all-pervading spirit, mystically indwelling in all men, or at least in the elect, uniting them to Himself, obliterating their individualities, "and so after justification they put a Christian in such an estate of sanctification as that he is a mere patient . . . like a weathercock which hath no power at all to move, but as the wind blows it, good or bad." Both of them, in short, forgot the distinction between God's ordinary and extraordinary dispensations, Arminians taking His revealed commandments for eternal laws by which He Himself was bound, so that He had of necessity to reward the obedient, and Antinomians assuming that His essential presence, by which He is everywhere and in everything, was the same as His special presence, by which in particular and in a peculiar way He inspires the elect. The piety of irresistible conversion and the morality of judicious reason parted company to form the two half-truths of Antinomianism and Arminianism, thereby illustrating the difficulties which beset men of the early seventeenth century in their effort to conceive of God as a perfect balance of all attributes. The more closely they reasoned, the more they became involved in the problems of morality and sanctification, of assurance and the nature of grace, the more they were tempted to solve their difficulties by the easy method of accentuating one quality of the divine Being at the expense of another, by presenting Him as more rational than arbitrary, or more inspirational than sane. Therefore, the doctrine of the Covenant of Grace, if it were to provide grounds for moral obligation and for individual assurance, had to set forth something more to the point than the traditional theology. If the moral law were to be upheld, men must know what part it played in God's design; if men were to know the conditions upon which they could base their assurance, they must be shown that God would abide by those conditions, that He would not override them in an impulse of whimsy or caprice. And yet the essential mystery of the Godhead, His unfathomable unity and His simultaneous possession of all perfections, no matter how incompatible they might seem, this mystery could not be sacrificed to men's desire for a universe after their own liking. "The secresie of God does drive men to much trouble," said Hooker; "It is like an unbeaten way to the Seamen, they must sound every part of it." They must not make a chart of God from their own notions, but mark the existing reefs and shoals. The theory of the Covenant resulted from the Puritan effort to sound this secrecy in the early seventeenth century, to find where lay the submerged grounds for moral obedience and for an assurance of any man's salvation.

The names of those who formulated the theory have frequently appeared on these pages, for they were among the authors most widely studied in New England: Perkins, Ames, Preston, Sibbes, Ball, Baxter, and Gale. It can hardly be said that Perkins invented it (except possibly in the Ramist sense of the word!), for it had figured in the writings of earlier reformers, but his works were the first in England to give it the stress which became overwhelming in the sermons of Preston.[11] Many of these men were acquainted with one another and with the clerical leaders of the Great Migration; the list coincides partially with the lists of those who worked out the scheme of Congregational church polity[12] and of those who adhered to the Ramist logic. I cannot say that the three always went together; there were evidently Ramists who were not federalists, and federalists who were not Congregationalists, but the secret of the New England mind is simply that New Englanders were all three at once. Undoubtedly another influence in shaping the doctrine, perhaps indeed the most important, was the common law, for the concept was essentially legal, and some of the writers settled disputes by saying, "We will referre it to the Common Law, whether this way of reasoning will hold or no," or "our Lawyers . . . have given us Presidents . . ." It seems significant that Preston, who most decisively placed the theory in the foreground of theology and was its greatest popularizer, should have been, as Master of Emmanuel, the leading politician among Puritan divines just when the union between religious reformers and the lawyers was being cemented.[13] He died in 1628 at the age of forty-one, of overwork and tuberculosis, protesting that "some men lived as much in seven years, as others did in seventy." According to Dr. Neal, Bishop of Worcester, Preston was a man who "talked like one that was familiar with God Almighty,"[14] and his works, the voluminous fruit of his talking, were edited by John Davenport, Richard Sibbes, and Thomas Goodwin, who in one preface said that Preston had spent his thoughts "in unfolding and applying, the most proper and peculiar Characters of Grace, which is *Gods Image;* whereby Beleevers come to be assured, that *God* is their *God,* and they in covenant with him." This description is apt for all his volumes, though his principal treatment of the subject was *The New Covenant, or the Saints*

Portion, published by his editors in 1629, many copies of which were in New England libraries. Almost as influential in the colonies was John Ball's *A Treatise of the Covenant of Grace,* 1645, though after the 1640's New Englanders had works by their own parsons in which to study the doctrine.

The substance of the federal theory can be stated briefly, though its implications could be investigated indefinitely. By the word "covenant" federal theologians understood just such a contract as was used among men of business, a bond or a mortgage, an agreement between two parties, signed and sworn to, and binding upon both. It was usually defined as "A mutual agreement between parties upon Articles or Propositions on both sides, so that each party is tied and bound to performe his own conditions." In his *Cases of Conscience,* Ames described the ordinary contract, emphasizing that its essence was voluntary engagement. It was, he said, a free consent, a treaty arrived at by the participants without constraint, each of whom honestly intends to live up to the terms and who, to record his willingness and his obligations, expresses them by an outward sign, by a document attested and sealed. Because each enters the pact of his own volition, each has a right to expect from the other a fulfillment to the letter; "the forme doth require internall, and essentiall the upright dealing of the Contractor, to bee true, and sincere." Always the fundamental point, insisted upon *ad nauseam,* was the voluntaristic basis of the undertaking: "Where two Parties do stand mutually obliged one to another in a voluntary Agreement, there is a Covenant." None ever need exist unless both signatories wish it; before it, they are free as the air, but once having set their hands to it, they are no longer at liberty, they are irrevocably shackled. "Natural Necessity destroys the very nature of a Covenant," said Willard, for it must be "a voluntary obligation between persons about things wherein they enjoy a freedom of Will, and have a power to choose or refuse," it must be "a deliberate thing wherein there is a Counsel and a Consent between Rational and free Agents." Because a man takes a covenant upon himself, it is the strongest tie by which he can ever be bound. In a covenant he is infinitely more liable than in a promise, more obligated than by a law, more involved than in a testament, more answerable than for his oath. An oath may attest a mistake, but a covenant guarantees truth. A promise calls for some future good, a law for some performance, but a covenant calls for both. A law depends upon the sovereignty of the law-giver, who is able to save or destroy and is under no compulsion to do the one rather than the other; a testament is grounded on the will of the testator, who gives without the consent of his beneficiaries; but a covenant "differs from them both, in this, that it requires the consent and agreement of both parties, and therein each party binds himself freely to the performance of several conditions each to other." An absolute monarch can change his laws every day, forswear his oaths, make promises and break them by the score, rewrite his testament as often as he pleases, but once he enters a covenant, though with but the humblest of his peasants, he is held as with hoops of steel. One who owes a debt of money may abscond, or of friendship may prove false, the day laborer may go elsewhere tomorrow; but when a man has made a covenant with his landlord, his friend, or his employer, he can never escape his commitment. Starting from absolute independence, the covenant leads to mutual subjection; in a universe where nothing seems certain, it alone produces certainty; in a society where men cannot be relied upon, it creates reliability. It is the only point at which might and weakness can meet on a footing of right.

The federal theology appropriated this concept and fastened it upon both God and man. "We must not make Gods Covenant with man, so far to differ from Covenants between man and man, as to make it no Covenant at all." It found in the idea a key to the history of the universe, the innermost meaning of divine revelation, the foundation of law in the apparent lawlessness of nature. It held that man, viewed simply as part of creation, is the serf of his lord, the subject of his prince, but that viewed as the rational part of that creation, he stands also in relation to God as one man in covenant with another. He who creates is under no obligation to those whom he creates; God might slay His creatures, or torture them, or forget them, and none could call Him to account, but in the Covenant He has voluntarily tied His hands, willingly agreed to a set of terms. There have been "as it were indentures drawne betweene God and man, conditions on both sides agreed upon," and in place of an ontological relation, a connection determined by brute necessity and the ineluctable order of things, is substituted an equally certain but more honorable relation of assent. God forgoes what is His by right divine, preferring a spontaneous to an enforced service. His gesture is pure graciousness. Covenants between men concern things "which either were not due before, or were not thought to be due, which are made firme, stable and due by the very Covenant, so that by the Covenant new right is acquired or caused, either to one or both, who Covenant betwixt themselves of any matter." Out of His mere pleasure, God in the Covenant gives men something new, something over and above their mere existence, something gratuitous, and then by affixing his seal to the grant translates the bestowed privilege into a right. He who might rule by fiat limits Himself to a contract; He who could exact tribute to the last farthing consents to parliamentary taxation. The covenant between God and man is an agreement of unequals upon just and equal terms, "in which God promises true happinesse to man, and man engages himself by promise for performance of what God requires." It may be, as Preston said, a difficult point to grasp, "yet you must know it, for it is the ground of all you hope for, it is that that euery man is built vpon, you haue no other ground but this, God hath made a Couenant with you, and you are in Couenant with him."

According to the federalists, God has never dealt with mankind except in this way. "As soon as God had Created man, he plighted a Covenant with him." He proposed that if Adam would perform certain things, Adam and his posterity should be rewarded with eternal life, and He laid down the specific conditions in the moral law, which He implanted in Adam's heart. Hence the terms of this first covenant, the Covenant of Works, are what we know as the law of nature, and by failing to keep them, Adam, and we as his posterity, incurred the just penalty. But God did not rest there. Beginning with Abraham, He commenced a new covenant, the Covenant of Grace, which is a true contract of mutual obligation, but this time the condition for the mortal partner is not a deed but a faith: "sayth the *Lord,* this is the Covenant that I wil make on my part, *I will be thy God* . . . you shall haue all things in me that your hearts can desire: The *Covenant* againe, that I require on your part, is, that you be *perfect with me,"* but the perfection required is in the heart rather than in the hands, "so that though a man be subiect to infirmities, yet, if he haue a single heart, an vpright heart, the *Lord* accepts it." Because fallen man is unable any longer to fulfill the moral law, God in the person of Christ takes the task upon Himself; the Covenant of Works is not recalled but kept by God in the place of man, while in the new Covenant those who will believe in the Redeemer have His righteousness ascribed to them and so are "justified" according to the new terms. Recognizing the now bankrupt condition of the tenant, the landlord guarantees in a new lease to provide him the wherewithal to pay his rent and keep a roof over his head, provided he will believe in the landlord's goodness and show what gratitude he can. "In the Covenant of workes, a man is left to himselfe, to stand by his own strength; But in the Covenant of grace, God undertakes for us, to keep us through faith." We have only to pledge that, when it is given us, we will avail ourselves of the assistance which makes faith possible, and Sibbes therefore defined the Covenant of Grace in terms common to all the writers:

> It has pleased the great God to enter into a treaty and covenant of agreement with us his poor creatures, the articles of which agreement are here comprised. God, for his part, undertakes to convey all that concerns our happiness, upon our receiving of them, by believing on him. Every one in particular that recites these articles from a spirit of faith makes good this condition.

If a man can believe, he has done his part; God then must needs redeem him and glorify him.

The new Covenant was first propounded, according to these theologians, to Abraham; the seventeenth chapter of Genesis was their key text, upon which most of their works were a commentary,[15] and Deuteronomy they called "The Book of the Covenant." The condition for Abraham was faith, exactly as for us, though he was required to believe that Christ would come; since the resurrection, we have merely to believe that He has come and that

He is "surety" for the new Covenant. But from Abraham to the settlers of New England, there is one and the same bond between God and man. "We are the children of *Abraham;* and therefore we are under *Abrahams* covenant." Abraham, according to Joshua Moody, "was the *Great Pattern Believer,"* and Cobbett spoke of the Covenant of Grace as "the old Charter of *Abrahams* covenant." The transaction upon the plain of Mamre in Hebron was not a mere promise on God's part, it was a complete commitment, for to these authors the idea that God merely promised was not enough. "It is impertinent to put a difference betweene the promise and the Covenant . . . The promise of God and his Covenant . . . are ordinarily put one for another." The Covenant, its origin, its progressive unfolding, its culmination, was thus the meaning of history, that which made intelligible the whole story of mankind. It was "the very Basis on which all that follows is built, and unto which it must be referred"; God never does anything for His people unless "he doth it by vertue of, and according to his Covenant," and the number of the saints is accomplished, not merely through the means, but through the means as agents of the Covenant:

> God conveys his salvation by way of covenant, and he doth it to those onely that are in covenant with him . . . This covenant must every soule enter into, every particular soul must enter into a particular covenant with God; out of this way there is no life.

So Puritan divines of the seventeenth century, perceiving the amplitude of this doctrine, broke like Cotton into hymns of delight: "This is such an Argument as the strength and wisdome of men and Angels cannot unfold," and then, like good Puritans and good Ramists, set themselves to unfolding it "(as the Lord hath revealed it) I mean, plainly and familiarly."

It may seem at first sight that some over-ingenious lawyer and no man of deep piety constructed this legalized version of Biblical history, and we may pardonably wonder how much it really clarified the murk of Calvinism. But Puritan divines had not studied dialectic for nothing; give them this broad premise, backed with copious Scriptural warrants, and they were ready to deduce from it the most gratifying conclusions, for it offered what no other single doctrine could provide, a scheme including both God and man within a single frame, a point at which, without doing violence to their respective natures, both could meet and converse. The Covenant was a gift of God, yet it entailed responsibility on Him as well as upon men. If the orthodox could answer Arminians and Antinomians only when they had set forth the character of God with greater precision, and if they could lay to rest doubts about moral obedience and personal assurance only when they had shown how each was compatible with the facts of human depravity and irresistible grace, then the covenant theory responded perfectly to their necessities. As for the nature of God, the concept of voluntary limitation did away with all difficulties, and as for morality and assurance, the concept of a covenant with conditions answered the objections of all heretics.

The God of the Covenant was still the ancient Puritan Jehovah, still a hidden and inexpressible essence, still an impenetrable "secresie", but the covenant theology seized avidly upon the distinction, always so precious to Augustinian thinking, between His secret and His revealed will. Arminius mistook His enacted moral statutes for His innermost being, and Antinomians confused His emanation with Himself; both forgot that He has first an "absolute" and then an "Ordinate Power," that the second is not so much different from the first, "but the former considered, as God hath pleased to set limits or bounds to it by the Decree." He has an "essential" justice, which is in Him necessarily and by which He can do no wrong, but also a "relative" justice, "which is in him freely, that is, it hath no necessary connexion with the Being of God," and from which "flows his proceeding with men according to the Law of righteousness freely constituted between him and them." The heretics forgot that while He rules the cosmos by His absolute power and His essential justice, He promulgates commandments or bestows grace by a special extension of Himself over and above the ordinary, by a power of specific ordination and a justice relative to circumstances. By the concept of a voluntary contract the theologians sundered the outward manifestation from the inner principle, and confined it in an irrevocable bond, so that the finite could thereafter treat with the infinite. They achieved this remarkable feat without dethroning His omnipotence, without circumscribing His sovereignty, by the plausible device of attributing the instigation of the deal to Him. He alone, of His own unfettered will, proposed that He be chained. "It's Gods usual way so to deal, not that he is tyed, or hath tied himself to this manner of dealing upon necessity, but that he hath expressed it to be his good pleasure so to dispense himself." In Himself He remains an unknowable transcendence, but in His Covenant He freely takes upon Himself a local habitation and a name; outside the pale He is wholly irresponsible, but within it He has placed Himself under a yoke. In His nature He remains above all law, outside all morality, beyond all reason, but in the Covenant He is ruled by a law, constrained to be moral, committed to sweet reasonableness. God as the source of all being, not only of things that are, but of all those things that might be, the boundless realm of possibility, was the starting point of piety, of physics, and of technologia, but simple piety had nothing more to build upon than the particular articles He had arbitrarily revealed, physics could merely report the order it had pleased Him to create, technologia could arrange in the arts just such actualities as He had despotically selected out of the unnumbered potentials, whereas the federal theology founded its doctrine upon the immovable basis of a sealed covenant, upon a just agreement eternally sanctioned, from which the supreme power of the universe could never depart by a hair's breadth. Dialectic invented whatever arguments were embodied in things and arranged them in imitation of factual dispositions; it was fortunately able to describe a rational universe, but the rationality was wholly fortuitous. As far as logic itself could tell, the logic of the universe was a happy incident in God's decree, and at any moment, by a flicker of His hand, He might send it sprawling into chaos. But in His Covenant the kaleidoscopic world came to rest. God gives some amount of certainty by His Word, and "not onely his bare Word, but a binding Word, his promises," but the ultimate certitude is not "onely Promises, but his Covenant, founded upon a full satisfaction made to his justice." Within the Covenant, as "in all other royall patents, and grants of princely grace, and bounty," permanence reigns. Within this circuit, infinitesimal as compared with His essence, but spacious enough to include all humanity, two and two will always equal four, a cause will have its effect, and the fulfillment of conditions never fail of the assured reward. Within this circumference, God speaks no longer with unpredictable fury, but in words of comfort:

> I will not onely tell thee what I am able to doe, I will not onely expresse to thee in generall, that I will deale well with thee, that I haue a willingnesse and ability to recompence thee, if thou walke before mee, and serue mee, and bee perfect; but I am willing to enter into Couenant with thee, that is, I will binde my selfe, I will ingage my selfe, I will enter into bond, as it were, I will not bee at liberty any more, but I am willing euen to make a Couenant, a compact and agreement with thee.

Thus we may cease being apprehensive over His hidden terrors, and may assume that in our experience He will abide by definite regulations. He will no longer do all the unimaginable things He can do, but "all things which he hath promised to doe." As John Cotton said, professing all reverence, God has "muffled" Himself as with a cloak, "He cannot strike as he would . . . he is so compassed about with his nature and property, and Covenant, that he hath no liberty to strike." Hooker joined the chorus: "We have the Lord in bonds, for the fulfilling his part of the Covenant: He hath taken a corporall Oath of it, that He will do it." Because the Covenant of Grace, said Willard, "ariseth from, or is grounded upon the occasions of dealing or trading between one and another," it too demands perfect sincerity of the contractors, and "each Party may be secured from suffereing any damage by the other; but may be able to claim and recover the performance." Having created the universe, the creator takes His place within it upon the same level with His creatures, becoming morally responsible and liable, should He ever take unfair advantage of His might, to be arrested, prosecuted, and fined.

Meanwhile, the balance of His attributes was impeccably preserved. His sovereignty was not infringed, for He entered the Covenant under no other pressure than His free assent. He was still the absolute monarch, although He had given His subjects a bill of inviolable rights. He remained thoroughly just, exacting the full penalty for transgressions of the first Covenant, and yet showed Himself in the second Covenant extravagantly merciful. "It is not in our reach to understand how ever this could have been done declaratively . . . but in the way of a Covenant." In fact, it almost seems as though Puritan theologians, having dwelt for years upon the implacable rigor of divine justice and being forced, in spite of the balance, to present sovereignty as the dominant attribute, were intensely relieved to come upon the covenant doctrine as at last something tangible to adduce in pleading that God was also gracious. A God who condescends to treat with fallen man as an equal is indeed kindly and solicitous. If we stop to consider, urged Preston, it is an exceedingly great mercy: "He is in heauen, and wee are on earth; hee the glorious God, we dust and ashes; hee the Creator, and wee but creatures; and yet he is willing to enter into Couenant, which implyes a kinde of equality betweene vs." One might almost suspect that the Covenant God was over-solicitous. He tried the Covenant of Works with Adam, and it failed; instead of leaving man to take the consequences, He bethought Himself of this ingenious scheme, that He should fulfill that Covenant Himself in order to save His own face and not let His justice go unavenged, and that He might then begin anew by offering man easier terms. It is richly eloquent of the temper of these theologians that they openly called their doctrine a clever arrangement: "never was there such a Wise Contrivance heard of in the World." Who but a most tender-hearted divinity "could have devised a way whereby the *Law* should be made more Honourable and Glorious than if man had never sinned, and yet guilty Creatures made to inherit Eternal Life: that *Mercy* should be magnified in the pardoning of many Crimes, and yet *Justice* fully satisfied too!" The Covenant was frankly "a Way found out by God, and discovered to Man, by which the Sinner may escape the suffering of this Wrath & Curse," as though God had been compelled to accommodate His ways to the intransigence of mankind. "There was no other way to make mankinde partaker of the Couenant of Grace, but onely by faith." We might well exclaim with Thomas Shepard:

> Oh the depth of Gods grace herein . . . that when he deserves nothing else but separation from God, and to be driven up and downe the World, as a Vagabond, or as dryed leaves, fallen from our God, that yet the Almighty God cannot be content with it, but must make himselfe to us, and us to himselfe more sure and neer then ever before!

We actually find the deity, as it were, pursuing men and begging them not to cast Him off: "The Lord can never get neer enough to his people, and thinks he can never gett them neer enough unto himselfe, and therefore unites and binds and fastens them close to himself, and himselfe unto them by the bonds of a Covenant." He is so anxious to win the love of mortals that He will consent to a union upon any terms, upon conditions dictated not by Himself but by mortal reason: "God will deal with Man in a way agreeable to his nature," and since man is "a reasonable creature, and a cause by counsell of his own actions," the distraught divinity "treats by making proffers to him, propounding fair and rationall Conditions, and adding gracious encouragements," while "for the full, cleer, and unfailing performance of all, Jesus Christ stands ready as an undertaker for the carrying on, and full accomplishment of the whole business." Not only does He shrink Himself into the terms of reason, but to insure the success of His "business" He unfolds the Covenant gradually, not frightening Abraham by presenting it point-blank, but introducing it by degrees, educating men up to it. Though from Abraham to the present has been but one Covenant, said Ames—who seems largely responsible for developing this point—"yet the manner of the application of Christ or of administring this new Covenant, hath not alwayes beene one and the same, but divers, according to the ages in which the Church hath been gathered." Other writers distinguished the stages of the administration differently, but all agreed that God had allowed the Covenant to grow with time, first dispensing it through conscience, then through the Prophets and ceremonies, and now through Christ, the preaching of the Word, and the sacraments. He has done this out of delicate consideration for human weakness; had the whole thing been enunciated to Abraham, it would have over-strained his faith, already burdened by the effort to believe that Sarah would conceive. "Dr. *Ames* saith well," Bulkeley wrote, "the Church was then considered . . . partly as an heire, and partly as an infant." This long period of tuition, by which the church was gradually enabled to grasp the idea of the Covenant clearly and distinctly, was a necessary concession to the nature of man, which "is so exceeding opposite to the doctrine of Christ and the Gospel" that had the Covenant "not been long framed by the tutoring of many hundred yeers by the Law," men would never have given it credence.

For Puritans the instruction provided by the Covenant of Grace upon the nature of God was merely preliminary to its instructions concerning salvation and ethics. The essential point was that it made possible a voluntary relation of man to God, even though man's will was considered impotent and God's grace irresistible. He who by His absolute dominion might "have dealt with Men in a way of Soveraignty only, requiring Duty and Obedience from them, without any promise of reward," nevertheless "has seen Good to transact with them in a Covenant way." He now occupies, not the throne of a tyrant, but the seat "of a righteous Judge, and cannot dispense with his own Law, because his Truth and Righteousness engage him to it." Therefore He fixes upon this scheme that there should be on the side of man a voluntary return, a sincere pledge that will have some elements of spontaneity. He made both the Covenants "conditional", that of Grace no less than that of Works, so that they would be relations founded upon mutual stipulations, not upon brute fact. He forewent his "unconfined prerogative" and "voluntarily obliged himself in the threatning annexed to his own Command"; does it not follow, then, that there is a double engagement, "by the one we are bound to God, and by the other God is bound to us"? As creator He is absolute, "but yet that man might not think much to yield obedience, God is pleas'd to engage himself to a recompense." The all-important fact for the Puritan parson, as each Sabbath he ascended his pulpit steps, was that he could promise the recompense to an active and generous obedience.

Even so, the good parson had his work cut out for him. His congregation knew, if they knew nothing else, that salvation by faith and not by works was orthodoxy, and that any hedging of this point was heresy. He had to explain to them that when faith was viewed not as a simple act of belief, but as the condition of a covenant, it became in itself, as it were, a "work", involving in the inward act an obligation to external behavior. He explained the connection a thousand times over, so insistently that we may suspect he was none too confident of his own logic. He put this construction upon faith by commencing always with the distinction between God's natural rule and God's special dispensation. In the natural rule, where God does everything "absolutely and simply without any condition, as the creation and regiment of the world," He acts as in the pestilence and the hurricane. Were men regenerated under this rule they would fall as ripe fruit to the ground or be driven as dead leaves before the wind. But when God acts by his "signifying" will, He "willeth some things for some other thing, with condition, and so we say, because that the condition annexed is a signe of the will, that God doth so will." He is equally sovereign in either manifestation, but whereas in the first He merely says, "Let the hurricane strike," in the other He says, "I will save those that believe." Thus belief, although given by His grace, is not quite the same thing as understood by unlearned piety; it does not merely regenerate man's faculties, but also enables the revived faculties, the reason and will, to believe, and through believing to give free, rational, and voluntary consent to a contract. In other words, sanctification was not expected to follow upon justification automatically, it was not left for God to work while the man stood idly by, but the will was enlisted and pledged, according to the stipulation, to see that all the faculties bestirred themselves. The covenanted saint does not supinely believe, but does the best he can, and God will not hold his failures against him; having pledged himself, the saint has taken the responsibility upon himself and agreed to coöperate with God in the difficult labor. He is not as a child to whom for no reason a fatuous parent gives a shilling, but as one informed by a wise father that he may have a penny if he washes his face and hands and improves his manners. Man does not recline and say, "Let God do it," but reflects, "I am engaged by my own consent, I must try to make good my word." The grace which enables some to try, and without which the others will not attempt anything creditable, is wholly an arbitrary favor dispensed in a way of sovereignty to those whom God has forever predestined to election, yet to the elect it is also dispensed in a way of free compact, so that they treat about it with God upon a voluntary basis. Hence they are covenanted to sainthood, not forced into it, and they are to be saved for trying, not for succeeding, whereas the reprobate are eternally damned, not for failing, but for not trying.

In order that men should not presume upon the "Absolute Promises" of the Covenant to give over trying, the federal God, who is exceedingly shrewd, perfected the adroit device of incorporating the Covenant of Works into the Covenant of Grace, not as the condition of salvation but as the rule of righteousness. No man can any longer be saved by fulfilling the law, even should he be capable of it, for the Covenant of Works is not now in force between God and man, and God is not bound by it. But the law, which was the condition of that Covenant, remains "as the unchangeable rule of life and manners, according to which persons in Covenant ought to walke before and with the Lord, and in this sense it belongs to the Covenant of grace." It is no longer one of the terms of the pact, but it is there as the "schoolmaster" of the new terms, to teach the goal toward which a believer must incessantly strive, even while knowing that he cannot encompass it. Man still owes a debt to the law; he who borrows money "stands bound to the Creditor to answer the Debt, though his state alter, and he be impoverished, and made unable to pay, yet his Bond for payment continues in full force against him, and he will be constrained to make it good." The faculties, restored by grace to some semblance of their original liberty, are not kept in ignorance of their duties: "For the Morall Law, the Law of the ten Commandements, we are dead also to the *covenant* of that law, though not to the *command* of it." Even before conversion, even while we are still impotent, the law is our schoolmaster, teaching what we should do, whether we can or not. It is indeed a rigorous pedagogue; we stand in relation to the law, said Hooker in one of the commercial metaphors so constantly employed in all preaching of this doctrine, as a tenant to a landlord, to whom the tenant owes rent for many years' occupancy and to whom, as he is about to be put out, he offers a half-year's fee:

> Will this man thinke that he hath now satisfied his Land-lord? if he should say, now Land-lord, I hope you are contented, and all is answered & I have fully paid all that is betweene you and mee, you Land-lords would be ready to reply thus, and say, This satisfies me for the last halfe yeare past, but who payes for the odde hundreds?

Realizing that we cannot fulfill the law, that we cannot pay for the odd hundreds, we flee to Christ for the assistance of grace. Knowledge of the law is thus for the unregenerate a "means" of conversion; it sets "home the burden of their sins unto their souls, thereby to drive them to feel their great need of the Lord." Once again God is dealing with man as a reasonable creature, giving him a rule that can be known in the understanding and embraced in the will. But according to the federal theology, conversion is synonymous with taking a covenant; we do not merely flee to Christ from the terrors of the law, but we strike a bargain with Him, and if we turn to Him in acknowledging our inability otherwise to pay our debt to the law, then with the help of His grace we should naturally undertake to fulfill our obligation. That we should use grace to satisfy the law would certainly be one of the conditions of the Covenant of Grace: "For God never calleth any unto fellowship with himself in a Covenant of Grace, but ordinarily he first bringeth them into a Covenant of Works." God as sovereign may do what He will, but He "doth not absolutely promise life unto any, he doth not say to any soule, I will save you and bring you to life, though you continue impenitent & unbelieving," but He commands us to repent and believe, "and then promises that in the way of faith and repentance, he will save us." So for us who have faith and have repented, "He prescribes a way of life for us to walk in, that so wee may obtaine the salvation which he hath promised." Thus the Covenant of Grace becomes a "conditional" covenant; the condition is faith, but covenant-faith has in the law a way prescribed for it to walk in, and faith as the fulfillment of a covenant obliges the believer so to walk, whereas unsophisticated piety naïvely supposes that faith in itself is adequate for salvation regardless of how it walks.

Once more we may marvel at the ingenuity of a contrivance which manages to demand what men cannot give and yet not punish them for failing, which forgives the wrong-doer and yet does not ask the law to go unsatisfied. The Covenant, as Willard professed, "hath declared a way which God hath found out to cover the imperfections, and accept of the sincerity of such as are in it, consistent with the Justice of God, and for the manifestation of his *Grace*." Thus the Covenant of Grace makes rationally comprehensible, if we can follow the federalists' reasoning, why saints should remain imperfectly sanctified and yet be assured of salvation. If their hearts are sealed, the rebellion of some lesser faculty cannot destroy the bond:

> If there be a Covenant made betweene two States, as suppose betweene France and England, if the Princes of both States keepe Covenant, it is not some lawlesse subject or Pirat on either side that breaks the League, so long as the Princes doe their best endeavours to punish it; so is it in the League made between God and my heart, it is not any disordered affection that breaks the league, but the sin that dwels within us.

No matter what his occasional lapses, he who is within the Covenant of Grace "doth not feare condemnation from his disobedience." A single violation destroyed the Covenant of Works, "but the Covenant of grace is not broken asunder by many transgressions, so long as we follow God in a way of faith and repentance." God has pledged Himself to save those that believe; if we believe, "we ought not to thinke, because we are not exact in keeping all the Commandements of *God* . . . that therefore *God* reiects vs." Since no man will ever be perfect in the flesh, faith will result in a continual purging of impurities; there is always a scum arising in pots that boil upon the fire, but good housewives "watch it, and as the scum riseth up, they take it off and throw it away, happily more scum will arise, but still as it riseth they scum it off." The scum of depravity must come to the surface occasionally even in the holiest; there is always some particular lust which cannot be rooted out of our natural constitution, which "the occasions offered in the Providence of God, or the affairs that we are employed in, do stimulate us to; and we are more easily won to hold correspondence with it." Though justification itself admits of no degrees, "every man that is justified in Christ, is within the Covenant," yet a man's sanctification may be more or less, and many saints, judging themselves by their behavior, will fall under "dismal apprehensions about themselves," being ready at times "to account themselves *Hypocrites,* and to Despair of Salvation thro' the horrid workings of Inherent Corruption." However, they should never despair; they must remember that God does not expect them to do all things, that the Covenant perfectly explains why assurance does not require absolutely perfect sanctification. Neither may the unregenerate take comfort from the imperfections of Christians: "I tell thee this, the Saints of God shall commit greater sinnes and goe to Heaven, when thou lesser and goe to Hell." All must know that natural men are finally to be judged by the natural covenant, the Covenant of Works, which requires exact conformity to the law, but those in the Covenant of Grace have a much less exorbitant demand laid upon them. It is indeed a little surprising to the modern student to find how much of Puritan sermons was actually devoted to telling the people that they should not let themselves be overwhelmed with too great a grief for their sins: it is a wile of the Devil, said Hooker, to keep us poring upon our misdeeds; "While the soule of a man is daily plodding upon his owne misery, and distempers . . . wee stop the streame of Gods promise . . . And . . . wee set open the streame and fludgate of corruption." The ministers seem to have been fully aware that the stark predestination of early Calvinism was too often driving the devout to distraction, and that it needed somehow to be softened. Hence they said again and again that there might be little visible difference between saints and sinners, that the difference would be in the aims and aspirations, in the earnestness of the effort. "God accepts at our hands *a willing minde,* and of childe-like indeavours; if we come with childe-like service, God will spare us; a father will accept the poor indeavours of his childe for the thing it self."

The all important point was not the success but the "indeavours". The essential concept was obligation to the law along with commutation of its sentence; the saint may be very imperfectly sanctified and still assured as long as his heart is sealed, yet all is lost if the heart is not engaged. Though the children of God "be not under the Covenant of the Law, yet [they] take themselves to be bound to the obedience of it." When the Covenant of Grace provides the spirit that enables them to keep the law, "though not perfectly, yet sincerely, then they take themselves bound to obey the Law." They are saved because they carry a constant purpose of heart to do it and never give over striving. If they assume that because they are in the Covenant of Grace they will not be damned, no matter what their wickedness, and relax their endeavors, they are surely hypocrites and undoubtedly will be damned; if they keep up the good fight, no sin they actually commit is enough to drag them down. The difference is entirely a matter of the will, and the Covenant of Grace is founded not upon morality but intention. Though it is "conditional", it is not Arminian conditionality, not a simple matter of God's saying, "If you do thus and so you will be saved," and then leaving it to you to do or not to do. It is a more complex procedure, in which He gives to the elect the grace enabling them to believe, and contracts to reward whosoever believes by giving them an assurance of their salvation despite their sins, while those who believe, by accepting grace as part of the contract, commit themselves on their side voluntarily to struggle for holiness as an indispensable part of believing. The conditions are not, in the jargon of theology, "antecedent and meritorious," not "the procuring cause of God's Love and Favour"; they are not causal but "declarative", making "manifest who be those true believers"; they are "as evidences and signes of those that do believe unto life." The duties of the Covenant are "connex and consequent, only pointing out unto us the way in which the free blessing of Grace is to be obtained by Mankind"; they are the terms we must accept and observe in order to receive in return the benefits pledged by God. Modern minds will sympathize with the puzzled John Fry, who complained that the ministers condemned Arminianism, "but for all this in the very same breath they will tell you, you may be holy and repent if you will, and 'tis your fault if you do not believe"; they told him even that man was a "Co-adjutor with God in the work of Conversion and Sanctification," that God had done His part and it was up to him now to do his. If this were not to say "our works are meritorious, I marvail with what face men can challenge God as they do, and how People can take such expressions in any other sence." But it was in another sense that New England divines took these expressions, thanks to the distinction between conditions which are causal and meritorious, and conditions which must be fulfilled because they "declare" who is and who is not regenerate.

Thus it followed, as day the night, that sanctification became a very handy evidence of justification; since it is a blessing of the Covenant, "it is a warrantable and safe way for a man by and from his sanctification to take an evidence of his justification." Both forgiveness and holiness are gifts of the Covenant, but because the will of man is engaged after the gift of forgiveness to help himself to the gift of holiness, sanctification is his work as well as God's. "Being justified and made acceptable, the Lord requires, that we expresse the Covenant, and walk answerable unto it, & expresse the virtues of him that hath called us." This was not legality, but it was not passivity. "Tho' help & strength to perform them, must come from the Spirit of God, yet the things themselves must be performed by us." The Ten Commandments are in the articles of faith, and a man of faith must respect the whole Covenant, "respect the whole word of commandement, hee doth not else beleeve rightly which doth not desire and indeavour this." We cannot take the promise of a covenant without submitting to the duty of it, though if we had merely a promise, not sealed in a bond of mutual stipulation, we might trust the promise and forget the duty. When God regenerates us by taking us into a covenant instead of merely acting upon our souls, "he doth not then leave us at liberty to live as we list; but he binds us by Covenant to himselfe." Peculiar though the Covenant of Grace may appear as compared with a league of princes or a lease of land, still it has the essential characteristics of any such agreement, conditions on both sides which the signers pledge themselves in all sincerity of heart to observe toward each other:

> The reason is this, for I would have nothing untouched that you may be wise and understanding Christians, because of the likeness betweene, and the resemblance of a Covenant that is made betweene two parties, and the Law, which is the Covenant which is given us of the Lord: In a Covenant, first there must be conditions and Articles of agreement betweene the parties offered and consented unto: and secondly, a binding one another to the performance thereof by Bond, perhaps a paire of Indentures are drawne betweene them, wherein is declared, that they mutually agree . . . It is just so here: Marke the agreement betweene us and the Lord: he propounds the Law, and saith, That if we will keepe the Law, he will blesse us abundantly in all things, house, and land . . . Then the people they agree, and say, Content Lord, whatever thou saist, we will doe.

Hence we must do. Here was the point to which the covenant theology returned again and again, the point that was accentuated every week from New England rostrums to a people who were to be saved for their faith and not for their good deeds. Richard Sibbes summarized in one short sentence what the whole intricate argument amounted to: "Though God's grace do all, yet we must give our consent."

Thus it was easy to see where Antinomians and Arminians went astray: Antinomians expected God's grace to do all, Arminians attributed everything to our consent. The covenant theology held to both the grace and the consent, to the decree of God and the full responsibility of man, to assurance in spite of sin and morality in spite of assurance. It ought to have been easy for poor Mistress Hutchinson to understand the true basis for assurance; it was not an immediate revelation, an inward ecstasy or some ineffable prompting of the soul, it was a hard and mathematically calculable test. He who fulfilled the condition of the Covenant could gain assurance, and the condition was belief followed by a conscious effort toward sanctification. Not the least useful service of this theology to Puritanism was its providing a definite criterion for telling sheep from goats, definite enough at any rate to permit the restriction of church membership to the visible elect. The end of any covenant is "to give the greater security to those transactions that are between men"; the end of the Covenant of Grace is to give security to the transactions between God and men, for by binding God to the terms, it binds Him to save those who make good the terms. Were it not for the Covenant we could never have any certain hope, for "the absolute promises do not describe the persons to whom the blessings of the Covenant do belong; onely the conditionall promises do point out the persons to be saved, as the absolute do shew the cause of our salvation." While the horrified ghost of Calvin shuddered to behold his theology twisted into this spiritual commercialism, New England parsons confidently asserted, "He who performs the condition of the general Gospel Promise, doth in so doing make the good of it so to become his own by promise," and thus does, "as it were bind the Covenant, and bring Christ himself into Bonds; so that God can as well deny himself, as refuse to justifie such." Therefore union with God promised to be no more a torturing uncertainty, not a ravishing of the surprised soul by a terrifying power, but a definite legal status, based on *quid pro quo*. Once in the Covenant we are safe: "If we be hemm'd in within this Covenant, wee cannot break out." If you have the seal set upon your heart, "that there is a change wrought in thee by the covenant, then thy election is sure." If our sanctification wavers, if we fall into vice and wonder whether after all we are hypocrites, we can always test ourselves: "We must then turne to the conditionall promises, trying whether the graces expressed in them, be wrought in us." If we honestly find them in us, we may go to God and *demand* our salvation of Him. This final deduction might seem to us one of the more breath-taking of human discoveries, but the theologians, carried along by their logic, saw in it nothing audacious. "You may sue him of his own bond written and sealed," said Preston, "and he cannot deny it." No Puritan was going to surrender himself, even to God, without getting something in return: "We require this back againe of God, that as we give up our selves a sacrifice to him, so that the Lord Jesus Christ be imputed unto us." Therefore once you are on sure ground, "take no denyall, though the *Lord* may defer long, yet he will doe it, he cannot chuse; for it is a part of his Couenant." With a genius for understatement which in their works upon the Covenant these divines exhibit as nowhere else, Preston informs us, "This is a very comfortable doctrine, if it be well considered."

Nevertheless, it was not comfortable enough for Anne Hutchinson. It left her in anxiety, unable to learn from her obedience whether she was fulfilling covenant conditions or merely improving "common graces". It seemed to her that all the ministers except John Cotton juggled with words, preaching salvation by faith, but immediately translating faith into federal terms, and so turning it into works. They spoke like Peter Bulkeley, who said that God promises mankind to save them for His Son's sake, and that this absolute promise is "a ground for the faith of adherence to cleave unto," but that in addition He gives "conditionall promises", addressed to specific individuals and telling them the conditions:

There be also conditionall promises, *(He that believeth shall be saved)* by meanes of which (we having the experience and feeling of such grace in our selves) we grow to an assurance that we are of those that he will shew that free grace upon.

Was it not enough, Mistress Hutchinson was asking, that we have the experience and the feeling? Did we need to study our behavior to grow into the assurance? Whether she herself perceived it or not, the more experienced divines recognized at once that her version could be maintained only upon the supposition of a union of the believer with Christ so intimate and so perfect that the believer would be exempted from all considerations of conduct. Yet they knew that even good Christians needed to give much thought to these matters, that weak Christians needed to give even more, and that wicked men would use her argument to escape all morality. If it were true that "God and any Creature do really participate in one common Nature, so as to be properly reduced to one head of distribution," Mrs. Hutchinson might have argued her case; but Protestantism had long before judged this conclusion pernicious and intolerable. Consequently, all Protestants had striven to define regeneration as a union, but not as a blending, as an infusion of divine energy which yet did not obliterate the will of man. Federal theologians thought they had the perfect solution in the covenant doctrine, in a theory of supernatural regeneration that preserved intact the will of man, his responsibility, and his moral obligation. Mrs. Hutchinson put the doctrine to the test, and the divines came out of the ordeal more than ever convinced of its truth and its value. God corroborated their feeling by delivering Mrs. Hutchinson over to the tomahawk, and Peter Bulkeley could draw the obvious moral: "Let her damned heresies shee fell into . . . and the just vengeance of God, by which shee perished, terrifie all her seduced followers from having any more to doe with her leaven." Thomas Shepard denounced all those who had to do with her leaven, those who "deny the use of the Law to any that are in Christ," and who "will not take any comfort of their good estate, from any conformity of their hearts to the Law of God"; hence they become, he said, "Patrons of free vice, under the mask of Free-grace," and pretending to be immune to the law, give their consciences full liberty to break every commandment with impunity. This was the result of not comprehending the subtle doctrine of the Covenant, and John Cotton, to whom Mrs. Hutchinson had first looked as the sole spokesman of the spiritual interpretation, seeing at last the terrible consequences for social morality of her theories, and incidentally the possible loss of his social position in Massachusetts Bay, turned upon her with the rest:

> If any therefore shall accuse the Doctrine of the Covenant of free grace, of *Antinomianisme,* . . . and if they commit any sin, they plead they are not bound unto the Law . . . the children of the Covenant of grace will onely tell you, that they are free from the Covenant of the Law, but not from the Commandment.

It was Cotton who had written that the faith of Christians "is not grounded upon the sight of their sanctification, but is revealed in an Absolute Promise of free grace"; when his brilliant parishioner concluded from his words that she would trust only the revelation of an absolute promise and not heed the conditional, when her doctrines caused others to feel that "to be solicitous about sanctification and inherent grace is too troublesome; to seek God diligently in the use of all means, in a daily and hearty performance of holy duties . . . must be laid by as a legal business," then it was time for John Cotton and the orthodox leaders of New England to commit Massachusetts and Connecticut to a firm stand upon the federal theology, and for the later divines to continue indoctrinating New Englanders with the concepts of a mutual stipulation and an irrevocable compact, by which devolves upon man the responsibility for fulfilling moral terms in return for irresistible grace, and by which the regenerating effects of divine grace could be distinguished from a merging of the human person with the Holy Ghost.

After the New England divines had weathered the storm of 1637–1638 they were never seriously threatened by any form of Antinomianism, though they were horrified by the sectarian outbursts in England during the 1640's and magnified the few Quakers who ventured within their jurisdictions into serious dangers against the established order. Spokesmen for the Antinomian view were seldom learned enough to challenge the orthodox divines in argument, and if ever they promised to become too formidable, the ministers could always appeal to "the very light of nature" which taught all nations "that mad men acting according to their frantick passions are to be restrained with chaines, when they can not be restrained otherwise." But Arminians were a different story. The Dutch and English heretics were among the most erudite and skillful scholars of the age, and to some of them, like Grotius, even the New England divines acknowledged an intellectual debt. Furthermore, the Arminian position was so natural a response to certain questions posed in orthodox theory, it grew so logically out of certain fundamental propositions, that divines were troubled by it even when not called upon to debate it, and had always to be on guard lest their congregations drift insensibly into it.

They often endeavored to answer the Arminians without invoking the Covenant, though generally they found it the most convenient stick for beating this particular dog. It gave them their most effective argument: moral obedience bears the same relation to salvation in God's special dispensation that second causes bear to their effects in God's ordinary concurrence. A cause is decreed by God to come before the effect "in the order of nature," and though it precedes, it does not in itself engender the effect; each is separately created and sustained by God, who also maintains the order of the occurrence. So in salvation, it is God who gives both the power of obedience and the redemption, but He ordains that an earthly obedience should anticipate the translation into heaven. Thus good works are, as we have seen, a condition of the Covenant not causally but "declaratively", just as fire is the condition of heat merely because God has enacted that it should ordinarily be concomitant. Deeds do not merit the salvation, but they must accompany it, and so, as Bulkeley explained, the grace of the Covenant is free notwithstanding the condition, "because we doe not put any condition as antecedent to the Covenant on Gods part, whereby to induce and move the Lord to enter into covenant with us, as if there were any thing supposed in us, which might invite and draw him to take us into covenant with himselfe." The condition is then merely antecedent to our being given the promise of life, "which condition we are to observe and walke in; and in the observation thereof to expect the blessing of life which the covenant promiseth." Arminians erred in making the obedience entirely an affair of man's good pleasure, whereas it is God who works in us a power to obey as well as rewards us with eternal life. The obedience must be hearty and voluntary on our part, but it is not and it never can be "meritorious". In the Covenant of Grace "workes are not set as the causes of our salvation, but as evidences and signes of those that do believe unto life." Sanctified works follow upon faith, are the fruits of election, and faith must go before "in order of Nature." This truth, the federal theologians believed, was not anywhere weakened by the covenant theory, which only made explicit the fact that after a saint receives faith, it behooves him to work for as much sanctification as his abilities and the providence of God make possible.

With Arminius thus disposed of, at least to their own satisfaction, the federal theologians perfected a philosophy of the Covenant that gave more and more scope to the moral will and put upon men's own shoulders the responsibility for their fates. They attacked the problem of the lassitude that always threatened to follow among Calvinists from the fatalistic doctrine of predestination. Conceiving of grace as the proffer of covenant terms, they could argue that all who live within hearing of any Christian preaching are invited to take up the bond. "It is offered universally to all wherever it comes, and therefore personally to every man." Hence when the Covenant is presented, through the means of a sermon, to a particular individual, and he does not take it up, or attempt to take it, he must be resisting it. You should take heed, said these theologians, of refusing the overture, for "there is a certaine acceptable time, when God offers Grace, and after that hee offers it no more." Though grace and faith come entirely from God, yet because they are tendered through natural means and reasonable inducements, which all can grasp through the senses and comprehend in their understandings, men have of themselves the power to turn their backs upon the grace of God, to refuse to be convinced by the most unanswerable demonstrations, to sneer at the minister and resist faith. By dealing through a covenant, God is able to present His case so that no man of ordinary intelligence should continue unconverted, if only on the grounds of self-interest: He tries to bring men "under a new Covenant Relation, and the promise that is revealed in it, is the great encouragement of the Covenant, giving men to understand what shall be the advantage that shall accrue to them by putting of themselves under it." A man must have God's assistance to accept the Covenant, but still it is thrust upon him so persuasively that as long as he retains the faculties of reason and will he is accountable for not accepting. "There is no man exempted, no man debarred, no man hindered to take grace upon those tearmes, if he will condescend to Gods conditions" —so runs the astounding exhortation of New England predestinarians; no matter what a man's condition or spiritual poverty, "if he will but choose and prize Christ above all other things, he shall receive him, and grace, and salvation by him." At any rate, the damned cannot curse God for their fate, "there is no backwardnesse on Gods part, God doth freely will that every soule that heareth the Word of God and hath Christ offered, that they should receive the Lord Iesus." When they come to die, the reprobate shall hear God remonstrating with them, "the time was, when I cryed to you by the Ministers, and you would not heare"; they will know then that the decree is passed against them, and that whether the cause be their works or the sovereign ordinance of Christ, they deserve their reprobation for having refused the easy and rational terms of the Covenant.

Thus the covenant theory was an extremely subtle, possibly an over-subtle, device within the framework of predestination for arousing human activity; it permitted man to conceive of divine grace as an opportunity to strike a bargain, to do himself a good turn, to make a sure profit, as an occasion that comes at specific moments in time through the agency of natural means, through the ministry and the plain, demonstrative sermon. Ergo, whoever does not close the deal when he has a chance cannot blame God for his own stupidity. "The Lord is a suitor to many a man that never gives himself to him." The Lord pledges Himself in the Covenant to do all that can rationally be expected of Him, to provide the means; He "is bound by *Covenant,* that they shall not for want of means perish: nor upon such grounds as are far above the *nature* of creatures to reach unto." Therefore, even though a man needs supernatural help to achieve faith, yet he lives of his own will, he may go to the sermon and listen to convincing arguments; if then he does not believe, it is his own doing, "as a man that is drunke, though he is not able to understand the commands of his Master, yet because he was the first Author of the drunkennesse, (which caused such sottishnesse), he is inexcusable." God is meeting us more than half-way when He arranges the method of conversion so that "hee will not doe it without us, because wee are reasonable men and women, and God affords us meanes." It was clear, then, that whatever theology might say about the futility of human efforts, covenanted Christians could use the means, because God appointed them precisely on the "condition" that they be used. "His promising includeth their endeavouring, and upon their endeavouring in the use of the meanes that God hath appointed, he hath promised to enable them to doe what he hath commanded." Because God has promised to assist those who do what they can "towards the performing the condition of the Covenant, we may well conclude, that there is no Man under the Gospel, doth perish, but through his own fault and neglect." Again and again, federal theologians come triumphantly to this moral: "It will therefore be your own fault if at last you shall go without it." We see others around us converted by the same means under which we live; is it not obvious that we too would have been enlightened had we not despised the light? It was not God who prevented us, but ourselves. There is nothing contradictory in His promising to work faith in men and yet blaming them for not profiting, "for he was willing to work it in them, but they resisted his holy Spirit in the Ministery." It is the fault of man if he does not take the Covenant, and it is his fault again if, having taken it, he does not keep it. "To transact with the Infinitely Holy God, in a way of Covenant, is a very Awful thing," and requires "the greatest care imaginable, to comply with our Engagements." Because, as we have seen, to covenant with God is to take up the moral obligation, then it "doth imply a professed subjection to the revealed will of God." Just as a servant, bound by an indenture, is to obey his master, "so a Covenant People have promised submission to the will of God." The unregenerate, to whom a covenant is offered through the means, justly excite God's anger when they refuse: "Nothing sooner, or more provokes God then the abusing or not well improving of visible Covenant-priviledges"; but He becomes still more furious, and with even better cause, when men already in the Covenant, when those who "are under such strickt solemn tyes, and obligations to service and obedience," who are "tyed up so short, so chained, so bound with the bonds of the Covenant, that their hands are so manicled that they cannot act as they would, feet so fettered that they cannot walk as they please," when these nevertheless struggle to escape. The afflictions which fall upon Christian communities thus become explicable: they are punishments either for an initial refusal of the people to take the Covenant when it is offered, or for their more willful efforts to extricate their engaged wills from the bond of the Covenant.

The covenant doctrine did not at any of these points intend to depart from essential Calvinism; it did not openly inculcate free will. But by conceiving of grace as a readiness of God to join in covenant with any man who will not resist Him, the theory declared in effect that God has taken the initiative, that man can have only himself to blame if he does not accede to the divine proposal. This was indeed a marvelous stratagem for getting around an immovable obstacle in theology. Calvin had simply disregarded this obstacle by asserting that though God elects or rejects according to His pleasure, the responsibility for damnation is man's own, but the generation of Cotton, Hooker, and Bulkeley could no longer accept so brusque or unsophisticated a solution. They were under greater compulsions to clear God of the charge of arbitrary government and to place the onus for success or failure upon men. The result was this conception, not of conditional election, but of conditional covenant, set up by the absolute decree of God and yet requiring the self-directed activity of man. Accordingly the federalists betrayed a marked tendency to reduce the actual intrusion of grace to a very minute point. Some of them, notably Hooker and Shepard, not only insisted that the tiniest particle was sufficient to start a man on the road to salvation, but even argued that before any faith was generated, before God gave the enabling grace, merely from the incentives of the means, a man could at least "prepare" himself for receiving the faith, though out of this argument were to grow conclusions still further removed from the pure doctrine of Calvinism. The final outcome in all New England preaching of the covenant theory was a shamelessly pragmatic injunction. It permitted the ministers to inform their congregations that if any of them could fulfill the Covenant, they were elected. The way to find out was to try. "Therefore goe on boldly, God hath promised to heare you, hee cannot deny you." Always you should go on. God may decree, but you can bargain with Him: "As he maketh a covenant with you, to give himselfe wholly to you: so do you devote and consecrate your selves, your wit, strength, gifts, and all to be wholly for him." John Preston summarized the ultimate spirit of these theologians, the practical point of their intricate system, in one amazing sentence: "The way to grow in any grace is the exercise of that grace."

Here then was a revision of Calvinism which by skillful dialectic preserved the essential tenets of piety—the absolute God, the depraved man, the redeeming and unmerited grace—and yet contrived at the same time that justification by faith should not produce a moral laxity. It aimed throughout to prove that faith without performance was impossible, a contradiction in terms, that the performance required is stated in the moral law, in the Ten Commandments, which are also the law of nature, the law of that which is good in itself. In dogmatic piety morality could exist only as a series of random fiats, it had no other basis, and to Calvin it had needed no other. The covenant theology was a later recognition that this basis was inadequate, that it reduced morality to arbitrary edict, that it offered humanity no other inducement to obedience than the whip and lash. Consequently, in New England morality was established, not so much on the decrees of God as upon the terms of the Covenant, and man's will was engaged to it, not so much out of his fear of the Lord as out of respect for his own given word. The law to which he had pledged himself was what he as a rational, logical being, possessed of all faculties, a student of nature and of the liberal arts, could see was inherently just, and he could not complain against being asked to observe it.

To say this much concerning the principal doctrine in the theology of early New England, the one tenet upon which all other theories were made to hang, is to restate a conclusion we have already had occasion to note: at the time New England was settled, the Puritan leaders and people were still children of Augustine, still men of piety, and their life, on the conscious level, was still dominated by spiritual considerations, but nevertheless their piety was on the wane. Even at its highest intensity, Puritanism had never cast off a rich and complicated intellectual heritage, though it had tried to simplify certain departments; Puritans still believed not only in their religious creed, but in reason, logic, and the arts. The more minutely we examine their thought, the more it becomes clear that the emotional drive of the piety was, as a matter of fact, already lessening at the time the colonies were founded, and that the colonists thenceforward were progressively more swayed by factors in the intellectual heritage than by the hunger of the spirit. A wise man, said William Hubbard—expressing the canniness we have often had occasion to note in the Puritan character—is he who knows how to accomplish his design with a full view of the circumstances, "for many times the circumstances may much alter a case." The

God of the Covenant was, in this sense, very wise, and He seems to have learned that He must wear gloves in handling so thorny a blossom as man. In the federal theology the Old Testament Jehovah begins the metamorphosis, which has proved an unforeseen result of the Reformation, from a mail-clad seigneur to a skillful teacher who contrives that pupils be brought to truth not by compulsion but by conviction, from the God of the whirlwind to the gentle father sorrowing for His lost children, to the God of eighteenth-century benevolence and Newtonian physics. The covenant doctrine might, therefore, be held the capital instance of the Puritans' deliberate effort to combine their piety with their intellectual concepts, to preserve the irrational force of revelation and yet to harmonize it with the propositions of reason and logic, of the arts and of physics, of psychology and of the causal effect of the means. And finally, as we have found repeatedly suggested by the tenor of this argument, the doctrine must bear some intimate relation to contemporaneous social history, to the points of view which Puritans were defending in the political and economic struggles of the century, to the alliance of Puritanism and the common law. Perhaps it would not be amiss to say that though the covenant doctrine was elaborated by orthodox Puritans against Arminianism and Antinomianism, yet in their attempt to fend off these heresies the orthodox took up many ideas not so much for theological as for social and economic reasons. When the federal theologians are viewed historically, they seem to have served not so much the cause of their creed as of their party, and since their party dominated the scene in New England, their theology becomes of most lasting importance as an aspect of the political and social order.

CHAPTER XIV

THE SOCIAL COVENANT

A historian of New England could easily overstate the importance of the federal theorists in European affairs. They were a special and restricted group, with a theory too complex and recondite to be accepted even by all Puritans, and only in Massachusetts and Connecticut, where theologians and politicians were able to treat it as the theoretical foundation of the state as well as of salvation, did the theology succeed for a time in uniting a whole thought upon a single concept. The importance of the doctrine is thus immense for the intellectual history of America, but in Europe it remained merely one among several abortive attempts to harmonize the irreconcilable ideas which were abroad in the seventeenth century. Nevertheless, when considered as a phenomenon of the period, as a symptom rather than as a cause, it takes on the deepest significance for our study, and the very fact that at the beginning of the next century it proved inadequate to cope with the intellectual situation causes it the more pertinently to set forth the elements of that situation.

Through the maze of dialectic with which the covenant theologians rephrased conventional tenets runs one consistent purpose: they were endeavoring to mark off an area of human behavior from the general realm of nature, and within it to substitute for the rule of necessity a rule of freedom. They were striving to push as far into the background as possible the order of things that exists by inevitable equilibrium, that is fulfilled by unconscious and aimless motions, that is determined by inertia and inexorable law, and in its place to set up an order founded upon voluntary choice, upon the deliberate assumption of obligation, upon unconstrained pacts, upon the sovereign determinations of free wills. They were struggling to extricate man from the relentless primordial mechanism, from the chains of instinct and fear, to set him upon his own feet, to endow him with a knowledge of utility and purpose, with the faculties to implement his knowledge, so that he might rationally choose and not be driven from pillar to post by fate or circumstance. They were inspired, even though but half conscious of their motive, with a desire to transform the concept of duty from something imposed brutally and irrationally by an ultimate datum into something to which man himself rationally and willingly consented. Obedience was no longer to be wrung from subjects by might, but accepted as a spontaneous token; a man was to be good or bad, not because he could never have been otherwise, but because he whole-heartedly preferred his course. Certainty in human affairs was to rest not upon inexplicable decrees but upon the seal that attested the sworn covenant and insured the fulfillment of covenant terms.

This is to say that the federal theology was essentially part of a universal tendency in European thought to change social relationships from status to contract, that it was one expression of late Renaissance speculation, which was moving in general away from the ideas of feudalism, from the belief that society must be modeled upon an eternally fixed hierarchy to the theories of constitutional limitation and voluntary origins, to the protection of individual rights and the shattering of sumptuary economic regulations. There can be no doubt that these theologians inserted the federal idea into the very substance of divinity, that they changed the relation even of God to man from necessity to contract, largely because contractualism was becoming increasingly congenial to the age and in particular to Puritans. If we are to seek ultimate causes for the federal doctrine in historical terms, we must undoubtedly resort to such considerations, yet there are two cautions to be observed in correlating too glibly the federal theology with the drift of contemporaneous social thinking. First, the authors themselves reached their conclusion by starting from the words of the Bible and deducing consequences according to the logic of Ramus, the rhetoric of Talon, the psychological assumptions of Aristotle; they may have been driven unwittingly to satisfy the interests of their class, of merchants and capitalists, but they had to observe the limits imposed by their authority, and by their instruments for interpreting it. They could develop the covenant only so far as the Bible permitted, or could be made to permit. Second, they were formulating the doctrine in the early seventeenth century, when contractualism was new, when the full implications of the covenant idea remained unexplored. They crystallized not its final result but its initial phase; they mark a transition, but they look backward as well as forward. They reflect the revolution in society, but not the direction of the revolt; they could never carry the theory of bilateral compact to the explicit rationalism and constitutionalism it ultimately became, and they were foredoomed to the exciting but hopeless task of stabilizing it along with their inherited belief in unilateral authority and divine revelation. The history of New England, from Winthrop to Otis, from Cotton to Emerson, is implicit in these latent antagonisms, and the intellectual career of the communities might be most succinctly described as a progressive disintegration of the federal theology.

To begin with, this theology was concerned not so much with framing a bill of rights against superior powers, either celestial or earthly—though this was indeed among its objects—as first and foremost with finding proofs for voluntarism, with showing that rulers have agreed to a pact and that subjects have willingly consented to assume their duties. Its primary interest was explaining that although God is absolute and His decrees final, nevertheless the reprobate go to hell of their own volition and the elect are saved by their own free option, while even God and Christ fulfill their appointed functions in the cosmic drama by virtue of contractual commitments. Men of the seventeenth century could not organize their church and state upon the premise of voluntary relations until they had found a larger sanction for voluntarism than economic interest; not until they had secured a contractual basis for damnation and salvation, and even for the most transcendent of Christian mysteries, for the very Trinity itself, could they venture to look for a similar foundation for the commonwealth.

The aim of the theologians was writ large in their version of the doctrine of original sin. Traditional piety, following the teaching of Augustine and re-instructed by Calvin, held that the depravity of Adam was communicated to his descendants as an inherited taint, a disease contained in the protoplasm, a violent contagion. "From a putrefied root, therefore, have sprung putrid branches, which have transmitted their putrescence to remoter ramifications." [1] Federal Puritans were not able entirely to overlook this interpretation, for it was firmly settled in the Augustinian tradition, but by deduction from the Covenant they were able to devise another theory which in effect nullified the Augustinian. If the sin of Adam were regarded as the violation of a contract, it could, as it were, become externalized, forensic rather than internal, a punishable crime rather than an infinite sin. Seen in this light, the disobedience would amount to a bond broken, a lease violated, and would call for punishment in the form not of deterioration of mind and body but of infliction of a judicial sentence:

> Thus man hath lost his freehold by his ill:
> Now to his Land Lord tenent is at Will.
> And must the Tenement keep in repare
> Whate're the ruins, and the Charges are.[2]

In the covenant theology, man has been expelled for non-payment, he is not spiritually polluted. Original sin is such disability as a criminal suffers under sentence for embezzlement, not the stench of a corpse. Adam had stood as the agent, the "federal" head of the race; when he, the spokesman for all men in the Covenant, broke it and incurred the penalty, the guilt was "imputed" to his constituents as a legal responsibility, not inherited as a cancer or a leprosy. Although the writers could not openly deny that all men by birth were actual participants in Adam's apostasy, they were inclined to touch lightly upon the historic theory of transmission and concentrate upon their own version of legal imputation. They argued like Preston that men are corrupt because, as the heirs of Adam, the debt of Adam is laid at their door:

> There being a compact and covenant betweene God and him, that if *Adam* stood, all his seed should stand with him; but if he fell, then that all that were borne of him should by vertue of that covenant, compact, or agreement have his sinne imputed to them, and so should be corrupted, as hee was, and die the death.

Hooker, who preached both the older and the newer versions, explained the constitutional character of the new in significantly political imagery: "*Adam* in innocencie represented all mankind, he stood (as a Parliament man doth for the whole country) for all that should be born of him." The preachers insisted that their aetiology had in it more justice, more "equity" than any other; "It being just," as Shepard explained, "that as if he standing, all had stood, by imputation of his righteousness, so he falling, all should fall, by the imputation of his sin." The addition of this version to the original may seem at first sight no very radical departure, yet by maintaining that inherent depravity was no injustice to the depraved because they had underwritten their agent and therefore could be called upon to make good his misdemeanor, the new version took sin from the plane of nature, of physics and of birth, and translated it to the plane of guilt, of responsibility and restitution. "So that all Humanity being contracted in our first Parents, humane nature became Guilty in and with them, as it was naturally derivable from them." It was not enough for Puritans that human nature be punished merely because it was derived by propagation from Adam, since it could not choose to be otherwise derived; but when in addition humanity could be shown to have assumed of itself the obligation to stand or fall by Adam's conduct, then indeed might it be held responsible. Such a gloss seemed to these lawyerlike theologians more intelligent, more in keeping with the manners of a God who deals with men in covenants, and they preached it exultingly, in spite of Baxter's ominous warning to beware lest they "bring the Doctrine of Original Sin it self into doubt, by laying all upon Covenant-Relation, and denying, or overlooking the *Natural proofs*." To them original sin became more comprehensible, one might even say more useful, when it meant that man was born owing God a debt, that his creditor had generously compounded with him, making a new arrangement out of consideration for his bankrupt state, and that when he fulfilled the easier terms, the debt would be canceled. In this formulation, the debt remained a serious hindrance to man's free action, but it was not an utterly crushing burden, and it did not obliterate the faculties of reason and will which man possessed as essential elements of the image of God. Therefore these faculties remained free enough to render their possessor inexcusable for neglecting God's law, potent enough to leave him no defense for failing in moral endeavors, because God in the Covenant had condescended to adapt Himself to them, had ordered the scheme of salvation in such a fashion that the reason might comprehend, the will follow, and the affections cleave to it. He had made the terms of salvation just, merciful, and reasonable, so that a reasonable creature could have no reason for rejecting them.

Whenever Puritans spoke of the natural man in purely pietistic terms, they emphasized his irremediable depravity and found in him nothing whatsoever that was good, but whenever they spoke in the language of formal logic or of psychology, they made the most of what remained of the divine image and built as much as possible upon the innate law of nature or the inborn light of reason. The covenant theology, with its theory of original sin by judicial imputation, fell in with the disposition, allowing greater vitality to the natural faculties and harmonizing still further the processes of damnation and regeneration with the methods of reason and freedom. A man would still need supernatural help in order to take up the Covenant of Grace; yet it was possible for theologians to demonstrate that, the terms of the Covenant being eminently rational, no being of understanding and of will could be exonerated for refusing them, and that consequently in the Covenant God provides plausible grounds for what would otherwise be a wholly accidental selection of the elect from the reprobate. With the notion of a covenant to assist them, theologians could give reasons for what physicists could but lamely assert, that in a universe governed by God's providence and sustained by His concurrence, the will of man remains free. The Covenant first made an entire separation of God's special manifestation in a mode perfectly adapted to negotiating with man, who in the great chain of being occupies the place of the creature with reason and will, who is required to fulfill the divine plan by acting on his own volition. "From this speciall and proper way of governing reasonable *Creatures,*" said Ames, "there ariseth that covenant, which is between God and them." Inferior creatures may be ordered through natural laws and unreflecting instincts, but God has created man as a rational creature, "able to know and chuse his own actions, and thereby capable of being treated with in the way of a Covenant, and, having so made him, He thus dealt with him."[3] Thus in a predetermined universe there is room for freedom, and the sovereign determiner, who might have bound all His creatures without bothering about their consent, withholds His might and converses with men in a covenant way, "unto which the Election and Consent of the Creature is essentially required." He conducts the affair in a manner "answerable to the nature of man, not with blowes, but with reasonings and disputes," and puts the final touch to His accommodation by acting in regeneration as though He were suing men in a court of common pleas. "He, as it were, enters a Law Case with the poor sinnefull sonnes of men, and proceeds in a judiciall course to recover a poore sinner from the pathes of death wherein he straied . . . as yee see men goe to Law." Certainly when God takes the trouble to hail a man before the bar of the Covenant, when He goes to the lengths of appearing upon the same level with His creature to collect by law what He might appropriate by force, and when all the time He is suing the creature not for life or estate but for the privilege of redeeming him, then at least it must follow that those have only themselves to blame who refuse to be convicted. "Hereby Men that slight and despise the Means, are rendered inexcusable, because the Offers made to them, were most highly Rational."

Thus the predestinating decree of Jehovah was in New England two very different things, depending upon whether conceived by piety or by metaphysics; for the pious heart it was the inescapable fact of nature, the cruel and ruthless imposition which all men suffer from their characters, their heredities, or from circumstance, but at the same time, for the intellect trained in logic, rhetoric, and physics, it was a rational judgment inflicting upon responsible individuals just such a sentence as they asked for. This was not to say with Arminius that their conduct was the cause of their sentence, but it was to say that justice was done, that none of the condemned could complain of being incarcerated for crimes of which they were innocent. Had God concealed within His impenetrable secrecy all clues as to who were to be saved, had He sphinx-like uttered no hint concerning the grounds for His selections, there could be no question of justice in the choosing, because there would be no known rule making it possible to distinguish the elect, who embrace Him, from the reprobate, who reject Him. But through the covenants His hidden and terrifying intentions are brought into the open, and His terrors turned into reasons; the rule of salvation is made explicit and the elect may now prove the justice of their redemption by freely accepting the reasonable Covenant, while the reprobate will vindicate the righteousness of their condemnation by their unreasonable and obstinate refusal. God's eternal purposes were originally sealed, and the full accomplishment of them will not for many centuries be experimentally felt, but the Covenant openly declares the purposes and guarantees the accomplishment. Whatever He does by absolute sovereignty must indeed be just, for God is the sum of all excellence and as He is just in His own nature, "so he is just in all his works and doings to his Creatures, and therefore in His Works of Judgments to his People"; the people could have had no cause for complaint had He chosen to judge them only by His secret rules, but they would never have seen the justice, and therefore out of His great mercy He binds Himself in the Covenant to try them by the rule of His relative justice, by the explicit terms of the Covenant.

> His Law considered as a Covenant, as 'tis under the Sanction of Promises and Threatnings, is the Rule according to which his own People may expect he will dispense Justice unto them, in the way of his Judgments. Against this Rule there is no exception to be made by us; no not against his Judgment of eternal Condemnation upon the Reprobate who perish, being Reprobated according to the Will of God; for their eternal Reprobation, and so their Condemnation it is according to this righteous Rule of Justice between God and man.

Arminianism was heresy, not because it tried to make God just, but because it secured His justice at the expense of His essential power, forcing Him to solicit the help of man, holding Him powerless to change a man who chooses to be evil. It was wrong to say that God expects anything from man in the sense of leaving any decree uncertain or dependent upon man's doing, as though God has to wait before He can tell whether the creature will fulfill the expectation, but it was correct to say that in the Covenant He expects a return from those whom He foreknows will give it. That He expects fulfillment of conditions from men "must be interpreted of his *revealed will,* in respect of the transactions that have past between God and his People: for, as he treats with them as men, so he is said to look for this or that from them, after the manner of men." One good Puritan who could not follow this seductive logic, Dr. Twisse, the troubled moderator of the Westminster Assembly, entered into debate with John Cotton and tried to defend the pure Calvinist position that God elects or condemns "meerly according to the good pleasure of his owne will," not out of His goodness or His wisdom but out of His "absoluteness", doing good "to none but what he will, and what he does is, *ipso facto,* good." Cotton admitted openly that for his part he intended "to clear the Orthodox Doctrine of Predestination from such harsh consequences, as are wonted to be derived from absolute Reprobation," and so declared to Twisse's horror that as "it is a greater honour to a Prince to be gratious and just, than to bee wise and powerfull," so God in his special government of mankind "aimed chiefly at the manifestation of his grace and justice, above the manifestation of his power and dominion." Therefore, said Cotton, God resorts to government by consent, even though He Himself has to supply His subjects with the ability to consent, so that the forms of justice may be fully observed. We must not say that He sends the reprobate to hell after offering them "life upon such condition which hee knew was impossible for them to keep"; on the contrary, in the Covenant of Grace He presents the issue so squarely that all can be said to have had revealed to them enough "to bring them on to see their impotency in themselves, and to stirre them up to seeke for help, and strength, and life, in him where it is to be found." If thereafter they neglect or despise the Covenant, as did the Pharisees, "God and his Covenant are blameless, in offering them life, and the meanes of it; their destruction is of themselves." Twisse frantically objected that a conditional covenant in this sense was a farce, because even if it enabled the damned to realize their impotence, it gave the power to perform the indispensable conditions to none but those who had been arbitrarily predestined; and he roundly declared,

There never was any such Covenant of God with man; I meane, in such sort conditionate: and consequently, there never was any purpose in God to make any such Covenant with man . . . For, since the Fall of *Adam* all being borne in sinne, there is no place for such a Covenant.

However Twisse might cry, and the modern reader may concur, that by the ingenious covenant theory "God is nothing at all advantaged hereby in his reputation, but onely in words, which is no reall reliefe to his honour, but the adding of another injury (if that bee an injury unto him, as you conceive;) namely, to mock him also," but he fulminated in vain, for he was one of the few who retained the strong theological stomach of the sixteenth century and who had not found in their experience any cause for "the manifold odious imputations of strange harshnesse layd upon Gods proceedings."[4] Cotton, stern Puritan though he is popularly imagined to have been, spoke for the more humane side of the seventeenth century, which would no longer bow abjectly before God in fear and trembling. So he was driven, even while remaining officially loyal to the theology of election and reprobation, to soften it, to smuggle into it the elements of abstract justice, at least a partial reassurance that the award of life or death was not given with an utter disregard of moral endeavors.

Not content with resting salvation upon a compact between man and God, the federal theologians were soon reinforcing the justice, the rationality, and the permanence of the Covenant of Grace with the hypothesis of another and a previous covenant between God and Christ, so that they made God not merely bound by His pledge to the creature, but still more firmly tied by a compact with Himself. Theologians called this pact the Covenant of Redemption, and posited it as the prerequisite, the foundation of the Covenant of Grace. Obviously it was necessary that Christ exist, that He fulfill the Covenant of Works and atone for the sin of man, so that God, His justice at last placated, could mercifully receive the saints for their faith; theologians had always agreed upon this necessity, and Anselm had proved that the necessity was ontological, that salvation could not be extended to any until divine justice had been satisfied. The federal theologians now introduced into theology a novel interrogation: which was more noble, that the Redeemer should be dispatched whether He would or no, or that He come of His own free and generous volition? "If we look upon Christ as God-man, or Decreed to be so, we must conceive that he hath voluntarily Undertaken it, for he was not so necessarily," said the New England parson, while the greatest of Puritan poets represented the Savior in the very act of undertaking His mission:

> I for his sake will leave
> Thy bosom, and this glorie next to thee
> Freely put off, and for him lastly die
> Well pleas'd . . .

And since heavenly persons do not take foolhardy risks, what more wise than that Christ should insure the success of His endeavor by binding God in a covenant to bestow grace upon those for whom He was about to die? As the imputation of Adam's sin to posterity results from his being the federal representative of mankind in the Covenant of Works, so the imputation of Christ's righteousness to the elect results from His being accepted by God in the Covenant of Redemption as their federal representative; once God has thus covenanted with His Son, He is committed to carrying out the Covenant of Grace. Christ may be called the covenant, "because all the promises in the Covenant are his, and made to him, and in him, and through him only conveyed to beleevers." The federal theologians, starting from the simple notion of a covenant between God and man, found the concept so attractive that they immediately extended it further, and supposed an anterior compact within the Godhead, *"An Everlasting Compact clearly made, and firmly Ratified, between God the Father, and God the Son, about the Redemption and Salvation of a number of the Children of Men."* We have no grounds for any certainty in the traditional doctrine of the Trinity, and Anselm's arguments become valid only if there is visible evidence of a divine consent to the scheme. The Covenant of Redemption is that evidence, showing the two persons in the act of making their purpose explicit and committing themselves eternally to achieving it. The Covenant of Grace could not otherwise exist, for it demands a previous willingness of the Son to assume the rôle of scapegoat. Thus the Covenant of Redemption "may be looked upon as the *procuring cause* of the Covenant of Grace: it opened the door to it, removed the obstructions that would else have impeded it, and made the way for God to be gracious to poor sinning man, and save him, without any injury done to his justice, or violence offered to his law." The justice of God was captured in a pledge from the beginning of time, even before the transaction with Abraham:

> God covenanted with Christ that if he would pay the full price for the redemption of beleevers, they should be discharged. Christ hath paid the price, God must be unjust, or else hee must set thee free from all iniquitie.

To the curious historian this audacious intrusion into the holy sanctuary of the Trinity seems one of the more shocking exhibitions of Puritan effrontery, a conformation of the supreme irrationality of Christianity to the prosaic cadences of common sense, blasphemous degradation of the tripartite divinity into a joint stock company. Yet to the theologians the charms of volition were so immense that the idea of binding God and Christ together in a covenant was to them an enhancement of the Trinity rather than a vulgarization. The "great Affair," said Willard, is most suitably represented to us under the notion of a covenant, "which being of so much use among men, is the more easily understood: and because it carries in it the strongest confirmation of things that Humane Nature is capable of, must needs be most accommodated to the establishing of our Faith." Indeed, the divines often announced with disarming frankness that we must conceive the atonement as the result of a covenant, "else we can have no rational and regular notion of a person sending, and of a Person sent." It was exceedingly necessary for English Puritans that their notions be rational and regular, and to them the relationship of Father and Son, creator and preserver, stood upon a more regular footing when it was a mutual covenant than when, in some fashion forever beyond the compass of rationality, it was a mysterious union of the two natures in one personality. In the community of a covenant the two formed not a monstrosity but a reliable corporation for underwriting the Covenant of Grace, for insuring the constant maintenance of covenant justice, for guaranteeing that those who readily fulfill the conditions will not miss the reward.

Thus the federal theology surveyed the entire field of purposive or moral action, tabulated all the varieties of behavior that do not follow automatically or recurrently from the plan of creation and that are independent of physical law. Having enumerated them, the theology classified them into two categories, virtuous if they were voluntary executions of a contract, sinful if they were willful repudiations. It found abundant opportunity in the universe for acts of deliberate choice, for the exercise of a liberty to do either one thing or another, notwithstanding the absolute sovereignty of God, but it found nowhere any intelligent conduct without some relation to a precedent contract. It asserted that every being higher in the chain of being than the animals, every agent capable of rational selection or to whom the word duty could have any application, was implicated in an explicit indenture. Every power able to consent or resist had already consented to live according to some particular terms. The discourse of reason was made syonymous with the domain of liberty, and liberty was conformed to law through the assent of reason. God was tied by a double covenant, angels had their conventions, all mankind were under the Covenant of Works and the elect engaged afresh in the Covenant of Grace. To give a systematic texture to their philosophy, Puritans had first to construct the whole cosmos upon a covenant; only then could they come down to earth and investigate the foundations of government. Had salvation been distributed by an iron law of necessity, had men been foredoomed by rigid fate, absolutism would infallibly have reigned in civil polity; a voluntary compact could never be negotiated by automatons nor a free society be composed by slaves. God was desirous that His will be done on earth as it was in heaven, and by creating in men the faculties of the rational soul, by dealing with them reasonably through means and in covenants, He had sufficiently defined His will. If He did not ask men to obey even His laws before securing their assent, if He stooped to give them reasons for compliance and to show what it should profit them, surely no earthly power had any absolute title to the support of its subjects. "No common weale can be founded but by free consent,"[5] asserted John Winthrop, who held it "clearely agreed" that states originate in a voluntary subjection of the citizens to rules and laws for the sake of the common welfare, "for no man hath lawful power over another, but by birth or consent, so likewise, by the law of proprietye, no man can have just interest in that which belongeth to another, without his consent." When the magistrates were accused of illegally extending their power, Winthrop commenced a pamphlet in their defense by acknowledging completely, "The foundation of the peoples power is their liberty," and explained that men were not to be brought under any rule otherwise "then accordinge to their will, & Covenant."[6] When he himself was accused of tyranny, he replied by describing arbitrary power as "where a people have men sett ouer them, without their choyce, or allowance: who haue power to governe them, & Judge their Causes without a Rule," and he publicly professed that since God alone could pass sentence without a rule—His will being "a perfecte Rule, & Reason it selfe"—for a man to usurp such prerogative was impiety. The ministers were equally certain that the sanction for community existence was a covenant; there are certain duties, said Hooker, that flow from the nature of things, so that quite apart from the Covenant of Grace man would owe homage to the creator, but "*this* relation from a rule of *nature,* it hath nothing to do with a *free covenant,* that must come between the persons and their duties." No mortal has authority over others from any "impression of nature" except fathers over their children, none from any "rule of providence" or "appointment of God," now that God no longer informs prophets and kings by direct revelation; hence "there must of necessity be a mutuall ingagement, each of the other, by their free consent, before by any rule of God they have any right or power, or can exercise either, each towards the other." This truth was for Hooker exemplified "in all covenants betwixt *Prince* and *People, Husband* and *Wife, Master* and *Servant,*" and though each relationship entails its special duties, "yet it is certain, it requires that they should *first freely ingage* themselves in such covenants, and *then* be careful to fulfill such duties." Throughout the large design of Puritan thinking was endlessly repeated the pattern of the covenant, of a mutual engagement between two independent parties, who, once they have given their oath, are eternally bound.

This compact to attend to such terms, to walk in such orders, said Hooker, gives being to every corporate body, this is "that *sement* which soders them all, that *soul* as it were, that acts all the parts and particular persons so interested in such a way"; outside of it "there is no man constrained to enter into such a condition, unlesse he will," and he who will enter "must also willingly binde and ingage himself to each member of that society to promote the good of the whole, or else a member actually he is not." With this doctrine ready to hand well before the colonies were settled, the leaders were prepared to organize their commonwealths and furthermore to acknowledge by force of logic several of the deductions which were later to furnish the political wisdom of a Locke or a Jefferson. That magistrates were limited by the compact, that government should be by laws and not by men, that the covenant was annulled by any serious violation of the terms, and that the people possessed a right to resist all such infringements —these principles were declared no less emphatically in Puritan theory than in the Declaration of Independence. The so-called theocracies of New England never lost sight of them, and whenever their own deeds were called in question they endeavored, after the example of John Winthrop, to exonerate themselves according to the first principles of contractualism. John Cotton put the case for the limitation of rulers as bluntly as any radical of the eighteenth century: neither magistrates nor ministers, he said, should "affect more liberty and authority then will do them good, and the People good," and so it is necessary "that all power that is on earth be limited." There were those who thought it dangerous to limit prerogatives, but he would say, "it is a further danger, not to have them limited." The people, "in whom fundamentally all power lyes," should give as much power to their rulers as God allows, but also the magistrates "should desire to know the utmost bounds of their own power," and both should know that "All intrenchments upon the bounds which God hath not given, they are no enlargements, but burdens and snares." The grim tread of Cromwell's troops sounds in his metaphor: "If you tether a Beast at night, he knows the length of his tether before morning; he will goe to the end of it before he have done." The *Body of Liberties* adopted in 1641 reflects with equal vividness the Puritans' resolve to defend the privileges of their compact against unlimited prerogative, as it asserts that the free fruition of such immunities, "Without impeachment and Infringement, hath ever bene and ever will be the tranquillitie and Stabilitie of Churches and Commonwealths." We uncover certain well-springs of the Puritan movement when we find that the first formulated code of Massachusetts, a colony designed to realize definite ideals of church order and holy living, was not a declaration of righteousness but a prevention of abuses, protecting the rights of Englishmen and forbidding that any man be tried or taxed "unlesse it be by vertue or equitie of some expresse law of the Country waranting the same." [7] Almost every election sermon throughout the century gave at least passing endorsement to the truisms of constitutional government; John Norton exclaimed, "We must do nothing but according to the Patern," the younger Shepard warned that "presidents of Arbitrary rule" would bring tyranny and woe, and Willard at last fitted several pages into *A Compleat Body of Divinity* to prove, "Where there is Government there must be a Rule."

Following this reasoning, New England discourses developed many other implications of the compact, ideas which were to become commonplace in the next century, but which then seemed novel and revolutionary. Repeatedly the authors asserted, "The people are not for the Rulers, but the Rulers for the people, to minister to their welfare," and ministers frequently admonished the most orthodox of magistrates, "It is impossible that any thing should be truly right, that is destructive to the common good." Though the clergy exercised discretion, not wishing unnecessarily to antagonize royal sensibilities, still they never left the people in doubt about their right to resist rulers who transgress the agreement. He who tells a king's subjects that they must obey "contrary to the stream of Law," said Cotton, is a criminal flatterer of the king and no proponent of true obedience; though private persons are not to rebel at every injustice, yet when the body of the people find their rulers "to have broken the fundamental Articles of their Covenant," they are released from any further loyalty. Not merely when rulers make war against the true religion, but when they violate "the way of Justice and happinesse, which they are sworn to maintain; now in such a case as this, It is . . . lawfull to take up armes of defence."

If we were to read these passages by any other light than that of the federal theology, we should find inexplicable their frequent anticipations of pages in the *Treatises* of Locke. We might predict that Puritan parsons would want to delimit secular rulers by the laws of Scripture or would preach the right of revolution against Papists, but we are the more astonished that they demanded limitation of civil officers by "right Reason and Equity." The rule of "Salus Populi Suprema Lex," said Jonathan Mitchell, "was never doubted nor denied by any that held but to Rational and Moral Principles," and hence the light of nature alone is sufficient to prove this rule binding upon all rulers and to teach that their disregard of it absolves the conscience of the people from obedience. Such incorporations of merely natural, reasonable, or equitable laws into the social covenant appear less inconsistent with the religious temper as we call to mind the Puritans' attitude toward classical learning, their belief that the laws of nature were enacted by God and that the light of reason was what remained in fallen man of the image of God. Yet these conventional tenets of theology would hardly in themselves have led to so tremendous an emphasis upon the rational principles of society had they not been effectively augmented by the less conventional federal theology. By reducing original sin to legal imputation and by turning redemption into a rational transaction, the doctrine was bound to enhance the value of natural capacities. A strange passage prefaced to the codified laws of 1648 exhibits the ingenious logic by which federal ideas contrived for the natural reason a larger influence upon social legislation than a literal application of the dogma of innate depravity could have permitted: indubitably, the preface states, God was more present in the laws of Israel than in others; nevertheless, He has never been wholly absent from the councils of all nations, particularly because of the covenants.

> There was also somwhat of equitie in their lawes, for it pleased the Father (upon the Covenant of Redemption with his Son) to restore so much of his Image to lost man as whereby all nations are disposed to worship God, and to advance righteousnesse.

Unfortunately the Gentile commonwealths, receiving only a portion of the original image, often abused God's mercy and corrupted the ordinances, religious or judicial, which He had bestowed upon them through the light of reason, and thereupon God quite justifiably "withdrew his presence from them proportionably, whereby they were given up to abominable lusts." Thus no nation has ever been punished by God without desert, for even peoples who had no revelation still had His basic precepts in the law of nature, thanks to the Covenant of Redemption! They could always have secured some blessing by observing these precepts as well as they were able: "Wheras if they had walked according to that light & law of nature they might have been preserved from such moral evils and might have injoyed a common blessing in all their natural and civil Ordinances."[8] The implication of this marvelous logic for a Christian people was unmistakable: if pagans gained favor and prosperity by writing the laws of nature into their compact, obviously a nation in the Covenant of Grace was all the more obligated to observe in its compact the laws of nature as well as the special enactments of Scripture.

The motives behind this political theory are not difficult to guess, nor the persons at whom it was aimed. James I said that kings are "the authors and makers of the Lawes, and not the Lawes of the kings," and contended gravely that though a good king would frame his actions according to the law, "yet is hee not bound thereto but of his good will."[9] Here was precisely the concept of power that Puritans were resolved to destroy. Against it they bent their every resource, not the least of which was their logical acumen, by which they managed to arraign the Stuart kings of England not alone for opposing the true welfare of the nation but for flouting the true nature of godly royalty. Charles I was tyrannical because he broke the compact, violated immunities, and invaded rights sealed in the agreement, but also he was impious because he pretended to a prerogative to which only God was entitled, but which God Himself scorned to exercise. A parliamentary orator in 1625, surveying apprehensively the growth of absolutism in continental monarchies, exhorted the Commons, "We are the last monarchy in Christendom that maintains its rights."[10] In order that Englishmen might have a weapon for maintaining their rights, Puritan ministers turned the grindstone while lawyers sharpened the edges of contractual theory.

At the same time, the ministers had other ends in view besides curbing the power of James and Charles. Had their political doctrine been inspired by no more aggressive ideal than checkmating royal prerogative, it would have developed at once into what it took several decades to become, and the New England colonies would have commenced by believing what was not to be generally current until the time of Mayhew and the Adamses. To Puritan thinking, limitation of tyrants and the protection of unalienable rights were not the end-all and be-all of the state; it had a positive as well as a negative function, and the covenant theology endeavored to designate both with equal clarity. Puritan theorists were not yet prepared to see the state as wholly secular, divorced from the church, unconcerned with righteousness; they would have won nothing worthwhile by proving that voluntarism might flourish in earthly covenants if the covenants were devoted to none but earthly ends. Therefore, after establishing society upon a covenant, with rights and equitable terms, they were obliged not to leave it to itself, but to identify the covenant of the people with the Covenant of Grace, to insert the terms of salvation into the political incorporation and to unite the duties of civil obedience with the duties of Christian worship.

We could more clearly ascertain the complex character of Puritan contractual theory could we trace its genesis. We can in a manner follow the growth of the theology itself through the published treatments, yet even these are not so plentiful as to tell in detail how the authors first came upon their ideas. It is still impossible to decide the primary question, whether Perkins, Ames, and Preston deliberately extended the idea of compact from their social to their religious thinking, or whether they worked their way from theology to social theory. We know that continental Protestantism had arrived at an idea of a compact between people and kings long before English Puritanism devised the compact of men and God, the classic statement being published as early as 1579 in the *Vindiciae Contra Tyrannos*.[11] It is also clear that the social contract was known in England before 1600, as is most notably attested by Richard Hooker. Furthermore, many later New England writings upon the theology, by their constant habit of finding analogies for the Covenant of Grace in the covenant of society, suggest to a more critical generation that what they offer as example must in fact have been exemplar. When John Cotton, for instance, describes three kinds of earthly covenants, friendship, marriage, and the covenant "between Prince and People," the last of which, he explains, "is usually in all well governed Common-wealths, unlesse the King come in by way of Conquest and Tyranny, but in well settled Common-wealths, there is a Covenant and oath between Prince and People," and declares the Covenant of God similar to all three, we may pardonably wonder if he had not acquired his conception of divine procedure from the human. His argument for the necessity of moral obedience in the elect looks as though it had originated in statecraft and then migrated to divinity:

> Look what a King requires of his People, or the people of a King, the very same doth God require of his people, and the people of God . . . that is, a Governor, a Provider for, and a protector of his people . . . and the people undertake to be obedient to his Lawes, to whatever he declares to be the counsell of his will.

Thomas Hooker seems to give the game entirely away by picturing God in negotiations with the covenanted people as though He were an ideal English king: "As in a Parliament Consultation, they must propound all to the King, and he must ratifie, and confirme it." By taking the Covenant upon Himself, God had become the kind of sovereign every Puritan in the House of Commons was hoping to behold in Westminster.

> The Covenant which passeth betwixt God and us, is like that which passeth between a King and his people; the King promiseth to rule and govern in mercy and in righteousnesse; and they againe promise to obey in loyalty and in faithfulnesse.

It would thus appear likely, to say the least, that social theory gave impetus to the religious, and that the federal theology was the lengthened shadow of a political platform. Nevertheless, it could not have been merely a subtle rationalization of that platform, because it clearly served other purposes in addition to justifying parliamentary opposition. It helped meet the theological crises precipitated by Arminius and by the Antinomian sects, and for the New England leaders it served most importantly for setting forth the positive ideals of the enterprise, for harnessing the free wills of men to the social chariot, for enlisting the voluntary powers of the citizens and marching them to an energetic pursuit of holiness in the state as well as in their private lives.

If there is difficulty in retracing the steps by which the theology was first propounded, there is still more in discovering those by which theology and political theory were united. Early treatments touch upon the political covenant only in passages so exasperatingly fugitive as to throw little light upon the question of whether the social deductions were clear from the beginning or grew imperceptibly into recognition. The sequence of events might be briefly recounted in some such fashion as this: at the end of the sixteenth century, English Protestantism, already imbued with the idea of social compact, was becoming aware of weaknesses in the creed which had been assumed to be the belief of the Church of England; between 1590 and 1600 began the division between English "Arminians" and Puritans over the theological issue, widening still further the breach between supporters of the established order and the Puritans; certain Puritans then developed the covenant theology in an effort to remedy creedal imperfections and to counteract Arminianism; meanwhile, all Puritans, becoming more deeply tangled in the constitutional struggle, advanced with increasing earnestness the thesis that government originates in a compact of the people and is limited by the terms of the agreement. At this juncture, for those Puritans who had devised a covenant between God and man similar to the hypothetical covenant of king and people, who had defined the relative justice of God in the language of a common law contract and thus secured the theoretical necessity for man's obedience, what more natural than that the two covenants should coalesce, that God should be made a party to the contract of ruler and subject, and that the moral duties nominated in the bond should include not merely those of civil life but those of the regenerate will?

This much is indubitable, that when New England was settled the two covenants, the religious and the social, had become one in the minds of the leaders. No political writing of seventeenth-century Massachusetts and Connecticut can be fully understood without reference to the whole system; the authors could see only one way to arrive at the principles of civil government, which was to begin with the Covenants of Redemption and Grace, and from them to deduce the rules of the social covenant. This method not only had the virtue of conforming to Ramus' golden rules, but it gave logical form to the historical narrative of the Book of Genesis. The Covenant of Grace is first propounded in Scripture to Abraham as an inward and personal bond, but from the very beginning it includes Abraham's "seed", upon whom is to be continuously devolved his ability to take up the Covenant and who will successively stand to the identical engagement. The children of Israel are chosen first as individuals, but since all, or almost all of them, are in covenant with the God of Israel, bound by their own consent to discharge His law, it becomes apparent that the Covenant of Grace is a covenant for the group as well as for individuals. As the family of Abraham grows more numerous, his progeny either must disperse themselves, thus losing the advantage of the means without which the covenant cannot survive, "or else be brought under the Covenant of

God into a state and national Church." The Old Testament abounds with instances, generally moments of crisis, where the inward covenant is publicly acknowledged by the whole community, and each man, swearing by virtue of the freedom acquired in the Covenant of Grace, takes it upon himself to carry out in society the articles of a divine agreement. These corporate registrations of the Covenant thus become mutual stipulations not merely of the persons with God but with each other and with their rulers. Out of the religious compact emerges in Judea the compact of society, as for instance, when Jehoiada "made a covenant between the Lord and the king and the people, that they should be the Lord's people; between the king also and the people." Richard Mather's gloss upon this text exposes completely the workings of the New England mind; the theorists read their Bibles in the light of the federal theology, and from their readings arrived at a political philosophy:

When *Jehojada* made a Covenant between the King and the people . . . that Covenant was but a branch of the Lords Covenant with them all, both King and people: for the King promised but to Rule the people righteously, according to the will of God: and the people to be subject to the King so Ruling. Now these duties of the King to them, and of them to the King, were such as God required in his Covenant, both of him and them.

In Massachusetts the clergy played the rôle of Jehoiada, the magistrates of the king, and the inhabitants of the people; in the migration to Massachusetts all entered into a covenant, among themselves and with the Lord. In the one compact the people were dedicated both to theological and to social duties. So John Cotton, preaching the farewell sermon to the departing fleet in 1630, Thomas Hooker, delivering an address before his flight from England in 1633, and John Winthrop, expounding the purpose of the migration aboard the *Arbella* in 1630, replying to Antinomians in 1637, or at last in 1645 describing the character of covenant liberty to the General Court—these leaders were fully equipped from the beginning with a consistent doctrine, sustained by logic and studded with Biblical proofs, which reached from the throne of God to the deliberations of the General Court of Massachusetts Bay, which conceived of their society as in covenant with God like Israel of old, which supplied meanings and directions not alone for theological speculation but for the civil polity as well.

As the future was indeed to certify, contractual theory was not in every respect ideally adapted to advancing piety. By building upon the rational choice of men, it asserted in effect that they were naturally good enough, intelligent and able enough, to ascertain what society should be, while at the same time it in effect declared that they had a right to make the society almost anything they happened to find convenient. By inference it denied original sin, proclaimed the competence of human reason, and allowed the autonomous individual a self-interest prior to all other moral concerns. It was voluntarism, but in its bare political form it was voluntarism with a vengeance, and though no Puritan voiced such forebodings, the more perceptive of them might have realized that they were playing with fire. With the best will in the world, Puritans would have needed time to digest these radical ideas, and particularly would they have been troubled over reconciling them with conceptions of society inherited from the past. The intellectual heritage had already bestowed upon Protestantism a philosophy of society in which two distinct views had for centuries been more or less perfectly joined, both of which were equally antagonistic to the tenor of contractualism.[12] One of these regarded the community as an organism, man a naturally political animal, and government an indispensable and perpetual necessity, a fact in nature along with earth and air. This view has been named "Aristotelian", though it was embedded in the Puritans' consciousness less because they studied it in the *Politics* than because they, just emerging from feudalism, were still a folk rather than an aggregation of disparate individuals, still possessed by a deep, an ingrained sense of the community that sometimes seems atavistic. The situation in New England at first did everything to accentuate this primitive tribal instinct, to underline the analogy with the people of Israel, to make the unit of thinking the race and not an atomic individual, to give practical point to Winthrop's injunction, "In such cases as this the care of the publique must oversway all private respects . . . for it is a true rule that perticuler estates cannott subsist in the ruine of the publique." At once the frontier began to teach one of its lessons, "Wee must be knitt together in this worke as one man," reinforcing the conviction already profoundly rooted in the Puritan mind, "Society in all sorts of humane affaires is better then Solitariness." Though Puritan theorists talked freely about the compact, the older idea persisted that "a family is a little common wealth, and a common wealth is a greate family." Along with the intellectual belief in contractualism survived a more elemental sense of the organic body, with "eache parte soe contiguous to [the] other[s] as thereby they doe mutually participate with eache other, both in strengthe and infirmity[,] in pleasure and paine." Contractual theory was pointing towards liberalism and individualism, permitting a difference of power and riches to different abilities and opportunities, without regard to the welfare of the race, but Puritanism was still unready to give up the belief that no man should become more honorable or wealthy than another "out of any perticuler and singuler respect to himselfe but for the glory of his Creator and the Common good of the Creature, Man." Consequently, the Puritan theory of a social covenant could advance ideas of constitutional limitation and protection of personal rights, but could never phrase them so as to lose all sight of God's glory and the common good of the clan.

The other attitude enshrined in the inherited philosophy was Stoic, Christian, and medieval, though it may for convenience be called "Augustinian" since it was supremely well expressed in *The City of God*. It viewed the earthly state as a consequence of the fall; it saw government as a counsel of desperation, not arising from a natural social virtue in men, but from the necessity of curbing their lusts and restraining overt expressions of their depravity. Had Adam not fallen, his descendants would have been just to each other without the supervision of a magistrate, but in their lost condition they have to be whipped into the forms of civility by a coercive power, or they will steal each other's goods and murder their neighbors. Without government, "there would be no living together for Mankind, but Humane Societie must disband; Murder, Adulteries, Rapine, and all manner of Oppressions would rage; and there would be less of Order in the Habitable World, then in Hell it self." In Eden, the "state of nature" meant peace and righteousness, but since the expulsion it has signified a state of war. "The name of Magistrate came in by sin, not by nature." The judge, the gaoler, and the soldier were necessary to prevent humanity from dissolving into chaos, and without the improvement of military weapons in the hands of authorities, it was evident "that all Civil and Sacred Liberty would soon be ravish'd by Unreasonable men; that Violence, Oppressions and Rapine would universally and unavoidably prevail; that Humane Societies (as things now are) must disband." According to this logic, to grant the people a right of revolution would be fatal, for depraved men would thereupon pretend that any curtailment of their deviltry was a violation of the covenant, and would revolt in order to have free play for their concupiscence. This view of society had always been a factor in Christian thought; it had always made the state a terrible necessity, required an almost abject surrender to whatever powers that were, even a submission to injustice, and had generally tended to support absolutism. According to Calvin, except when the magistrate imposed laws that endangered a man's salvation, no matter how tyrannical they might otherwise be, he had to submit. Much of this moral was inevitably a part of the Puritan ethic as long as Puritans sincerely entertained the doctrine of original sin. As long as they were men of Augustinian piety they had to agree that God enjoined obedience to magistrates as a religious duty, that civil powers were divinely appointed to keep the world from becoming "a great Den of Thieves and Robbers," and that but for them, *"Might would bear down Right.* Men, like Dogs, would try their titles with their teeth; and all difference between *Meum* and *Tuum* would be abolished." Thus the Puritan theorist always confronted the possibility of a serious conflict between his social and religious tenets. The ministers would frequently, like Thomas Shepard, deliver at colonial elections passages of this sort:

Sins of men are like raging Sea[s], which would ouerwhelm all if they haue not bankes; the bankes are wholesome lawes[,] these bankes will breake down vnles some keepe them[,] h[ence] magistrates; so that magistrates must either not restrayne & then all goes to ruine or restrayne & then the Sea rageth against her own bankes & weary of her own magistracy which god hath set ouer them . . .

How in the face of such dicta could the ministers also maintain that laws were the terms of a compact freely entered into by rational beings?

Yet when we consider the values which were obviously dear to Puritans, the standards they upheld in their conception of human nature, the care they took in expounding natural philosophy to show that rational creatures were not caught in any web of physical necessity, their veneration for logic and their theory of means, when we remember the elaborate effort of the federal theology to equate morality and free will, we can recognize that neither of the two traditional theories of society could be any longer wholly satisfactory. Puritans could not get rid entirely of the Aristotelian tradition that man was naturally a political animal, nor could they entirely forget that sin was a cause of the state, but both of these explanations made the state an unalterable and universal phenomenon, a sociological necessity with no place in it for human volition. In either case man had no choice; his obligations in society were not moral duties to which he had consented, but exactions laid upon him by a power he could not question, to whom his consent was superfluous. Clearly neither view would very much help Protestant minorities in the sixteenth century, still less aid seventeenth-century Puritans to resist the Stuarts. But still more important than the political deficiencies of traditional philosophies were their religious inadequacies: neither made possible a positive dedication of the state to righteous ends. Each was politically fatalistic, each left the state a secular, natural agency, occupied with civil justice and the bodies of men; neither brought into its jurisdiction their souls and their wills, neither gave it any power to guide men to the kingdom of heaven. Thus when English Puritans turned to the theory of contract, it was only in part to protect their rights against absolutism; it was also to justify them in subordinating individuals to the state, once the ideals of the state had been rightly conceived and the power of enforcing them placed in the correct hands. In New England, after a company of Puritans solved the problem of limiting King Charles's prerogative by migrating beyond his reach and secured their privileges by their charters, the constitutional aspect of the theory could be subordinated to the religious. Contractarian doctrine in New England therefore contributed to liberalism only inadvertently and accidentally; its deliberate aims were authoritarian and intolerant.

The Puritan state was seen by Puritans as the incarnation of their collective will; it was driven by an energy they had acquired in their conversion, it was the embodied image of their power, of their resolution, of their idea. John Winthrop, standing upon the deck of the *Arbella,* thinking himself another Moses in a new Deuteronomy, outlined in advance the basis of New England politics: Adam had not merely reft himself from the creator but had sundered man from man, so that everyone is born in nature full of self-love, with a selfish pride that may be chastened, yet can never be expunged by natural means; but when Christ takes possession of his soul, a man conceives a great love not only to God but to his fellows. "Each discernes by the worke of the spirit in his own Image and resemblance in another, and therefore cannot but loue him as he loues himselfe." Out of this love among the regenerate is born the community, the pledge of their common affection, the symbol and bond of their unity. Every state in the world, according to the theory we have noted in the preface to the laws of 1648, was to some extent a similar merging of many wills into one, for after the Covenant of Redemption God allowed all men some power to perceive justice by the law of nature and to frame a code of good laws by the light of right reason. As far as any state proceeds from a free compact, as far as it incarnates the principles of reason and equity, to that extent it derives from God. But if pagans thus engendered a government by free association, and if its living spirit was pumped through their wills from the reservoir of the spirit in heaven, how much more should a state created by Israelites be an emanation from God! He graciously permitted a Solon or Lycurgus some access to the law of nature, but for His own people He opened the floodgates of His spirit and filled their souls with the exuberant vitality of heaven. "When the Spirit is poured out upon a people, All, or the generality of them, or at least very many among them will be either enquiring for, or walking in the way to Zion with their faces thitherward." New England political theory made the state almost a kind of second incarnation, a Messiah fathered by God and born of the people. Mortal men, being visited by God in the Covenant of Grace, conceive a will to moral obedience; when they covenant among themselves, when they combine their several regenerate wills into one all-inclusive will, the state becomes another savior, the child of God and man, leading men to righteousness and preparing them for the final reckoning. The cohabitation of a people gives being to the state, but they can no more order it to suit their mere convenience than parents can predetermine the sex or complexion of their children. Indeed, God does permit men to settle the particular form of the government according to circumstances and their practical discretion, but the magistracy itself is divine, even though it be brought into existence by a covenant of men. "The being of Magistracy is from God immediately . . . This or that Form of Civill government, is of God mediately, i.e. by the means of man." A government needs the consent of the people in order to be, but a people cannot make any government they list out of their lawless and corrupted imaginations; they must find the one government God has decreed. The ministers told Roger Williams that no magistrate in a free state has power over the bodies or goods of the people but by the people's free consent, yet because all men, regenerate men in particular, are in this world to be "stewards" over their bodies and estates and to improve them for God's glory, "they may not give their free consents to any Magistrate to dispose of their bodies, goods, lands, liberties at large as themselves please, but as God (the soveraigne Lord of all) alone [pleases]." There is, said Hooker, "a double Covenant in the frame *of Scripture,"* the internal covenant of salvation between the soul and its God, and the consequent covenant of external obedience: "the Lord requires that we should walke in new obedience before him, and answerable to that grace bestowed . . . and this is the covenant . . . which the Lord reveals, requires, and exacts of all that have given their names unto him." As soon as "those whom he hath taken into Covenant with him, to be a peculiar people to himself," become numerous enough to form a nation, they perceive that as a peculiar people they are all alike dedicated to godliness. By the power of regenerating grace in their wills, they foresee the advantages that would accrue to godliness from their setting up a government of their own determination, and thus they determine precisely such a government as God desires:

> Where the Lord sets himselfe over a people, he frames them unto a willing and voluntary subjection unto him, that they desire nothing more then to be under his government . . . When the Lord is in Covenant with a people, they follow him not forcedly, but as farre as they are sanctified by grace, they submit willingly to his regiment.

Both in church and state the regenerate willingly submit to His regiment; they are eager, said John Eliot, to "enter into covenant with the Lord to become his people, even in their Civil Society, as well as in their Church-Society." They must submit to God in the civil society even though they themselves have created it. They draw up the contract in terms which they intend to observe, yet the terms are not formulated by them but dictated by God, and "it is no impeachment of Christian Liberty to bow to Christian Lawes." As soon as the spirit quickens us, it "draweth us into an holy Confederacy to serve God in family, Church, & Common-wealth." As soon as the will of man is liberated from sin it seizes the opportunity to subject itself once more, but this time to a moral obedience, which is a rule for social relations as well as for private meditation. The personal covenant with God is impaled on the same axis as the social, like a small circle within a larger.

So God creates the state, yet not directly, not by His own immediate institution. He acts through human freedom exactly as in working an effect He employs a cause. He might in either case dispense with the means and order the effect by fiat, but He prefers to work more rationally. Meanwhile, no means is ever the all-sufficient cause of any effect, it is merely "in order to it." As John Davenport explained, in one of the best discussions of the theory, his election sermon of 1669, "The orderly ruling of men over men, in general, is from God, in its root, though voluntary in the manner of coalescing." God may commission a magistrate directly, just as He can reveal certain truths in the Bible, or He may empower him "mediately" through the election of the people, just as He reveals other truths through natural laws or through the deductions made by natural logic from Biblical premises. In either case the magistracy is equally a divine appointment. The power entrusted to a ruler comes from the people, and he therefore exercises a power which was not inherently in him—"Nor doth a Community, in chusing Civil Rulers, surrender so much their right and liberty to their Rulers, as their Power, both Active to do, and Passive to suffer unjust violence." Nevertheless, the power communicated to magistrates was God's before it was the people's, and was given them by Him, so that by choosing a man to office they issue him a divine commission. "In regular actings of the creature, God is the first Agent; there are not two several and distinct actings, one of God, another of the People: but in one and the same action, God, by the Peoples suffrages, makes such an one Governour, or Magistrate, and not another." By His power over the people through the Covenant of Grace, God regulates their choosing; hence they elect whom they think best, and give to him no more authority than they believe right, and so they fulfill God's will in every election and every relation. God approves of their setting limits to the grant, and they give it "conditionally . . . so as, if the condition be violated, they may resume their power of chusing another." In this way the Puritan state could be wholly contractual, it could be the product of men's volition, and subject to the laws of their reason, and yet be directed and ruled by God. In society as in physics, free will and absolute decree went hand in hand. The Aristotelian and Augustinian ideas were not displaced, but coördinated in a new and subtler theory. Society still originated from the nature of man as God had created it and also from an ordinance for restraining the violence of depravity, but at the same time from a compact of the citizens. Just so much constitutionalism as was required to justify Parliament against the king was proved to be the law of the universe; all magistrates, though appointed by God, were shown to be limited by fundamental law and the people invested with a right of revolution. But also, by the terms of the compact, a Christian people were committed to walking before God in active holiness and positive fulfillment of His commands, and the government was to see that they kept their word. The work we have in hand, explained Winthrop to the voyaging emigrants, "it is by a mutuall consent through a speciall overruleing providence, and a more then an ordinary approbation of the Churches of Christ to seeke out a place of Cohabitation and Consorteshipp vnder a due forme of Goverment both ciuill and ecclesiasticall." The free consent of regenerate men was not given merely to what suited their interests, nor were they protected simply in rights which were of commercial value; they were also pledged by their own consent to seek a "due forme of Goverment," a form to be settled by the eternal and objective rules of God, whether found in the Bible or in right reason.

The colony of Massachusetts Bay, being founded upon a theory that for the comprehensions of ordinary men proved, to say the least, difficult, was supremely fortunate in having in John Winthrop not only a resolute statesman but also a philosopher and stylist. For fifteen years he was spokesman for the magistrates in a tense struggle with the lower house of the General Court, with the deputies who were, according to him, actuated by a "democratical spirit." From the very first, the freemen strove to confine the magistrates within explicit limitations, and from Winthrop's point of view were ready to sacrifice the Bible commonwealth for a mere constitutional republic, as though "magistracy must be no other, in effect, than a ministerial office, and all authority, both legislative, consultative, and judicial, must be exercised by the people in their body representative." The citizens showed what they took the covenant to mean in Massachusetts by insisting that the magistrates be drastically pinioned to definite rules, by demanding strict observance of the charter, asserting that no powers or offices should exist "but such as are commanded and ordained of God," forcing the publication of a written code of laws even though the magistrates thought the time not yet ripe, endeavoring to fix specific penalties for all offenses and to leave magistrates no discretion to vary any punishment to fit the crime, and at last by trying to deprive the magistrates of their power to negate acts of the lower house. The Puritan leaders, having taught in England that the state was created by a confederacy of people and that governors should be held to the terms of federation, had to reckon in New England with the consequences of their own teaching. They were hard pressed to explain why what had been sauce for Charles I should not also be sauce for themselves.

The details of the conflict need not here detain us, except in so far as out of them emerged more precise definitions of the political theory. At each crisis in the struggle Winthrop set forth the arguments by which the leaders finally won their case. The hardest task he ever confronted was persuading the rank and file that though they made the compact, they had yet to accept their superiors' interpretation of it rather than to insist upon definitions of their own. He had to prove that though a people create their government when they "come together into a wilderness, where are nothing but wild beasts and beastlike men, and there confederate together in civil and church estate," nevertheless the government is not their creature nor is it at their beck and call. He found that his case could be maintained only by proofs fetched from fields other than purely contractual theory, for had the dispute been restricted wholly to the political covenant of magistrates and people, the deputies would have won every engagement just as they gained their demand for a written *Body of Liberties*. But Winthrop drew with subtle skill upon all departments of the intellectual heritage, and particularly upon logic and the federal theology; he cowed the yeomanry of New England with the logical axiom that deductions are as valid as premises, and with the theological axiom that those who sign a covenant must abide by its conditions. In the debate over the negative vote he once angered the deputies by remarking that ordinary men should not overbear men of wisdom, thus seeming to imply that the magistrates had a monopoly of this commodity, and he was obliged to apologize that some deputies might not be inferior to the magistrates. Yet he never surrendered his essential point, that the laws recorded in any compact must be general and must hold the magistrates to only certain broad limitations. The indentures of the social compact were precisely analogous to the verses of the Bible, they would always need to be "opened" by human learning. John Cotton described as a fact what Winthrop was determined to maintain: "Our people here (whose government is elective) make choice of men of greatest worth for wisdome, for sufficiency, for birth"; Cotton also informed the people that it was "more safe" to entrust power "in the hand of the Magistracy then in the Commonalty," although he also declared it evident "by the light of nature, that all civill Relations are founded in Covenant." In order that the theory of its contractual origins might not turn Massachusetts into a democracy—which Cotton declared God did never "ordeyne as a fitt government eyther for church or commonwealth"—Winthrop and the leaders took unto themselves the tremendous prestige which a Puritan laity accorded to learning, scholarship, and academic training. Winthrop traded upon this prestige in order to convince common men that after they had become parties to the compact they were to be content with general regulations and to entrust administration to men wiser than they, to men capable, as they were not, of deducing logical conclusions from the general to the particular.

If this argument would not subdue the "commonalty"—and there were moments when it seemed inadequate—then Winthrop was capable of proving more explicitly how little the people comprehended the nature of a free covenant. In 1637, for instance, during the stress of the Antinomian affair, the General Court passed a law prohibiting strangers from entering the colony unless approved by two magistrates. Harry Vane[13] attacked this as tyranny according to the theory of compact, for it allowed the magistrates an "illimited consent or dissent" over admissions, without regard to the basic laws of the community, which were, Vane said, the royal charter and the rules of Christ. Asking a rhetorical question which he knew would ring convincingly to the ears of those who had resisted Charles I, he demanded, "Now is it sufficient for those who are betrusted with the execution of this law to follow their perswasions, judgments and consciences, except they be rightly ruled by the word of truth [?]" Winthrop again stepped into the breach, and answered that Vane's idea of the social compact made it a much too strict and literal demarcation of the magistrates' office, giving them so rigid a commission that they could exercise no discretion whatsoever. Yet for a Puritan compact, which demanded not alone that the rights of the people be protected but that all occasions be improved for advancing God's glory, it was absolutely essential that the leaders possess such discretion. The magistrates were not in Winthrop's view potential tyrants to be prevented from doing mischief, but an integral part of a unified community, the guardians of its ideals and purposes. They were triply bound because as members of the churches they were signers of the church covenant, as freemen they had sworn to the social covenant, and by their oaths of office were engaged in the covenant between rulers and people, "regulated by their relation to the people, to seeke their wellfare in all things." Hence the magistrates spoke for the inner will of the community; they were not lackeys appointed to stand in one place and perform only menial services. They were endowed with the heavenly gifts of wisdom, sufficiency, and birth, by which they could judge the equity of laws and apply them to particular cases. The society had agreed to a compact, and in order to insure success must appoint men of probity and logical wit to superintend it, just as God, having delivered His Word, must raise up ministers with good hearts and dialectical accomplishments to interpret the Word in relation to circumstances. This kind of discretion was not Stuart prerogative, for it did not pretend to be above the law or itself the source of law: it was an exercise of rational discipline, of logic and human wisdom, within the broad limits of fundamental law, exactly as orthodox theology was the exercise of logic and intelligence within the confines of revelation. Correspondingly, Winthrop argued against Vane that whatever wise magistrates brought out of the social compact by "rationall inference," that too was part of the original compact. With the magistrates sufficiently limited "both by their church covenant and by their oath, and by the dutye of their places, to square all their proceedings by the rule of Gods word, for the advancement of the gospell and the weale publick," it followed that whatsoever sentence any magistrate gave according to his rational discretion, as long as it was within these limitations, "the judgment is the Lords, though he do it not by any rule particularly prescribed by civill authority." His argument reappeared ultimately as the official position of the colony, and was succinctly stated in the preface to the codified laws of 1648:

That distinction which is put between the Lawes of God and the lawes of men, becomes a snare to many as it is mis-applyed in the ordering of their obedience to civil Authoritie; for when the Authoritie is of God and that in way of an Ordinance *Rom.* 13. 1. and when the administration of it is according to deductions, and rules gathered from the word of God, and the clear light of nature in civil nations, surely there is no humane law that tendeth to common good (according to those principles) but the same is mediately a law of God, and that in way of an Ordinance which all are to submit unto and that for conscience sake. *Rom.* 13. 5.

Thus in New England, thanks to the people's awe of logic and the ministers' teaching that logical consequences were as authoritative as first principles, thanks to the theologians' identification of the light of nature and the word of God, of the common political good with the glory of God, it could be consistently maintained both that free Christians were "the first subject of ciuill policy and power," and that the compact of free Christians was not to provide them civil immunities but rather to further the cause of Christ. Christians agreed in their covenant to Christ's terms, not to any of their own invention, and they created a commonwealth to embody their devotion and to supervise their obedience. A Puritan state would give adequate liberty to its citizens if, after insuring the obvious rights of trial by jury and *habeas corpus,* it guaranteed them the ordinances of Christ, the means of conversion, faithful preaching and the sacraments. Civil law should be not so much a protection of subjects' rights as an instrument by which the state defines their social duties and directs the exercise of their liberty.

Winthrop's final triumph in his protracted bout with the "democratical spirit" came with his oration of 1645. Historians have rightly seen in this discourse the culminating expression of the Puritan ideal in New England, and justifiably dwelt upon the dramatic circumstances of its delivery. He had interposed as a magistrate to keep the peace during a disputed militia election at Hingham; his enemies accused him of exceeding his office and raised again the cry of tyranny. When they committed the tactical blunder of impeaching him, he stood his trial and forced the freemen to acquit him; then he drove home the lesson of their folly by telling them a few simple truths about the covenant. Much as historians have praised his speech, few have yet done justice to the large sweep of his argument, and we can appreciate his great artistry only when we remember that his audience had been thoroughly indoctrinated by their parsons with the theology of the covenant. He was deliberately playing upon ideas so fixed in the minds of the populace that they could not possibly be challenged. He first explained the nature of a covenant as it exists between rulers and subjects, and then as between men and God. Under the first head, he pointed out that though the citizens call magistrates to office, the office itself is divine and has its authority from God. "The covenant between you and us is the oath you have taken of us, which is to this purpose, that we shall govern you and judge your causes by the rules of Gods laws and our own, according to our best skill". The deputies might have replied that, being themselves parties to the covenant and not utterly devoid of skill, they too had a liberty to judge their causes, but Winthrop anticipated their remonstrance as he informed them of the true nature of covenant liberty. When he distinguished between natural and civil liberty, and defined the natural as that which men have in common with the beasts, as a liberty to do what they list, evil as well as good, the hearts of the democratical spirits must have sunk. They saw him identifying their agitations with the sort of natural liberty which, since the fall of Adam, had become a deliberate malignancy. Unless they were prepared to question the doctrine of original sin, the deputies had no choice but to agree with Winthrop that such liberty was inconsistent with authority, that the exercise of it made men worse than beasts, and that all the ordinances of God were bent to restrain and subdue it. On the other hand, they could not pretend that their opposition to magisterial authority had been an act of regenerate liberty, for Winthrop clinched his argument by defining civil liberty upon the model of Christian liberty, merging the political covenant with the Covenant of Grace, and civil obedience with moral observance.

> The other kind of liberty I call civil or federal, it may also be termed moral, in reference to the covenant between God and man, in the moral laws, and the politic covenants and constitutions, amongst men themselves. This liberty is the proper end and object of authority, and cannot subsist without it; and it is a liberty to that only which is good, just and honest.

His hearers could not help perceiving that he granted them a power to consent to the covenants, both spiritual and political, merely to assure them that, having consented, they were now bound to behave in one way only, with a dutiful subjection to the eternal law of God as expounded by those upon whom God had bestowed the gifts of exposition. Winthrop was imposing submission to the rule of public morality, to that which was intrinsically good, just, and honest, by the same invincible arguments with which theologians proved the law of God just in and for itself, and imposed submission upon the elect through the assumption of their free consent. Just as the covenant between God and man was an agreement to terms, but terms dictated by absolute moral standards and not by the convenience of the contractors, so the articles of the social compact are first good, just, and honest in themselves, not from the compact. Men agree among themselves to create a state, but the rule of righteousness exists as an archetypal idea apart from all agreements; they covenant with themselves and with God in a single act, and thus agree among themselves and with Him that they will conform themselves to the preexisting pattern. They freely incorporate the rule of righteousness into their contract, which thereafter binds them less because it is inherently right than because they have consented. Whatever crosses this obedience, said Winthrop, is not liberty, but a corruption of it; civil liberty is maintained only by way of subjection to authority, and therefore, O citizens of Massachusetts:

> If you stand for your natural corrupt liberties, and will do what is good in your own eyes, you will not endure the least weight of authority, but will murmur, and oppose, and be always striving to shake off that yoke; but if you will be satisfied to enjoy such civil and lawfull liberties, such as Christ allows you, then will you quietly and cheerfully submit unto that authority which is set over you, in all the administrations of it, for your good.

After this, the deputies could no longer obstruct their authorities unless they were ready to confess openly that they were acting in a way of natural liberty and corruption, an admission they could never afford to make.

There was nothing new or original about Winthrop's speech. He repeated merely what the ministers were saying in their expositions of the "conditional" covenant. Liberty, said one of them, was a freedom from "any external restraint, or obstruction on mans part, to walk in the Faith, Worship, Doctrine and Discipline of the Gospel, according to the Order of the Gospel"; it is not, said another, "liberty to sin, but to be holy; liberty to *run the wayes of Gods commandments.*" Winthrop's discourse was unique simply for the dispatch with which he transposed the covenant theory from the soul to the state, and spectacular because he used it to quell an uprising of citizens. He delivered it with such smashing force that for several decades the democratical spirit was hardly anywhere to be seen in Massachusetts Bay.

Thus the Puritan populace discovered after they had migrated to Massachusetts or Connecticut that they had not simply fled from illegal exactions, but had given themselves by their own consent to the quest for a due form of civil government, which they were not of themselves to determine but were to accept. They could perceive the practical importance of "humane learning" when they saw that not alone was it a help to divinity but that, since it expounded the laws of Scripture and reason, it also legislated for their compact. Voluntarism did not mean license; it meant knitting the whole body together as one man to achieve God's design:

> Look as in a Common-wealth or Kingdome, none hath the benefit of the Law, but those that subject themselves to the Law: none have the protection of authority, but those that obey it . . . If we will have God to be our God to pardon us, and to blesse us, wee must have him a God over us to govern us after his own will.

Every society must have an orderly form and it must act, but "action without knowledg is reprehensible and order unprofitable," and so "understanding" is essential to the being of commonwealths. The theocracies of New England have become a by-word in history as societies founded upon the Bible, yet when we review their political discussions, particularly the election sermons, we discover that a large portion of the political morality, as of the theology, was preached either on the authority of logic, which made supposedly infallible deductions from revealed precepts, or frankly on the authority of nature and right reason. All good laws, said Shepard, "are either expressly mentioned in the word, or are to be collected and deducted from the word, as being able to give sufficient direction herein." By this logic the laws of a community could be declared in accordance with the Bible not merely when corroborated by specific texts, but also "when they command or forbid such things as really advance or tend to promote the public good." As long as the magistrates were orthodox in religion, they were to rule by their intelligent conception of the public good as well as by the Bible. William Hubbard, for instance, in an election sermon of 1676, developed a large discourse upon the need for "order" in society—by which he meant subjection of inferiors to superiors—almost wholly on the grounds of nature, with the help of a few Biblical verses which were obviously incidental to his reasoning. "For Order is as the soul of the Universe, the life and health of things natural, the beauty and strength of things Artificial." Things natural prove that everyone must keep to his due and proper place, and that

> the like is necessary to be observed in the rational and political World, where persons of differing endowments and qualifications need a differing station to be disposed into, the keeping of which, is both the beauty and strength of such a Society.

The life of New England was molded by ideas deriving from the intellectual heritage as much as by the ideals of religion, and in some respects even more so. Differences in position and wealth within the social hierarchy were ordained by God, but these decrees, like His decrees in physics and in conversion, were thoroughly reasonable and just, and were accomplished through natural methods. Social classes were not irrational accidents or corruptions of God's primitive design:

> It is not then the result of time or chance, that some are mounted on horse-back, while others are left to travell on foot. That some have with the Centurion, power to command, while others are required to obey. *The poor and the rich meet together, the Lord is the maker of them both.* The Almighty hath appointed her that sits behind the mill, as well as him that ruleth on the throne.

In appointing men to various stations God did not simply follow His arbitrary pleasure, but "herein hath he as well consulted the good of humane nature." By the light of nature it is fully evident that nothing could be "more remote either from right reason, or true religion, then to think that because we were all once equal at our birth, and shall be again at our death, therefore we should be so in the whole course of our lives." It would thus appear by reason alone that "whoever is for a parity in any Society, will in the issue reduce things into an heap of confusion." Whether arguing from right reason or from the law of Scripture, Puritan leaders came to the same conclusion, to an authoritarian state, a society of distinct classes, ruled by a few basic laws administered by the wise and learned of the upper class through their mastery of logic, their deductions from the basic laws being as valid as the laws themselves, and resistance to their conclusions being the most exorbitant sin of which the lower classes were capable.

Puritan theory therefore was only in a slight degree progressive; it was for the most part the elaborate restatement of a medieval ideal, and for many years retained such medieval aims as fixing just prices, preventing usury, and prescribing wearing apparel according to social status. Yet the New England theorist was confident that he had improved immeasurably upon authoritarian philosophies of the past, for he had contrived that men should obey civil laws and the Ten Commandments not merely because the rules were right but because the men themselves had agreed to obey them. New England leaders did not come before the people as conquerors or dictators, but as judges; they did not sentence any offender for a crime he could not help committing, but for his willful refusal to do what he had promised and was thoroughly competent to perform. Contractualism in New England was almost a theoretical trap, a ruse for convincing men that they were engaged to support whatever learned ministers and magistrates could show was just, right, and honest. It avoided imposing obedience from without, but it convinced men from within that they had no other choice; it taught them to follow Christ not forcedly but to submit willingly to His regiment. The leaders knew that not all men would let themselves be convinced, and that original sin would harden some spirits into obstinacy who would need to be restrained by the sword, but they expected that the others, especially those who purported to be saints, could be dealt with as though they were pledged of themselves to the cause. They could be made to believe that they were volunteers and not victims of the press gang, and their officers could demand that they keep discipline in the ranks of Zion's army.

Yet calling the contractual element in Puritan theory a ruse does not mean that it was a malicious conspiracy of the magistrates and clergy. They were not necessarily dishonest or disingenuous because they found the origin of the society in a compact of the people and yet forced the people to submit to the rule of the good, the just, and the honest. When we examine their political theory in conjunction with their other ideas, we find in it the same dual tendency, the same confusion and latent contradiction, for it also was a part of their attempt to reconcile piety and the intellect, spirit and reason. It incarnated anew their effort on the one hand to cling to authority, revelation, and dogma, and yet on the other to permit an appeal to nature, reason, and logic. It shows at once both a Calvinist sense of the absolute divine sovereign and a humanistic respect for man's dignity. Their endeavor to unite cosmological and social theory shows them still scholastics, yet their desire to achieve the synthesis through a concept of volition shows them responding to forces that eventually were to shatter all scholastic unities. Theology demanded predestination, but contemporaneous social and economic conflict demanded freedom; freedom was essential for resistance to the Stuarts, but too much freedom might lead men to forget theological and social orthodoxies, might give rise to Antinomians, democratical spirits, and Levellers. The ideals of orthodoxy were absolute dicta, but if they remained simple absolutes, men might become satisfied with formal acknowledgments and never be incited to more active cultivation. Puritan leaders in the early seventeenth century devised a complex theory to meet a complex intellectual situation: they had to provide arguments that would allow constitutional resistance to the King but would not lead to political confusion; they had to furnish such proofs for freedom as would not tempt men to assert their independence of all law or of the rule of righteousness. In order to justify parliamentary opposition in England, they had to enjoin that rulers should seek the common welfare, but in order to maintain a Bible commonwealth in New England, they had to identify the common welfare with the glory of God. They had to demand that rulers look after the good of the people, but that God and not the people determine the good. All these pressures and urgencies came together in the federal theology and the covenant theory of the state. The formulation delivered in New England was an unstable balance, marking by its very complexity the shifting factors of a transitional age. Beguiled by circumstances into adopting contractual theory, Puritans were yet unable to give up inherited ideas of status, of the state as an organism or as an ordinance of God for restraining human depravity; the contractual idea presented priceless opportunities to inspire in men an energetic devotion to orthodoxy and to provide the state with a clear right to punish heresy and sin as well as crime and injustice. All the desired ends seemed to John Winthrop well accomplished, and the dangers circumvented, when he summarized the philosophy in his speech on liberty. The rules of reason and of piety seemed triumphantly combined to the compilers of the laws of 1660, who declared in one breath that laws are the people's birthright, that lawmakers are the parents of a country, that the light of nature taught heathens to account both rulers and laws sacrosanct and inviolable, that considerations of religion and civil polity ought to make a still deeper impression upon Christians, and finally that men should submit "to every Ordinance of man for the Lords sake." This mingling of nature and religion, of civil law and divine law must have seemed a final synthesis to the authors of this passage. They could hardly have realized the extent to which they were testifying that theology had lost its self-confidence, that even they, for all their religious devotion, were no longer ready to rest their case solely upon faith. They had to secure the aims of faith by proving that men had rationally consented to them in a covenant, and that magistrates and ministers were to expound them by logic. They believed they had thus shown the findings of reason to be one with the tenets of faith. They could not foresee, even in 1660, how short the time would be, once men had commenced thinking in this fashion, until the findings of reason would suffice of themselves, until the compact and the deductions of logic would provide the content of political wisdom, and politicians would no longer be obliged to heed the requirements of faith.

CHAPTER XV

THE CHURCH COVENANT

"God sifted a whole nation to bring choice grain into the wilderness," said the Puritan historian, never doubting that he was setting down the "cause" of the Great Migration. He would have acknowledged that social pressures at home or the promise of financial reward in a new country had been inducements, but he would never have called them the cause; they were at best "means" employed by God to bring His people together in a holy commonwealth, natural methods for working a special providence. A later age, less wont to distinguish the hand of God in history, finds itself unable to ascertain precisely how or to what extent the more mundane influences operated upon particular emigrants. Our researches into economic and geographical origins have not as yet made clear why this or that man, or this or that group, migrated, while their neighbors, equally Puritanical and subject to the same compulsions, stayed at home. Recent disclosures, however, have pointed to one previously neglected factor that must now be allowed as much influence as hostility to the personal rule of Charles I or the depressed state of the wool industry: long before they left England, a large number of those who ultimately became leaders of the colonies were known to each other. Many of the clergy were united by friendships formed at the universities, or by their common allegiance to a few great theologians, particularly Ames and Preston. The civil leaders were friends of the clergy, and often acquainted with one another before they began to purchase shares in the Massachusetts Bay Company. It would be an exaggeration to say that, before the departure, all the ministers and magistrates had become an organized band or that the settlement was a matured conspiracy to which every settler was an accessory, yet a sufficient number of connections can be traced among the principal figures to suggest a sharing of principles, of definitions, and of purposes. Whatever social and economic forces brought these individuals together, it seems probable that they also came to a fairly definite community of belief and a substantial agreement upon a program of action. Largely because they were Cambridge men, they were generally students of Ramus; as disciples of Ames and Preston they were federalists in theology; and above all they were consciously united, almost to a man, in the conviction that the form of church order decreed explicitly by revelation from heaven was Congregational.

This ecclesiastical doctrine was the unique and distinguishing feature of New England Puritanism, setting it off not alone from Anglicanism but from other Puritanism and from continental Calvinism. The fact that all except five or six of the New England ministers were seeking this particular "due forme" of church government indicates that the migration was not alone propelled by political or economic adversity—though the importance of such motives should not be minimized—but was undertaken as a positive crusade for an idea. It was an expedition headed by theorists with ambitions so well formulated and so radical that they had perceived the utter impossibility of realizing them in Europe. In 1684 William Hubbard, looking back upon 1630, declared that when the fathers approached these shores their minds "were as *Rasa Tabula,* fit to receive any Impression from the spirit of truth, either as to Doctrine or Worship." He was certainly wrong concerning their lack of preconception in doctrine, and most probably incorrect in the matter of worship. A Presbyterian author in 1645 hit more nearly upon the truth when he noted that English Independents such as Nye and Goodwin were advocating the identical church order outlined by John Cotton, and commented that the English propagandists could not have been "strangers to the plot of this Authour, either before or since his going over." Beyond all doubt, this "plot" was a large part of the Puritan intention, in the eyes of many the predominant concern. Jonathan Mitchell, who sat at the feet of the first ministers, declared in 1662, when some of them were still alive, "The Latter Erecting of Christs *Kingdom* in whole *Societies* . . . was our Design, and our Interest in this Country: tho' with Respect to the *Inward* and *Invisible* Kingdom, as the Scope thereof." To understand the Puritan mind we must endeavor to comprehend how the two kingdoms, the inward and the social, were for that mind forever inseparable. The leaders, if not the followers, arrived already possessed of a definite plan, with at least the outlines of an "ectypal" pattern for the order of the visible church, which they were resolved to make "entypal". When they came ashore they did not for the first time open their Bibles to spell out the "archetypal" polity of the Apostles. They had long since "invented" the ecclesiastical arguments of the Bible, "opened" every text, and explained away discrepancies. We today may stare in amazement at what they devised, and marvel anew at the ingenuity of their brains, but they saw nothing amazing or ingenious about it. They proceeded to put their program into effect, never doubting that it was of divine authority or that it would succeed.

Though we have hitherto spoken of New Englanders as "Puritans", and generalized about their thinking on the basis of all Puritan expression, we must henceforth bear in mind that the New Englander was *sui generis* even among Puritans. Very shortly after 1630 divines in England began to be disturbed over the strange practices reported from the colonies, and in the 1640's, when the Independents were preventing new presbyters from succeeding to the power of old priests, Presbyterian leaders directed a voluminous pamphlet onslaught toward New England as the source of the schism.[1] The colonial clergy were sadly troubled, since they held many beliefs in common with their critics. Presbyterians also had opposed Charles I and suffered in order that a church patterned upon the Word of God might replace the Babylonish hierarchy; they too were faithful preachers in the plain style, and many were theologians of the Covenant. But on the question of ecclesiastical polity, they and the New Englanders came to a parting of the ways. "Those godly learned Divines, who doe thus argue," said John Cotton in 1645, "wee doe soe highly esteeme, and so deeply reverence in the Lord, that were the cause our owne, and not the Lords, we should rather let it fall, then defend it, by opposition to the grave judgements of such holy Saints." But more than fifteen years before, the New England divines had elected to obey the express command of Christ and not the opinions of men, even of such holy men as Ball, Rathband, and Rutherford, and for those fifteen years had been following it to the letter. They were therefore obliged, as Cotton put it, "to excuse our selves from submitting to their judgements in this cause, which yet generally in others wee yeeld unto them." By 1650 the New Englanders were an isolated faction, even though they constantly professed their doctrinal solidarity with all Puritans at home; not only did the Presbyterians look upon them with horror, but English Independents like Nye or Goodwin, who in 1640 undertook to spread the New England system in England, were turned aside by the unforeseen course of the wars and forced to preserve their lives in an unholy alliance with the sects upon a platform of toleration. Meanwhile, being left to follow their own devices, New Englanders were able to concentrate all their intellectual resources upon justifying their peculiar establishment. They put inherited disciplines and arts to a final and, to them, ultimate employment in expounding their church; they used logic to derive its principles from the Bible, physics to explain its place in the natural world, psychology to prove its suitability to man, the concept of means to elucidate its function, rhetoric to give it a voice, the federal theology to supply its theoretical foundations, and the doctrine of the state to protect and advance it, while at the same time it stood in their eyes the preëminent monument to their profound piety. The church incarnated upon earth the entire pattern of the New England idea; it was the emotional center and the intellectual synthesis for this particular school of Puritans.

The heart of the church theory was the church covenant. Regenerate men, the theory ran, acquire a liberty to observe God's commanding will, and when a company of them are met together and can satisfy each other that they are men of faith, they covenant together, and out of their compact create a church. Therefore each society is an autonomous unit, and no bishops and archbishops, no synods and assemblies, have any power, either from the Bible or from nature, to dictate to an independent and holy congregation. The members, from whom the church originates, perpetuate it by receiving into the fellowship those whom they judge, as far as one man can judge another, to be within the Covenant of Grace, and also protect the society by expelling those in whom they have been deceived and who violate the compact. Participation in the covenant must throughout be limited to those who, appraised by the rule of "rational charity," appear authentic saints, and these, being the source of church power, elect ministers and officers, appropriate funds and determine all policies by suffrage. It is not enough that men be thrown together as neighbors or by circumstance, that they be driven to the church by law or revere a minister put over them without their consent; there can be no true church until there is a covenant of the saints, submitting to the rule of Christ in public observance out of their free and regenerated wills. This was the meaning of a church in New England: "A company of People combined together by holy Covenant with God, and one with another." Richard Mather defined the covenant more copiously thus:

> A solemne and publick promise before the Lord, whereby a company of Christians, called by the power and mercy of God to fellowship with Christ, and by his providence to live together, and by his grace to cleave together in the unitie of faith, and brotherly love, and desirous to partake together in all the holy Ordinances of God, doe in confidence of his gracious acceptance in Christ, binde themselves to the Lord, and one to another, to walke together by the assistance of his Spirit, in all such wayes of holy worship in him, and of edification one towards another, as the Gospel of Christ requireth of every Christian Church, and the members thereof.

Puzzled opponents read Congregational writers with incredulity, for the church covenant seemed to Anglicans like William Lucy a fantastic "conceit"; he could hardly believe his eyes when he studied Thomas Hooker's *Survey:* "Some such Covenant (if I can reach his sence) is that which gives to the receivers an Obligation and bond, and it is in Conscience one towards another, which bond is the formal Essence and being of a Church."[2] Lucy was reaching Hooker's sense accurately. Richard Mather put the theory in the language of physics by calling the "matter" of a church the collection of visible saints and the "form" a covenant, which unites or knits the saints into one visible body:

> Some union or band there must be amongst them, whereby they come to stand in a new relation to God, and one towards another, other then they were in before: or els they are not yet a Church, though they be fit materialls for a Church; even as soule and body are not a man, unlesse they be united; nor stones and timber an house, till they be compacted and conjoyned.

It was of the essence that the membership be carefully selected and that only those be admitted who were evidently converted, for none but saints could really exercise free will or stand to the terms of a pact. Only those able to discern false doctrines and false teachers could choose pastors wisely or administer excommunication justly. We may not add to the church those whom God does not include:

> Ought not the Lords Stewards to be faithfull in Gods house, and to doe nothing therein, but as they see the Lord goe before them? receiving whom he receiveth, and refusing whom he refuseth.

A holy congregation, already within the circle of the Covenant of Grace, united publicly in a bond to which they have sworn of their sovereign volition, confederated "for the carrying on of Church power and order, and ordinances of Christs ends"—this was the special and specific goal, social and spiritual, of the Puritan theorists as they cast off an England in which they saw no hope for it and became Americans in order to achieve it.

Their Presbyterian brethren preached the theological covenant, but this notion of a particular church founded upon a public covenant appeared as much nonsense to them as to Anglicans. A church, they said, must include the whole nation, everyone living under one civil government, and nothing more should be required of the people than belief in the main points of Christian faith and a formal submission thereunto. "Neither is it requisite that they should be truly godly, to make them members of a visible Church, for then no man could tell whose child were to be baptized, or who are members of a Church, or when he is in a true Church." But the New England contention was exactly that the members should be truly godly and that godliness could be detected. The question at issue, said Thomas Shepard, was this: did Christ ordain "an universall visible Church" or did he give the administration of His ordinances only "to particular visible Churches," which become visible by their covenants? The question may seem to us technical and fruitless, yet when we consider the larger philosophical implications of the difference, the arguments by which New Englanders defended their system, by which they limited membership to the visible elect and turned each congregation into a small independent commonwealth founded upon a compact, become of far-reaching importance for the future.

Of course, they argued that the system was Biblical. They attacked the Church of England for not conforming to the Word, they haggled with Presbyterians over the riddles of the New Testament, and they published their platforms with a full complement of Biblical annotations at every proposition. As Cotton emphatically declared:

Our principall care and desire is to administer and partake *in all,* and *no more then all,* the ordinances of Christ himselfe, and in all those (so farre as the Lord hath lent us light) in their *native puritie* and *simplicitie,* without any dressing or painting of humane inventions.

In civil or philosophical affairs Puritans allowed the authority of natural reason or the law of nature, but they said that in the sphere of ecclesiastical government these powers were wholly subordinate to revealed mandates. The light of nature, wrote Willard, may suggest to us "a convincing reason of the equity and suitableness of the Institution," but the institution itself must come entirely from Christ; the realm of the church is entirely separate from the realm of nature, and to decide upon its laws Christ consulted only His pleasure. An ecclesiastical ordinance "hath no foundation necessary in the nature of the thing, cannot be inferred and concluded from our way of reasoning." If there were any department of Puritan thought where logic or the arts gathered by reason from nature seemed to have no relevance, it was ecclesiastical doctrine, which purported to stem directly from the particular enactments of the New Testament.

Nevertheless the Presbyterians, who knew their Bible at least as well as the Boston parsons, could discover no church covenant in it: "I finde no mention of any such Covenant, besides the general imposed on Churches, nor example or warrant for it in all the Scriptures, and therefore cannot account it an Ordinance of God." As a matter of fact, the Presbyterians insisted, it was simply "a prudential humane device to keep the members together, which in some places and cases may haply be of good use," but for any to make it an absolute article of faith, an indispensable observance of Christian life and a condition of salvation, when it was a mere social expedient, what was this but to add unto God's worship, to impose rites or forms "according to Principles of State-Policy, or Humane Prudence," exactly as did the Anglicans? How could Richard Mather assert that Christ requires the consent of every church to a covenant when the Apostles never demanded it of churches in the New Testament? How, indeed, without turning to exegetical methods, to "equity" and "humane learning", without going beyond the literal text and coming to this crucial doctrine not upon the explicit authorization of God but upon the strength of reason and dialectic, by invention and syllogism and by analogy with the social theory? Even granting, said Mather in what seems to us a startling concession, that "there were not pregnant places for it in the New Testament, yet it is not enough to prove the same unlawfull," because whatever ordinances of the Jews were not repealed by Christ, whatever are of moral and perpetual "equitie", are still binding upon us. Since the church covenant is in the Old Testament, and is not denied in the New, ergo, it is still the revealed will of God:

And the New Testament hath nothing to the contrary, and they are all according to morall equitie and reason, and therefore they are to be observed from the Scriptures of the Old Testament, as the revealed will of God, though there were nothing expressely for them in the New.

John Cotton would assert that the ordinances of Christ should not be dressed or painted with "humane inventions", but it was no human invention for a Ramist logician to explain on historical grounds why the church covenant was not called by name in the New Testament:

Let no man wonder why there is so little expresse mention of the peoples taking hold of the Covenant in the new Testament, when this promise commeth to be accomplished. In the *old Testament,* where the *Church* and *Commonwealth* grew up together in divine institution and administration, there is expresse mention of this Covenant, and the Church being nationall, and all the *Magistrates* being members of the Church from the first plantation of it, the Covenant of the Lord with his Church was not at all *suspitious* to them, (who were parties to it themselves) but very acceptable; but in the dayes of the *new Testament,* the *Magistrates* and Princes of the earth being *Aliens* and *enemies* to the Church, the Apostles thought it meete to speake of this Covenant not *plainly,* but as it were in *Parables and similitudes,* as knowing the name of *Covenants* and *Covenanters* might breed no small *jealousies in Civill States,* as seeming most dangerous to civill peace, but yet in apt similitudes they so describe the estate of Churches as doth necessarily imply a joynt Covenant, both *betweene the Lord, and them one with another.*

We can sympathize, as we read such a passage, with Lucy's bewilderment before the New England mastery of "conceit". Cotton is picturing the Apostles as though they were English Puritans and the Caesars as though they were Stuarts; he assumes that the epistles had to be written in a sort of code lest the emperors wax as furious at the discovery of a covenant as James I at the mention of Scotch covenanters. Yet having thus acquired his premises, he feels perfectly secure in arguing therefrom by the necessary implication of similitudes, according to the laws of rhetoric! As I have already had occasion to mention, much of the dispute between Congregationalists and Presbyterians was conducted in the jargon of dialectic, the great points contested between Thomas Hooker and Samuel Stone on the one side and Samuel Hudson on the other being whether individual churches were primary artificial arguments or "argumenta a primo orta," whether the churches taken together were a "totum universale" (in which the parts give being to the whole) or a "totum integrale" (in which the whole gives being to the parts). They fought up and down the field of logic over the wholly abstract question, is the church a genus? and each answered "by the definition of a *genus* both according to the *Ramists* and *Aristotelians*." Hooker's *Survey,* the ablest theoretical exposition of the system, is today unreadable to one not at home in Ramus' *Dialecticae,* and even then the Presbyterian Hudson declared that Stone's defense of Hooker was "a logical Lecture, and of so abstruse and sublime a subject, that as it was little taken notice of, so it was less understood by any, but those schollars that were versed in those studies." Had the divines employed only arguments understood by scholars, none but scholars would have come to New England; yet the fact remains that every exposition of the system, even for the benefit of the folk, was to some degree a "logical Lecture," though most of them were fortunately less abstruse than Stone's. In other words, the so-called Bible commonwealths of New England were Biblical only in so far as an intellectual heritage, which was not Calvinist nor even Christian in origin, determined the meaning of the Bible. They were based on the Word of God—as interpreted by logic, physics, psychology, rhetoric, and theology, and nowhere was this qualification more true than in the church, which was the one feature in the regime supposedly dictated word for word by the Bible, without any intermediacy of the arts or human reason. Being men of piety, the Puritans frequently humbled themselves in the dust before the majestic God, and called themselves worms; at the same time they were giving a breath-taking exhibition of self-confidence: absolutely assured that their understanding of Scripture was correct, and that their logic was invincible, they erected a commonwealth and a state church upon deductions. Few logicians have ever put so much trust in logic.

The practical result of their deductions in New England was this Congregational system, unlike anything the world had ever beheld. The core of each town was a church, composed of those who had given proof that they were visibly sanctified, joined together by a covenant into which they entered of their own will, who elected the minister and voted upon admissions and excommunications. Surrounding these saints were the body of "inhabitants", persons of whom the best that could be said was that they had not yet shown signs of being regenerated. They were expected to attend church services, to listen to the sermons, and to pay taxes for support of the minister, though they had no voice in his selection or in the conduct of the society. In order to insure the continued devotion of the colony to holy ends, Massachusetts and New Haven restricted the franchise to church members; the Connecticut settlements did not expressly confine the vote to church members, but provided for a ministerial supervision of the electorate that achieved by less obvious means the same control. Those without the pale, who under the first charter of Massachusetts Bay amounted to some four fifths of the total population, might have a vote only in town meetings, but otherwise were to submit to the rule of the saints and attend submissively upon divine ordinances, in which, unless they were suddenly to receive regeneration by the means, they could not actively participate.

If we in New England cannot make good our church government, wrote John Cotton, let it be published abroad that "we live not by faith in Church-order, but by fancie." He invited trial because he was confident that God Himself "will bear witnesse from heaven to that government, which his Gospel hath taught us," yet to our eyes, his conclusions generally seem a far cry from the verses of the New Testament, and the elaborate chains of deduction by which he and his colleagues attached a heavenly authorization to every minute provision of a highly idiosyncratic system are not convincing. Were we to take them at their word, and assume that the only determinants in their thinking had been the Bible and logic, we should be justified in dismissing the whole enterprise as an eccentric, fantastic, and absurd perversion of Holy Writ. But as we have already seen, the logical method by which they worked out the system is itself worth examination, not for its eternal and timeless truth, but for what it reveals of the Renaissance mind, and the same point of view must be brought to an analysis of the church covenant. Although the men themselves believed in all sincerity that the Gospel taught their church polity, the historian must note that the real sources seem rather to lie in certain ideas of the contemporaneous world, that the system testifies not so much to a profound reading of the New Testament as to a profound response to several forces molding the thinking of all men in the seventeenth century. When the doctrine of church covenant is considered in the setting of its period, its ingenuity no longer seems excessive, for in it were curiously mingled at least three distinct aspirations, all dear to the Puritan heart and yet extremely unsuited to simultaneous achievement. Flowing from the piety, from the tremendous thrust of the Reformation and the living force of the theology, came a desire to realize on earth the perfect church order, cleansed of corruption and purified of all unregeneracy. At the same time, springing from the traditions of the past, from the deep and wordless sense of the tribe, of the organic community, came a desire to intensify the social bond, to strengthen the cohesion of the folk.[3] And finally, prompted by the newer political and economic forces, fathered by the disruptive impulses which even then were smashing the last segments of medieval unity, came the powerful sense of the individual, of the supreme importance of the will, of the motives which were producing in England the theories of constitutional limitation and government by consent. The Congregational theory emerged in an age of transition, and showed the impress of shifting, of contradictory tendencies. It was ingenious because the situation which it had to meet was not intellectually simple: it had to provide a mechanism for constituting a church only of saints, it had to knit the saints together as one man, and yet it had to bring them into the church by their own decision. In comparison, both Anglicans and Presbyterians appear entirely traditional, medieval, unresponsive to newer developments. They did not believe that the church could afford to rely upon the perseverance of the saints, and both were agreed, in spite of their differences, that if the institution were built upon the voluntary consent of even the best of men it would collapse. They were quite content with a national church imposed upon the whole people. "Seeing the subjects of Christs Ecclesiastical Kingdom runne parallel further with the subjects of a civil Kingdom, they all being Christians, Why may not the combination also run parallel?" The majority of Englishmen saw no necessity in this world for aspiring to unworldly perfection, or for paying so exaggerated a respect as did the Independents to the sanctity of the individual will. "The Magistrate may civilly in his way compel to the means of Salvation," said Rutherford, "the baptized ones especially, both to hear, and to eat and drink at the Lords Table." It was all one to Presbyterians, for practical purposes, whether men were in the church by compulsion or by choice as long as they were in it; the one sort would go to perdition, the other to heaven, but meanwhile the problem was ruling the people. If a man sits down within the civil limits of a parish, the officers ought to take charge of him "whether he will or no." Consequently, neither Anglicans nor Presbyterians could see the point, even when they accepted the federal theology, in setting up an additional and public covenant as the basis of the visible organization. Was it not enough if the church as an institution professed Christian faith and if men belonged to it because they were commanded? For New Englanders, this was definitely not enough; their opponents seemed to sunder inward sincerity from outward order, to imply cynically that there was no need for a correspondence, that the church would remain sound even if full of devils forced to attend the Lord's Supper by the sword of a civil magistrate. But on the other hand, the New England leaders could not give over the idea of a state church, of a society in which religion inspired the government, where men were ruled for their spiritual as well as for their physical and civil prosperity. In their belief it was still the function of government to lead men to the good life. "It is a carnall and worldly, and indeed, an ungodly imagination, to confine the Magistrates charge, to the bodies, and goods of the Subiect, and to exclude them from the care of their soules." The settlers of New England were to some extent in the party of the future, in that they could not endure a social system in which the assent of the members was not regarded, but they were still so far children of the past that they were unable to go the whole way with voluntarism and entrust the churches entirely to the good motions of individual wills. The result of their entertaining these several ambitions at once was Congregationalism, speaking for the Reformation in limiting its membership to the saints, retaining the past in its conception of the social function of the church, pointing to the future in its attempt to found the visible government upon a free consent of the governed.

The outlines of Congregational theory were worked out explicitly by William Ames, who declared that a church must be recruited from believers "because that same thing in profession doth make a Church visible, which by its inward and reall nature doth make a mysticall Church, that is, Faith." The distinction, he said, between the visible and the mystical churches, between the militant and the triumphant, is not between two distinct bodies, but between modes or "affections", between "accidental formes" of the same essence. John Cotton enlarged upon Ames's logic, saying that the "distribution" of churches into the visible and the invisible "is not into divers kinds of Churches, nor into divers kindes of Members of the same Church, but into divers Adjuncts of the same Members of the same Church." The members should, ideally speaking, have faith in their hearts and profession on their tongues; Christ perceives the first and so they become joined with Him, but an outward profession, "visible to men," is necessary for their joining with one another. The covenant of a society was the formal ceremony for such profession; a church was not just any number of people thrown together by chance or birth within the geographical confines of a parish, it was a deliberate creation of the regenerate acknowledging their faith to each other. The covenant of the church united the material and mystical bodies, and Samuel Hudson was essentially correct when he declared that Cotton's description "seems to me to belong to an invisible Church and not to a visible." Presbyterians raised the cry of "Donatism", but New Englanders could repudiate the label even while accomplishing the end. The earnestness of their piety would not let them rest easy if the church were one thing and salvation something apart. They were unable to conceive that a man's inner and personal religious life could or should be kept silent and private, and therefore saw no reason why the public order should not be adjusted to personal righteousness, or why those obviously deficient in righteousness and probably not destined to be saved should be taken into the sanctuary.

"Donatism" was a serious charge, for it was an insinuation that the endeavor to identify the visible and invisible church was one with the crack-brained schemes of enthusiasts and sectaries, of Anabaptists, Millenarians, and Levellers, who believed that they too were setting up congregations of the holy. The Congregational idea was undoubtedly inspired in part by a similar spirit; the surge of religious conviction carried the sober theologians and solid magistrates of New England to the very brink of frenzy, but their strong sense of social responsibility, their profound communal instinct, counterbalanced the intoxication of piety. They were eager to fashion the natural order upon the spiritual, but they were certain that it must be an order, a regulated, a disciplined and a steady commonwealth. New England piety was intense, but in the seventeenth century it did not often become delirious, and the ecclesiastical system expressed both the religious inspiration and the corporate solidarity. Except for some rather desultory efforts at converting a few Indians—to be cited in justifying the colonies at home—the New England brand of Christianity was not a missionary creed; it did not drive men into the trackless wilderness, but called them to their places within settled associations. Its first aim was sorting out the elect from the mass, and its second providing a method whereby both could live in stable concord under the rule of the elect. The church was the center of a communal system, and the process of conversion was always to take place within a rigid frame of public observance. Grace like love was to grow and be consummated within legal forms. Although men ought to be saints before being received as members, said Cotton, "yet we beleeve this Saintship and Regeneration is wrought ordinarily not without the Church, but within the Church; that is to say, wrought in such, as in the Assembly of the Church doe attend upon the meanes of grace dispensed by the Ministery of the Church." If the New England system be considered by purely sociological criteria, it becomes a fascinating scheme for securing rectitude in a community without sacrificing cohesion. Within the church the fraternity was made one by their mutual and irrevocable pledge; the members entered "all of them together (as one man) into an holy covenant with himselfe, To take the Lord (as the head of his church) for their God, and to give up themselves to him, to be his Church and people"; by the power of their oath they must cleave one to another "as fellow-members of the same body in brotherly love and holy watchfulnesse unto mutuall edification in Christ Jesus." The children of the fraternity, growing up under the seal of baptism, by which they were taken into covenant with God at their birth, were also incorporated into the visible institution; when their baptism became, as was believed it always would become, the "means" of their regeneration, they automatically became active participants in the federation. And finally, those outside the church, the environing ring of inhabitants, were not left at loose ends, but were mobilized into an audience, bound to the church as the center both of their expectation and their township, whence alone they could hope to receive the vital current of regeneration. The theory of church covenant fused the saints into one conventicle, while the theory of the means tied the unregenerate to it no less firmly. The keys to the kingdom of heaven were the ordinances: the sermon and the Lord's Supper for the visible elect, the sermon and baptism for their children, and the sermon alone for the non-members. "By the opening and applying of these, both the gates of the Church here, and of heaven hereafter, are opened or shut to the sons of men." Whoever received grace obtained it through the agency of ordinances; those not yet converted should therefore attend upon them and not slight ordained ministers and public forms. "Faith comes not by reading, but by hearing." We have seen that throughout the fabric of New England thought the warp of piety was woven with the woof of rationality; we have traced a sustained effort to merge the law of heaven and the law of nature, the edicts of God and the eternal principles of justice. In the church system the coincidence of heaven and earth was believed to be made visible and institutional. When the true platform of God's idea was put into effect, and the hierarchy of status replaced by the hierarchy of contract, when the classes of nobles, bishops, priests, and laity had been altered into the distinctions of magistrates, elders, freemen, and inhabitants, the society fell into orderly procession at the meeting-house door, and within its walls took their places accordingly, the elect to have their faith made stronger by the means of a plain sermon, the others to hear doctrines and reasons adapted to their understandings and to listen for uses that might arouse their wills and affections.

The supreme achievement of the New England doctrine was not merely that it embodied the true church in the earthly without overturning the reign of law and political order, but that it achieved this end in a church constituted through the consent of mankind. It not merely obeyed God's command, but won a willing compliance; it secured liberty, but "civil liberty," and contrived that the rule of the good, just, and honest should be served by the positive election of the citizens. To prove this point, the clergy brought forth the usual array of Biblical passages, yet neither they nor John Winthrop could have wrung from the Bible the moral they desired had they not read it in the light of the federal theology. The ultimate triumph of the New England mind was, to use the language in which it conversed, the discovery that the Covenant of Grace included and generated the covenant of the churches.

Two simple syllogisms were most frequently used to extend God's transaction with Abraham in the seventeenth chapter of Genesis so that it could become the constitution for churches in Boston and Hartford. According to the federal doctrine, faith was interpreted as man's acceptance of terms. The first syllogism therefore ran roughly thus: God has commanded his children to form churches, the saints in covenant with God obey His commands, therefore the saints form churches. Putting the obligation within the terms of a conditional covenant rather than of mere submission to fiat secured an all-important advantage: obedience flowed from spontaneous effort and the church was brought into existence by men acting at their own discretion. Because a man has acquired an interest in the Covenant of Grace and received "spirituall illuminations, and consolations, and quicknings promised," is he to cast off all visible observances? "This Scripture ground . . . might now be urged: Thou shalt therefore, even because of the promise and covenant, keepe my covenant, saith the Lord." As soon as true faith is stirring, "it longs and desires much after the strongest, purest, and liveliest Ministery, and every Ordinance in the greatest purity." Were faith merely a passive reception of divine illumination, a man might go apart by himself in silent ecstasy, but since it is also a covenant, an agreement to accomplish certain ends, the inward "quickning" must cause a corresponding declaration, "when men do profess before all the world that they are and would be the Lords Servants." None may enter the church before they are called by Christ, for their vocation is the necessary qualification, yet because Christ has ordained churches and committed His ordinances to them, "it will be needfull for every good Christian, to whom God giveth opportunity, to joyne himselfe to some one or other church of Christ, that so he may not deprive himselfe of the benefit and comfort of any of Gods holy Ordinances." The Covenant of Grace gives men liberty, but again it was Winthrop's "civil liberty," a freedom to do only the good and the honest, which by any definition certainly included participation in the church.

The second syllogism contains in the minor premise an assumption which in many quarters today would hardly be accepted, but which to Puritans, with their inability to conceive of the church except as an integral part of the state, was as plain as day: In the Covenant of Grace God requires as a condition of salvation that men perform duties to other men as well as to Himself; in the church covenant they undertake to perform social duties; ergo, the saints must undertake the church covenant. "Watchfulnesse and duties of edification one towards another, are but branches of the Lords Covenant, being duties commanded by the Law." The revealing trait of the Puritan mind is this certainty that men could not exercise watchfulness and edification one towards another outside the church. Yet once more the necessary duties were not simply imposed from on high. Men took them upon themselves, and so had to subscribe a formal and public registration of their intention. The church covenant was their act of confession, not merely of their faith but of their social conscience, and so it was an inescapable consequence of the Covenant of Grace. By assuming the obligations of believers, the regenerate come under the necessity of taking active part in the fellowship. Having subscribed the covenant of heaven, they must seek admission to the covenant of the fraternity; in order to live eventually with angels they must for the present dwell justly and righteously among men. The church covenant is drawn up like the social compact with men and with God. "When we enter into Church covenant, we binde our selves to God, and to our Bretheren, to walke with God and one with another, according to the rules of divine politie." The compact of the congregation "is not another Covenant contrary to the Covenant of Grace, which every beleever is brought into at his first conversion, but an open profession of a mans subjection to that very Covenant, specially in the things which concerne Church estate." God, being a God of order and not of confusion, brings His people "to such mutual covenanting together, as is necessary for the orderly discharge of the several duties that are to be performed by vertue of such a state and relation." That which must be comes about through choice, and God's design is fulfilled as always by men exercising their free and unconstrained wills; but in the order of the church, the wills of men are consciously devoted to the task, whereas in the order of nature God must adroitly contrive things so that in spite of the evil doing of the unregenerate His decrees shall prevail.

Presbyterians said that they could not object if the New Englanders, for reasons of policy, gathered a people and a pastor together to draw up a deed of incorporation, "You shall be our pastour, &c. and we will be your people"; they would not criticize the use of a covenant to secure the people's assent to the New England form of the church, even though they believed the Congregational form was erroneous. But they were bound to object when the New England theorists, admitting that the church covenant served these material and strategic ends, also declared it a part of the Covenant of Grace and a necessary condition of salvation. "When an expresse vocall covenant is held forth, and with all eagernesse pressed on us, and on all churches as a Divine Ordinance . . . without which there is no true church, but all societies are whores and concubines," it was no marvel if the idea should meet with opposition. New Englanders replied patiently to such attacks with still more minute logical distinctions. If the word "covenant" be taken "in the narrowest acceptation," said Hooker, for merely the inward and invisible covenant of the Gospel, "betwixt God and the soul only," it does not necessarily include the covenant of the church. Hooker seemed to recognize, in other words, that the essence of the federal idea is a mystical relationship, made firm and continuous by a formal bond between God and the soul. In relation to this inward covenant, the covenant of the church is simply an "ordinance". It is a command of God which the elect must endeavor to obey, though imperfections in their performance will not stand in the way of their ascension to heaven. A lone saint, for instance, brought by the providence of God to dwell among pagans, would have no chance to join a church; he would be saved by the Covenant of Grace though he never realized God's ecclesiastical commandments. Or when a church is dissolved and scattered through persecution, the members are automatically absolved from the duties of confederacy. "In Propriety of speech," Hooker would admit, the church covenant is not the Covenant of Grace nor is it absolutely requisite, and salvation is possible without it; yet in settled Christian communities, where the church is established and the means of grace are available, there God demands that the covenanted saints become churchmen. In that sense, the ecclesiastical compact "is within the verge, and contained within the compasse of the Covenant." When God by His providence removes all outward obstacles, the inward reception of grace and the outward act become one, and the impact of grace is translated in one uninterrupted motion to the deed. The institution materializes from the spirit imparted to the saints. "The Covenant of grace is ever included and presupposed in the Covenant of the Church." Men may reach heaven by the invisible covenant alone when there is no opportunity of their joining in a visible; still it is certain that providence will place few in such a predicament, just as it will not permit too many to be born blind. Richard Mather most ably summarized the New England logic by commencing with the premise that all covenants contain a promise to bless on the part of God and a restipulation "or binding of man unto dutie back againe on his part"; the Covenant of Grace is first "personall, private and particular, between God and one particular soule," but it too demands duties back again, duties to men as well as to God, and so requires that several particular souls undertake them jointly:

> A Covenant taken thus generally when it respects spirituall blessings, and spirituall duties, in the Communion of Saints, is that which is called Church-covenant, which Church-Covenant differs not in substance of the things promised from that which is between the Lord and every particular soule, but onely in some other respects; as first, the one is of one Christian in particular, the other of a company joyntly together. Secondly, if right Order be observed, a man ought not to enter into Church-Covenant, till he be in Covenant with God before, in respect of his personall estate. Thirdly, The one is usually done in private, as in a mans Closet between the Lord and his soule, and the other in some publick assembly. Fourthly, The one in these dayes is of such duties as the Gospel requires of every Christian as a Christian, the other of such duties as the Gospel requires of every Church and the members thereof.

That which made New Englanders unique in all seventeenth-century Christendom, which cut them off from all reformed churches and constituted them in truth a peculiar people, was their axiom: "The Covenant of Grace is cloathed with Church-Covenant in a Politicall visible Church-way." They held that the love of God reached not merely into their souls, but that it pervaded their community. "God delights in us, when we are in his Covenant, his Covenant reacheth to his Church, and wee being members of that Church: Hence it comes to passe, that we partake of all the pleasant springs of Gods love." Technologia explained that the visible universe corresponded to the archetypal pattern of divine ideas, but close as was the natural relation of the thing to the idea, the relation of an institution deliberately created by regenerate men to the divine exemplar would be certain to surpass any exactitude of correspondence in nature. The church militant and the church triumphant, the seen and the unseen, both proceeding from the one Covenant of Grace, were to become effectively one in the covenants of particular New England churches, for the first time since the churches of the Apostles.

At the same time, being founded upon a compact of the saints, the church militant sprang from the militant wills of men, not from brute necessity or irresistible compulsion. Divinely ordained though the system was, socially expedient though it was to become, it was also sanctioned by the eternal and rational principles of contractualism. No more astonishing pages are to be found in the ecclesiastical monographs of New England, written ostensibly to prove that the church system was an absolute mandate of revelation, than those which frankly justify it by appeal to the theses of the political revolution. While God was represented as commanding the churches by fiat, while an established ecclesiastical regime was proclaimed indispensable to the being of a good society, nevertheless the authors asserted without hesitation that among men "whatever power one hath over another, if it be not by way of conquest or naturall relation . . . it is by covenant," and so took the church out of the realm of conquest or natural relation. Powers not based upon contract, said Shepard, "are but usurpations." There was still a third syllogism in the New England argument, far more important for the intellectual future of the region than either of the others: "If a true Church be a Citie of God, then a Church becomes a Church by Covenant: But every true Church is a Citie of God; *Ergo*." The assumption, said Mather, is proved by Scripture, Psalms 87.3, and Ephesians 2.9, but the consequence of the assumption, that a church becomes a church by covenant,

> is plaine in reason, for every Citie is united by some Covenant among themselves, the Citizens are received into *jus Civitatis,* or right of Citie priviledges, by some Covenant or Oath; And therefore it is so likewise in this Citie of God the Church; and men become Citizens of the Church by solemne Covenant.

To John Cotton also it was "evident by the light of nature, that all civill Relations are founded in Covenant," and he could conceive of no other way whereby a people "free from naturall and compulsory engagements, can be united or combined together into one visible body, to stand by mutuall Relation, fellow-members of the same body, but onely by mutuall Covenant," a truth which appeared most clearly, he added, in the relation of "Magistrates and subjects in the Common-wealth." John Davenport agreed: "For as all Citizens are admitted into *jus Civitatis,* and become free Denizens, by voluntary entering into the common engagement and covenant, whereby they become a Political-body; so it is in the Church." Natural relations, as between children and parents, require no stipulations, "there is no

Covenant to make a man a Parent, or a childe," nor do relations of violence, of conqueror to conquered, require a treaty, but all voluntary subjections of one rational creature to another must follow upon a compact. Presbyterians asked if it was not sufficient that a man come into the Covenant of Grace without being required to profess public submission to the institution: "He hath a right to all Ordinances whereever he finde them, being a member of Christ." They asserted that neither his duty to be a member nor the church's to admit him were matters for human determination, but that both obligations proceeded "from a Divine Law, or the general Covenant, which requires the one to joyn, and the other consequently to receive." But the New England mind was determined, at whatever dialectical expense, to play down the concept of stark command, to hold in abeyance the absolute power of God; it was unresponsive to any scheme of life that omitted the power of rational choice, but it quickened to the idea of an order based upon volition. When a godly Christian comes "into these parts," said Cotton, no minister "can *usurpe Pastoral authoritie over him,* unlesse that Christian *call him thereunto,*" nor can he expect any ministerial care "unless the Minister see just cause to *accept such a charge, and professe so much.*"

> The Churches receiving a beleever . . . implyeth and presupposeth his *offering* and *giving up* of himselfe unto them, in a *professed subiection* to the Lord, and unto them, according to the will of God; and their *receiving* of him, implyeth and holdeth forth no lesse then their *professed acceptance* of him unto all those holy liberties with them, and performance of all such spirituall duties to him, which belong to all the fellow-members of the same body; and let men call this expression of mutuall agreement by what name they please, this is no other then what wee call *Church-Covenant.*

According to Presbyterians, men of godly demeanor, being presumably in the Covenant of Grace, should be counted by the authorities as "implicitly" within the church and be ruled accordingly, but New Englanders could never see any charms in an "implicite faith." Over and above the implicit and the secret belief, they required of men "their open profession of their Faith in the God of *Israel,* and open binding of themselves by Covenant to all such duties of faith and obedience, as God required of the Church of *Israel,* and the members thereof." New Englanders were men of piety, but definitely not quietists. However tortuous or suspect might be their logic, even when their writings achieved a subtlety that verges upon the specious, they held firm their grip upon this great and revolutionary idea, that no force but the will of man can bring order out of the chaos of human depravity, though they did not always appreciate exactly how great or revolutionary it was. There could be no other reason for the church-state, said John Eliot, "but the consent, concurrence, confederation of those concerned in it"; nature or violence could not create churches, baptism could not fill up its ranks, for baptism was not the cause but an effect of membership, nor could mere profession. A church had to be "a voluntary thing." It was "against reason," said Increase Mather, that simple "Cohabitation should doe it." The founders of New England clearly understood "that a particular Church is constituted by the Covenant, or agreement of Saints to walk with God, and one another, according to the Order of the Gospel." The future of the New England mind—and of the society—was bound up with the life of this idea.

When critics of the New England way, of whom the Presbyterians of the 1640's were the most vociferous, attempted to avoid the highly theoretical plane upon which Hooker and Stone pitched the argument, they generally advanced two practical objections. If the churches were founded on covenants, they asked, and all ecclesiastical power was attributed to the consent of the people, would not the people rule within each church? The result, it seemed to English and Scotch Presbyterians, was bound to be "democracy", which all the world abhorred. Secondly, what of the vast majority of the people who were not permitted to become members? How could the authorities tell, to begin with, that these men were not in the Covenant of Grace? And then, how were they to be governed? Were they to be left under no religious supervision, to become pagans and beasts? To such critics the Congregational system promised nothing but anarchy, both within and without the churches.

On the first score, Rutherford declared that the brethren, "being often unlettered Tradesmen, and many of them dull and rude, though believers, are most unfit persons to judge of sound and unsound Doctrine, and of controverted points," yet according to Thomas Hooker these are "to judge and try the learning, ability of Pastors, unsoundness in Socinian, Antinomian, Popish, Arminian &c. Tenets, though they know no more the Tongues, Arts nor Sciences, than some Priests who can scarce reade the Mass-book in Latine." New Englanders profess to despise popular government, Rathband contributed, "but what can be more popular then this, wherein all have equall power to decree, and any of them may be used to act as well as the officers, and the officers are used as meer servants to the body, which is the Mistress?" Answering this attack proved no great hardship to the colonial leaders, who did indeed condemn popular government and were certain that Congregationalism would never become democratic. The political theory supplied them at once with arguments for precluding such developments; by a similar use of human learning in the conduct of church government and by defining the church covenant after the analogy of the social compact they reproduced in miniature within each society their philosophy of the state. The articles agreed upon in the confederations were not simply what the people might desire but the laws of God. The congregations had "no power to make Lawes for themselves or their Members, but to observe and see all their Members observe those Laws which Christ hath given and commanded." Winthrop put drastic limitations upon the covenants of civil societies, but even they were permitted an immense freedom in determining their laws and forms as compared with churches. "In this Spiritual Kingdom of Christ, men may not alter the kind or Form of Church, which Christ hath Instituted, but must preserve inviolate the Laws, Administrations, Priviledges, and Church-Government ordained by him, without Addition, Diminution, or alteration." Consequently, having professed subjection to a definite platform, the people stand in constant need of learned men to interpret it. The elders' work, said Richard Mather, "is to teach and rule the Church by the Word and lawes of Christ . . . and unto whom so teaching and ruling, all the people ought to be obedient and submit themselves." Characteristically, the Puritan leaders assumed, as though it were a matter beyond question, that learning would forever be respected and heeded in a consociation of saints, that the people would never themselves presume to judge any tenet but would wait upon the judgment of the properly qualified. There are always one or two men in every congregation, said Richard Mather, "who doe not want all humane learning, but have been trained up in Universities," and with Harvard College in existence there seemed no reason to fear a future deficiency. Furthermore, those who "are fit matter to bee combined into a Church-body" will never be so hopelessly illiterate "but they have learned the Doctrine of the holy Scripture." The prestige of learning in a Puritan world was in itself sufficient promise that "a Government meerly Popular or Democraticall . . . is farre from the practice of these Churches," but in addition the covenant itself, when interpreted according to Winthrop's definition of "civil liberty," would absolutely assure it. The saints, being instructed in the doctrine of the holy Scripture, would understand that when they chose pastors and teachers, they were merely agents through whom God did the selecting. Every proper election was a special providence, in which the fraternity, their wills engaged to God by inward covenant, became the means for issuing a divine commission. Though the minister was called "by his church," yet the summons was "from Christ," and the vote of the people no more made him "the servant of the Church, then a Captain (by leave of the Generall) chosen by the Band of Souldiers is the servant of his Band." In the conduct of church government, policies "ought not to be determined meerly by multitude or plurality of Votes, but by rules from the word of Christ." The fundamental law, enacted in the church covenant, secured certain liberties for the fraternity and prescribed limits to the power of the elders—a restriction which seemed dangerous to Presbyterians, though Congregationalists were confident that in practice it would bind both fraternity and elders all the more firmly to the predetermined pattern since both were freely sworn to maintain it.

Neither the *Elders* nor the people doe rule with Lordly and Princely rule, and Soveraigne authority and power; for that is proper to Christ over his Church . . . They are not so to rule, as to doe what themselves please, but they must do whatsoever *Christ* hath commanded.

Even if the government were democratical ("as it is not," said Cotton) there could be "no tumultuous disorder, where not the *will* of each man beareth the sway, but the voice of Christ alone is heard, who is the Head and wise Monarch of the Church"—the voice of Christ, that is, as expounded by learned elders. Samuel Stone hit happily upon a perfect description of the Congregational ideal, "a speaking *Aristocracy* in the face of a silent *Democracy*," nor was he describing only the theoretical goal. For the first few decades practice in the main followed theory, and the skillful ministers, backed by firm magistrates, kept the democracy silent while the aristocracy spoke the will of God. Only in the last decades of the century, after the ministers themselves had become of several minds concerning some important particulars in the will of God, or after the concept of His will began to lose the sharp precision of the first days, only then could the democracy show signs of insubordination and tumultuous disorders break out in particular Congregational churches.

Both for theory and practice the problem created by the physical presence in the colonies of unregenerated inhabitants was more menacing. Not that there was much apprehension, at the beginning, over the possibility of distinguishing between the converted and the unconverted. The Covenant of Grace could be trusted to furnish reliable tests. If the elect were bound to do the will of God, and only the elect would have the power to do it, then those who had the power were the elect. "A willing subjection of a mans self to Christ in this Covenant," said John Eliot, "is some hopeful sign of some degree of faith in Christ," whereas, said Richard Mather, "willingly not to doe this is a secret disparagement to the wisdome of God." Willingness being the gift of the Covenant, a capacity to will became the trial of the sanctuary. A church restricted to visible saints was feasible because God would no more keep the names of His chosen hidden in His own breast than true saints would conceal their being chosen. He disclosed His favors, and so a man, "being in the covenant of grace, is to be judged according to rationall charity." Of course, the congregation might now and then be deceived, but God permitted them to proceed by "the rule of Reason and love," to pick the men who had sworn to the Covenant of Grace and had thus acquired the strength to swear to the covenant of the congregation. Presbyterians were profoundly skeptical of this rule of reason and love.

They thought it safer to gather everybody into the fold by the rule of force and leave the selection to God. William Rathband described how in New England the ministers put a poor candidate on trial, examined his life and knowledge before the congregation, and required "a verball declaration (either made by a mans selfe, or else drawne out of him by interrogatories) touching the manner of his Conversion from point to point, and what evidences he can shew of the truth of his grace, of his sound faith, and sincere repentance." To this monstrous practice Rathband objected that few men can remember exactly how or when they were converted, that even the holiest saints, being imperfectly sanctified, are subject to doubts and despairs, that some never know whether they ever were converted, that many good souls cannot speak in public, that hypocrites with a gift of speech may give satisfaction where shy Christians stand tongue-tied; he said that this examination gave the congregations more power to pry into men's private affairs than the bishops ever dreamed of, and that they, being no better than mobs, would be influenced by ulterior partialities. By all such comments the New England leaders remained unmoved, for as long as they took the Covenant of Grace for a fact, they were convinced that every sound conversion would make a sound candidate for a church. Because grace was not merely regeneration but was also a compact binding the regenerate to hasten their sanctification, every saint would exhibit some token measurable by the rule of rational charity. "So profession of his Faith, and of his subjection to the Gospel, and the Churches approbation, and acceptance of him (which is the summe of Church-Covenant) is the formall cause that gives him the being of a member." The church covenant was therefore no newfangled "humane dressing," but an orderly accomplishment of articles agreed upon in the spiritual covenant, while the fact that the spiritual covenant was an affair of articles demanding fulfillment furnished objective grounds for deciding who was within it.

Consequently, for the early leaders there was no problem in separating the sheep from the goats; the real difficulty was preventing the goats from running wild once they were shut out of the fold. Winthrop could afford to hold the deputies to a standard of civil liberty, for they were church members and their wills were competent to embrace the good, just, and honest; the fraternity could be required to submit to learned ministers, for they had received enabling grace. But how could strangers to the Covenant of Grace be expected to exercise any but a "natural liberty" or to act otherwise in the churches than in "tumultuous disorder"? What became of the principle of voluntarism when four fifths of the people were pronounced incapable of holy volition, when the overwhelming majority, unless forcibly restrained by the civil authority, would become worse than brute beasts? To the modern mind this question often supplies an indictment of the Puritan regime; our ideas of justice and honesty are outraged by a system in which four out of five persons were forced to attend divine services and support the minister even while they were denied membership and informed that they were probably destined to perdition. The leaders seem to us guilty of gross inconsistency when they attributed their society to a compact of the people, and yet confined the powers of legislation and election to a hand-picked minority of those who favored their own policies. We cannot help asking how the many who were thrust out because they were pronounced deficient in virtue could have put up with the Pharisaical arrogance of the few, or why they, Englishmen as freeborn as the visible elect, permitted themselves to be relegated to political impotence. We imagine that humanity should have risen in justifiable wrath, that many must have shared William Blackstone's disgust on finding, after fleeing Lord Bishops, that he was now to be bullied by the lord brethren. Recent historians have stressed the several instances in court records of non-members being presented and punished for insults to the elders or the saints. We understand the language of the lawyer Thomas Lechford, who declared of Massachusetts Bay that "three parts of the people of the Country remaine out of the Church," and noted, "The people begin to complain, they are ruled like *slaves*." The modern student, assuming that human nature of the seventeenth century was essentially human nature as he knows it in the twentieth, concludes that the regime must have been maintained by force and characterizes it as a dictatorship of the righteous, the tyranny of a party, a totalitarian theocracy.

No doubt there were some who objected, like Blackstone, to being ruled as slaves, yet it is hard to discover among the victims of Puritan justice in the seventeenth century any who were protesting solely on grounds which the modern democrat or liberal would expect. Though the remonstrance of Dr. Robert Child in 1646 asked that "civil liberty and freedom be forthwith granted to all truely English," it is doubtful if he was making a stand for the rights of Englishmen rather than maneuvering to arouse the then Presbyterian Parliament against the Congregational power.[4] Most of the persons haled before the county courts whose offenses bear any relation to the law of exclusion seem to have been ignorant bumpkins or shrews, guilty of scurrilous speeches or some crude form of Antinomianism or Anabaptism, rather than of a liberal attack upon exclusive church membership and the restricted franchise. Even Roger Williams' assertion of toleration came not from a political or constitutional scruple but from a conception of the spiritual life so exalted that he could not see it contaminated by earthly compulsion. In other words, the long struggle in the seventeenth century for what Brooks Adams called "the emancipation of Massachusetts" was fought not by persons who objected on principle to the dictatorial or undemocratic rule of the saints, but by adherents of religious views at variance with the established orthodoxy. The deputies may have been actuated by a "democratical spirit," but they confined their agitation within the General Court; they showed no disposition to extend their democratical sympathies and take the visibly unregenerate into their ranks. If we search among the excluded and the disfranchised for signs of protest against ecclesiastical despotism, we forget that when New England was settled the Civil Wars had not yet taught Puritans to put questions of political and social rights before the single-minded pursuit of religious ideals, and Englishmen in general had not then imagined that a voice in the churches or a vote in the government was the due of every man. At the time of the migration, Puritan leaders were still thinking more of the will of God than of the social compact and the bill of rights, and had come to entertain the political ideas chiefly because these promised to be the means to religious ends. As long as theology predominated in the minds of the people over political economy, as long as they could be made to prize the law of God over the laws of nature, so long could they be brought to believe from their own experience that the ministers had taken the correct line, even if some apparent consequences of the law of nature were thereby curtailed. They could be persuaded that the rights of Englishmen went no further than the *Body of Liberties,* and that membership in the churches or a vote in the government should properly be granted only to the probable elect. Thus they could be brought to accede to their own elimination.

This is not to say that the regime could have succeeded without using force. Journals and court records, particularly the frank admissions of William Bradford in the year 1642, reveal that among the mass of settlers there was still plenty of what Puritans called "the old Adam," that the multitude were not universally holy and probably had no great comprehension of the complex theory. Many, perhaps the majority, migrated for material rather than spiritual reasons, and their energies were certainly much taken up, once they had arrived, with physical tasks. In order to keep them in line, to secure from them the very minimum of religious observance, the governments had to stand firmly behind the colonial ministers and implement the theology with fines, prisons, the ducking stool, and the noose. The point is, I believe, not that the theological definition of aims was sufficient to gather everybody into the enthusiasm of the crusade, but it was enough to prevent purely political objections to the theological order from gaining headway, indeed from ever arising. If an ordinary yeoman reached the point of demanding why he was debarred from membership or from citizenship, he encountered the clergy's explanation that the fault was entirely his own, that he had willed his predicament and could justly be deprived of these privileges, which did not pertain to his condition. He might not have followed all the steps in the demonstration, but he would have known no way to rebut it; so long as the religious spirit retained something of the first vigor, the democracy could not overcome the religious reasoning that preserved a limited church membership and made the church covenant the prerequisite for citizenship.

Christian theologians had always striven by whatever logic they possessed to prove that the reprobate work evil of their own free choice. No matter how vivid their sense of divine sovereignty, how explicit their recognition of predetermination and the enslavement of the moral will, Augustinians and Calvinists averred that none go to hell without deliberately entering upon the descent. The exclusive system of church polity in New England and the restricted franchise in Massachusetts Bay were applications of this tenet to society, but the principle could hardly have been applied so literally, the mass could not have been so confidently ruled out of the fold, had not the federal theology furnished more tangible grounds for alleging the willfulness of the unregenerate than was provided in traditional doctrine. When humanity is pictured as languishing in a dungeon, and only those liberated to whom the keeper arbitrarily grants a reprieve, it is difficult to see how the others can be accused of remaining on their own volition. But when regeneration is conceived as the offer of a covenant, through means suited to human faculties, when it comes not as an unruly descent of the Holy Ghost but as the chance to strike a profitable bargain with a minimum of risk, then those who let it pass must be consciously recalcitrant. Churches and the state can have only one responsibility toward the refractory: to see that they are brought into the precincts of the means, that they are exposed to the rational discourses of faithful preachers and taught sound doctrine. If they will listen and be convinced, they may become members. There can be no such thing as their believing without their taking the formal covenant. How can a man pretend to be in the Covenant of Grace and not be ready to manifest it in his conduct, and how can he manifest it toward those of his fellows to whom he is obliged by the Covenant to join himself except by covenanting with them?

> If any should have claimed Church-fellowship, saying, I beleeve the promises, but would not binde himselfe to any duties of Evangelicall obedience, this had been a taking hold of the Covenant by the halves, a taking of one part of it in seeming and pretence, and a leaving of another; but it would not have been sufficient to have brought a man into the fellowship of the church.

From the theory of regeneration according to the federal theology it followed that Christian society was a consequence of faith, all the more mandatory for being undertaken by the free consent of believers. "Those that were in Christ, and believers in Him, were not wont to abstaine from joyning to some particular Congregation or other; . . . as they were in Christ by their Faith, so by such joyning they became also to be within the visible Church." Inasmuch, therefore, as the church covenant involved no more than what the Covenant of Grace required, "inasmuch as entring into Church-Covenant is nothing else but a solemne promise to the Lord, before him and the Church, to walke in all such wayes as the Gospel requireth of Church Members," for any to reject the ecclesiastical bond, whether they were unable or unwilling, "this would be an evidence against them, of their unfitnesse for Church priviledges." All who have an opportunity to hear sermons and who receive the good effects of the means, "whose setled abode is in a place where Churches are gather'd and order'd according to Christ," and who yet do not join in the church covenant, can hardly be accounted true believers. "The fear of God, and Faith of those men, may be justly doubted." We refuse admission to no man of approved piety, said John Cotton, "if he be willing to accept it." The qualification was willingness, not birth or class or wealth, and the fact seems to be that four fifths of the people were not sufficiently willing, and yet were unable to attribute their lack of will to any other cause than that given by the ministers. If they were unhappy over it, they could only hope and pray; if they said, what care I for God's ordinances or His people? "Certainly this is to cast off Christ's power; and if continued in, the salvation of your souls is also cast off." And should a holy enterprise, seeking the due forms of government, a city set upon a hill to be an example for all mankind, permit the obstinately unrighteous to share in the church or to determine civil policy? The answer to this question being so obvious, the New England authorities had no qualms over the justice of their regime, while the non-freemen were so incapable of avoiding the logic by which the question came to be posed that even had they wished, they could have presented no organized resistance to it.

The civil magistrates of New England, conceiving of themselves as the executives of Christian states, took unto themselves powers to which every European government of the early seventeenth century assumed it was entitled, to expel or execute heretics and to punish disturbers of the ecclesiastical peace. They felt themselves obliged by their office not to tolerate errors, to forbid within their jurisdictions all churches except the orthodox. They were to look after "the *establishment of pure Religion, in doctrine, worship, and government,* according to the word of God." There was nothing exceptional for the times in the main principles of the New England theory; all religiously minded persons in Europe, Protestant or Catholic, were certain in the year 1630 that the state and church should be "reciprocally helpfull to each other; The Civill polity ratifying the Churches cases, by Civill Laws and punishments, the Ecclesiasticall polity lending help to State and Common-wealth cases, by declaring the Laws and rules of God." On all sides there was agreement that the function of a state was to lead its members to the good life.[5] The colonies were remarkable merely for the consistency with which they were able to enforce uniformity and suppress dissent within their boundaries at a time when larger empires were finding themselves physically unable to reduce all citizens to complete conformity. So successful were Massachusetts and Connecticut in vindicating the rules of intolerance and coercion that they were extremely reluctant to abandon them, even after English non-conformists during the Restoration turned to toleration as a *modus vivendi*. Yet the special ecclesiastical order of these colonies introduced from the beginning a peculiar qualification into their concept of the church-state relationship, which can hardly be paralleled in any other nation of the century. The problem for a European prince or republic under the law of uniformity and intolerance was not only suppressing heresy and collecting tithes, but constraining all citizens to be members of the established church. But in New England the ecclesiastical system translated the abstract theology of the Covenant of Grace into the concrete covenants of churches. The immediate result was the creation of two distinct classes of persons, visible saints and those of whom no more could be said than that they were not yet evidently regenerate, and these new divisions cut across conventional class lines. The basis for distinction was an act of will, an aptitude for faith. The regime therefore was committed to maintaining this distinction; the "due forme" of government amounted to a mechanism for permitting the two sorts of men to be discriminated. Where other governments strove to gather everyone into the churches and keep him in, the colonial authorities had to separate saints from sinners, and while suppressing notorious heretics by force, had yet to allow free play for the human will to range itself among the one or the other. They could force none to assume the obligations of a member who was unwilling to take them upon himself. The "end and instigation" of all outward government, said Thomas Shepard, "was to set up and help forward the inward"; the external ordinances were nothing in themselves "but as they were appointed and sanctified for this end." The state, therefore, had to accommodate itself to the Covenant of Grace. It had a dual responsibility: to the visibly regenerate it had to guarantee the ordinances of Christ in all their purity, particularly faithful, orthodox, and learned preaching of the Word, but for those not yet called it could properly do no more than provide for them to attend the preaching so that they would be in a position to hear the call when and if it came. Massachusetts and Connecticut were coercive theocracies, as consistently intolerant as any absolute monarchy, and yet they were strangely compelled by their own assumption to mark off and preserve inviolate a sphere of human volition, a field of action in which they had to permit individuals a fundamental freedom, even the freedom to go to the Devil. The magistrates were to be "nursing Fathers" to the church and to exercise "a *co-active power* to compel the Church to execute the ordinances of Christ, according to the order and rules of Christ"; they were to defend the purity of God's worship and ways "against all Infesting, infringing, Impugning or Impairing principles," to protect the saints in the enjoyment of their exclusive spiritual privileges. But at the same time, as regarded those who were not saints, they could act only as a "means" of giving assistance to rational beings, helping them to make up their minds but not compelling them. The civil ruler could force them to go to church and listen, but he could not require that they believe. He could draw them on "by all meanes he can, by his proclamations, lawes, and examples"; if they violated the rules of law and decency he could put forth his coactive power against them, but otherwise he could do no more than take care "that the best means be seasonably and wisely used with them, according to their capacities, to bring them first to the knowledge of the true God, and of his word, and to convince them of the falshood & vanity of their gods." He could lead them to the water but not make them drink. He might, said Hooker, compel the unregenerate to attend the ordinances "and force them to use means of *information* and *conviction* . . . *But* the civill Magistrate is to leave the Church to follow the *rule* of Christ in her *Admissions*." The difference between this Congregational theory and the compulsive philosophies of the Stuarts, of the Presbyterians, may seem slight, particularly as the New England colonies held out to the bitter end against the idea of toleration. Voluntarism did not make at once for liberalism, if anything it contributed to authoritarianism. And yet the church theory testifies once more to the shifting influences in seventeenth-century Puritanism, to the fashion in which rationalism and freedom were finding a place in the very citadel of theocracy. *"Christ's people are a willing people;* faith is not forced." As long as the settlers of New England could be kept up to something like the first pitch of religious intensity, men could be rejected from the churches on the assumption that they were unwilling to join, and the ecclesiastical order would not suffer. But trouble was brewing for the New England way if ever the day came when the distinction between saint and sinner should not be easy to find, when a social system devised to sever the children of God from the sons of Belial should discover itself unable to tell one from the other. Should the posterity become unwilling to carry on the covenant of their fathers, either some means not envisaged in the original scheme would need to be created to incite them, or the covenant would have to be abandoned and the theory of church and society be reorganized on wholly different grounds.

In the first years, such prospects seemed exceedingly remote. The ranks of the saints were sound and vigorous, Winthrop and the magistrates suppressed disorders, and most of the unregenerate fell into line with astonishingly little complaint. The future was secured by the sacramental system; the children of the members had the seal of the covenant upon them, and God would surely in the fullness of time bring them to participation in its gifts. They were given to God, "to be nursed up by him, and wee beleeve for them, that there is that in Christ for them which they stand in need of and therefore we beleeve in their behalfe, that God will be gracious to them, for his Covenants sake." Meantime the all-important point was gained: the platform of revealed ideas was made to coalesce with the pattern of reason. The unification of piety and intellect, for which Puritanism strove on every occasion, was obtained most spectacularly in the ecclesiastical doctrine, for this was no mere abstraction but was triumphantly carried into practice. The seventeenth-century preoccupation with "method" was vindicated when it led to a successful method for society, when it did away at once with both metaphysical and political obstacles. Orthodox Puritans, both Presbyterian and Independent, rallying to the defense of learning in the 1650's against fanatical sectaries, declared that if human reason were entirely banished from the church, so that it had to depend upon nothing but revealed fiat and the inspiration of the spirit, it would become an anarchical and spasmodic irruption in society. They advanced the thesis that there were many points in common between assemblies of Christians and civil societies, "Churches being humane Societies as to the matter of them, i.e. partaking of this general nature of being a Collection of rational Creatures: and that whatever is applicable to humane Society in general, belongs to Churches as contained under that larger notion," particularly the use of wisdom and discretion. While the shade of Richard Hooker smiled ironically, Thomas Hooker wrote that the Congregational government shared "with other[s] of the like rank, in the generall nature common to them and it, and thence may (as it is) truely be called, an Art or Policy, as Civil governments are stiled: and there be a like parity and proportion of reason, in regard of the nature of the work." From some points of view the New England way, as against English Presbyterianism, seems to have more in common with the sectaries' enthusiasm, but as against the sectaries themselves it remained solid and orthodox, staunchly resisting the heresies of Antinomianism and Arminianism, and the dangerous polities of Anabaptism, Quakerism, and Gortonism, condemning all proposals for a church ruled by an inner light without regard to reason and the law of nature. The New England apologies contain countless passages asserting that "nothing is more naturall or agreeable to morall equitie" than the New England establishment; John Cotton would plead three sanctions: "The light of Nature, the law of *Moses,* the Gospel of Christ, do all of them make a ready answer for us." Presbyterians also opposed enthusiasts and dogmatists, and endeavored to prove that their polity was ratified by the light of nature, but they often felt that New Englanders overdid the appeal to reason. The Congregationalists, said Thomas Edwards in 1641, teach that in such particulars as are common to the church with other societies the light of nature should prevail, and insist upon this principle so strongly that it "is brought as the maine ground for their Church covenant (though there be neither precept nor practice of it, in the Word) namely the Lawes and rules of Nature which doe run along with, and are alike common to things Spirituall and Humane, so farre as both are found to agree in one common nature together." There are times when the student may find in this comment the all-sufficient key to the thought and expression of New England, the final insight into the real meaning of the Congregational polity. As Lord Clarendon observed, the English Independents triumphed in the "pulpit skirmishes" of London by 1647 because they "were more learned and rational."[6] The colonial leaders believed that they had Scripture on their side, yet careful analysis of their arguments shows again and again that the polity was established upon the Bible only at several removes, only after the Bible had been pressed by logic to yield up deductions which are not always obvious in the texts, or else that it was established openly upon the laws of reason and nature, upon the political ideals of contract and government by consent. The crucial influence exerted by the intellectual heritage upon a society and upon a mind avowedly regulated by the Word of God is seen when John Davenport, most exacting of the first generation of divines, argues "from the Analogy and agreement that is between the Spiritual power of a Congregational Church of Christ, and the civil power of the most free and perfect Cities," and offers as authorities for his definition of the legitimate powers of both a church and a city—Grotius and Thucydides!

At no point in their thinking did the New England divines practice deliberate duplicity. They deduced their tenets, so they believed, straight from Holy Writ, and were prepared to submit their reasonings to the inspection of the learned. We can hardly appreciate how sincere they could be in extracting their particular beliefs from the Bible, or how naturally they might read their preconceptions into it, unless we recur to the then state of historical scholarship and the absolute confidence of the age in the infallibility of logic. With the Bible narrative not yet looked upon as an historical document, to be read in relation to times and places, but as absolute and timeless, and with logic regarded as that which proceeds by infallible degrees from certain premises, the New Englanders could take their polity as well as their creed from the Bible without any sense whatsoever that they were exceeding warrantable meanings. But while they were sincere, precisely because their sincerity was uninhibited by any "higher criticism" or by any sense of the relativity of logic, they proceeded all the more freely to interpret the Bible with methods supplied by the intellectual heritage. In this way they were able to refashion the articles of their piety, the tenets of divine sovereignty, human depravity, and irresistible grace, and make a place beside them for the articles of reason and humanism, for the sanctity of the human will and the power of consent. Therefore in their church polity they identified the Covenant of Grace, which was of the soul, with the covenant of the church, which was of the community. Along with a theology that conceived of man as a sinful creature who had mortally offended an almighty and irresistible sovereign, against whom he had no rights whatever and from whom he had no reason to expect anything but the most summary treatment, the divines managed to erect a church wherein man was a responsible being, free and independent, who could not legally be compelled to submit to any exactions but those to which he consented. In the federal theology the two views were mingled, for in the concordat of grace God remained sovereign, but He consented to terms; in the Congregational church, built upon the Covenant of Grace, the two orders, spiritual and natural, were still further united because the men agreed to a confederacy in accordance with the principles of nature and yet depended on God for the empowering spirit. By its inherent nature, grace was a capricious and chaotic visitation; the ecclesiastical theory transformed this anarchic flame into a voluntary and sober subjection to order. It asserted the continuity of inward rectitude with outward conduct, causing that illumination which transcends the earth to produce on earth a law-abiding society, harnessing man's most acute sense of life and liberty to a sense of civic duty. Out of a piety in which the individual was the end of creation, it deduced a social philosophy in which he was subordinate to the whole. The theologians proved by meticulous logic what visionaries had failed to convey in poetry and allegory, that fact could be made one with the ideal. In their churches they could be both utilitarians and idealists, because, as Samuel Willard put it most succinctly, the design of God in all His relations with man is man's salvation, "which, because God will have it be advanced by means suitable to the Nature of Man, he hath ordained, that there shall be an orderly Combination of Men professing it, among whom these Means may be enjoyed."

CHAPTER XVI

GOD'S CONTROVERSY WITH NEW ENGLAND

Greek and Roman historians never ceased to marvel that so small a band as charged at Marathon or manned the ships at Salamis overcame the Persian hosts. Being pagans, and knowing nothing of the providence of the true God, they ascribed the victory to fortune, but we, said Increase Mather, who have the Scripture to instruct us, know the real cause of those astounding triumphs: angels fought in the ranks of the Greeks. Just as Homer described a physical presence of the Gods in the battles before Troy, so the pastor of the Second Church in Boston conceived that the Grecians "were secretly and invisibly animated by Angels." By such lights did Puritans read history. The record of humanity was to them a chronicle of God's providence, exactly as occurrences in nature or in the heavens were significations of His governing will. Nothing that men had ever done was without a spiritual import, for the power that created the world continually guided and directed all worldly events; though men acted of their own volition, they always fulfilled His intentions. Even events which at first sight seemed contrary to God's interests proved, upon closer analysis, to have served His ends. The onslaught of the Turks might appear to the casual or atheistical student a victory for the powers of darkness, but to Increase Mather the finger of God was obvious even in their successes. When the Holy Roman Emperor "was minded to destroy his Protestant Subjects, God let loose the great Turk upon the Empire, and so diverted the evil designs against his people, which had been long preparing, and were become ripe for execution." The Puritan scholar studied all history, heathen or Christian, as an exhibition of divine wisdom, and found in the temporal unfolding of the divine plan that the entire past had been but a sort of prologue to the enactment of the New England commonwealths.

Puritans recognized, as we have seen, that the problem of determinism, the danger of the will's relapsing into passive dependence upon God's decrees, was not confined to the private spirit; it threatened the state as well as the saints, and just as the federal theorists endeavored to prevent the lessening of individual exertions by propounding to the elect a covenant which was conditional without being meritorious, so the New England ministers extended the same covenant to include their political and ecclesiastical institutions. But even after they had thus secured a theoretical frame for the social order, they confronted the question of the future, of how long the perfect society would endure, of what sanctions could be applied to insure continued rectitude among their posterity. At this point the conventional religious interpretation of history obtruded itself, since what was to be in a determined universe could be forecast only in the light of what had been, and many lessons of the past, as learned by piety, boded ill for the long endurance of any earthly holiness. Without ever becoming more than half-conscious of their motives, the New England divines turned to the logic of the federal theology for an escape from the logic of time. Once more they were striving to extricate themselves from the round of necessity, from the dead level of material and implacable fact, and to assure themselves and their people that not only was Christian history coming to its foreordained climax in their Jerusalem, but that theirs would be an exception to all the cities that ever before had been set upon a hill, and would resist degeneration with the sustaining help of the Covenant of Grace.

Strictly speaking, there was no place for contingency, fortune, or accident either in the past or in the future, and no nation could ever attain to a destiny other than what had been appointed. The "great line of time" had been plotted by God before the commencement of time. The future was as secure and as unalterable as the past; from the creation to the day of judgment every event was arranged, the rise of empires, revolutions, and the decline of churches. The whole of time was an elaborate and figured pattern, the portions yet in the future covered by a shadow, those of the past brilliantly revealed; yet the contours still undisclosed were fixed and to some extent discernible through the darkness. In broad outline, the future was as predictable as the past was recordable. For this reason the prophecies of Scripture were possible, for they were insights into what was inevitably to happen. "*Prophesie* is History *antedated;* and History is *Postdated Prophesie:* the same thing is told in both." The chief task of him who studied former times was not to furnish entertaining reading but to discover "near what *Joynt* in that *Line of Time,* we are now arriv'd," exactly as a man traveling from one known place to another uses a map to calculate how far he has yet to go before reaching his destination. There might be doubt as to exactly when the universe would be rolled up like a scroll, whether next year or a thousand years hence, but to the Puritan there had been a definite beginning and there was to be a precise ending. History was an inevitable progression from one limit to the other, as immutable beyond the point at which any man was living as behind it.

Since God created, determined, and regulated temporal events, no one epoch could be intrinsically any better than another. The course of nature was uniform; there could be no fading of God's influence, no fluctuations in His control. "In Civil matters there be the like manners of men now as of old; the like causes and successes of warre and peace." A knowledge of former ages was "behovefull", as Cotton expressed it, because of the eternal sameness of things and the perpetual recurrence of manners and causes. To the Puritan mind, ideas either of a decay of nature or of a law of progress were inadmissible, for both insinuated imperfections in the providential power of an absolute God. However, to say that history told of the eternal sameness of things was not to say that things were eternally one and the same. The essential continuity of the divine plan permitted surface variations from age to age. God was, to say the least, too competent an "artist" to embody in time a monotonous chronicle without relief or interest.

> The principal cause of all passages in the world: which is not mans weaknesse, or goodnesse, but chiefly the wise and strong and good providence of God: who presenteth every age with a new stage of acts and actors . . . And if a Poet would not present his spectators but with choyce variety of matters, how much lesse God?

To furnish the necessary variety within the fundamental unity, God inspired among His creatures at certain junctures greater recognition of Himself than at others. One century might be spiritually dead, and the next witness a great revival, though the cause of either condition was the same decree of God. "The barrenesse and fruitfulnesse of severall ages, depend meerly upon Gods good pleasure; who opens and shuts the womb of truth from bearing, as he sees fit, according to the counsell of his own will." Truth does not change, "but the alteration grows, according to mens apprehensions, to whom it is more or lesse discovered, according to Gods most just judgement, and their own deservings." Consequently there were limits beyond which neither spiritual declension nor religious revival could go. If men plunged too deeply and disastrously into idolatry, the scheme of redemption would miscarry; if they all achieved and sustained perfection, the scheme would lose its point. Therefore piety of the sort we have called Augustinian gave rise to a kind of cyclical theory of history, to a concept of mankind as perpetually alternating between eras of widespread corruption and periods of reform, with each extreme followed by a turn in the contrary direction. Successive oscillations between phases of degeneracy and of righteousness were abundantly illustrated by the history of the Jews, and to James Allen it seemed clear that we should not find either in the Scriptures or in the subsequent experience of the churches "that the next Age after any considerable progress in Reformation, did go beyond the first, but the contrary . . . There have been gradual declinings till that light hath almost been extinguished; then the Lord hath raised a new spirit of Reformation, to whom he hath given & revealed more of his will, & further knowledge of his truth." The centuries were all manifestations of God's providence, but they were not all as like as peas in a pod. Yet if piety alone were to determine the philosophy of history, and the past was to be understood simply as a drama written and directed by an absolute sovereign, the diversity of events could never amount to more than a vibration between two fixed poles. When the last scene in the human performance had been completed, the whole play would appear to have been full of pulsations but to have remained essentially static. This version of history might well be heartening to those living, as they believed, at a point in time when the line was about to turn upwards from the nadir of depravity, but for conscientious souls born when the pendulum had swung to the other extreme, and the human race was falling backwards once more, the prospect would be profoundly discouraging. Urian Oakes was gloomily reflecting in 1677 that this ebb and flow affected politics no less than religion, and though at certain times, he said, when wise men and good men stand up for their country and its liberties, there will be a concurrence of forces to aid them, yet "at another time, they may endeavour it, and the Times frown upon them, the Spirit and Humour of the People is degenerated; and they swimm against the stream, & are lost in the Attempt." That God had set a boundary to the defeats and disappointments of the saints was a comforting reflection in days of adversity, but the corresponding knowledge that He had circumscribed the duration of success was a cause for anxiety to the successful. New England being settled in the flood tide of reformation, by men aiming in state and church at the highest perfection to which men had aspired since the Apostles, was it not inevitable that immediately thereafter a decline should set in? Was there a further level of holiness to which the children could progress beyond that attained by the first settlers, and if there were none, could the later generations conceivably remain poised at the same pitch of virtue? And surely if the line once began to fall from so immense a height, the momentum of the descent would carry it proportionately low before there could be any hope that it would again remount. The terrifying reflection that haunted leaders of New England was an almost inescapable consequence of their fundamental beliefs, and unless they could find somewhere a mechanism compatible with those beliefs which would also rescue New England from the ceaseless undulations of vice and virtue, they would have to face the fact that by a law as inexorable as that which caused the moon to wax and wane their holy experiment was bound to fail.

That their experiment was the very apex of a reforming era was to them altogether obvious. No one could review the history of Europe since the death of the Apostles and come to any other conclusion. The centuries between the first and the fourteenth had been one long swing downward, the lowest depths of human depravity being touched in the church of the thirteenth. The declension had begun, according to Puritan calculations, in antiquity itself, so that Puritan scholars were always distrustful of the Fathers. Cotton would profess to acknowledge with thankfulness and reverence "the Labors of these ancient Divines," yet deem it "partiality" to say that they interpreted Scripture correctly; when Anglicans or Presbyterians cited patristic writings, Cotton replied that if a doctrine "have no higher rise than the Fathers, it is too young a device," and protested that "later Writers had a clearer discerning, therefore it will be of more use to read wholsome later Writers." The total eclipse of true Christianity set in for the Puritan historian with Constantine, who "enebriated the Church with wealth and honour, and hereupon the Church falleth into a long sleepe, which shee shook not wholly off for many ages." What we now call the Middle Ages Puritans accounted a long night—"*Reader,* wilt thou not give thanks to God that thou wast not born in *those* days," for then "Clouds of thick Barbarity enveloped and overwhelmed all *Schools of Literature,*" and Popes dominated over princes "by Matchivilian policy." Puritans considered Machiavelli a very evil man, but his word was adequate testimony for John Cotton to prove that medieval religion had been "meer jugling, to fill the Popes Coffers, and keep his Kitching warm by purgatory and pardons"; Machiavelli perceived this much, but did not therefore turn to the true faith, thus illustrating the wickedness of Popery, which "leads simple men to superstition, and understanding men to Atheisme." The great event of modern history, second in importance in all history only to the appearance of Christ and perhaps to the Puritan mind really more engrossing, was the Reformation. This was certainly the work of no one man, but was inspired by God and was brought on by degrees, God here duplicating the technique He had employed throughout the Old Testament in unfolding the Covenant of Grace. Leaders arose independently, for whenever the tide of religion has receded as far as God will permit, He enlightens His servants, "though farre distant one from another, with the same beams of light of Divine Truth." Puritans never looked upon Luther as more than one among several reformers and by no means the first. The harbinger of reform was "Petrus Waldus, a Citizen of Lions." About the year 1300, according to Cotton, God began to summon His servants to testify for Him, and Cotton's list of these proto-Protestants is an interesting commentary on the Puritan's conception of his tradition, particularly for his mingling of early humanists with late medieval theologians as though all had been engaged upon the same work: "*Dantes, Marcillius, Potavinus, Ocham, Gre-*

gorius, Ariminensis, Petrarchus, Wickliffe, and many moe, whose Ministry brought on so many, that some have counted it the first resurrection." John Huss and Jerome of Prague marked the second period of reform, Savonarola—"a Godly learned Preacher in *Florence,* a man endued with a Prophetical Spirit"—inaugurated a third, so that by 1500 "the Regions were white and ready to the harvest, else *Luther* had not found such good successe in his Ministry." God's subtle management of the action was to be seen in His contriving that the avarice and ambition of the Papacy, exhibited in the sale of indulgences, should become the occasion of its downfall. But Luther was not the greatest or the final figure; Cotton deplored that "the pregnant strength, and glorious lustre of many heroicall and excellent gifts of *Luther* had bin so idolized, that many and great Nations followed him in some notorious errors of his way," and found further degrees of perfection achieved in Geneva, Holland, and England. Yet even in these nations there were still notorious errors. However pure they became in doctrine, they failed to grasp the idea of the church covenant, and until they came to this understanding the Reformation would remain incomplete. "The *Reformation* which was no where fully *perfect,* had in several Nations, various degrees of its *perfection;* some went much further than others in restoring of *Primitive Christianity,* and reforming of all things, according to the *word of Christ.*" But none by 1630 had restored the form of church government according to the Word; clarification of doctrine had necessarily preceded the work of polity, yet until at least one nation had erected the Biblical system to guide all subsequent ages, the cycle of reform would not be brought to its inevitable completion. Quite apart from the particular commands of God, which were nominally obligatory at all times, history showed that specific times must run their irresistible course, and the movement begun in the fourteenth century must come somewhere in the seventeenth to its organic fulfillment.

However, the sad fact was clear by 1630 that Geneva and Holland had proved incapable of the final effort, as also had the Huguenots of France in spite of Ramus' informing them of the correct Congregational platform. For a time it seemed that God had selected England as the country in which the reform would find its certain consummation, and New England Puritans, even after the Restoration, never lost their expectation that the Established Church would some day be broken up and reorganized into independent, covenanted congregations. But though the English Reformation commenced auspiciously, God was pleased for reasons of His own that it should prove abortive. Henry VIII and Elizabeth "cut off the head of the Beast," but they preserved the body of the beast in the canons of their church. "There was an unsafe principle in their hearts," and they took unto themselves the impious title which the Pope had usurped, though "the truth is, neither the Pope, nor King hath power to make Laws to rule the Church, but it must be by the Laws of Christ." For three generations "many eminent Divines and many gracious Christians" strove to inculcate "a forme of knowledge and of government in *England,"* but for all their labors, though the doctrine became good, the administration still was "deaded with the inventions of men," and in the opinion of Puritans, "if you look upon the government of Churches, you will find little difference between Episcopacy and Popery." In the decade of 1620 to 1630 the cause of true churches in England seemed hopeless, while the Protestant forces of Germany and France were being routed, and all over Europe the lights were going out. "Consider the present time of the Church," exhorted the great John Preston with his dying breath, "consider how soone the times may come upon us, when we shall be put to it, for now things are in praecipitio; hasting downe to the bottom of the hill." Hitherto religion and peace had managed to walk together in England, but "these times are growing and daily gather strength more and more; therefore let us strengthen our faith, and prepare for a tryall." Events had come to such a pass that gallants were deliberately profaning the Sabbath in order not to be counted as Puritans; England was bent on destruction, while in Bohemia and Denmark "what shall you see, nothing else but as Travellers say, Churches made heaps of stones, and these Bethels wherin Gods name was called upon, are made defiled Temples for Satan and superstition to raigne in." In Germany "you cannot goe two or three steps, but you shall see the heads of dead men, goe a little further, and you shall see their hearts picked out by the fowles of the ayre, whereupon you are ready to conclude that Tilly hath been there." Thomas Hooker was asking, "Those Churches are become desolate, and why not England?" His last sermon in his native country, entitled *The Danger of Desertion,* dwelt not on the danger of England's leaving God, but of God's deserting England. Was the period of reform approaching its end prematurely and would the nations once more revert to barbarism and superstition before any one of them attained to the pure form of church government? Would God permit the age to miss its destiny?

At this very moment the hand of God was stretched forth and the choicest of His saints led out of Egypt to the new land of Canaan, the one place indubitably provided in which the Reformation might not fall short, where "the world might see a *Specimen* of what shall be over all the Earth in the Glorious Times which are Expected." What was wanting in Europe should be supplied in America; God's servants having made clear the laws of the covenant, and the pious care of the magistrates being enlisted for their enforcement, "this wisdome will by the blessing of God be established; that that which other Nations have not attained to this day, may by the blessing of God be reached by us." We can appreciate the New Englanders' sense of their own rôle in the cosmos only when we realize that they believed the Reformation to be a cumulative and still expanding force in the seventeenth century, but were also convinced that in Protestant countries of Europe it had not gone more than half way and could proceed no further until it received further guidance. For the moment, the first onslaught having dislodged erroneous doctrines, the Protestant ranks were in confusion and were losing their advantage; they were falling into the anarchy of Anabaptism and Antinomianism or being betrayed by Arminianism into a disguised Popery. In order that the disorganized troops of righteousness might be rallied anew and the lines reformed, there was desperate need of a plan of battle. The doctrinal positions won by Luther and Calvin had to be reinforced by the more concrete program of polity, and New England had been reserved in the divine strategy to furnish Protestantism with a model for the final offensive of the campaign. If the New Englanders' estimate of their own importance seems ludicrous or pathetic to us, we must remember that we no longer read history in the light of piety, and we forget that from their point of view several thousand years of human experience pointed unmistakably to their existence and defined their task. They did not, at least in the first settlements, regard themselves as fleeing from Europe but as participating to the full in the great issue of European life; they did not set out to become provincial communities on the edge of civilization but to execute a flanking maneuver in the all-engrossing struggle of the civilized world. The Lord was granting them the greatest opportunity afforded to any people since the birth of Christ, the chance "to enjoy Churches, and Congregational Assemblies by his Covenant, to worship him in all his holy Ordinances," such a privilege indeed as "for 1260 years, the Christian world knew not the meaning of it . . . but this the Lord vouchsafeth to us this day, above all Nations that have power of the civill sword." We, the people of New England, wrote Peter Bulkeley, "are as a City set upon an hill, in the open view of all the earth, the eyes of the world are upon us, because we professe our selves to be a people in Covenant with God." Our function is to walk so that all the nations will say, "Onely this people is wise, an holy and blessed people"; the Lord has purposely kept us few, weak, and poor, so that we may excel in grace and holiness alone. John Cotton called Davenport to New England because here "the Order of the Churches and of the Commonwealth was so settled, by common Consent; that it brought to his mind, the New Heaven and New Earth, wherein dwells Righteousness." New England's obligation to righteousness was not alone the ordinary and universal duty of all Christians to glorify God and enjoy Him forever; it was in addition a special appointment, a definite and concrete mission "of enjoying Christ in his Ordinances, in the fellowship of his people." In order that the whole world might be instructed and a particular phase of history be accomplished, the towns of Massachusetts and Connecticut had to be settled; they were not designed to become mere abodes of prosperity and contentment, to give men land and crops, peace and security. They were to demonstrate to England and Europe what yet remained to be achieved, and their appointed task was as clear to the eye of reason, studying the pages of history, as to the eye of faith perusing the pages of revelation.

The magistrates and ministers of the first generation believed that they accomplished what was expected of them. "It is for us to doe all the good we can, and to leave nothing to those that shall come after us, but to walk in the righteous steps of their fore-Fathers." Cotton felt he might affirm without vanity or vainglory that "a greater face of reformation" was to be seen in New England than anywhere else in the world, that here at last was simplicity. "Whatever men say, yet the Lord may say here is wisdome, and here is neither marke, nor name, nor number of name, but all carried according to the laws of the 12 Apostles." The great Junius, distressed by the insufficiencies of the Dutch reform, had cried out, "What I pray may be expected in future times, if the best Church and the best Common-wealth grow up together?" Thomas Shepard informed the General Court in 1638 that Massachusetts had realized Junius' dream. New England was set in the right way, having had "the help of all the former ages, and other Nations as well as our own, Godly and Learned Divines in them, to take pattern and example from, in the laying our first Foundation, both of Religion and Righteousness, Doctrine and Discipline, Church and Commonwealth." Indeed, Thomas Hooker could not help speculating, before his death, whether truth had not now fulfilled her appointed months of travail, "the instant opportunity of her deliverance drawing on apace," whether the day of judgment were not at hand, for with the erection of the New England way it seemed that truth had made the last disclosure conceivable within the frame of time. New England was the *ne plus ultra*. Any further discovery would surpass the possibilities of earth and commence the reign of eternity.

But no sooner was the divine order completed, and the ultimate work of reformation performed, than the first signs of faltering appeared among the people. The younger generation, according to Cotton, were coming of age in the 1640's without coming into their fathers' spirit, and young men were manifesting their irreverence by wearing their hats when the Word was read in the congregations; but still worse, the founding saints themselves were proving to be "not so lively in their profession as they were wont to be many yeares agoe." Some who for piety had been "marvellous eminent in our native Country" were discovering, often to their genuine distress, that here they could not pray so fervently or hear the Word with so much profit: "They wonder what is become of their old prayers . . . and of their lively spirits in holy duties." In the 1640's there commenced in the sermons of New England a lament over the waning of primitive zeal and the consequent atrophy of public morals, which swelled to an incessant chant within forty years. By 1680 there seems to have been hardly any other theme for discourse, and the pulpits rang week after week with lengthening jeremiads. We have precious little evidence from which to reconstruct the ordinary daily life of the communities, yet we can in effect trace the chronology of their social and material growth, of their economic evolution, through the expanding array of vices, sins, and naughty practices enumerated by the ministers. From Cotton's mild complaint of disrespectful hats and his deploring the dry springs of fervor, the list of evils accumulated into a staggering index of criminality: worldliness, fornication, uncleanness, drunkenness, hypocrisy, formality, oppressing of debtors by creditors, usury and profiteering, the wearing of wigs and luxurious clothes, Sabbath-breaking and cock-fighting, rudeness and incivility among the young, and a general "degeneracy from the good Manners of the Christian world." Horror was piled upon horror when the people wished, like dogs returning to their vomit, to celebrate Christmas, when fortune-tellers could make a living in New England, and when at last there were rumors of a brothel in Boston. In 1662 Michael Wigglesworth achieved his best verse in a work entitled *God's Controversy with New-England,* representing the monarch of creation wringing His hands in unavailing distress over the languishing state of New England: could these be the men, He marveled, who at His command forsook their ancient seats to follow Him into a desert?

> If these be they, how is it that I find
>   In stead of holiness Carnality,
> In stead of heavenly frames an Earthly mind,
>   For burning zeal luke-warm Indifferency,
> For flaming love, key-cold Dead-heartedness,
>   For temperance (in meat, and drinke, and cloaths) excess?

The profanation was not confined to the unregenerate, according to Joshua Moody, for the saints themselves, being shaken by constant bickerings and squabbles, "do cause more *filth* and *froth* to rise then either themselves or others thought to have been there," and by 1682 Increase Mather had found that "as to the company which men keep there is little difference to be observed between some Professors and the profane," so little that if a man should seek for certain of the visible elect, "he must look for them in some Tavern, or in some publick house, and there he shall find them amongst *vain persons,* mispending their precious time." The holy commonwealth had become, in Mather's estimation, "like the rest of the Nations, being grown into the same conformity to the World, with other Plantations." That Massachusetts Bay should become one in manners and morals with Virginia—"Be astonished at this, O ye Heavens!"

In one sense, however, the heavens had no cause to be astonished. They knew, and the Puritan clergy had learned, enough of the influence of material circumstances upon the spirits of men to perceive physical reasons for the retrogression. When there is a storm at sea, said Shepard, every man is ready and will be pulling his rope, "but when a calm, they go to their cabins, and there fall asleep"; in England the storm of conflict had aroused every man of faith to mighty exertions, but in New England, after the first hardships of settlement were over, "We have all our beds and lodgings provided, the Lord hath made them easy to us." At home, when the saints were being deprived of true ordinances, they had longed after them with lively hearts, but now that "the Lord hath freed us from the pain and anguish of our consciences," they were taking sermons and lectures for granted. It had become especially appropriate, John Cotton asserted in his last years, to preach in Boston upon Ecclesiastes and to drive home its refrain of the vanity of earth, because men "that have left all to enjoy the Gospel, now (as if they had forgotten the end for which they came hither) are ready to leave the Gospel for outward things." That success breeds sloth, that prosperity relaxes spiritual efforts, were lessons of experience even to Puritans. It was a melancholy fact, according to Cotton, that rich men have always eaten up the estates of poor men by oppression, "and even Christian men, if they be not the more watchfull, will be so eaten up with their businesse as they have no leisure to feed on the Lord." In a copy of Jonathan Mitchell's *Discourse of the Glory to which God hath Called Believers,* on the margin of a page which exhorts believers to press on to heaven and be as strangers in the world, a contemporaneous hand has written a couplet,

Some doe Walk & som runn,
It is for money when all is done.[1]

Yet such cynicism can hardly be construed as a cryptic revolt against the doctrine of the ministers, for they themselves gave full recognition to the growing absorption of the saints in business and commerce: "In Wares, Merchandize and Trading, a gaining what they can possibly, as if Justice had set them no bounds, but to gain what they can is their professed justice; and their gain is their godliness." The preachers made very clear that a simultaneous pursuit of riches and of godliness was extremely difficult. "There is so much rooting in the Earth," said Oakes, "that there is little growing upward," and Samuel Willard laid down the rule that when men acquire great estates their possessions are apt to prove the greater security for sin: "It is a rare thing to see men that have the greatest visible advantages for it, to be very zealous for God." The past was strewn with instances to justify Eleazar Mather in admonishing that were he to point out a people from whom God is departing, "it would be this, Such people as can make up that they want in God, with the presence of the Creature," and to the pious at the end of the seventeenth century New England seemed to be progressively lacking in God and proportionately compensating itself with the creature.

Yet much as Puritans acknowledged the truth of these saws, even while seeing the unavoidable connection between ownership of the world's goods and a worldly spirit, they could not blame material prosperity itself for the collapse of virtue. Even when the clergy most vehemently arraigned the economic expansion of the colonies as the occasion of the people's depravity, they could not call it the cause, for financial success was given by God. Affluence was the reward of New England's virtue. As Michael Wigglesworth's Jehovah reflects upon His controversy, He asks Himself,

> Is this the people blest with bounteous store,
> By land and sea full richly clad and fed,
> Whom plenty's self stands waiting still before,
> And powreth out their cups well tempered?
> For whose dear sake an howling wildernes
> I lately turned into a fruitfull paradeis?

It was God's doing that men in New England had houses and lands, lots and farms and outward accommodations; He had liberally provided for them in order to encourage them in His service. Consequently, the unhappy clergy could not set themselves in the path of progress and oppose New England's getting on in the world. They could not regard the deleterious consequence of opulence merely as an effect of environment upon an organism, but were compelled to see it rather as a symptom of innate depravity. Even the best of saints were imperfectly sanctified, and men could be brought only so far towards perfection. Certainly no people at large, as theology declared and history corroborated, could ever be sustained indefinitely upon the heights of altruism and spiritual dedication. The more trading, buying, and selling, the less the praying, watching over the heart, and close walking. The rising action of reform in every nation was always followed by the falling action of degeneration, not because reformation itself created security and carelessness, but because God blessed reformed men and thereupon they, being still susceptible to the temptations of the flesh, proved incapable of showing the proper gratitude for their advantages. The law of periodic decay was not so much a rule of physics as a consequence of sin, and it could hardly be abrogated, even in New England, unless the people of New England were then and there to become full inheritors of the saints in light; yet to suppose such a thing possible while they were still in the flesh was to give way to the insane delusions of Antinomians and Muggletonians. God might indeed have sifted the choicest grain of the Reformation to be planted in America, but as long as the seed was put into the soil and took its sustenance from the earth, just so long would some taint of mildew be bound to appear upon the harvest.

Traditional theology thus accounted for the inability of reformations to endure forever. Yet for the New England leaders this explanation left much to be desired; it made the rise and fall of godliness mechanical and irresistible, it involved the saints in a vicious circle from which there seemed no escape, and implied that men were as actively fulfilling the will of God when they degenerated as when they improved. It seemed to say that the law of life runs in this fashion: a nation reforms with the aid of divine grace; God rewards its efforts with material prosperity; the reformed are then seduced by their security and in three generations the nation is back where it started. The New England clergy could not demand that the people stay poor, for their economic opportunities were specifically opened by the providence of God; on the other hand, they could not quietly acquiesce in letting New England go the way of all flesh. Even if the declension could not be arrested, they had to have at least the satisfaction of fixing the responsibility upon the people, of placing the blame squarely upon human shoulders. They could not deliver to their congregations the simple dictum that those who drove a roaring trade would be doomed. They could not confess that there was no help to be had.

The federal theology solved this ministerial dilemma and so provided a framework for New England sociology. From the beginning of the enterprise the leaders were conscious of a similarity between New England and the Jews: "Let *Israel* be the evidence of the *Doctrine,* and our glass to view our Faces in," said the ministers, while the irreverent Peter Folger threw the idea into satirical verse,

> *New-England* they are like the *Jews,*
> as like, as like can be.

Anyone who reads the history of Israel in the light of the covenant doctrine sees at once the reason for Israel's many afflictions. God sealed the bond with Abraham and his seed; the seed became a nation, and were therefore committed not merely as individuals but as a whole country to making good the conditions of the covenant. A nation as well as an individual can be in covenant with God—here was the outstanding moral of Old Testament history to Puritan readers, for from this assertion there followed, by the same logic which proved the moral obligation of the individual in the Covenant, that a nation could be constrained by its own assent to obey the laws of God. There was a social as well as a private responsibility, which was founded upon a specific treaty, an engagement between God and the nation as though the nation were one will and one man. No matter if this or that believer fulfilled his particular duties, if the nation failed it could be held to account. When the people of Israel violated their covenant, "God was wont to deliver both them and their Governours, into the hands of their Enemies, that they might learn to rule with God, and to bee faithfull with his Saints." The dealing of God with His chosen was always full of "equitie", and the veriest heathen by-stander, judging simply by the light of nature, could see the justice in it and say, "The Lord is just, for they have forsaken the Covenant of the Lord their God." A people that have sworn in unison to stand upright before God, and whom God has promised to reward for their righteousness, may be given riches without any necessary endangering of their sanctification. They are not caught in an irresistible succession of poverty and wealth; their outward state is a sign of their inward health and will vary only as their spirit alters. They receive affluence upon an explicit understanding, and they are furnished an ability to enjoy it with weaned affections; there is no intrinsic reason why they, as distinguished from nations outside the covenant, should not manage simultaneously to prosper in trade and to grow in spirit, and whenever they yield to the temptations of riches and luxury, they do not fall by an inexorable law, but by their own deliberate act.

To watch the emergence of this conception among Puritan writers of the early seventeenth century is a fascinating study. Obviously it could be conceived only by those already versed in the doctrine of the Covenant. By the strenuous decade of the 1620's several preachers were making heroic efforts to apply the concept to England itself, especially John Preston, who here again appears to have pointed the way to New Englanders. He endeavored to interpret the disasters of the time as a divine chastisement upon a nation that was not making good its covenant with God. Both Cotton and Hooker had come to a full definition of the idea before they left England; in a sermon delivered at Dedham in Essex, Hooker expounded its essence:

> The Lords people take a corporall oath, and a Curse upon themselves, if they doe not keepe Covenant with the Lord. This belongs to us at this day, for we entred into a Curse, and desired that all the plagues and curses written in the Booke of God, might light upon us if we keepe not the Commandements.

England having abandoned the covenant, God was justified in deserting England. Yet there were difficulties in maintaining that the whole people of Britain had ever been in covenant with the Lord. There was nowhere recorded a negotiation between some patriarch of England and his God as there was between Abraham and Jehovah; the country showed no signs of ever having been unanimously involved in such a treaty, and the religious theorists could not so conveniently as Locke and the Whig politicians push their covenant far back into a hypothetical past, for it then ceased to be real or urgent to the people. Try as they would, Puritans could never convince themselves, let alone others, that the English people were united in a single public engagement, as were the Scots; with the miscarriage of the Solemn League and Covenant the idea of the nation bound as one personality in covenant with God, liable to physical punishment should it violate the bond and assured of material blessings for observing it, died a natural death in England.

But in New England the settlement was a deliberate act. The men gathered together, made a decision, took part only after thought and deliberation. The greatness of Winthrop's address aboard the *Arbella,* the daring flight of his imagination, consists precisely in the genius with which he applied this part of the federal theology to the migration of these new Israelites. The act of migrating he made one with the taking of a covenant, and the will to leave England he identified with a willing submission to the terms of a bond. He tied heaven and earth to his enterprise: God has given us, he declared, a special and unique commission, which he expects us strictly to observe.

Thus stands the cause betweene God and vs, wee are entered into Covenant with him for this worke, wee haue taken out a Commission, the Lord hath giuen vs leaue to drawe our owne Articles wee haue professed to enterprise these Accions vpon these and these ends, wee haue herevpon besought him of favour and blessing: Now if the Lord shall please to hear vs, and bring vs in peace to the place wee desire, then hath hee ratified this Covenant and sealed our Commission, [and] will expect a strickt performance of the Articles contained in it, but if wee shall neglect the observacion of these Articles which are the ends wee haue propounded, and dissembling with our God, shall fall to embrace this present world and prosecute our carnall intencions, seekeing greate things for our selues and our posterity, the Lord will surely breake out in wrathe against vs[,] be revenged of such a periured people and make vs knowe the price of the breache of such a Covenant.

If we keep this covenant, Winthrop assured his people, "wee shall finde that the God of Israell is among vs," but if we deal falsely with our God, we who are appointed to show to the whole world the final meaning of the Reformation, we who are to be a city upon a hill with the eyes of all people upon us, we shall shame the faces of God's servants "and cause theire prayers to be turned into Cursses vpon vs till wee be consumed out of the good land whether wee are goeing." New England was the ultimate perfection of the Reformation not because it was carried passively on the crest of a wave, but because it knowingly and rationally undertook the task and bound itself by an explicit commitment. That which the others maintain in their churches by profession, the New Englanders have promised God to bring into familiar and constant practice, to observe all His laws not simply as laws but as "the Articles of our Covenant with him that wee may liue and be multiplyed, and that the Lord our God may blesse vs in the land whether wee goe to possesse it." Unlike Protestants elsewhere, New Englanders could be exhorted to cleave to God for life and prosperity, for they alone were in a legal compact with Him, and by their cleaving to Him they would infallibly gain prosperity, while should they fail Him, they would as infallibly procure losses by land and sea, defeats at the hands of their enemies, and massacre by the Indians.

This concept of a communal covenant grew apace through the sermons and discourses of later New Englanders; it ceased very soon to be a mere adjunct of the doctrine of the Covenant of Grace, but commenced to thrive as a self-sufficient principle, and became before the end of the century a dominant idea in the minds of social leaders in Massachusetts and Connecticut. The intellectual history of the seventeenth-century colonies might be said to consist primarily of a luxurious foliation of the federal theory, a separation of several compacts, to all of which God was a party, which were mutually interrelated, but which were capable of being severally considered. By 1700 the ministers were speaking familiarly of the Covenant of Grace, by which they meant the secret transaction of the individual and God, of the covenant of baptism, which pledged the children of saints to the church on the assumption that they were included in the Covenant of Grace, of the church covenant, of the social or political covenant, and lastly of this national covenant, the engagement of the people as a whole with God, apart from the social compact, concerning the purpose of the society and its moral responsibility.

In a curious way the national covenant reproduced some features of the Covenant of Grace. It too put restraints upon the absolute sovereignty of Jehovah, not by presumptuous imposition from without, but upon the hypothesis of His having voluntarily restricted Himself. God spoke in His own person through the verses of Michael Wigglesworth, declaring that it was the New England people

> With whom I made a Covenant of peace,
> And unto whom I did most firmly plight
> My faithfulness, If whilst I live I cease
> To be their Guide, their God, their full delight;
> Since them with cords of love to me I drew,
> Enwrapping in my grace such as should them ensew.

God having agreed with His chosen, He had to abide by the terms of the bond. It was true, as the ministers took care to qualify, He reserved a sovereignty to Himself in dispensing grace and mercy; He might vary the circumstances of His dealing "without either infringing his Covenant, or rendring to the creature a Reason of that variety." Nevertheless, in the public covenant He had declared His "ordinary way" of treating His people: "as to the essence of the Covenant, he thus far stands positively engaged to reward obedience, and to punish disobedience." With a heathen world he might do what He pleased "upon his meer Prerogative"; if He spared them, it was sheer indulgence, and if He afflicted them, He need give no reasons, "whereas he treats with a Professing People, who are in visible

Covenant with him, according to the tenour of that Covenant, in which there are Conditionate Promises and Threatnings." Again, just as an individual in the Covenant of Grace lived in the world but was not of it, a covenant people carried on their political and social life, but not upon the usual conditions; just as there was a distinction to be observed between God's general presence, His common and universal government, "by which he is intimately present with all creatures," and His special presence, which was over and above the plane of nature, which was unique and particular, so among the nations, there were those living by the law of nature alone, and the occasional covenanted people, Jews or New Englanders, who were required for the time being to observe natural laws and necessities, but were supernaturally directed by an especial communication from God, "inwardly by his spirit, outwardly by his Ordinances, and Providences." Unregenerate nations frequently discovered that He blessed their observance of the law of nature, although He was under no obligation to do so: "Now, if it might have been so with the nations who were so much strangers to the Covenant of Grace," declared the colony of Massachusetts Bay in the preface to its laws, "what advantage have they who have interest in this Covenant, and may injoye the special presence of God in the puritie and native simplicitie of all his Ordinances by which he is so neer to his owne people?" [2] The good or evil fortunes of all others depended upon the arbitrary caprice of God and the accidental circumstances of their situation, but the chosen race alone knew upon what conditions its fortune was to be had. Only they could be certain that if they were virtuous they would blossom like the rose, no matter in what economic soil they were planted, for as long as they observed the covenant God would be obliged to create providential opportunities for their advancement.

However, the communal covenant, as compared with a purely personal one, had of necessity to be in one or two particulars somewhat special. The Covenant of Grace was founded upon the timeless decree of predestination, and the individual who was once effectively admitted to it could never again be cast out. He might yield to temptations, but he was assured that he would be supported through his lapses and infidelities. An individual was united irrevocably to God, both inwardly and publicly, both spiritually and, as the word was, "foederally". Consequently, though his sanctification might be deficient, he could be confident of his justification, for salvation was given for faith and not for works. But a nation, as such, has no life beyond this world; a whole people are not saved in a lump for believing, but only particular persons. A community cannot migrate *en masse* to the celestial pastures as the Puritans moved to Boston. A society cannot make a treaty involving its salvation or damnation hereafter, but only concerning its present existence; it cannot be in bond with God otherwise than "foederally". If God made a treaty with New England, He had to propose such terms as New England could observe, not terms suited to an immortal spirit. "Now what concerns such a People as they are a Body, or a Company of Professors standing under the Obligations of such a Covenant, referrs unto this life and the Affairs of it, for they will not be considered or treated after this life as a people." Therefore it followed that the articles of this covenant were to be fulfilled in time, that the rewards were to be tangible and immediate, the punishments consequent upon misdeeds; a nation would continue in the grace of God, unlike a man or woman, only so long as it observed the conditions, and would be utterly cast off when it abused them. In the purely spiritual covenant, William Stoughton told the General Court in 1668, a sufficiency of grace was absolutely engaged for the believer, to enable him to keep its laws and to prevent it from ever being disannulled, "but as to that external political Covenant, which takes in *A Body of People,* here there is no such engagement of grace sufficient, infallibly to be bestowed for the keeping of the same." Stoughton denied emphatically that there was anything of "merit" in the "foederal" covenant, but he and all writers made it hinge purely and simply upon performance. "The Covenant which God makes with men as to the external dispensation of it," said Willard, "hath its conditions with which the promises of it are connected; and the performance of them can be in no other way challenged, then according as the tenour of the *Covenant* in which they stand." Persons internally and sincerely in partnership with God never lose their interest, said Increase Mather, but a folk may let it slip; as long as they do not forsake their pledge, "the Lord blesseth them visibly, but if they degenerate, then blessings are removed, and woful Judgments come in their room." Or again, as the Reverend John Rogers of Ipswich explained in an election sermon of 1706, God administers His providence promiscuously upon particular persons in this world, afflicting saints in order to try them or prospering evil men in order eventually to cast them down; He can afford to allow discrepancies between their spiritual assurances and their worldly conditions because everything will be rectified in the future. But a body politic has no such future:

God does not deal thus with Nations, because . . . Publick Bodies & Communities of men as such can only be rewarded & punished in this World . . . This being the only Season for National Rewards and Punishments, it seemeth Reasonable and necessary in some degree, for a present Vindication of the Honour and Majesty of the Divine Laws, that a People should be prosperous, or afflicted, according as their general Obedience or Disobedience thereto appears.

Arminianism was damnable heresy in the realm of the individual's walk with God, but something so much like Arminianism that to the eyes of the uninitiated it can hardly be distinguished was the rule of national welfare: "A people in visible Covenant stand upon their good behaviour, as they carry it so they may expect it shall go with them." As John Rogers professed, this principle as applied to God's public dispensations was both necessary—and reasonable!

Thus it was no accident that New England grew fat and comfortable, beyond even the most extravagant dreams of the founders. Yankee farms have become a by-word for scanty yields and back-breaking stones, but to English immigrants in the 1600's the land appeared rich and flowing, while the sacred cod soon proved an inexhaustible mine of wealth. John Ball had written in England that through His covenant God promised not only to write His laws on our hearts, "but also to conferre temporall blessings, as they shall be seruiceable to vs in our iourney towards Heaven," and John Cotton preached in Boston, "Christ having made a Covenant with us, he gives the Inheritance of the world to such as beleeve on him." In America He proved as good as His word, and what the saints accounted a sufficient inheritance of the world was accordingly made over to them. Yet the gifts of "health, maintenance, credit, prosperous successe in our callings and lawfull dealings, deliuerances out of troubles, and such like," were not as in other countries merely the natural results of diligence or of luck. New Englanders were expected to be diligent, but not to look to the natural profits of their diligence, and in their economy luck was entirely eliminated. They did not gain "competent provision" so much from their own labors in field and counting house as from their submission to the covenant; earthly blessings were bestowed upon them primarily as signs of love and mercy, "as gifts of the couenant, tokens of free grace, and by a supernaturall prouidence eleuated to spirituall vse, in which sence they are promised and vouchsafed vnto them that feare God and walke in his wayes." It was lawful for the saints to endeavor "prudently" to advance their estates, not because good husbandry would always get a larger return than bad management, but because "this *Prosperity* is one of the Promises of the Covenant, and we may Pray for it." Riches being a reward of godliness, they "are consistent with *Godliness;* and the more a Man hath, the more Advantage he hath to do Good with it, if God give him an Heart to it." As long as men kept their hearts right, they could grow wealthy without endangering their souls.

So New England, though confessedly born of the Reformation, was not in its own opinion a child of history; the national covenant exempted it from the normal operations of cause and effect, and secured it upon the pinnacle of ecclesiastical perfection. It could stand there forever if it wished, beyond any doubt that God would provide the wherewithal to support it. But—as Hooker declared in Essex and every minister reiterated in New England—"If people sin, God will proceed in wrath against them." The best of saints, as God learned from bitter experience in Palestine, cannot be trusted too long with material favors; they let themselves become ensnared and wax wanton and secure. In individuals such declensions can be forgiven in the name of Christ, but when a whole people abuse their blessings, they must be punished, and a nation can be dealt with only here and now. A people in agreement with the Lord have "bound themselves to yield obedience to all his commands," and consequently "when . . . they depart from his obedience . . . they therein depart from their Allegiance." We cannot assume that God's children are at fault because they meet with afflictions in their particular concerns, "for the design of these is very often for their trial," but "when God brings sore and wasting Calamities of Sickness, Famine, and War, on a professing people . . . God is not angry without a cause." Personal dispensations are on a level of grace, where justice is replaced by mercy, but for an entire community within a covenant, the law of justice is still in effect. A good covenanted society prospers in this world, a bad one gets what it deserves.

The very light of natural conscience, let alone the light of grace, said Willard, would easily satisfy men "in the reason and equity of such Providences as these are." As the ministers developed the idea of national covenant they so perfected the reason and equity of it that at last they were representing God as meticulously suiting the national chastisement to the crime, although they acknowledged that in the eyes of sincere piety the slightest affront to His spotless majesty was as reprehensible as the largest insult. An individual deserved damnation for a peccadillo as much as for parricide, yet individuals were either inside the Covenant of Grace or outside, there being no intermediate status; nevertheless a nation could be within the national covenant to the extent that it was virtuous. God treated the unregenerate as damned and the saints as saved, but He treated "a Sinful People of God, as they are a Body Politick," neither in the one way nor the other, rather as physicians treat the sick. He put them in "a way of Physick." His judgments and afflictions, such as property losses, crop failures, storms, fires, Indian outrages, or epidemics, were "his Physick," and proportionately as the nation's misdemeanors became more severe He proceeded "like a wise and considerate Artist . . . from those Medicines which are more gentle and easy, unto those that are more strong and potent; as if He would at length come to the use of such as will certainly kill or cure; mend us, or end us." Particular men, once definitely passed over, could never hope for pardon, but a covenanted nation, even though it had sunk almost to the lowest depths, might recover; if it would allow the "physick" to work, if it would learn from affliction and return to the diet of the fathers, prosperity and health would revisit the body politic. "This is the priviledge of a People in visible Covenant with God, that there is no threatning denounced against them, but with a gracious reserve and room to reverse it in case of Repentance." Up to a certain point, up to the very end, God offered the folk a chance to mend, though the ministers were forced to admit by the inescapable logic of the idea, that somewhere there had to be a limit, an extremity of depravity which finally and irrevocably broke the bond and relieved God of any further responsibility toward them. Once they went beyond the pale, God was no longer obliged to practice toward them the rational and contractual rule of rewards and punishments. If the people of New England were to fall at last to the very bottom, the treaty would be canceled, and they would stand before God upon the same footing with other plantations, to receive blessings or curses according to His mood, having no grounds for complaint against His justice.

New England ministers denounced the sins of the land and expanded the list of its crimes until the by-stander, judging by the light of reason, might well have supposed the limit to be exceeded. The clergy were less ready to draw such an inference; they would prophesy that the time was at hand when the Lord would bring His controversy with New England to a crisis, and constantly warned their congregations that this or that moment was the last opportunity to save themselves by repentance and reformation, but they could not announce flatly that the time had passed and that all hope should be abandoned. If they were ever publicly to make this admission, they would be surrendering their reason for being; having commenced on the assumption that they were leading a covenanted people, and that a covenanted community could win God's favor by its moral efforts, the churches could not, during the seventeenth century, confess that there was no longer any reason why this particular community should strive to be holier than others. The great end toward which the theory aspired, the moral which the leaders worked to instill into the minds of the people, citizens or inhabitants, was the principle of communal responsibility. When a commonwealth breaks covenant with God, Thomas Shepard declared, it casts Him off, and a people taken together as a commonwealth are able so to cast Him off, though the grace imparted to individuals is irresistible. A fellowship can forsake the covenant of its own volition, and does so whenever it fails to keep touch "with God, in sincere, exact, and holy obedience, answerable to the means and mercy he bestows upon us, and the care and kindnesse of the Lord towards us." Well into the eighteenth century the notion was still being dinned into the ears of legislators, as when Grindal Rawson in 1709 explained to the General Court that while the privileges of a people in compact with God are great, "so also are their Duties and Obligations," that where others might just as well sin to their hearts' content because they would gain little in the way of public good by their virtues,

A Covenant People are not left at their Liberty, whether they will Love, Fear, Serve and Obey the Voice of God in his Commands, or not. They are under the highest, and most awful Obligations imaginable to the whole of Covenant duty; not only from Gods express Command and Precept, who is their King, Lord, and Lawgiver; but also, by virtue of their own Professed Subjection unto

God . . . They are therefore most Solemnly cautioned to take heed to themselves, and beware, lest they should forget and forsake the Lord, his Worship, Fear and Service; because by this means they would assuredly forfeit all those desirable blessings, which a course of Obedience would crown them with, and pull down upon themselves the just rebukes, and terrible revenges of Heaven.

The people of New England could thus survey the past in the light of their tribal covenant, see the course of history coming to a predestined climax in themselves, and yet argue that they were not necessarily fated to follow the pattern into an equally inevitable decline. They could assert that the first generation had done all the good that was ever to be done, and yet reasonably expect the children to walk faithfully in the righteous steps of the fathers. A society, considered apart from its component individuals, was lifted by its covenant out of the flux of nature, set above the laws of physics, an exception to the cycles of history. Others acquired wealth where it was to be found and depended on circumstance; New England was assured in advance that the land and sea would offer them possibilities for exploitation, "let all the whole course of second causes bode never so ill." God's word had been passed, "and he will never recede from it." Others might grow rich, and thereby become depraved; New Englanders were awarded riches for their holiness, and were under no necessity of being corrupted. They were swinging free in time and space, masters of their own destiny, their fate in their own hands to make or mar at will. In a universe created by absolute power, ruled by unlimited prerogative, founded upon a perfect and immutable pattern of ideas, in which grace alone could extricate men from the web of necessity—grace which was dispensed regardless of merit—in such a universe an entire people could still be informed that they had taken upon themselves an agreement with the Lord and that their physical and material career depended from day to day upon their moral conduct. Success and morality here were linked together as nowhere else in the world by a specific promise of the same God who elsewhere regulated success or failure without the slightest regard to civic virtue.

With this description of the communal covenant we have, as I believe, completed our enumeration of the major intellectual achievements of Puritanism in seventeenth-century America. I originally set out to follow what seemed a logical method of topical organization, commencing with the basic theological doctrines and inherited philosophies, from which there promised to be a natural progression to a study of the cosmological system, cosmology in turn promised to lead to the conception of man as an integral part of the universe, and the doctrine of human nature to furnish the foundations for theories of human association in church and state. At this point I have become belatedly conscious that the procedure has consistently created one impression which was not previsioned and which is far from being historically accurate, for each remove in the presentation has carried us a step further from the heart of the piety, from the burning conviction of man's irreparable sin and of God's stainless purity, which was the first subject of our investigation. Assuredly in the doctrine of the Covenant of Grace, and more particularly in this shrewd application of it to the nation, in this "foederal" compact of God and the community upon the terms of a downright commercial bargain, we might justifiably decide that the last vestiges of religious sincerity, of anxiety over human weakness and reverence for divine majesty, had become utterly dissipated. The sense of sin and the magnificent vision of cosmic optimism have here become transformed into a local Pharisaism and provincial smugness, even when, paradoxically, the ministers are denouncing the vices and declensions of New England. Quite apart from our astonishment at the naïve egotism implicit in the Puritans' view of history and their staggering notion that all recorded events had been managed to provide them with a dramatic entry upon the stage, we are warrantably aghast at their reduction of God to the rôle of an economic schoolmaster, rewarding His good pupils for their model deportment and punishing His bad ones for neglect of their lessons. We might well put our finger upon this belief, and declare that here were lost the last elements of the spiritual grandeur and self-abnegation of Augustine.

However, should we close our study upon this ironic note I feel that we should be doing the early New Englanders a grave injustice and should miss the most valuable point of our research. For we must remember that from the very authors who most clearly voiced the commercialism of the national covenant, from those who insisted most alarmingly upon the limitations of God in the Covenant of Grace, could also be extracted a series of quotations freely and truthfully expressing the piety without a mention of the covenants. We have seen on almost every point that there were latent oppositions among ideas entertained simultaneously and often successfully by the Puritan mind, oppositions that appear obvious to our critique because we know that some of the inherited ideas had formerly been in serious conflict, or else that other tensions were to develop into open hostilities in the next century. The contrast between the strictly theological conception of God and the God of the covenant is to our eyes probably the most striking of these implicit antagonisms in the whole range of New England thought, but the violence of the contradiction should serve the more trenchantly to illustrate the fundamental problem of the age, not to furnish an indictment of Puritans for hypocrisy and mendacity. Were we to glance for a moment at more sophisticated speculations among contemporaneous philosophers we should find them struggling to reconcile opposing values which correspond roughly to those clothed for the Puritans on the one hand in the theology of piety and on the other in the theology of the covenant. Within the framework of their thinking, the colonial parsons were responding to the same impulses that were prompting Bacon, Descartes, and Locke. They were seeking to understand, to draw up explicable laws, to form clear and distinct ideas, to maintain order and logic in the universe. They could not separate theology from life, as did Bacon, exalt divinity so far above the plane of reason as to leave it suspended in the empyrean, and thus leave the field of nature free for purely secular induction; they could not reduce the universe to extension and movement with Descartes, or share without reservations in Locke's confidence that the world was constructed on the principles of a rational, uniform, and smoothly running machine. They still had too vivid a sense of the arbitrary Jehovah, of the *Deus Absconditus,* of the God of the whirlwind, ruling the world by irresistible might and wrenching the course of events to suit His pleasure, for them to indulge as yet in such assertions as the more advanced philosophers would hazard. However, even while paying the proper respect to the terror and the fury of God, they could contrive to take many steps in these directions as soon as they had seized upon their brilliant discovery that the absolute monarch had voluntarily engaged Himself to regular procedures and bottled up His prerogative in a covenant. The rest followed surely and easily from this premise: the validity of logic, the identification of the divine ideas with the arguments of dialectic, the veracity of the liberal arts and the perfection of technologia, the regularity and sequence of secondary causes, the coincidence of supernatural grace with the natural processes of psychology and the consequent effectiveness of rhetoric, the responsibility of man under the means, the rational foundations of holy commonwealths and churches. When they confounded their fate with the preservation of Christianity, and their colonies with the hope of mankind, the Puritans appear to us guilty of arrogance, but they were simply endeavoring to explain themselves in relation to a reasonable pattern of history; they heeded the inward call of faith, but wanted to make sure that it summoned them to no insane adventure. A man who looked over Europe in 1630 with the eye of a sincere Protestant might well have resolved on the grounds of evidence and common sense that the only hope for the Reformation lay in an escape of some saints to a haven where they could not be prevented from fulfilling God's injunctions. The clergy may seem to have transformed the Deity by their federal covenant into an agent of the community welfare, a sort of bookkeeper and paymaster, but at the same time they were endeavoring, as far as possible within the confines of their creed, to show that prosperity on this earth was no longer an arbitrary award of despotism and ignorance, but that it might take on the indelible characters of justice and reason.

Nor must we suppose that the Puritans were restrained from embracing a wholly rationalistic or naturalistic philosophy merely out of a calculated and insincere respect for the letter of orthodoxy. I have frequently remarked that by logic or rhetoric or the federal theology they managed to support the principles of reason and intellect in spite of their absolutist doctrines, but we should not so misread their minds as to decide that they had no genuine allegiance to the absolute ideas, or that these were not sincerely felt. They achieved marvels by their artful device of securing God's assent to His own delimitation, and by their still more daring stratagem of inveigling Him into partnership with the nation upon the condition that it be rewarded and punished here and now and according to its deserts. Yet in the seventeenth century no Puritan entirely forgot that God was transcendent and omnipotent, that He was not completely and finally to be fathomed or understood by men. He had condescended in some particulars to speak their language, but the undiscoverable essence, the living principle of the universe, was not to be circumscribed by human devices and clever stratagems. The Puritans might argue that the Covenant of Grace, or the various subsidiary covenants which they manipulated out of the spiritual compact, offered them pragmatic assurances that God's justice was to most intents and purposes the same as human equity, but they could not say outright that it was invariably the same. Behind phenomena, behind the Covenant of Grace, the church covenant and the federal covenant, behind the explicit word of the Bible, loomed the inconceivable being about whom no man could confidently predict anything, who was not to be relied upon or perfectly trusted, who might day in and day out deal with men in stated forms, and then suddenly strike without warning, scatter the world into fragments with a casual sweep of His hand. Puritans, as long as they remained Puritanical, could never banish from their minds the consciousness of something mysterious and terrible in life, of something that leaped when least expected, that upset all the regularities of technologia and circumvented the laws of logic, that cut across the rules of justice, of something behind appearances that could not be tamed and brought to heel.

Though our survey has shown the great care and effort of the Puritan mind to resist vitalism and enthusiasm, to guard religious conviction from becoming frenzy and hysteria, we must not therefore jump to the conclusion—which many in our age find congenial—that Puritanism systematically stifled its own intensity. Because it was highly intellectual and abstract did not mean that it was any less passionate and vehement. Because it loved logic and the arts, conceived of nature as causal and sequential, maintained the distinction of bodily faculties even in the act of conversion, and established reasonable conditions for salvation, we must not infer that it was giving merely lip service to the doctrines of innate depravity, absolute grace, and salvation by faith. The machinery of second causes conformed in the main to law, yet it depended upon the first cause in every operation, upon Him who not merely stirred up efficient agents to their work but directed them to their ends and determined their effects:

He can stop the Sun in its course, and cause it to withdraw its shining; He can give check to the Fire, that it shall not burn; & to the hungry Lions, that they shall not devour . . . Though He hath set an Order among his Creatures, this shall be the cause of that effect, &c. yet He himself is not tied to that Order; but Interrupts the course of it, when He pleases. The Lord reserves a Liberty to Himself to interpose, and to Umpire matters of Success and Event, contrary to the Law and common Rule of Second Causes. And though He ordinarily concurreth with Second Causes according to the Law given and Order set; yet sometimes there is in his Providence a Variation and Digression . . . Herein the absolute Soveraignty and Dominion of God appears.

If systematic physics rested so precariously upon the unhampered pleasure of God, how much more had the method of regeneration, for all its orderly constitutions and natural means, to wait for success or failure upon His mere will? A plausible and psychological narrative of conversion through means could always be supplied, yet "when we have searched into all the causes of Regeneration . . . we must ultimately determine it hither: we are made to partake in this Grace, because God hath appointed us to it; and the reason why we were so appointed, was because it so pleased God." In a manner of speaking, God was irrevocably captured in the Covenant of Grace—but "howsoever God will bestow what he hath promised, yet hee reserves the time to himselfe, and what time he will doe it, and after what manner, and by what means, that is onely of Gods free will." A covenant with the Lord could never be quite so firm or so reliable as a covenant among men, for it was not an agreement of equals. Though it observed the forms of a contract, it depended upon the formless will of an absolute sovereign:

As the heavens are higher then the earth, so are the wayes of God higher then our wayes . . . and in speciall the wayes of his grace, and of the Covenant thereof, with men indeed mutuall agreement and consent is necessary to a Covenant, but with God, Gods appointment maketh a Covenant, whether the Creature consent to an agreement or no.

The Covenant was but a glove upon the hand of iron. Even though it was an agreement, a deed, a legal transaction, yet the ability which enabled any man to take it up was in the gift of a fitful and desultory power; God could do what He would with His own and yet do wrong to none, so that in spite of flourishing ordinances and vigorous means, of societies in sanctified compacts, assiduous in the cultivation of civil and legitimate liberties, "he denyes pardon and acceptance to those who seek it with some importunity and earnestness . . . and yet bestowes mercy and makes known himself unto some *who never sought him.*" And likewise in the national compact, if we will examine carefully the well-chosen words of the ministers, we shall find that God was not held down to quite the degree of servility that might at first sight appear. After all, it was He who gave the grace that enabled men to earn the prosperity, and He either provided a further supply empowering them to resist the insidious temptations of wealth, or else by withholding His influence He made certain that they would bring down merited punishment upon the society.

God is therefore then for a People, when he helpeth them to comport with the terms on which he hath promised them so to be: for it must be of him to enable and assist them, that so they may keep close to their duty. And consequently, the first step to his being against them, is when he deserts them, so as to suffer them to depart from him. But when he gives them the Grace to perform the condition upon which the Promise is secured, it is because he hath a love for them, and purposeth to do them good, and not hurt.

The reins were still in the hands of God. Many long pages in the New England sermons were devoted to exhorting the people to reform in order to gain material blessings, or to pointing out that their physical castigations had resulted from their willful defaultings, but somewhere in almost every such discourse there was hidden an admission, however it might be smoothed over, that a people's reformation or declension depended on God's pleasure. "When God purposeth to bestow His everlasting Mercies upon a People, He shews it by enabling of them to keep His Covenant . . . If He withhold this Grace, the most excellent Priviledges of a People are to them Judicial." In other words, if God chose not to give New Englanders His grace, their precious covenant privileges became the instruments of their destruction, for they then did no more than to guarantee that New England, unlike the heathen parts of the world, would not alone be damned hereafter but would be scourged and smitten immediately and remorselessly.

When we thus refresh our memory of the piety, of the true fear of God which was always an element in Puritan theorization, when we reflect that even while Puritans were extending their logical and contractual concepts over the face of nature and imposing them upon the divine being Himself, they had not closed their eyes to the illogical and unconfinable terrors of the universe, I believe that then we may get some insight into the depths of their thinking. We may then grasp at significances which we can hardly understand by historical analysis, economic interpretation, or philosophical rephrasing, but for the comprehension of which we must also appeal to psychology and to such techniques as the twentieth century has so far discovered for dealing with the unconscious and inaccessible depths of the human spirit. The Puritans were gifted—or cursed—with an overwhelming realization of an inexorable power at work not only in nature but in themselves, which they called God; whatever may have been the factors in their society and their experience that so sharpened the edge of their awareness, the acuteness and poignancy of the awareness are phenomena which psychology will recognize though it cannot explain, and which history must take into account. And by a necessity which both students of the soul and students of the past must endeavor to comprehend, whenever men conceive, in whatever guise, that they confront this gigantic power, either in the visible world or in their souls, they invariably must find means of coming to terms with it, of bringing it into friendship, for the furtherance of their common interests and for their respective sanctifications, not merely for that of humanity but for that of the lawless, brutal force itself. "Need human and need divine," says Thomas Mann, "here entwine until it is hard to say whether it was the human or the divine that took the initiative." The Puritan sense of life was different from ours, or to speak more accurately, different from what ours became in the course of the eighteenth and nineteenth centuries, because Puritans had a particularly clear, an almost abnormally intense vision of man hemmed in between God and nature, at the mercy of malevolent forces and crushing objects. They saw so cogently the weakness of man's condition, the frailty of his body and the stupidity of his mind, that they bent every effort thereafter to protect and preserve him. They surrounded God with the integument of the Covenant, they disciplined nature into conformity with a logical pattern of ideas. As long as both God and nature still threatened to close in upon the human figure, just so long were Puritans doomed to recognizing that God was hidden, but to strive nevertheless to pin him in the bond, or as John Cotton said, to cloak him and muffle him in the covenant.

In one final particular it should be mentioned that the topical method of this volume has inevitably falsified certain perspectives; it has most notably obscured the chronology of the situation. The idea of the national covenant was planted in New England by the founders, but this particular seed grew as fast, if not faster, than any others of their sowing, and produced the most luxuriant fruit. Though I have said that authors at the end of the century who wrote upon the federal concept also composed passages which illustrate the deep piety of New England, yet it is also true that among New England sermons, those at the end of the century rather than at the beginning contain the more confident descriptions of God as tied by the agreement with the nation and as forced to wait upon the deeds of the folk with rewards and punishments in order to secure their respect and worship. In short, with the economic development, with the lessening of man's direct dependence upon the capricious forces of nature for a bare subsistence, with the expansion of the new science and the beginnings of its conquest of nature, with all the intellectual and social developments upon which we have touched and that constitute the history of the European mind in the seventeenth century, the immediate and desperate pressures, both of God and of nature, were gradually and insensibly removed. As the created universe yielded its secrets to Boyles and Newtons, while trade flourished and banks arose, while God was becoming more genial and more remote as the scientific regularity of the cosmos made His presence or His interference superfluous, the urgencies that produced Puritan theology, with its peculiar mixture of religion and intellect, dogma and logic, piety and covenant, were relaxed. New England was founded as a Puritan commonwealth and was intended to be a holy and unique corner of the world, but it went into the eighteenth century well prepared in the terms of its own tradition to keep pace with the intellectual and emotional alterations of a new era, with both the emergence of an Age of Reason and the newer religious mood that was to arise in the reaction against reason.

APPENDIX A

THE LITERATURE OF RAMUS' LOGIC IN EUROPE

There is crying need for a full study of Ramus and his influence. I have not attempted more than a cursory survey, nor checked all the editions, and offer this summary provisionally as an aid to further investigation.

Much of the contemporaneous writing upon Ramus is rhetorical exercise or vituperation, of the sort familiar to students of English literature in Milton's vilification of Salmasius. No doubt passions were running high, but much of the vehemence becomes merely tiresome to modern readers. Ramus' enemies shrieked with horror that he should so much as intimate anything disrespectful of the canonized Aristotle: "Dare you call him sophist whom Plato, of whom you profess to be a disciple, called the philosopher of truth? . . . Have you dared, I will not say to violate most abominably, but to presume to term him religionless, whom all ages, all men of letters, and all men until you, have held in highest veneration? Who is so great a madman as this?" (Govéa, *Pro Aristotela,* 57 Recto). Ramus was compared to Phaeton attempting to drive the chariot of the sun; his followers were chastised for their arrogance and conceit, and the judgment of God invoked upon them for frivolity and irreverence. The friends of Ramus celebrated him in terms no less extravagant. "You are unconquerable, O Ramus," wrote Freigius, "for you have the strength of twice two men, of Socrates, Euclide, Tully and Aristotle; in art you are Aristotle, in method Plato, in speech Tully, in genius Euclide;—O Ramus, what is there more?" (Beurhusius, *In. P. Rami,* last page). Broscius suggested (*Apologia,* B 1) that Ramists exercise upon panegyrics of this nature something of the critical severity which Ramus applied to Aristotle, but the Ramists were not to be restrained. They compared him to Prometheus, restoring the sacred fire of logic after the Aristotelians had suffocated it in obscurities and sophistical darkness; Rodingus said he spoke but moderately when he declared that the head of Ramus rises above all others as the cypress surmounts the sluggish pines (ed. *Dialecticae,* 1579, pp. 5-7). At times Ramists uttered stirring sentiments for "freedom" in philosophy, attacked authoritarianism and excessive veneration for any man, argued that all philosophers including Aristotle should be "not lords but leaders". Ramus himself framed eloquent statements which, taken out of their context, sound like charters of liberalism, as when he berated an opponent because in an oration, "in all the explicating analytics, you appear to have proposed no other truly philosophical principle, no other law of judging than the authority of Aristotle or than the authority of Galen. For these authors alone and perpetually you bring forth for all principles, for all problems and theorems" (*P. Rami et Jacobi Schecii,* A 2 Verso). But such speeches must be read in relation to the times and not invested with meanings congenial to the twentieth century. Rennemannus insists, "Disciples ought not to be credulous," but his veneration for the master was little short of idolatry, and his demands for freedom were based upon the assumption that "there stands but one rule of truth, which Logic reveals," that this one rule is the system of Ramus (*Dissertatio,* pp. 115, 119). Mulhemius admitted that the system was the absolute perfection of logic, that as Helen was the supreme simulacrum of beauty, gathering into herself the beauty of all women, so the logic of Ramus was the exemplar of all natural and human reason (*Logica,* A vi).

Furthermore, the literature of the controversy is given over excessively to the peculiar hair-splitting and verbal quibblings in which men of the Renaissance took great delight. Thus Ramus named his logic "dialectic", and thereupon thousands of wearisome pages were devoted to haggling over the word. When he defined dialectic as "ars bene disserendi", he started a furious debate on the question of whether the word "bene" should be included in the definition or whether it was sufficiently implied in the word "ars". The pedantic aspects of the issue were satirized in Ramus' lifetime by Rabelais (*Pantagruel,* I, iv) and by Du Bellay (*Satyr de Maistre Pierre Cuignet sur la Petromachie de l'Universite de Paris;* the "Petromachie" was the contest between the two Pierres, Ramus and Gallandius). Ramus was no Bacon but a complete academic; the whole reform was an episode in the history of humanism, deriving its doctrines or its inspiration from Erasmus, Cicero, Quintilian, Lefèvre d'Etaples, and in particular from Rudolph Agricola and Johann Sturm (Cf. Ramus, preface to *Scholae in Liberales Artes,* for specific expression of indebtedness to Agricola and Sturm). At best, the program was a reorganization, and often a mere renaming, of the academic curriculum, and the fury of the contest is testimony not so much to the profundity of Ramus' thought as to the intensity of sixteenth-century feeling in matters of education. As Saisset notes, the Ramist logic was not a reform of philosophy but of pedagogy and rhetoric. For all his eloquent attacks, Ramus was not fundamentally opposed to Aristotle, and though careful students may believe that Ramus cast aside much that was truly Aristotelian, Ramus himself thought he was freeing Aristotle from the crabbed perversions of the Aristotelians; in the first pages of his last important work, he announced that "the principal battle will be for Aristotle against the interpreters of Aristotle" (*Scholarum Dialecticarum,* p. 32). To read such a book as Piscator's *Animadversiones* is to marvel anew at the gusto which the Renaissance brought into scholarship, for only a great zest for the subject could have carried the author or his readers through such arid wastes of verbal quibbles. Temple and Piscator debated interminably such questions as whether the precepts of logic are its "matter" and disposition its "form", whether a positive statement should be called an axiom "affirming" or an axiom "affirmed". The literature must be read, if it is ever to be read, with copious allowance for the intellectual habits of the period.

It should also be said that throughout all the controversy the system of Aristotle figures as that which men of the late Middle Ages thought was his, not what we today believe was his true meaning. Very little profit is to be derived by comparing either the Aristotelians or the Ramists with the Stagirite himself; each side thought they understood him thoroughly, and each side, in the light of modern criticism, was equally unable to read him correctly.

The principal sources for the life of Ramus are three biographies by devoted disciples: Johann Thomas Freigius, in the preface to his edition of Ramus' *Praelectiones in Ciceronis Orationes Octo Consulares,* published at Basle in 1575; Theophilus Banosius, in the preface to *Commentariorum de Religione Christiana,* 1577; and Nicholas Nancel, *Vita,* Paris, 1599. Of modern treatments the best is still Charles Waddington, *Ramus, sa vie, ses écrits et ses opinions,* Paris, 1855, which contains a bibliography. Frank Pierrepont Graves, *Peter Ramus and the Educational Reformation of the Sixteenth Century,* 1912, follows Waddington much too closely. There is a useful article in Bayle; also helpful are Charles Desmaze, *Ramus,* Paris, 1864, and the few pages on Ramus in Hardin Craig, *The Enchanted Glass,* New York, 1936.

The works of Ramus which are of most general interest and in which his teachings can best be studied are:

The two volumes published in 1543, which initiated the controversy and were burned by the decree of Francis I: *Dialecticae Partitiones sive Institutiones,* 1543 (other eds. 1547, 1549; edited by Omer Talon as *Institutionum Dialecticarum libri tres,* 1552, and issued frequently under this title; edited by Freigius at Basle, by Beurhusius in 1581, by Piscator in 1583, by Temple in 1591), and *Aristotelicae Animadversiones,* 1543 and 1545 (reissued as *Animadversionum Aristotelicarum libri xx,* 1548, and frequently thereafter).

A collection of orations delivered by Ramus, Talon, and Bartholomao Alexander in 1544, setting forth the ideals of the reform, *Tres Orationes a Tribus Liberalium Disciplinarum Professoribus.*

His discourse upon taking charge of the Collège de Presles in 1546, *Oratio de Studiis Philosophiae et Eloquentiae Conjungendis,* and his discourse upon becoming Regius Professor, *Oratio Initio Suae Professionis Habita,* 1551.

His only important work in rhetoric, *Rhetoricae Distinctiones,* 1549; however, the compact *Rhetorica,* 1567, by Ramus' alter ego, Omer Talon, must be listed in the bibliography of Ramus, for it was the necessary counterpart to Ramus' own work, and accompanied the Ramist logic everywhere that the doctrine exerted any influence.

The central document for the movement, the fifty-page summary of the art of logic, was issued first in French, *Dialectique,* 1555, and in Latin, *Dialecticae libri duo,* 1556. There were possibly a hundred or more editions of this work within the next century, and many of the books of Ramus' disciples were no more than commentaries upon it. The French version of 1555 has an important preface, containing Ramus' view of the history of logic and a statement of his own aims (reprinted in Waddington, *op. cit.*, pp. 401-407); the edition of 1576 contains in final form the preface which generally appears in all republications after Ramus' death, and also an important treatise on "use" or practical application, giving Ramus' doctrine of genetical and analytical methods.

His educational program, found in his report on the state of the University, published in French and Latin in 1562, the French title being, *Advertissements sur la Réformation de l'Université de Paris, au Roy.* A further statement is in his *Oratio de Professione Liberalium Artium,* 1563.

Ramus' version of the quarrel with Charpentier, *Remonstrance au Conseil Privé,* 1567.

His treatment of metaphysics, *Scholarum metaphysicarum libri quatuordecim,* 1566, edited by Piscator, Frankfort, 1583, 1610.

The most readable work, *Scholae in Liberales Artes,* Basle, 1569; this was edited by Piscator and issued twice at Frankfort in 1581 under the titles, *Scholarum dialecticarum, seu Animadversionum in Organum Aristotelis libri xx,* and *Scholae in Tres Primas Liberales Artes;* under the latter title it was reissued at Frankfort in 1595.

His debate with Jacob Schegk or Schecius, *Epistolae, in quibus de artis logicae institutione agitur,* also published at Basle during Ramus' visit in 1569; a further argument against Schecius is *Defensio pro Aristotele adversus Jac. Schecium,* Lausanne, 1571.

His great work on theology, published posthumously, *Commentariorum de religione Christiana libri quatuor,* Frankfort, 1576, 1577, 1583; this work is well expounded in P. Lobstein, *Petrus Ramus als Theologe,* Strassburg, 1878.

The enemies with whom Ramus contended at Paris published many attacks. Pierre Galland, principal of the Collège de Boncour was leader of the assault; one of his orations, *Literarum Latinarum Professoris Regij,* appeared in 1560, though he fought Ramus more effectively by inciting his own students: Joachim Périon, who replied to Ramus' first publication with *De Dialectica Libri III* in 1544, and later attacked Ramus' edition of Cicero in *Pro Ciceronis Oratione;* Antoine de Govéa, who joined Périon with his *Pro Aristotela responsio* in 1544; and Jacques Charpentier or Carpentarius, *Animadversiones,* 1555, *Orationes tres,* 1566, *Oratio Habita initio Professiones,* 1566. Pierre Danès was another opponent, a memorial of whose opposition appears in Génébrard, *Oraison funebre de Pierre Danès,* 1577. Adrien Turnebus joined the attack over the edition of Cicero, *Disputatio ad libram Ciceronis de fato,* 1556, and was answered by Talon's *Admonitio* in the same year.

Outside of Paris opponents gave more serious discussion to the system itself; among these may be noted Cornelius Martin, *Commentariorum Logicorum adversus Ramistas, Libri V,* 1623; Johannes Regius, *Commentariorum ac Disputationum Logicarum,* 1583; I. Broscius, *Apologia pro Aristotele et Euclide,* 1652; and John Case, *Summa Veterum Interpretum in Universam Dialecticam Aristotelis,* 1593. The hostile opinion of the great Ursinus is found in a letter to Frederick III, Elector Palatine, printed in *Organi Aristotelei,* 1586. The most prominent opponents of Ramus in the seventeenth century were Keckermann and Piscator. Keckermann discussed Ramus throughout the *Operum,* 1624, especially pp. 60-65, 78-89, 98-136, 420-423; Piscator edited many of Ramus' works and appended criticisms to every passage. He issued the *Dialecticae* at Frankfort in 1583 with Talon's notes and his own replies to both Ramus and Talon, thus swelling Ramus' volume of fifty pages to over four hundred.

Ramus' outstanding friend and champion was Omer Talon. Almost as stalwart a defender in the 1560's was Arnaud de Ossat, who was later to have a distinguished career at the Papal Court, who argued for Ramus even after Ramus had become a Protestant, in *Expositio in Disputationem Jacobi Carpenterii de Methodo,* and *Additio ad Expositionem,* 1564. The great jurist, François Hotoman, in his *Dialectica Institutiones,* 1573 (also, *Opera,* Geneva, 1599, I, 1129–1271), shows clearly the influence of Ramus, though he was not an uncritical disciple. In the year of Ramus' death Henry Schorus published *Specimen et forma legitime tradendi sermonis et rationis disciplinas, ex. P. Rami scripta collecta,* a treatise on preparing sermons and orations according to the principles of the logic, which is in fact a summary of the whole Ramist theory of education, dedicated to the great Sturm, who replied with a praise of the author. When Ramus visited Basle in 1569 he met Freigius, who thereafter was an energetic champion. In *De Logica Iureconsultorum,* 1582, Freigius applied the logic to the study of law, and in 1586 he edited *P. Rami Professio Regia. Hoc est septem artes liberales . . . in tabulas perpetuas,* a volume of "tabulae" in which all the seven liberal arts are diagramed according to Ramist principles; Freigius declared that he prepared the work "ad publicum omnium Ramae Philosophiae studiosorum usum," and the preface was signed by several Ramists; it is probably the most compact form in which the doctrine can be surveyed. William Rodingus edited Ramus' *Dialecticae* along with the commentary of Talon at Frankfort, 1576, 1579, and later; Mulhemius brought out at Frankfort in 1584 a *Logica Ad P. Rami Dialecticam Conformata,* with the places and figures illustrated by Biblical passages; at Basle, Andrea Kragius published the logic with illustrations from Horace, *Q. Horatii Flacci Ars Poetica ad P. Rami Dialecticam & Rhetoricam resoluta,* 1583. Nathaniel Baxter, an Englishman, published at Frankfort *In Petri Rami Dialecticam Quaestiones & Responsiones,* 1588. Rudolph Snell, a Dutch physicist, wrote voluminously, treating his subject according to the method of Ramus; typical is his *Partitiones Physicae, Methodi Ramae Legibus Informatae,* 1594. Henning Rennemannus edited Ramus in Germany and wrote much in his defense, most vigorously in *Dissertatio pro Philosophia Ramea, adversus Peripateticas,* 1595, and *Responsio Apologetica ad Dissertationem pro Philosophia Peripatetica aduersus Ramistas.* In *Triumphus Logicae Ramae,* published at Basle and reprinted in London, 1583, William Scribonius surveyed and answered objections. A particularly able defender was Frederic Beurhusius, many of whose works were reprinted in London. His three-volume treatise on the teaching of logic was a standard guide for Ramist educators: *In P. Rami Dialecticae . . . explicationum quaestiones,* London, 1581; *De P. Rami Dialecticae praecipuis capitibus disputationes scholasticae,* 1578, and London, 1582; *Ad P. Rami Dialecticam, variorum et maxime illustrium exemplorum,* 1583. The last two, running to a thousand pages each, rifle the literature of classical antiquity to prove the correctness and justice of the system. Beurhusius also edited the *Dialecticae* with an added *Defensio eiusdem dialecticae,* which was published in London in 1589; he demonstrated the application of the logic to divinity with an analysis of the New

Testament, proving that the Apostles wrote as Ramists, *Analysis Epistolarum et Euangeliorum dominicalium scholastica,* 1585. A late recension of Ramus, widely used in New England, was Marcus Fredericus Wendelinus, *Logicae Institutiones Tironum adolescentum,* first edition Amsterdam, 1654, and frequently republished during the next forty years; it made some concessions to the Aristotelians and rephrased many of Ramus' most important ideas, but it always gave the original terms and was in fact no more than a paraphrase of the *Dialecticae.*

Circumstances often produced peculiar chapters in the history of the logic. Because Ramus opposed Beza over ecclesiastical polity, the system was not welcomed at Geneva; it was, however, taken up with enthusiasm at Basle, and Frankfort seems to have been the continental center. In Holland, the Arminians embraced it, and consequently orthodox Calvinists condemned it; the Estates ordered all schools to study logic from Franconus Burgersdicius, *Institutionum Logicarum Libri Duo,* 1632. This work was used in New England and in 1697 was translated into English, "By a Gentleman," under the title *Monitio Logica;* to compare it with Ramus' *Dialecticae* is perhaps the best way to perceive concretely the differences of the two logics. In Germany, where controversy over the system was exceedingly intense, the Calvinists were in general inclined to Ramus and the Lutherans to Aristotle, but not invariably so. An interesting example of the tone of controversy along the Rhine can be seen in the published correspondence of Nicodemus Frischlin, who opposed Ramus, and Conrad Neubecker, who defended him: *Nicodemi Frischlini Poetae, Oratoris, et Philosophi Caesarii Dialogus Logicus,* Frankfort, 1590. In Germany there was an attempt to combine the two logics, to harmonize Ramus with Melanchthon's version of Aristotle; this school was known in the seventeenth century as "Philippo-Ramist", and some of their works were owned in New England. The combination was usually effected by enumerating the categories at the beginning of a book and then proceeding serenely with the Ramist scheme. Andrea Libavius, in his *Dialecticae Emendatae Libri Duo,* 1595, took over the substance of Ramus' system, but attacked him no less furiously; he was answered by Johann Bisterfeldus, *Defensio Pro Antapodixi Ramea,* 1596. Both Keckermann and Piscator, although they fulminated against Ramus, owed much to him and were regarded in their day as tinged with Ramism. The great *Encyclopaedia* of Alsted, which was of immense importance in shaping the New England mind, was organized on Ramist principles and frequently quoted Ramus; the section on logic is basically Ramist, with some Aristotelian additions. In the *Encyclopaedia* and in his other works, notably his *Physica Harmonica,* 1616, Alsted groups his materials into Ramist dichotomies. The most popular of Philippo-Ramist textbooks were: Amandus Polanus, *Logicae Libri Duo,* 1590, which is almost entirely Ramus, and Conrad Dietrich, *Institutiones Dialecticae ex Probattissimis Aristotelis et Rami Interpretibus Studiose Conscripta,* 1631, frequently republished, which boasted that the mode of treatment was "neither purely Aristotelian nor purely Ramean, but mixed." Beurhusius was regarded in his day as a Philippo-Ramist, though it is clear that his sympathies were almost wholly with the "purely Ramean"; his principal effort toward the reconciliation appears in his edition of the *Dialecticae* with a supplement, *Et his e regione comparati Philippe Melanthonis Dialecticae Libri Quatuor,* Frankfort, 1588 and 1591.

In England the first traceable publication of Ramus was a translation of the *Dialecticae* in 1574, *The Logicke of the Most Excellent Philosopher P. Ramus Martyr,* purporting to be done by "M. R. Makylmenaeum Scotum". The Latin text was published in 1576. At least two volumes of Beurhusius' work on the teaching of logic were printed in London in 1581 and 1582, while the *Dialecticae* with Beurhusius' important *Defensio* was reprinted in 1589; Scribonius' *Triumphus* was issued twice in the year 1583. The system was established at Cambridge, and identified with Puritanism, principally through the work of the great commentators. The first of them, Sir William Temple, later Provost of Trinity College, Dublin, was fellow of King's and tutor in logic in the 1580's. His controversy with Piscator was the greatest of the pamphlet battles waged after Ramus' death. It began in 1580 when Everard Digby, fellow of St. John's, attacked Ramus with *De Duplici Methodo libri duo, vnicam P. Rami Methodum Refutantis,* arguing that the method of formal logic could not be based upon natural habits of thought, that the proper procedure should be not from universals to particulars but from particulars to universals. In the same year Piscator published on the continent, *Animadversiones Ioan. Piscatoris Arg. In Dialecticam P. Rami* (3rd edition, Frankfort, 1586). Temple then took up the cudgels against Digby, but published under the assumed name of "Francis Mildapettus", describing himself on the title page as "Navarrene", referring to the Collège de Navarre, where Ramus had been a student; the work was dedicated to Philip Howard, Earl of Arundel, and entitled, *Ad Everardum Digbeeum Admonitio de Unica P. Rami Methodo,* London, 1580. This was a passionate celebration of Ramus' reform of logic—"laborem hercule gravissimae contentionis & invidiae"—and at the end endeavored to crush Digby by calling the roll of great and good men who were Ramists, including Freigius, Schorus, Scribonius, Beurhusius; Temple insinuated that the logic had a foothold at Oxford, asserted that it flourished at Cambridge, and capped the climax by pointing to the young Earl of Essex, who was at that moment studying Ramus! Digby apparently replied, for Temple continued the debate under his own name with *Pro Mildapetti de Unica Methodo Defensione contra Diplodophilium* (i.e., Digby), London, 1581, republished at Frankfort, 1584. To this work Temple added an appendix against Piscator's *Animadversiones;* Piscator replied in *Gulielmi Tempelli Philosophi Cantabrigiensis Epistola De Dialectica P. Rami,* 1582, and Temple countered with *Epistolae de P. Rami Dialectica contra Iohannis Piscatoris Responsionem,* Cambridge, 1584. In 1584 he also published at Cambridge *P. Rami Dialecticae Libri duo, Scholliis G. Tempelli Cantabrigiensis illustrati,* dedicated to Sir Philip Sidney, to which was appended a still further refutation of Piscator; this was Temple's most important service to the cause, and was reprinted on the continent at Frankfort in 1591. Temple became involved in another controversy by writing a preface to James Martin, *Disputatio de Prima Simplicium et Concretorum Corporum Generatione,* 1584, to which Andrea Libavius replied, *Quaestio Physicarum,* Frankfort, 1591. Martin was a Scot, who became a professor of philosophy at Paris while Ramus was still active; he was later at Turin, where his book apparently was published in 1577; it was reissued with Temple's preface at Frankfort in 1589. Temple's last work on logic was an endeavor to follow the master's injunction that the system be applied to theology: *A Logicall Analysis of Twentie Select Psalmes,* published in 1605.

The second of the great English commentators, George Downame, later Bishop of Derry, was fellow of Christ's College in 1585; significantly enough, he was a Calvinist, and one of his sermons against Arminianism was suppressed in 1631 by Laud. At Cambridge he delivered a commentary upon Ramus and an oration in his praise; the commentary was published in 1610, and thereafter most students at Cambridge and in New England read the *Dialecticae* in editions bound up with Downame's commentary. This was in print as late as 1669. The third of the commentators was by far the most original of the three, and is yet the most obscure: Alexander Richardson was a tutor at Queen's College; his lectures were thronged and notes upon them were circulated in manuscript among Puritan students in England and New England. The notes were published under the title, *The Logicians School-Master,* in 1629, and reissued with the addition of notes on other subjects by Samuel Thomson in 1657. This is undoubtedly the most important Ramist work in the background of New England thought.

There were many other publications of Ramus in England during the period. One of the most interesting is Abraham Fraunce, *The Lawiers Logike,* London, 1588; Fraunce declares that he first became interested in Ramus by discussions with Sidney; he translated the *Dialecticae,* but instead of retaining illustrations from classical literature he devised new ones, taken either from the common law—thus following in English the example of Hotoman and Freigius—or from *The Shepheards Calender.* Nathaniel Carpenter's *Philosophia Libera,* Oxford, 1622 and 1636, was an attack on Aristotle, obviously borrowing much from Ramus, though not itself a Ramist work. Anthony Wotton, Puritan divine, who was a student of Temple's at Cambridge, translated the *Dialecticae* under the title, *The Art of Logick . . . Gathered out of Aristotle and set in due forme, according to his instruction by Peter Ramus,* published by his son, Samuel Wotton, London, 1626; it gave new examples for the places, especially from Scripture. Thomas Spencer issued *The Art of Logick Delivered in the Precepts of Aristotle and Ramus,* 1628, and Robert Fage translated Ramus again as *Peter Ramus of Vermandois the Kings Professor, his Dialectica,* London, 1632. William Ames, who was a principal influence upon the thought of early New England, is said to have written a commentary upon the *Dialecticae,* published in 1672, though I have not seen a copy of it. The last important publication of Ramus in England was in the year 1672 and involves a still greater name: John Milton probably did his reworking of the *Dialecticae* much earlier in his career, but it was published thus late as *Artis logicae, plenior institutio, ad Petri Rami methodum concinnata* (reprinted *Works,* ed. John Mitford, London, 1851, VII, 1-185).

Students in the early seventeenth century found bibliographical guidance for the study of logic in several works which were known in New England. Henry Diest in *De Ratione Studii* (pp. 69-72, 146) described the schools, advised students of divinity to remain neutral and to use all systems; Ramus, he said, was briefer and more useful for analysis and accurate method, but Aristotle better for accurate disputation, dexterous judgment, and acumen of wit. He recommended Snell and Downame for the study of Ramus, Polanus and Dietrich for the Philippo-Ramists, and Keckermann for the Peripatetics. In *Bibliotheca Classica* (1611), Draudius listed over three hundred items on dialectic, providing an excellent bibliography of the three schools. Adrien Heereboord, in his "Consilium de ratione studendi philosophiae," published in *Meletemata Philosophica,* 1659, pp. 27-28, and at the end of *Philosophia Naturalis,* 1660, gave suggestions for the study of logic according to the systems of Aristotle, Ramus, and Descartes; he sought to combine the best features of all three and praised the Ramist method for its doctrines of analysis and genesis, but his work marks the point at which the memory of Ramus began to pale before the brighter light of Descartes, and foreshadows his ultimate displacement by Locke.

For the vogue of Ramus in New England, see Morison, *Harvard College in the Seventeenth Century,* Chapter VIII. Almost all the principal works of Ramus appear in the New England lists; the *Dialecticae* was in John Harvard's bequest (A. C. Potter, "Catalogue of John Harvard's Library," *Publications of the Colonial Society of Massachusetts,* XXI [1919], 220), and several copies can be identified as belonging to Harvard undergraduates (A. O. Norton, "Harvard Text-Books . . . of the Seventeenth Century," *Publications of the Colonial Society of Massachusetts,* XXVIII [1935], 424). In 1684 John Ive imported thirteen copies (Worthington C. Ford, *The Boston Book Market,* p. 131). Two titles of Beurhusius were owned by Harvard students (*Publications of the Colonial Society of Massachusetts,* XXVIII [1935], 388); Piscator's discussion of Ramus was in the Harvard College library. Both Elder Brewster and Increase Mather owned Temple's application of the logic to the Psalms (H. M. Dexter, "Catalogue of Elder Brewster's Library," II *Proceedings of the Massachusetts Historical Society,* V, 69; Julius H. Tuttle, "The Libraries of the Mathers," *Proceedings of the American Antiquarian Society,* New Series, XX [1910], 282), and Increase Mather owned Temple's commentary (*Proceedings of the American Antiquarian Society,* New Series, XX [1910], 288). Milton's edition was obviously one of the most popular texts of the later seventeenth century; both John Ive and John Usher were importing copies in 1685 (Ford, *The Boston Book Market,* p. 147; Leon Howard, "Early American Copies of Milton," *Huntington Library Bulletin,* No. 7 [1935], 170), and copies are mentioned on many other lists. Most important of all, Alexander Richardson's *The Logicians School-Master* appears again and again (A. O. Norton, "Harvard Text-Books . . . of the Seventeenth Century," *Publications of the Colonial Society of Massachusetts,* XXVIII [1935], 425; Morison, "The Library of George Alcock, Medical Student, 1676," *Publications of the Colonial Society of Massachusetts,* XXVIII [1935], 355; Charles F. and Robin Robinson, "Three Early Massachusetts Libraries," *Publications of the Colonial Society of Massachusetts,* XXVIII [1935], 133; J. H. Tuttle, "The Libraries of the Mathers," *Proceedings of the American Antiquarian Society,* New Series, XX [1910], 288, 292; *Catalogus Librorum Bibliothecae Collegii Harvardiani . . .,* Boston, 1723; *Catalogue of . . . Books of George Curwin . . . to be sold at Auction,* Boston, 1718, p. 6; *A Catalogue of Curious and Valuable Books, Being the greatest part of the Libraries of . . . Mr. Rowland Cotton . . . and Mr. Nathanael Rogers . . .,* Boston, 1725).

APPENDIX B

THE FEDERAL SCHOOL OF THEOLOGY

The history of the covenant doctrine can be traced through successive publications, though the following list represents merely the limits of my own reading. Undoubtedly further research in the welter of seventeenth-century religious literature will discover other treatises.

It is highly improbable that the English Puritans originated the fundamental idea of the covenant, which, after all, is found in the Old Testament in a sense not too remote from that in which they took it (Cf. Sir James George Frazer, *Folk-Lore in the Old Testament,* London, 1918, I, 391-429, III, 93-111). The English were in the vanguard of the movement, but they were also participants in an international development of European Calvinism. Sibbes could write as early as 1623, on the supposition that his readers were already familiar with the doctrine: "It supposeth a reader grounded in the knowledge of the nature and properties of God, or Christ and his offices, of the covenant of grace, and such like" (Preface to Ezekiel Culverwell, *Treatise of Faith*). The Covenant of Grace was, of course, an old catchword in theology, which had long served as a descriptive for the scheme of redemption; more concretely, it had been used to signify an agreement made between God and Christians in the sacrament of baptism. Richard Hooker employed it in the conventional sense when he said that baptism implied "a covenant or league between God and man," wherein God bestows remission of sins, "binding also himself to add in process of time" sufficient grace for the attainment of life hereafter. But however the idea first became transformed from this loose concept into the specific doctrine of the federalists, it is certain that the English theologians were active in the process and that the three great names in the early development were Perkins, Ames, and Preston. Perkins wrote no one treatise directly upon the doctrine, but passages can be found throughout his *Workes,* published in three volumes, 1609–1617, and again 1626–1631. Ames's contribution must be extracted from the pertinent sections of the *Medulla Theologiae* of 1623 or its English translation, *The*

Marrow of Sacred Divinity, London, 1643, and of the work which was translated as *Conscience With the Power and Cases thereof,* London, 1643. His treatment of the theme can also be seen in his writings against Arminius, *Coronis ad Collationem Hagiensem,* London, 1630, and *Christianae Catecheseos Sciagraphia,* Franeker, 1635. The idea runs through all of Preston's many works; one volume in particular is devoted directly to the subject, *The New Covenant, or the Saints Portion,* London, 1629. The constituents of the federal doctrine also appear throughout the writings of Richard Sibbes, which can be conveniently consulted in the edition of Alexander Grosart, Edinburgh, 1862; in particular should be noted a sermon, "The Faithful Covenanter," in Volume VI.

William Ames taught the elements of the conception at Franeker and among his students was a Dutchman known to history as Cocceius, who became the founder of a school which took the covenant as its central doctrine and which, throughout the seventeenth century, disturbed the Dutch churches almost as much as did the Arminians; these federalists developed the theory in the main along lines parallel to the English, though they accentuated some features in a manner peculiar to themselves. Thus, from its appearance in the works of Perkins, the doctrine had a sort of triple life: in England it continued to be preached by various theologians; in Holland it became the doctrine of the Cocceian faction; and in New England it was from the beginning a fundamental tenet, the basis for much thinking which was ecclesiastical, political, and social as well as theological.

The chief seventeenth-century English works upon the subject, in addition to those already mentioned, are, chronologically: John Downame, *The Christian Warfare,* first edition 1604, and frequently thereafter; [Anon.] *The Covenant Betweene God and Man Playnely declared in laying open the chiefest points of Christian Religion,* 1616; George Downame, *The Covenant of Grace or An Exposition upon Luke 1.73.74.75,* 1631; John Ball, *A Treatise of Faith,* 1632; Robert Harris, *A Treatise of the New Covenant,* 1632, reprinted in *Works,* 1654; Tobias Crisp, *Christ Alone Exalted,* 1643, and frequently thereafter, in 1690, ed. Samuel Crisp; John Arrowsmith, *The Covenant Avenging Sword Brandished in a Sermon Before the Honourable House of Commons,* 1643; John Brinsley, *The Saints Solemne Covenant with their God,* 1644; Thomas Blake, *The Birth-Priviledge; or, Covenant-Holinesse of Beleevers,* 1644; and *Infants Baptisme Freed from Antichristianisme,* 1645; James Ussher, *A Body of Divinity,* 1645; John Ball, *A Treatise of the Covenant of Grace,* 1645; Edmund Calamy, *The Great Danger of Covenant-Refusing, and Covenant-Breaking,* 1646; probably by Calamy, *Two Solemne Covenants Made Between God and Man,* 1647; Thomas Blake, *Vindiciae Foederis,* 1653; and *The Covenant Sealed, or a Treatise of the Sacraments of both Covenants,* 1655; Edward Leigh, *A System or Body of Divinity,* 1654; and *A Treatise of Religion and Learning,* 1656; William Strong, *A Treatise Shewing the Subordination of the Will of Man unto the Will of God,* 1657; Obadiah Sedgwick, *The Bowels of Tender Mercy Sealed in the Everlasting Covenant,* 1661; William Allen, *A Discourse of the Nature, Ends, and Difference of the Two Covenants,* with a preface by Richard Baxter, 1673; John Owen, *The Doctrine of Justification by Faith,* 1677; William Strong, *A Discourse of the Two Covenants,* with a preface by Theophilus Gale, 1678; [Anon.] *The Covenant of*

Grace Effectually Remembred, 1682. After 1690 a new phase in the history of the idea was inaugurated with the republication of Crisp's *Christ Alone Exalted* and the beginning of the so-called "Crispian controversy" (Cf. Olive M. Griffiths, *Religion and Learning,* Cambridge, Eng., 1935, Chapter VII); in anticipation of that controversy the wholly different treatments of the covenant idea given by Bunyan and Thomas Boston should be noted: Bunyan, "The Work of Jesus Christ As An Advocate," *Works,* ed. George Offor, 1843, I, 151-202, and "The Doctrine of the Law and Grace Unfolded" (1660), *Works,* I, 492-576; Thomas Boston, "The Marrow of Modern Divinity," *Whole Works,* ed. Samuel M'Millan, Aberdeen, 1850, VII, 146-491; "A View of the Covenant of Grace from the Sacred Records," VIII, 379-604, XI, 178-343.

The history of the concept in Holland can be pursued in: Johannes Cocceius, *Summa Doctrinae de Foedere et Testamento Dei,* 1648, 1654; *Collationes de Foedere et Testamento Dei,* 1648; *Summa Theologiae ex Scrituris Repetita,* 1669; Franciscus Burmannus, *Synopsis Theologiae & Speciatim Oeconomiae Foederum Dei,* 1677; Hermann Witsius, *De Oeconomia Foederum Dei cum Hominibus,* 1677, 1694, translated by William Crookshank, *The Oeconomy of the Covenants between God and Man,* London, 1758, 3 vols.; William Momma, *De Varia Conditione & Statu Ecclesiae Dei sub Triplici Oeconomia,* 1673, 1683; Johannis Braunius, *Doctrina Foederum,* 1688, 1692. Cf. also, M. Joncourt, *Entretiens sur les Differentes Methodes d'expliquer l'Ecriture & de prêcher, De ceux qu'on appelle Cocceiens & Voetiens Dans les Provinces Unies,* Amsterdam, 1707; Gottlob Schrenk, *Gottesreich und Bund im älteren Protestanismus, vonehmlich bei Johannes Coccejus,* Guterslah, 1923.

New Englanders received constant instruction in the federal doctrine from the theological textbooks used throughout the century, Ames, *Medulla,* Wollebius, *The Abridgment of Christian Divinity,* Ursinus, *The Summe of Christian Religion,* and Petro van Mastricht, *Theoretico Practica Theologia.* The works of Perkins, Ames, Preston, and Sibbes appear in every booklist; John Downame's *The Christian Warfare* is found repeatedly, and one copy, which was in John Harvard's bequest to the college, is today the sole surviving work from that library. Of the English titles, mention is made of those by Ball, Harris, Crisp, Blake, Ussher, Leigh, Sedgwick, Owen, Strong; of the Dutch federalists, many copies can be traced of Cocceius and Witsius.

The idea and philosophy of the covenant run through almost the entire output of the New England writers. The outstanding work specifically on the subject is Peter Bulkeley, *The Gospel-Covenant,* 2nd ed., 1651; also important are: Thomas Cobbett, *A Just Vindication of the Covenant,* 1648; John Cotton, *The Covenant of Gods Free Grace,* 1645; *The Grounds and Ends of the Baptisme of the Children of the Faithfull,* 1647; *Of the Holinesse of Church-Members,* 1650; *The New Covenant,* 1654; *A Treatise of the Covenant of Grace,* 1659; John Davenport, *The Power of Congregational Churches,* 1672; Thomas Hooker, *The Faithful Covenanter,* 1644; *The Covenant of Grace Opened,* 1649; George Phillips, *A Reply to a Confutation,* 1645; Thomas Shepard, *The Sincere Convert,* 1640; *The Sound Beleever,* 1645; *The Church-Membership of Children,* 1663. The relevant sections of Willard's *A Compleat Body of Divinity* should also be consulted; later discussions in New England were usually involved with the question of the Half-Way Covenant and will be noted in my next volume; I have based the discussion in this work upon a more technical study of the idea, "The Marrow of Puritan Divinity," *Publications of the Colonial Society of Massachusetts,* XXXII, 247-300.

NOTES

Unless otherwise indicated, works of New England authors were printed at Boston.

Citations of Harvard theses from the commencement of 1642 refer to Appendix D of Samuel Eliot Morison, *The Founding of Harvard College* (Cambridge, 1935). Theses and quaestiones from later commencements through 1708 are taken from Appendix B of Morison, *Harvard College in the Seventeenth Century* (Cambridge, 1936).

Chapter I

1. Cf. Adolph Harnack, *History of Dogma* (Boston, 1899–1902), V, 77-92.

Chapter II

1. The best places in which to study the attitude of the New England Puritans toward the future life are: Jonathan Mitchell, *A Discourse of the Glory To which God hath called Believers by Jesus Christ* (London, 1677); and Leonard Hoar, *The Sting of Death and Death Unstung* (1680).

2. Cf. Adolph Harnack, *History of Dogma* (Boston, 1899–1902), VI, 110ff., VII, 209ff.; cf. William Ames, *Conscience with the Power and Cases Thereof* (London, 1643), bk. IV, p. 6.

3. Thomas Hooker, *The Application of Redemption* (London, 1659), p. 376; cf. John Rogers, *The Doctrine of Faith* (London, 1629), pp. 361ff.; John Cotton, *Christ the Fountaine of Life* (London, 1651), pp. 92-160; Samuel Lee, *The Joy of Faith* (1687), pp. 122-127; Samuel Willard, *A Compleat Body of Divinity* (1726), pp. 801ff.

4. Cf. Hardin Craig, *The Enchanted Glass* (New York, 1936), p. 25.

Chapter III

1. Owen's *Animadversions on a Treatise Intituled Fiat Lux* was in the possession of both Increase and Cotton Mather and was listed in the Harvard College Library Catalogue of 1723 (Julius H. Tuttle, "The Libraries of the Mathers," *Proceedings of the American Antiquarian Society,* New Series, XX [1910], 287, 314; *Catalogus Librorum Bibliothecae Collegii Harvardini . . . ,* Boston, 1723).

2. Thomas Hall, *Vindiciae Literarum* (London, 1655), p. 68; "How the Cobler" was Samuel How, one of the first sectarians to turn the enthusiasm of Puri-

tanism against the orthodox divines. In 1639 he published *The Sufficiencie of the Spirits Teaching without human learning: or a Treatise tending to prove humane Learning to be no help to the spirituall understanding of the Word of God*. Cf. William Haller, *The Rise of Puritanism* (New York, 1938), pp. 267-268.

3. The principal works of William Dell in the controversy were: *The Stumbling-Stone* (London, 1653); *The Tryal of Spirits* (London, 1653); and *A Plain and Necessary Confutation of Divers Gross and Anti-Christian Errors, Delivered to the University Congregation . . . by Mr. Sydrach Simpson* (London, 1654). Significantly enough, a copy of his *Tryal of Spirits* was owned by Roger Williams; Williams also testifies in a letter dated February 15, 1655, that copies of *The Tryal of Spirits* were publicly burned in Massachusetts Bay (Thomas G. Wright, *Literary Culture in Early New England, 1620–1730*, New Haven, 1920, p. 35; IV *Collections of the Massachusetts Historical Society*, vi, 291). Though Dell was recognized as an enemy by the Massachusetts orthodoxy and was answered by President Chauncy of Harvard College in *Gods Mercy, Shewed to his People* (Cambridge, 1655), it is impossible to ascertain the truth of Williams' remark. However, the Massachusetts General Court, on August 22 and again on October 18, 1654, did order the burning of books by Muggleton and Reeves (*Records of the Governor and Company of Massachusetts Bay in New England*, ed. N. B. Shurtleff, 1853–54, III, 356; IV [pt. I], 204). Possibly the authorities identified Dell's position with that of the Muggletonians, in which case his books might have been burned also, and Chauncy's attack on Dell would have been particularly timely.

The principal works of John Webster were: *The Saints Guide* (London, 1653); and *Academiarum Examen* (London, 1654).

4. Principal defenders of learning against Webster and Dell were: John Hall in *An Humble Motion to The Parliament of England Concerning The Advancement of Learning* (London, 1649); Edward Waterhouse in *An humble Apologie for Learning and Learned Men* (London, 1653); Joseph Sedgwick in *A Sermon Preached at St. Marie's* (London, 1653), and in *Learning's Necessity to an Able Minister of the Gospel* (London, 1653); Seth Ward in *Vindiciae Academiarum* (Oxford, 1654); Thomas Hall in *Vindiciae Literarum* (London, 1654); and Edward Reynolds in *A Sermon Touching the Use of Humane Learning* (London, 1658).

Of these works, at least one copy of Waterhouse is known to have been owned in New England (Edward Waterhouse, *Apology for Learning*, listed in *A Catalogue of Curious and Valuable Books, Being the greatest part of the Libraries of . . . Mr. Rowland Cotton, . . . and Mr. Nathanael Rogers . . .*, Boston, 1725, p. 9.

5. Samuel Eliot Morison, *The Founding of Harvard College* (Cambridge, 1935), p. 361.

Chapter IV

1. Perry Miller and Thomas H. Johnson, *The Puritans* (New York, 1938), pp. 829-831.

2. John Cotton, *Gospel Conversion* (London, 1646), p. 30. This work must be used with caution for illustration of the orthodox position. It was published by a friend of Sir Henry Vane, probably without Cotton's consent, and represents

Cotton's views before he was forced by the Antinomian crisis to exercise caution. The book was obviously popular among English sectarians and was published as *A Conference Mr. John Cotton held at Boston with the Elders of New England* (London, 1646), and again as *Severall Questions . . . propounded by the Teaching Elders unto Mr. John Cotton with his respective answer to each question* (London, 1647).

3. Cf. William Hubbard, *The Happiness of a People in the Wisdome of their Rulers Directing* (1676), p. 35: ". . . Why else doe wee in New-England that profess the doctrine of Calvin, yet practise the discipline of them called Independant, or Congregational Churches, but because the authority of the Countrey is perswaded, that to be most agreeable to the mind of God." See also Richard Bernard, *The Faithfull Shepherd* (London, 1621), pp. 126-127.

4. William Ames, *The Marrow of Sacred Divinity* (London, 1643), p. A 3 verso; cf. the praise by the Presbyterian, Samuel Hudson, in *The Essence and Unitie of the Church Catholike Visible* (London, 1645), p. 12: "he the most rigid in discipline, and exact in Logicall divisions and deductions."

5. John Wollebius, *The Abridgment of Christian Divinity* (tr. Alexander Ross, 3 ed., London, 1660), p. A 2 recto. Naturally copies of Wollebius are found listed in the Harvard College Library Catalogue of 1723 and in many other places. See for example Julius H. Tuttle, "The Libraries of the Mathers," *Proceedings of the American Antiquarian Society,* New Series, XX (1910), 355; Arthur O. Norton, "Harvard Text-Books and Reference Books of the Seventeenth Century," *Publications of the Colonial Society of Massachusetts,* XXVIII (1935), 434; Robert F. Seybolt, "Student Libraries at Harvard, 1763–1764," *Publications of the Colonial Society of Massachusetts,* XXVIII (1935), 461; Worthington C. Ford, *The Boston Book Market, 1679–1700* (Boston, 1917), pp. 127, 143.

6. Zacharias Ursinus, *The Summe of Christian Religion* (tr. Henry Passy, London, 1633), p. 443. Copies of Ursinus were easily available. See for instance: *Catalogus Librorum Bibliothecae Colegii Harvardini . . .* (Boston, 1723), p. 97; *A Catalogue of Curious and Valuable Books, Being the greatest part of the Libraries of . . . Mr. Rowland Cotton, . . . and Mr. Nathanael Rogers . . .* (Boston, 1725), p. 2.

7. Van Mastricht was in the Harvard College Library Catalogue of 1723.

8. Theophilus Gale, *Philosphia Generalis* (London, 1676), pp. 686-689; Gale's work was in the Harvard College Library. Cf. Increase Mather, *Angelographia* (1696), p. 90; Benedictus Aretius, *S.S. Theologiae Problemata* (1604), p. 3.

9. Jonathan Mitchell, *A Discourse of the Glory To which God hath called Believers by Jesus Christ* (London, 1677), p. 129. For knowledge of classical literature in the New England colonies, see Samuel Eliot Morison, *Harvard College in the Seventeenth Century* (Cambridge, 1936), pp. 164, 178, 197ff. Note specific defense of classical learning in John Hall, *An Humble Motion to The Parliament of England Concerning The Advancement of Learning* (London, 1649), pp. 8-22.

After Plutarch and Seneca, classical authors most cited were Horace, Virgil, Cicero, Plato, Aristotle, and even Aristophanes.

10. Porter G. Perrin, "Possible Sources of *Technologia* at Early Harvard," *New England Quarterly,* VII (1934), 724.

11. For the use of Alsted's *Encyclopaedia* at Harvard, see Morison, *Harvard College in the Seventeenth Century,* p. 158; it was the mainstay of many New England libraries, as for example: Charles F. and Robin Robinson, "Three Early Massachusetts Libraries," *Publications of the Colonial Society of Massachusetts,* XXVIII (1935), 172; Arthur O. Norton, "Harvard Text-Books and Reference Books of the Seventeenth Century," *Publications of the Colonial Society of Massachusetts,* XXVIII (1935), 383; Julius H. Tuttle, "The Libraries of the Mathers," *Proceedings of the American Antiquarian Society,* New Series, XX (1910), 282; Thomas G. Wright, *Literary Culture in Early New England, 1620–1730* (New Haven, 1920), p. 59; *Catalogus Librorum Bibliothecae Collegii Harvardini . . . ,* p. 3; Dean Fenn's MS. card catalogue of quotations of Cotton Mather in the *Magnalia.*

12. For the use of Keckermann at Harvard, see Morison, *Harvard College in the Seventeenth Century,* p. 158. Either Keckermann's complete works or copies of separate works appear in almost all New England lists; for example: Franklin B. Dexter, "The First Public Library in New Haven," *Papers of the New Haven Historical Society,* VI (1900), 312, 313; Thomas H. Johnson, "Jonathan Edwards' Background of Reading," *Publications of the Colonial Society of Massachusetts,* XXVIII, 197; Henry M. Dexter, "Catalogue of Elder Brewster's Library," II *Proceedings of the Massachusetts Historical Society,* v (1890), 42; Samuel E. Morison, "The Library of George Alcock, Medical Student, 1676," *Publications of the Colonial Society of Massachusetts,* XXVIII, 354; Alfred C. Potter, "Catalogue of John Harvard's Library," *Publications of the Colonial Society of Massachusetts,* XXI (1920), 211; "Books given to [Harvard] Library by John Harvard, Peter Bulkley, Sir Kenelme Digby, and Governor Bellingham," *Bibliographical Contributions* (Harvard University Library), No. 27 (1888), p. 10; Arthur O. Norton, "Harvard Text-Books and Reference Books of the Seventeenth Century," *Publications of the Colonial Society of Massachusetts,* XXVIII, 412, 413, 414; Charles F. and Robin Robinson, "Three Early Massachusetts Libraries," *Publications of the Colonial Society of Massachusetts,* XXVIII, 127, 152, 159; Julius H. Tuttle, "The Libraries of the Mathers," *Proceedings of the American Antiquarian Society,* New Series, XX (1910), 281, 288, 307; *Catalogus Librorum Bibliothecae Collegii Harvardini . . . ,* pp. 20, 83; *Catalogus variorum & insignium librorum . . . D. Guilielmi Amesii . . .* (Amsterdam, 1634); *A Catalogue of Curious and Valuable Books, Being the greatest part of the Libraries of . . . Mr. Rowland Cotton, . . . and Mr. Nathanael Rogers . . . ,* pp. 9, 14; *A Catalogue of Curious and Valuable Books, Which mostly belonged to the Reverend Mr. George Curwin . . .* (Boston, 1718), pp. 10, 11; *The Library of . . . Mr. Samuel Lee . . .* (Boston, 1693), p. 15; *Catalogue of Rare and Valuable Books . . . of Joshua Moodey, and . . . Daniel Gookin* (Boston, 1718); Dean Fenn's MS. card catalogue of quotations of Cotton Mather in the *Magnalia.*

13. For the use of these works at Harvard, see Morison, *Harvard College in the Seventeenth Century, passim.*

14. Magirus' *Physiologiae Peripateticae* appears in many book lists, e.g.: Arthur O. Norton, "Harvard Text-Books and Reference Books of the Seventeenth Century," *Publications of the Colonial Society of Massachusetts,* XXVIII, 417; Alfred C. Potter, "Catalogue of John Harvard's Library," *Publications of the*

Colonial Society of Massachusetts, XXI, 214; Charles F. and Robin Robinson, "Three Early Massachusetts Libraries," *Publications of the Colonial Society of Massachusetts,* XXVIII, 152, 175; *Catalogus Librorum Bibliothecae Collegii Harvardini . . . ,* p. 84; *Catalogus variorum & insignium librorum . . . D. Guilielmi Amesii . . . ; A Catalogue of Curious and Valuable Books, Being the greatest part of the Libraries of . . . Mr. Rowland Cotton, . . . and Mr. Nathanael Rogers . . . ,* pp. 9, 14, 16; *A Catalogue of Curious and Valuable Books, Which mostly belonged to the Reverend Mr. George Curwin . . . ,* pp. 8, 11; *Catalogue of Rare and Valuable Books . . . of Joshua Moodey, and . . . Daniel Gookin;* "Library of John Winthrop, Jr.," *Catalogue of The New York Society Library* (New York, 1850), p. 499.

These particular works of Zanchius and of Burgersdicius also appear in the lists, e.g.: Arthur O. Norton, "Harvard Text-Books and Reference Books of the Seventeenth Century," *Publications of the Colonial Society of Massachusetts,* XXVIII, 396, 434; *A Catalogue of Curious and Valuable Books, Being the greatest part of the Libraries of . . . Mr. Rowland Cotton, . . . and Mr. Nathanael Rogers . . . ,* p. 7.

15. Draudius was in the Harvard College Library.

16. *Bibliographical Contributions,* Harvard University Library, No. 27 (1888), p. 13; Morison, *Harvard College in the Seventeenth Century,* p. 641.

17. Aretius, *S.S. Theologiae Problemata,* pp. 446-451. Aretius was recommended highly by Cotton Mather in the *Manuductio,* and copies of his work were circulated in New England (*A Catalogue of Curious and Valuable Books, Which mostly belonged to the Reverend Mr. George Curwin . . . ,* p. 6).

18. Petro van Mastricht, *Theoretico-Practica Theologia* (1699), p. 3; cf. also Henry Diest, *De Ratione Studii Theologici* (2 ed., Amsterdam, 1654), pp. 20-21, 24-40.

19. Edward Reynolds, *A Sermon Touching the Use of Humane Learning* (London, 1658), pp. 12-13, 17; Magirus, *Corona Virtutum Moralium* (Frankfort, 1601), pp. 2-3.

20. Charles Morton, MS. *Compendium Physicae* (copied by Jeremiah Gridley; Massachusetts Historical Society), Preface.

21. Etienne Gilson, *The Spirit of Mediaeval Philosophy* (New York, 1936), p. 37.

Chapter V

1. For bibliography of this chapter, see Appendix A.

2. Charles Morton, MS. *System of Logick* (Massachusetts Historical Society), p. 49.

3. Samuel Eliot Morison, *The Founding of Harvard College* (Cambridge, 1935), pp. 333, 337, 434, 436; *Harvard College in the Seventeenth Century* (Cambridge, 1936), pp. 185ff.

4. Harriet Beecher Stowe, *Oldtown Folks* (Boston, 1897), p. 224.

5. For authorities on his life, see Appendix A.

6. Samuel Clarke, *A Generall Martyrologie* (London, 1651), p. 13.

7. Thomas Lawson, *A Mite into the Treasury* (London, 1680), p. 16.

8. Morison, *Founding of Harvard College,* pp. 132ff.

9. Cf. Abraham Fraunce, *The Lawiers Logike* (London, 1588), p. A 1 recto. He and Sidney were drawn together "to a greater liking of, and my selfe to a further trauayling in, the easie explication of Ramus his Logike."

10. *Samuel Johnson* (ed. Herbert and Carol Schneider, New York, 1929), II, 60.

11. For records of Ramus' works in New England, see Appendix A.

12. Massachusetts Archives, CCXL. 141. 5a.

13. Charles Waddington, *Ramus, sa vie, ses écrits et ses opinions* (Paris, 1855), pp. 135-136, 240-247; Frank P. Graves, *Peter Ramus and the Educational Reformation of the Sixteenth Century* (New York, 1912), pp. 74-75, 199-201; Emile Saisset, *Précurseurs et disciples de Descartes* (Paris, 1862), p. 78n.; cf. also P. Lobstein, *Petrus Ramus als Theologe* (Strassburg, 1878).

14. See below, Chapters VI and VII.

15. Instead of dividing logic into argument, axiom, syllogism, and method, Brattle called for Descartes' perception, proposition, discourse, and method. Although he professed to justify these divisions by Aristotle and Descartes, he treats them in an essentially Ramist manner. The principal change is a substitution, in accordance with Cartesian doctrine, of the concept of perception for the Ramist idea of invention. Again, under the influence of Descartes, the chapter on method is expanded beyond anything to be found in Ramist works.

16. Quotations used in this work are from the copy in the Massachusetts Historical Society.

17. Francis Bacon, *Works* (ed. Spedding, Ellis, and Heath; London, 1857–74), I, 663; cf. III, 530.

18. Theses logicae, No. 14, 1670; cf. Jonathan Mitchell, MS. dissertation: "Various testimony is of worth through the various artificials of the assumption."

19. Richard Hooker, *Of the Laws of Ecclesiastical Polity*, I, vi, 4; I, iii, 4.

20. Mass. Archives, CCXL. 141. 1a.

21. Thomas Shepard, Jr., "My logicall and physicall synopses," MS. dated 1655 in the Massachusetts Historical Society.

22. Mitchell MS., Mass. Archives, CCXL. 141. 4a; 141. 5.

23. Hardin Craig, *The Enchanted Glass* (New York, 1936), pp. 140-158.

24. Bartholomäus Keckermann, *Operum Omnium Quae Extant* (Geneva, 1614), I, "Praecognitorum philosophei," pp. 60-65; "Praecognitorum logicorum tractatus tres," pp. 78-89, 110-129; "Gymnasium logicvm," pp. 420-423.

25. William Rodingus, ed., Ramus' *Dialecticae Libri Duo* (Frankfort, 1579), pp. 5-7.

Chapter VI

1. Gosivino Mulhemius, *Logica ad P. Rami Dialecticam Conformata* (Frankfort, 1584), pp. A4 recto-A4 verso; cf. Henningus Rennemannus, *Dissertatio pro Philosophia Ramea, adversus Peripateticas* (Frankfort, 1595) pp. 30-31.

2. Theses technologicae, No. 4, 1670. Cf. mock theses technologicae, No. 3, 1663: "Encyclopaedia is the sphere of rational activity."

3. Theses technologicae, No. 15, 1678; see Samuel Eliot Morison, *Harvard College in the Seventeenth Century* (Cambridge, 1936), pp. 253-254; cf. E. K.

Rand, "Liberal Education in Seventeenth-Century Harvard," *New England Quarterly,* VI (1933), 534.

4. Morison, *Harvard College in the Seventeenth Century,* p. 278.

5. Theses technologicae, No. 1, 1653 (Aug. 9); No. 7, 1678; cf. definition of dialectic in Shepard's MS. synopsis of logic: "Dialectic is the art or rule by which the reasons of things are administered to their eupraxia."

6. Cf. theses technologicae, No. 2, 1678: "Art primarily consists in theoretics, and secondly of practice."

7. *Samuel Johnson* (ed. Herbert and Carol Schneider, New York, 1929), II, 62-68; cf. theses technologicae, No. 3, 1719: "All discipline is both archtype and ectype."

8. William Ames, *The Marrow of Sacred Divinity* (London, 1643), pp. 24-25; cf. further: "In us the things themselves are the example, platform or copy, and our knowledge is the Image: but in God the Divine knowledge is the coppy-platforme, and the things themselves the Image, or expresse likenesse of it."

9. Samuel Willard, *The Doctrine of the Covenant of Redemption* (1693), p. 70; cf. Willard, *The Checkered State of the Gospel Church* (1701), pp. 37, 39; *A Compleat Body of Divinity* (1726), pp. 102, 151.

10. Cf. Ames's discussion, *Philosophemata* (Leyden, 1643), pp. 15-18, 70-72.

11. Alexander Richardson, *The Logicians School-Master* (London, 1657), pp. 23, 134; Ames, *Philosophemata,* pp. 57, 145.

12. Ames, *Philosophemata,* pp. 37-52, 81, 100; cf. especially p. 148: "Comprehension of all these arts by which things emanate from some primary being and at last return to him is called encyclopaedia: of which circular chain the first link is dialectica and the last theology." Cf. Richardson, *Logicians School-Master,* pp. 31-33; Alsted, *Encyclopaedia,* I, sections entitled "Technologiam" and "Archelogiam."

13. Jonathan Mitchell, MS. notebooks, Massachusetts Archives, CCXL. 141. 6; Quaestiones, No. IV, 1659.

Chapter VII

1. Pascal, *Pensées,* No. 284.

2. *Paradise Lost,* bk. XII, ll. 474-476.

3. For the best discussion of this point, see William Ames, *The Marrow of Sacred Divinity* (London, 1643), pp. 60-63.

4. Calvin, *Institutes,* II, ii, 18.

5. William Brattle, MS. abstract of Henry More, *Enchiridion Ethicum* (Massachusetts Historical Society), p. 6; cf. Samuel Eliot Morison, *Harvard College in the Seventeenth Century* (Cambridge, 1936), pp. 258, 263.

6. Willard discusses this theme in several connections. Cf. especially his analysis and definition of justice, pp. 75-77; his endeavor to identify the punishment of Adam with natural justice, pp. 190-194; his concept of sin as "a swerving of the reasonable creature from the law of God," pp. 209ff.; pp. 560ff.; his definition of the "moral law" and his distinction between natural and positive law, pp. 649ff.; and his constant assertion, as for example p. 573, that "Man was made a reasonable Creature, and God [will] treat him in a rational way." Cf. also Willard, *The Doctrine of the Covenant of Redemption* (1693), pp. 78-79.

7. Cf. in particular Mulhemius, *Logica ad P. Rami dialecticam conformata* (Frankfort, 1584); Beurhusius, *Analysis epistolarum et evangeliorium* (Mülhausen, 1585); Daniel Hofman, *De usu et applicatione Notionum Logicarum ad res Theologicas* (Frankfort, 1596). Cf. also Abraham Fraunce, *The Lawiers Logike* (London, 1588), p. 4 recto: "Logike is necessary for a diuine, yet Logike yeeldeth no diuinitie: but when a Preacher hath by continuall perusing of the sacred Scriptures furnished himselfe with store of matter, then Logike wil teach him how to teach others, & not onely that, but also how to learne himselfe, to defend, to confute, to instruct, to reprehend. . . ."

8. Sir William Temple, *A Logicall Analysis of Twentie Select Psalmes* (London, 1605), "Dedication"; this dedication is an essential document for understanding the effects of the Ramist system on English thinkers. It is a summary of the ideals, the methods and the certainties of the Ramist school, expressing above all the assurance that when arguments were once clearly distinguished the discourse would organize itself by a marshaling of each argument in its proper rank and place.

9. Cf. Morison, *Harvard College in the Seventeenth Century,* pp. 268ff.

10. John Norton, *The Heart of N-England rent at the Blasphemies of the Present Generation* (Cambridge, 1659), pp. 9-10, 11; it should be noted that New England divines explicitly declared that the doctrine of the Trinity rested not upon any literal authorization of the Scripture but wholly on logical consequence. Cf. Thomas Cobbett, *A Just Vindication of the Covenant and Church-Estate of Children of Church-Members* (London, 1648), pp. 130-131.

Chapter VIII

1. Charles Morton, MS. *Compendium Physicae* (copied by Jeremiah Gridley; Massachusetts Historical Society), Preface.

2. Hardin Craig, *The Enchanted Glass* (New York, 1936), pp. 198-202.

3. Roberto Almagià, *La dottrina della marea nell' antichità classica e nel medio evo* (Rome, 1905), pp. 454-455, 506ff.; John Kirtland Wright, *The Geographical Lore of the Time of the Crusades* (New York, 1925), pp. 25-26, 190ff.; Lynn Thorndike, *A History of Magic and Experimental Science* (New York, 1923–34), IV, 612. I am indebted to my colleague, Professor Dana B. Durand, for calling my attention to this background material.

4. Samuel Eliot Morison, *Harvard College in the Seventeenth Century* (Cambridge, 1936), Chapters X and XI.

5. *Letters of John Davenport* (ed. Isabel MacBeath Calder, New Haven, 1937), pp. 133-134.

6. Morison, *Harvard College in the Seventeenth Century,* p. 233; cf. Adrian Heereboord, *Philosophia Naturalis* (1663), pp. 1-3.

7. Kenneth B. Murdock, *Increase Mather, the Foremost American Puritan* (Cambridge, 1925), pp. 147-148.

8. Samuel Willard, *A Compleat Body of Divinity* (1726), p. 137; cf. pp. 38, 134, 136; also John Cotton, *A Briefe Exposition with Practicall Observations upon The Whole Book of Ecclesiastes* (London, 1654), pp. 64-65, and James Fitch, *The first Principles of the Doctrine of Christ* (1679), p. 23: "Natural

causes which he guides by the Law of nature to their inferior ends, . . . they act by power, or principle arising out of nature, *natura est res nata ex principiis,* as water cooleth and fire burneth. . . . Hence this cause acts to the uttermost of its power if not hindred by an external power over-ruling. . . . Nature is in all Creatures, and God as a God of nature over-ruleth them, therefore this is called a common government."

9. John Davenport, *The Knowledge of Christ Indispensably required of all men that would be saved* (London, 1653), p. 70; cf. John Richardson, *The Necessity of a Well Experienced Souldiery* (Cambridge, 1679), p. 6: "We in these days have no promise of such a miraculous & immediate assistance; God works now by men and meanes, not by miracles."

Chapter IX

1. The contemporaneous theory of human psychology can best be studied in certain works specifically devoted to psychological investigation which were published or circulated in England in the sixteenth and at the beginning of the seventeenth century. Those which I have found particularly useful for this chapter are: Timothy Bright, *A Treatise of Melancholy* [1 ed., 1586] (London, 1616); Otho Casmannus, *Psychologia Anthropologica* (Hanover, 1594); F. N. Coeffeteau, *A Table of Humane Passions* (London, 1621); Sir William Cornwallyes, *Essayes* (London, 1610); John Huarte, *Examen de Ingenios* (London, 1596); Philippe de Mornay, *The True Knowledge of a Mans Owne Selfe* (London, 1602); Pierre de la Primaudaye, *The French Academie* (London, 1602–05, 3 vols.); Edward Reynolds, *A Treatise of the Passions and Faculties of the Soule of Man* (London, 1658); J. F. Senault, *The Use of Passions* (London, 1649); Thomas Wright, *The Passions of the minde in generall* (London, 1604).

Of these works, traces of Reynolds' book can be found in New England (*A Catalogue of Curious and Valuable Books, Being the greatest part of the Libraries of . . . Mr. Rowland Cotton, . . . and Mr. Nathanael Rogers . . .*, Boston, 1725, p. 8; *Catalogus Librorum Bibliothecae Collegii Harvardini . . .*, Boston, 1723, p. 28), as also the *Essayes* of Sir William Cornwallyes (Henry M. Dexter, "Elder Brewster's Library," II *Proceedings of the Massachusetts Historical Society,* v, 74; George E. Bowman, "Governor Thomas Prence's Will and Inventory and the Records of his Death," *The Mayflower Descendant,* III [1901], 209). In New England, as in England, perhaps the most popular was *The French Academie,* copies of which were owned by William Bradford and the Harvard College Library (George E. Bowman, "Governor William Bradford's Will and Inventory," *The Mayflower Descendant,* II [1900], 232; *Catalogus Librorum Bibliothecae Collegii Harvardini . . .*, p. 57; Alfred C. Potter, "Catalogue of John Harvard's Library," *Publications of the Colonial Society of Massachusetts,* XXI [1920], 196; Will of Miles Standish, *New England Historical and Genealogical Register,* V [1851], 337; *A Catalogue of Curious and Valuable Books, Being the greatest part of the Libraries of . . . Mr. Rowland Cotton, . . . and Mr. Nathanael Rogers . . .*, p. 3). These works are testimonies to widespread preoccupation with the problems of the soul which characterized the whole Renaissance and which found expression also in the works of Ludovico Vives and in Melanchthon's *De Anima,* and which culminated at last in the psychological analyses of Descartes, Hobbes, Spinoza, and La Rochefoucauld.

I have depended on histories of psychology, particularly George Sidney Brett, *A History of Psychology* (London, 1912–21, 3 vols.) and H. M. Gardiner, Ruth Clark Metcalf, John G. Beebe-Center, *Feeling and Emotion; a history of theories* (New York, 1937), and furthermore have been guided in my study of the psychological background by much good work now being done by students in Renaissance literature, particularly by the relevant pages in Hardin Craig, *The Enchanted Glass* (New York, 1936), Murray Wright Bundy, *The Theory of Imagination in Classical and Mediaeval Thought* (University of Illinois Studies, Urbana, 1927), Ruth Leila Anderson, *Elizabethan Psychology and Shakespeare's Plays* (University of Iowa Studies, Iowa City, 1927), Lily B. Campbell, *Shakespeare's Tragic Heroes, Slaves of Passion* (Cambridge, 1930), and by the advice and counsel of my colleague, Professor Theodore Spencer.

2. Calvin, *Institutes,* I, xv, 6; II, ii, 3.

3. The psychological doctrine can be found most compactly expressed in the relevant sections of the following textbooks, all of them used in New England throughout the seventeenth century: Alsted, *Encyclopaedia* and *Physica Harmonica;* Zanchius, *De Operibus Dei* (1597), especially bk. III, pp. 680-850; Heereboord, *Philosophia Naturalis;* Keckermann, *Operum Omnium Quae Extant;* Rudolph Snell, *Partitiones Physicae;* and probably the most useful of all, Magirus, *Physiologiae Peripateticae.* The doctrine can also be found in Charles Morton's MS. *Compendium Physicae,* and is treated at length in Zanchius' *The Whole Body of Christian Religion,* which was generally available to New England ministers.

4. Etienne Gilson, *Etudes sur le rôle de la pensée médiévale dans la formation du système cartésien* (Paris, 1930), pp. 22-25, 143-144, 153; Bundy, *Theory of Imagination,* pp. 67-70.

5. Brett, *A History of Psychology,* II, 161.

6. Morton, MS. *Compendium Physicae* (copied by Jeremiah Gridley; Massachusetts Historical Society), p. 145.

7. John Preston, *The New Creature* (London, 1633), p. 41; the functions of the human reason and its relation to the sensible soul are set forth in the technical language of the day in Morton's *Compendium,* pp. 184-186.

8. Thomas Aquinas, *Summa Theologica* (tr. the English Dominican Fathers, London, 1912–22), IV, 296.

9. This quotation is from the yet unpublished poetry of the Reverend Edward Taylor of Westfield, whose works have been discovered in the library of Yale University, and are shortly to be published by Dr. Thomas H. Johnson. Through his kind permission I have been able to use and quote from the manuscript.

10. Brett, *A History of Psychology,* II, 19-21; it is worth noting that the Elizabethan psychologists, particularly Senault, quote extensively from Augustine.

11. Gardiner et al., *Feeling and Emotion,* pp. 97-99, 120; Lily B. Campbell, *Shakespeare's Tragic Heroes,* pp. 93ff., 157.

12. John Donne, *Poetical Works* (ed. H. J. C. Grierson, Oxford, 1912), I, 36.

13. *Paradise Lost,* bk. XI, ll. 515-525.

14. Bundy, *Theory of Imagination,* pp. 66-67.

15. Brett, *A History of Psychology,* II, 76.
16. Bundy, *Theory of Imagination,* pp. 166-172.
17. *Ibid.,* pp. 177-179, 199-210.
18. Brett, *A History of Psychology,* II, 163-164.
19. Gilson, *Etudes sur le rôle de la pensée médiévale dans la formation du système cartésien,* pp. 32-33; cf. pp. 10-20, 26-27.
20. *Ibid.,* p. 36.
21. *Ibid.,* pp. 201, 288, 294.
22. Descartes, *Discours de la méthode,* deuxième parti.
23. Edward, Lord Herbert of Cherbury, *De Veritate* (tr. with an introduction by Meyrick H. Carré, University of Bristol, Eng., 1937), pp. 132, 235, 282.
24. See pp. 156-160.

Chapter X

1. John Preston, *The Position of John Preston* (London, 1654), pp. 5-10; I have summarized in this paragraph a long argument which deserves more careful study and is the best study of regeneration in psychological terms which I have encountered.
2. From the Taylor MS.
3. From the Taylor MS.

Chapter XI

1. William Perkins, "The Art of Prophecying," in *Workes* (London, 1626–31), II, 671; William Ames, *Conscience with the Power and Cases Thereof* (London, 1643), bk. IV, p. 74; Ames, *The Marrow of Sacred Divinity* (London, 1643), p. 159; Increase Mather, *The Life and Death of . . . Richard Mather* (Cambridge, 1670), p. 31.
2. John Preston, *Sinnes Overthrow* (London, 1635), p. 102; cf. p. 103: ". . . he that useth Eloquence in the Preaching of the Word, doth nothing else but draw the heart away from affecting the pure Word, unto that which hath no vertue in it to save. . . ."; Preston, *The New Creature* (London, 1633), p. 163: "If we had al the wit in the world to set the Word of God in it, it is better than that in which it is set; as the Diamond is better than the Gold in which it is set."
3. Samuel Butler, *Hudibras* (ed. A. R. Waller, Cambridge, Eng., 1905), p. 16.
4. Michael Wigglesworth, "The Prayse of Eloquence," MS. notebook in the New England Historical and Genealogical Society.
5. Cf. John Cotton, *A Practical Commentary . . . upon The First Epistle Generall of John* (London, 1656), p. 76: "A Minister that delivers an old Doctrin, and known to the people, yet he must bring it in in a new manner, that it may affect them the more, being drest after a new manner, the appetite desires new dishes more, as for our Saviour, he taught no new Doctrin, but he spake it in such a manner, in such Parables, that it seemed strange to them."
6. Cf. W. Fraser Mitchell, *English Pulpit Oratory from Andrewes to Tillotson* (London, 1932), p. 68.
7. John Huarte, *Examen de Ingenios* (London, 1596), p. 128; cf. J. F. Senault, *The Use of Passions* (London, 1649), pp. 170-174; Francis Bacon, "Advance-

ment of Learning," in *Works* (ed. Spedding, Ellis, and Heath; London, 1857–74), III, 389-391, 409ff.

8. Alexander Richardson, "Grammatical Notes," in *The Logicians School-Master* (London, 1657), pp. 1-2; cf. p. 8: "Grammar carrieth the matter in a budget neither too big or too little, like one of these Irishmen with Breeches without pockets. *Rhetorica* carrieth it in a fine bag full of laces. . . ."

9. Cf. Cotton, *The Way of the Churches of Christ in New-England* (London, 1645), p. 72; Increase Mather, *The Blessed Hope, And the Glorious Appearing of the Great God our Saviour, Jesus Christ* (1701), p. 8; Samuel Willard, *The Barren Fig Trees Doom* (1691), p. 261; Willard, *The Fountain Opened* (1700), p. 8; Henry Diest, *De Ratione Studii Theologici* (2 ed., Amsterdam, 1654), pp. 16-28.

10. Copies of Farnaby were obviously in use in New England; cf. Robert F. Seybolt, "Student Libraries at Harvard, 1763–1764," *Publications of the Colonial Society of Massachusetts,* XXVIII (1935), 454; "Catalogue of Mr. Wigglesworth's Books Taken Oct. 22, 1705," in John W. Dean, *Memoir of Rev. Michael Wigglesworth* (2 ed., Albany, 1871), p. 152; Samuel E. Morison, "The Library of George Alcock, Medical Student, 1676," *Publications of the Colonial Society of Massachusetts,* XXVIII, 357; Julius H. Tuttle, "The Libraries of the Mathers," *Proceedings of the American Antiquarian Society,* New Series, XX (1910), 289, 327; *The Library of . . . Mr. Samuel Lee . . .* (Boston, 1693), p. 13; *Catalogue of Rare and Valuable Books . . . of Joshua Moodey, and . . . Daniel Gookin* (Boston, 1718); Worthington C. Ford, *The Boston Book Market, 1679–1700* (Boston, 1917), p. 85.

11. For the place of Keckermann in rhetorical theories, see M. Gibert, *Jugemens des savans sur les auteurs qui ont traité de la rhétorique, avec un précis de la doctrine de ces auteurs* (Paris, 1713–19, 3 vols.), II, 369-377.

12. Copies of Vossius were obviously circulating in New England; cf. Julius H. Tuttle, "The Libraries of the Mathers," *Proceedings of the American Antiquarian Society,* New Series, XX, 353; *A Catalogue of Curious and Valuable Books, Being the greatest part of the Libraries of . . . Mr. Rowland Cotton, . . . and Mr. Nathanael Rogers . . .* (Boston, 1725), p. 14; *A Catalogue of Curious and Valuable Books, Which mostly belonged to the Reverend Mr. George Curwin . . .* (Boston, 1718), p. 13.

13. For an estimate of Vossius' place in the history of rhetoric see Gibert, *Jugemens des savans,* III, 1-20.

14. Separate copies of Talon's *Rhetorica* appear on New England lists; e.g., Julius H. Tuttle, "The Libraries of the Mathers," *Proceedings of the American Antiquarian Society,* New Series, XX, 289; Arthur O. Norton, "Harvard Text-Books and Reference Books of the Seventeenth Century," *Publications of the Colonial Society of Massachusetts,* XXVIII, 430; Alfred C. Potter, "Catalogue of John Harvard's Library," *Publications of the Colonial Society of Massachusetts,* XXI (1919), 220; "Books given to [Harvard] Library by John Harvard, Peter Bulkley, Sir Kenelme Digby, and Governor Bellingham," *Bibliographical Contributions* (Harvard University Library), No. 27 (1888), p. 12.

15. Cf. Gibert, *Jugemens des savans,* II, 212-220, 299-315.

16. Vossius devotes several pages specifically to refuting Ramus' division be-

tween rhetoric and logic; *Rhetorices Contractae* (Oxford, 1651), pp. 9-12, 116-117.

17. Ramus' Preface can be found in any edition of Talon; I have used that of Frankfort, 1589.

18. Foster Watson, *The English Grammar Schools to 1660* (Cambridge, Eng., 1908), p. 449.

19. John Brinsley, *Ludus Literarius* [London, 1612] (ed. E. T. Campagnac, Liverpool, 1917), p. 203.

20. In addition to the sections on rhetoric in the *Encyclopaedia* (1649 ed., I, 372-404), Alsted published separately two works on rhetoric, *Orator* (3 ed., 1616) and *Rhetorica Quatuor Libris Proponens* (1616), the first of which circulated in New England: *A Catalogue of Curious and Valuable Books, Which mostly belonged to the Reverend Mr. George Curwin . . .*, p. 9; *A Catalogue of Curious and Valuable Books, Being the greatest part of the Libraries of . . . Mr. Rowland Cotton, . . . and Mr. Nathanael Rogers . . .*, p. 15.

21. Another useful example of the Philippo-Ramist school is Cunrad Dieterich, *Institutiones Oratoriae* (Utrecht, 1688).

22. A copy of Butler was listed in the Harvard College Library Catalogue of 1723.

23. Cf. *Hoskins' Directions for Speech and Style* (ed. Hoyt H. Hudson, Princeton Studies in English, 1935); Louise Brown Osborn, *The Life, Letters, and Writings of John Hoskyns* (New Haven, 1937).

Dugard must have been extensively used in New England and very possibly was the principal work through which the influence of Talon was exerted on New England writings. It is found in student libraries (Robert F. Seybolt, "Student Libraries at Harvard, 1763–1764," *Publications of the Colonial Society of Massachusetts,* XXVIII, 454; "Account of Books William Adams took to Yale College . . . ," IV *Collections of the Massachusetts Historical Society,* i, 44) and was imported wholesale by booksellers—15 copies were received at Boston in 1682, John Ive received 10 copies in 1684 and 10 more in 1685 (Ford, *The Boston Book Market,* pp. 90, 126, 150).

Dugard was constantly in print during the latter half of the seventeenth and the first quarter of the eighteenth century. The seventh edition was published in 1673; a fifteenth in 1721.

24. Smith's book must have been almost as popular as Dugard's; John Ive imported 10 copies in 1684 (Ford, *The Boston Book Market,* p. 126), and 2 copies are noted on the Ratcliff Invoice in 1688 (Howard J. Hall, "Two Book-Lists: 1688 and 1728," *Publications of the Colonial Society of Massachusetts,* XXIV [1923], 66).

25. Brinsley's *Ludus Literarius* was in the Harvard College Library.

26. Theses rhetoricae, No. 1, 1643; No. 1, 1653 (Aug. 10); No. 3, 1691; cf. Bernard's instructions in *The Faithfull Shepherd* (London, 1621), p. 222, that the preacher should contrive "by the obiect of the eyes, the affections of the heart may come to bee mooved"; or Samuel Willard in *The Truly Blessed Man* (1700), p. 424: "For goodness is the proper object of the will, which exerts it self by the affections."

27. From the Taylor MS. Meditation 44, second series.

28. John Donne, *LXXX Sermons* (London, 1640), p. 149.

Chapter XII

1. W. Fraser Mitchell, *English Pulpit Oratory from Andrewes to Tillotson* (London, 1932), p. 365.

2. John Donne, *Works* (ed. Henry Alford, London, 1839), VI, 266.

3. The works of William Perkins are found in practically every book list in early New England; cf. in addition to *The Art of Prophecying,* his treatise on pastoral care, *Of the Calling of the Ministrie.*

4. Copies of Bernard existed in early New England: Charles F. and Robin Robinson, "Three Early Massachusetts Libraries," *Publications of the Colonial Society of Massachusetts,* XXVIII (1935), 126, 155.

5. The Aristotelian method of sermonizing can also be studied in Gulielmus Bucanus, *Ecclesiastes* (1604), and Nicholaus Caussinus, *De Eloquentia Sacra et Humana* (3 ed., Paris, 1630).

6. W. Fraser Mitchell, *English Pulpit Oratory,* pp. 94-98.

7. Compare Perkins' definition of the interpretation of a text: "*Opening* of the words and sentences of the Scripture, that one entire and naturall sense may appeare," "Art of Prophecying," in *Workes* (London, 1626–31), II, 651.

8. W. Fraser Mitchell, *English Pulpit Oratory,* pp. 91-92; cf. Perkins, "Art of Prophecying," in *Workes,* II, 656-659.

9. William Chappell, *The Preacher* (London, 1656), p. 26; the pronounced Ramist character of Chappell's method can be seen clearly in his classifications of the kinds of axioms in which a doctrine is to be stated, which follow word for word the classifications of Ramus; furthermore, he exhibits the characteristic Ramist preference for positive axiomatic statement as against the syllogism; if a text can be adequately analyzed, he says, "according to the axiomatical judgement . . . and that the full sense of the place may be had by it; it will not be necessary to resolve the Text into a Syllogistical consideration, every time as we shall have power so to doe." *The Preacher,* pp. 116ff.

10. Alexander Richardson, *The Logicians School-Master* (London, 1657), p. 275. From the point of view of the Ramist logicians the "use" of a sermon was an inevitable consequence of the doctrine itself, exactly as the praxis of any art followed inescapably from its propositions; cf. Chappell, *The Preacher,* p. 133: "As the Arguments or places of invention, representing unto us the various affections of things amongst themselves doe yeeld foundations of deductions, so the force of affections the firmnesse and necessity of the same."

11. From a MS. sermon of William Brattle, 1696 (Massachusetts Historical Society); cf. Thomas Cobbett, *A Fruitfull and Usefull Discourse* (London, 1656), p. A3 recto: "Who knoweth not, that mans dull and deceitfull heart, will not oftimes be moved with generals, and common heads of holy doctrine, or practice, lightly touched upon, but when drawn out into particulars, and these being distinctly handled, wisely applyed, and strongly urged and pressed upon the conscience, the strong holds of sin and Satan, in man, come to be thrown down. . . ."

12. W. Fraser Mitchell, *English Pulpit Oratory,* p. 116.

13. *Ibid.,* pp. 78-79.

14. *John Saffin, His Book* (ed. Caroline Hazard, New York, 1928), p. 47; Saffin could find authority in Bacon as well as in Ramist rhetoric for the Puritan

stylist ideal, e.g., his entry, pp. 60-61, under the heading "Sundry Reading Epitomiz'd": "It was well said of Themistocles to the king of Persia that Speech was Like Cloth of Arras opened and put abroad; whereby the Imagery doth appear in figure whereas in Thoughts they Lye out as in packs out of view."

15. Donne, *LXXX Sermons* (London, 1640), p. 145.

16. Thomas Adams, *The White Devill* (London, 1621), p. 34.

17. Cf. James Allen, *Serious Advice to delivered Ones from Sickness* (1679), and *New Englands choicest Blessing* (1679), "To the Reader."

18. W. Fraser Mitchell, *English Pulpit Oratory,* p. 104.

19. Donne, *Works* (ed. Henry Alford, London, 1839), I, 216.

20. From the Taylor MS.

Chapter XIII

1. For bibliography for this chapter, see Appendix B.

2. Calvin, *Institutes,* II, ii, 1.

3. *Ibid.,* III, xxiii, 12.

4. John Fry, *The Clergy in their Colours* (London, 1650), p. 26.

5. Cf. Thomas Hooker, *A Survey of the Summe of Church-Discipline* (London, 1648), p. a 2 recto: ". . . their factours and followers the *Arminians,* who receive their errours by whole-sale from them, and retail them out again in their particular treatises."

6. Calvin, *Institutes,* III, xxi, 1.

7. Thomas Maule, *Truth held Forth and Maintained* ([New York] 1695), Preface.

8. *Ibid.,* p. 44.

9. *Ibid.,* p. 53.

10. John Ferriby, *The Lawfull Preacher* (London, 1652), p. A 3 recto; cf. Theophilus Gale, Preface to William Strong, *A Discourse of the Two Covenants* (London, 1678), p. A 3 recto.

11. William Perkins, *Works,* I (London, 1626), pp. 32-71, 164-165; for Ames's contribution to the development of the federal theory, see in particular *The Marrow of Sacred Divinity* (London, 1643), pp. 101-103, and *Coronis ad Collationem Hagiensem* (London, 1630), pp. 377, 400-401.

12. Perry Miller, *Orthodoxy in Massachusetts* (Cambridge, 1933), Chapter IV.

13. It is significant that Chappell in his bibliography for ministerial candidates recommended first on the question of the Covenant the works of Preston and in addition those of the New Englanders Cotton and Bulkeley.

14. For the life of Preston, cf. John Ball, "The Life of Dr. Preston," in Samuel Clarke, *A Generall Martyrologie* (London, 1651); James Bass Mullinger, *The University of Cambridge,* Vol. II (Cambridge, Eng., 1884), pp. 478-486, 520, 554-560, 569-572; William Haller, *The Rise of Puritanism* (New York, 1938), pp. 70ff. For his rôle in the New England imagination, see for example Increase Mather, *Practical Truths tending to promote the Power of Godliness* (1682), p. 30.

15. Cf. Cobbett's characterization of Genesis 17: ". . . a place that in these later dayes, hath been through mens distempers like *Isaacs* well, an *Esek* for conten-

tion about the waters in it." *A Just Vindication of the Covenant and Church-Estate of Children of Church-Members* (London, 1648), p. 37.

Chapter XIV

1. Calvin, *Institutes,* II, i, 7-8.

2. From the Taylor MS.

3. Samuel Willard, *A Compleat Body of Divinity* (1726), p. 213; cf. p. 153: ". . . as a Reasonable Creature, Man was capable of Transacting with God in the way of a Covenant; he was able to understand, and subscribe to the Articles, to give his free Consent, and set his Seal to them."

4. William Twisse, *A Treatise of Mr. Cottons, Clearing certaine Doubts Concerning Predestination. Together with an examination thereof* (London, 1646), *passim.*

5. *The Hutchinson Papers (A Collection of Original Papers Relative to the History of the Colony of Massachusetts-Bay)* (The Prince Society, Albany, 1865), I, 80.

6. Robert C. Winthrop, *Life and Letters of John Winthrop* (Boston, 1869), II, 432.

7. *The Colonial Laws of Massachusetts. Reprinted from the Edition of 1660* (ed. William H. Whitmore, Boston, 1889), p. 33.

8. *The Laws and Liberties of Massachusetts. Reprinted from . . . the 1648 edition . . .* (ed. Max Farrand, Cambridge, 1929), Preface.

9. *The Political Works of James I* (ed. Charles H. McIlwain, Cambridge, 1918), pp. 62, 63.

10. Charles Harding Firth, *Oliver Cromwell and the Rule of the Puritans in England* (London, 1900), p. 13.

11. J. W. Gough, *The Social Contract* (Oxford, 1936), Chapter V.

12. Cf. *ibid.,* pp. 37ff.

13. Cf. *Hutchinson Papers,* I, 79-113.

Chapter XV

1. Principal titles in this list are: [Anon.], *Vindiciae Clavium* (London, 1645); [Anon.], *A Censure of that Reverend and Learned Man of God Mr. John Cotton Lately of New-England* (London, 1656); Robert Baillie, *A Dissvasive from the Errours of the Time* (London, 1645); John Ball, *A Tryall of the New-Church Way in New-England and in Old* (London, 1644); Daniel Cawdrey, *The Inconsistencie of the Independent way* (London, 1651), *Independencie a great schism* (London, 1657), *Independency Further proved to be a Schism* (London, 1658); Thomas Edwards, *Reasons against the Independent Government of Particular Congregations* (London, 1641); Samuel Hudson, *The Essence and Unitie of the Church Catholike Visible* (London, 1645), *A Vindication of the Essence and Unity of the Church Catholike Visible* (London, 1650), *An Addition or Postscript to the Vindication of the Essence and Unity of the Church-Catholick visible . . .* (London, 1658); William Rathband, *A Briefe Narration of some Church Courses Held in Opinion and Practise in the Churches lately erected in New England* (London, 1644); Samuel Rutherford, *The Due Right of Presby-*

teries, or a Peaceable Plea for the Government of the Church of Scotland, wherein is examined 1. The Way of the Church of Christ in New England, etc. (London, 1644), *A Survey of the Survey of that Summe of Church-Discipline Penned by Mr. Thomas Hooker . . .* (London, 1658).

2. William Lucy, *A Treatise Of the Nature of a Minister* (London, 1670), p. 158.

3. I am in part indebted for my conception of conflicting forces in Congregational polity to an unpublished thesis by Mr. Alan Geismer, entitled "Messianic and Millenarian Activity in the Seventeenth Century."

4. Perry Miller, *Orthodoxy in Massachusetts* (Cambridge, 1933), pp. 298-309.

5. I am much indebted for my understanding of New England political theory to an unpublished essay by Mr. Edmund S. Morgan.

6. Edward Hyde, Earl of Clarendon, *The History of the Rebellion and Civil Wars in England* (ed. W. Dunn Macray, Oxford, 1888), IV, 311.

Chapter XVI

1. Cf. p. 242 of the copy in the Harvard College Library.

2. *The Laws and Liberties of Massachusetts. Reprinted from . . . the 1648 edition . . .* (ed. Max Farrand, Cambridge, 1929), Preface.

INDEX